# Encyclopedia
# of Angels

# Encyclopedia
# of Angels

*Rosemary Ellen Guiley*

☑®

Facts On File, Inc.

**Encyclopedia of Angels**

**Copyright © 1996 by Rosemary Ellen Guiley**

Facts On File, Inc.
11 Penn Plaza
New York NY 10001

**Library of Congress Cataloging-in-Publication Data**

Guiley, Rosemary.
    Encyclopedia of angels / Rosemary Ellen Guiley.
      p. cm.
    Includes bibliographical references and index.
    ISBN 0-8160-2988-1
    1. Angels—Dictionaries. I. Title.
BL477.G87    1996
291.2′15′03—DC20               96-12009

Facts On File books are available at special discounts when purchased in bulk quantities for businesses, associations, institutions, or sales promotions. Please call our Special Sales Department in New York at 212/967-8800 or 800/322-8755.

You can find Facts On File on the World Wide Web at **http://www.factsonfile.com**

Cover design by Dorothy Wachtenheim

Front cover art: Detail from *Ascension of Mary* (Perugino, 1500). Courtesy of the Galleria dell' Academia, Florence / AKG, London

Printed in the United States of America

VB INNO 10 9 8 7 6 5 4 3 2

This book is printed on acid-free paper.

# CONTENTS

For Lynne Hertsgaard

# ACKNOWLEDGMENTS

My deepest appreciation and gratitude go to Rosemary McMullen and Joanne P. Austin, who were instrumental in researching and compiling portions of this book.

# FOREWORD

The angel is a mystery, one that we have attempted to explain for more than two thousand years. The study of angels is vast and complex. Thousands of angels (and demons) are cited in lore and literature. However, contradictions abound concerning name spellings, functions, duties and identities. In fact, one can become submerged in minutiae about angels that does little to shed light on their true essence.

For *Encyclopedia of Angels* I have chosen to cover angels by topic. Many significant angels and demons are listed by name and by group. Otherwise the characteristics, functions and nature of angels, and our beliefs about them and experiences with them, are covered under general subject headings and under biographical profiles of mystics, theologians, philosophers and others. I also compare angels to similar beings in non-Western religions. The collection of these entries provides what I hope will be for the reader a fascinating journey into the evolution of the angel in Western thought. This evolution has been shaped largely by visionary experience. What we know about angels comes through our otherworldly contact with them.

My own interest in angels was sparked in the mid-1980s (before angels became the darling of the media), when I began having archetypal dreams that included a mysterious figure I identified as an angel. This figure served as a psychopomp into the reaches of inner space, leading me through a psychic transformation from one life-stage of consciousness to another, which unfolded over time. Earlier in life I had received no particular religious indoctrination about angels, and felt rather neutral about the question of their existence as portrayed in text and art. However, it was obvious to me that I was nonetheless tapping into an archetypal form that exists in the collective unconscious regardless of my own personal views. This is an ancient archetype, shaped by countless experiences, which in turn shaped beliefs, which revolved to shape experience. And now this archetype was breaking through the *unus mundus*, the undifferentiated whole of the universe, in response to my own psychic need. I found that the more I accepted this angel, the more the archetype became energized in my life, expressing itself not only through dreams but through inspiration, creativity, intuition and even visionary experience. In the ensuing years I have found myself in the company of numerous angelic presences.

Do I believe in angels? The answer must of course be yes, although even after years of study on the subject, I remain open as to their exact nature. I do not believe there are easy answers. Under the ANGEL entry, I have given the definition traditional to our mythology: "a supernatural being who mediates between God and mortals." Do they exist in their own right, in celestial realms? Perhaps so. Or perhaps there is an energy, a vibration of love and light from the Godhead, which becomes an "angel" when it interacts with human consciousness, taking on a form that we can comprehend and integrate into our spiritual and cosmological outlooks. Perhaps it is our need for semidivine messengers, for spiritual companions, protectors and guides, and for divine beauty in our own likeness, that draws to us what we call the angel. Our monotheistic God is imageless, abstract and remote. The angel, upon whom we project a form that is an exalted image of ourselves, helps us to feel closer to the Source of All Being.

The world's mystical traditions teach oneness, that everything is part of everything else. Quantum physics tells us that there is no separation between object and observer, that we are inexorably bound up in what we think we merely observe. Consequently we and the angels are part of each other; the good angel can be seen as an expression of our higher self (and the demon as an expression of our lower nature). The dynamics between the two, high and low, are what psychic integration and spiritual growth are all about.

The angel is a profound mystery, as deep as the mystery of the soul, as limitless as the mystery of infinity and eternity. This is a puzzle we may never be able to solve, but our probing of the mystery yields endless permutations that deepen our insights into ourselves. The experience of an angel—an ANGELOPHANY—is just as powerful today as it was for the visionary prophets of the biblical era. The prophets were escorted to a state of consciousness called heaven and were given the word of God in the form of laws and moral codes. Today the epiphanies are more personal, but just as life-changing. Via the angel we glimpse the unknown, and we are encouraged to press on.

—Rosemary Ellen Guiley
Annapolis, Maryland

**Abaddon (also Apollyon)** An angel of death and destruction, whose name literally means "the destroyer." In REVELATION, Abaddon (the Hebrew version of Apollyon) is king of the abyss, the bottomless pit of hell (Revelation 9:10), and also is the angel who possesses the key to the bottomless pit and binds Satan and throws him into it for one thousand years (Revelation 20:1–3).

Sometimes Abaddon also is equated with SATAN and SAMAEL. His name is used in conjuring spells for malicious intent.

**Abraham** The patriarch of the Hebrews was a frequent recipient of instructions and interventions from Yahweh and the Angel of Yahweh, otherwise known as the ANGEL OF THE LORD.

Although the text of Genesis often reads "Yahweh said," Genesis 15:1 reads "it happened . . . . that the word of Yahweh was spoken to Abram in a vision." (Abram was Abraham's original name before God made him founder of the Hebrew nation.) When Abram's concubine Hagar gave birth to a son and was expelled from the household by Abram's childless wife Sarai, "the angel of Yahweh met her" and spoke to her. The angel foretells Hagar's numerous descendants and tells her to name her son Ishmael. She calls the angel "El Roi," the God of Vision, and the well where this meeting took place was renamed Lahai Roi (Genesis 16:7–14). Hagar's mistaking an angel for Yahweh was the first of many confusions about the identity of the Angel of the Lord.

Later, Yahweh makes a covenant with Abram, promising him the birth of a son to the by-now-elderly Sarai, and also land. He instructs Abram to circumcise himself and all in his household. Abram's name from now on will be Abraham and Sarai's will be Sarah (Genesis 17).

One midrash (rabbinical text) says that Isaac's birth was announced three days after Abraham's circumcision of his entire household, and that God commanded MICHAEL, GABRIEL and RAPHAEL to comfort Abraham, who suffered great pain, as always happens on the third day of circumcision. The archangels protested: "Would you send us to an unclean place, full of blood?" God answered: "By your lives, the odor of Abraham's sacrifice pleases me better than myrrh and frankincense! Must I go Myself?" Then they accompanied Him disguised as Arab wayfarers. Michael was to announce Isaac's birth; Raphael to heal Abraham; and Gabriel, to destroy the evil cities of SODOM AND GOMORRAH.

The midrash above ties in with the story that follows, the most often-discussed angel episode in the Abraham story,

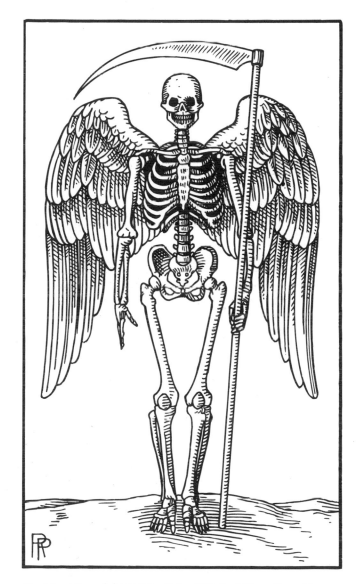

Abaddon (Copyright 1995 by Robert Michael Place, from *The Angels Tarot* by Rosemary Ellen Guiley and Robert Michael Place. Reprinted courtesy of HarperSanFrancisco)

Genesis 18 and 19. In this story the confusion between God and angels becomes readily apparent. The text says, "Yahweh appeared to him at the Oak of Mamre while he was sitting by the entrance of his tent during the hottest part of the day. He looked up and there he saw three men standing near him. As soon as he saw them he ran from the entrance of the tent to meet them, and bowed to the ground." This was not a sign of adoration but a sign of respect. At first Abraham sees his guests as mere human beings and welcomes them warmly. Their superhuman character is only gradually revealed. Abraham hurries to get a meal prepared and stands by them while they eat under the tree. They ask where Sarah is and Abraham says she is in the tent. Then one says he will come and visit in a year and Sarah will have a son. Sarah overhears and laughs. The guest asks why Sarah laughed, when is anything too wonderful for Yahweh?

"From there the men set out and arrived within sight of Sodom, with Abraham accompanying them to show them the way. Now Yahweh had wondered, 'Shall I conceal from Abraham what I am going to do?' " Yahweh is referring to his plans for Abraham's line to live in his righteous way. He says, "How great an outcry there is against Sodom and Gomorrah," and says he will go and investigate. "The men left there and went to Sodom, while Abraham remained standing before Yahweh" (Genesis 18:22). They convince Yahweh to spare the city if he finds ten righteous men there. Chapter 19, verse 1 reads "when the two angels reached Sodom that evening. . . ." Then follows the account of the destruction of Sodom and Gomorrah, the escape of Lot and his daughters, and the changing of Lot's wife into a pillar of salt. Chapter 19, verse 5 reads, "when dawn broke the angels urged Lot . . . ."

Maimonides used this passage to illustrate his conception that "whenever seeing, or being addressed by an angel is mentioned, this refers to prophetic vision or to a dream. It makes no difference whether this fact is explicitly stated or not. . . . In such a prophetic vision or prophetic dream the prophet sometimes sees God speaking to him . . . or he may see an angel who speaks to him" (*Guide of the Perplexed*, XLII).

God advises Abraham to expel Hagar and Ishmael (Genesis 21: 12–14), and again divine intervention occurs. "But God heard the boy wailing, and the angel of God called to Hagar from heaven." Hagar is told to hold up the child to be blessed, for he will lead a great nation. "Then God opened Hagar's eyes and she saw a well . . ." (Genesis 21:15–19).

M. J. Field's theory that angel messengers in the early Old Testament could well have been remnants of stories of visitations and encounters with desert holy men who were using their dramatic and occult arts to intervene in the spiritual development of the Hebrew nomads can be applied to this episode, including a postulate that one of them might have impregnated Sarah and applied herbal or other aids to bring the pregnancy to term (see ANGEL OF THE LORD).

Again, with the story of the sacrifice of Isaac in Genesis 22, Abraham's first instruction to take Isaac to the land of Moriah and offer him as a burnt offering comes from "God," yet who intervenes at the last minute to prevent Abraham's knife from killing Isaac? "The angel of the Lord called to him from heaven." (See ISAAC.)

The rabbis writing the Seypher Hayashar add this to the story. As Abraham and Isaac ascend Mount Moriah, the fallen angel SAMAEL steals up in the shape of a humble graybeard and says: "Can a command to kill the son of your old age proceed from a God of mercy and justice? You have been deceived!" Abraham sees through the disguise and drives him away; but he reappears in the shape of a handsome youth to Isaac, whispering, "Wretched son of a wretched mother! Was it for this she awaited your birth so long and patiently? Why should your besotted father slaughter you without reason? Flee, while there is yet time!" Isaac repeats these words to Abraham, who curses Samael and sends him away.

The Book of Jubilees, a pseudepigraphical work, presents a different version of events with Abraham, focusing on the promise of progeny and land. It does not mention the theophany (manifestation of God), nor the angels' eating of food. The angels, who are not specified by number, do tell Sarah that she will bear a son, and they give her son-to-be the name of Isaac.

Theologians and philosophers have examined and debated the story of Abraham for centuries. Was his original vision a theophany or an ANGELOPHANY (manifestation of an angel)? Did the angels, whom Abraham initially assumed were mortal, really eat food or only appear to eat food? It was established early that the vision was an angelophany, and that the angels, being incorporeal, only gave the appearance of eating.

See also ANGEL OF DEATH; EATING; TREES.

**Further reading:**
Field, M.J. *Angels and Ministers of Grace*. New York: Hill and Wang, 1971.
Graves, Robert, and Patai, Raphael. *Hebrew Myths*. New York: Doubleday Anchor Books, 1964.
Maimonides. *Guide of the Perplexed*. Abridged. Introduction by Julius Guttmann. London: East and West Library, 1952.

**Abraxas**  An ancient name attributed to a god, a sun, an angel, and a devil. Abraxas was the name of a sun mounting an ouroboros (a snake biting its tail) held by the highest Egyptian god, Isis, the creator of the sun and mistress of all the gods. Isis mythology found its way deeply into GNOSTICISM, in which Abraxas is the name of the ruler of the 365th (highest and final) AEON, or sphere, ascending to the unknowable God. Abraxas thus became the Gnostic demigod or Aeon or the High Heaven.

Abraxas also was associated with the Mithraic mystery religion of Persian origin, the chief rival of Christianity in Rome in its first 400 years. Like Gnosticism, Mithraism featured a complex astrology and numerology. Numerical values of Mithra's and Abraxas's names each total 365.

Abraxas was assimilated into the Gnostic "Lord of the World," the Old Testament God (really a creation/son of SOPHIA, a high Aeon) who created the material world and had demonic qualities. Orthodox Christians came to view Abraxas as a demon. In turn, Abraxas became a favorite deity of heretical sects of the Middle Ages.

Abraxas appears in the works of Carl G. JUNG. The father of depth psychology wrote a vast amount of material on his personal visionary experiences, little of which has been released by his heirs. One such document, reported by Jung to have been composed on three nights between December 15, 1916 and February 16, 1917, entitled *Seven Sermons to the Dead*, purports to be written by the Gnostic teacher Basiledes in Alexandria; several of the sermons feature Abraxas.

Abraxas (Copyright 1995 by Robert Michael Place, from *The Angels Tarot* by Rosemary Ellen Guiley and Robert Michael Place. Reprinted courtesy of HarperSanFrancisco)

heart and the universal heart, the sun, invoked by chanticleer; the human torso embodies the principle of logos, or articulated thought; the snake legs indicate prudence, whereby the dynamic rulership of universal being governs its own all-powerful energies; the shield is symbolic of wisdom, the great protector of divine warriors, while the whip denotes the relentless driving power of life and the four horses the tetramorphic (four elements, Jung's four functions) forces of the universal libido or psychic energy. The number 365 appears again, for in both Greek and Hebrew the seven letters of the name Abraxas yield 365 numerologically, and the seven letters correspond to the seven rays of the planetary spheres, according to Gnostic principles.

Jung calls Abraxas "the truly terrible one" because of his ability to generate truth and falsehood, good and evil, light and darkness with the same word and in the same deed. Jung also refers to the divine Abraxas as "hybrid," the living and symbolic refutation of the philosophical attitude of the excluded middle, the Western "either-or" by which all things are categorized absolutely and polar opposites abound. In the Fourth Sermon, Abraxas is mentioned as "the activity of the whole," thereby indicating that it is energy, or force, that characterizes this principle most clearly, the life-force, élan vital.

In Jungian psychology there is no easy way out of psychic conflict; one must not only fight on the side of the angels, but occasionally join the host of the fallen angels. Author and Jungian expert Stephan Hoeller writes in *The Gnostic Jung and the Seven Sermons to the Dead*:

> Not a few alienated persons of modern culture are indeed in need of discovering Abraxas power within themselves, somewhat after the fashion of Hesse's *Steppenwolf*. As the fear of God has been envisioned as the beginning of wisdom, so the fear of Abraxas is said by Jung to be wisdom. This fear, as a holy comixture of awe and caution, will prevent the individual from either underestimating or foolishly provoking the titanic forces resident in the nucleus of the atom of the soul. The most important injunction to be found in Jung's sermon, however, is: "Not to resist him means liberation." To resist Abraxas, means invoking the supreme disaster. The fierce dynamism of life will not be denied; it will break into the field of consciousness by some means or other. . . . Acceptance of and permeability toward the promptings and designs of the unconscious is the way to liberation, individuation, Gnosis, or whatever word may apply to describe it.

In spite of the controversy Jung's Abraxas figure caused among orthodox theologians, it is very strong evidence of his modern Gnostic leanings.

Another reference to Abraxas appeared in Nobel Prize—winning writer Herman Hesse's first successful novel, *Demian*, published in 1919 under the pseudonym Sinclair. Hesse utilizes many Gnostic themes in the novel. One of the characters says Abraxas is the "name of a godhead whose symbolic task is the uniting of godly and devilish elements."

**Further reading:**

Hoeller, Stephan A. *The Gnostic Jung and the Seven Sermons to the Dead.* Wheaton, Ill.: Quest Books, 1982.

In contrast to Helios, the god of light, and the Devil, god of darkness, Abraxas appears as the supreme power of being in whom light and darkness are both united and transcended. He is also defined as the principle of irresistible activity and is a close approximation of an active manifestation of the Pleroma (state of oneness or wholeness). Gnostic talismans bearing the figure of Abraxas were saved because they were carved into valuable stones, usually oval. They show a figure with a human body, the head of a rooster (or, more seldom, of a hawk), and legs fashioned like serpents. The god's hands hold a shield and a whip, the shield usually inscribed with the name IAO, reminiscent of the Jewish four-letter name of God. Often he is mounted on a chariot drawn by four white horses, with both sun and moon, gold and silver, masculine and feminine, overhead.

The symbolism usually is explained as follows: the rooster represents wakefulness and is related to the human

**aeon** In GNOSTICISM, both a celestial plane and the ruler of that plane. The Gnostics conceived of the heavens as a series of concentric spheres called aeons. Basilides enumerated 365 aeons, though others counted far fewer—thirty or less. The chiefs of the aeons are called aeons themselves. They are emanations of God and approximately comparable to seraphim (see CHOIRS) in closeness to the Godhead. ABRAXAS is chief among aeons. SOPHIA rules the thirtieth aeon, the highest level of the Pleroma, which are the thirty aeons closest to earth and which form earth's celestial heavens. Before the angelic hierarchy of PSEUDO-DIONYSIUS became established, aeons were counted among the orders of angels as a tenth level.

**Aeshma**   See ASMODEUS.

**aethyr**   See MAGIC, ANGELS IN.

**Ahriman**   See Rudolph STEINER; ZOROASTRIANISM.

**Ahura Mazda**   See ZOROASTRIANISM.

**Amahrasp and (Amesha Spenta)**   See ZOROASTRIANISM.

**Anafiel**   An angel associated with the prophet ENOCH and the angel METATRON. The name means "branch of God."

Anafiel is one of the angels identified as the one who carries Enoch to heaven. He also is the angel chosen by God to punish Metatron on one occasion with a flogging of sixty lashes.

Anafiel also is the keeper of the keys of the heavenly halls, and is cited in the Merkabah, early Jewish mystical tradition, as chief of the eight great angels of heaven.

**angel**   A supernatural being who mediates between God and mortals. Angels are held to minister over all living things and the natural world, and also all things in the cosmos. The term *angel* comes from the Greek *angelos*, which means messenger. Similarly, the Persian term *angaros* means courier. In Hebrew the term is *malakh*, which also means messenger. The name refers to one of the angel's primary duties: to shuttle back and forth between realms, bringing human prayers to heaven and returning with God's answers. Angels also mete out the will of God, whether it be to aid or to punish humans. Angels are specific to Judaism, Christianity and Islam; however, they are derived from concepts of helping and tutelary spirits that exist in mythologies the world over.

The Western concept of the angel evolved primarily from the mythologies of Babylonia and Persia. ZOROASTRIANISM developed a complex angelology that influenced the Hebrews. The angel also absorbed characteristics from Sumerian, Egyptian and Greek beings. The Hebrews in turn influenced the Christians, and the Jews and Christians influenced the Moslems.

The Bible presents angels as being representatives of God. The term "Angel of the Lord" appears frequently, and may refer either to an angel or to God himself. Angels

**Angels (Gustave Doré)**

exist in a celestial realm. They are incorporeal, but have the ability to assume form and pass as mortals. They also appear as beings of fire, lightning and brilliant light, sometimes with wings and sometimes not (see WINGS). Various classes of angels are mentioned in the Bible; by the sixth century these were organized into hierarchies (see CHOIRS).

In the Bible, angels are main players on the stage of life, and in the working out of humanity's relationship to the Divine. With a few exceptions, they are never referred to with proper names. MICHAEL and GABRIEL are the only two angels mentioned; RAPHAEL appears in the apochryphal Book of Tobit. However, numerous angels are mentioned by name in the APOCHRYPHA and PSEUDEPIGRAPHA. By the Middle Ages, midrashim, kabbalistic writings and other sources had cited thousands of angels by name (see NAMES OF ANGELS).

The ranks of heavenly angels have evil counterparts in the fallen angels of hell. The fallen angels became demons (whose ranks also include the demonized gods of pagan cultures). The role of demons is to tempt humankind into sin and to steal souls into hell, the kingdom of SATAN, the prince of all evil, according to Christianity. (See also HELL and LUCIFER).

The church fathers of Christianity gave extensive consideration to the duties, nature, numbers, abilities and functions of angels. This theological interest peaked in the Middle Ages and began to decline in the Renaissance. The scientific revolution forced angels offstage, though devotional cults kept their interest alive. Angels made a comeback in popularity in the late twentieth century, due in part to a widespread spiritual hunger for personal relationships with the Divine and for the comfort of ready supernatural assistance and guidance. Popular thought has tended to sanitize the angel into a "best friend" mold, ignoring the angel's history of sternness and impartiality (See GUARDIAN ANGEL).

For descriptions of the evolution of various angelologies, and for comparisons to other religions, see the entries on GNOSTICISM, JUDAIC ANGELOLOGY, ISLAMIC ANGELOLOGY, PROTESTANT ANGELOLOGY, MORMONISM, HINDUISM, TANTRIC BUDDHISM and ORISHAS. Other major overviews are provided by the entries on ART, ARCHITECTURE AND RITUAL; FILM, DRAMA AND TELEVISION; LITERATURE; and MUSIC. There also are entries on SEX AND ANGELS and EATING. The entries on angelophanies and DREAMS discuss the many ways in which angels manifest.

**Angel of Death**  The angel charged with announcing death and taking the soul either to heaven or hell. The Angel of Death is known by various names in different traditions. In his true form, the Angel of Death has a terrible countenance, but he is able to manifest in any pleasing form in order to trick or calm the living into giving up their souls to him.

The archangel MICHAEL, whose duties include leading the souls of the dead to the afterlife (i.e., playing the role of psychopomp), is called the Angel of Death. Likewise GABRIEL, as the guardian of the underworld, bears this title. The fallen and evil angels SATAN, SAMAEL and IBLIS are the Angel of Death as well. In rabbinic writings, at least a dozen angels are named as the Angel of Death; among these (beyond those already mentioned) are METATRON, Azrael, Apollyon, ABBADON, Hemah, Kafziel, Kezef, LEVIATHAN, Malach ha-Mavet, Mashit, Yehudiah and Yetzer-hara. In

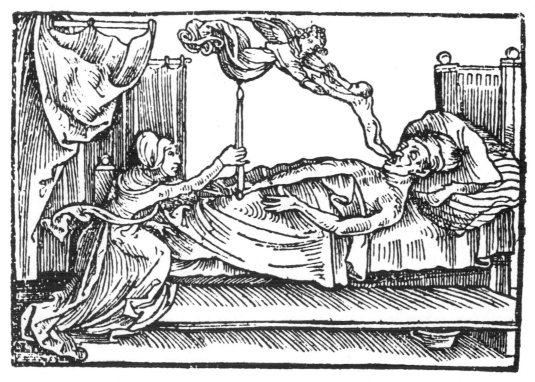

Angel of Death taking a soul, in the form of a child, from a dying man (Reiter, *Mortilogus*, 1508)

Arabic lore, Azrael and Iblis fill this role, and in Zoroastrianism, it is Mairya. In folktales, the Angel of Death frequently is not named.

Stories about the Angel of Death are common in folklore; the following examples come from Jewish lore.

The Testament of Abraham, a pseudepigraphical work, relates the story of Abraham's encounter with the Angel of Death. The story begins when Abraham is 175 years old and at the end of his life. Curiously, both his wife Sarah and son Isaac figure in the story, despite the contradictions in Genesis that Sarah's death preceded that of Abraham, and that Isaac was married to Rebecca when his father died.

God sends MICHAEL to Abraham to tell him it is time to die. Abraham still lives by the oak tree at Mamre, where he had earlier in his life served and fed three visitors who were angels in disguise (see ABRAHAM). Abraham sees Michael approach him, and although he looks like a splendid warrior, Abraham does not recognize him as an angel. He invites Michael to come with him, and the two walk back to Abraham's house. Isaac, recognizing Michael as an angel, falls at the angel's feet. He tells Sarah that Michael is an angel.

Abraham has Isaac fetch water, which he uses to wash Michael's feet. He begins to weep, and sees that Michael weeps tears of precious stones. Abraham then orders Isaac to prepare a room for a banquet.

Michael excuses himself and goes immediately to heaven, where he has a conversation with God. Abraham is so righteous, he says, that he cannot pronounce death upon him. God decides to send a prophecy of death in a dream to Isaac, which Michael can then interpret.

Michael also wonders how he will be able to eat food. God says he will send an all-devouring spirit to consume the food and protect Michael's identity. (In Genesis, the visiting angels are offered food by Abraham and give the appearance of eating.) Michael goes back to Abraham and joins him in the meal. They pray together.

When Isaac goes to sleep, he dreams the death prophecy and awakens weeping. Michael also weeps. Sarah attends them, and realizes that Michael is one of the three mysterious visitors from before. She quietly lets Abraham know. Abraham hears Isaac's dream, and Michael interprets it.

Abraham persuades Michael to admit that he is an angel, and to reveal the purpose of his visit. Abraham refuses to die. He discusses death with God, and Michael takes him on a tour of the cosmos.

God then sends the Angel of Death to Abraham at Mamre, and he reveals his true appearance: "Then Death made his appearance dark and more fierce than any sort of beast . . . and he showed Abraham seven fiery heads of dragons, fourteen faces of the most flaming fire . . . and a gloomy viper's face. And the face of a terrible precipice, and the fiercer face of an asp, and the face of a fearsome lion . . . and he also showed him the face of fiery sword . . . and another face of a wild sea raging and a river rushing and a fearsome three-headed dragon and a mingled cup of poisons." Death prevails in the end, and Abraham dies.

The Angel of Death manifests in a much friendlier form in the Hasidic folk tale (Eastern Europe, nineteenth century) of the esteemed rabbi Reb Pinhas. The angel appears as a visiting Hasid, and politely presents a petition of death to Reb Pinhas, which reveals his true identity. The rabbi answers with his own petition: he will be happy to go wherever the Angel of Death wishes to take him, but if he could have a choice, he wishes to go to Gehenna (the Jewish hell), because he wishes to be of service to the souls there and work for their release.

This places the Angel of Death in a predicament, for he has been ordered not to deny Reb Pinhas any wish. Yet, he cannot bring himself to take the rabbi to hell. Like Michael, he goes back to heaven to ask God what to do. He is given an answer, whispered through a curtain.

The angel goes back to Reb Pinhas and presents him with a petition, to which has been appended a single word inscribed in black flames. The petition tells Reb Pinhas that he has been given a holy name that will take him either to Paradise or to Gehenna, depending on how the name is pronounced. The true pronunciation is so secret that only the angel METATRON knows it. Not even the Angel of Death can help.

Reb Pinhas, still intent on going to hell, studies the word but ultimately must guess at its pronunciation. He winds up in heaven, illustrating that there is no escape from one's fate. You cannot go to hell when you deserve to go to heaven, and vice versa.

A rabbinic tale from Babylon in the fifth century illustrates that there is no escaping the Angel of Death. One morning King Solomon hears birds chirping, and because he understands the language of birds, he learns that the Angel of Death plans to take two of his closest advisers. He tells them, and they beg him to help them escape their doom. He urges them to flee to the enchanted city of Luz, which the Angel of Death is forbidden to enter.

(Luz, according to the Talmud, is a secret city where everyone remains immortal as long as they do not venture outside the gates. Solomon knows the location. Also, in Genesis 28:19 Luz is the city cited as the place where JACOB had his dream of the ladder.)

But the Angel of Death knows all, and when the men arrive at the city gates, they find the angel waiting for them just outside, barring their way.

This and other tales about the Angel of Death show that mortals cannot escape fate and that once God has decreed it, Death always has the last word. However, another rabbinic story tells that Rabbi Joshua ben Levi outfoxes the Angel of Death by talking the angel into letting him hold his sword. He refuses to give it back, and leaps straight into the Garden of Eden while he is still alive.

The Beit ha-Midrash tells the story that Moses wrote thirteen Torahs on the day he was told he was going to die, as a means of preventing the Angel of Death from taking him. According to lore, one cannot die while one is studying the Torah. The thirteen Torahs included one for each of the twelve tribes of Israel, plus a celestial Torah (the best of the lot) that was taken to heaven and used by the angels. (According to legend, the archangel GABRIEL gave this Torah to Rabbi Meir ben Baruch of Rothenburg, a leader of German Jewry in the thirteenth century who spent much time in prison, and copied the Torah during his confinement. He put the copy in a casket and sailed it off down the Rhine, to be discovered by Jews.)

Still another Jewish story demonstrates how angels exert free will, and how God can change his mind and retrieve the Angel of Death. A mystical tale from Yemen in the fourteenth century tells about the fate of the bride and bridegroom. An old man, Reuben, sins once in his life by rebuking another man for sitting in his place at the synagogue. God decides to punish him by sending the Angel of Death to take away his son, who is about to be married. Reuben pleads with the angel to spare his son until he is married and has tasted the joy of life. Moved with pity, the angel agrees.

God rebukes the angel for disobeying him. Chastened, the angel decides to revenge himself by taking the son with the same tremendous anger shown him by God. The prophet Elijah tells the son that at his wedding, an old man in rags will appear, and it will be the Angel of Death.

Sure enough the angel appears, and Reuben offers himself as a surrogate. The angel displays his faces of cruelty, anger, wrath and severity, and draws his sword to cut off Reuben's head. Reuben flees. Similarly, Reuben's wife offers herself, and then flees in terror.

Finally the bride offers herself, and does not flee. The Angel of Death sheds a tear of mercy. God, watching from heaven, has pity and orders the Angel of Death to retreat. He grants both bride and bridegroom seventy more years of life.

See DEATHBED VISIONS; IZRA'IL.

**Further reading:**

Davidson, Gustav. *A Dictionary of Angels*. New York: The Free Press, 1967.

Schwartz, Howard. *Gabriel's Palace: Jewish Mystical Tales*. New York: Oxford University Press, 1993.

## Angel of the Lord (also Angel of Yahweh)

An angel especially associated or identified with God. While any angel sent to execute the commands of God might be called the angel of the Lord (II Samuel 24:16; I Kings 19: 5, 7), mention is made of an angel under circumstances that justify one in always thinking of the same angel, who is distinguished from Yahweh, and yet is identified with him: Genesis 16:7–14; 18:1–4, 13–14, 33; 21:17; 22:11–12, 15–16; 31:11, 13; Exodus 3:1–6; 23:20–24; Numbers 20:16; 22:21–35; Joshua 5:13–15; 6:2; Judges 2:1–5; 5:23; 6:11–24; 13:1–25; 1 Samuel 29:9; 1 Chronicles 21:15–30; Zechariah 1:10–13; 3:1–2. This is an angel who revealed the face of God (Genesis 32:30), in whom was Yahweh's name (Exodus 23: 21), and whose presence was equivalent to Yahweh's (Exodus 32:34; 33:14; Isaiah 63:9). The "angel of the Lord" thus appears as a manifestation of Yahweh himself, one with Yahweh and yet different from him. Sometimes the angel of the Lord may be described as a floating conception, at one moment an angel, at another the Lord.

Whether or not these passages indicated a direct visitation or manifestation of God, God appearing through an angel, God giving an angel more direct power than usual, an angel taking the form of a man, or some other phenomenon was a question regularly taken up by Judaic and Christian commentators (see ORIGEN and St. AUGUSTINE on theophanies). One modern scholar, M. J. Field, has argued well for a reading of the earliest angel messengers, particularly in Genesis, as men appearing to be angels. According to Field's thesis, the unschooled Hebraic nomads could well have been

Angel appearing to Zacharias

guided and led to make decisions through the intervening powers of holy men of the deserts who were interested in drawing these people toward monotheism. Field spent many years in Africa witnessing the magical and persuasive powers of men and women hermits who exerted "spiritual oversight" over tribes. Field notes that these people often are adept in "special effects" such as fire, sparks and smoke, and ventriloquism, like the voice in the burning bush (Exodus 3:2). Their luminosity, dignity, powers and charismatic presence would derive from years of spiritual practice. There is no doubt that such "saints," individuals who practiced spiritual discipline, existed in the lands and especially the deserts of the Bible. In fact, they were the instigators of western monasticism.

Maimonides (see JUDAIC ANGELOLOGY), writing in the twelfth century C.E., read the same passages quite differently. He interpreted the angelic appearances, which usually conveyed announcements or instructions, as prophetic visions or dreams. According to Maimonides's cosmology, angels were indeed intermediaries between God and man, but they operated through the visionary imaginative plane in the human mind to convey God's wishes to the patriarchs and prophets. Maimonides explains:

It is all the same whether the particular passage says first that he saw an angel, or the phrasing implies that he thought at first it was a human being and then in the end he realized it was an angel. Whenever it turns out in the end that what he saw, and was addressed by, was an angel, you must accept it as true that this was from the outset a prophetic vision or prophetic dream. In such a prophetic vision or prophetic dream the prophet sometimes sees God speaking to him . . . or he may see an angel who speaks to him, or hear someone speak to him without seeing anyone speaking, or he may see a human being speaking to him and afterwards he realizes that the one who spoke to him was an angel (*Guide of the Perplexed*, ed. Guttmann, Ch. XLII).

He goes on to decipher passages about such encounters by ABRAHAM, JACOB, and Balaam.

In the New Testament, angelic voices and dream visions surround the birth and early lives of John the Baptist and JESUS. In fact "the angel of the Lord" who appeared to Zechariah (Luke 1:11–20) says "I am Gabriel, who stands in God's presence." The angel of the Lord continues to be a standard title applied to any unnamed angel throughout the Gospels, including those present at the tomb on Easter morning. But the angel of the Lord came to be identified with Christ himself early in church writings. This controversy in Christian theology appears not to have been resolved even in the late twentieth century.

Justin Martyr (100?–165? C.E.) was the first to advocate that the angel of the Lord was none other than a pre-incarnate appearance of Christ under the guise of an angel. Others attracted to this concept found Old Testament "angel of the Lord" passages and intruded Christ. It was Christ who wrestled with JACOB, according to Clement of Alexandria (150?–220?). Hilary of Poitiers (315?–367) took Jesus' words in John 8:56 ("Abraham saw my day") to mean he was one of the three angels who visited Abraham (Genesis 16:10). Augustine was acutely aware of the dangers of embracing the idea that Christ had been corporeal prior to the incarnation and stated his opinion that the Trinity was incorporeal in the Old Testament. Nevertheless, he broadened the idea of "angel"/messenger to include the Holy Spirit. Augustine's calm view dissipated the controversy for over a millennium. Aquinas did not pursue the issue.

It arose again in the Reformation. Calvin in the *Institutes* committed himself to a descent of the non-yet-incarnate Christ "in a mediatorial capacity, that he might approach the faithful with greater familiarity" (1.13.10; 14.5). The Lutherans deemed it heresy to deny that "the angel of the Lord" was Christ (Calovius, *Consensus*). Calvin in his list of accusations against Servetus indicted him for heresy in not holding that the angel was Christ (*Institutes* 1.13.10). Eventually it was shown that every theophany in the Old Testament was a "christophany" by the angel-Christ advocates. They argued that because these angels were sometimes worshiped, or that people who saw them believed they had seen God, that they were indeed God. They held that the Old and New Testaments must be mediated by the same source in name, form and substance, i.e., to prove that Christ was the Messiah and true God. If their point were taken, the storehouse of data on the historical Christ would be amplified by large amounts of material from the Old Testament. Major nineteenth-century Christologists maintained the angel-Christ identification, and many of the twentieth do not question it.

Scholar William G. MacDonald argues against this wholesale acceptance of the angel of the Lord as Christ, mainly on the grounds that pre-incarnation appearances of Christ make it impossible theologically to reconcile the full deity of Christ with the full humanity of Christ. He brings linguistics to bear in the context of cultural considerations. For example, *malak*, the Hebrew word for angel, means not only "messenger" but "agent." Servants had full authority to carry on their masters' business. MacDonald says "the Semitic *malak* idea was perfectly adaptable to the monarchical order. One is not surprised to find in the celestial court of Yahweh an array of angels waiting like royal ministers to magnify his presence throughout the earth. A dispatched angel would arrive anonymously (in terms of his own name), because coming in the name of God, i.e. as *malak* Yahweh ["angel of the Lord"] or *malak* Elohim ["the angel of God"], his sole concern was to speak or act for God as the situation required and to receive man's response to God." He finally asks the obvious: On what basis were the Old Testament personages and writers supposed to be capable of distinguishing one supernatural being from another, that is "the Son of God" from a seraph? If one adds M. J. Field's argument that the angel messengers could have been more clever and gifted human beings practicing drama and occult arts, the question is broadened to: Could the Old Testament "witnesses" distinguish magic from supernatural phenomena, much less God from an angel?

**Further reading:**

Field, M. J. *Angels and Ministers of Grace: An Ethno-Psychiatrist's Contribution to Biblical Criticism*. New York: Hill & Wang, 1971.

Heick, O. W. *A History of Christian Thought*. Philadelphia: Fortress Press, 1965.

MacDonald, William Graham. "Christology and 'The Angel of the Lord.'" *Current Issues in Biblical Patristic Interpretation*. Ed. G. F. Hawthorne and Merrill Tenney. Grand Rapids, Mich.: Erdman, 1975.

Maimonides. *Guide of the Perplexed*. Abridged. Introduction by Julius Guttmann. London: East and West Library, 1952.

**Angel of Yahweh**    See ANGEL OF THE LORD.

**angel wreath (feather crown)**    In the folklore of the Ozarks area of the United States, angel wreaths are lumps of feathers formed into wreath shapes, which are found inside bed pillows. According to lore, an angel wreath found inside the pillow of someone who has just died is a lucky omen that the person is saintly and has gone to heaven. The wreath is a symbol of the golden crown the person will wear in heaven.

Angel wreaths vary in shape and size. Some are tightly bunched and others loosely formed. They resemble rings, buns, caps and balls, and generally are from two to six inches in diameter. Most likely the wreaths form naturally from pressure and handling of the pillow. The feathers become attached by the minute barbs on the quills.

Folkloric tradition holds that the feathers inside the pillow of a deceased person should be searched for signs of an angel wreath. If one is found, the family is relieved. Angel wreaths have been preserved in families as lucky charms.

In earlier times, the discovery of an angel wreath was worthy of mention in the town newspaper. Angel wreaths once were so highly prized that they were stolen or secreted into pillows. Sometimes people would ask to be buried with the angel wreaths of their deceased spouses or relatives. It was widely believed that the wreaths were not made by humans or by chance, but were of divine origin.

Conversely, Ozark superstition also holds that angel wreaths are not from heaven but from the Devil, and are a sign of witchcraft at work. Thus, feather pillows should be regularly searched, and any partially formed wreaths destroyed.

**Further reading:**
Randolph, Vance. *Ozark Magic and Folklore.* New York: Dover Publications, 1964. First published 1947.

**angelic hierarchy**   See CHOIRS.

**angel-man**   In German folklore, the angel-man is an effigy representing the solar fire, which traditionally was burned at celebrations of the summer solstice. The burning of fires once was a widespread practice in honor of the solstice and to help the sun, at its peak power, change its course in the sky. Scriptures and other sacred writings describe angels as "burning" and "clothed in fire." Thus, an angel became an appropriate image in some seasonal fire festivals.

The German ritual was called "beheading the angel-man." It was performed on Midsummer Day, at least up through the early twentieth century and perhaps later. The angel-man was an effigy made of a stump driven into the ground, wrapped in straw and fashioned into a crude human figure with arms, head and face. Wood was piled around the effigy. Boys armed with swords covered it with flowers. The wood was lit. When the angel-man burst into flames, the boys attacked it and cut the burning figure into small pieces. They then jumped backwards and forwards over the fire.

Straw effigies of humans—usually a man but sometimes a woman—commonly were burned as a part of summer solstice festivals.

**Further reading:**
Frazer, James G. *The Golden Bough.* New York: Avenel Books, 1981. First published in 1890.

**angelophany**   The experience of perceiving an angel with one or more of the five senses. The characteristics of angelophanies differ, probably in accordance with cultural conditioning, expectations, and acceptance or rejection of such experiences.

Ancient angelophanies found in the Bible, APOCHRYPHA, PSEUDEPIGRAPHA and rabbinic literature focus on visionary experiences and DREAMS, which were the customary media for prophecy. The great prophets, such as EZEKIEL, MOSES, ISAIAH and ENOCH were treated to grand visions of angels and transport to heavenly realms. They reportedly saw angels, were guided by them, beheld the throne of God and were anointed as holy messengers to return to their people and disseminate the word of God through warnings and moral and ethical codes. They heard the voices of angels and the voice of God. Such visions involved common elements of brilliant light, fire and lightning, and sounds of thunder and earthquakes. The angels were described as having the forms of men and being clothed in brilliant light or garments. Sometimes they were said to have wings; other times wings are not specified.

The dramatic nature of such visions may have been necessary to gain the attention of people; the angelophanies—and theophanies, or experiences of God—certified the prophets as official agents of the Lord. Such visions—especially that of Ezekiel—also formed the basis for early Hebrew mysticism in which one rode to the heavens via prayer and meditation to attain access to God, much as Ezekiel did when he rode up to heaven in his "throne-chariot."

On some occasions in early writings, angels pass for mortals, and seem to have the ability to disguise their heavenly light. In Genesis, ABRAHAM is so fooled when three men visit him on the plains of Mamre and partake of a feast he offers them in hospitality. They even converse with him. Similarly, the archangel RAPHAEL appears as a mortal man in the Book of TOBIT, and acts as a guide on the journey of Tobias.

Angels were not always seen when they manifested in early descriptions. Often percipients described hearing angelic voices (and sometimes singing).

In Catholicism, angels are considered to be pure spirits who have the ability to take the form of men and women. They intervene to help people fulfill their spiritual and temporal needs.

The literature of the saints is replete with angelophanies. Saints have regularly seen, heard and smelled angels, who often leave distinctive, sweet perfumes in the air. Literally scores of saints reportedly were guided by their GUARDIAN ANGELS or other angels in their quest to perfect their souls. Stories of the early Christian martyrs tell of angels who comforted them during their tortures and gave them courage, and who stood ready to take their souls to heaven upon death. Some of these are legend and have not been historically substantiated, but some later saints had angelophanies in the presence of witnesses who—even if they could not sense what the saints were experiencing—could at least document what they observed in the behavior of the saints. Visions, voices, singing and odors are common in hagiographies. Although names of angels are important in esoteric and mystical literature (see NAMES OF ANGELS), the angels manifesting to saints do not give names. Some identify themselves by class (seraphim, cherubim, archangel, etc.), but usually they are referred to only as "angel" or "guardian angel." The Catholic church forbids the use of proper angel names other than the three mentioned in Catholic canon: MICHAEL, GABRIEL and RAPHAEL.

St. Simeon Stylites (390–459), who was one of the oddest of the martyrs, spent the last thirty-seven years of his life confined of his own accord to the top of a sixty-foot-high pillar. His disciples gave him food and removed his waste with buckets and ropes. Even this deprivation was not enough for him, however, so he had himself bound to the platform so tightly that the ropes cut into his flesh and maggots began to eat at the wounds. It was documented that he was often and visibly visited by his guardian angel, who devoted many hours to teaching him the mysteries of God. The angel also foretold his death.

St. FRANCIS OF ASSISI beheld an angel who played the violin for him, filling him with such joy that he thought his soul would leave his body. A seraph also gave him his stigmata. St. FRANCES OF ROME was able to see and hear a guiding angel for the last twenty-eight years of her life.

St. Gemma Galgani (1878–1903) had a rich visionary life, recorded in detail in her diaries and letters. She saw her guardian angel and heard his voice. Her conversations with her angel were observed and recorded by others who could

*Portrait of St. Francis Xavier* (Bartolomé Esteban Murillo, c. 1670; reprinted courtesy of the Ella Gallup Sumner and Mary Catlin Sumner Collection Fund, Wadsworth Atheneum, Hartford, Conn.)

only hear one side of the conversation—hers. Her spiritual director commented that whenever she saw or listened to her angel, she entered into an ecstatic state of consciousness, lost in another world; as soon as she turned her eyes away, she resumed her usual personality.

Gemma's angel was her constant companion, so familiar that she often treated him like a brother. She was once admonished by Father Germano, her spiritual director—who overheard one of her one-way conversations—that she should treat him with more respect. She agreed, and vowed to remain one hundred steps behind the angel whenever she saw him coming.

Whenever Gemma was plagued by evil spirits, she called upon her angel. In 1900 she recorded an episode in which she was harassed for hours by the devil in the form of a horrible "little fellow." She was assaulted by blows upon her shoulders while she prayed. Her angel appeared and, curiously, attempted to beg off her request to stay with her all night. He told her he had to sleep. When she replied that the "Angels of Jesus do not need to sleep," he said he still needed to rest. Nonetheless he remained, and spread his wings over her while she slept.

Sometimes the angel was severe with her, in word or expression, as a way of trying to keep her on the straight and narrow spiritual path. He would find fault with her, and tell

her he was ashamed of her. If she strayed from the path, he would depart from her presence for a while (this departure of divine grace, either in the form of the presence of an angel or the presence of God, appears often in the literature of saints).

Perhaps the most remarkable trademark of Gemma's angel was his couriership. She would send him off on errands to deliver verbal messages to people in distant places, and return with their replies. Gemma considered this angelic postal service to be a natural thing. Others reportedly received the messages. Sometimes replies were delivered back to her by the guardian angel of Father Germano. When some suggested that this was the work of the devil, Father Germano subjected Gemma to various spiritual tests, asking for irrefutable signs, and got them.

On June 8, 1899, when Gemma was twenty-two, she received the stigmata. Her angel then helped her climb into bed.

Gemma was visited by other angels as well, and often by Father Germano's guardian angel, who, she said, had a brilliant star over his head. No thought or deed of hers ever escaped angelic attention. If she was distracted in prayer, her angel would punish her. If she did not feel well, or if she would not eat enough, the angel exhibited a tender side, inquiring after her welfare and urging her to eat.

Modern angelophanies differ significantly from those described in the past. In the modern West, the culture does not support grand prophetic visions in the style of the Old Testament prophets; however, the NEAR-DEATH EXPERIENCE incorporates many of the same elements (guiding beings of light, visions of heaven, prophetic visions of the future, warnings about the present course of humanity).

Nor do many people in the modern West in the secular world report constant communication with angels in the fashion of the saints. Jayne M. Howard, author of *Commune With the Angels*, is an "open channel" with the angelic realm, and receives constant communication and guidance from a variety of angels and archangels. Howard hears angels and visually perceives them as ripples and waves of light, and also in human form. She senses angels with inner eyes and inner ears, yet says she sees and hears them as if they were people present speaking to her.

Modern research shows that for many people, an angelophany is a once-in-a-lifetime event, usually in response to a crisis or severe psychological need. Angels are most likely to appear as mortals, either adult or child (see MYSTERIOUS STRANGER). Other visual perceptions are of balls, clouds and pillars of light (in Exodus, the Israelites are led out of Egypt by a pillar of cloud in the day and a pillar of fire at night, widely interpreted as angels). If angels manifest as being of light, they invariably have a beautiful human form and countenance; rarely are wings ever reported (see WINGS). Many people believe that angels have appeared to them in the form of animals. Some people have experiences that could be classed as angelophanies, though they do not identify any presences as "angels" (see Charles LINDBERGH). This may be due to cultural conditioning in which individuals do not believe in "real" angels or in the possibility of encountering angels.

Many angelophanies take place on the inner planes, without phenomena perceived by the external senses. People who attempt to cultivate communication with angels do so in meditation and prayer; many feel they receive spiritual guidance in return.

A modern trend has been to name angels who manifest regularly or who seem to be guardian angels. This is due in part to a belief that names have power, and also to a desire to feel personally close to angels.

For many people, an angelophany bolsters spiritual faith, or jolts one on to a spiritual path.

**Further reading:**

Adler, Mortimer J. *The Angels and Us.* New York: Collier Books/ Macmillan, 1982.
Connolly, David. *In Search of Angels.* New York: Perigee Books, 1993.
Gordon, Anne. *A Book of Saints.* New York: Bantam Books, 1994.
Guiley, Rosemary Ellen. *Angels of Mercy.* New York: Pocket Books, 1994.
Parente, Fr. Pascal P. *The Angels: The Catholic Teaching on the Angels.* Rockford, Ill.: Tan Books and Publishers, 1973. First published 1961.
Parisen, Maria (comp.) *Angels & Their Co-Creative Power.* Wheaton, Ill.: Quest Books, 1990.
O'Sullivan, Fr. Paul. *All About the Angels.* Rockford, Ill.: Tan Books and Publishers, 1990. First published 1945.

**angels of destruction**    Angels who function as the "Sword of God," and who are dispatched to mete out punishment to humans. Punishment can be in the form of illness, plague, pestilence, misfortune or death.

Angels of destruction specifically named are URIEL, Harbonah, Azrael (the ANGEL OF DEATH), Simkiel, Za'afiel, Af, Kolazonta, Hermah and Kemuel. Various sources cite either Kemuel or Simkiel as chief of the group. Other angels not specifically "angels of destruction" also carry out God's orders of punishment. The archangel GABRIEL sometimes is cited as the angel dispatched to destroy the wicked SODOM AND GOMORRAH. Accounts of destroying angels often do not give names of the angels.

Numbers of angels of destruction also vary according to source, ranging from 40,000 total to 90,000 in hell alone.

**The Destroying Angel (reprinted courtesy of U.S. Library of Congress)**

Numerous incidents of angelic punishment are cited in Scripture and other religious tracts. The *Zohar*, a kabbalistic work, observes that there is no act of annihilation or punishment that does not involve a destroying angel.

Besides the destruction of Sodom and Gomorrah, biblical accounts of punishing angels include a number of episodes, among them the following.

In 2 Kings 19, King Hezekiah battles the Assyrians, and is assured by God that not a single Assyrian arrow will be shot into Jerusalem. A lone destroying angel visits the Assyrian soldiers one night, and the next morning all 185,000 of the troops are found dead.

However, God is not so pleased with Jerusalem, because King David has displeased him (1 Chronicles 21). SATAN incites David to number (count) Israel against God's orders. God gives David a choice of punishments (1 Chronicles 21:11–12): "Take what you will: either three years of famine; or three months of devastation by your foes, while the sword of your enemies overtakes you; or else three days of the sword of the Lord, pestilence upon the land, and the angel of the Lord destroying throughout all the territory of Israel." David opts not to be punished by his mortal enemies. God sends the pestilence and the destroying angel. David sees the angel, stretched between heaven and earth, ready to smite Jerusalem with his sword, and begs for mercy. The angel instructs him to set up an altar. David does so, and offers a sacrifice to God. The Lord accepts, and orders the angel to stay his hand.

One of the best-known accounts is that of the destroying angel who slaughters the firstborn of Egypt in the Passover, recounted in Exodus 12:18–30. God warns the Israelites held captive in Egypt that he will pass judgment on the land. The faithful are told to smear blood on their lintels and doorposts as a sign. At midnight on the appointed night, the destroying angel sweeps over Egypt and kills the firstborn of man and beast in every household except those houses whose lintels have been marked by blood.

In Job 2, Satan again functions as an angel of destruction when God, seeking to test Job's faith as a righteous man, delivers Job into Satan's hands. Satan smites Job with "loathsome sores" (boils) all over his body, but Job only curses the day of his birth, and not God. Eventually, God restores Job to favor and rewards him with prosperity.

Punishing angels appear in the New Testament as well. In Matthew 13, Jesus goes out into a boat and addresses a large crowd on shore, speaking in parables. In 13:47–50, he describes the kingdom of heaven as like a net thrown into the sea, which gathers every kind of fish. Fishermen must sort out the good from the bad. "So it will be at the close of the age," he explains. "The angels will come out and separate the evil from the righteous and throw them into the furnace of fire; there men will weep and gnash their teeth."

Acts 12 tells of the punishment of King Herod. Herod is angry with the people of Tyre and Sidon. A group of them come to him and ask him for peace, because their people depend on his country for food. Herod dons his royal robes, ascends his throne and delivers an oration to them. They cry out, "The voice of a god, and not of man!" (Acts 12:22). Acts 12:23: "Immediately an angel of the Lord smote him, because he did not give God the glory; and he was eaten by worms and died."

REVELATION, a vision of the end of times, is filled with angels of destruction who obliterate sinners. Revelation 8 describes seven angels who blow their trumpets, raining down upon the earth hail and fire mixed with blood, turning part of the sea into blood, dimming the sun, moon and stars and wreaking tremendous havoc. A host of angels unleash pestilence, plagues, searing fires and earthquakes upon the earth. The angels promise to torture with fire and sulphur anyone who worships "the beast" (the Devil). The author of Revelation is assured that Jesus has sent his angel to reveal the prophecies, and to remind people that he is "coming soon, bringing my recompense, to repay everyone for what he has done. I am the Alpha and the Omega, the first and the last, the beginning and the end." (Revelation 22:12–13)

The concept of angels of destruction conflicts with certain modern and popular ideas about angels as beings solely of goodness, protection and beneficence. The body of early lore on angels presents them as neither intrinsically "good" nor "bad," but as capable of acting out in either "good" or "bad" ways as seen from the perspective of the human recipient. Angels are charged with carrying out the instructions of God, whether they be to reward or punish. The New Testament gives us the concept of evil, or "fallen" angels, thrust out of heaven and into hell; these became synonymous with DEMONS, malicious beings which exist in all mythologies.

**Further reading:**

Davidson, Gustav. *A Dictionary of Angels*. New York: The Free Press, 1967.

Graham, Billy. *Angels: God's Secret Agents*. New York: Doubleday & Co., 1975.

Guiley, Rosemary Ellen. *Angels of Mercy*. New York: Pocket Books, 1994.

**angels of the elements**    See ELEMENTAL.

**angels of the presence**    A group of exalted angels who are close to God. According to the Book of Jubilees, a pseudepigraphical work dating to the mid-second century, the angels of the presence, along with other angels, were created by God on the first day.

Traditionally, there are twelve angels of the presence: MICHAEL, METATRON, SANDALPHON, URIEL, JAHOEL, Suriel, Astanphaeus, Saraqael, PHANUEL, Zagzagael, Yefefiah and Akatriel. Rabbinic lore also describes seventy tutelary angels as "angels of the presence."

The angels of the presence keep the cosmic secrets. According to Jubilees, it is one of these angels (not named) who orders MOSES, when he is atop Mt. Sinai, to take down every word that God speaks. The *Zohar* says that these angels were expelled from heaven when they revealed the mystery of God's purpose.

Another term for angels of the presence is "angels of the face."

**angels of the winds**    See NATURE SPIRIT.

**Anpiel**    In kabbalistic lore, the angel who protects birds. Anpiel resides in the Sixth Heaven. He wears seventy crowns, crowns all prayers sent up from earth and sends them up to the Seventh Heaven. In *The Legends of the Jews*, Anpiel is credited with taking ENOCH to heaven.

The Angel of Prayer (reprinted courtesy of U.S. Library of Congress)

**Apocalypse**    See REVELATION, BOOK OF.

**Apocrypha**    Additional, or "hidden," books of the Old Testament, which are excluded from the Hebrew canon and from some versions of the complete Bible. Some apocryphal writings contain important information about angels, which continues to influence modern thought.

All Bibles contain the same twenty-seven books of the New Testament, and the thirty-nine books of the Old Testament that are part of the Hebrew canon. In addition there are fifteen books or portions of books sometimes appended to the Old Testament. These comprise the Apocrypha, a word that means "things that are hidden." Two interpretations can be made of the term. One is that the books were deliberately hidden from all but initiates because of their profound esoteric lore. The other is that the books were hidden because they were heretical.

Lists of the Apocrypha vary. *The New Oxford Annotated Bible* gives these:

1 Esdras
2 Esdras
Tobit
Judith
Additions to the Book of Esther

The Wisdom of Solomon
Ecclesiasticus, or the Wisdom of Jesus the Son of Sirach
Baruch
The Letter of Jeremiah
The Prayer of Azariah and the Song of the Three Young Men
Susanna
Bel and the Dragon
The Prayer of Manasseh
1 Maccabees
2 Maccabees

Eastern Orthodoxy also considers 3 Maccabees, 4 Maccabees, and Psalm 151 to be part of the Apocrypha (4 Maccabees is placed in an appendix).

Acceptance or rejection of the Apocrypha has varied over the centuries. The texts were written primarily between 200 B.C.E. and 200 C.E. Though they are not part of the Hebrew canon, many of the Old Testament books refer to the Apocrypha. None of the New Testament books do, however.

The Septuagint, the Greek version of the Old Testament, includes the Apocrypha. Thus, most of the early fathers of the Christian church accepted the Apocrypha as Scripture. In the fourth century, the great biblical scholar St. Jerome was commissioned by Pope Damascus to prepare a standard Latin version of the Bible. Jerome's version, known as the Latin Vulgate, included the Apocrypha, but noted that they

Angels gazing toward the world of archetypes, with correspondences in Sphere of Nature below (Malachias Geiger, *Microcosmus Hypochondriacus*, 1652)

belonged in a separate category from the Old Testament. This distinction was a subtle one to many, and the Apocrypha generally were considered to be part of the Scriptures up through the Middle Ages.

The first English version of the Bible, translated from the Latin Vulgate near the end of the fourteenth century, includes all of the Apocrypha but 2 Esdras, but makes a distinction between the Apocrypha and other Scriptures. The Protestant Reformation saw numerous disputes over doctrine. English Protestants eventually rejected the books as sources of doctrine, and excluded them from The Revised Standard Version of the Bible.

In response in part to the Reformation, the Apocrypha were officially declared part of the Christian canon in 1546 by the Council of Trent, and anyone who did not accept them was declared anathema. However, the books are given a lesser status than the rest of the Scriptures.

In angelology, the most important apocryphal work is the Book of Tobit, which tells the story of the blind man Tobit, his son Tobias, and the archangel RAPHAEL (see TOBIT). It is considered to be an historically based novel, the purpose of which is to impart lessons on righteousness and morality, and to teach occult lore concerning healing and exorcism.

Despite their troubled standing in doctrine, the Apocrypha nonetheless have wielded a tremendous influence upon the arts, especially poetry, drama, music, literature, sculpture and painting. Shakespeare may have been familiar with the Apocrypha—the matter is debated by scholars—and Handel definitely was influenced. Depictions of Raphael and Tobias, painted by the old masters of the Middle Ages and Renaissance, hang in most art galleries in Europe and America.

See also PSEUDEPIGRAPHA.

**Further reading:**
*The New Oxford Annotated Bible with the Apochrypha.* Herbert G. May and Bruce M. Metzger, eds. New York: Oxford University Press, 1977.
*The Lion Encyclopedia of the Bible.* Pat Alexander, ed. Batavia, Ill.: Lion Publishing Corp., 1986.

**Apollyon** See ABADDON.

**Apsara** See HINDUISM.

**Aquinas, St. Thomas** (1225–1274) The great medieval scholar and "Doctor of the Church," St. Thomas Aquinas is still considered the chief synthesizer of philosophy and theology for the Catholic church. The 1917 Code of Canon Law lists only Aquinas as being required for the training of priests "according to his method, doctrine and principles," and the 1983 Code states that Aquinas is to be taken "in particular as their teacher." Catholic children are taught to invoke St. Thomas at the beginning of study. In his forty-six years, at a phenomenal rate, Aquinas synthesized in the light of *sacra doctrina* (God's truths revealed in Scripture) Plato, Aristotle and their interpreters; the other classical Greek and Roman thinkers; all preceding Christian fathers and contemporary theologians; Arab and Jewish philosophers and texts. His early death may have been caused by overwork. About a thousand years following AUGUSTINE's *City of God*, Aquinas provided the church with a second grand synthesis: a system

of *sacra doctrina* in the context of all knowledge available in the West at the time, coupled with a strong method of ordering, reason and argument. Thomistic angelology became that of the Catholic church, and remains so.

### A SUMMARY OF AQUINAS'S LIFE

Aquinas was born Tomasso Aquino into the central Italian local gentry in Roccasecca near Aquino. At the age of six he was sent to study at the famous Benedictine monastery at Montecassino. When he was fourteen he entered the University of Naples, known for being innovative and for being one of the first conduits of Aristotle's complete works, which had only recently entered the Western world via Arabic translations. At eighteen Aquinas decided to join the Dominicans, a new order of mendicant monks especially committed to study, teaching and preaching. His family attempted to foil this decision by detaining him for almost two years, but they failed to deter him.

He rejoined his Dominican brethren and soon was sent to Paris, where he transcribed the lectures of the Dominican scholar Albert (St. Albert the Great) on Dionysius the Areopagite (see PSEUDO-DIONYSIUS), a strong influence on Aquinas's angelology. From 1248 to 1252 Aquinas lived at the priory of the Holy Cross in Cologne, studying with Albert especially the works of Aristotle, impressing his teachers and superiors. Tradition says he was called "the dumb ox" because he was physically heavy and had a silent, reserved manner. Albert reportedly told his classmates: "We call this lad a dumb ox, but I tell you that the whole world is going to hear his bellowing!"

Aquinas was then sent back to Paris to prepare to teach Dominicans. He received a license to teach in 1256 and first worked as an apprentice professor lecturing on Scripture. Next he was promoted to teach on the official university textbook for theological instruction, the *Sentences* of Peter Lombard. Throughout his years of official teaching and writing, Aquinas carried on a "moonlighting" project: his line-by-line commentary on Aristotle's texts. In 1257 he was made a professor of theology and for the next few years lectured on the Bible and worked on a series of discussions based on classroom debates. These became some of his earliest written works, the so-called Disputed Questions, one *On Spiritual Creatures*, his earliest comment on angels. From 1258 to 1269 Aquinas taught in various cities in Italy: Naples, as Dominican preacher general; Orvieto, in the curia of Pope Urban IV; and in 1267–68 at Viterbo, with Pope Clement IV. In 1269 he returned to Paris to resume his teaching post, and wrote volumes. In addition to his incessant work, he was devoted to prayer and to the life of his religious order.

Aquinas's complete writings include biblical commentaries, his series on Aristotle, and polemical tracts. His most famous works are two enormous treatises covering the whole range of Christian doctrine and its philosophical background: the *Summa Contra Gentiles* ("on the truth of the Catholic faith against the unbelievers," supposedly commissioned as an aid to Dominican missionaries); and the *Summa Theologica*, ranging over God, creation, angels, human nature and happiness, grace, virtues, Christ, and sacraments. Begun in 1266, it remained unfinished at his death. The *Summa Theologica* amazed Aquinas's own and subsequent generations with its orderly system, unflagging intellectual eagerness, and sustained clarity. He acquired a reputation for supernormal mental capacity. One report said that he dictated to more than one secretary on different subjects at the same time; another insisted that he composed even in his sleep.

In December 1273 he suddenly abandoned his usual routine and neither wrote nor dictated anything else. When urged by his serving companion to return to work, he reportedly replied: "No, Reginald, I cannot, because all that I have written seems like straw to me." He may have been affected by a dream. Or, he may have suffered a stroke or breakdown from nervous exhaustion caused by overwork. Soon he was called to attend the Second Council of Lyons as Dominican theologian. He set out in late December, and became ill on the way. He lodged with his niece in Maenza, but after two months it is said he told her, "if the Lord is coming for me, I had better be found in a religious house than a castle." He was taken to a nearby Cistercian monastery, where he died in a guest room on March 7.

When it was protested at the canonization proceedings for Thomas Aquinas that few miracles were attributed to him, Pope John XXII declared that every proposition he wrote was a miracle. He was canonized in 1323, named *Doctor Angelicus* of the church by Pius X in 1567, and declared patron saint of the Catholic schools by Leo XIII in 1880.

### THOMISTIC METHOD

It struck Aquinas in his early study of Aristotle that philosophers had arrived at truths about God which are equivalent to some revealed truths. The first question that Aquinas takes up in *Summa Theologica* is: What need is there for any science other than those that make up philosophy? The question makes sense only if one knows those philosophical sciences. The answer is: We cannot arrive at the revealed content of Christian faith merely by philosophical argument. Philosophical argument, however, is the most convincing way to present all truths. Aquinas's reasoning and communication method was firmly grounded in Aristotle's, and his major teacher, Albert, was an Aristotelian thinker as well. In short, he approaches theological issues like a philosopher.

Aquinas's treatment of angels fits into the schematic typical of all his thinking and writing: a synthesis of *sacra doctrina*—what can be assumed true from Scripture as revealed by God (theology)—and what can be assumed true on the basis of common experience of the world (philosophy). He applies to angels the same grid he applies to God, creation, the soul, etc., involving language and distinctions common to philosophic discourse: cause and effect, general and principal causes, matter and form, essence and being.

### EXISTENCE OF ANGELS

Aquinas believed and proved that the world, including matter itself, was created by God. Angels are creatures whose existence can be demonstrated. In certain exceptional cases they have even been seen, which Scripture attests. To disregard them destroys the balance of the universe considered as a whole. God's principal end in creation is the supreme good constituted by assimilation to God. God produces creatures by intelligence and by will. Thus the perfection of the universe demands the existence of intellectual creatures. Since the object of the intellect is the universal, and the particularity of bodies does not fulfill that object, there should be some

intellectual creatures that do not have bodies. This amounts to saying that the perfection of the universe demands the existence of creatures totally stripped of matter or of body. Otherwise, the general plan of creation would show an obvious gap if there were no angels in it, since the hierarchy of beings is continuous.

In addition, the nature and operation of inferior creatures such as human beings can be placed in perspective by comparison and contrast with angels. Among the many forms of being, the human soul has just that degree of perfection or actuality whereby it is able to subsist apart from matter but is not able to do so in full possession of individual and specific being. The forms of being above humankind (i.e., the angels) are pure forms, unmixed with matter. Every angel is a complete species of being in itself, a single pure form which actualizes in its own individuality the full perfection of a whole species. Since it can so exist, it does not need to be repeated over and over in matter in order to fill out a specific degree of perfection (*Summa Theologica*, I, 76, 5).

The human soul, on the contrary, is specifically incomplete; it is a form, but not a species. It becomes a species through the principle of matter, involving repetition and numerical multiplicity; the species is a composite of human souls and bodies. The human intelligence issues from its senses, which are lodged in the body. Below humans are living beings without intellect; why not intellectual beings without bodies above humans? The imperfect in any genus always points to the more perfect in that genus, and ultimately to the absolutely perfect. Therefore it is impossible to believe that the human intellect, the most imperfect conceivable, should be the only intellect, or even the only created intellect. Intellect and matter are the opposite poles of being, and if, as in humanity, intellect is found united with matter, then most surely it exists also separate from matter. Consequently, the existence of angels is perfectly credible on grounds of natural reason alone. (*Summa Theologica*, I, 50, 1, 2; *Contra Gentiles* II, 91; *Spiritual Creatures*, V).

### THE NATURE OF ANGELS

The attributes of angels are enumerated in *Summa Theologica* Ia, 54–60. Aquinas demonstrates that these are consistent with what he has established as the angels' being: pure spirits, immaterial intelligence. Space does not here allow more than a one- or two-sentence presentation of key features. Mortimer J. Adler's *The Angels and Us* is a useful follow-up; he pursues in depth and puts into context many of Aquinas's most pertinent ideas on angels.

The angels are most probably more numerous than all material things. The angels cannot die, decay, break up or be substantially changed, since they are incorruptible substances. Angels are pure spirits without bodies, but angels assume bodies as instruments through angelic power, as when the archangel RAPHAEL accompanied Tobias, but they are not exercising the true functions of a bodily life. An angel is not in a place as contained by a place, but as containing a place; angels are present definitively. To show what that means, Aquinas makes an admittedly imperfect comparison of sunlight being in a room and beyond the room too. An angel cannot be in several places at once, nor can two angels be in the same place at the same time because there cannot be more than one complete cause of the same effect. Angels do not have to move through space to get from one place to another; they exercise their power to be in one place and are there. But they can move in time instantaneously from one to another place, though not measurably by our minutes and seconds.

Humans have an active and passive intellect, whereby they process their sense experience, but angels have their knowledge directly from God at creation; thus, they need not learn nor work anything out. However, they can have knowledge of the material things which human beings know by the senses. The degrees of knowledge in angels follow a hierarchy. Each angel receives what is fitting depending on its status and service. Aquinas compares these degrees of knowledge to light (God's knowledge) passing through successive panes of glass.

Can angels know the future? Yes, for the operation of existing and necessitating causes. Yes, conjecturally (following from logic). No, they cannot know future events themselves. Only God knows this. Humans also can have future knowledge of the first two kinds, but angels possess it far more perfectly. An angel cannot know the secret thoughts or will of humans or another angel. They must be "spoken to" by both humans and other angels. Angels do not know the workings of divine grace *de natura* (by virtue of their very nature), but higher angels impart their knowledge of such mysteries to the lower angels. The angelic mind is like a clear mirror that takes in the full meaning of what it turns upon. Angels also know how humans go about composing, dividing and reasoning, though they do not do so themselves. A good angel knows no falsehood, nor errs; the fallen angels are totally divorced from divine wisdom, and so are prone to err in things supernatural. Aquinas agrees with Augustine's distinction between angelic "morning" and "evening" knowledge, the former being of the thing as it is in God, and the latter being as it is in its own nature.

Angels have free will and exercise it more perfectly than humans, since they have no outside influences from senses. Where there is will, there is love; therefore the angels have love. Angelic love is knowledge of an intellectual order and involves not only inclination but choice. Angels love themselves both by natural tendency and by choice. Since angels are all of the same nature, they love one another. (Though they are generically one—same genus—they are specifically distinct—different in essential kind.) By natural love, angels love God more than they love themselves.

God alone exists from eternity. It is most likely that angels and the bodily world were created at the same time, not angels first. Angels were created in heaven, with happiness *de natura*, but not in glory, the possession of the beatific vision. Angels were created with sanctifying grace, leaving them free to choose love of God, but not confirmed in that choice, because some angels fell. Those who chose God gained the beatific vision, and they enjoy it according to their status in the hierarchy. Beatified angels cannot sin. There is no evolution in their degree of beatitude, since a capacity that is perfectly filled up cannot be made more full.

The sinning angels are guilty of all sins, in that they lead men to commit every kind of sin, but they have no tendency to fleshly sins themselves. They commit only two sins: pride and envy. LUCIFER wanted to be as God, a prideful sin because he knew that equality with the creator was impossible,

(self-deception being impossible for angels, even Lucifer). He wanted to be like God in a way not suited to his nature. The evil angels are not naturally evil, nor created in wickedness. But they sinned immediately after creation, rejecting the good that was meant for them. Lucifer probably was highest of the angels before his fall. But some say he was only the highest of the angels who fell. He attracted the others, who fell by bad example, and to this extent he was the cause of their sin.

There are more good angels than fallen angels, because sin is contrary to the natural order. The fallen angels lost neither their natural knowledge nor their angelic intellect by their fall. They are unrepentant and inflexibly determined in sin, since a being of immaterial spirit is necessarily final and unchanging. There is sorrow in them, though not repentance, in knowing that they cannot attain beatitude though humans may get to heaven. The fallen angels are engaged in battling against human salvation and in torturing lost souls in hell. Wherever they are, they endure the pains of hell.

### THE DIVINE GOVERNMENT

Another chapter of *Summa Theologica* (Ia, 103–119) is devoted to the order of the cosmos, ruled by God's divine goodness. God directly preserves all that he created; otherwise it would fall back into nothingness. He does not delegate. He is in all conserving forces such as air, light, warmth. He does not annihilate anything, since that would be contrary to divine wisdom. God works in all things in such a way as suits the operation natural to each thing. An effect produced in the bodily universe outside of this natural order of creation is a miracle.

Superior angels can enlighten inferior angels but cannot influence their will. The higher the angel the more it partakes in the divine good, and the more it gives. They remain superior even when they give all their knowledge, for the lower angels have less capacity than the superior.

Angelic speech has nothing to do with sounds or words and is not impeded by time or distance. An angel speaks by directing its thought to another angel. Angels "speak" to God by consulting his divine will and contemplating him.

Just as there is human hierarchy so there is angelic hierarchy, according to the three grades of angelic knowledge. Each hierarchy has three orders. In all there are nine orders of angels (specifics on these nine orders follow). The fallen angels have hierarchy insofar as some subjugate others. They (demons) do have speech like beatified angels, but they do not enlighten their inferiors. The nearer creatures are to God, the greater is their rule over other creatures. Therefore the good angels rule and control the demons.

### ANGELS, DEMONS, GUARDIAN ANGELS IN THE BODILY WORLD

Superior rules inferior, therefore angels rule the bodily world in the sense that they can stir bodily agencies to change. They cannot of themselves work miracles, which is God's proper work, but they do serve as ministers or instruments in working miracles. As angels are superior to humans, they can act upon the human intellect by strengthening awareness and understanding. They cannot influence human will, but both good and bad angels can indirectly affect human will by stirring up images in the human imagination. Angels also can work upon the human senses, either outwardly by assuming some visible form, or inwardly by disturbing the sense functions themselves; for example, by making one see what is not there.

God sends angels to minister to his purposes in the bodily world. Only five orders of angels are sent for the external ministry; the superior angels are never sent. Aquinas agrees with St. Jerome's commentary on Matthew 18:10 that each human soul has a GUARDIAN ANGEL.

This office is taken by the ninth order, the angels. The guardian angel comes at the moment of birth, not at the moment of baptism. In hell, each fallen human soul will have a fallen angel to punish him. Angel companions will be given to the human who gains heaven, a different kind from the angel guardian. Guardian angels never fail or forsake their charges. Humans cannot teach or enlighten angels, but through speech or prayer can make known to angels their thoughts and wishes, which the angels would not otherwise know. The guardian angels do not will the sin their wards commit, nor directly will their punishment. They do will the fulfillment of divine justice, which requires free will; hence sin is probable followed by trouble, including punishment. All angels are in perfect accord with the divine will insofar as it is revealed to them, but there may arise conflict between them because their revelations of the divine will differ.

God gives humans the requisite aid to resist the temptations of demons; God permits sin and turns it into human benefit and opportunity. The devil (Satan, the fallen Lucifer) plans exclusively all the campaigns and assaults on mankind. In a strict sense, humans can sin on their own, out of their weakness and inordinate appetites, without any temptation by a demon. After an assault God's mercy provides, so it seems, a breathing space; because the demon cannot return at once to strike again. Angels cannot perform miracles, and neither can demons, but they can do astonishing things, and cause real havoc.

### THE TRIADIC HIERARCHY

The three tiers of the angelic hierarchy seem at first glance to be arranged paradoxically. Quality equals simplicity; the lower the nature of intelligence, the more numerous its means of knowing. What constitutes relative superiority among created beings is their greater or lesser proximity and resemblance to the first being, God. God's total fullness in knowledge is all together at one point, His Essence, in which he knows all things. The closer the creature is to His Essence, the less differentiated will be its intelligence. The first triad know intelligible essences as preceding from the first principle. The second triad know intelligibles as subjected to the most universal created causes. The third triad know intelligibles as applied to singular beings and dependent upon particular causes. Scholars have noted that Aquinas followed closely PSEUDO-DIONYSIUS's system in *The Celestial Hierarchy*. In *Summa Contra Gentiles*, Aquinas states his own thoughts before acknowledging Dionysius's points regarding each of the nine orders. Those texts are quoted below at the beginning of each order. The nine orders of angels, their names and features, have appeared in many cultures with many forms, some of which differ from Aquinas's scheme. Aquinas also treats the angelic hierarchy in *Summa Theologica* Ia, 108; additional comments on the hierarchies are summaries from this source. (See also separate listings for each order.)

### First Hierarchy (1); First Order: Seraphim

"Those who see most clearly are called seraphim, the ardent and burning ones, because to be designated in terms of fire associates one with the depth of love or of longing, and love and loving are directed toward the ultimate role. Therefore Dionysius the Areopagite says that this name indicates both their ardent immutability in regard to the Divine and their versatility in guiding those below them to God as the ultimate goal."

Angels of this hierarchy consider the highest end of the universe, which is the goodness of God. Those who see it most clearly are called seraphim because they are aglow, on fire with love for this object which they know with an exceedingly perfect love.

### First Hierarchy (2); Second Order: Cherubim

"The second rank fully acknowledge the ground of providence in the essential form of the Divine itself. They are called cherubim, which may be interpreted as 'fullness of knowledge,' in other words, knowledge is fulfilled through the essential form of the knowable. Therefore Dionysius says that this designation means that they are observers of the primal creative power of divine beauty."

The other angels of the first hierarchy contemplate the divine goodness not directly and in itself, but insofar as it is Providence. They are called cherubim, that is, fullness of science, because they see clearly the first operative principle of the divine model of things.

### First Hierarchy (3); Third Order: Thrones

"Those of the third rank contemplate the enactment of divine justice. They are called thrones, for the power of judgment is shown by the throne. Hence Dionysius says that this designation means that they are bearers of God and wholly capable of undertaking all that is divine."

### Second Hierarchy

"Among the lower spirits who receive from the higher spiritual beings a full knowledge of the divine order that they are to accomplish, there must be a hierarchy."

The second hierarchy does not know the reasons of things in God Himself, as in a sole object, but in the plurality of universal causes. Thus its proper object is the general disposition of means in view of their end. This supposes the existence of many directors.

### Second Hierarchy (1); Fourth Order: Dominations

"For providence is enacted through many agents; through the order of dominations. It is the concern of those who exercise dominion to command what others should do. Hence Dionysius says that the name "domination" indicates leadership in one's own right, removed from all serfdom and subjection."

### Second Hierarchy (2); Fifth Order: Virtues

"Second, the enactment of providence . . . is extended through many agencies, and through the power of VIRTUES. This order, as Dionysius says, indicates courage and maturity in all godly action, that no godly movement may languish in inertia. Clearly the primal ground of comprehensive action belongs to this order of angels. Therefore it would seem that this order is entrusted with the movement of the heavenly bodies. From them as from inclusive causes there derive the particular operations of nature; hence they are also known as the 'heavenly powers,' meaning that the celestial powers will be shaken (Luke 21:26). . . . Anything else that is inclusive and primary among the divine tasks . . . falls by rights to the lot of this order of angels."

The general directives issued by dominations are received by Virtues, who multiply them and channel them according to the various effects to be produced. They confer on the general causes the energy required for their numerous operations.

### Second Hierarchy (3); Sixth Order: Powers

"Third, the general order of providence, once it has taken effect, is unerringly preserved, and whatever could disturb that order is prevented. This is the concern of Powers. Hence Dionysius says that the name 'Powers' means well-ordered and precise enactment of what has been received from God."

### Third Hierarchy

"The lowest order among the higher spirits are those who receive the order of divine providence from God, so far as it is recognizable in its particular causes. These spirits are placed directly over human affairs . . . all lower beings and especially causes which are ordered in regard to man and serve the purposes of men. And among these spirits too there is a hierarchy."

The third hierarchy knows the order of Providence, not in itself nor in its general causes, but as it can be known in the multiplicity of particular causes; thus they are placed in immediate charge of the administration of things human.

### Third Hierarchy (1); Seventh Order: Principalities

"In human affairs there is a general good which is the welfare of the state or nation. That would seem to be the concern of the order of Principalities. Hence Dionysius says that the name 'Prince' indicates rule together with holy order. . . . Hence the order of kingdoms and the transitions from one tribe to another must be part of the work of this order of angels. It would also seem to be the office of this order to instruct those who are among men about all that concerns the exercise of rule."

### Third Hierarchy (2); Eighth Order: Archangels

"There is also a human good which is not located in the community but concerns the individual man in himself, but which is nevertheless of use not merely to one but to many men, as for instance that which is to be believed and followed by all as well as the individual; i.e., the worship of God. . . . That is the concern of the Archangels who, Gregory says, announce the highest things. Hence we call GABRIEL the Archangel because he announced the incarnation of the only-begotten Word, in whom all men must believe."

### Third Hierarchy (3); Ninth Order: Angels

"But other matters have more to do with the individual. They are the concern of the order of angels. Gregory says that they have to impart lesser things. They are also known as the guardians of men, in accordance with Scripture: 'For he has charged his angels to guard you wherever you go' (Psalms 91.11)."

**Further Reading:**
Adler, Mortimer J. *The Angels and Us.* New York: Macmillan, 1982.
Clark, Mary T. *An Aquinas Reader.* New York: Fordham University Press, 1988.
Davies, Brian. *The Thought of Thomas Aquinas.* Oxford: Clarendon Press, 1992.
Gilson, Etienne. *The Christian Philosophy of St. Thomas Aquinas.* Trans. L. K. Shook. New York: Random House, 1966.
McInerny, Ralph M. *A First Glance at St. Thomas Aquinas.* Notre Dame, Ind.: Notre Dame University Press, 1990.

**archetypes**    Universal primordial images and instincts that reside in the collective unconscious, and are expressed in behavior and experience. Archetypes have existed since the dawn of humanity. Mythologies, religions, sacred rites and folktales are especially rich in archetypal themes and characters (for example, the hero, the trickster, forces of nature, the elements are all archetypal representations). Angels are representations of archetypes.

Carl G. JUNG developed, but did not originate, the concept of archetypes. Heraclitus was the first to view the psyche as the archetypal first principle. Plato articulated the idea of archetypes in his Theory of Forms, which holds that the essence of a thing or concept is its underlying form or idea. The term "archetype" occurs in the writing of Philo Judaeus, Irenaeus, and PSEUDO-DIONYSIUS. The concept, but not the term, is found in the writings of St. AUGUSTINE.

Jung first wrote of primordial images in the unconscious of his patients in 1912. He first used the term "archetype" in 1919, in order to distinguish between the archetype itself and the archetypal image which is perceived on a conscious level.

*The Archangel Gabriel* **(Masolino da Panicale, c. 1420–30; reprinted courtesy National Gallery of Art, Washington, D.C., Samuel H. Kress Collection)**

Archetypes are without end, created by the repetition of situations and experiences engraved upon the psychic constitution. They are forms without content—they wait to be realized in the personality, and are recognizable in outer behaviors.

Archetypes are a means through which the *unus mundus*, the unitary world or undifferentiated whole, can express itself in our conscious reality. The *unus mundus* is found in all spiritual traditions and is lawfully ordered by a transcendent plan that links everything together. This order is of such a sublime nature that it is beyond sensory perception but can be grasped through expressions of archetypes. The expressions themselves are not archetypes but representations of archetypes. All psychic imagery, such as is found in dreams and sacred art and ritual, is archetypal to some extent.

Historian Mircea Eliade observes that human history is governed by archetypes, and is a reflection of celestial archetypes; thus, myths and symbols share similarities among diverse cultures. Cities, temples and houses represent the sacred center, for example, and the cross of Christianity represents the Cosmic Tree.

Thus it can be seen that angels are representations of the positive-negative polarity, the yin and yang, the light and dark, the good and evil. They also represent the ability of the human soul to ascend to heaven or descend to the underworld, as well as the immortality and inherent divine nature of the soul. The functions and characteristics ascribed to individual angels all express archetypes.

The stronger and more active is the belief in archetypal representations, the stronger they become in the collective unconscious and the more they express themselves by impinging on the outer world through such things as synchronistic events (in the case of angels, these would be an array of angelic interventions). The pagan deities of the classical world have lost strength due to neglect over ensuing centuries; meanwhile, the archetypal forces serving newer religions, such as Christianity, have gained strength. Angels reached a peak of popularity in the Middle Ages and then fell into disuse as a force active in the psyche. As of the late twentieth century, the angel archetypal force has been reactivated in Western consciousness.

**Further reading**
Eliade, Mircea. *The Myth of the Eternal Return.* Princeton: Princeton University Press, 1971. First published 1954.
_____. *Images and Symbols.* Princeton: Princeton University Press, 1991. First published 1952.
Jung, Carl G. *The Archetypes and the Collective Unconscious.* 2nd ed. Bollingen Series XX. Princeton: Princeton University Press, 1968.
Little, Gregory L. *People of the Web.* Memphis: White Buffalo Books, 1990.

**architecture**    See ART, ARCHITECTURE AND RITUAL, ANGELS IN.

**archons**    Ruling angels of the heavens and underworld, and also of nations. They are sometimes equated with AEONS and archangels (see CHOIRS).

In GNOSTICISM, Sophia's son IALDABAOTH creates archons to rule over all the hierarchies, but gives them lesser powers so that he can rule over all of them.

*The Hypostasis of the Archons* ("The Reality of the Rulers") is an anonymous Gnostic work that gives an esoteric interpretation of Genesis 1–6. Its date of origin is unknown, but it was originally written in Greek, probably in Egypt. Its contents show a Hellenistic syncretism. The document declares that archons are not imaginary, but are real. The archons generally exhibit arrogance, cruelty and base behavior; they are called the Rulers of Darkness and Rulers of Unrighteousness.

Norea, the daughter of Eve, cries out to God to be rescued from the clutches of the Rulers of Unrighteousness, and is immediately visited by Eleleth, the Great Angel who stands in the presence of the Holy Spirit. He says he is one of the Four Light-givers. None of the Rulers has true power here, he tells Norea, because they cannot prevail against the Root of Truth. He tells her the story of how the androgynous Ialdabaoth came into being, and how he created the archons, seven in number and all androgynous like himself. He proclaims himself "God of the entirety," which angers Zoe, the daughter of Sophia. She breathes fire into his face, and the fire becomes an angel and casts Ialdabaoth into the underworld (Tartaros).

His offspring Sabaoth repents and condemns his father and his mother (Matter), and Sophia and Zoe lift him up to the seventh heaven, where he rules in splendor. Ialdabaoth becomes jealous, and this is the origin of Envy. Envy engenders Death, and Death creates the offspring of Chaos (similar to the fallen angels). The lesson of the story is that when humans discover the Spirit of Truth, they will exist deathless. When Death is conquered, the archons (Authorities) will come to an end as well, and angels will weep over their destruction. Humanity will become the Children of Light.

**Further reading:**
Barnstone, Willis. *The Other Bible.* San Francisco: HarperSanFrancisco, 1984.

**Ariel (also Arael, Ariael)**    Angel whose name means "lion of God." Ariel appears in biblical, aprochryphal, Gnostic, Coptic and occult literature in a variety of guises, both angel and demon.

The apochryphal book of Ezra calls Ariel an angel. In the Old Testament, the book of Isaiah refers to Ariel as an altar, man and city. This was echoed by the Renaissance occultist Henry Cornelius Agrippa von Nettesheim, who referred to Ariel as a demon, angel or city. In Hebrew lore, Ariel is a name for Jerusalem, and in kabbalistic lore it is the name of a virtue. Ariel is ranked among the seven princes by Thomas Heywood in *The Hierarchy of the Blessed Angels*. In the Coptic *Pistis Sophia*, Ariel rules the lower world, and in GNOSTICISM he is associated with the creator god IALDABAOTH. In ceremonial magical texts, Ariel is described as a lion-headed angel.

Shakespeare named a fairy Ariel in *The Tempest*. Ariel also figures in Gaelic prayers of protection for the home and hearth.

**Further reading:**
Davidson, Gustav. *A Dictionary of Angels.* New York: Free Press, 1967.

**Aristotle**    See INTELLIGENCES.

**art, architecture and ritual, angels in**    Human fascination with angels, demigods, and daemons is augmented by the imagery that has been associated with art, places of worship, and ritual—sacred drama—from time immemorial. Artisans among tribal peoples and every sect worldwide—Hindu, Taoist, Buddhist, Zoroastrian, Sumerian, Egyptian,

Judaic, Christian and Islamic, as well as practitioners of various Hermetic and esoteric magic arts—memorialized the qualities and stories, archetypes and myths, of their spiritual allies and foes. Their iconography and imagery are preserved in ancient and medieval structures, museums, rare books and the field reports of archaeologists and anthropologists; much of it continues to be used and appreciated daily in millions of places of worship.

The sites and particulars of temples, churches, monastaries, and mosques were often dictated by gods/angels to the devotees who supervised their construction. Certain physical sites were considered "doorways" through which higher realms might be glimpsed or attained. The sea-girt island of Mont Saint-Michel, off the coast of Brittany in France, where a Cistercian monastery was constructed, carried just such a connotation. When stained glass came into use in Gothic cathedrals, the windows embodied this belief literally; sacred geometry expressed the divine emanational order of creation, including the ranks of angels. The architects of Chartres cathedral in particular were preoccupied with the alchemical notion of *anima mundi*, the world soul as link between God and creation. To the degree that the cathedral embodied the world soul on earth, reflecting its sacred laws of creation, harmony and proportion, it could mediate God and the human mind and spirit, just as angels do. In this sense the cathedral itself could become the holy alchemical "grail," the vessel of transformation. Sculpted and painted images and icons were also considered empowered, spiritual "windows" between this world and the others. Eastern orthodox icons still hold awe for this reason.

Rituals too were enacted in that liminal space, the threshold where humans ascend, God and the angels descend to become actors in sacred "play." Muhammad learned the words and gestures of the Islamic ritual prayer by observing the angels at worship. Rituals recreate the activities of angels in heaven, brought to humanity by prophets and seers who ascend to heaven, or angels who descend to earth. Art historian Peter Lamborn Wilson says that "ritual, by definition, must be Angelic because it belongs properly neither to 'this world' nor to the divine Essence beyond form, but plays an intermediary role between the two. Ritual is a Jacob's Ladder, and its celebrants climb, meeting the descending Angels halfway."

Liturgies often codify images as well as rituals for a congregation, according to its founder's visions. The Mevlevi Sufi order, "the whirling dervishes," conduct a sacred inner journey to the source of Being, to the point where one is closest to the Divine. The dervishes see themselves as participating in the music of the spheres, the Great Chain of Being, each in rapport with their holy teacher and with the enlightened state of the whole spiritual lineage, including their founder, the great mystic poet Mevlana Jalaluddin Rumi (1207–1273) and Muhammad. Various saints reported angels assisting or co-celebrating the Mass. Hermetic iconography, rituals and music were believed to have been brought to humanity by Hermes himself in a time before time. (See MUSIC AND ANGELS and LITERATURE AND ANGELS.)

### THE WING MOTIF

Wings indicate mystic travel when appended to beings, not birds. India's Garuda, the golden-winged sun bird, was a mysterious figure similar to the Persian *simurgh*. Garuda was variously pictured as a man, a bird, a man riding a bird, or a curious combination of human and avian characteristics. Though probably older than the religion of Vishnu, Garuda is now regarded as the vehicle of Vishnu, bearing the god either within or upon his back. In Egypt, the *ba* was one of each person's seven souls. Its usual form was that of a human-headed bird, and linked to the ancient worldwide concept of ancestors and ancestral divinities in bird shapes. The hawk was the totemic form of the god Horus, shown as a man's body with a hawk's head. Thoth, the Egyptian god comparable to Hermes, god of magic, spells, writing and record keeping, was depicted with the head of an ibis.

In about the eighth century B.C.E. the figure of a lordly helmeted four-winged man carrying corn and oil, called a "genius of blessing" by historians, was carved and painted in the Assyrian palace of Sargon and now rests in the Louvre. In the same museum stands a bronze statue of a demon with a similar wing arrangement from the same area and period. In Persepolis appears Ahura- Mazda ("Lord Wisdom") in a stone relief, the upper half of a man on a winged sun-disc. Winged lions, griffins, sphinxes, centaurs, bulls, enthroned or standing guard, abound in the ancient Middle East, along with bird-headed demons with wings. Wings can often be found on East Asian gods and demons.

Greek myth provided many winged images. A winged siren-handled cauldron dates from the eighth century B.C.E., a winged sphinx from 560 B.C.E. Nike, the victory aspect of Athena, was always pictured or sculpted winged. EROS, son of Aphrodite, like the angels of the Kabbalah, is a winged messenger, both Ancient of Days and naked graceful boy. In other contexts, like winged shamanic figures from diverse cultures, he acts as guide of the soul, the guardian or spiritual double of man, representing both spiritual master and beloved, and also trickster and magician.

Some of these qualities and many more were ascribed to Hermes (a universal Indo-European god much older than Greece, the original Hermaphrodite), whose iconography called for a helmet with wings and wings on the feet of his naked body. Dark-winged figures include the Furies, also called the Eumenides and the Erinyes, the personification of the vengeful aspect of Demeter, the "great lady who sends black-winged dreams" (Euripedes, *Hecuba*). Descriptions of winged harpies and fairies worldwide fall under the Greek rubric of imaging local daemons, "genii" of forests, wells, rivers, villages and homes.

In the *Phaedrus* Plato associated the wing with qualities that apply ubiquitously to angelic figures as symbols of spiritual ascent:

> The wing is the corporeal element which is most akin to the divine, and which by nature tends to soar aloft and carry that which gravitates downwards into the upper region, which is the habitation of the gods. The divine is beauty, wisdom, and the like; and by these the wing of the soul is nourished, and grows space. . . .

He added the aspect that became important to the concept of angelic INTELLIGENCES:

> The mind of the philosopher alone has wings; and this is just, for he is always, according to the measure of his abilities, clinging in recollection to those things in which God abides,

and in beholding which He is what He is. And he who employs aright these memories is ever being initiated into perfect mysteries and alone becomes truly perfect. But as he forgets earthly interests and is rapt in the divine, the vulgar deem him mad, and rebuke him; they do not see that he is inspired.

In Rome, Mercurius (Hermes), the "genii" of the seasons and the four directions, Fate and Victory, continued to be winged. Winged figures were painted on the walls of Pompeii. Since all pagan sects used wings for their gods, demigods, and demons, Christianity for several centuries eschewed the winged motif when depicting angels. The Divine Will was symbolized by the Hand of God in early iconography and was supplanted by angels, usually human bodies with accompanying attributes signifying their functions. A staff, as an indication of a messenger on a mission, was the sole attribute of an angel at first. An important early appearance of these creatures is on the chancel arch of St. Mary Major in Rome (c. 440 C.E.). *The Celestial Hierarchy* of Dionysius the Areopagite (see PSEUDO-DIONYSIUS) was influential in shaping the orders in Byzantine art (where the costumes of the angelic choirs represented the various grades of court attendants to the emperor). It was translated in the ninth century and used as an authority by St. Thomas AQUINAS in the thirteenth. This teaching was set forth at length in a popular form in Jacobus de Voragine's *Golden Legend* and became the chief reference for medieval artists. (See also WINGS.)

### CHRISTIAN ICONOGRAPHY OF ANGELS

Among the Greeks, the seraphim have six wings of fiery red and bear a flaming sword; their feet are bare. Cherubim have two blue wings and shod feet. Thrones are two fiery wheels with four eye-filled wings each. Dominations, virtues and powers are two-winged, wear long albs, golden girdles, and green stoles, hold the seal of Jesus Christ in their right hands, and a golden staff topped by a cross in their left hands. Principalities, archangels and angels appear as soldiers with two wings, golden belts, and lance-headed javelins.

Among Western images, certain other features distinguish the choirs. Cherubim can hold open books representing their fullness of knowledge, and stand on wheels. Thrones carry thrones or scales representing divine justice. Dominations have royal garments and crowns, carry scepters, orbs, swords or books. Virtues are vested in the garments of high ecclesiastics and carry liturgical items, lilies or red roses symbolic of Christ's passion. Powers sometimes hold rods or swords, wear knightly armor, and lead demons in chains. Principalities wear princely robes over armor, with crowns and sword or scepter. Archangels are shown as warriors in armor or deacons in albs.

Angels wear ecclesiastical garments and frequently wear a diadem with a cross in the front. A late medieval variation was to show them in clothing made of feathers. They carried many objects: candles, musical instruments, scrolls and inscribed shields. In the earliest Eastern icons, there are naked angels on the model of Eros and Hermes, a motif not to reemerge until the Renaissance PUTTI or so-called cherubs. The Renaissance started the stylization of angels that remains in Western art: the idealized human form, winged, rendered somehow more genuinely mystical. Boticelli, Raphael, Fra Angelico (given his name for his seraphically beautiful subjects), Titian, Tintoretto, Veronese, Perugino, Murillo, Rembrandt, Rubens, El Greco and legions of others created the images that come to mind when we think of angels in modern times.

MICHAEL, who in his office of "prince" of the Hebrew nation became, after Christian revelation, the guardian of the Church Militant in Christendom, is invariably depicted as young, beautiful and powerful, most often clothed in a coat of mail with sword, spear and shield, wings rising from his shoulders and sometimes wearing a jeweled crown. Frequently he is battling with Satan, represented as a dragon, serpent or demon. Medieval and Renaissance paintings also depict his intercession in the Old Testament in scenes from ABRAHAM, JACOB, MOSES and the battles led by Joshua. He plays an important role in the legends of the Virgin, as it was Michael who was sent to announce to the Virgin her approaching death and he who carried her body to heaven.

GABRIEL is the guardian of the celestial treasury, the Angel of Redemption and the Chief Messenger, with this latter role the most prominent in the series of artistic renderings of his delivering messages to DANIEL, Zechariah (see JESUS), and most notably, as the angel of the Annunciation, to Mary (Luke 1:26–28). Gabriel is a majestic, beautifully androgynous figure who wears a crown and is richly robed. He evokes purity by carrying a lily.

RAPHAEL, the guardian angel of all humanity, is represented as a benign friend and fellow traveler, protector of the young and innocent, rendered in episodes from the Book of TOBIT. He is dressed as a pilgrim, wears sandals and carries a staff and some supplies on his belt or slung over his shoulder. When he is portrayed as a guardian spirit he is richly dressed, has a casket of provisions and holds a sword in one hand, and makes a gesture of warning with the other. Christian tradition relates that it was Raphael who announced to the shepherds the arrival of the Savior on Christmas night: "Fear not; for behold, I bring you tidings of great joy. . . ." (Luke 2:10).

URIEL appears less frequently. Early legend states that it was Uriel who, as ambassador of Christ, appeared to the disciples at Emmaus (Luke 24). In art, Uriel usually is represented as carrying a scroll and a book indicating his role as interpreter of judgments and prophecies.

### ISLAMIC IMAGES OF ANGELS

Islam, contrary to popular opinion, does not prohibit images. In Sufi iconography ISRAFIL, the Angel of the Day of Judgment, has hairs and tongues over which are stretched veils. He glorifies Allah with each tongue in a thousand languages, and Allah creates from his breath a million angels who glorify Him. Israfil looks each day and each night toward Hell, approaches without being seen and weeps. His trumpet or horn has the form of a beast's horn and contains cells like a bee's honeycomb, in which the souls of the dead repose. Mika'il (Michael) has hairs of saffron from his head to his feet, and his wings are of green topaz. On each hair he has a million faces and on each face a million eyes, from which fall 70,000 tears each, and a million tongues, which speak a million languages. The tears become the

Kerubim, who lean down over the rain and the flowers, the trees and fruit.

Jibra'il (GABRIEL) has 1600 wings and hair of saffron. The sun is between his eyes. Each day he enters the Ocean of Light 360 times. When he comes forth, a million drops fall from each wing to become angels who glorify Allah. When he appeared to MUHAMMAD to reveal the Koran, his wings stretched from the East to the West. His feet were yellow, his wings green, and he wore a necklace of rubies or coral. Between his two eyes were written the words: "There is no God but Allah, and Muhammad is the Prophet of God." In icons and late medieval paintings he takes his more usual shape, that of a delicate and beautiful youth. One Sufi vision of Jibra'il shows him "like a maiden, or like the moon amongst the stars. His hair was like a woman's falling in long tresses. . . . He is the most beautiful of angels. . . . His face is like a red rose."

Azrael, the Angel of Death, is veiled before the creatures of God with a million veils. His immensity is vaster than the heavens, and the East and West are between his hands like a dish on which all things have been set, and he eats what he wishes. He has four faces, one before him, one on his head, one behind him, and one beneath his feet. He has four wings, and his body is covered with innumerable eyes. When one of these eyes closes, a creature dies.

**Further reading:**
Cavendish, Richard. *Visions of Heaven and Hell*. London: Orbis Publishing, 1970.
Cicciari, Massimo. *The Necessary Angel*. Albany: State University of New York Press, 1994.
Halewood, William H. *Six Subjects of Reformation Art*. Toronto: University of Toronto Press, 1982.
Wilson, Peter Lamborn. *Angels*. New York: Pantheon, 1980.
———. *Angels: Messengers of the Gods*. London: Thames and Hudson, 1980, 1994.

**Asmodeus**   A fallen angel who became the demon of lechery, jealousy, anger and revenge. The goals of Asmodeus are to prevent intercourse between husband and wife, wreck new marriages and force husbands to commit adultery. He also is frequently blamed in cases of demonic possession.

In the lore of fallen angels, Asmodeus is regarded as one of the most evil. He is usually portrayed as having three heads: that of an ogre, a ram and a bull, all sexually licentious creatures. He also has the feet of a cock, another sexually aggressive creature. He has ugly wings, rides on a dragon (a Christian symbol of Satan and evil) and breathes fire.

Asmodeus has his roots in ancient Persian mythology. He is identified with the demon Aeshma, one of seven archangels. The Hebrews absorbed him into their mythology, where he attained the highest status and most power of his legends. According to the Hebrews he is the son of Naamah and Shamdon. He was part of the seraphim, the highest order of angels, but fell from grace when LUCIFER was cast from heaven. In other Hebrew legends he is either associated with, or is the husband of, LILITH, the demon queen of lust. He also is said to be the offspring of Lilith and Adam.

In other lore, King Solomon, using his magic ring, forced Asmodeus and other demons to build his magnificent tem-

Asmodeus (Francis Barrett, *The Magus*, 1805)

ple. Asmodeus managed to obtain the ring, force Solomon into exile and become king himself. He threw the ring into the sea. But Solomon found the ring in a fish belly and gained back his power. As punishment, he put Asmodeus in a jar.

In the apocryphal Book of TOBIT, Asmodeus plagues a young woman named Sarah by killing her husbands on their wedding nights in the bridal chamber, before the marriages can be consummated. Sarah loses seven husbands before being rescued by Tobias, a young man who is aided by the archangel RAPHAEL, disguised as a man. Raphael instructs Tobias to take the liver, heart and gall of a fish and burn them to make a foul incense that will drive away Asmodeus. Tobias is dubious, but Raphael assures him that the trick will work and Tobias will be able to claim Sarah as his wife. Tobias becomes betrothed to Sarah and, on their wedding night, prepares the foul smoke to repel Asmodeus. The demon is driven out and flees to Egypt, where he is bound up by another angel.

Asmodeus appears in Christian demonology as one of Satan's leading agents of provocation. Witches in the Middle Ages were said to worship him, and magicians and sorcerers attempted to conjure him to strike out at enemies. Medieval *grimoires* (textbooks of magical instruction) sternly admonish anyone seeking an audience with Asmodeus to summon him bareheaded out of respect. According to Johann WEYER, a sixteenth-century physician and demonologist, Asmodeus also ruled the gambling houses.

Asmodeus was one of the infernal agents blamed for the obscene sexual possession of the Louviers nuns in seventeenth-century France, during the height of the witch scare that ran through Europe. The incident occurred at a convent in Louviers in 1647, and involved eighteen nuns who allegedly were possessed through the bewitchments of the nunnery's director and the vicar of Louviers. According to confessions—most extracted under torture—the possessed nuns committed unspeakable sexual acts with the Devil and demons; attended witches' sabbaths where they ate babies; and uttered obscenities and spoke in tongues. The nuns were subject to public exorcisms. The vicar, Father Thomas Boulle, was burned alive. The body of the nunnery director, Mathurin Picard, who died before sentencing was passed, was exhumed and burned. A nun who leaked the story to authorities, Sister Madeleine Bavent, was sentenced to the dungeon.

See DEMON.

## Further reading

Guiley, Rosemary Ellen. *The Encyclopedia of Witches and Witchcraft.* New York: Facts On File, 1989.

May, Herbert G. and Bruce M. Metzger (eds.) *The New Oxford Annotated Bible with the Apocrypha.* Revised Standard Version. New York: Oxford University Press, 1962.

Ronner, John. *Know Your Angels.* Murfreesboro, Tenn.: Mamre Press, 1993.

**Astaroth**   In Hebrew lore, Astaroth was a seraph and a prince of thrones, but he cast his lot with Satan and was thrown out of heaven. In hell, according to demonologist Johann WEYER, he reigns as a "grandduke." He commands forty legions of demons, and serves as great treasurer.

Of Syrian origin, Astaroth is a demonized version of the goddess Astarte. He is described as both an ugly and a beautiful angel who rides a dragon and holds a viper in his left hand. He encourages slothfulness and laziness. He believes he was punished unjustly by God, and that someday he will be restored to his rightful place in heaven.

**asura**   See HINDUISM.

**Augustine, St.** (354–430)   The most comprehensive and influential of the early church fathers. Augustine is remarkable in the array of Catholic saints for having been in his youth an unmitigated sinner who wrote a detailed account of his conversion, the *Confessions,* addressed to God. The influence of this book on subsequent generations of Christians is incalculable.

At about age 72, Augustine sat down to review his writings and put them in chronological order, and was astounded at the quantity. His complete works, written in Latin, are about the size of an encyclopedia. The generations of scholars following him have dutifully consulted Augustine. Whereas the *Confessions* constitute his intimate spiritual autobiography, *The City of God* is, in the words of Thomas Merton, "the autobiography of the Catholic Church."

The tension in the will that characterized Augustine's early life became the basis of his theology which, because of his great influence, also became the core of Christian doctrine. Augustine devotes much attention to angels: how they were created, how they differ from demons, how they operate in expediting the progress of the human soul to holiness.

### A SUMMARY OF AUGUSTINE'S LIFE

Augustine was born on November 13, 354 in Tagaste, North Africa. His mother Monica was a Christian, and his father Patricius a pagan, whom Monica eventually converted by her patience and example. Augustine was not baptized as an infant, but his mother enrolled him as a catechumen in the Catholic church. He studied Latin and Greek grammar and literature in his boyhood, complaining about rough treatment by his schoolmasters.

After his father died in 370, Augustine went to Carthage to study rhetoric as the first step in preparing for a public life. There he met a young woman at a church service, began to live with her, and fathered a son named Adeodatus ("God's gift"). With the coming of adolescence, he confides to God in the *Confessions,* "both love and lust boiled within me, and swept my youthful immaturity over the precipice of evil desires to leave me half drowned in a whirlpool of abominable sins. . . . My soul was sick, and broke out in sores,

Holy Face of Christ displayed by two angels (Albrecht Dürer, 1513)

whose itch I agonized to scratch with the rub of carnal things," including stage plays, "with the mirror they held up to my own miseries and the fuel they poured on my flame."

Augustine was still making those judgments twenty years later. But during the years in Carthage he was probably embroiled in tensions set in motion by conflicting explanations of the human condition offered by his mother's and his father's behavior (his father was guilty of marital infidelities) and religions. This tension also was at the base of the Manichean religion, which Augustine joined in 373. The Manichees taught that there are two supreme gods, one good and one evil, and similarly two competing souls within the human person. For nine years he maintained interest in this cult. After his move to Rome in 383, to teach a better class of rhetoric students, he became the guest of a Manichee and socialized with many prominent members of the sect.

In the next year, 384, he won an appointment as a professor of rhetoric in Milan. In the two years following he abandoned Manicheism and gradually came under the influence of his Christian mentors: Ambrose, the influential local bishop, and Simplicianus, a wise elderly former bishop. At the same time he wanted to advance himself in position and possessions, so marriage seemed the logical next step. His mother had by now joined him, and she helped him to arrange a marriage to a girl who was not yet twelve, so he agreed to wait two years. Augustine's mistress of many years had to leave him as part of this marriage plan, which threw Augustine into emotional turmoil. "My heart which had held her very dear was broken and wounded and shed blood," he wrote. "She went back to Africa, swearing that she would never know another man, and left with me the natural son I had of her. . . . I was simply a slave of lust. So I took another woman, not of course as a wife; and thus my soul's disease was kept alive as vigorously as ever." He was tormented both by the loss of his former lover and the hopelessness for him of a life of continence, which ran in circles alongside his growing seriousness in reexamining Christianity.

In a touching scene in a garden (described in Book VIII of *Confessions*), he experienced a striking conversion, in which his self-doubt was expelled and "the light of utter confidence shone in all my heart." His mother was exultant. Augustine decided to give up his teaching position and was baptized along with his son Adeodatus and another close friend on Easter 387. About a year later the group was at the port of Ostia, on their way home to Africa, when Monica died. She and Augustine had shared an ecstatic experience five days previously (described in Book IX of *Confessions*), after which she had told him that all her prayers had been answered in superabundance and she no longer hoped for anything in this world.

When Augustine finally returned in 388 to Tagaste in North Africa, he set up a sort of monastery on his family land with his close friends. His son Adeodatus died within a year, aged sixteen. (In *Confessions*, Book IX, Augustine reveals his love for his son, crediting God entirely for the boy's many virtues and intelligence. He notes that his book *De Magistro* is a dialogue between the two, and "that all the ideas . . . put into his mouth were truly his, though he was but sixteen.") Augustine soon gave away his possessions, and for the rest of his life lived simply as a monk in community with men.

In 391 he was ordained a priest in Hippo by Bishop Valerius, who permitted Augustine to begin preaching almost immediately. Upon Valerius's death in 396, Augustine became Bishop of Hippo; he was to serve there for 35 years. He composed the Rule that the Augustinian Order follows to this day. In the 390s he started a convent for women following the Rule. He preached almost daily and wrote incessantly: theological treatises, letters, polemics against heresies, the *Confessions* (finished in 400) and *The City of God*, written in installments between 413 and 426. He died on August 28, 430, while the city of Hippo was under siege by the Vandals.

### THE CITY OF GOD

When Rome was sacked by the Goths under Alaric in 410, many intellectuals made accusations that Christianity had debilitated the Empire, exhausted and softened it for the kill by the barbarians, so to speak. *The City of God* is Augustine's response to that charge. His defense of Christian doctrine was informed by politics and history, full of direct references to pagan philosophers from Plato to his contemporaries.

The fall of the earthly city of Rome was the inevitable result of the sinful wills of its rulers and citizens; at the same time the rise of the city of God (the Catholic church) was a process that had begun before time and was infused with grace, personified by Jesus Christ. This concept of the two cities is eloquently summarized in a famous passage from Book XIV: "Two loves have built two cities: the love of self, which reaches even to contempt for God, the earthly City; and the love of God, which reaches even to contempt for self, the heavenly City. One glories in itself, the other in the Lord. One seeks its own glory amongst men; the greatest glory of the other is God, witness of its conscience. One, swollen with pride, uplifts its haughty head; the other cries out to God with the Psalmist: 'Thou art my glory, it is Thou who dost lift up my head.'"

Duality is intrinsic to human souls and by extension to angelic spirits which dwell on a middle ground between God's eternal immutable perfection and the lowest level of bodily mutable mortality. Humans can look upward to God and the eternal truths (the *conversio ad Deum*) or downward to mutable creatures (the *pervasio animae*). The upward gaze of the soul contains the workings of the *ratio superior*; in the downward glance, the *ratio inferior*. These are not two faculties of the soul, but are two dispositions of one and the same mind. The soul is not divided, but the being is. It is on the same basis that the two "loves" are distinguished, and so two societies of intellectual creatures. Augustine makes a similar distinction of time and eternity, a topic dear to him.

Augustine shows in Books XI and XII how the good and bad angels had inaugurated the two cities on the basis of the two loves. He proceeds carefully through the opening of Genesis, examining possible interpretations. Though there is no explicit verse saying how and when the angels were created, Augustine concludes that in "Let there be light, and there was light" "we are justified in understanding in this light the creation of the angels." He says "they were created partakers of the eternal light which is the unchangeable Wisdom of God." Whereas "the true Light, which lighteth every man that cometh into the world" (John 1:9) "lighteth also every pure angel, that he may be light not in himself but in God. . . . If an angel turn away, he becomes impure, as are all those who are called unclean spirits, and are no longer light in the Lord, but darkness in themselves, being deprived of the light eternal. For evil has no positive nature; but the loss of good has received the name 'evil.'"

In Books XIII and XIV, Augustine explains how this error was repeated by Adam and Eve. This brought humanity into a state of original sin, which Augustine boldly calls a fortunate fall, because we are redeemed by the intervention of Christ. From God, our first parents received a free will capable of loving Him. But as the bad angels at the instigation of their leader Satan had already done, they preferred to love themselves by wishing to live not according to the love of God but according to a law of their own, thereby establishing themselves at the same time in pride and falsehood.

The angels who remained blessed enjoyed uninterrupted and unchangeable connection with God with no doubt whatsoever; the others "of their own will did fall from the light of goodness." Augustine considers whether the fallen angels may have enjoyed something on this level before their fall, and says it is possible but not accompanied with foresight of their eternal felicity that the good angels had. "If it is hard to believe that they were not all from the beginning on an equal footing, . . . it is harder to consider that some good angels are now uncertain of their eternal felicity. . . . For what catholic Christian does not know that no new devil will ever arise among the good angels, as he knows that this present devil will never again return into the fellowship of the good?"

Augustine does not talk about the leader of the fallen angels per se, but after this passage (Book XI, 13) cites several words of Christ from the New Testament as clues to understanding how and when this sin of the angels occurred. "He was a murderer from the beginning, and abode not in the truth." Augustine takes it to mean "from the beginning of the human race, when man, whom he could kill by his deceit was made." He refutes the interpretation that this passage indicates that the devil was flawed from his very creation, as the Manichees posited. On this same ground he refutes that interpretation of the Apostle John's comment "the devil sinneth from the beginning" (1 John 3:8), citing "prophetic proof": "How art thou fallen, O LUCIFER, son of the morning" (Isaiah 14:12), by which, Augustine says "it is meant that he was some time without sin."

Augustine leaves the perennial question "How could a good God create beings whom He knows will become evil?" in a rhetorical circle (XI, 17). God "makes good use of evil wills." Accordingly, He caused the devil (good by God's creation, wicked by his own will) to be cast down from his high position and to become the mockery of His angels—that is, He caused his temptations to benefit those whom He wishes to injure by them. In Book XII, 9, Augustine returns to the subject and offers this conclusion: The bad angels "either received less of the grace of the divine love than those who persevered in the same; or if both were created equally good, then while the one fell by their evil will the others were more abundantly assisted, and attained to that pitch of blessedness at which they became certain they would never fall from it. . . . We must therefore acknowledge, with the praise due the Creator, that not only of holy men, but also of holy angels, 'the love of God is shed abroad

in their hearts by the Holy Ghost', . . . [and] not only of men, but primarily and principally of angels it is true, as it is written, 'it is good to draw near to God.' And those who have this good in common, have, both with Him to whom they draw near, and with one another, a holy fellowship, and form one city of God—His living sacrifice, and His living temple."

Augustine also works with a two-tiered elaboration of the two-cities idea: "The city of God, not in its state of pilgrimage and mortality, but as it exists ever immortal in the heavens." There is an imperfect city of God on earth and an imperfect city of God in heaven flawed by the defection of the bad angels; the present earthly city has no connection with God. Wicked angels are stirring up persecutions of Christians, constantly seducing those in power over nations, and otherwise setting the struggle in motion on a temporal-political as well as an individual-spiritual and -psychological level. But the church can raise the earthly city up, an ascent accomplished through the ministry of angels and aspiring humans.

A just man seeking to accomplish this is therefore without doubt much higher than a reprobate angel. "All who understand or believe them to be worse than unbelieving men are well aware that they are called 'darkness.' . . . We understand these two societies of angels—the one enjoying God, the other swelling with pride; the one to whom it is said 'Praise ye Him, all His angels,' the other whose prince [Satan] says [to Jesus, Matthew 4:9] 'all these things will I give Thee if Thou wilt fall down and worship me;' the one blazing with the holy love of God, the other reeking with the unclean lust of self advancement."

Another way to look at this is that there are only two cities, each containing angels and men; the city of God contains good men and angels, while the city of man contains both kinds of reprobate creatures, man and angels. Augustine says something most significant in his design for the practice of a good life: the nature of the good angels ("the holy angels who maintain their allegiance to God, who never were, nor ever shall be apostate, between whom and those who forsook light eternal and became darkness, God . . . made at the first a separation") determines the nature of the subsequent city of God by providing the earthly city with a prototype; all Christians must try to be like good angels.

But those who succeed will actually *become* angels. Augustine delineates how angelic operations pertain to man in his spiritual quest. In the Rule he wrote for his order, this point is elaborated (see MONASTICISM, CHRISTIAN). The angels form the link between the two manifestations of the *civitatis Dei*, the earthly and the heavenly. Together the angels and the elect comprise the one city of God. The fall of the reprobate angels left gaps in the celestial court. God desires to fill these openings with His elect. The city of God in heaven will remain imperfect and unfulfilled until the temporal city of God reaches heaven after the Parousia (the Second Coming of Christ). Man's plight here below is temporary, since his goal is to resume his place next to his co-citizens in heaven. Aspiring humans are obligated to yearn to return to the voids reserved exclusively for them. Here on earth they are expected to behave in a manner befitting potential neighbors of the angels. The angels participate in this passage by assisting the elect in their pilgrimage toward the perfect homeland above.

However, Augustine warns that devils can imitate angels. "As Satan, as we read [2 Corinthians 11:14] sometimes transforms himself into an angel of light, to tempt those whom it is necessary to discipline, or just to deceive, there is great need of God's mercy to preserve us from making friends with demons in disguise, while we fancy we have good angels as friends; for the astuteness and deceitfulness of these wicked spirits is equalled by their hurtfulness" (XIX, 9). This is part of human misery, and indeed the saints themselves are often tempted in this manner.

Men and angels are thus joined symbiotically, each being dependent on the other. The angels need humans to fill their depleted ranks; humans long to rise to the occasion; angels assist them both in practical terms and by offering their example. The office of assistance by the good angels pertains only to the earthly elect, not to the reprobate men who also reside in the church universal. Finally, humankind's moral obligation to follow the angelic example inspired a practice of trying to become angels here on earth, a key inspiration behind Augustinian monasticism.

The earlier books of *The City of God* are devoted primarily to refuting the arguments of pagan philosophers. Here Augustine's early education across the classical gamut is evident, as well as his skill in rhetoric. He expends great effort in looking at their beliefs seriously in order to show how the coming of Christ must change them. This labor is a reminder of the difference between the thousand-year monolith of Christianity (which Augustine was largely responsible for creating) and the diversity and complexity of religion in his own and earlier times: the subtleties of words and names; the profundity and mystery of the basic questions on the soul, God and the creation of the world; the attractions of certain personalities and their arguments; the seductiveness of magic. In constantly interposing the new cosmology introduced by Christ, Augustine tries through careful, sustained argument to overthrow the practices and psychological residue left by millennia of polytheism.

Here is one example of this polemical aspect of *The City of God*. Augustine is well aware that many pagans consider demons (or daemons) to be the mediators between gods (immortals) and mortals. He explains (IX, 14) how Christ alone is the mediator between God and man. There is "a wicked mediator [the evil angels or Satan] who separates friends, and a good Mediator [Christ] who reconciles enemies. And those who separate are numerous. . . . The evil angels being deprived, they are wretched, and interpose to hinder rather than to help this blessedness, and by their very number prevent us from reaching that one beatific good." By becoming mortal Christ showed us that "in order to obtain that blessed and beatific good, we need not seek mediators to lead us through the successive steps of this attainment, but . . . having Himself become a partaker of our humanity, has afforded us ready access to the participation of His divinity. For in delivering us from our mortality and misery, He does not lead us to the immortal and blessed angels . . . but he leads us straight to that Trinity, by participating in which the angels themselves are blessed.

Therefore, when He chose to be in the form of a servant, and lower than the angels, that He might be our Mediator, He remained higher than the angels, in the form of God—Himself at once the way of life on earth and life itself in heaven."

Another theme that Augustine addresses several places in *The City of God* is the invocation of demons in many magical practices (see MAGIC, ANGELS IN). In X, 9, he states that miracles in the Bible were wrought "for the purpose of commending the worship of the one true God, and prohibiting the worship of a multitude of false gods." They were "wrought by simple faith and godly confidence," not by "a criminal tampering with the unseen world." There is no distinction between theurgy (practiced by honorable people) and necromancy (practiced by magicians "addicted to the illicit arts") because "both classes are the slaves of the deceitful rites of the demons whom they invoke under the names of angels." On the other hand, Augustine holds that good angels minister to perform miracles (X, 12) and that "the place and time of these miracles are dependent on His [God's] unchangeable will." Angels will never demand sacrifices or worship for themselves (X, 16) but instead inspire us to worship and serve God.

### OTHER WORKS

Several of Augustine's other works include some fascinating explanations of angels.

In *On Genesis Against the Manichees* he states that the ultimate destiny of humankind is a "renewal," a "liberation," which he terms a "change into angelic form." This constitutes a restoration to our original status lost by sin.

In *De Quantitae Animae*, a dialogue with his friend Evodius, he agrees with Evodius's firm conviction that he is "soul," but adds a corollary: "our souls are not *in* bodies." He tells his friend that the soul is by its nature "equal of the angel," any present inferiority being a consequence of its sin. Such distinctions were to be taken up in great depth by the medieval church fathers, notably St. Thomas AQUINAS.

Augustine's prescription for each Christian to live on earth by emulating angels, in preparation for taking on angelic status in the City of God, was written some years after *Literal Commentary on Genesis* (410/414). One can see his devotion to Scripture mix with his mystical vision to create his angelology in this treatise, where Augustine says much on angels' involvement with creation and the administration of it.

He states that every being is first made in the eternal uttering of its idea in the Word of God; he parallels this stage with the phrase from Genesis "Let there be." Then according to the phrase "and so it was made," the angels receive knowledge of the things, still to be created, in its idea within the Word; finally, with the phrase "and so God made," the thing takes on its finite actuality (II, 6, 10–7, 15). This does not mean that the angels are the mediators of creation; God is the sole creator, the one who makes things in their separate existence. But Augustine thinks further that no creatures beneath the angels were created "without their knowledge" (IV, 22, 39). This introduces a kind of symmetry into the entire creative process, since the angels themselves have been brought to full actualization through their own knowledge of the Divine Word.

In Book IV, Augustine comments on the six days, each with its evening and morning. He notices that the text speaks not of "the first day" but "one day" and reinforces a passage of Ecclesiastes (18:1) which Augustine translates to say that God created all things *simul* (altogether). Creation does not take place in six days then, but is completed in the first moment of time. What, then, are the six days?

Augustine draws a parallel between two kinds of knowledge and evening and daylight, and postulates that this might be what "day" means in Genesis. When things are known directly in themselves as parts of creation they are known dimly, as if seen in the partial darkness of the evening. When the same things are known in their eternal principles (*rationes aeternae*), as they are in the Word of God, they are known clearly, in the full light of day. Thus, there is in the spiritual order a very real succession of night and day. The ordinary mode of knowledge which the angels enjoy, for instance, is that of spiritual daylight; they see the *rationes* of things in the Word of God.

Since the angels have direct knowledge (though inferior to God's) of creation subsequent to themselves, the six days could be thought of as a recapitulation of the process by which this happened. The evening which concludes each day is the angels' looking in turn at each realm (first themselves, then the firmament, and so on) as it is completed and stands forth in its own being, the outcome of God's creative intention, yet inferior to what it remains in the *rationes aeternae*. The morning which follows is the referring of these various creatures to the praise of their Creator; and the new day reaches its full brightness in their looking to the divine ideas to see what next is to be created. The angels are connected to God without interruption, therefore their knowledge is "day." But they also know created things as they are in themselves, and this looking downward is "evening." If they should turn away from "day" knowledge (as Lucifer did), then their knowledge turns into that of the "evening."

The day and evening hues of knowledge are understood to be mystical, but the significance is finally practical, with cosmic import, for the angels are not only specially privileged observers of the creation but are brought into its administration as the chief agents of the ruler. The angelic community is present to all these realms in these two ways. Augustine uses the word "presence" (*praesentia*) repeatedly in Book IV, 21 and 35, in the sense of the proper mode of relation of soul to body, remaining sovereign to it and not being drawn into excessive involvement with it. The angels' presence in the corporeal world follows this prescription. They are present to created things in two ways: first looking to the ideal pattern in the divine mind, and then only on that basis looking as they are in themselves, with their own places in the texture of events.

In the huge treatise *De Trinitatae*, devoted to distinguishing the Father, Son and Holy Spirit, Augustine discusses in Book IV the whole question of divine theophanies, the various appearances of God on earth. Could the Father have been sent to earth? Are all the Divine Persons (of the Trinity) equally invisible? Were the angels used as instruments in these appearances? Was it the voice of the Father who spoke to ABRAHAM? What Person appeared to MOSES in the burning bush? To DANIEL? In answer to these and similar questions, Augustine suggests that apart from those pertaining to

**Angel keeping demons at bay**

Christ Himself, all the other appearances of God to man may have effected through the intervention of angels. He distinguishes between "words or sensible appearances ... wrought before the Incarnation ... by angels" and after the Incarnation "a voice of the Father ... or corporeal appearance by which the Holy Spirit was manifested ... done through the creature." The tongues of fire at Pentecost would be an example of the latter (II, 5, 10).

There is always tension between two in Augustine: between the two loves, the two cities, the two kinds of knowledge for the angels, between finite beings inferior to divine things and the divine ideas and beings superior to the created things, which are nevertheless oriented toward their realization. The tension is not to be resolved by fleeing into the eternal and forsaking the temporal, but by setting them in their intended relationship. Augustine credits the holy angels with having accomplished precisely this: engaged in both cities, never losing connection with the infinite eternal God and referring all things toward their source.

**Further reading:**

Augustine, *The City of God*. Translated by Marcus Dods, George Wilson and J. J. Smith. Introduction by Thomas Merton. New York: Modern Library, 1950.

Augustine, *Confessions*. Translated by F. J. Sheed. New York: Sheed and Ward, 1943, 1970.

Brown, Peter. *Augustine of Hippo*. Berkeley: University of California Press, 1967.

Bourke, Vernon J. *Wisdom from St. Augustine*. St. Thomas, Texas: Center for Thomistic Studies, 1984.

Battenhouse, Roy W. Ed. *A Companion to the Study of St. Augustine.* New York: Oxford University Press, 1955.

TeSelle, Eugene. *Augustine the Theologian.* New York: Herder and Herder, 1970.

**Avicenna**    See ISLAMIC ANGELOLOGY.

**Azael**    One of the principal evil angels who cohabited with mortal women. The name means "who God strengthens." According to lore, Azael slept with Naamah and spawned Assyrian guardian spirits known as *sedim*, invoked in the exorcism of evil spirits. As punishment, Azael is chained in a desert until Judgment Day. In magical lore, he guards hidden treasure.

See SONS OF GOD.

**Azazel**    One of the chief SONS OF GOD who came to earth and was corrupted by cohabitation. Azazel (whose name means "God strengthens") brought aggression (by teaching men to make swords and shields) and vanity (by teaching women how to use cosmetics). The Book of Enoch cites Azazel as among twenty-one chiefs of two hundred fallen angels.

In Judaic lore, Azazel figures prominently in folktales, along with another fallen angel, SEMYAZA (Shemhazai). He is sometimes described as demonic in appearance, with seven serpent heads, fourteen faces and twelve wings.

In Islamic lore, Azazel refuses to bow down to Adam, and so God casts him out of heaven and changes him into IBLIS.

**Further reading:**
Davidson, Gustav. *A Dictionary of Angels.* New York: The Free Press, 1967.

**Azrael**    See ANGEL OF DEATH; IZRA'IL.

**ba**  In Egyptian mythology, the *ba* is the soul, represented in art as a human-headed bird. As the winged, eternal part of a person, it provided an early inspiration for the image of the winged angel.

The Egyptians associated the *ba* with the *ka*, or the person's double, and the *ib*, or heart. The *ba* is invisible and does not permanently leave the body upon death, but remains with it in the tomb, sometimes coming out at night with a lamp to roam a bit and then returning to the tomb. The body must remain intact in order for the *ba* to return to it (hence the need to preserve the corpse by embalming). The *ba* is fed cakes and is cared for by the sycamore tree goddess.

The Egyptians left small openings in the pyramids so that the *ba* would have easy access. Small ledges inside were built for the *ba* to stand upon.

The ancient Egyptians believed that the stars were *ba*, lit by their tomb lamps.

See WINGS.

**Baal (also Bael)**  Many small deities of ancient Syria and Persia bore this name, which means "the lord," but the greatest Baal was an agricultural and fertility deity of Canaan. The son of El, the High God of Canaan, Baal was the lord of life, and ruled the death-rebirth cycle. He engaged in a battle with Mot ("death") and was slain and sent to the underworld. The crops withered until Baal's sister, Anath, the maiden goddess of love, found his body and gave it proper burial. The Canaanites worshipped Baal by sacrificing children by burning. According to the *Zohar*, Baal is equal in rank to the archangel RAPHAEL.

In Christian demonology, Baal became one of the fallen angels and descended to hell, where he governs sixty to seventy legions of demons. Baal is portrayed as triple-headed, with a cat's head and a toad's head on either side of his human head. In ceremonial magic, he is conjured to impart visibility and wisdom.

See DEMON.

**Balaam**  An Old Testament sorcerer whose eyes are opened by an angel and his ass. The story is told in Numbers 22:21–35. The moral of the story concerns seeing what one cannot or will not see.

Balaam, renowned for his effective curses, is summoned by Balak, the king of Moab, to curse Israelites camped in the wilderness. Balaam is reluctant to do so, but receives a dream in which God tells him to go, but to do only as God bids him to do.

Balaam saddles up his ass and goes off with the princes of Moab, intending to curse the Israelites. This makes God angry, and he sends an angel to stand in Balaam's way in the road, with sword drawn. Balaam does not see the angel, but the ass does. Three times she tries to avoid the angel, twice by swerving and once by falling at Balaam's feet. Each time he beats her severely with his staff.

After the ass falls, God speaks through her and says, "What have I done to you, that you have struck me these three times?" (Numbers 22:28) Balaam replies that the ass has made sport of him, and if he had a sword, he would kill her.

God then lets Balaam see the angel. Balaam falls on his face in humility. The angel tells Balaam that he has come to withstand Balaam because his way is perverse, and if the ass had not turned aside three times, the angel would have killed Balaam and spared the ass. Balaam says he has sinned, and will return if the angel bids him to do so. The angel tells him to proceed on, but to speak only the words he is instructed to speak.

Numbers 23 and 24 tell that when Balaam reaches Balak, he prepares a sacrificial altar, and tells the king that he cannot curse those whom God has not cursed. Twice more, Balak orders him to curse the Israelites, but Balaam can only bless them. He prophesies the destruction of Moab at the hand of the Israelites. Balaam returns to his own place, and Balak goes his own way to his own destiny.

**Further reading:**
Margolies, Morris B. *A Gathering of Angels*. New York: Ballantine Books, 1994.

**Beelzebub**  Originally, a Syrian god, who became demonized in Judaic and Christian demonologies. According to the Kabbalah, Beelzebub was the prince of demons who governed the nine evil hierarchies of the underworld. In Christian demonology, he is second to Satan among the fallen angels, the prince of devils and chief of demons.

Also known as Baal-zebub, "the lord of the flies," the name is a distortion of Baal-zebul, the chief Canaanite or Phoenician god meaning "lord of the divine abode" or "lord of the heavens." Beelzebub has always been considered a demon of great power, and sorcerers have conjured him at great risk. Most depictions show him as an enormous fly.

Many of the Pharisees, trying to cast doubt on Jesus' power to cast out demons, accused Him of being possessed by Beelzebub. The incident is recounted in Matthew (12:24–29), Mark (3:22–27) and Luke (11:14–22).

And the scribes which came down from Jerusalem said, he hath Beelzebub, and by the prince of devils casteth he out devils. And he called them unto him, and said unto them in parables, "How can Satan cast out Satan? And if a kingdom be divided against itself, that house cannot stand. And if Satan rise up against himself, and be divided, he cannot stand but hath an end. No man can enter into a strong man's house, and spoil his goods, except he will first bind the strong man; and then he will spoil his house." (Mark 3:22–27)

This incident also presents the idea of binding (adjuring) Satan to the will of God before he can be thrown out of the "house," or the body of the possessed victim.

During the time of ELIJAH, the god Baal was the main rival to the Israelite god Yahweh (Jehovah). King Ahab was not constant in his faith and had allowed his wife Jezebel to introduce the worship of the Canaanite Baals into Israel. In I Kings 18:20–40, Elijah challenges the 450 prophets of Baal to a contest to see which god is greater. The prophets prepare a sacrificial bull and place it on a pyre but do not light the fire. Elijah does the same. The prophets of Baal call on their god all day, but to no avail. Elijah taunts the prophets, suggesting that Baal has gone on a journey, or perhaps is asleep or even tending to bodily functions.

Elijah then take twelve stones representing the twelve tribes of Israel and places them near the bull and altar. He digs a small trench around the altar and fills it with water, drenching the pyre as well. Water is added a second time. Then Elijah calls on the Lord to show that He is God, and the pyre and all the stones and water are consumed by flame. Elijah captures the 450 prophets of Baal and assassinates them.

During the witch hunts of the Inquisition, Beelzebub was regarded as one of the chief demons over witches. At sabbats, witches supposedly denied Christ in his name, and chanted it as they danced. Numerous accounts attest to Beelzebub copulating with witches in wild orgies.

Beelzebub also was among the demons blamed for the demonic possession cases. In 1566 he tormented a young girl named Nicole Obry in Laon, France. Her daily exorcisms before huge crowds were used by the Catholic church, embroiled in religious struggles with the French Huguenots, as examples of the church's power over the Devil. Through Obry, Beelzebub claimed the Huguenots as his own people, gleefully noting that their supposed heresies made them even more precious to him. The demon was exorcised through the repeated administration of holy wafers.

Beelzebub also was blamed for the bewitchment of nuns of Loudon, Louviers and Aix-en-Provence in the late sixteenth and early seventeenth centuries, leading to the fiery deaths of his accused lieutenants, Fathers Louis Gaufridi and Urbain Grandier.

One of the demon's most notorious appearances in the twentieth century was as the possessing devil of Anna Ecklund of Wisconsin. He entered the young woman at the behest of her father Jacob, angry that Anna would not engage in incestuous sex with him. She became totally possessed in 1908. The demon left on December 23, 1928, in a terrible roar of "Beelzebub, Judas, Jacob, Mina [Anna's aunt and Jacob's mistress]" followed by "Hell, hell, hell" and a terrible stench.

See DEMON.

**Further reading:**
Elledge, Scott, ed. *John Milton: Paradise Lost, An Authoritative Text.* New York: W. W. Norton & Co., 1975.
Guiley, Rosemary Ellen. *The Encyclopedia of Witches and Witchcraft.* New York: Facts On File, 1989.
May, Herbert G., and Bruce M. Metzger, eds. *The Oxford Annotated Bible with the Apocrypha, Revised Standard Version.* New York: Oxford University Press, 1965.

**Behemoth**   The male counterpart to LEVIATHAN, one of the fallen angels and a demon of the deep. Like Leviathan, Behemoth is associated with RAHAB and the sea, and is personified variously as a whale, crocodile and hippopotamus. He also is associated with the ANGEL OF DEATH.

The Book of Enoch, an apocryphal work, says that Behemoth and Leviathan were separated by God at the creation, with Leviathan being sent to the sea and Behemoth being sent to an immeasurable desert named Dendain. In the Bible, Job 40:15–24 describes Behemoth as a mighty beast, "the first of the works of God" (40:19). Rabbinic lore holds that on the Day of Judgment, he will slay and be slain by Leviathan. His fate is to furnish meat for the Messiah's feast, and his flesh will be distributed to the faithful. Another rabbinic legend says that God destroyed Leviathan on the day he created both monsters, but placed Behemoth, in the form of a giant ox, on enchanted mountains to fatten him up. There he eats the grass of one thousand mountains each day; the grass grows back each night. Behemoth is doomed to remain there alone until the end of time, because God realized that such a monster could not be loosed upon the world.

In Christian lore, Behemoth is considered one of the prime representations of evil. The demonologist Johann WEYER, who catalogued the ranks of hell, did not include Behemoth in his list, but did include him in another work, *Praestigiorum Daemonum*, in which he suggested that Behemoth represents Satan himself. Other demonologists of medieval times did include Behemoth in their rankings.

Behemoth is sometimes described as being overweight and stupid; thus he encourages gluttony and the pleasures of the belly. He shapeshifts to various animal forms, and often is depicted as an elephant with a huge stomach.

**Further reading:**
Hyatt, Victoria, and Joseph W. Charles. *The Book of Demons.* New York: Fireside Press, 1974.

**Belial (also Beliar)**   A fallen angel and one of Satan's most important and evil demons, who is deceptively beautiful in appearance and soft of voice but full of treachery, recklessness and lies. He is dedicated to creating wickedness and guilt in mankind, especially in the form of sexual perversions, fornication and lust.

Belial's name probably comes from the Hebrew term *beli ya'al*, which means "without worth." The ancient Hebrews believed that Belial was the next angel created after Lucifer and was evil from the start, being one of the first to revolt against God. After his fall from heaven he became the personification of evil. St. PAUL considered him to be chief of demons. According to lore, Belial danced before King Solomon, and was among the demons who worked under the king's command, ruled by Solomon's magical ring.

The demonologist Johann WEYER said that Belial commands eighty legions of demons and serves as infernal ambassador to Turkey. Medieval magicians believed that sacrifices and offerings were necessary to invoke him. Belial was reputed to break his promises to magicians, but those who managed to gain his true favor were handsomely rewarded.

Belial's name is sometimes used as a synonym for Satan or the Antichrist, the epitome of evil. In the Old Testament, the phrase "sons of Belial" refers to worthlessness and recklessness.

**Bernard of Clairvaux, St.** See MONASTICISM, CHRISTIAN.

**Blake, William** (1757–1827)   English poet, artist, engraver, mystic and iconoclast, William Blake received little appreciation for his work during his lifetime but fascinates readers and art lovers today. He often depicted angels in his engravings and poems, finding them to be excellent representations of authority, power and divinity.

Born in London on November 28, 1757, Blake had little formal schooling until his father sent him as a teenager to the Royal Academy to study art. He had read extensively as a young man and was well versed in literature, philosophy and religion. From an early age, Blake experienced extraordinary visions of angels and other religious figures. He claimed to have talked to GABRIEL, EZEKIEL, the Virgin MARY and others. At age eight, Blake saw a tree filled with angels whose bright wings covered the tree boughs like stars.

In 1772 he became apprenticed to an engraver and began to earn a living in the trade at age twenty-two. He developed a technique called "Illumined Printing" in 1788, whereby illustrations and print could be engraved simultaneously, but it was so costly that he did not reap the financial rewards that he had expected. Blake continued to use the technique for his own work, however.

Heavily influenced by the more spiritual movements of his day, such as Swendenborgianism, Blake rebelled against the eighteenth century's emphasis on reason versus the "natural" pull of feeling and emotion. He especially detested Newtonian physics as an example of life following orderly precepts. Nearly all his poems and engravings depict his mistrust and disdain of Reason, finding it responsible for poverty, racism, the denigration of women, sexual repression, and any and all ills of the period.

Although Blake communicated with angels, he depicted them in his early works as servants of the enemy Reason. They represented absolutism, political empire and the exercise of pure power. Even so-called "good" angels were not so; the angels who clothe Adam and Eve in Blake's engraving "The Angel of the Divine Presence Clothing Adam and Eve with Coats of Skins" represent cold reason and repression against divine Innocence.

In his poem "I Asked a Thief" (1795), Blake sarcastically describes an angel as being an eighteenth-century version of a modern corporate baron, one who can have it all:

> I asked a thief to steal me a peach,
> He turned up his eyes;
> I ask'd a lithe lady to lie her down,
> Holy & meek she cries.

> As soon as I went
> An angel came.
> He wink'd at the thief
> And smild at the dame—

> And without one word said
> Had a peach from the tree
> And still as a maid
> Enjoy'd the lady.

Blake particularly chafed at his society's conventions against women and sexual freedom, and often portrayed his men and women in relatively graphic sexual poses.

Later in life Blake's philosophy changed, and he came to rely on the supremacy of imagination over anything in nature. Additionally, he believed that when man begins to imitate divine images (represented by angels) in his life and art, he can begin to realize his own divinity.

By the early nineteenth century, Blake had honed his engraving into the style of romantic classicism. He saw such art as the ultimate example of beautiful, specific detail, enabling any practitioner to achieve a divine vision of Innocence. Blake maintained that the human form must be carefully drawn and delineated in art, emphasizing every particularity, in order to sanctify every inch, limb and part of the divine whole.

Blake's great epic poem, "Jerusalem," summed up his final philosophy: that traditional, orthodox Christians have per-

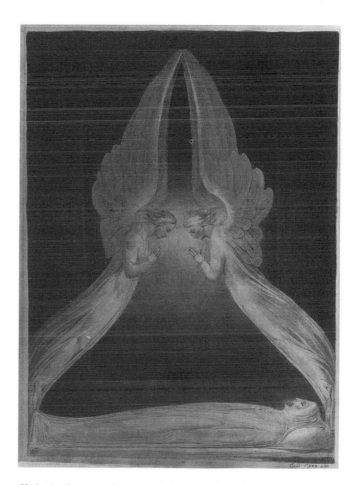

**Christ in the sepulchre, guarded by angels (William Blake; reprinted courtesy of Victoria and Albert Museum, London)**

verted Christ's forgiving love into a system that vengefully punishes sin and rejects sexual pleasure and love. He depicted this evil as a Covering Cherub, the very description of Lucifer before his fall. He is the Antichrist incarnate: a hermaphroditic, hypocritical, egotistical entity that incorporates all the Pharisees, scribes and Sadducees of ancient Jerusalem. He has a contracted and constricted body that portrays an outward show of pomp and ceremony but in reality serves the Whore of Babylon. In other words, the figure is a grotesque rendering of the Human Form Divine.

Such ideas were beyond the comprehension of most of Blake's contemporaries or audience, and he died in 1827, unappreciated and in poverty.

See LITERATURE AND ANGELS.

**Further reading:**

Allison, Alexander W., et. al. *The Norton Anthology of Poetry*, Third edition. New York: W. W. Norton & Co., 1983.

Cavendish, Richard, ed. *Man, Myth & Magic: The Illustrated Encyclopedia of Mythology, Religion and the Unknown*, Vol. 11. New York: Marshall Cavendish Ltd., 1985, p. 2963.

Mellor, Anne Kostelanetz. *Blake's Human Form Divine*. Berkeley: University of California Press, 1974.

**Blavatsky, Helena Petrovna**   See DEVA.

**Bodhisattva**   See TANTRIC BUDDHISM.

**Boehme, Jakob** (1575–1624)   An autodidact Bohemian shoemaker who began circulating writings derived from his mystical experiences, Jakob Boehme gained an eminent following in his lifetime and in the generations to come. His principal works are *De signatura rerum* and *Mysterium magnum*.

Among Boehme's admirers have been the scientist Isaac Newton, the English theologian William Law (1686–1761), the German philosopher Friedrich W. J. von Schelling (1775–1854), and the poets William BLAKE, Johann Wolfgang von GOETHE (1749–1832) and Samuel Taylor Coleridge (1772–1834). Carl G. JUNG considered Boehme a modern Christian Gnostic. He noted that Boehme's life-cycle, which moves through seven "Forms" or "properties" of Nature, creates a Gnostic mandala holding threefold "hellish" or dark elements (attraction, expulsion and the wheel of anguish) and "heavenly" or light elements (light or love, intelligible sound and the all-embracing Reality) in balance, with lightning sparking between them, much like the Gnostic figure ABRAXAS.

In Boehme's visionary scheme, all seven Forms are found within all things, even in God's name. The same forces operating above in the celestial world also operate below, in stones, earth and plants. The overall paradigm of Boehme's Christology draws upon meteorological, astrological, alchemical, mechanical and psychic prototypes. The shapes of individual beings are ruled by the angels, what we would call the individualized ideas of God in His Wisdom. Originally they existed in two forms only and were created from the first principle, being of Light's matrix. States Boehme: "They are the essence of both the inner internal fires. Their powers are from the great emanating names of God. All have sprung from the Yes and been led into the No, in order that powers might become manifest." Thus, angels

*Of Divine Revelation* (Jakob Boehme)

are the formed powers of God's Word, His outspeaking, His Thoughts.

Angels help God rule the world; they are His instruments by and through which He reveals His powers, numbering a thousand times ten thousand, unequal in rank, ranged in three realms and seven dominions, according to the seven Forms of Nature, with each having a throne with seven princely hierarchies. As free angels, they have a possibility of falling. Before Lucifer's fall they were able to imagine themselves into the world of matter. Each angelic realm is ruled by a prince: LUCIFER, MICHAEL or URIEL. Of these Lucifer is the most beautiful of all heavenly creatures ruling the second kingdom. Angels as such do not fall, but humble themselves before God's great majesty so that the eternal No may not gain dominion over them. The ensemble of stars represents the totality of divine forces. The stars also "mean" the angels.

Within each angelic creature the divine forces are incessantly exciting one another, harkening to the music of eternity, receiving impulses from without and rising up to sing. In each angelic body the seven spirits forge the five senses and coordinate the consensual and expressive faculties. Embodying pure force and pure sensory awareness, the angels are wholly alive, unlike the human "half-dead angel" that has fallen from grace.

The great mystery to Boehme was the human creature. He believed that angels are brethren to humans in looks because they too were created in the image of God, with hands, feet, mouth, nose; they eat paradisiacal fruit of the divine power of God's Word. Matter, like the flesh, is a garment put on or congealed by the fallen will, and a medium in which the eternal wisdom of God is mirrored. Spirit, as conscious life, is the ascending, sublimated aspect of the root torment of the will. Even the basest sexual desire is a longing for something higher, a longing for the eternal light and a flight from death and darkness. From the human vantage point, the angels represent the fulfillment of all betterment, be it of the soul in need of redemption or of the world in need of improvement.

All of Boehme's work set out to explain the contradiction inherent in reality, "to grasp the possibility, indeed the necessity of evil in the highest Good." He found that "in the being of all being, there is strife and opposition"; any revelation is possible only in division. The will of the Nothing looks out in search of Something as light (love), and having achieved self-revelation in the Son, draws it back to itself in desire as fire. Yet the two exist in union. They are a coincidence of opposites. God rests, as Boehme puts it, in love-play. All of life is endowed by an imprint, which is no less present for being concealed. The Kaballah calls it Tav, the mark of the Shekinah, or divine presence in the world. Boehme called it *Signatura rerum*, the seal or signature of the eternal within things. The rediscovered harmonies of nature are a model for restoring harmony to the strife-torn world, a theme which, a few generations later, would be taken up by the Romantic philosophers and poets.

**Further reading:**
Stoudt, John Joseph. *Jacob Boehme: His Life and Thought.* New York: Seabury Press, 1968.
Weeks, Andrew. *Boehme: An Intellectual Biography.* State University of New York Press, 1991.

**Bonaventure, St.**   See MONASTICISM, CHRISTIAN.

**Byron, Lord**   See LITERATURE AND ANGELS.

# C

**Caddy, Eileen and Peter**   See FINDHORN.

**Calvin, John**   See PROTESTANT ANGELOLOGY.

**Candomblé**   See ORISHAS.

**Catherine of Siena, St.**   See MONASTICISM, CHRISTIAN.

**Cayce, Edgar** (1877–1945)   American psychic, called "the sleeping prophet," renowned for his readings from an altered state of consciousness in which he diagnosed illness and prescribed remedies, discussed past lives and spiritual wisdom. Edgar Cayce had only a grammar-school education, but from an altered state he could accurately prescribe treatments. His calling was initiated by an angelophany, and occasionally presences identified as angels transmitted through him.

Cayce was born on March 18, 1877, in Hopkinsville, Kentucky. He had psychic powers from an early age, among them the ability to see nonphysical beings, who were his childhood companions, and the auras of everyone.

As a child, Cayce received religious instruction, and attended the Liberty Christian Church in Hopkinsville. He was given a Bible at age ten and quickly read it in its entirety over and over again. His biblical background formed the foundation for the spiritual work of his adult years, and is evident in his readings.

One of Cayce's favorite activities was to go off alone into the woods to read. One afternoon, he did just that with the Bible. He suddenly became aware of a woman standing before him. At first he thought it was his mother; then he noticed that something on her back was making shadows shaped like wings. "Your prayers have been heard," the woman said to him, in a voice that sounded like music. "Tell me what you would like most of all, so that I may give it to you." Frightened, Cayce could barely respond: "Most of all I would like to be helpful to others, and especially to children when they are sick." The woman vanished, and Cayce ran home. He shared the story with his mother, who accepted it.

The next day, Cayce—who was a poor student—heard the woman's voice as he struggled with his spelling lessons. She told him, "If you can sleep a little, we can help you." Cayce put his spelling book beneath his head and fell asleep. When he awoke, he discovered that he mysteriously knew his lessons. He began to sleep with all of his schoolbooks beneath his head. He always would awaken with the contents learned. This ability faded within months.

Edgar Cayce (photograph copyrighted 1978, Edgar Cayce Foundation Archives. Used by permission)

Cayce's diagnostic and remedial powers date from March 1900, when he was twenty-one and working as a salesman. He suffered from a persistent hoarse throat and intermittent laryngitis, which resisted medical treatment and forced him to give up his job. In 1901, as last resort, he tried hypnosis. He could not be hypnotized, and so he asked to put himself to sleep. He then was asked for the cause of his affliction and a cure. He gave the answers, and at the end of the session had his voice back. He gave his first formal readings—for patients of Dr. Al C. Layne—on March 31, 1901.

On June 17, 1903, he married Gertrude Evans, with whom he had two sons, Edgar Evans and Hugh Lynn.

Cayce's success was so great that thousands eventually sought him out for help. He could read for anyone anywhere in the world—he needed only a name and address.

In a 1911 reading he made his first reference to "transmigration" as a cause of physical ailment, but this escaped notice. In 1923, during an attempted horoscope reading, he spoke of reincarnation. He sometimes spoke about the fabled civilizations of Lemuria and Atlantis, and how the latter's inhabitants had misused their high-tech power. He came to believe in reincarnation, and his readings revealed that among his own past lives, he had been one of the first celestial souls to project into matter prior to Adam and Eve; an Atlantean; Ra-Ta, a high priest in Egypt 10,600 years ago; a Persian ruler; a Trojan warrior; Lucius of Cyrene, mentioned in the New Testament as a minor disciple of Jesus; and various others. He believed that his scientific knowledge in readings had come to him from a former life as a chemist in Grecian Troy.

Cayce and his family moved to Virginia Beach, Virginia, in 1925. In 1928 he established a hospital, and in July 1931 established the Association for Research and Enlightenment (A.R.E.). On July 15, 1928, at a trance session with his study group, the archangel MICHAEL made an appearance, speaking through Cayce: "I am Michael, Lord of the Way! Bend thy head, O ye children of men! Give heed unto the way as is set before you in that sermon on the mount, in that on yon hill this enlightenment may come among me . . . for in Zion thy names are written, and in service will come truth!"

The hill referred to the site of what was to become the headquarters for the A.R.E., which was officially founded in 1931.

Michael made 19 appearances in 14,306 documented Cayce readings. His voice was so loud and booming that dishes rattled in the kitchen. Son Hugh Lynn asked his father who was Michael, and received the answer: "Michael is an archangel that stands before the throne of the Father . . . Michael is the lord or guard of the change that comes in every soul that seeks the way, even as in those periods when His manifestations came in the earth" (Reading 262–28, Par. 18-A).

The gist of Michael's messages was that the people present at the sessions had been chosen for service in a time when spiritual renewal was needed. He admonished people to hold to high spiritual values, and said he would protect those who sought to know the face of God. He was not tolerant of using readings for material gain.

The angel sometimes was harsh. In one of the last readings of Cayce's life, when his health was rapidly failing and his staff was quarreling, Michael lashed out, "Bow thine heads, ye children of men! For I, Michael, Lord of the Way, would speak with thee! Ye generation of vipers, ye adulterous generation, be warned! There is today before thee good and evil! Choose thou whom ye will serve! Walk in the way of the Lord! Or else there will come that sudden reckoning, as ye have seen! Bow thine heads, ye who are ungracious, unrepentant! For the glory of the Lord is at hand! The opportunity is before thee! Accept or reject! But don't be pigs!"

In the mid-1930s, Cayce's study group began to compile material from the readings that eventually was published in the two-volume work *A Search for God*. A new angel, which identified itself as Halaliel, manifested through Cayce with a commanding tone that made some of the group uneasy. "Halaliel," whose name does not appear in any of the

angelology writings of old, identified himself as an angel who defied ARIEL in the heavenly rebellion led by Satan. (Ariel—"lion of God"—is both an angel and a demon in lore.) The inference was that Halaliel was an archangel who fought on Michael's side.

(The name "Halahel" does appear in the magical text *The Lemegeton*, and is described as a spirit who is part good and part evil, and under the rule of Bael. In the *Zohar*, Bael is equated with the archangel RAPHAEL, but in the demonology of Johann WEYER, he is a king of hell. There is no certainty that Halaliel and Halahel are synonymous, but often many variations in spellings are given for angels' names in the literature.)

Halaliel indicated to the study group that he had been appointed to teach and guide them, and that their acceptance of him would mark a change in the course of the group. However, warnings surfaced in readings not to accept any other than Jesus Christ. Bitter arguments ensued over Halaliel but ultimately the group voted to reject him.

Cayce also gave twenty-four readings dealing with the Book of Revelation. Essentially, he interpreted the symbols described by John of Patmos as representative of forces that war within the human psyche. The fallen angels represent fallen ideals, which are necessary in order to attain the "new Jerusalem" of a higher state of spiritual consciousness.

Cayce prophesied the Second Coming of Christ for 1998, accompanied by cataclysmic earth changes.

Cayce drove himself to try to keep up with the demand for readings. In August 1944, he collapsed from exhaustion. He went to the mountains near Roanoke, Virginia, to recuperate, returning home in November of that year. On January 1, 1945, he told friends he would be "healed" on January 5, and they took it to mean his death. He died peacefully on January 3, 1945, at the age of 67. Gertrude died the following April 1. The A.R.E. is now under the direction of Cayce's grandson by Hugh Lynn, Charles Thomas Cayce.

In addition to the A.R.E., three other organizations are dedicated to Cayce's work. Atlantic University, chartered in 1930 in Virginia Beach, offers graduate-level transpersonal studies. The Edgar Cayce Foundation, chartered in 1948 in Virginia Beach, provides permanent custodial ownership for the Cayce readings and their supporting documentation. The Harold J. Reilly School of Massotherapy was opened in 1986 under the auspices of Atlantic University. It offers a diploma program certified by the Commonwealth of Virginia in massage, hydrotherapy, diet and preventive health-care practices based on the Cayce readings.

**Further reading:**
Grant, Robert J. *Are We Listening to the Angels?* Virginia Beach, Va.: A.R.E. Press, 1994.
Sugrue, Thomas. *There Is a River.* New York: Holt, Rhinehart & Winston, 1942.

**Cellini, Benvenuto** (1500–1571) Celebrated goldsmith, sculptor and author during the Renaissance, who credited his guardian angel with saving his life.

Benvenuto Cellini tells in his flamboyant autobiography, *The Life of Benvenuto Cellini* (published posthumously in 1728), how an angel rescued him while he served time in prison. Cellini, a hotheaded man, was constantly engaging in scrapes and fights with other people. On several occasions he was imprisoned, and once was condemned to death. He was absolved once for murder, by Pope Paul III.

In 1535, he was jailed in Rome on charges of stealing the jewels of Pope Clement. Cellini was incarcerated high in the towers of the Castel Sant'Angelo. He made a daring attempt to escape by scaling down the castle walls on a rope made of bedsheets tied together. He suffered a broken leg, was captured and thrown into a wretched dungeon. The dungeon lay below a garden that was filled with water, and Cellini's cell was damp and populated by "big spiders and many venomous worms." His mattress quickly became water-soaked. A tiny shaft of sunlight trickled through a narrow opening for about an hour and a half every day, enabling him to read his Bible.

In these horrible conditions, Cellini sank into despair and resolved to kill himself. As he wrote:

> Once, notwithstanding, I took and propped a wooden pole I found there, in position like a trap. I meant to make it topple over on my head, and it would certainly have dashed my brains out; but when I had arranged the whole machine, and was approaching to put it in motion, just at the moment of my setting my hand to it, I was seized by an invisible power and flung four cubits from the spot, in such terror that I lay half dead. Like that I remained from dawn until the nineteenth hour, when they brought my food.

Upon reflection, Cellini said, "I came to the conclusion that it must have been some power divine and my good guardian angel."

This angel manifested several times to Cellini while he was in prison:

> During the following night there appeared to me in dreams a marvellous being in the form of a most lovely youth, who cried, as though he wanted to reprove me: "Knowest thou who lent thee that body, which thou wouldst have spoiled before its time?" I seemed to answer that I recognized all things pertaining to me as gifts from the God of nature. "So then," he said, "thou hast contempt for His handiwork, through this thy will to spoil it? Commit thyself unto His guidance, and lose not hope in His great goodness!" Much more he added in words of marvellous efficacy, the thousandth part of which I cannot now remember.

Cellini took the angel's advice to heart. He began to ignore his suffering and to sing the praises of God throughout the day and night instead. His good spirits continued, despite the fact that his teeth were rotting and falling out, his gums perforating and bleeding, and his nails growing so long that he wounded himself every time he touched himself.

Cellini's good humor confounded his jailors. Once a party came to visit him:

> They found me on my knees; I did not turn at their approach, but went on praying my orisons before God the Father, surrounded with angels, and a Christ arising victorious from the grave, which I had sketched upon the wall with a little piece of charcoal I had found covered up with earth. This was after I had lain four months upon my back in bed with my leg broken, and had so often dreamed that angels came and ministered to me, that at the end of those four months the limb became as sound as though it had never been fractured.

Cellini said he prayed daily, and every night was visited by his guardian angel in his dreams. He told the angel that he had but one request, to see the sun again, and then he would be content to die. On October 3, 1539, he awoke to be taken away by his invisible angel, who was like a whirlwind. A vision then unfolded: Cellini was taken by the angel first to a large room and then into the sunlight. An image of Christ upon the cross formed itself out of the light, followed by a Madonna and child. Cellini basked in the vision for about fifteen minutes, he said, before it faded.

According to Cellini, these celestial visitations and visions sustained him through the darkest period of his imprisonment. Not long after the sun-vision, he was released from the dungeon by the pope on the personal request of a cardinal. He went on to become one of the most celebrated artists of the Renaissance.

The tone of Cellini's autobiography is florid, and some scholars opine that he exaggerated, or perhaps even fabricated, some of the events he related. Whether or not the angel episodes were experience or exaggeration remains unknown.

**Further reading:**
Cellini, Benvenuto. *Autobiography*. New York: P.F. Collier, c. 1910.

**cherubim**   See CHOIRS.

**choirs**   Ranking of angels into a hierarchy of tiers and groups. The most accepted arrangement is of nine groups, or choirs, arranged in three tiers. "Choirs" means "bands of

Ministering angels saving souls (reprinted courtesy of U.S. Library of Congress)

singers," which is somewhat of a misnomer, since angelic duties go far beyond heavenly music and singing.

In the Christian church there is disagreement over the structure of the angelic hierarchy, and which groups of angels are included in it. The Bible gives the names of nine groups of angels—angels, archangels, principalities, powers, dominions (dominations), virtues, thrones, cherubim and seraphim—but does not specify their respective rankings or their celestial duties. Those details have been filled in by theologians, philosophers and artists.

The best-known hierarchy was elaborated by PSEUDO-DIONYSIUS, a Greek writer dating to the fifth or sixth century C.E. Pseudo-Dionysius was heavily influenced by Platonic thought, and also by some of the opinions expressed in previous centuries by early church fathers. St. Ignatius Martyr, who died in 107 C.E., made direct reference to ranks and hierarchies of angels.

Saints Jerome, Ambrose and Gregory the Great wrote about the rankings of angels, but did not concur among themselves. St. Ambrose organized the nine groups in ascending order from angel to seraphim. St. Jerome specified only seven choirs, leaving out principalities and virtues, and wondered about the real differences between ranks. The *Apostolic Constitutions*, which also predate Pseudo-Dionysius, list ten choirs, adding aeons and hosts but omitting dominions, and at another time give eleven choirs, adding dominions back in. St. AUGUSTINE said that he did not know the difference between the ranks of thrones, dominions, principalities and powers.

Other church fathers argued over whether or not Scripture had included all of the choirs, pointing to a vague statement by St. PAUL. In Ephesians 1:21, Paul refers to Christ sitting at God's right hand "far above all principality and power and virtue and dominion, and above every name that is named, not only in this age but also in that which is to come. . . ." Some argued that the statement implies an infinite number of angelic choirs, while others have argue that Paul didn't know all of the choirs and mentioned only those that he did know. Still others have suggested that Paul deliberately concealed the true numbers of choirs.

Pseudo-Dionysius's angelic hierarchy became the accepted standard. Pseudo-Dionysius said that the hierarchy implies a holy order that aims to achieve the greatest possible assimilation to and union with God. Only God can know the true number of angels, their ranks and duties, he said.

The higher choirs possess all of the wisdom, abilities and illumination of the lower tiers, which in turn depend upon the immediate higher choirs for dispensation of the light and love of God. The highest tier of seraphim, cherubim and thrones receive illumination directly from God and send it down through the layers. The second tier consists of virtues, dominions and powers, and the third and lowest tier consists of principalities, archangels and angels.

The following are descriptions of each choir of angel (for Pseudo-Dionysius's descriptions, see PSEUDO-DIONYSIUS).

The *seraphim* rank first and are closest to God. Their name means "firemakers," "carriers of warmth" or "ardor." Seraphim are the created representations of Divine Love, the fire of which consumes them and keeps them close to the throne of God. In fact they are the only angels to actually stand above the throne.

The seraphim constantly glorify God by chanting "holy, holy, holy." They set up the vibration of love, which in turn creates the field of life. They purify all, and dispel the shadows of darkness.

Seraphim are of such subtlety that they rarely are perceived by human consciousness. When they so choose, they can manifest in a humanlike form with four heads and six wings—two for flying, two to cover the face, and two to cover the feet. They are able to shed their skin and appear in their true, brilliant form.

Rulers of the seraphim are Seraphiel, JAHOEL, METATRON, MICHAEL and SATAN prior to his fall from heaven.

ENOCH declared that there are only four seraphim, one for each cardinal direction.

The name *cherubim* comes from the Hebrew *kerub,* which means either "fullness of knowledge" or "one who intercedes." The cherubim are the voice of divine wisdom, possessing a deep insight into God's secrets. They enlighten the lower levels of angels. They emanate holiness through the universe in order to ensure the success of universal truths. Cherubim also function as charioteers to God, and stand beside his throne. They also personify the winds.

The name *kerub* is derived from the Akkadian term *kari-bu,* a winged guardian being of Assyria. *Kari-bu* had the bodies of sphinxes or bulls and the heads of humans. They originally guarded entrances to buildings.

In early lore of the Israelites, cherubim were not angelic, but gradually acquired angelic status. They are the first angels to be mentioned by their group name in the Bible, appearing in Genesis 3:24. God places them at the east entrance to the Garden of Eden, guarding it with flaming sword. Cherubim make various appearances by name throughout the Old and New Testaments. In Exodus 25:18, God tells Moses to have made two cherubim of hammered gold for the mercy seat of the Ark. In Ezekiel 10:14 they are described as having four faces: a cherub, a man, a lion and an eagle. In Revelation 4:8, they are "living beasts" with many eyes and six wings, who ceaselessly praise God.

Chiefs of the cherubim are Ophaniel, Rikbiel, Cherubiel, RAPHAEL, GABRIEL, Zophiel and SATAN before his fall.

According to the Koran, the tears Michael cries over the sins of the faithful form the cherubim.

The *thrones,* also known as *ophanim* (*offanim*) and *galgallin,* are creatures that function as the actual chariots of God driven by the cherubs. They are characterized by peace and submission; God rests upon them. Thrones are depicted as great wheels containing many eyes, and reside in the area of the cosmos where material form begins to take shape. They chant glorias to God and remain forever in his presence. They mete out divine justice and maintain the cosmic harmony of all universal laws.

The *dominions* (also known as dominations, lords, lordships and *kuriotetes*), regulate the duties of the angels, making known the commands of God. They also are channels of mercy.

The *virtues* are angels who carry out the instructions of the dominions. Through them God governs the seasons, elements and heavens, though lower orders of angels have direct responsibility for those tasks. Virtues are in charge of miracles and provide courage, grace and valor. They sometimes are referred to as "the shining ones" or the "brilliant ones." The angels of the ascension were virtues. According to

Cherub with thrones depicted as wheels with eyes. (Copyright 1995 by Robert Michael Place, from *The Angels Tarot* by Rosemary Ellen Guiley and Robert Michael Place. Reprinted courtesy of HarperSanFrancisco)

the Book of Adam and Eve, a pseudepigraphical work, two virtues and twelve other angels helped Eve to prepare for the birth of Cain.

The *powers*, also called potentates, dynamis and authorities, fight against evil spirits who attempt to wreak havoc through human beings. They protect the divine plans initiated by the dominions and carried out by the virtues. However, St. Paul alludes to their capability for both good or evil, and Pope Gregory believed they presided over demons. Their chief is said to be either SAMAEL or Camael, both angels of darkness. The *Excerpt of Theodotus* says that powers were the first created angels.

The *principalities*, are beings which have "princely powers" and watch over the actions of the Earth's nations and cities—the visible world of humankind. They also govern and protect religion on this planet. Their chiefs are Requel, Anael, Cerviel and Nisroc.

The *archangels* are liaisons between God and mortals; they are in charge of Heaven's armies in the battle against hell;

and they are the supervisors of the guardian angels. They themselves are guardian angels to great people, such as heads of religions and states. They carry the divine decrees of God.

The most significant archangel for the Catholic church is MICHAEL, the ruling prince of the order, who defends the church against the forces of darkness. Michael is the only angel named in the Bible who is specifically called an archangel (Jude 1:9). In Daniel (10:13, 21), he is called "one of the chief princes" and "your prince," implying to some that he is an archangel.

There is only one other biblical reference to an archangel, but no names are given. In speaking about the Second Coming, I Thessalonians 4:16 states: "For the Lord himself will descend from heaven with a cry of command, with the archangel's call, and with the sound of the trumpet of God."

Revelation 8:2 speaks of "seven angels who stand before God," but again no names are given. Elsewhere in Revelation (12:7), Michael is named only as an angel. The seven who stand before God are widely interpreted to be archangels.

The Book of Tobit, part of the Catholic canon but otherwise considered apochryphal, features RAPHAEL as a central figure. (See TOBIT.)

The Book of Enoch names the seven as URIEL, RAGUEL, Michael, Seraquel, GABRIEL, Haniel and Raphael (also said to be the prince of the order of archangels). Various other writings in the PSEUDEPIGRAPHA and APOCHRYPHA present other candidates for the title of archangel, such as PHANUEL (as a substitute for Uriel), Oriphiel, Zadkiel, Anael, Jehudiel, Sealtiel and Barachiel.

Catholicism considers Gabriel and Raphael to be archangels, and has elevated these two angels, along with Michael, to sainthood. There are numerous devotions to these three angels (see DEVOTIONAL CULTS).

In Islam, the Koran acknowledges the existence of four archangels but names only two: Jibril (Gabriel), the angel of revelation, and Michael, the warrior angel. It is likely that the other two are Azrael, the angel of death and ISRAFIL, the angel of music.

The *angels* are those closest to the material world. They are couriers of heaven, delivering prayers to God and God's answers, as well as other messages, to humans. They mirror the will of God.

**Further reading:**

Davidson, Gustav. *A Dictionary of Angels*. New York: The Free Press, 1967.

Godwin, Malcolm. *Angels: An Endangered Species*. New York: Simon & Schuster, 1990.

Humann, Harvey. *The Many Faces of Angels*. Marina del Rey, Calif.: De Vorss Publications, 1991.

Parente, Fr. Pascal P. *The Angels: The Catholic Teaching on the Angels*. Rockford, Ill.: Tan Books and Publishers, 1973. First published 1961.

*St. Michael and the Angels*. Rockford, Ill.: Tan Books and Publishers, 1983. First published 1977.

**Christian angelology**   See St. Thomas AQUINAS; St. AUGUSTINE; MONASTICISM, CHRISTIAN; PROTESTANT ANGELOLOGY; PSEUDO-DIONYSIUS.

**Coleridge, Samuel Taylor**   See LITERATURE AND ANGELS.

# D

**daemon (also daimon)**   In Greek mythology and religion, the term *daemon* was ubiquitous, referring to supernatural agents or intelligences, lower in rank than a god and holding a middle place between gods and humans, such as the Corybantes, Curetes, Dactyls, Satyrs and Sileni. Spirits of forests, rivers, glades and mountains, as well as cities presided over public and family life and were also referred to as daemons. Daemons could be either good or evil, but even good ones were believed to be capable of evil acts if angered by humans.

Daemons could also be ministering spirits, god like beings, souls of dead persons, or familiars (companion or helping spirits that take on animal forms). Generally they were considered by the Greeks to be protective and/or attending spirits much like guardian angels or Plotinus's notion of tutelary spirits (see INTELLIGENCES). In addition, gods themselves are invoked as daemons in certain texts.

Belief in daemons dates to ancient Mesopotamia. The Babylonians had an elaborate daemonology, in which daemons were organized into armies and hierarchies, and like angels had specific duties.

The Greeks also had a large daemonology. Their term *daimon* originally meant "divine being," and was not always distinguished from the term *theos* for "god." It was not until the Hellenistic period that the two terms became distinctly different.

Daemons were said to haunt locales, take over human bodies in the form of possession (especially for oracular prophecies), and also to possess humans in order to cause physical and mental illness. Some were vampiric in nature (see LILITH).

In particular, daemons were associated with the dead. The ancients believed that the remains of dead people retained for a time a spark of life force, which could be conjured in magical practices. Such daemonic entities could be asked for advice or dispatched on errands.

Other daemons were akin to angels and were associated with stars and planets and the plants and minerals of the earth. In the Hellenistic period there was a popular belief in a good daemon, called an *agathodaimon*, who functioned as a kind of guardian angel. An evil daemon was referred to as a *kakodaimon*.

Plato, in *Laws* II. 914b, warns pious Greeks not to disturb abandoned property, as it is guarded by the spirit of the wayside. In *Laws* V, he reminds his fellow countrymen not to mistreat aliens, as they are protected by the demigod Zeus Xenios.

Plato's works add a complex texture to the senses in which ancient Greece conceived of the three worlds of gods, daemons and humans. In *Epinomis* 984–985 he distinguishes the order and characteristics of the gods, various immortals under the rubric daemons, naming first the

> stars as visible gods . . . ; after them and below them, come in order the daemons and the creatures of the air, who hold the third and midmost rank, doing the office of interpreters, and should be peculiarly honored in our prayers that they may transmit comfortable messages. Both sorts of creature, those of aether and those of air, who hold the rank next to them, we shall say, are wholly transparent; however close they are to us, they go undiscerned. Being, however, of a kind that is quick to learn and of retentive memory, they read all our thoughts and regard the good and noble with signal favor, but the very evil with deep aversion. For *they* are not exempt from feeling pain, whereas a god who enjoys the fullness of deity is clearly above both pain and pleasure though possessed of all-embracing wisdom and knowledge. The universe being thus full throughout of living creatures, they all, so we shall say, act as interpreters, and interpreters of all things, to one another and to the highest gods, seeing that the middle ranks of creatures can flit so lightly over the earth and the whole universe. As for the fifth and last of our substances, water, the safest guess would be that what is formed from it is a demigod. . . .

Plato concludes "these five sorts of creatures must surely exist, when it comes to beliefs of individuals or whole societies originating in the intercourse of some of them with us—appearance in dreams of the night, oracular and prophetic voices heard by the whole or the sick, or communications in the last hours of life—and those have been, as they will be hereafter, the resources of many a widespread cult. . . ." He adds that rulers need to be sensitive to these worship needs, "inherited usages. . . ."

In *Cratylus* 397–398, Socrates begins a definition of daemons as "the golden race of men who came first" by quoting Hesiod's *Works and Days* 121: "But now that Fate has closed over this race,/ They are holy daemons upon the earth,/ Beneficent, averters of ills, guardians of mortal men." He explains that "golden" meant "good and noble" and not really gold, and says

> I have the most entire conviction that he [Hesiod] called them daemons, because they were daemon, [meaning knowing or wise] . . . and other poets say truly that when a good men dies he has honor and a mighty portion among the dead, and becomes a daemon . . . signifying wisdom. And I say too, that every wise man who happens to be a good man is more than human both in life and death, and is rightly called a daemon.

In *Apology* 26–27, Socrates defends himself against a charge that he does not believe in daemons, or demigods, by explaining that daemons are to gods as flute-playing is to flute-players, or horsemanship is to horses, therefore belief in supernatural and divine activities implies belief in supernatural and divine beings, and vice versa.

In *Phaedo* 107–108, Socrates discusses the immortality of the soul and explains that when anyone dies, the GUARDIAN SPIRIT, which was given charge of him in life, tries to bring the deceased to a place of assembly for judgment, and then sets out to Hades in the company of a guide whose job it is to escort souls from this world to the other. The soul, which is deeply attached to the body, will not leave readily, and only after much resistance and suffering is it at last led forcibly away by its appointed guardian spirit.

In *Statesman* 274, Plato retells a creation and fall myth which suggests that humankind's failings are explained by its presence in a cycle "bereft of the guardian care of the daemon who had governed and reared us up, . . . [and regressed to] become weak and helpless. . . ." In *Timaeus* 41 Plato recasts another creation myth, saying, in the voice of the creator of the universe speaking to the first gods, that their job is to create three tribes of mortal beings, but "the part of them worthy of the name immortal, which is called divine and is the guiding principle of those who are willing to follow justice and you—of that divine part I will myself sow the seed, and having made a beginning, I will hand the work over to you. And do ye then interweave the mortal with the immortal and make and beget living creatures. . . ."

Plutarch developed a complex daemonology that assigned daemons functions traditionally assigned to gods. Daemons were spiritual beings that lived for centuries, he said, and their thoughts were so intense that vibrations were created that could be picked up by other spiritual beings and highly sensitive humans as well.

St. AUGUSTINE devoted several chapters of Books 8 and 9 of *The City of God* to Greek and Neoplatonist beliefs and practices with regard to daemons, still flourishing in his own day, with the objective of discrediting them and implying through rhetorical parallelism the superiority of Christian cosmology and theology. The blanket condemnation of all pagan daemons was complete by medieval times, though the church continued to believe implicitly in their existence. Demons, as they became known, were usually considered to be messengers and assistants of a single devil, in the same relationship to the Devil as the angels to God.

According to St. Thomas AQUINAS, all bad weather and natural catastrophes are brought about by demons. He said "it is a dogma of faith that demons can produce wind, storms, and rain of fire from heaven." Pope Eugene IV issued a bull against human "agents of Satan" who controlled weather-demons, and Pope John XXII complained of wizards trying to kill him through the agency of demons sent into inanimate objects.

See DEMON.

**Further reading:**

*A Plato Reader*. Trans. B. Jowett., ed. Ronald B. Levinson. Boston: Houghton Mifflin, 1967.

Luck, Georg. *Arcana Mundi: Magic and the Occult in the Greek and Roman Worlds*. Baltimore: Johns Hopkins University Press, 1985.

**Daniel, Book of** Daniel is second only to REVELATION in apocalyptic tone and arcane imagery, with many striking variations on familiar (MICHAEL and GABRIEL) and unfamiliar angels. It was one of the last books to be included in the Old Testament canon, about 165 B.C.E., and depicts some of the sufferings of the Jews under Hellenic domination, especially the pressure to conform to idolatry. Daniel is purported to be present at the court of Nebuchadnezzar (604–562), but much of the historically allegorical prophecy actually describes events that were well past by the second century B.C.E. The opening of the book is in Hebrew, but in 2:4 it switches abruptly into Aramaic until the end of Chapter 7, and so into the remaining chapters in Hebrew. This would suggest two documents of different periods combined by an editor, but scholars have not come up with a convincing explanation of the duality of language, because there is a unity in the literary devices and habits of thought throughout.

The crises of the first few chapters occur when Daniel, Hananiah, Mishael and Azariah—young Hebrews who have been educated and found favor in the Babylonian court and have been given the Babylonian names respectively of Belteshazzar, Shadrach, Meshach and Abednego—are pressured to worship idols or ordered not to worship any god besides the king. Shadrach, Meshach and Abednego are thrown into a fiery furnace, which is so hot that servants stoking it are burned up, but the ANGEL OF THE LORD keeps the Hebrews cool and unscathed (3:19–20). While in the furnace the three sing a beautiful song praising all the works of the Lord. When Nebuchadnezzar sees what is happening he is amazed and says he sees four men in the furnace "and the fourth looks like a son of the gods" (3:25).

The Aramaic word used in 3:25 is *ir*, usually translated "watcher," a term for angels that appears in the Apocrypha—but only in Daniel in the canonical Bible. This word was associated in the ancient [Aramaic] Ugaritic language with *irim*, local protecting gods. The Israelite monotheists transformed these watchers into angels, and their old name, its meaning lost, came to be understood as "wakeful." It was interpreted by some to mean archangels, not infrequently fallen archangels in the Apocrypha. In later tradition the "watchers" became guardian angels. Nebuchadnezzar himself declares that God has sent his angel to protect the three (3:28). In 7:16 it is "one of those who stand by" (a watcher) who interprets a complex dream for Daniel.

The Hebrews remain safe and rise to great prominence in Babylonia while Nebuchadnezzar lives. Daniel, however, who has gained tremendous prestige in Nebuchadnezzar's court because he has managed to interpret the king's dreams when no one else can, is thrown into a lion pit by the next ruler for praying to his own god instead of to him. Daniel is protected. "My God sent his angel who sealed the lions' jaws, they did me no harm, since in his sight I am blameless, and I have never done you any harm either, O king" (6:22–24). The villains who plotted to trap Daniel are thrown to the lions and eaten immediately.

Chapter 7 recounts a complex apocalyptic vision with four beasts, the "Ancient of Days," and in 7:13–14 a much-discussed manlike figure:

I gazed into the visions of the night, and I saw, coming on the clouds of heaven, one like a son of man. He came to the one of great age and was led into his presence. On him was conferred sovereignty, glory and kingship, and men of all people, nations and languages became his servants. His sovereignty is an eternal sovereignty which shall never pass away, nor will his empire ever be destroyed.

In all the Old Testament, Jewish and Talmudic literature, heavenly beings do not emerge from the transcendent sphere on clouds except to show themselves to man. Some have taken this manlike figure to represent (the faithful of) Israel, and others have taken it to be the Messiah. But some modern scholars now parallel the theophany of God to the earth (the Ancient of Days) with this one, a theophany of his agent, that is, an angel. In 7:15–18 "one of those standing" (a "watcher") interprets this for Daniel, saying "those who are granted sovereignty are the saints (holy ones) of the Most High." Some linguists assert that the Aramaic word for "saint" normally denotes supernatural beings (e.g., Psalms 89:5–7; Zechariah 14:5; Deuteronomy 33:2; and in Daniel 4:13 and 8:13), and note that in the Qumran literature this is the title par excellence given to angels. It is suggested therefore that verses 14 and 18 refer to the kingdom given to the angelic hosts; the world is now ruled by the powers of heaven instead of the evil powers. It is even conceivable that the manlike figure is MICHAEL, leader of the hosts of heaven and representative of the saints on earth. This reading of the passage is by no means shared by all.

Another vision puzzles Daniel, and as he tries to understand it "I saw someone standing before me who looked like a man. I heard a man's voice cry over the Ulai [a gate], 'GABRIEL, tell him the meaning of the vision!' He approached the place where I was standing; as he approached I was seized with terror and fell prostrate" (8:15–17), and Gabriel interprets for him. This experience ends with Daniel falling into unconsciousness and being ill for several weeks (8:27). This illness makes sense in the context of what Maimonides says about Daniel: "The speech of the angel to him and his setting him upright, all this happened in a vision of prophecy. In a state such as this the senses too cease to function, and the overflow in question comes to the rational faculty and overflows from it to the imaginative faculty so that the latter becomes perfect and performs its function" (*Guide of the Perplexed*: II, 41; 385). When things happen through the agency of angels, and when God is said to have spoken to someone, these events all take place "in a dream or in a vision of prophecy."

In a later incident, while Daniel is in prayer, "Gabriel, the being I had seen originally in a vision, flew suddenly down to me at the hour of the evening sacrifice. He said to me, Daniel, you see me; I have come down to teach you how to understand. . . . You are a man specially chosen. Grasp the meaning of the word, understand the vision" (9:20–23). In other apocalyptic visions it is a "man in white linen" who explains them to Daniel. In 10:5–6 he sees

> a man dressed in linen, with a girdle of pure gold round his waist, his body was like beryl, his face shone like lightning, his eyes were like fiery torches, his arms and his legs had the gleam of burnished bronze, the sound of his voice was like the noise of a crowd. I, Daniel, alone saw the apparition; the men who were with me did not see the apparition, but so great a trembling overtook them that they fled to hide. I was left alone, gazing on this great apparition; I was powerless, my appearance altered out of all recognition, what strength I had deserted me.

A cherub (Toome, in Heyward's *Hierarchy of the Blessed Angels*, 17th c.)

When this apparition speaks, Daniel falls to the ground unconscious, but then he feels a hand touching him and setting his knees and hands trembling. Daniel is told again that he is specially chosen to receive the prophetic news about the times to come.

He tells about a battle that has been going on for twenty-one days between him and "the prince of Persia" and "Michael, one of the leading princes, came to my assistance" (10:13). He says a bit later that Michael is the guardian angel of the people of God (10:21). In this vision the man dressed in white linen shows to Daniel: "In all this there is no one to lend me support except Michael your [Daniel's] prince." Scholars have found references in the Dead Sea Scrolls to this "supreme angel" who relates the military situation to Daniel here. He is probably the "army's Prince" referred to in an earlier vision (8:11). The "Prince of Light(s)" (also with other names in the Dead Sea Scrolls) has a similar military office. The literal translation of 1QM17, 6–7 shows that he is not Michael but assists Michael and Israel.

In 12:1 another prophecy is given to Daniel of "the time of the end." "At that time Michael will stand up, the great prince who mounts guard over your people" (cf. Exodus 23:20ff). The prince of Persia in 10:13 is apparently one of the guardian angels of the nations (these also are associated with principalities—see ORIGEN, PSEUDO-DIONYSIUS, St. Thomas AQUINAS). This championing of opposed sides by different angels signifies that the fate of nations is a secret awaiting God's revelation and hidden from the angels themselves, and also parallels Michael's functions in REVELATION.

**Further reading:**

Beasley-Murray, G. R. "The Interpretation of Daniel 7," *The Catholic Biblical Quarterly*. Vol. 45, No. 1. January, 1985.

Maimonides. *Guide of the Perplexed*. Ed. and Trans. S. Pines. Chicago: University of Chicago Press, 1963.

Introduction and notes, *Jerusalem Bible*. Garden City, New York: Doubleday, 1966.

**dakini**   See TANTRIC BUDDHISM.

**Dante Alighieri** (1265–1321)   Dante generally is considered one of the greatest poets and writers of the late Middle Ages. T. S. Eliot remarked once that Shakespeare and Dante divide the modern world between them, allowing no third. Dante's epic *The Divine Comedy (La Divina Commedia)* established his Tuscan dialect as the literary tongue of Italy and gave readers a detailed exposition of medieval man's conception of God and His perfect, changeless universe. Dante's travels into Hell, Purgatory and finally Heaven not only glorify God but serve as a chatty tabloid of the follies and sins of past and present political and church figures, clarify the Catholic church's position on supposed heresies of the day, and extol and sanctify the memory of Beatrice Portinari, Dante's greatest love.

Born in Florence in 1265 to a noble but impoverished family, Dante studied at the university in Bologna. Around the year 1295 he began to take an active interest in the byzantine world of Florentine politics, siding with the Guelphs, or the bourgeoisie, in their struggles against the aristocratic Ghibellines. When the Black Guelphs defeated the White faction in 1302, Dante was banished to Ravenna, where he wrote *The Divine Comedy*.

He first met Beatrice at the age of eleven in 1274, encountering her again in 1281 and again in 1283. Even though Dante married Gemma Donati in 1284, his unrequited but pure passion did not die. Beatrice died in June of 1290.

Virgil, the ancient Roman poet, accompanies Dante on his journeys through the *Inferno* and *Purgatorio*, but the angelic Beatrice guides his voyage into Heaven's holy spheres in the *Paradiso*. Along the way she introduces him to various biblical and contemporary spirits who have earned the right to approach God as the center of the universe, populating several lower spheres and ascending to the highest sphere or Empyrean.

When Dante and Beatrice arrive at the Ninth Sphere, or the Primum Mobile, Dante sees a brilliant point of light surrounded by nine spinning, dazzling spheres. The closer spheres are more radiant than those further away, leading Beatrice to explain that they are more brilliant because of their absorption of God's essence.

These nine spheres are the Angel Hierarchy, organized into the nine ranks of traditional medieval thought: seraphim, cherubim, thrones; dominions or dominations, virtues, powers; principalities, archangels, angels. The angels are too numerous to count, as they concentrate on God and sing and praise His name. Beatrice explains that Love created the angels as "pure act" without potential for further greatness.

Since according to Beatrice, all Creation occurred simultaneously, Lucifer's fall from grace happened before a person could count to twenty. Dante calls him a principality, or Prince of Heaven, instead of an archangel. He fell because of pride, she explains to Dante, and those angels that remain do so because they are humble and undemanding, and possess a higher vision illumined by grace.

**Beatrice and Dante before the Empyrean (Gustave Doré)**

Totally focused on God's light and secure in their own eternity, these angels have no understanding, memory or will, as man comprehends these attributes. Their eyes never turn from God.

Proceeding upward into the lower levels of the Empyrean, Dante learns that the angels he first saw are what Beatrice describes as the "sacred soldiery": those mortal souls who, through their sanctity, encircle God the Father within their nine spheres. Beatrice sits as a throne in the third sphere.

Within the Empyrean are the Angelic Host: those angels created by God who never left Paradise. Instead of encircling the Father they fly rapidly back and forth between God and His Son, represented by a Mystic Rose, much as bees swarm between the hive and the flowers. Dante's translator and critic, John Ciardi, describes this swarming as taking the sweetness of God's hive to the flowers and returning to God the bliss of Heaven's souls.

In Dante's vision, then, as opposed to Milton's in *Paradise Lost*, there are two angelic congregations: one created by God and one dedicated to God. Both, however, appear as beautiful, shining, gold-winged and dazzling creatures. And all receive their happiness and grace through the redeeming ardor of Love.

Dante also was an accomplished painter and sculptor. He writes in *La Vita Nuova* (c. 1294), a work preceding *La Divina Commedia*, that as he reflected on Beatrice's ascension into heaven, "among the angels in the realm of peace" (Chapter XXXI), he was painting angels on boards. Ciardi speculates that these angels were part of a larger work commissioned for a church.

See LITERATURE AND ANGELS.

**Further reading:**

Arthos, John. *Dante, Michaelangelo and Milton*. London: Routledge and Kegan Paul, 1963.

Dante Alighieri. *La Vita Nuova*, translated by Barbara Reynolds. Harmondsworth, Middlesex, England: Penguin Books, 1969.

———. *The Divine Comedy*, translated by John Ciardi. New York: W. W. Norton & Co., 1961.

Elledge, Scott, ed. *John Milton: Paradise Lost, An Authoritative Text*. New York: W. W. Norton & Co., 1975.

Levey, Judith S. and Agnes Greenhall, eds. *The Concise Columbia Encyclopedia*. New York: Columbia University Press, 1983.

**days of the week, angels of**   Various angels are associated with the days of the week in occult magical lore. Their names are to be invoked in rituals.

In addition to days, the angels also have other associations: the seven major planets of the ancient world, the air, the directions of the wind and different levels of heaven. Within each level of heaven are four directions, each associated with angels. Each day is ideal for different activities. Duplication among angels occurs.

The associations, drawn from *The Magus* by occultist Francis Barrett (1801) are as follows:

### SUNDAY

Chief angel: MICHAEL
Other angels: Dardiel, Huratapel
Angels of the air: Varcan, king, and his ministers Tus, Andus and Cynabal
Wind: North
Heaven: Fourth
Angels of the east: SAMAEL, Baciel, Abel, Gabriel, Vionatraba
Angels of the west: Anael, Pabel, Ustael, Burchat, Succratos, Capabili
Angels of the north: Aiel, ARIEL, Aquiel, Masgrabiel, Saphiel, Matuyel
Angels of the south: Haluliel, Machasiel, Charsiel, URIEL, Naromiel
Planet: Sun
Favorable activities: acquiring gold and gems (wealth), seeking favor and honors, dissolving ill will, eliminating infirmities

### MONDAY

Chief angel: GABRIEL
Other angels: Michael, Samael
Angels of the air: Arcan, king, and his ministers Bilet, Missabu, Abuhaza
Wind: West
Heaven: First
Angels of the east: Gabriel, Madiel, Deamiel, Janak
Angels of the west: Sachiel, Zaniel, Habiel, Bachanae, Corobael
Angels of the north: Mael, Uvael, Valmuum, Baliel, Balay, Humastraw
Angels of the south: Curaniel, Dabriel, Hanun, Vetuel
Planet: Moon
Favorable activities: procuring silver, conveying things from place to place, disclosing secrets of people both present and future, making horses swift

### TUESDAY

Chief angel: SAMAEL
Other angels: Satael, Amabiel
Angels of the air: Samax, king, and his ministers Carmax, Ismoli, Paffran
Wind: East
Heaven: Fifth
Angels of the east: Friagne, Guel, Damael, Calzas, Arragon
Angels of the west: Lama, Astagna, Lobquin, Soneas, Jazel, Isael, Irel
Angels of the north: Rhaumel, Hyniel, Rayel, Seraphiel, Fraciel, Mathiel
Angels of the south: Sacriel, Janiel, Galdel, Osael, Vianuel, Zaliel
Planet: Mars
Favorable activities: bringing or causing war, death, infirmity and combustions (fire)

### WEDNESDAY

Chief angel: RAPHAEL
Other angels: Meil, Seraphiel
Angels of the air: Mediat, king, and his ministers Suquinos, Sallales
Wind: Southwest
Heaven: Second
Angels of the east: Mathlai, Tarmiel, Baraborat
Angels of the west: Jerusque, Merattron
Angels of the north: Thiel, Rael, Harihael, Venahel, Velel, Abuiori, Ucirmiel
Angels of the south: Milliel, Nelapa, Calvel, Laquel
Planet: Mercury
Favorable activities: procuring all sorts of metals, revealing all earthly things past, present and future, pacifying judges, giving victory in war, teaching experiments and sciences, changing things alchemically, procuring health, raising the poor and casting down the rich, binding or loosing spirits, opening locks and bolts

### THURSDAY

Chief angel: Sachiel
Other angels: Cassiel, Asasiel
Angels of the air: Suth, king, and his ministers Maguth, Gutrix
Wind: South
Heaven: None, because there are no angels of the air above the fifth heaven (instead of prayers to angels, prayers are directed to the four directions)
Planet: Jupiter
Favorable activities: procuring the love of women, causing merriment and joy, pacifying strife, appeasing enemies, healing the diseased, procuring things lost

### FRIDAY

Chief angel: Anael
Other angels: Rachiel, Sachiel
Angels of the air: Sarabotes, king, and his ministers Amahiel, Aba, Abalidoth, Blaef
Wind: West

Heaven: Third

Angels of the east: Setchiel, Chedusitaniel, Corat, Tamuel, Tenaciel

Angels of the west: Turiel, Coniel, Babiel, Kadie, Maltiel, Huphaltiel

Angels of the south: Porosa, Sachiel, Chermiel, Samael, Santanael, Famiel

Planet: Venus

Favorable activities: procuring silver and luxuries, causing marriages, alluring men to love women, causing or removing informities, and doing all things which have motion

### SATURDAY

Chief angel: CASSIEL

Other angels: Machatan, Uriel

Angels of the air: Maymon, king, and his ministers Abumalith, Assabibi, Balidet

Wind: South

Heaven: None; same as Thursday

Planet: Saturn

Favorable activities: sowing of discord, hate, evil thoughts and irritations, maiming and murdering

**Further reading:**

Barrett, Francis. *The Magus*. Secaucus, N.J.: The Citadel Press, 1967. First published 1801.

**deathbed visions**  Dying persons who retain consciousness as they near death sometimes report seeing and communicating with angels, gods, religious figures and apparitions of the dead. Such deathbed visions have been recorded since antiquity and share common characteristics regardless of racial, cultural, religious, educational, age and socioeconomic factors.

The first scientific study of deathbed visions was done in the early twentieth century by William Barrett, an English professor of physics and psychical researcher. Barrett became interested in deathbed visions in 1924 when his wife, a physician specializing in obstetrical surgery, told him about a woman patient who spoke of seeing visions of a place of great beauty, and of her dead father and sister, shortly before she died. The visions were real to the patient, and transformed her into a state of great radiance and peace. Barrett was struck by the fact that the woman had not known that her sister had died about three weeks earlier.

Several decades later, Barrett's research interested Karlis Osis, then director of research for Eileen Garrett's Parapsychology Foundation. Under the auspices of the Foundation in 1959–60, and later the American Society for Psychical Research in 1961–64 and 1972–73, Osis collected information from doctors and nurses on tens of thousands of deathbed and near-death experiences in the United States and India. The Indian survey (1972–73) was conducted with Erlendur Haraldsson. Of those cases, more than a thousand were examined in detail. The findings of these studies confirmed Barrett's findings, as well as research of the NEAR-DEATH EXPERIENCE (NDE) and research with the terminally ill.

Deathbed visions usually come to individuals who die gradually, as from terminal illness or injuries, rather than those who die suddenly, as from heart attacks. The majority of visions are of apparitions of the dead, who usually are

Angel taking away the soul of a child (reprinted courtesy of U.S. Library of Congress)

close family members and appear to be glowing and dressed in white. Other apparitions are of angels and other religious figures, such as Jesus, the Virgin Mary, and gods and semidivine beings pertinent to a person's background.

The primary purpose of these apparitions is to beckon or command the dying to come with them; thus, they are frequently called "take-away apparitions." The dying person usually is happy and willing to go, especially if the individual believes in an afterlife. (However, deathbed visions do occur to people who do not believe in an afterlife.) If the person has been in great pain or depression, a complete turnaround of mood is observed, and pain vanishes. The dying one literally seems to "light up" with radiance. Osis and Haraldsson, in their book *At the Hour of Death*, relate this story:

> The condition of one man, suffering from a heart attack, had been serious for the last few days. Suddenly he gained consciousness. He looked better and cheerful. He talked nicely to his relatives and requested them to go home. He said, "I shall go to my home. Angels have come to take me." He looked relieved and cheerful.

Other persons present usually cannot see the apparitions. Sometimes people see a cloud or mist form over the patient at the moment of death, and usually interpret it as the soul leaving the body.

Angel guarding a tomb (author's collection)

Approximately one-third of deathbed visions involve total visions, in which the patient sees another world—heaven or a heavenly place, such as beautiful gardens or alpine meadows. Some people also see gates, bridges, rivers and boats, which are symbolic of transition, as well as castles and beautiful cities. Sometimes these places are filled with angels or glowing souls of the dead.

Such visions are resplendent with intense and vivid colors and bright light. They either unfold before the patient, or the patient feels transported out-of-body to them. As with apparitional figures, visions of ethereal places fill the person with radiant joy and anticipation. Interestingly, few total visions conform to religious expectations about the nature of the afterlife. Researcher Osis found only one case of a vision described as hell, from a Catholic woman who seemed to be carrying a great burden of guilt about her "sins."

A small number of persons in the Osis-Haraldsson research reported hearing heavenly or angelic music. The incidence of music is higher in cases collected around the turn of the century by earlier psychical researchers, and may reflect the different tastes in music then.

Most deathbed visions are short: approximately 50 percent last five minutes or less; 17 percent last from six to fifteen minutes; and 17 percent last more than one hour. The visions usually appear just minutes before death: approximately 76 percent of the patients studied died within ten minutes of their vision, and nearly all of the rest died within one or several hours. The appearance of the vision seems to have little connection with the physical condition of the patient. Some who seemed to be recovering, then had visions, quickly fell into comas and died. Consider the following anecdote from *At the Hour of Death*, involving a girl of ten dying from pneumonia:

> The mother saw that her child seemed to be sinking and called us [nurses]. She said that the child had just told her she had seen an angel who had taken her by the hand—and she was gone, died immediately. That just astounded us because there was no sign of imminent death. She was so calm, serene—and so close to death! We were all concerned.

Natural explanations of deathbed visions include drugs, fever, disease-induced hallucinations, oxygen deprivation to the brain, wish-fulfillment and depersonalization. These factors can cause hallucinations, but rarely do the hallucinations concern the afterlife. The Osis-Haraldsson research found that deathbed visions are most likely to occur in patients who are fully conscious.

Deathbed visions are significant to thanatology, the scientific study of death and dying, and also provide evidence in support of survival after death.

The literature on Christian saints includes numerous accounts of saints who saw and heard angels prior to their deaths; sometimes the angels were heard or witnessed by others. St. Vincent Ferrar, a Dominican, was able to see and converse with the Guardian Angel of Barcelona, which caused a devotional cult for that angel to spring up there. Upon St. Vincent's death, a multitude of angels gathered at his deathbed in the form of beautiful white birds. The birds vanished at the moment the saint expired.

Many of the early martyrs, persecuted by the Romans, credited angels with providing comfort during their unspeakable torture, and with standing by as they faced death. St. Lawrence was being beaten and stretched on a rack when a voice suddenly boomed out of nowhere that he was reserved for still greater trials. The voice, attributed to an angel, surprised bystanders and convinced at least one soldier, Romanus, to convert to Christianity. St. Lawrence was then roasted slowly on a gridiron, and died. St. Eulalia, who was only twelve when she was threatened with horrible tortures if she did not renounce her faith, was consoled by three angels who told her to suffer with courage. She was burned alive, and angels reportedly took her soul to heaven.

See ANGEL OF DEATH.

**Further reading:**

Barrett, William. *Death-Bed Visions: The Psychical Experiences of the Dying*. Wellingborough, Northhamptonshire, England: The Aquarian Press, 1986. First published 1926.

Osis, Karlis. *Deathbed Observations by Physicians and Nurses*. Monograph No. 3. New York: Parapsychology Foundation, 1961.

Osis, Karlis and Erlendur Haraldsson. *At the Hour of Death*. Rev. ed. New York: Hastings House, 1986.

O'Sullivan, Fr. Paul. *All About the Angels*. Rockford, Ill.: Tan Books and Publishers, 1990. First published 1945.

**Dee, John** (1527–1608)   English alchemist, mathematician, astronomer and astrologer, who devoted most of his life to trying to communicate with the angelic realm. He was a credulous man, and his desire to speak with angels, coupled by his failure to do so on his own, made him a gullible target for fraudulent mediums.

John Dee exhibited scholastic brilliance at an early age; he was made one of the original fellows at Trinity College at Cambridge. He was a respected lecturer at home and abroad. He was fascinated by the occult and magic, and was well versed in Neoplatonic, Hermetic and kabbalistic philosophy. He was sometimes called "the last royal magician" because of his astrological services to Queen Elizabeth I. His occult interests, however, landed him in trouble. In 1555 he was imprisoned on accusations that he had cast death spells on Queen Mary I. In 1583, a mob whipped up by witch-frenzy ransacked his home in Montlake, burning many of his valuable books. Queen Elizabeth reimbursed him for some of the £2,000 in damages. He was able to salvage some 3,000 books, most of which are currently in British museums.

Dee suffered from continuous financial problems, and turned to alchemy for a solution. He desired to contact angels who would help him find the philosopher's stone (a mysterious substance that allegedly could turn base metals into silver and gold) or else discover buried treasure. He was influenced by Cornelius Agrippa's *Three Books of Occult Philosophy*, which describe the cosmic ladder of angels (see JACOB) and how one might ascend to the level of angels through magic. Dee also paid great attention to his dreams and to scrying with a mirror of black obsidian.

Dee could not cultivate his own mediumistic ability, and so he advertised for mediums. His first partnership was with a young man named Barnabas Saul, who got into trouble with the law after a few months. His second partner was Edward Talbot (who became known as Edward Kelly), a hot-tempered Irishman who'd lost his ears as punishment for forgery. Kelly came to Dee's house and demonstrated his ability by scrying into a stone. After about fifteen minutes he said he could see an angel, who identified himself as URIEL. Dee felt uneasy about Kelly, and dismissed him. But Kelly persisted, and Dee then relented. For seven years, the two had an uneasy partnership which Kelly dominated and for which Dee paid Kelly a salary.

Kelly would gaze into a crystal stone and summon spirits with incantations, or "calls" in a complex and secret magical language, Enochian, of unknown origin. It is a real language with its own grammar and syntax, and similar in sound to Sanskrit, Arabic or Greek. Many believe Kelly and Dee invented it. Dee would ask the spirits questions and Kelly, as the medium, would relay their answers, which Dee took down in dictation. They conjured the angels with the Nineteen Calls or Keys of Enochian. The first two keys conjured the element Spirit, and the next sixteen keys conjured the four Elements of nature, each of which was also subdivided into four classes. The nineteenth key invoked any of thirty "aethyrs" or "aires" which they never defined, but which probably represent levels of consciousness, or are comparable to the aeons of GNOSTICISM.

When the angels appeared in Kelly's crystal, he communicated with them in Enochian by using charts of squares either filled with letters or left blank. The angels would spell out messages by having Kelly point with a rod to various squares.

To further add to the air of mystery that he liked to engender, Kelly claimed the messages were always dictated backwards, because to communicate them directly would unleash dangerous and powerful forces beyond control. When the messages were finished, he and Dee rewrote them in reverse order.

In one of Dee's own, few psychic experiences, he saw Uriel floating outside his window, holding a pale pink crystal about the size of an orange. The archangel MICHAEL appeared and told Dee to use it for scrying. This crystal, and Dee's obsidian "magic mirror" and other instruments, are in the British Museum.

Dee's *Spiritual Diaries* form an intriguing, firsthand account of alleged communication with angels. Many encounters are suspect; the angels wax on at great length, and some of the entries appear to have been rewritten in a neat, not scribbled, hand. Curiously, Dee, who professed be on a search for spiritual truth, peppered the angels with the most mundane and trivial questions, of the kind one might pose to a fortuneteller. The occasional mystical philosophies and revelations of the angels seem to be regurgitations of material that could have been found in magical and kabbalistic texts available at the time.

Kelly exhibited an unbalanced personality and was prone to fits of rage and darkness, which were reflected in his sessions with the spirits. He offered up dark prophecies—many of which never came to pass—and descriptions of horrible, demonic beings. Sometimes he said he felt possessed by demonic beings and wanted to be exorcised of them. Dee, a devout Christian, was often wary of Kelly's visions. Concerned that he might be tricked by evil spirits, he put various tests to screen them out. However, if Dee thought that Kelly was accessing good angels, he tended to accept whatever was transmitted without question.

Dee and Kelly sold their services to a variety of noblemen, including Count Albert Laski of Poland, who brought them to Poland. From 1585 to 1589 Dee, Kelly and their families toured the Continent, performing for royalty and nobility, but with only modest success. Whenever Dee and Kelly quarreled, Kelly would stop scrying for a time. The pope accused Dee of necromancy (conjuring the dead), and they were thrown out of Prague. Kelly and Dee parted company shortly after Kelly announced that Madimi, one of their chief spirits, had ordered them to share wives, and that if anyone objected, God would strike them dead. Both wives were hysterical at the idea, and Dee himself was not pleased. Nonetheless he acquiesced, and convinced his wife to do the same. But before the swap could be consummated, Dee and Kelly split up. The Dees returned to England and Kelly remained in Europe. He was killed in 1595 while trying to escape from prison in Prague.

Back in England, Dee found a new medium partner, Batholomew Hickman. Queen Elizabeth made Dee warden of Christ's College in Manchester in 1595, but Dee did not like the job. In 1604, he unwisely challenged James I, successor to Elizabeth, to try him for sorcery, but nothing happened. He was however, dismissed from his college post a years later in 1605. He died in poverty and obscurity in 1608. His story has been resurrected in more recent times by historians of the Western magical and mystery tradition.

The language Enochian sank into oblivion until the nineteenth century, when it was revived by the Hermetic Order of the Golden Dawn, a magical order in England. Enochian also was studied at length by Aleister Crowley, who said the Keys were genuine, and worked. Crowley said that only properly initiated adepts could invoke all of the aethyrs in the Nineteenth Key (he claimed to be able to do this himself), which would produce visions of spirits and astral beings.

Enochian magic as a path of inner work continues to be practiced by magical adepts who use the Keys for astral travel to different levels of consciousness. (See MAGIC, ANGELS IN.)

**Further reading:**
Cavendish, Richard. *The Black Arts.* New York: Perigee Books, 1967.
Gilchrist, Cherry. "Dr. Dee and the Spirits," *Gnosis*, No. 35, Summer 1995, pp. 33–39.
Guiley, Rosemary Ellen. *The Encyclopedia of Witches and Witchcraft.* New York: Facts On File, 1989.

**demiurge**   See GNOSTICISM.

**demon**   A lesser spirit, usually regarded as malevolent. Pagan demons, called daemons, were both good and evil according to their inherent nature, and included a broad range of beings, from spirits of the dead to gods. But the Christian view, condemning all pagan spirits as evil, regards demons as agents of the devil whose purpose it is to ruin souls and condemn them to hell.

Judaic demonologies have long and complex histories, and distinguish between classes of demons. According to the Kabbalah, evil powers emanate from the left pillar of the Tree of Life, especially from Geburah, the *sephira* of the wrath of God. By the thirteenth century the idea had developed of ten evil *sephiroth* to counter the ten holy *sephiroth* of the Tree. Another system of demons distinguishes those born of night terrors (see LILITH), and describes demons that fill the sky between the earth and the moon. There are demons who, with angels, are in charge of the night hours, and interpretations of diseases, and those who have seals that may be used to summon them. The *Zohar* states that every pollution of semen spawns demons.

In Christian demonology, demons are associated only with evil and the Devil. By the end of the New Testament period, demons were synonymous with fallen angels, the one-third of the heavenly host cast out of heaven along with LUCIFER (later identified as SATAN), who all descended into hell. As Christianity spread, the ranks of demons swelled to include the gods and demons of the ancient Middle Eastern and Jewish traditions, and all pagan deities and nature spirits.

The fall of Satan and his angels is related in the Book of REVELATION: "And the great dragon was thrown down, that ancient serpent, who is called the Devil and Satan, the deceiver of the whole world—he was thrown down to the earth, and his angels were thrown down with him." (Revelation 12:9)

St. AUGUSTINE attributed this fall to pride and will: "Good and bad angels have arisen, not from a difference in their nature and origin . . . but from a difference in their wills and desires. . . . While some steadfastly continued in that which was the common good of all, namely, in God himself, and in His eternity, truth, and love; others . . . became proud, deceived, envious."

The story of the fallen angels was popularized in literary works, especially by John MILTON and DANTE (see also LITERATURE AND ANGELS.)

During the Middle Ages demons became associated with witches, who also were regarded as agents of the Devil. Much was written about the specific ways in which demons tormented humans, especially through sexual assault. Male demons (incubi) and female demons (succubi) were believed to visit people in their beds at night to copulate with them. Monstrous births were explained away as being the products of human–demon intercourse.

The preeminent guide of the day, *The Malleus Maleficarum* ("The Witch Hammer"), goes into great detail about the offenses of demons and witches. Written by two Dominican inquisitors, James Sprenger and Heinrich Kramer, *The Malleus Maleficarum* was first published in Germany in 1486, and quickly spread throughout Europe in dozens of editions.

The book is divided into three parts. Part I is concerned with how the devil and his demons and witches, with God's permission, perpetrate a variety of evils upon men and animals, including sexual assaults, instilling hatred, obstructing or destroying fertility, and changing humans into beasts. According to the authors, God permits these acts, otherwise the Devil would have unlimited power and destroy the world. Part II provides details of how witches cast spells and

**Demons (Gustave Doré)**

bewitchments—such as conjuring and controlling demons—and of how these actions may be prevented or remedied. Part III sets forth the legal prodecures for trying witches, including the taking of testimony, admission of evidence, procedures for interrogation and torture, and guidelines for sentencing.

### SEX WITH DEMONS

Inquisitors often sought confessions of sex with demons. Demons with appetites for intercourse with humans exist in demonologies around the world, and were part of the mythologies inherited by the Christian movement. However, the church denied the possibility of intercourse with demons prior to the twelfth century. But as the Inquisition gained force, the idea of intercourse with demons became accepted by the fourteenth century. Enemies of the church were said to not only have sex with demons, but to copulate wildly and frequently with them and to worship them. In many cases the distinction between the devil himself and demons was blurry. Such tales served the church's purpose of consolidating its power over the populace by branding all pagan deities and rites, and all acts of magic and sorcery as instruments of the devil.

Sex with demons invariably was portrayed as unpleasant and painful. Sometimes demons deceived people by appearing in the forms of spouses or lovers. After copulation they would reveal their true identities and blackmail the victims into continuing the sexual liaison.

Incubi were especially attracted to women with beautiful hair, young virgins, chaste widows, and all "devout" females. Nuns were among the most vulnerable, and could be molested in the confessional as well as in bed. While the majority of women were said to be forced into sex by the incubi, it was believed that some of them submitted willingly and even enjoyed the act. Incubi had huge phalluses, sometimes made of horn or covered with scales, and ejaculated icy semen. When they appeared as demons and not as human imposters, they were described as ugly, hairy and foul-smelling.

Incubi were believed to have the ability to impregnate women. They did not possess their own semen, but collected it from men in nocturnal emissions, masturbation, or in coitus while masquerading as succubi. The demons preserved semen and used it later on one of their victims.

Succubi were less prevalent (women were considered morally weak and therefore more licentious than men). If a man was assaulted by a succubus, it was most likely not his fault. The sex act with a succubus was often described as penetrating a cavern of ice. There are accounts of men being forced to perform cunnilingus on succubi, whose vaginas dripped with urine, dung and other vile juices and smells.

The wild copulation between witches (usually female) and demons was lamented in *The Malleus Maleficarum*, which noted that "in times long past the Incubus devils used to infest women against their wills [but] modern witches . . . willingly embrace this most foul and miserable servitude." Some incubi served as familiars to witches, who sent them to torment specific individuals.

The church prescribed five ways to get rid of sexual demons: sacramental confession, making the sign of the cross, reciting the Ave Maria, moving away, and exorcism. Reciting the Lord's Prayer and sprinkling holy water also were effective.

Sexual molestation by demons continues to be reported in modern times, often in connection with hauntings and poltergeist activities.

See also SEX AND ANGELS.

**Further reading:**
Connolly, David. *In Search of Angels.* New York: Perigee Books, 1993.
Guiley, Rosemary Ellen. *The Encyclopedia of Witches and Witchcraft.* New York: Facts On File, 1989.
Kramer, Heinrich and James Sprenger. *The Malleus Maleficarum.* London: John Rodker, 1928.
Remy, Nicolas. *Demonolatry.* Secaucus, N.J.: University Books, 1974. First published in 1595.
Russell, Jeffrey Burton. *A History of Witchcraft.* London: Thames and Hudson, 1980.

**destroying angel**   See ANGELS OF DESTRUCTION.

**deva**   An advanced spirit or god-being who governs the elementals and the well-being of all things in nature. In Sanskrit, *deva* means "shining one."

In Hinduism, the term *deva* has various meanings. It is a brahman in the form of a personal God. A brahman is an abstract concept expressing absolute being or absolute consciousness, a state of pure transcendence that defies precise description. A deva also is a mortal who has attained a state of divinity, but remains mortal. And a deva also is an enlightened person who has realized God.

In Buddhism, a deva is a god who lives in one of the good celestial realms (there are twenty-eight altogether). Such devas enjoy a long and happy life in these realms as a reward for having lived good lives while mortals. However, they are subject to the wheel of reincarnation. Their very happiness in their realm is an obstacle to their enlightenment, for they cannot come to terms with the truth of suffering, one of the four noble truths that form the basis of Buddhist philosophy. The truth of suffering holds that everything is suffering: birth, illness, death, dislikes, desires and attachments of the personality.

## DEVAS IN THEOSOPHY

The concept of devas was introduced to the West largely through the writings of Helena P. Blavatsky, cofounder of The Theosophical Society. According to Blavatsky, devas are types of angels or gods who can neither be propitiated nor worshipped by men. She quoted an Ascended Master, one of her mentors, as describing the devas, also called "Dhyan-Chohans," as progressed entities from a previous planetary period. In the evolution of new solar systems, the devas arrive before either elementals or man, and remain dormant until a certain stage of human evolution is reached. At that time the devas become an active force, and integrate with the elementals—(spirits of nature) to further the development of man. In classical Greece, Blavatsky said, a class of devas became symbolized by Prometheus, symbol of the purely spiritual man.

Theosophists believe that all religions stem from the same roots of ancient wisdom, and they find a belief in angels common to many religions. In fact the gods of ancient Greece and Rome, Assyria and Mexico, and those worshipped today by Indians, Native Americans and practitioners of Vodun, Santería and Candomblé, may actually be angels. Such beings are rays or emanations of the Divine Absolute, an impersonal, eternal ONE much different from the intensely personal God of Judeo-Christian tradition.

The idea of Divine Breath, of a sending forth of the Word of God, does not differ from the Logos doctrine of Christianity, however:

> In the beginning was the Word, and the Word was with God, and the Word was God. He was in the beginning with God; all things were made through him, and without him was not anything made that was made. In him was life, and the life was the light of men. . . . And the Word became flesh and dwelt among us, full of grace and truth.
>
> John 1:1–4, 14

According to Blavatsky in her book *The Secret Doctrine*, creation is the utterance of the Word, the Great Breath of the Absolute, into nothingness. The Divine Idea subdivides into three aspects—masculine, feminine and androgyne—eventually forming great patterns, called Archetypes, which are the basis of all life. These archetypes first become the Archangels, who transmit the Divine Will and Intelligence and serve as Lords of the planetary systems.

As energy is sent outward, and an organized hierarchy of devas, nature spirits, humans, animals, plants and minerals eventually forms under the ministry of the Archangels. This vast army of solar and planetary angels is called the Army of the Light, or the Hosts of the Logos. Each plant, each solar system, each type of being has an archangelic regent, supported by legions of lesser devas. Eternal emanations of the Word are continually transmitted, organized and refined by the Archangels and angels. Geoffrey HODSON, a Theosophist and clairvoyant, described this process of creation as a performance by the celestial symphony, conducted by the ONE as Divine Musician.

Devas appeared before the creation of man and are not the spirits of former humans. They are the ministers and messengers of the Absolute and have no personality separate from the Divine Will. Although they were patterned after the same archetypes as humans, devas have no clearly defined bodies or gender, differing solely by the order to which they belong.

There are orders of devas or gods responsible for every minute thing in the universe. Mountain Gods preside over the peaks, while Landscape Angels rule over the divisions and areas of the earth's surface. Builder Angels use the archetypes to create the lesser spirits, humans, animals, plants and rocks. Guardian Angels watch over humans, their homes, children and endeavors, while Healing Angels tend the sick, heal the wounded and console the bereaved. Ruler Angels guide and direct nations in the fulfillment of their destiny. Devas of Nature provide the spark of life to the Builders' creations and nurture each being's existence. Within this category are the nature spirits who tend the earth, air, fire and water, as well as the gods of storms, fire and weather. Devas of Art and Beauty lift up the beautiful in all things, while the Angels of Music bear the Voice of God, in all its complicated melodies, to mankind.

Borrowing from the Hebrew Kabbalah, Theosophy also organized the devas into seven *sephiroth*, usually designated the first emanations from the Divine ONE. These Seven Sephiroth are called the Archangels of the Face, the Mighty Spirits Before the Throne, the Seven Viceroys, the Cosmocratores. Along with the Three Supernal Aspects or the Trinity—the Masculine, Feminine and Androgyne; the Father, Mother and Holy Spirit—the Seven become the Ten.

The first three sephiroth are the primary ones, as follows:

1. *The Sons of Will*. Imbued with omnipotence, the First Sephira includes the agents of Manifested Will. They are robed in white radiance and are also called the Morning Stars. By directing creation's rays they bring those forces together and atoms into being.

2. *The Sons of Wisdom*. The Second Sephira forces embody and manifest cohesion, balance and harmony. They also direct the vitalizing current of solar energy by which substances and forms are given coordination and life. They preserve the balance of Nature and are forever wise.

3. *The Sons of Intelligence*. The Third Sephira forces order the patterns of formation and fashion the forms according to transcendental dreams. They are the artists and craftsmen of the universe, producing innumerable progeny of lesser devas and the nature spirits. They mold Nature according to the Archetypes and control thought and law.

Skipping to the secondary sephiroth:

5. *Fifth Sephira*. This order conceives of evolving forms. Through this emanation, Divine Ideation goes from the Archetype to the concrete. Whereas the Ideation, or Thought, was eternal in the First Sephira, everlasting in the Second and durational in the Third, it is controlled in the Fifth by Time. The Fifth Sephira is the soul of the Third, containing many gods and devas in perpetual creative activity and represented by fire.

6. *Sixth Sephira*. This order, like the rhythmic waves of the ocean, constantly expresses the One Life at the lower levels, including the physical world, saturating it with divine, vitalizing fluid. The Sixth Sephira corresponds to the Second as the sustaining life-blood of Nature and is represented by air and water.

7. *Seventh Sephira*. This order is the Lord of all Nature and the physical universe. The angels of this group are responsible for matter and the construction and maintenance of physical forms, representing the Logos in physical substance, and are symbolized by earth. The Seventh Sephira expresses the Immanence of God, the Indwelling Presence, while the other six show God's Trancendence.

The Fourth Sephira links the primary and secondary orders, acting as a powerful intermediary to maintain the Archetypes. All the powers, offices and attributes of the other six sephira must be mastered by the fourth. It is the Center.

As noted above, the gods or devas, in one way or the other, are associated with all major religions and the practice of many lesser faiths. To the ancient Mayans of Pre-Columbian Mexico, Ekxhuah was the god of travelers, a name quite similar to the Exus of Brazilian Candomblé and the Eshus of Santería. In Hindu India, the *devarajas* are worshipped as gods or goddesses, but may also be considered angels. All these religions share a belief in an all-powerful, distant Absolute, but invoke the intervention of lesser gods or angels to deal with the more mundane affairs of humans. Angels will respond to any human, religious or not, who calls them through prayer, study and meditation, and the practice of ceremony and ritual.

### MODERN CONCEPTIONS OF DEVAS

Through Theosophy, devas came to be regarded as high-level nature spirits. Modern views vary as to whether devas are part of, or work under, the angel kingdom. Channeling messages from devas increased during the latter twentieth century, as part of the New Age movement. Such messages have tended to focus on the devas' displeasure with humanity's pollution of the earth and disrespect for nature.

The concept of devas as nature spirits received a tremendous boost from the activities at FINDHORN, a community in northern Scotland that became renowned in the 1970s for spectacular produce grown with the advice of devas. The primary channel for the devic advice was Dorothy MACLEAN, one of the founders of Findhorn. Maclean, not certain what to call the beings with whom she communicated, settled on the term "deva" as personally preferable to "angel." However, she used the terms "deva," "angel" and "nature spirit" interchangeably when referring to the beings. The main contact was a being she called the "Landscape Angel." She never saw these beings with external vision, but sensed them on the inner planes. They were of awesome scope, she said. Their duties were to hold the archetypal pattern of all material things in place—even manmade objects such as machines—and to offer love to humankind.

Publicity about the devas at Findhorn elicited a huge public response. Maclean and others discovered that numerous other persons around the world said that they too had established contact with the devic realm, but had remained quiet about it out of fear of ridicule. By the last decade of the twentieth century, rapport with devas had become a norm in certain New Age circles. Findhorn became the model for other similar gardens and communities, such as PERE-LANDRA, near Washington, D.C., and GREEN HOPE FARM in New Hampshire.

Descriptions and impressions about devas are, like angels, subjective, and dependent upon the experiencer. Some individuals perceive detailed hierarchies of beings, while others say that devas, angels and nature beings are facets of a whole—like a diamond—and resist categorization. Devas themselves may remain invisible to the percipient, or manifest as humanlike bodies of light, balls or points of light, or diffuse fields or grids of energy. They communicate via mental impressions, intuitions, the inner voice, or sometimes a clairaudient external voice, much like the DAEMON who whispered in Socrates' ear.

Gardeners who know devas consider them to be "architects" of nature; one is assigned to every living thing, even the soil. Devas design blueprints for all living things, and orchestrate the energies necessary for growth and health. Devas dispense advice on planting, fertilizing, watering and general plant care, as well as how to eliminate pests such as moles and worms without killing them. However, the relationship with devas is perceived to go much deeper, to include a heightened respect for all livings things and for nature, to work with unseen realms in love and cooperation, and to realize the interconnectedness of all things and to God.

See ELEMENTAL; NATURE SPIRIT.

**Further reading:**
Blavatsky, H. P. *The Secret Doctrine.* Pasadena, Calif.: Theosophical University Press, 1977. First published 1888.

Findhorn Community. *The Findhorn Garden.* New York: Harper & Row Perennial Library, 1975.

Hawken, Paul. *The Magic of Findhorn.* New York: Bantam Books, 1976.

Hodson, Geoffrey. *The Brotherhood of Angels and Men.* Wheaton, Ill.: The Theosophical Publishing House, 1982.

———. *The Kingdom of the Gods.* Adyar, Madras, India: The Theosophical Publishing House, 1972.

Maclean, Dorothy. *To Hear the Angels Sing.* Hudson, N.Y.: Lindisfarne Press, 1990. First published by Lorian Press, 1980. 2nd ed. by Morningtown Press, 1988.

May, Herbert G. and Bruce M. Metzger, eds. *The Oxford Annotated Bible with the Apocrypha,* Revised Standard Version. New York: Oxford University Press, 1965.

Wright, Machaelle Small. *Behaving As If the God in All Life Mattered.* Jeffersonton, Va.: Perelandra, 1987.

**devotional cults** Special devotion and veneration of the angels have been permitted, even sometimes encouraged, in the Christian church since its beginnings. Devotional cults are most prominent in Catholicism. Catholic tradition regards angels as conscious beings of high intelligence, not bound by the limitations of physical laws, who can be of help to humanity—but who must not be worshipped or adored, or placed above Christ or God. Devotion to angels centers on imitating them, for they in turn imitate God. Veneration of saints is closely associated with angelic devotion, for saints are considered to be the real friends of angels and models of piety to men and women.

The early Christian Church looked to St. PAUL as setting the standard for veneration of angels. On various occasions, Paul referred to angels within a context of respect and veneration. In 1 Corinthians 11:1–16, Paul discusses proper ways

Angel guarding a cathedral (author's collection)

to worship. Women should worship with their heads covered, he says in 11:10, "because of the angels." In this way, they would show respect for the divine order, which is administered by angels (also, women are assigned a lower status than men, whose heads signify Christ; men should not worship with their heads covered).

Early church fathers were sometimes cautious about encouraging veneration of angels out of fear that it would lead to idolatry. The celestial intermediaries proved convenient substitutes for pagan gods and daemons, but the fathers did not wish to see worship of pagan gods transferred to angels. Consequently, angel cults were occasionally suppressed. St. Justin Martyr defended veneration of angels, and the philosopher Celsus declared that angels were different from gods, else they would be called demons.

ORIGEN took pains to distinguish between worship of God and devotion to angels. In his *Contra Celsum* (IV, 5), he states:

> We indeed acknowledge that Angels are ministering spirits, and we say they are sent forth to minister for them who shall be heirs of salvation, and that they ascend, bearing the sup-

plications of men, to the purest of the heavenly places in the universe, or even to the supercelestial regions purer still, and they come down from these, conveying to each one, according to his deserts, something enjoined by God to be conferred by them upon those who are to be the recipients of His benefits. . . . For every prayer and supplication and intercession is to be sent up to the Supreme God through the High Priest, who is above all the Angels, the living Word and God. . . . It is enough to secure that the holy Angels be propitious to us, and that they do all things on our behalf, that our disposition of mind toward God should imitate, as far as possible for human nature, the example of these holy Angels, who themselves imitate the example of their God.

St. AUGUSTINE was among those who feared that veneration of angels would be confused with worship of pagan gods. "We honor them out of charity not out of servitude," he said primly in *De Vera Religione*.

Once the celestial hierarchy of PSEUDO-DIONYSIUS became established and accepted, veneration of angels achieved a level of comfort in Christianity. From about the sixth century on, devotion to the angels grew steadily. St. Benedict and Pope St. Gregory fostered this practice. By the eighth century, however, angels were so popular that prayer to them was discouraged, again out of fears of idolatry. Devotion to the angels still climbed, and reached a height during the Middle Ages; St. Bernard of Clairvaux was especially ardent about the GUARDIAN ANGEL. Citing Psalm 90:11, which states, "God has given his angels charge over thee, to keep thee in all thy ways," Bernard advocated lavishing great respect, gratitude and love upon angels.

Besides in liturgy and prayer, devotion to angels has been expressed in the dedication of churches; many of these dedications sprang from apparitional experiences (see MICHAEL; VISIONS). In Constantinople, a shrine to the archangel Michael was erected outside the city, and fifteen churches within city limits were dedicated in his honor. In Rome, Michael had seven churches dedicated to him by the ninth century.

Catholics observe a number of feast days in honor of angels. Only three individual angels are thus honored: the archangels Michael, GABRIEL and RAPHAEL. There are feast days for guardian angels in general and all angels in general, but no feast days for any of the orders in the celestial hierarchy, such as seraphim, cherubim, etc.

The feast of the guardian angels (October 2) once was not separate from the feast of Michael (September 29 in the West and May 8 in the East). The custom began in Spain and spread. In 1518, Pope Leo X issued a bull creating a special office in honor of the guardian angels. The office was raised in rank by Pope Clement IX in 1667, Pope Clement X in 1670, and Pope Leo XIII in 1883.

In places where veneration of the angels is particularly high, feasts also are held in honor of the guardian angel of the place.

Names of angels have always been held in high regard for the power they invoke (see NAMES OF ANGELS), but the Catholic church has not encouraged litanies, in which the names of all the CHOIRS of angels are invoked. Litanies were even forbidden in earlier centuries (such as by Pope Clement VIII and Pope Benedict XIV in the seventeenth and eighteenth centuries, respectively). However, certain litanies of the angels are allowed for private use if approved by a local bishop.

Veneration of the angels also led to the establishment of confraternities, legal and approved associations whose purpose is work of piety or charity and advancement of public worship. The first Archconfraternity of Saint Michael was established in 1878 in Italy (an archconfraternity has the right to afilliate other confraternities). Confraternities were particularly popular during the nineteenth century; they have had renewed interest in the latter twentieth century.

In 1950, Philangeli was established in England with Episcopal approval, and has spread worldwide. Members seek to become real friends with angels.

The Opus Sanctorum Angelorum ("The Work of the Holy Angels") is one of the newer Catholic movements intended to renew and bolster belief in guardian angels and to foster a collaboration between angels and humans for the glory of God, the salvation of humanity, and the regeneration of all creation.

The Opus Sanctorum Angelorum was sanctioned by Pope Paul VI in 1968, who probably was influenced by POPE PIUS XII, who advocated a renewal of devotion to angels. Other sources of inspiration are the experiences of Padre Pio, and the appearance of the angel in Fatima, Portugal (see MARIAN APPARITIONS).

The goal of the Opus is a divine conjugation—a *hieros gamos*—between humanity and the angelic kingdom. The Opus teaches that the guardian angel will "ward off danger to body and soul; prevent Satan's suggestion of evil thoughts; remove occasion of sin; enlighten and instruct; offer our prayers for us; correct us if we sin; help us in the agony of death; conduct us to God or purgatory at death."

Initiates are guided by priests who are part of the Opus. There are three phases.

In the first phase, "the Promise," initiates make a promise to God and their angels that they will love their guardian angels and will respond to their instructions when heard through the voice of conscience. The Promise is done in the presence of a priest. This initial phase lasts for one year, during which time the initiates strive to learn to hear the voice of their guardian angels.

The second phase involves a consecration to the guardian angel. The initiates participate in a candlelight ceremony in the presence of the Blessed Sacrament, in which they consecrate themselves to their "holy guardians." They pledge to become like angels, and to venerate angels, who have been given to humanity by God "in a very special way in these days of spiritual combat for the Kingdom of God." The initiates ask their angels to obtain for them "a love so strong that I may be inflamed by it."

In the third phase, the initiates participate in a ceremony of consecration to all the angel kingdom, which will enable the initiates to live in sacred communion with all things.

What the Opus accomplishes is the bringing to life of powerful psychic forces within the individual—the unmanifest creative potential.

**Further reading:**
Grosso, Michael. "The Cult of the Guardian Angel," in *Angels and Mortals: Their Co-Creative Power*, compiled by Maria Parisen. Wheaton, Ill.: Quest Books, Thesophical Publishing House, 1990.

Parente, Fr. Pascal P. *The Angels: The Catholic Teaching on the Angels.* Rockford, Ill.: Tan Books and Publishers, 1973. First published 1961.

**directions, angels of**   See NATURE SPIRITS.

**djinn**   See JINN.

**dominions (dominations)**   See CHOIRS.

**dreams**   Angels appear in dreams, usually as messengers of important information, as vehicles of divine inspiration, and as harbingers of healing. Essentially, the angel is a representation of divine wisdom.

Dreams were especially important for divination and prophecy in the ancient cultures of Egypt, Babylonia, Greece, Rome and the Middle East. The divine will was held to be constantly revealed in dreams, and incubation procedures were followed to obtain dream answers to questions. Because of the connection between dreams and idol priests (who incubated and interpreted dreams, and who also practiced magic), the Israelites were warned against them. Nonetheless, God revealed himself through dreams—sometimes using angels as the messengers—on a number of significant occasions.

Genesis relates the story of JACOB, son of ISAAC and Rebekah, who was hunted by his twin brother, Esau. Jacob

*The Vision of St. Joseph* **(Philippe de Champaigne; reprinted courtesy of the National Gallery, London)**

escaped to his uncle. En route, he had a dream of angels ascending and descending a ladder to heaven. God promised him and his descendants the land upon which he slept. "I will not leave you until I have done all that I promised you," God said (Genesis 28:15). An angel again addresses Jacob in a dream in Genesis 31:11–13, instructing him to return to the land of his birth.

Joseph, husband to MARY, the mother of JESUS, similarly was given important messages by angels in dreams, according to the Gospel of Matthew. While betrothed to Mary, Joseph learned of her pregnancy, and resolved to divorce her quietly. Before he did so an angel appeared to him in a dream and said, "Joseph, son of David, do not fear to take Mary your wife, for that which is conceived in her is of the Holy Spirit; she will bear a son, and you shall call his name Jesus, for he will save his people from their sins" (Matthew 1:20–21).

Joseph followed the angel's instructions. After Jesus was born, Joseph was again contacted by an angel through his dreams. The angel told him to take Mary and Jesus and flee to Egypt until the angel instructed otherwise, for King Herod was intent on searching for the child and destroying him (Matthew 2:13). Joseph followed directions; they remained in Egypt until Herod was dead. An angel reappeared in a dream to Joseph, telling him Herod that was dead and he should take his family and return to Israel (Matthew 2:19–20). Other passages in Matthew (2:12 and 2:22) refer to Joseph receiving warnings in dreams, but do not state that the messages were delivered by angels.

Divine inspiration from an angel also struck MUHAMMAD (*c.* 570 or 571–632), the founder of Islam, who received the revelations that became the Koran in a series of angelic visions. In 610, Muhammad was forty years old and living a life of asceticism when, one night in his dreams, the archangel GABRIEL appeared and gave him the first revelation of the Koran, the holy book that contains the doctrine of Islam.

Modern researchers of angelology, prayer and healing have found anecdotal cases of dream angels being instrumental in a healing process. People who pray to be healed of an illness or problem sometimes have dreams in which angels tell them they are healed, or give them encouragement or information to help them heal. In *The Miracle of Prayer: True Stories of Blessed Healings*, the author tells the story of "Joan," who was semi-paralyzed and could not get up out of bed or walk unassisted. She experienced a dream in which an angel told her to get up. Joan arose and walked around her house without crutches for the first time in a year. She returned to bed. But when she awoke, she found herself still semi-paralyzed. However, the dream demonstrated to her that healing was possible. With renewed determination, she pursued therapy and complementary healing, and restored her ability to walk. Angelic presences continued to manifest to her after the healing. Her psychic abilities also opened.

The appearance of angels in dreams can be interpreted from different perspectives. Many societies have, since ancient times, considered dreams to be not imaginary, but real events occurring in a separate reality. The early Greeks and Romans believed that the soul traveled while the body was asleep. The soul would go to otherworldly realms, wherein dwelled those lesser spirits who mediated between humans and the gods. Plato called this realm "the between." Here the human soul had experiences and encounters that had the same validity as experiences had during waking life. In dreams it was possible to meet the gods, to see the distant past or future and to be healed of illness and disease.

Depth psychology would call the dream angel a manifestation of the higher self, imparting wisdom already within and known to the dreamer, but buried. The angel is an archetypal image that makes it possible for the dreamer to access this buried wisdom.

See FLAMEL, NICHOLAS.

**Further reading:**
Engle, David. *Divine Dreams*. Holmes Beach, Fla.: Christopher Books, 1994.
Guiley, Rosemary Ellen. *Angels of Mercy*. New York: Pocket Books, 1994.
———. *The Miracle of Prayer: True Stories of Blessed Healings*. New York: Pocket Books, 1995.

**eating**   The question of whether or not angels eat food has been addressed by Christian and Jewish theologians. Because angels are incorporeal, the conclusion is that angels do not eat food in the same manner as mortals. How, then, to explain texts in which angels eat food with mortals? The accepted answer is that they only *appear* to eat, which is sometimes necessary to protect their disguise as humans.

In Genesis 18, ABRAHAM is visited by three angels, who partake of a feast of food and drink he prepares for them (he mistakes them for men). In the apocryphal Book of Tobit, RAPHAEL, in the guise of a man, eats food with his mortal companion and charge, Tobias (see TOBIT). In The Testament of Abraham, a pseudepigraphal work, MICHAEL arrives to fetch the soul of Abraham and is offered a feast.

In the latter work, Michael in a quick visit to God protests that he will not be able to eat; God says he will send an all-devouring spirit to enable Michael to give the appearance of eating. Similarly, theologians explain that the angels of Genesis (thought to be Michael, GABRIEL and Raphael) only appear to eat. In Tobit, Raphael explains that visions are created to give the appearance of eating; the angels actually consume manna, a special food of heaven.

Manna, a flaky substance like thin cakes of honey, also sustained the Israelites during forty years in the wilderness: "Then the Lord said to Moses, 'Behold I will rain bread from heaven for you'" (Exodus 16:4); "And the people of Israel ate the manna forty years." (Exodus 16:35) There may be a real manna—a substance excreted by plant lice on tamarisk shrubs (found in the Sinai wilderness), which hardens in the dry desert air.

Sometimes angels turn away food. In Judges 6:21, Gideon presents food to the ANGEL OF THE LORD, who promptly burns it up; this is a sign that the angel is who he says he is, and his instructions to Gideon must be followed. Also in Judges (13:15–16), an angel declines a kid offered by Manoah: "If you detain me, I will not eat of your food; but if you make ready a burnt offering, then offer it to the Lord."

Modern-day accounts of angelophanies tell of angels who seem to eat food.

**Further reading:**
Guiley, Rosemary Ellen. *Angels of Mercy*. New York: Pocket Books, 1994.
Ronner, John. *Do You Have a Guardian Angel?* Murfreesboro, Tenn.: Mamre Press, 1985.

**eblis**   See IBLIS.

**El Roi**   See ABRAHAM.

**elemental**   A lower order of spirit being that exists as the life-force in the natural world, whose task it is to maintain harmony. In occult lore, elementals are said to govern minerals, plants and animals; the four elements of earth, air, fire and water; the planets, stars, signs of the zodiac; and hours of the day and night. They are ruled by angels. Most are viewed as benevolent, though some are malicious or trickster-like in behavior.

The Neoplatonic Greeks grouped elementals according to the four elements of life. Earth elementals are gnomes, ruled by the angel ARIEL; air elementals are sylphs, ruled by Cherub; water elementals are undines, ruled by Tharsis; and fire elementals are salamanders, ruled by Nathaniel or Seraph. In the fifth century, Proclus added a fifth group which lives beneath the ground, and in the eleventh century, Psellus added a sixth group, the *lucifugum*, which means "fly-the-light."

The term "elemental" is applied to a broad range of spirit beings, also including elves, who live in the woods and along the seashore, and household spirits such as brownies, goblins, bogles and kobolds, and fairies.

Elementals appear in a variety of forms. Some are human-like, such as the dwarfish gnomes. Sylphs appear as butterflies and undines as waves. Some are more like angels, and are amorphous shapes of white light surrounded by flowing, colorful auras of energy. British Spiritualist Grace Cooke said that elementals enjoy human company, can understand human speech, and respond to music. They have their own karmic evolutions, progressing toward higher forms of life.

British medium Geraldine Cummins channeled information about elementals, purportedly from the deceased Frederic W. H. Myers, one of the founders of the Society for Psychical Research in London. In automatic writing, "Myers" described elementals as the essence which emanates from forms of life such as trees and plants, and which coalesces into a form perceived by the human mind as a sprite.

See DEVA; FINDHORN; NATURE SPIRIT.

**Further reading:**
Hall, Manly P. *Paracelsus: His Mystical and Medical Philosophy*. Los Angeles: The Philosophical Research Society, 1964.
Steiner, Rudolph. *The Influence of Spiritual Beings Upon Man*. Spring Valley, N.Y.: Anthroposophic Press, 1961.

**Elijah**   A prophet-angel of the Old Testament who is translated directly to heaven in a fiery chariot. The name means "my God is Jehovah." Elijah is the forerunner of the Messiah, preparing the way by spreading repentance, peace and justice among Israelites.

In the Old Testament (1 Kings), Elijah is a prophet in Israel during the reign of King Ahab. Ahab and his foreign wife, Jezebel, sin by worshipping BAAL and killing God's prophets. God sends Elijah to warn of punishment by drought.

Elijah departs the land, but returns in three years to find the drought still going on. Ahab accuses him of causing it. Elijah challenges the king's prophets to prove that their god, Baal, is real. Both they and Elijah will prepare sacrifices on Mt. Carmel. Whichever god sets the sacrifices afire will be declared the real God.

The prophets of Baal dance, pray and ritually cut themselves all day, but nothing happens to their sacrifice. When Elijah prays, God sends fire and burns his sacrifice. The people turn on the priests of Baal, and they and Elijah slay them.

The killings infuriate Jezebel, and Elijah flees for his life. After a day of wandering, he sits down and asks God to let him die. He sleeps, during which an ANGEL OF THE LORD appears and tells him to arise and eat. Elijah awakes to find a jar of water and a cake baked on hot stones. The angel urges him to eat and drink more in preparation for his journey. The food and water last him for forty days and nights as he journeys to Mount Horeb. God tells Elijah that he has much work to do: He must anoint a new king, and train the prophet Elisha to carry on his work.

Ahab is later killed in battle, and his son Ahaziah succeeds him to the throne.

In 2 Kings 2:9–11, Elijah passes his role to Elisha in a dramatic scene. He strikes the waters of the river Jordan with his rolled-up mantle, causing them to part. The two cross. A chariot of fire and horses descends from the sky, separating the two. It takes Elijah to heaven.

In Malachi 4:5–6, the prophet Malachi foretells the return of Elijah. In the New Testament, it is inferred that Jesus is "Elijah, who is to come" (Matthew 11:13). In Luke 9:28–33, Jesus, on the Mount of Transfirguration, appears to his disciples in a vision along with MOSES and Elijah.

In rabbinic lore, Elijah is credited with being an angel from his beginnings; he becomes SANDALPHON, the angel of prayer, in heaven. He also serves as a guide for the souls of the dead: he stands at the crossways of Paradise and helps the righteous find heaven. In midrashim (rabbinical texts), Elijah often is synonymous with the prohet ENOCH, who also translated directly to heaven, and became the angel METATRON.

In kabbalistic lore, the ANGEL OF DEATH is not happy with Elijah's translation, insisting that humans must die under his jurisdiction. God tells the angel that Elijah is not like other men, and can even replace the Angel of Death if challenged to do so. Elijah and the Angel of Death confront each other, but God holds Elijah back to prevent him from destroying the Angel of Death. God instructs Elijah to be the guardian his of children and to make himself known as God's messenger throughout the world. Elijah then receives the name Sandalphon.

In Talmudic lore, Elijah is a champion of the poor and the underdogs.

As the forerunner of the Messiah, Elijah will give three proclamations in Israel three days prior to the Messiah's appearance, according to Jewish lore. The archangel MICHAEL will blow a trumpet, and Elijah will appear and introduce the Messiah. During the reign of peace, Elijah will be one of eight princes in the Messiah's cabinet.

**Further reading:**
Alexander, Pat (ed.) *The Lion Encyclopedia of the Bible*. Batavia, Ill.: Lion Publishing, 1986.
Davidson, Gustav. *A Dictionary of Angels*. New York: Free Press, 1967.
Margolies, Morris B. *A Gathering of Angels*. New York: Ballantine, 1994.

**elohim**   See NAMES OF ANGELS; Rudolph STEINER.

**encounter phenomenon**   See EXTRATERRESTRIALS.

**Enoch**   Patriarch taken to heaven on orders of God, and transformed into the archangel METATRON to become a heavenly scribe. According to legend, Enoch's descriptions of the heavens and hells he encountered, and the angels therein, are given in the Book of Enoch, also called the "Chronicles of Enoch," pseudepigraphical writings not part of the canon.

According to the Bible (Genesis 5:18–24), Enoch was the seventh generation from Adam in the long-lived lineage of patriarchs. His father, Jared, was 162 years old when Elijah was born and lived for another 800 years. Enoch fathered Methuselah at age 65, and lived another 300 years before translating directly to heaven (although his fate is debated by scholars). Genesis 5:24 says that "Enoch walked with God; and he was not, for God took him."

The Book of Jubilees, a Jewish pseudepigraphical text from the second century B.C.E., says that Enoch was "conducted into the Garden of Eden in majesty and honor, and behold there he writes down the condemnation and judgment of the world."

Most likely the Book of Enoch was written by numerous anonymous authors around the last two centuries B.C.E. (some authorities say the first and second centuries C.E.), in Aramaic or Hebrew. They are attributed to the legendary figure Enoch. Whatever the sources, the writings carried great authority. Tertullian, a Roman Christian theologian of the late first and early second centuries C.E., said that the book was divinely inspired, and had either been preserved by Noah on the Ark during the Flood, or had been reproduced by Noah through the inspiration of the Holy Spirit. ORIGEN, a second-century Christian philosopher, gave the same weight to the Book of Enoch as he did to the Psalms. Clement of Alexandria, a Greek theologian who converted to Christianity and who died c. 215 C.E., referred to the Book of Enoch as a sacred text.

The chronicles were declared apocryphal in the fourth century C.E. by St. Jerome, a Father and Doctor of the Church. One of the chief objections to them was that they portray a multilayered heaven that contains hells populated by fallen angels—a concept contradictory to the heaven-above, hell-below model set forth in Christianity.

St. AUGUSTINE, a Doctor of the Church and a contemporary of St. Jerome, says in his opus *The City of God* that certain scriptures were declared apocryphal because their origins were obscure and their errors many. In Book XV, Chap. 23, Augustine states:

> We cannot deny that Enoch, the seventh from Adam, left some divine writings, for this is asserted by the Apostle Jude in his canonical epistle. But it is not without reason that these writings have no place in that canon of Scripture which was

preserved in the temple of the Hebrew people by the diligence of successive priests; for their antiquity brought them under suspicion, and it was impossible to ascertain whether these were his genuine writings, and they were not brought forward as genuine by the persons who were found to have carefully preserved the canonical books by a successive transmission.

Thus kept out of the canon—along with the Book of Jude, which quotes from it—the Book of Enoch subsequently fell into obscurity and became 'lost' for more than 1,000 years. Fragments of it allegedly were preserved. Three copies were discovered in 1773 by Scottish explorer James Bruce in Abyssinia (what is now Ethiopia). Bruce kept one and gave the other two to the Librairie Bibliothèque in Paris and the Bodleian Library in Oxford, England. The Bodleian copy was translated into English by Dr. Richard Laurence, archibishop of Cashel and a former professor of Hebrew at Oxford. Laurence opined that the book was written after the Christian era. A second edition was published in 1883. The book was translated into German in 1838 and 1853, and into Latin in 1840. Another version of the book, called the *Book of the Secrets of Enoch* or 2 Enoch, was discovered in a Belgrade library in 1886 and was translated in 1896. A third version, *Enoch III*, also exists and was translated in 1922.

Its reemergence brought it to the attention of occultists and esoteric orders, who reopened questions concerning its antiquity, authorship and symbolic meanings. Freemasons associated Enoch with the legendary Thoth of Hellenic Egypt, the god who taught mystical wisdom, magic, mathematics, writing and other skills to humanity; and with Hermes, the Greek god who is the patron of magic, messenger to the gods, psychopomp of souls and personification of universal wisdom. (These two deities formed a composite, Hermes Trismegistus, the legendary author of Neoplatonic, Christian and kabbalistic writings that form the foundation of the Western occult tradition.)

Madame Helena P. Blavatsky, cofounder of the Theosophical Society, considered the Enoch question in her greatest work, *The Secret Doctrine*, published in 1888. Blavatsky disputed the existence of Enoch as a single living man, it would be like accepting Adam as the first one, she said. She translated *Enoichion*, or the Book of Enoch, as "inner eye" in Greek, and in esoteric terms "Seer of the Open Eye." In Hebrew, she said, the term means "initiator" and "instructor," and is a generic title. Thus, Enoch was a generic title borne by scores of persons in all times and ages around the world, she said. There was no translation to heaven; the biblical statement about God taking Enoch referred to the disappearance of sacred wisdom from humanity and its preservation by secret colleges of priests.

Blavatsky also said that the writings of Enoch were allegorical and symbolical copies of the original records, or the philosophy of every nation that preceded the Deluge. These were produced by the early Third Root Race before the Fall, and were handed down orally to the Fourth Root Race—the root races being part of Blavatsky's cosmogenesis as given to her by the Ascended Masters.

According to the story told in the Book of Enoch, Enoch was 365 years old when two angels appeared and whisked him off to heaven. One day when he was asleep on his couch, a "great distress" came into his heart, which he could not understand. Two beings appeared before him, which he described as men:

> And there appeared to me two men, exceedingly big, so that I never saw such on earth; their faces were shining like the sun, their eyes too *were* like a burning light, and from their lips was fire coming forth with clothing and singing of various kinds in appearance purple, their wings *were* brighter than gold, their hands whiter than snow.

Enoch was frightened, but the angels told him to fear not—they had been sent by God to take him into heaven. They bore him up on their wings to the clouds of the first heaven. (In other accounts, such as in *The Legends of the Jews*, the angel ANPIEL alone took Enoch to heaven; or, in the same work, he was taken up in a fiery chariot similar to that in the experience of ELIJAH.)

In all, Enoch found seven heavens and seven corresponding earths, all united to each other by hooks. Beyond the seventh heaven there lay three more heavens.

The first heaven, ruled by GABRIEL, is the one closest to Earth, and contains the winds and the clouds. The angels who live here are astronomers, and rule the stars and heavenly bodies. There also are angels who are guardians of ice, snow, flowers and dew.

The second heaven is ruled by RAPHAEL and is a dark penal area where fallen angels await judgment. His guiding angels, said Enoch,

> ... showed me darkness, and there I saw prisoners hanging, watched, awaiting the great and boundless judgment, and these angels were dark-looking, more than earthly darkness, and incessantly making weeping through all hours.

Enoch was told that these prisoners were "God's apostates," fallen angels who had turned away from God with their prince, who was fastened in the fifth heaven.

The fallen angels asked Enoch to pray for them, but he wondered how he, a mere mortal man, could do what angels were supposed to do for humankind.

The third heaven is ruled by Anahel and is a land of contrasts. One part of this heaven, the northern section, is actually hell, ice-cold and sulfurous, filled with torturing angels who punish the evil souls who reside there. The condemned include those who dishonor God, sin against nature, and practice enchantments and witchcraft. However, the rest of this heaven is an Eden-like garden where manna is made and the souls of the holy—those who are righteous and compassionate—reside. Angels of light watch over this heaven.

The fourth heaven, under the jurisdiction of archangel MICHAEL, contains Holy Jerusalem and its temple, all made of gold, surrounded by rivers flowing with milk, honey, wine and oil. The Tree of Life is to be found in this heaven, as well as the sun and the moon. Here Enoch heard the singing of angels:

> In the midst of the heavens I saw armed soldiers, serving the Lord, with tympana and organs, with incessant voice, with sweet voice, with sweet and incessant *voice* and various singing, which is impossible to describe, and *which* astonishes every mind, so wonderful and marvelous is the singing of those angels, and I was delighted listening to it.

The fifth heaven is yet another prison, a fiery ravine where the angelic Watchers, or Grigori, are being imprisoned for marrying into the human race. (See SONS OF GOD.)

The sixth heaven is full of scholarly angels, studying astronomy, nature, and *homo sapiens*. Here Enoch found archangels, as well as angels who rule over all the cycles and functions of nature: the seasons, the calendar, the rivers and seas, the fruits of the earth, the grass, etc. There also are angels who record all the lives and deeds of every human soul, to set forth before God.

In the seventh heaven Enoch found the higher angels, such as the thrones, cherubim, seraphim and dominions, as well as "fiery troops of great archangels." These angelic hosts bowed down before the Lord, singing his praises.

Enoch's two angel guides left him at the end of the seventh heaven. He was terrified, but Gabriel appeared before him, caught him up as though he were a leaf caught up by wind, and transported him higher.

In the eighth heaven, called Muzaloth, Enoch saw the "changer of the seasons, of drought, and of wet, and of the twelve signs of the zodiac." The ninth heaven, called Kuchavim, holds the heavenly homes of the twelve signs of the zodiac.

Then archangel Michael escorted Enoch to the tenth heaven, where he be held the face of God. It was, said Enoch,

> . . . like iron made to glow in fire, and brought out, emitting sparks, and it burns.
>   Thus I saw the Lord's face, but the Lord's face is ineffable, marvelous and very awful, and very, very terrible. . . .
>   And I cannot tell the quantity of his many instructions, and various voices, the Lord's throne very great and not made with hands, nor the quantity of those standing round him, troops of cherubim and seraphim, nor their incessant singing, nor his immutable beauty, and who shall tell of the ineffable greatness of his glory?

God instructed Michael to "take Enoch from out of his earthly garments, and anoint him with my sweet ointment, and put him into the garments of my Glory." Enoch then took on a shining appearance, like the angels around him. One possible interpretation of this description is that Enoch was out of his physical body and in his "light body," or astral form.

God summoned the archangel PRAVUIL, "whose knowledge was quicker in wisdom than the other archangels, who wrote all the deeds of the Lord," to bring out the books of knowledge for Enoch to read.

After instruction from Pravuil, Enoch wrote 366 books in thirty days. He was then summoned by the Lord, who revealed to him the creation story, and that the world would end on the eighth day of creation (or after 8,000 years), when time would cease and the righteous and the wicked would be judged. Enoch was given all the rules of morality and righteousness for humans to live by.

After these revelations, Enoch was sent back to earth for thirty days, so that he could pass on the teachings to his sons and others. God then took Enoch back into heaven and transformed him into Metatron, giving him 365,000 eyes and thirty six pairs of wings. One of his functions as Metatron was to be the scribe of heaven.

**Further reading:**
Augustine, St. *The City of God*. New York: The Modern Library, 1950.
Blavatsky, H. P. *The Secret Doctrine*. Pasadena, Calif.: Theosophical University Press, 1977. First published 1888.
Laurence, Richard, (trans.). *The Book of Enoch the Prophet*. San Diego, Calif.: Wizards Bookshelf, 1976.

**Enochian calls**   See John DEE; MAGIC, ANGELS IN.

**Eros**   The Greek god of love (the name means "erotic love"), called Cupid by the Romans, is often mistaken for an angel because of his portrayal in art as an infant with wings, reminiscent of the Italian PUTTI. In mythology, Eros is the son of Aphrodite and Ares, and is married to Psyche (soul). His brother Anteros is the god of mutual love.

Eros often is portrayed as being about to shoot an arrow of love into a mortal. Once shot, the victim falls in love with the first thing he or she sees.

In ceremonial magic lore, the angel of love is Theliel. The invocation of Theliel's name will secure the love of someone desired.

**erotes**   Winged, boyish figures called erotes were a regular feature of Roman funerary art, and provided inspiration for the image of the winged angel.

Erotes are ministers of the dead, and help to transport the souls to the land of the dead or the Christian heaven. They are based on the myth of Psyche (soul), who marries Eros (erotic love). They function as "eros psychophoros," or escorts of the soul. Sometimes they are called *genii* (singular "genius," comparable to the DAEMON, though the association is not entirely accurate).

**Winged Eros served as a model for angel art (reprinted courtesy of U.S. Library of Congress)**

Erotes were common on sarcophagi and funerary altars into the early centuries post-Christ. They were portrayed in pairs, either standing or hovering, and carrying one of three items: a gorgoneion, or Minerva's shield with the severed head of the Gorgon, which was believed to be a powerful amulet against evil; an inscribed tablet; or an image of the deceased. Typically they were shown nude, with mantles reaching down to the feet.

Erotes often were depicted along with VICTORY, another early inspiration for the winged angel. They also were associated with the winged Roman goddess Aeternitas (Eternity), who functioned as a psychopomp to the dead.

See EROS; WINGS.

**Further reading:**
Berefelt, Gunnar. *A Study on the Winged Angel: The Origin of a Motif.* Stockholm: Almquist & Wiksell, 1968.

**extraterrestrials (ETs)** Since the advent of ufology around the time of World War II, hypotheses have been advanced that biblical descriptions of angels, and other ancient writings relating to shining beings and gods who come from the sky, were referring to extraterrestrial visitors from space. It is argued that advanced beings from other planets would have seemed godlike to earlier peoples, and their high-tech spacecraft would have been described in such nontechnical terms as "flying disks" and "wheels."

As a social phenomenon, ET encounters, which are reported worldwide, are as significant as encounters with the Devil or with angels, and reported sightings of the Virgin Mary throughout history.

The age of modern interest in ETs began in 1947. On June 26, a Boise, Idaho businessman and pilot, Kenneth Arnold, sighted a chain of nine bright objects while flying over the Cascade Mountains in Washington State. He estimated their speed to be at 1600 miles per hour. Arnold said the objects' motion resembled saucers that had been skipped over water, which gave rise to the popular term "flying saucer" to describe unidentified flying objects (UFOs).

Since then an estimated 70,000 sightings and encounters have been reported—probably a small fraction of the actual number. Approximately 95 percent of the cases have been explained as natural phenomena, aircraft, weather balloons or hoaxes. The U.S. Air Force set up a project in the late 1940s to analyze UFO reports; the project ended in 1969. It was advised by J. Allen Hynek, chairman of the Astronomy Department at Northwestern University. Even though most cases appeared to have natural explanations, the minority that did not eventually led Hynek to conclude that UFOs were a reality.

Parallels have been drawn between ancient descriptions of angels and aerial gods and modern-day descriptions of encounters with extraterrestrials; many modern encounters contain religious, especially Christian, elements. Passages in the Bible involving angels have been reinterpreted in modern ufological terms.

Among the parallels cited by some ufologists are the following: Visitations by both angels and ETs are preceded by brilliant light. The visiting beings also are radiant or are clothed in radiant garments. They have large, burning eyes. They are superior to humans and travel about in the sky. Parnormal phenomena occur (telepathy, levitation, psy-

chokinesis, out-of-body experience, etc.). Unusual physical effects occur (blindness, paralysis, heat, light, suspended animation, spontaneous healing, etc.). The beings present themselves as custodians who are always watching over the Earth, know what people are doing and can be anywhere instantaneously. The beings often seem to have a mission of imparting important information—moral codes, apocalyptic warnings—that must be disseminated to others. Sometimes people are taken away with the beings, instructed and then returned. The visiting beings may or may not be kindly. The encounters often have a dreamlike quality.

The characteristics of ET encounters have changed over the decades. Early encounters were more likely to include benevolent, beautiful beings with angelic characteristics. Or contactees who were unfamiliar with ufology interpreted visiting beings as angels. One of the most notable cases in ufology is that of Betty Andreasson Luca, who reported that her first encounter occurred in 1944 at the age of seven, involving voices and a ball of light. According to Luca, numerous subsequent encounters took place over ensuing decades, all with a broad purpose of anointing Betty as a messenger to the world. The key event took place in 1967, when several small beings came through the wall of her house. Betty, a devout Christian, assumed them to be angels. They took her aboard their saucerlike craft, where she underwent some highly symbolic and religious experiences. She entered rooms and tunnels full of crystals, and was shown a reenactment of the phoenix myth.

Eight years elapsed before Betty reported her experience to UFO researchers. Through hypnosis, details of that and other encounters were uncovered. Betty later referred to her visitors as "ETs." However, in their communication with her they exhibit knowledge of Christianity, and seem to approve of her Christian background. Their "message," like that of other ETs and otherworldly beings, is to wake up humanity to its multidimensional and spiritual nature, and to warn of dire apocalyptic events that will occur if people do not respond.

Since the late 1970s another type of encounter—decidedly unpleasant—has dominated ufology. Small beings with gray, rubbery skin and large, insectlike slanted eyes (called "the Grays") reportedly abduct humans and subject them to terrifying and painful medical procedures and forced sex with other humans. They also extract semen and ova, allegedly for the purpose of creating a hybrid race of half-human, half-alien beings.

Some ufologists equate these encounters with medieval stories of encounters with demons. The sexual cross-fertilization also is reminiscent of the fallen SONS OF GOD. A Christian spin on this scenario holds that these ETs are diabolical and are part of Satan's fallen angels, sent to Earth to corrupt humanity and steal souls. Their warnings and their messages of "salvation" are tricks to lure people into spiritual enslavement.

Another seemingly demonic aspect of ET encounters is a phenomenon called the "men in black." These are mysterious men who dress in disheveled, dark clothing and drive dark cars, who visit contactees, and warn them not to reveal what has happened. Men in black frequently exhibit a strange, robotlike demeanor. They often represent themselves as government or military agents. They bring with them a host of paranormal phenomena, especially polter-geist effects. They may repeatedly visit a contactee, or harass one by lurking about the home or workplace. Some contactees are intimidated by them, and suffer psychologi-cal deterioration.

The comparison between angels and demons and ETs is intriguing, but one that is widely rejected outside of ufology. The Reverend Billy GRAHAM, while lumping UFOs with occultism and interest in satanism in general, repudiates any connection between angels and ETs in his book, *Angels: God's Secret Agents.*

Another way of looking at the angel-ET connection is through the "encounter phenomenon" hypothesis. According to this view, all manner of encounters with otherworldly beings—regardless of type of being or culture—share funda-mental common characteristics that pertain to the psycho-spiritual evolution of humanity. The encounters occur in a mythic, alternate reality springing from the human uncon-scious. The particulars—types of beings, what happens, etc.—take on a framework that can be accepted by the society of the moment. Thus, it is argued, ETs, with their high technology, fit our present-day mindset.

According to the encounter phenomenon hypothesis, such encounters are need-driven, both on an individual and a collective level. Individuals may unconsciously seek an otherworldly event in order to enhance their sense of pur-pose and self-esteem, and give direction to their lives. On a collective level, these encounters may spring from the col-lective unconscious in answer to very deep longings for a sense of connection to the ineffable, and for spiritual devel-opment. It is interesting to note the apocalyptic nature of the messages imparted by a variety of beings. These harbingers of the "end times" may represent the evolutionary or para-digm shift in human consciousness. (See similarities in NEAR-DEATH EXPERIENCE.)

Carl G. JUNG considered the possibility that UFOs are truly extraterrestrial, but emphasized their psychological implications, observing that they are "a modern myth of things seen in the sky," a direct psychological consequence of man's intense interest in space. ET encounters cut across all social, educational and cultural lines, but so far as is known, occur only to individuals who already are aware of the possibility of ET existence and contact. Jung also said that UFOs are harbingers of collective psychic transforma-tion. (See ARCHETYPES.)

The numerous descriptions of ETs who resemble sick and starving children—such as the Grays, who are small beings with enlarged heads, big eyes and spindly limbs—can also be placed within the context of the encounter phenomenon hypothesis. Philosopher Michael Grosso suggests that ETs are mythical projections of the Child archetype, who in myth is the bearer of extraordinary powers, the harbinger of the future and always under threat. ETs, then, may be symptoms of a racial self-healing (human beings putting themselves on the operating table) and the emergence of a new mythology.

From the standpoint of the encounter phenomenon hypoth-esis, angels, demons and ETs may have much in common.

**Further reading:**
Bramley, William. *The Gods of Eden.* San Jose, Calif.: Dahlin Family Press, 1989.

Downing, Barry H. *The Bible & Flying Saucers.* New York: Lippincott, 1968.
Evans, Hilary. *Gods, Spirits, Cosmic Guardians: A Comparative Study of the Encounter Experience.* Wellingborough, Northamptonshire, England: The Aquarian Press, 1987.
Fowler, Raymond. *The Watchers.* New York: Bantam Books, 1990.
Godwin, Malcom. *Angels: An Endangered Species.* New York: Simon & Schuster, 1990.
Grosso, Michael. "UFOs and the Myth of the New Age," *ReVision*, Vol. 11, No. 3, Winter 1989, pp. 5–13.
Guiley, Rosemary Ellen. *Harper's Encyclopedia of Mystical and Paranormal Experience.* San Francisco: HarperSanFrancisco, 1991.
Little, Gregory L. *People of the Web.* Memphis: White Buffalo Books, 1990.

**Ezekiel**   One of the great Old Testament prophets, who was taken to heaven by cherubim and thrones. His account is one of the richest in angel lore.

Ezekiel lived in Jerusalem, and was taken captive by the Babylonians when Nebuchadnezzar invaded in 597 B.C.E. After about four years in Babylon, he received the call to be a prophet. In numerous visions and trances he received apoca-lyptic messages, with themes that were common among the Jews of the day. Ezekiel preached repentance; his main prophecy was that Jerusalem would fall because of the wickedness of its inhabitants (the city did fall eleven years later, in 586 B.C.E.). "Thus says the Lord God" became his sig-nature line.

Like many visions of antiquity, Ezekiel's visions are couched in a sort of coded language and are difficult to deci-pher. The book of Ezekiel opens with a dramatic description of Ezekiel taken up to heaven (4–14):

> As I looked, behold, a stormy wind came out of the north, and a great cloud, with brightness round about it, and fire flash-ing forth continually, and in the midst of the fire, as it were gleaming bronze. And from the midst of it came the likeness of four living creatures. And this was their appearance: they had the form of men, but each had four faces, and each of them had four wings. Their legs were straight, and the soles of their feet were like the sole of a calf's foot; and they sparkled like burnished bronze. Under their wings on their fours sides they had human hands. . . . [T]heir wings touched one another; they went every one straight forward, without turning as they went. . . .
> [E]ach had the face of a man in the front . . . the face of a lion on the right side . . . the face of an ox on the left side . . . the face of an eagle at the back . . . And their wings were spread out above; each creature had two wings, each of which touched the wing of another, while two covered their bodies. And each went straight forward; wherever the spirit would go, they went, without turning as they went. In the midst of the living creatures there was something that looked like burning coals of fire, like torches moving to and from among the living creatures; and the fire was bright, and out of the fire went forth lightning. And the living creatures darted to and fro, like a flash of lightning.

Ezekiel then sees four wheels beside each of the living creatures. They gleam like chrysolite and have rims full of eyes. They go in any direction without turning as they go. When the living creatures rise, the wheels rise with them. When the living creatures stand still, so do the wheels. The flapping of the wings sounds like many waters, like the thun-der of the Almighty.

Ezekiel's vision (17th c. Bear Bible)

There is a firmament over the heads of the living creatures, and there appears a throne like sapphire, and a human likeness seated upon it, glowing like fire and surrounded by a rainbow. This is the glory of the Lord. Ezekiel receives a scroll, which he eats and which tastes like honey, and also receives instructions to act as prophet. When the message is over, there is a sound of earthquakes, the cherurbim rise up, and Ezekiel is deposited back among the exiles in Babylon. "And I sat there overwhelmed among them seven days," he writes (3:15).

Ezekiel has other visions in which he is in the presence of God and is shown the evil ways of the Israelites. Once again he sees the winged cherubim and the whirling wheels, as well as a "man clothed in linen" who carries out the instructions of God (9:11ff) to punish wrongdoers on earth.

The four living creatures are also referenced in Revelation 4:7. The wheels are the thrones, third in the highest hierarchy of angels, who carry God (see CHOIRS). Four wheels also symbolize omnidirectional ability, and the four faces of the cherubim symbolize the ability to see in all directions at once. The man in linen is described also in DANIEL 10:5 and is probably a reference to an angel, perhaps the ANGEL OF THE LORD.

Ezekiel's vision formed a key element of the Merkabah tradition, Jewish mysticism dating from *c.* 100 B.C.E. to 1000 C.E. "Merkabah" means "God's Throne-Chariot," a direct reference to the vision. The goal of of Merkabah was to ascend through seven heavens to the throne world, a journey in which the mystic was assailed by evil spirits attempting to thwart his flight. The mystical names of God and angels were important for their power to protect against evil and to contemplate the mysteries of the throne. (See NAMES OF ANGELS.)

See also ANGELOPHANY.

**Further reading:**

Alexander, Pat, ed. *The Lion Encyclopedia of the Bible.* Batavia, Ill.: Lion Publishing, 1986.

*The New Oxford Annotated Bible with Apocrypha.* Herbert G. May and Bruce M. Metzger, eds. New York: Oxford University Press, 1977.

Scholem, Gershom. *Kabbalah.* New York: Dorset Press, 1974.

# F

**fallen angels**   See DEMON.

**feather crown**   See ANGEL WREATH.

**film, drama and television, angels in**   On screen or onstage, the appearance of an angel requires the special effects of an otherworldly aura in sound and sight. When it comes to stories about angels, filmmakers have fallen into several thematic patterns: the earth-heaven and heaven-earth trip of a dead person's soul to revisit and rectify errors with angelic help and perspective; direct angelic intervention by angels to inspire people, usually on spiritual matters; comic or ironic twists on situations from angelic lore, such as GABRIEL blowing the horn for the last judgment or SATAN trying to achieve a victory over a troubled soul.

The toll taken by World War II was felt deeply in the early 1940s, and Hollywood produced many films that dealt with death and bereavement and often managed to be patriotic at the same time. Critic James Agee wrote in *The Nation* in 1944:

> The real wonder is not that Hollywood is so eager to exploit the grief, anguish, fear, premonition and troubled spiritual apprehensions of everyone on earth it can reach, but that it has been so slow in recognizing the magnificence of its opportunity to do so. It is more than possible, too, that a good deal of this extremely lucrative exploitation is "sincere."

An early classic in the angel-come-to earth genre was *Here Comes Mr. Jordan* (Columbia, 1941). After boxer Robert Montgomery crashes his plane and a heavenly messenger escorts him to heaven, where an error is discovered, Mr. Jordan, the "man in charge" (Claude Rains), accompanies him back to earth to search for a suitable replacement body and uncover and rectify wrongdoings in his former lifetime. In 1947 Columbia released a musical sequel, *Down to Earth*, reprising several roles from *Here Comes Mr. Jordan*, featuring Rita Hayworth as the muse Terpsichore who comes to earth because she is dissatisfied with a Broadway producer's jazz treatment of the nine muses. *Heaven Can Wait* (Paramount, 1978) was a remake of *Here Comes Mr. Jordan*. The title came from the Henry Seegal play from which the 1941 movie had been adapted. In the Beatty version, Mr. Jordan (James Mason) is clearly identified as an archangel.

*Heaven Can Wait* (20th Century-Fox, 1943) is entirely different. Don Ameche plays a bon vivant reviewing his supposedly unworthy human existence on the doorstep of hell. In *Happy Land* (20th Century-Fox, 1943), Ameche plays a

father who has lost his son in the war. He is helped through his grief by his long-dead grandfather Harry Carey, a Civil War veteran who has received permission from "the authorities" to intervene.

*A Guy Named Joe* (RKO, 1943) adds patriotism to the angelic agenda of assisting humans through their time of bereavement. Pilot Spencer Tracy dies and becomes guardian angel of new pilots during World War II, including Van Johnson, with whom he fixes up his grieving girlfriend Irene Dunne. *Always* (Steven Spielberg, Universal, 1989), a remake of *A Guy Named Joe*, casts Audrey Hepburn as a guardian angel who assists dead pilot Richard Dreyfuss in fixing up his girlfriend with the right man. Many other spin-offs, adding cars to the "cinematic heaven-to-earth train" in the 1940s and 1950s, are not memorable.

Probably the most famous film with an angel in it is Frank Capra's *It's a Wonderful Life* (RKO, 1946). James Stewart depicts a man of moral worth rediscovering his own life at Christmas after his attempted suicide attempt is foiled by his guardian angel Clarence Oddbody (played by Henry Travers, who was in his seventies at the time), an apprentice trying to get his wings. When financially pressed, George declares, "I wish I had never been born." Clarence shows George what life in Bedford Falls would be like without him. *It Happened One Christmas* (1977), an ABC-TV movie remake of *It's a Wonderful Life* with a gender switch, featured Marlo Thomas as Mary Bailey Hatch. *Clarence*, a 1990 Family Channel Cable film, developed the character of Clarence Oddbody. This script added a new twist: Guardian angels get younger as they gain rank with every good deed, and reach the ultimate state of grace as cherubs.

*A Cabin in the Sky*, first a Broadway musical in the early 1940s, was produced by MGM in 1943 with an all-black cast including Ethel Waters, Lena Horne, Duke Ellington and Eddie "Rochester" Anderson. Lucifer and the Lord battle for a soul. *Liliom*, a 1921 Ferenc Molnár play, was adapted by Rogers and Hammerstein into their musical *Carousel*, which debuted on Broadway in 1945. 20th Century-Fox adapted it for film in 1956. Dead carousel barker Billy Bigelow gets permission from the Starkeeper in heaven to go help his family on earth.

*The Bishop's Wife* (RKO, 1947) features Cary Grant as Dudley, an angel who intervenes when an Episcopal bishop (David Niven) loses his faith at the Christmas season. In *One Magic Christmas* (1985), angel Gideon (Harry Dean Stanton, dressed as a cowboy who plays the harmonica up in a tree), stops time, saves lives, takes a little girl to the North Pole to see Santa Claus, and reverses history so as to rekindle the spirit of Christmas in an embittered midwestern housewife (Mary Steenburgen).

Some angel-plot films don't fall under established rubrics. A highly original Depression-era plot, *Gabriel over the White House* (MGM, 1933), tells the story of a comatose president who revives and becomes a benevolent dictator via Gabriel, who gets jobs for an army of unemployed, conquers crime, collects foreign debts, and dies after signing an international peace treaty.

*I Married An Angel* (MGM, 1942), a Jeanette MacDonald–Nelson Eddy musical based on a Hungarian play by Vaszary Janos, was adapted into a Rodgers and Hart musical for Broadway in 1938. A playboy dreams he is married to an angel, and wakes up to discover the love of a plain girl he has been ignoring. *The Horn Blows at Midnight* (1945) featured Jack Benny as Athanael, Angel junior-third-grade, a nightclub trumpet player who fights with two fallen angels to prevent the earth from being blown up by a trumpet blast. In *For Heaven's Sake* (20th Century Fox, 1950) Clifton Webb and Edmund Gwenn play disguised angels doing good on earth. In *The Angel Levine* (United Artists, 1970) Harry Belafonte plays a Jewish angel on probation. *Brother John* (Columbia, 1971) features Sidney Poitier as an angel or an even higher-ranking being who undose wrongs in a southern town full of bigotry and strife. In *Angels in the Outfield* (MGM, 1951, remade in 1993) angels intervene to assist a losing baseball team to victory. In *Two of a Kind* (20th Century Fox, 1983), four angels ask God to spare the earth if they can find two souls who will perform a great deed of sacrifice for one another. John Travolta and Olivia Newton-John play the two humans chosen at random to prove to God (Gene Hackman) that he should not destroy the earth with a second flood.

A spate of 1980s films about angels interacting with adolescents sought to appeal to the teenage marketplace: *The Kid with the Broken Halo* (1982), *Somewhere Tomorrow* (1983), *School Spirit* (1985), *Date with an Angel* (1987) and *The Heavenly Kid* (1985). *Earth Angel*, a 1991 ABC-TV movie, told of a prom queen killed in a car crash, who returns 28 years later to perform good deeds.

The angel-helper theme has been used as the basis of several television series. *Highway to Heaven*, starring Michael Landon, aired from 1984–1988. Landon played Jonathan Smith, an angel who was on probation in heaven, and was helping himself by helping people in trouble. The 1994 season brought *Touched by an Angel*, in which an experienced guardian angel mentors a new one through the learning loops of human assistance.

The bargain-with-the-devil theme achieved masterful treatment in Marlowe's *Doctor Faustus* and Goethe's *Faust* (see MUSIC AND ANGELS and LITERATURE AND ANGELS), which has been staged repeatedly and rendered into many operas. Stephen Vincent Benet's novel *The Devil and Daniel Webster* was adapted into a folk opera by Douglas Stuart Moore and a film in 1941 by William Dieterle. The film features Edward Arnold as the mid-nineteenth-century American statesman Daniel Webster undergoing Faustian despair and temptations at the hands of Mr. Scratch, played by Walter Huston.

Wim Wenders, an *auteur* rather than a movie-maker, released *Wings of Desire* (*Der Himmel Uber Berlin*, Road movies) in 1987, and *Far Away, So Close* in 1993. These films revisit via cinema certain literary themes involving angels (see LITERATURE AND ANGELS). Angels want to become more familiar with the world and with the people of Berlin. One falls in love with a trapeze artist and forgoes his immortality in order to be with her.

Another conceptually challenging modern work is Tony Kushner's *Angels in America*, which received Tony awards in 1993 and 1994. This first part of the musical the *Millennium Approaches* opened in London in 1991. The full work, adding part two, *Perestroika*, comprising a seven-hour epic in total, had its world premiere in Los Angeles in November 1992, and ran for two more years on Broadway. The play ranges from earth to heaven, politics, sex, and religion. It switches between realism and fantasy, treating the tragedy of AIDS and the death or at least the absence of God. The subtitle, "A Gay Fantasia on National Themes," summarizes its intellectual content: a critique of America's soul from a political perspective. One character says: "There are no angels in America, no spiritual past, no racial past, there's only the political."

At the heart of the drama of the lives of several mainly gay characters is Lucifer-figure Roy Cohn, the McCarthy-era lawyer and ruthless power broker, a vicious bigot who was secretly gay but persecuted homosexuals in public. When at the end of Part One the character with AIDS is visited by an angel who emerges from an unzipped earth and flies down to hail him as a new prophet, he gasps "*very* Steven Spielberg." In *Perestroika* the fantasia continues, with the angel revealing herself as the ANGEL OF DEATH. The task of the AIDS patient is to make sense of death and to "face loss with grace." Part of this grace is humor, moving toward resolutions that are darkly comic. Cohn is relentlessly conniving, even in death, bursting into the afterlife to offer his legal services to the runaway God.

**Further reading:**
Parish, James Robert. *Ghosts and Angels in Hollywood Films*. Jefferson, N.C.: McFarland & Company, 1994.

**Findhorn**   An experimental spiritual community in northern Scotland near the Arctic Circle, made famous in the 1960s and 1970s by the gardening guidance given by devas and nature spirits that yielded spectacular produce in inhospitable terrain.

Findhorn founders were Peter and Eileen Caddy, husband and wife, and their friend Dorothy MACLEAN. The three never intended to establish a spiritual colony. Findhorn came into being after they were all laid off from their jobs running a resort hotel in Scotland. Out of work and with nowhere to go, they banded together in the Findhorn Bay Caravan Travel Park, where the Caddys had their trailer. The trailer park was a desolate place, situated next to a rubbish dump and a rundown building. However, the Caddys had moved there because of spiritual guidance received by Eileen in meditation, suggesting that a purpose would unfold there.

The Caddys and Maclean had known each other for years, and had studied under the same spiritual teacher, a Quaker woman named Sheena Govan, who was Peter's wife for five years; she terminated the marriage, but they retained a close relationship. In addition Peter Caddy, a Royal Air Force officer, had studied Rosicrucianism. Maclean was steeped in Sufism. Both Eileen Caddy and Maclean had developed mediumistic gifts; of the two, Maclean's gift dominated at Findhorn.

Unable to find work, Peter Caddy turned to gardening in 1963 to pass the time, even though Findhorn was ill suited for it. The area is located on a narrow sandy peninsula jutting into the North Sea, and is exposed to near-constant winds from all sides. The soil is mostly sand and gravel.

In May of 1963, Maclean, while meditating, received a message from an angelic being—whom she later referred to as both "angel" and "deva"—instructing her to tune into the nature spirits so that a cooperation could begin. Maclean did so, and began to receive regular advice from an assortment of angelic spirits on how to cultivate the garden. Peter Caddy would pose questions for the devas, and Maclean would obtain the answers. The chief coordinating entity was a being Maclean called the "Landscape Angel."

Within a year, Findhorn was transformed. Cabbages, which normally reach four pounds at maturity, weighed over forty pounds. Broccoli grew so large that they were too heavy to lift from the ground. Flowers were nearly twice their normal size. Word of the Findhorn successes spread, but agronomists were at a loss to explain them.

In 1966 a friend of Peter Caddy's, the scholar R. Ogilvie Crombie, paid a visit to Findhorn, an experience that opened him psychically. Shortly afterward Crombie was sitting in the Royal Botanic Gardens, near his home in Edinburgh, Scotland, when he saw a nature spirit dancing in front of him. The three-foot-high, half-man, half-animal gave his name as Kurmos, and said he lived in the gardens and helped trees to grow. This meeting paved the way for a subsequent meeting with Pan, chief of the nature spirits. Pan told Crombie that he had been chosen to help renew the lost contact between mankind and the nature spirits. Crombie passed on to Caddy and the others at Findhorn what he learned from Pan about the spirits who lived and worked in the garden.

For several years the Caddys and Maclean were reluctant to talk about their invisible helpers, though word of their spectacular gardening successes spread. When the residents finally began to talk of the devas, they attracted disciples who wanted to live and work with them.

Over time Maclean sensed the creation of a new entity, the "Angel of Findhorn," which started as a nebulous impression and grew slowly over the years. The Landscape Angel told Maclean that the Angel of Findhorn was being fed by the growth in the gardens, as well as the love generated by the human beings present. Maclean clairvoyantly perceived this being developing almost like a fetus, until it had acquired sufficient power to open to all devic knowledge. The angel took on a masculine presence, and when it communicated with Maclean, described itself as "the Spirit of a place."

Findhorn became a model community for proponents of the New Age movement. By the early 1970s, its peak, it boasted more than three hundred people, among them the philosopher David Spangler, considered a respected New Age prophet in his native United States. Spangler arrived in 1970 with his spiritual partner, Myrtle Glines. Residents viewed themselves as the vanguard of a new society based on the principle of cooperation between man and the kingdom of nature.

After Spangler's arrival, an angelic presence called Limitless Love and Truth manifested. The being provided revelations that had first appeared, independently, to another man in Britain. Spangler published some of the transmissions in his book, *Revelation: the Birth of a New Age* (1976).

By 1980 the Findhorn community had declined, due in part to the departures of some of the principles, including Maclean, Peter Caddy (he and Eileen had divorced) and Spangler. Eileen remained, but took a background position so that Findhorn could be cared for by a new generation of residents. Without someone like Maclean as a focal point, interest and involvement in the nature kingdom faded. But a decade later, around 1990, interest returned, as part of a broader upswing in interest in human cooperation with the angelic and natural realms.

Findhorn continues on as a small community, and it provides a variety of spiritual workshops and seminars. It has served as a model for other similar garden enterprises and communities, such as PERELANDRA, near Washington, D.C., and GREEN HOPE FARM in Meriden, New Hampshire.

See DEVA; ELEMENTAL.

**Further reading:**

Findhorn Community. *The Findhorn Garden*. New York: Harper & Row, 1975.
Hawken, Paul. *The Magic of Findhorn*. New York: Bantam Books, 1976.
Maclean, Dorothy. *To Hear the Angels Sing*. Hudson, N.Y.: Lindisfarne Press, 1990. First published by Lorian Press, 1980. 2nd ed. by Morningtown Press, 1988.
Spangler, David. *Revelation: The Birth of a New Age*. Elgin, Ill.: The Lorian Press, 1976.

## Flamel, Nicolas (1330–1416)

French scribe, alchemist and adept, whose successful career as an alchemist was launched by an angel, according to legend.

Nicolas Flamel was born in 1330 in Pontoise, eighteen miles north of Paris, to a modest family. As a young man he set up business in Paris as a public scribe, copying and illuminating manuscripts and performing other publishing services. He enjoyed a good reputation. Through his work he met Madame Pernelle Lethas, an older woman who was twice widowed and left with comfortable means. He fell in love with her. They married, and led a quiet and thrifty life.

Alchemy, the transmutation of base metals to gold and silver, was popular at the time, and Flamel undoubtedly copied various alchemical manuscripts. He showed little interest in the subject, however, until he experienced a dream one night. An angel appeared to him and held out a beautiful book of obvious antiquity. The angel said, "Flamel, look at this book. You will not in the least understand it, neither will anyone else; but a day will come when you will see in it something that no one else will see." In the dream Flamel reached out to take the book, but both it and the angel vanished in a golden cloud.

Flamel paid scant attention to the dream until sometime later, in 1357, when an event occurred. For a mere two florins, he acquired from a vendor a mysterious gilded book that was large, very old, and made not of paper or parchment but from the thin bark of tender shrubs. Its cover was made of copper, and it was engraved with strange symbols. Its contents included equally strange drawings, and a claim that it was authored by Abraham Eleazar, or "Abraham the Jew," a prince, astrologer and philosopher. It also delivered curses against anyone who should set his eyes on the book, lest he be a sacrificer or scribe.

Feeling exempted from the curses, Flamel examined the book and determined that it was an alchemical text that told how to transmute metals into gold, so that Jews could pay levies due to the Roman empire. The secret remained hidden in the drawings, some of which were not accompanied by explanatory text. On every seventh leaf there was an illustration of one of three icons: a caduceus (staff) with intertwined serpents; a serpent crucified on a cross; or a snake-infested desert with beautiful mountains. Among other drawings was one of a winged Mercury with Saturn holding an hourglass and scythe, and a mountain with a rose (with a blue stalk and red and white flowers) blown in the north wind.

The book remained inscrutable to Flamel and his wife for years. In 1378, Flamel made a pilgrimage to Spain, hoping to meet a learned Jew who was versed in the Kabbalah who could help him to decipher the alchemical book. After a year of wandering he met a converted Jew, Maitre Canches, who identified copies of some of the drawings from the book as coming from an old Kabbalistic text, the *Asch Mezareph*, written by a Rabbi Abraham and believed to be lost. Maitre Canches decided to return to France with Flamel, but became ill on the journey and died when they reached Orleans. According to Flamel, Canches revealed enough secrets before he died so that Flamel could then decipher his book on his own.

Nonetheless, it still took Flamel, assisted by Pernelle, three years of hard labor to make a successful projection of the philosopher's stone. In 1382, Flamel claimed, they turned lead (according to some accounts it was mercury) first into silver and then, on a second occasion, into gold. Legend has it that they made three projections, which gave them a handsome amount of gold, so much that they founded and endowed fourteen hospitals, built three chapels, made generous gifts to seven churches, and paid for the repair of numerous church buildings. They made similar grants in Bologne, where Pernelle had been born.

Flamel wrote about his experiences in a book, but he gave away no secrets. In addition, he painted some of the drawings from the book as frescoes in an archway he had built in the Cemetery of the Holy Innocents in Paris. The painting symbolizes the Great Secret, and was the object of many pilgrimages by alchemists into the seventeenth and eighteenth centuries.

Pernelle died in 1397. Flamel died on November 22, 1416 (he is also said to have died in 1417 or 1418). His house was futilely ransacked by fortune hunters seeking the secrets of transmutation. It was widely believed by other alchemists that Flamel did achieve the philosopher's stone—the substance that transmutes metals into gold—but apparently his secrets died with him, and his success was not achieved by others.

Legend has it that Flamel did give some of his philosopher's stone to a nephew of his wife named Perrier, who passed it on to a Dr. Perrier. When he died, his grandson, named Dubois, found it among his effects. He took it to Louis XVII, and successfully transmuted some base metal into gold in the king's presence. The king asked him to make some more of the philosopher's stone, which Dubois promised but failed to do. He was hanged, according to the story.

Flamel and Pernelle entered legend, and reputedly attained immortality—the spiritual side of the philosopher's stone. Stories about them circulated for centuries. They were reported to be alive in India in the seventeenth century, and to have been seen attending an opera in Paris in 1761.

See DREAMS.

**Further reading:**
Burckhardt, Titus. *Alchemy: Science of the Cosmos, Science of the Soul.* London: Stuart and Watkins, 1967.
Grillot de Givry. *Witchcraft, Magic & Alchemy.* New York: Dover Publications, 1971. First published 1931.
Holmyard, E.J. *Alchemy.* Mineola, N.Y.: Dover Publications, 1990. First published 1957.
Seligmann, Kurt. *The Mirror of Magic.* New York: Pantheon Books, 1948.
Thompson, C.J.S. *The Lure and Romance of Alchemy.* New York: Bell Publishing, 1990. First published 1932.

**Frances of Rome, St.** (1384–1440)   Christian saint who was guided daily by angels. She reportedly was given two guardian angels at birth, but neither one of these presented themselves in a dramatic way. Rather, she was guided first by an archangel and then by a power.

Frances's frequent angelic visits began with the death of her first son, Evangelista, at age nine. Just before dying, he exclaimed that angels had arrived to take him to heaven (see DEATHBED VISIONS). On the one-year anniversary of his death, Frances had an extraordinary hour-long vision. Her oratory was filled with a brilliant light at dawn, and she beheld her son accompanied by a beautiful boy. Evangelista said that he now resided in the second choir of the first hierarchy of angels, and introduced his companion as an archangel who had a place above his. He told his mother that God was sending her this archangel, who would not leave her day or night, and that she would be blessed by seeing the archangel with her "bodily eyes." Evangelista then said he had to return to heaven, but the sight of the angel would always remind his mother of him.

Evangelista disappeared, never to manifest to Frances again. The angel remained, standing with arms folded across his chest. Frances fell to her knees, and begged for his help in guiding her spiritual growth and in defending against the devil. When she finally left the oratory the angel followed her, enveloping her in a halo of light. The angel, and this halo around Frances, could not be perceived by other people (see ANGELOPHANY).

Frances could not look upon the angel's brightness without its hurting her eyes, so, she looked upon the glow around him. Over time she was able to more directly see his features while she was at prayer; it seemed that the angel purposefully dimmed his own light to help her. He looked like a boy of nine, with sparkling eyes, an ever-present sweet expression upon his face, and his eyes turned constantly toward heaven. He wore a white robe covered by a tunic that reached to his feet. He was clear as light, and an ethereal color like sky-blue and flaming red. His hair, like spun gold, fell across his shoulders. The light coming from his hair was so bright that Frances frequently did not need a candle, even at night.

She wrote that the angel was never soiled by dirt or mud when he walked beside her. If she committed even the slightest fault, however, he disappeared from her sight, and would reappear only after she had confessed her transgressions. If she was plagued by doubts, he gave her a kind look that immediately made her feel better. When he talked, she could see his lips move; his voice was incredibly sweet.

Much of the angel's guidance centered around Frances's worries as head of a family. The angel assured her that she was not lost in God's sight. He also enabled her to supernaturally discern the thoughts of others. Thus she reportedly was able to short-circuit evil intent, reconcile enemies, and help wandering souls return to the fold.

Frances also was engaged in a constant struggle against evil spirits. Whenever the devil would particularly plague her, she would appeal to the archangel for help. Like Samson, the angel's power also lay in his hair, for when Frances asked him for protection, the angel shook his hair and frightened the evil spirits away.

The archangel—who never offered a name—stayed with Frances for twenty-four years. In 1436 she joined her own community and was granted a vision in which she saw God seated on a high throne and surrounded by myriads of angels. God appointed one of the high-ranking powers (see CHOIRS) to replace the archangel. In his human form, the power was even more beautiful than the archangel, and exhibited greater power and courage. He did not have to shake his hair to scare away evil spirits; his mere presence accomplished that. He carried in his left hand three golden palm branches, which symbolized three virtues that he helped Frances to cultivate: charity, firmness and prudence.

The power stayed with Frances for four years until she died. Her angelic experiences are characteristic of the literature of saints.

**Further reading:**

Parente, Fr. Pascal P. *The Angels: The Catholic Teaching on the Angels.* Rockford, Ill.: Tan Books and Publishers, 1973. First published 1961.

O'Sullivan, Fr. Paul. *All About the Angels.* Rockford, Ill.: Tan Books and Publishers, 1990. First published 1945.

**Francis of Assisi, St.** (1181?–1226) Often called the most Christ-like of all the saints, Francis of Assisi is known for his love of animals and for his stigmata, given to him by an angel.

Francis of Assisi was born in either 1181 or 1182 in the town of Assisi in Umbria, Italy, to Pietro Bernardone and his wife Pica. Although baptized Giovanni, or John, the boy was called Francesco, "the Frenchman," because his father was often in that country conducting his successful cloth trade.

Francis spent his early years in song, drink and extravagance, going through his father's money but showing no interest in his father's business. In 1201 war broke out between Assisi and neighboring Perugia, and Francis was captured. He languished for a year in prison, then suffered a long illness after his release. During his convalescence he kept receiving signs that he should change his ways. Upon recovery he outfitted himself to join the forces of Walter de Brienne, who was fighting in southern Italy, but instead ended up trading his fine clothes and armor for the rags of a poor former knight he met on his journey.

*The Stigmatization of St. Francis* (Stefano di Giovanni called Sassetta, reprinted courtesy of the National Gallery, London)

By 1204 he had stolen one of his father's horses and a large amount of cloth, which he sold to rebuild the ruined church of San Damiano de Assisi. His father tried everything to dissuade Francis from his "mad" ideas, including beatings and shackles, but Francis was immovable. By 1206 he had completely renounced his patrimony and had taken a vow of absolute poverty. He and his growing band of followers wore long, rough tunics of undyed wool, shaved the tops of their heads and preached as itinerants among the poor and sick, depending solely on the generosity of strangers.

St. Francis's commitment to Christ caught the imagination of his day. Familiar with court poetry and the songs of the troubadours, St. Francis introduced into medieval worship a love of nature and creation, of song and praise, and of higher chivalric love. His poem the "Canticle of the Sun" is still sung in Christian churches all over the world. He introduced a crèche at a Nativity Mass in Greccio in 1223, as a memorial to Jesus' humble birth. St. Francis's simple appeal and total devotion, as well as the stories of his prophecies and miraculous-healings, continue to attract followers to this day.

Perhaps his most unusual achievement was the acquisition of stigmata after an ecstatic vision in 1224. During the summer of that year, close to the Feast of the Assumption (August 15), St. Francis returned in seclusion to a tiny hut on

Monte La Verna, part of the property of Orlando, count of Chiusi. He intended to suffer a long fast in honor of the archangel Michael, requesting that he be left alone until the angel's feast day on September 29. St. Francis was then forty-two years old, racked with disease and fevers and quite thin from self-mortification.

On September 14, the Feast of the Exaltation of the Holy Cross, St. Francis continued his fasting and prayer by concentrating on Christ's sufferings on the cross. As described in the *Little Flowers of St. Francis of Assisi*, he was contemplating the Passion so fervently that he believed himself transformed into Jesus. While in such an ecstatic state, his vision continued with the appearance of a seraph. The angel's six fiery wings descended from heaven, and as they drew closer to St. Francis they revealed the crucified Jesus within their folds. St. Francis was filled with fear, joy and sorrow. When the vision ended, the saint found to his amazement that his hands and feet were marked with black excrescences in the form of nail heads and bent nails, and that a wound on his side—like the sword wounds suffered by Jesus—oozed blood frequently.

St. Francis was embarrassed and frightened by these stigmata, and for the remaining two years of his life kept his hands within his habit and wore shoes and stockings. He told none of his followers about the miracle, but they finally deduced the situation after finding blood on his clothing and after noting St. Francis's inability to walk without hobbling.

Modern research suggests that the marks were scar tissue from earlier, unknown wounds. In the days of the early church, any disfigurement was known as "stigmata." Today, stigmata are believed to result from the auto-suggestion of worshippers who brood intensely on Christ's sufferings. Yet several surviving accounts from various of St. Francis's followers refer to his bleeding wounds, the saint's inability to walk, and the blackness of the marks. St. Francis's biographer Thomas of Celano reported that black marks resembling nails even appeared on St. Francis's flesh after death. And two paintings of St. Francis, painted within ten years of his death, both show the stigmata.

St. Francis died on October 3, 1226 and was canonized two years later by Pope Gregory IX. There were no verified reports of stigmata before St. Francis's designation in 1224, and there have been very few since.

**Further reading:**

Cavendish, Richard, ed. *Man, Myth and Magic: The Illustrated Encyclopedia of Mythology, Religion and the Unknown*, Vols. 4 and 10. New York: Marshall Cavendish Ltd., 1985, pp. 1031–1032, 2698–2699.

Chambers, R., ed. *The Book of Days: A Miscellany of Popular Antiquities in Connection with the Calendar*, Vol. II. Detroit: Gale Research Co., 1967.

Oliphant, Mrs. *Francis of Assisi*. London: Macmillan and Co., Ltd., 1898.

*One Hundred Saints*. Boston: Bulfinch Press, 1993.

Walsh, Michael, ed. *Butler's Lives of the Saints*, Concise Edition. San Francisco: Harper & Row, 1985, pp. 314–320.

Wilson, Ian. *Stigmata: An Investigation into the Mysterious Appearance of Christ's Wounds in Hundreds of People from Medieval Italy to Modern America*. San Francisco: Harper & Row, 1989.

# G

**Gabriel** The angel Gabriel—given the rank of archangel in post-biblical lore—is one of the three principal angels of Christianity, and figures prominently in Judaic, Christian and Islamic angelology. The name means "hero of God" or "the mighty one" in Hebrew. Gabriel is the angel of revelation, wisdom, mercy, redemption and promise. He sits at the left hand of God.

Gabriel is mentioned four times in the Bible, and always in connection with important news. In the Old Testament he is named as Daniel's frequent visitor, bringing prophetic visions of apocalyptic proportion (Daniel 8:16, 9:21). Angelic attribution of the visions, which were treasonous at the time of the writing of the book of Daniel, might explain Gabriel's prominent presence. In the New Testament, Gabriel's name is given to Zechariah: "I am Gabriel who stand in God's presence" when he announces the coming birth of John the Baptist (Luke 1:19). Gabriel is once again cited in the annunciation to Mary (Luke 1:26) of the coming birth of Jesus.

Gabriel's messenger mission probably inspired his presence in the secondary Hebrew literature, where Gabriel figures in the stories of Adam's creation, the punishment of the fallen angels (see MICHAEL), the burials of Adam, Abel and ABRAHAM, and other events in Genesis. The angel figures in various Hebrew folktales as well.

Midrashim concerning Gabriel and a magical stone begin with Abram (later Abraham). Abram is left in a cave by his mother because of the slaughter of newborn males by King Nimrod. God sends Gabriel to tend the infant who feeds Abram with his thumb, through which milk and honey flow. This enables the boy to grow at the spectacular rate of a year a day. The archangel also talks with him, so that when his mother returns, she is amazed at her son's ability to speak.

On his third day in the cave, Abram finds a glowing stone, which Gabriel places around his neck. This is the Tzohar ("light" or "window"), the light of the Garden of Eden preserved by God after the fall of Adam and Eve. The Tzohar was given to Adam by the angel Raziel. Adam, in turn, gives it to his son Seth, who uses it to become a great prophet. Eventually the stone is given to ENOCH, who uses its light to read the Celestial Torah on his trip to the heavens. Enoch gives it to his son Methuselah, who gives it to his son Lamech, who gives it to his son Noah, who places it in the Ark. The story goes that after Noah lands on Mt. Ararat he celebrates with wine, gets drunk, and lets the Tzohar slip into the sea. It eventually finds its way into the cave in which Abram is being hidden.

Abraham wears the stone for his entire life, and all who look upon it are healed. He uses it as an astrolabe with which to study the heavens. He passes the stone to ISAAC, who passes it to JACOB, who wears it during his famous dream of the angels going up and down the ladder to heaven. Jacob gives it to his son Joseph, but does not tell him of its power. When Joseph's brothers take his coat of many colors and throw him into a dark pit, the stone begins to glow. Suddenly Joseph finds himself transported to an incandescent palace. Gabriel, a glowing being, announces himself and says that this is his palace, and Joseph will remain there as long as he is held prisoner in the pit. Gabriel creates a cloth woven from the stone's light, and so Joseph is clothed. Gabriel points to a window, and there Joseph sees revelations of future generations.

For three days and nights Joseph remains in the palace, studying the Torah and the future of Israel. At the end of the third day Joseph is rescued from the pit and sold into slavery. He keeps the Tzohar inside a silver cup, and prophesies the future and interprets dreams by gazing upon it. When Joseph dies the stone is buried with him, but MOSES recovers it and hangs it in the Tabernacle.

Gabriel's palace figures in another Jewish mystical tale from the oral tradition in Germany. According to the story, Rabbi Meir of Rothenburg is imprisoned and declines to be ransomed. Instead he asks only to be given scribe's tools, so that he can write down his thoughts on the Torah. One night his soul ascends to Gabriel's brilliant palace. Gabriel, also brilliant in light, introduces himself and says that Rabbi Meir has been brought here to receive a Torah. In fact he is getting one of the thirteen Torahs that Moses wrote before his death, the one that was intended for the celestial academy.

When Rabbi Meir awakens, he finds a Torah in his cell. He follows Gabriel's instructions and reads from it loudly enough for the heavenly host to hear him. When he does so, his cell fills with a holy light. He discovers numerous truths that can be obtained only from that celestial Torah.

Rabbi Meir copies the Torah. As soon as he is done, Gabriel comes in the night and takes the original back to heaven. Rabbi Meir seals his copy in a waterproof wooden ark and sets it afloat upon the River Rhine. It comes to Worms. Gentiles cannot catch it, and after Jews capture it, Gentiles cannot lift it or open it. The Jews open it. The Torah remains in the city for many generations. (See also ANGEL OF DEATH.)

According to several midrashim Gabriel is the angel that destroys Sodom. He is not specifically named in the Genesis account (see SODOM AND GOMORRAH).

In the courtship of Rebekah by Abraham's agent Eliezer, Gabriel is credited with exchanging a plate of poison food planned by Laban.

When Abraham dies, four archangels bury him. According to midrashim, MICHAEL and Gabriel witness the contract between Esau and JACOB when Esau sells his birthright to Jacob.

Like the angel SANDALPHON, who weaves garlands of prayers, Gabriel weaves shoes from the feet of Jews who dance to commemorate the Giving of the Torah. In the fervor of dancing, the shoes fly off to the Garden of Eden, where they are swept up by angels and delivered to Gabriel.

Gabriel also is among the candidates to be the dark angel who fought with JACOB.

It is in his role as annunciator of the coming of the birth of Christ to MARY that Gabriel is best known and best depicted in art. He is shown holding a lily, the symbol of purity. Luke 26–38 describes the encounter between Gabriel and MARY. He appears to her, tells her that she has found favor with God, and that she will become pregnant with a son who is to be named Jesus. When Mary wonders how this can happen since she is a virgin, Gabriel tells her that the Holy Spirit will come upon her and that the child will be holy. When she consents ("Behold, I am the handmaid of the Lord; let it be me according to your word."), the angel departs. Though the angel who announces the birth of Jesus to the shepherds (Luke 2:8–14) is called only an "angel of the Lord," Catholic tradition credits this as being to Gabriel.

Gabriel also is credited with other major acts of unnamed angels in the story of Jesus: as the angel who appears in a dream to Joseph, warning him to take his family and flee to Egypt to avoid Herod's hunt for the baby Jesus (Matthew 2:13); as the angel who appears in the Garden of Gesthemane to provide strength and support to Jesus in his agony (Luke 22:43); and as the "angel of the Lord" who has a countenance as lightning and a raiment as snow, who rolls back the stone from the tomb of Jesus and sits upon it (Matthew 28:2). In addition Gabriel is said to be the unnamed archangel in 1 Thessalonians 4:15, who sounds the trumpet of judgment and resurrection.

Gabriel has a prominent place in the Catholic devotion to angels, because of his role in the Annunciation. Gabriel's salutation, "Hail, full of grace, the Lord is with thee, blessed art thou among women" is reiterated in the Hail Mary. His feast day is March 24.

Because of his role in the Annunciation, other lore about Gabriel holds that he guides the soul from paradise to the womb and there instructs it for the nine months prior to birth.

Gabriel also figures prominently in ISLAMIC ANGELOLOGY, where he is equated with the Holy Spirit. It was Gabriel, with 140 pairs of wings, who dictated the Koran to MUHAMMAD, according to some accounts. In Islamic theosophy, the Angel Gabriel is the Angel of Knowledge and Revelation, to whom the philosophers trace back their active Intelligence. He is the personal Holy Spirit, the companion and celestial guide. (See INTELLIGENCES.)

Rudolph STEINER associated Gabriel with the "Christmas imagination" in an approach blending the senses, imagination, inspiration and intuition, and Steiner used imaging, poetry, and all the arts to express his teachings. In a series of lectures given in October 1923, he interwove details about Gabriel with the cosmic and natural processes indicated by the change of seasons.

At Christmas the birth of the Redeemer is celebrated. In the depths of winter the Earth, in relation to the cosmos, is self-enclosed, as if it were cut off from the cosmos. During the winter the Earth is wholly Earth, with a concentrated Earth-nature. In high summer, on the other hand, the Earth is open to the cosmos, lives with the cosmos, and in between, spring and autumn hold Earth in balance. When Earth is most herself, the Redeemer emerges from its juncture with heaven, and Gabriel, who has interacted with humans at phases of the preparation for this event, announces it to humankind surrounded by the heavenly host.

The depths of winter show that the Redeemer is literally connecting the cosmos with the birth-forces of the Earth, represented as the Madonna and Child: formed out of the clouds, endowed with the forces of the Earth, with the Moon-forces below, with the Sun-forces in the middle, and above, toward the head, with the forces of the stars. The depiction of Mary with the child arises out of the cosmos itself. Gabriel's is a mild and loving gaze, his gesture one of blessing.

**Further reading:**

Davidson, Gustav. *A Dictionary of Angels.* New York: The Free Press, 1967.

Graves, Robert, and Patai, Raphael. *Hebrew Myths.* New York: Doubleday Anchor Books, 1964.

O'Sullivan, Fr. Paul. *All About the Angels.* Rockford, Ill.: Tan Books and Publishers, 1990. First published 1945.

Schwartz, Howard. *Gabriel's Palace: Jewish Mystical Tales.* New York: Oxford University Press, 1993.

*The Annunciation* (Eustache Le Sueur, c. 1650; reprinted courtesy Toledo Museum of Art, Toledo, Ohio; gift of Edward Drummond Libbey)

*St. Michael and the Angels.* Rockford, Ill.: Tan Books and Publishers, 1983. First published 1977.

Steiner, Rudolf. *The Four Seasons and the Archangels.* Bristol, England: The Rudolf Steiner Press, 1992.

**Galgani, Gemma, St.** See ANGELOPHANY.

**genius** In Roman mythology, a genius ("guardian spirit") is comparable to a guardian angel, but differs in that it can be attached to people, places or things. The genius presides over the birth of a person, place or thing and shapes its character and destiny. If attached to a person, the genius stays with him or her through life, and becomes the person's living soul after death. The genius of a place is perceived as the living spirit that animates a locale and gives it its unique powers and atmosphere. The Romans used a figure of a human being to symbolize the genius of a person, and a serpent to symbolize the genius of a place.

See DAEMON.

**George, St.** See MONS, ANGELS OF.

**Gideon** The Book of Judges tells the story of Gideon and his encounter with the ANGEL OF THE LORD.

In Judges 6, Gideon is commissioned by God to deliver Israel from the Midianites, their greatest enemy at the time. He is threshing his wheat at Ophrah when the angel of the Lord appears and apprises him of his mission. Gideon protests that his clan is weak, and asks for a sign that it is the Lord who is speaking.

Gideon retires to his house, where he prepares food: a kid, unleavened cakes of bread, and broth. He returns to the angel and presents them. The angel tells him to place the meat and cakes on a rock and pour the broth over them. Judges 6:21: "Then the angel of the Lord reached out the tip of the staff that was in his hand, and touched the meat and the unleavened cakes; and there sprang up fire from the rock and consumed the flesh and the unleavened cakes, and the angel of the Lord vanished from his sight." This is proof to Gideon, and he builds an altar on the site.

To fulfill God's mission, he assembles an army of 300 men. Armed with trumpets, empty pitchers and torches, they storm the enemy at night, shouting, "A sword for the Lord and for Gideon!" (Judges 7:20) The Midianites fall into panic and flee. Under Gideon's rule, peace reigns for forty years until his death.

As in virtually all biblical encounters involving angels, there is ambiguity over whether the divine entity is an angel or the Lord himself. "Angel of the Lord" often is interpreted as being another description of God.

**Further reading:**
*Harper's Bible Commentary.* James L. Mays, gen. ed. San Francisco: HarperSanFrancisco, 1988.

*The New Oxford Annotated Bible with the Apochrypha.* Herbert G. May and Bruce M. Metzger, eds. New York: Oxford University Press, 1977.

**ginn** See JINN.

**Gnosticism** A popular cult of beliefs and practices more or less contemporary with early Christianity but with roots far older, traceable in Egypt, Babylonia, Persia, Greek philosophy and Semitic mythology. The term *gnosis* means knowledge and came to have a connotation of the restoration to a favored few of the truth of humanity's situation. Humans had become cut off from their real nature and from God by a series of developments told in many ways and in many stories, all comprising an elaborately rich mythology full of angels of many kinds and degrees. The entire Gnostic cosmology makes angels the key players. When the Gnostics viewed the night sky they saw the stars as angels who had erred, the heavens as a vault barring them from their soul's home. Not God, not man, but exalted higher beings are the forces that caused the Fall, created the world, and facilitated the means of redemption.

*BACKGROUND*

Gnosticism was driven forward by a radical questioning of current explanations for the presence and power of igno-

**Angel (Copyright 1995 by Robert Michael Place, from *The Angels Tarot* by Rosemary Ellen Guiley and Robert Michael Place. Reprinted courtesy of HarperSanFrancisco)**

rance, evil and suffering on earth. Its most notable proponents were Simon Magus (who meets Peter in Acts 8);
Basilides, who taught in Alexandria c. 120–140; and Valentinus, who was born Christian and who taught in Rome c.
140–160. ORIGEN and other church fathers dealt with
Gnosticism repeatedly in their writings, and not always to
refute them. Origen's commentary on the Song of Solomon
considers the Gnostic union of Logos and SOPHIA to be one
valid allegorical reading.

Gnosticism arose in the Hellenic Middle East, particularly
in Alexandria, an intellectual crossroads of cultures. Thus the
Gnostics were thoroughly familiar with the Scriptures of
Christianity and Judaism, Greek philosophy, Hermeticism
and probably the religions of the East. The Gnostics wrote
gospels and epistles and combined lore and practices from
many sources, expanding their limits as they wished.

Prior to the twentieth century, Gnosticism was studied
mainly from three perspectives. First, it was considered to be
a heresy by Christians from the second and third centuries
on, with some remnants of the heresy surviving into the
Middle Ages. Most early extant documents pertinent to
Gnosticism were writings of Christian fathers that examined
its tenets with a view to denouncing them. Second, it interested occultists fascinated with the Gnostics' reputation as
sorcerers. Third, scholars studied its relation to all of those
sources just mentioned that flowed into it.

In the twentieth century some new lines of development
opened up. In 1945 a cache of Gnostic documents was discovered in Nag Hammadi in Egypt; it took more than twenty
years for scholars to access, translate and begin to analyze
them. Having an all-inclusive bent from its beginnings,
Gnosticism can be interpreted as accommodating two millennia of developments in philosophy and psychology.
Modern theologians of all persuasions now approach
Gnosticism positively. June Singer observes that the Gnostics
would have been fascinated with Freud, "for all their cosmology and their anthropology bears the scars of this cosmic
traumatism caused by man's *premature* appearance on
earth." Carl G. JUNG studied Gnosticism thoroughly. He
states in *Aion*: "It is clear beyond a doubt that many of the
Gnostics were nothing other than psychologists."

There is no organized, clearcut statement of Gnostic
beliefs. Its several strains share a primary vision of the origin
of humankind as being inherently flawed by earthly elements, yet keeping a spark of divinity, a "touch of light"
from its exalted origin, and thus a breath of hope. Gnosticism
is similar to Hinduism and Buddhism and is poles apart
from most Western religions, in this negative view of the
material world and its yearning toward an unknowable mystery. Like Eastern religious practices, Gnosticism facilitated
many degrees of commitment and initiation. For some,
learning the magic names of some angels and partaking in
rituals was sufficient. (Basilides once required his advanced
students to spend five years in complete silence.) Another
modern appeal of Gnosticism is its apparent lack of gender-
bias for aspirants. In fact, the feminine principle was honored as integral in Gnostic belief.

### GNOSTIC ANGELOLOGY

Like the Platonists, the Gnostics viewed the cosmos as being
a series of concentric spheres. They called them *aeons*, each
with its own ruler or AEON (comparable to a very high angel).
The highest (365th) circle is ruled by ABRAXAS, the chief of the
heavens. At the summit or the center is the good God, otherwise called the Father, essentially unknowable to humans.
Aeons could combine and subdivide and multiply themselves in a process called *syzygy*. Descending in tiers down to
our own terrestrial world are thirty circles, which according
to Valentinus constitute the Pleroma (fullness).

SOPHIA was the Aeon of the thirtieth circle. Her story told
how she desired to contemplate on her own the splendor of
the Pleroma. This was an ill-fated wish, for when she crossed
the last circle she was dazzled by light and fell down to our
world. Sophia was made pregnant by the Pleroma and gave
birth to a creature, the Demiurge, who, after modifications
by the Aeons of the Pleroma, created humankind. Gnostics
associated their many versions of this "accursed god" with
the God of the Old Testament.

Another version says that Sophia (the active principle)
desired to create a work without her consort (the passive
Unknown good God). When she did so her thought became
a work, an image of heaven. But a shadow was cast; the
shadow was envious of heaven, being superior to itself. Thus
the beginning (*arche*) of envy entered all the regions in chaos
and became matter. This Demiurge, as it was called, had no
spirit. It created the visible world but withheld knowledge
from humanity, beginning with the warning to Adam and
Eve not to eat of the tree of knowledge of good and evil (Tree
of Gnosis). When Sophia saw the horror that had occurred,
out of compassion she breathed life into the world of matter.

An original Gnostic document recovered from Nag
Hammadi, the *Apocryphon Johannis*, supposedly a vision
given to the apostle John, gives another variation on this
story so far. It says that Sophia was the third Aeon of the
fourth light, and that without the consent of the spirit or the
approval of her partner she had a son, "Ialdabaoth" (literally,
"child, pass through to here") of whom Sophia was ashamed
because he was a being unlike her. She hid him in a cloud so
that the other aeons would not see him. He created his own
world with twelve angels, after the pattern of the immortal
Aeons, and subordinate angels for each of them. He also
appointed seven kings of the heaven and five to rule over the
chaos of the underworld, all the hierarchies of heaven
(archons). Some of their names were taken from the Old
Testament, some from magic, to crop up again in many
sources: Iao, Sabaoth, Eloaeus (Elohim), Adonaeus (Adonai),
Astapheus, Horaeus.

Ialdabaoth gave his creatures no part of the power that he
had inherited from his mother, however, and so could rule
over them. Ignorant of any higher being, he declared, "I am a
jealous God; beside me there is no other" (on which the
author comments: "Were there no other, of whom would he
be jealous?"). Both Valentinus and the *Apochryphon* continue
on from here in a similar vein. By the time Sophia reencoun-
ters Ialdabaoth, he is full of power in himself and has created
the lower heavens and earth and stated: "I have need of no
one. I am God, and there is no other apart from me." Sophia
cries out against him, "You are wrong, Samael."

SAMAEL means "the blind god." This passage is crucial to
comprehending the Gnostics, who regarded not sin but
blindness or ignorance as the seat of evil. Ignorance leads to
pride, vanity, greed, ambition, etc. From a psychological per-

spective, one could say that the Gnostics projected the evil in the human heart onto the archons, the bad angel rulers under Samael's thumb.

Valentinus's story continues with the archons abusing Sophia; she herself becomes blind. At length she comes to understand that all this has happened because she separated herself from her consort. She repents, asking the "Father" to hear her prayer. The highest God hears her and sends to Sophia redemption in the form of the Logos, who takes the form of Jesus. Jesus restores Sophia's sight with a touch, and she begins the process that will bring redemption to all mankind. This reunification of Logos (masculine) and Eros (feminine) is another great Gnostic theme, which recurs when the creation story moves to the Garden of Eden.

The Gnostics considered the first man, Adam, to be an earlier and superior being to the Demiurge. He traveled from the Unknowable God through the spheres, gaining more materiality at each stage. Adam is associated with the three-sonship scheme, wherein Jesus is superior to the Demiurge, but Adam has no real life in him until he is imbued with the pneumatic life substance by Holy Eve, the emanation of Sophia.

The *Apochryphon* says that the Father revealed to Ialdabaoth's seven archons his own image revealed in water, and they were so impressed that they resolved, "Let us make a man after the image and likeness of God." Each of them contributed of his own power, so that the new man incorporated in himself the powers of the seven, but he lay lifeless. Neither the archons nor their sixty angels could quicken him to life. The Mother, however, intervened with the Father, and he sent Christ with his four great lights to Ialdabaoth in the form of Ialdabaoth's angels. They advised him to breathe into the face of the new creature the power that he had inherited from his mother, He did so, and thus transferred to Adam this power, so that Adam became superior both to his creators, the seven archons, and to Ialdabaoth himself.

Ialdabaoth and his powers brought Adam down into the material world and fashioned him a body made of the four elements. But at this point God in his mercy sent him a helper (the soul or spirit within), the Epinoia (soul) of light, whom he called Zoe. This was hidden in Adam so that the archons would not become aware of it. Ialdabaoth set Adam in Paradise to deceive him, for its bliss was illusory. The Tree of Life was intended to lead Adam astray and to keep him from reaching perfection; the Tree of the Knowledge of Good and Evil (Tree of Gnosis) was no other than the Epinoia of light—hence the command from Ialdabaoth not to eat of it. According to the Gnostic version, it was Christ, not the serpent, who encouraged man to eat of it.

To prevent Adam from perceiving the truth, Ialdabaoth brought forgetfulness upon him, then created another human being in the form of a woman. Epinoia instigated them to eat of the Tree of Gnosis, and so they became aware of their true being. Realizing his failure, Ialdabaoth cursed man and expelled him. Ialdabaoth desired Adam's wife and begot two sons, the righteous Eloim and the unrighteous Jave, whom men call Cain and Abel. These he set over the four elements from which the material body of man had been made. Ialdabaoth also implanted sexual passion in Adam, whose son was Seth. According to the story, there are now two spirits in man, one divine and the other earthly. The for-

mer inspires him from his sleep and forgetfulness to Gnosis; the latter is the sexual instinct which serves the ends of Ialdabaoth.

Other versions emphasize Sophia's role, blending her with Epinoia and the Holy Eve. She hides herself in the Tree of Gnosis when threatened by the archons, seeking to escape domination by Adam. They seek to defile her so that they will have control over her children, but instead they defile an image of herself that she has created. It is the archons who tell Adam and Eve not to eat of the Tree of Gnosis, but the serpent intervenes and convinces Eve to eat. Therefore she gives gnosis to her husband and their understandings are opened. In dismay, the archons cast them out of paradise. Sophia drives the archons out of heaven and casts them down to become the wicked demons of the earth.

In one of Basilides's several versions of creation, the unknowable God desires to create a world in seed form via its spoken word, inherent in which is the threefold sonship that manifests in archons of greater and lesser purity; they brought matter into being, with angels emanating from them, creating spheres and ruling over their realms, eventually totalling 365. The Great Archon rules the Ogdoad (the eighth Aeon) and is the father of Jesus, who is superior to all other sons. The Holy Spirit emanates from the Ogdoad into the Gospel. From the least sons came the Demiurge, who rules the Hebdomad (seventh Aeon) and orders the earth. The Great Archon discovers from his son that he is inferior to him. In another version attributed to Basilides, the unknowable God (the Father) sends his first-born son Nous (Jesus) to confront the God of the Jews. He does wonders but does not suffer, since Simon of Cyrene has been transformed to take the place of Jesus at the Crucifixion.

Hierarchical switches and revelations, with different names in different spheres, pervade Gnosticism and vary from sect to sect. These not only make for difficult reading, but leave no hope of a definitive myth. Singer concludes that this nebulosity is part of the method of Gnosticism: Meaning goes far beyond the literal level, and human knowing by its very nature can never be complete. It is not difficult to understand Jung's fascination with the implications of these many archetypes, as well as with the constant mutability of the complex systems (very much in keeping with Jung's vision of human consciousness) that pervade the mythology.

Many Gnostics believed that prophesy was inspired by both creator angels (aeons) and Satan. They regarded Satan with ambivalence, fearing and hating him but also rather admiring him for the courageous way in which he had opposed the Old Testament God. The Gnostics' reputed sorcery arose from their ability to name and invoke various aeons and archons. There were spells and passwords by which the Gnostic was able to ascend through the aeons to the highest realms. These were secrets of initiation.

Also there were rituals to celebrate the union of Logos and Eros. Simon Magus and his companion Helen represented themselves, and were regarded by some, as the apotheosis of the Father and Mother of the Universe, Logos and Sophia. Like many Gnostics, Simon was an advocate of unbridled sexuality. Whereas the Christian fathers accused the early Gnostics of "free love," of impure acts and abominations, later Gnostics were to adopt a practice of total asceticism, a refusal to procreate. These polar-opposite positions provide a good indication of the Gnostics' ambivalence toward human behavior, and their belief that redemption comes through grace, not good works. Therefore either asceticism or debauchery might be the right path for an individual at a particular time, depending on the state of their Gnosis, their current holistic apprehension of existence.

The fact that the Gnostics were persecuted by the Romans along with the Christians led them to become more and more secretive. Their long-hidden documents have at last come to light, in an age that can appreciate and apprehend more clearly the forces activating the stories they used to explain life.

**Further reading:**

Jonas, Hans. *The Gnostic Religion*. 2nd. ed. Boston: Beacon Press, 1963.

Laccarriere, Jacques. *The Gnostics*. Translated by Nina Rootes. New York: City Lights, 1989.

Pagels, Elaine. *The Gnostic Gospels*. New York: Random House, 1979.

Robinson, James M. (ed.) *The Nag Hammadi Library in English*. San Francisco: Harper & Row, 1977.

Singer, June. *Seeing Through the Visible World: Jung, Gnosis, and Chaos*. San Francisco: Harper and Row, 1990.

## Goethe, Johann Wolfgang von (1749–1832)

Goethe's *Faust* ranks with John MILTON's *Paradise Lost* and DANTE's *Divina Commedia* as the spiritual manifesto of a great poet of an epoch. Goethe worked on *Faust* for sixty years, leaving parts of it to be revealed only posthumously. Its poetic heights, virtuosity, breadth and complexity, gripping drama, and philosophical vigor are unparalleled in the German language, and rank it among the world's greatest literary achievements. *Faust* is the story of a genius whom the devil can make sport of, who sells his soul, sins, repents, dies, and is finally redeemed. *Faust* projected a sublimely noble aspiration of the human spirit, but Goethe did not glorify him; nobody can miss his sinister side. Even before his association with the Evil One, Faust is labeled a "superman" (*Ubermensch*), deeply ironic given subsequent German history.

In a poem called "Dedication" at the head of his collected poems of 1794, the poet describes being dazzled by an apparition whom he recognizes as the Goddess of Truth, comparable to SOPHIA. She says to him:

> You see how necessary it was to reveal only a small part of my essence to you. . . . Scarcely having overcome the crudest error, scarcely having mastered thy first childish willfulness, thou deemest thyself straightway a superman who can afford to ignore the ordinary duties. Art thou really so different from the others? Get to know thyself. Live in peace with the world.

*Faust* acts out a next step toward the development of national self-consciousness, indeed of the self-consciousness of mankind. (Thomas Mann's esteemed novel *Doktor Faustus* [1945], composed during the final years of the Nazi era before the ultimate collapse of Germany, pursues the problematic identification of the Faust legend with both the German genius and the German nation, noted by Carl G. JUNG and others in a cautionary tone throughout the twentieth century.)

Like his English contemporary William BLAKE, Goethe's vision was iconoclastic in its approach to good and evil. The Prologue in Heaven (probably written in 1799, after Goethe had read *Paradise Lost*) shows God being presented by MICHAEL, RAPHAEL and GABRIEL with a sublime status quo. MEPHISTOPHELES enters as a court jester and asks the Lord about mankind's wretchedness. God mentions Faust, "my serf," and agrees to let Mephistopheles try to sway him. Faust is "doctor" of all knowledge of all the realms, but takes no solace from this fact.

Goethe's faith in the future of mankind was unshakable, but at the same time he was no sentimentalist. He saw the struggle between good and evil as engendering the forward direction of evolution; even evil can be a vehicle of objective progress. Mephistopheles says that he himself is "a part of that force which always wills evil and always produces good."

The seeds of good can lie hidden in evil, but at the same time, there can be something evil in the most lofty feeling. This balancing on the razor's edge is what constitutes the inner drama of *Faust*.

We meet Faust as he is falling into despair with weariness and emptiness, despite his possessing immense knowledge and magical power. He has been rebuffed by the Earth Spirit, the lesser deity that dwells in the earth. He is miffed that he, "godhead's likeness," "more than cherub," has been "withered" by the Earth Spirit's rejection. Faust is about to commit suicide when Easter bells and a chorus of angels interrupt him. When Mephistopheles arrives on the scene the seduction of Faust via his limitations begins, and they are off on their "superman" adventures, including: "the depths of sensual life" which eventually destroys Gretchen, an innocent woman who loves him (after a witch has restored youthful vigor to him); attending a Witches Sabbath; and watching Gretchen die and pray to the heavenly hosts for protection as a voice proclaims that she is redeemed even as Mephistopheles insists she is damned.

As Part II opens, it seems to be several lifetimes later. Faust wakes in a charming landscape with fairies and ARIEL (the same spirit of the air from Shakespeare's play). Mephistopheles next takes Faust to Greece for an inside view of an emperor's life, lovemaking with Helen of Troy, frolic among the gods, satyrs, fauns and nymphs. His steady movement to damnation contrasts with the glories of knowledge and sensuality. After Faust dies he is buried by angels and demons.

In Act V the heavenly angels confront Mephistopheles and his devils, to seize Faust's soul and carry it off to heaven. In the epilogue, male and female saints and blessed children sing of God's plan as the ranks of angels comment on the ascent of Faust's immortal essence. Gretchen is heard among the chorus of penitent women, and Faust's soul is received by the Sophia-like "Woman Eternal."

Both Goethe and his contemporary, the philosopher Georg Hegel, held the Enlightenment conviction that the human race would be capable of indefinite perfection once it had freed itself from the fetters of the Middle Ages. Goethe wrote in a letter: "Man must be ruined again. Every exceptional man has a certain mission. . . . Once he has done so, he is no longer needed on earth in this figure." Hegel wrote: "From the struggle, from the destruction of the particular, the universal results." So for Goethe and Hegel both, the unceasing progress of the human species results from a chain of individual tragedies. The tragedies occurring in the microcosm of the individual only serve to disclose in the macrocosm the ceaseless progress of the species. "Man ever errs the while he strives," says the Lord to Mephistopheles. This is the factor common to both Goethe's *Faust* and Hegel's *The Phenomenology of Mind.*

Mephistopheles is simply a subordinate representative of the libido (naked greed for gold, and naked sexuality), but precisely because he stands lower than Satan in the hierarchy of the netherworld he is more spiritualized than Satan. He must elevate the diabolical principles to a sufficiently high level of spirituality and sublimate them in order to tap into the inner problems of Faust. Mephistopheles transforms the satanic wisdom into human language, as when he says: I gave him to understand that life is properly given to us to live. . . . While we have life, let us be alive!" Or as Blake puts it: "Energy is eternal delight."

Like Blake, Milton and other great poets, Goethe too was a visionary. He said (in *Conversations with Eckermann*):

All supreme productivity, every important observation, every invention, every great idea that bears fruit and has lasting effect, stands not in anyone's power and is above earthly force. Man must regard these things as gifts from on high, as pure children of God, and he must receive and venerate them with joyful gratitude. It is related to the daemonic which can overpower him and do with him as it pleases and to which he gives himself up unconsciously, while believing himself to be active under his own power. In such cases man can often be regarded as the tool of a higher world government, as a vessel that has been found worthy to receive a divine influence. . . .

No doubt Goethe considered Faust a "higher tool."

**Further reading:**
Goethe, Johann Wolfgang von. *Faust.* Ed. Cyrus Hamlin., trans. Walter Arendt. New York: Norton, 1976.
Lukacs, Georg. *Goethe and His Age.* New York: Grosset and Dunlap, 1969.

## Graham, Rev. Billy (1918–   )

Prominent American Protestant evangelist, who has believed in angels and has spoken and written about them for years.

Reverend Billy Graham's classic book *Angels: God's Secret Agents*, written in 1975 and revised in 1986 (the second edition was republished in 1994 under the title *Angels*), outlines his belief that angels are with people at all times and all places. In it, Graham comments on the rise of evil, Satanism, UFOs and other supernatural phenomena, but bemoans the lack of interest—at least in the mid-1970s—in the existence and power of angels. Angels, he says, act on God's behalf to perform supernatural feats of healing and salvation, to provide comfort and guidance at death, to fight the Devil's evil intentions, to serve as God's messengers and to dispense justice as God's avengers. By 1995, the book had more than three million copies in print, in two editions.

Graham has been an evangelist nearly all his life. Born William Franklin Graham on November 7, 1918, he was ordained a Southern Baptist minister in 1939 and received his first church in Western Springs, Illinois, in 1943. Since that time Graham has founded various religious and evangelical organizations, written several books and columns, and produced the "Hour of Decision" radio broadcast. He has spoken to hundreds of thousands at Billy Graham Crusades over the years and reached millions more by television. He embodies Christian living for many, having never been implicated in the scandals that have soiled the reputations of other televangelists.

Graham uses Scripture to describe the angels' characteristics and how they differ from humans. He notes the ironic situation that while humans were created lower than the angels, the angels were created to serve humankind, who are the only real heirs to salvation. Graham asks how can angels— holy beings that know no sin—be redeemed at the Final Judgment by people who were first sinners? He comments that although the angels serve God and His son Jesus, they do not fully comprehend Jesus' power as Savior. Nevertheless, until that day, angels remain superior to humans.

Graham says that God is not "Father" to the angels because they cannot look to Him for redemption from sin: They are not sinners. And while there is eventual redemption for sinful man, the sinful angels were not enticed as Adam and Eve were into sin, so they cannot be forgiven their choice to defy God. As God's ministering spirits, angels will remain exalted at the Final Judgment, but only man, who has tasted death, can receive everlasting life. And while Graham reports that the angels rejoice each time someone accepts Jesus as his or her savior, they cannot personally attest to the saving grace of God, as they have never experienced the need for such salvation. Neither do they receive the Holy Spirit, for the same reason.

Based on Jesus' observation in Matthew 22:30 that at the resurrection men neither marry nor are given in marriage but become as the angels in heaven, Graham deduces that angels neither marry nor procreate. (Mother Ann Lee, founder of the United Society of Believers, or Shakers, used the same passage to convince her followers that humans should not marry or procreate.) Graham believes that since the obedient angels do not die, their numbers are fixed. Although medieval scholars tried hard to count them, Graham simply says that the host is innumerable. (See NUMBERS OF ANGELS.) They do not need food, but when occasionally in human form they eat and drink. (See EATING AND ANGELS.) Milton, on the other hand, had the angel RAPHAEL tell Adam that not only do angels eat and drink but they make love as well—an idea singular to the great poet.

Graham ascribes great knowledge and power to angels, but they are neither omniscient nor omnipotent. They cannot be in more than one place at one time. They do not know when the Lord will return to make His Final Judgment. But at that time, one angel, probably MICHAEL, will take a chain and bind SATAN, throwing him into the bottomless pit. And while the heavenly choirs may refer only to the various ranks of angels, Graham believes that the angels' capacity for praise does make them singers.

The angels' work is personal, Graham believes, ministering to a particular group or even one individual. He cites the biblical struggles of JACOB with angels, the angel who closed the lion's mouth and saved DANIEL, the angels who appeared to ABRAHAM and MOSES, the angels who ministered to the disciples after Jesus' resurrection.

Graham tells of a woman and her daughter who called on the angels for protection in the Nazi concentration camp at Ravensbruck. The angels, the woman believes, shielded her and her daughter and allowed them to keep their woolen underwear and a small Bible. While everyone else in line was searched, the guards appeared not even to see the woman and her daughter and their hidden "treasure."

Angels protect everyone, whether they are Christians or not, according to Graham. They also stand in judgment, warning of God's power, and carry out His dreadful commands against the wicked. Graham cites the near destruction of Jerusalem after David counted the Israelites, the angel who killed all the Egyptian firstborn before the Exodus, the angels who will separate the good from the evil at the Final Day.

Principally, however, angels are messengers. They brought the message of Jesus' conception, His birth, the birth of John the Baptist. They spoke to the apostles and directed them to people who were eager to accept the gospel of Jesus. Angels announced Jesus' resurrection to the women at the tomb, and explained the Ascension to the bewildered disciples. Graham says that angels also will prophesy and bring the message of upcoming salvation to a weary world.

Perhaps the angels' greatest ministry, according to Graham, is to help the dying cross over into their new life. Often described today as NEAR-DEATH EXPERIENCES, several stories of the dying seeing Jesus and a light ahead are recounted by Graham. Most often He is surrounded by angels. Angels also bring balm to the bereaved, helping them to deal with loss and giving them hope of the life to come.

Finally, Graham issues this warning: Remember that evidence of the Devil is everywhere, but do not let the sometimes overwhelming presence of evil lead man to forget the holy angels. They are a mighty force for good, and a bright promise that God's goodness and mercy will overcome.

**Further reading:**

Elledge, Scott, ed. *John Milton: Paradise Lost, An Authoritative Text.* New York: W.W. Norton & Co., 1975.

Gibbs, Nancy. "Angels Among Us," *Time.* December 27, 1993, pp. 56–65.

Graham, Rev. Billy. *Angels: God's Secret Agents.* Garden City, New York: Doubleday & Co. Inc., 1975.

Guiley, Rosemary Ellen. *Harper's Encyclopedia of Mystical and Paranormal Experience.* San Francisco: HarperSanFrancisco, 1991.

May, Gerbert G. and Bruce M. Metzger, eds. *The Oxford Annotated Bible with the Apocrypha*, Revised Standard Version. New York: Oxford University Press, 1965.

**Green Hope Farm**   Garden in Meriden, New Hampshire, similar in concept to FINDHORN and PERELANDRA, in that its activities are guided by intelligent forces in nature called variously devas, angels, nature spirits and elementals. The garden is privately owned and is sometimes open to the public.

Green Hope Farm was founded by Molly and Jim Sheehan. Molly Sheehan, a longtime gardening enthusiast who grew up on a farm in Connecticut, experienced a psychic opening in 1984, and began a spiritual quest that led to communion with the devic and angelic kingdoms. One day something shifted in her consciousness, and she began to receive "little messages" from the plants. She was then able to identify the voices as those of angels, devas and elementals, who began to give her gardening guidance. They told her what, how, and when to plant, how to cultivate, and also how to design gardens.

Sheehan prefers not to precisely define the beings—such terms as "angels" and "devas" are human labels, she says—but defines them only as "a spectrum of energy" whose nuances can be detected by shifts in vibrations. She senses that devas possess a "bigger" energy than do angels, and are more evolved. But there are contradictions, for the energy of the archangel MICHAEL is bigger yet.

Initially Sheehan spent hours in meditation in order to communicate with the intelligences. Over time she perfected her ability so that communication became easier, especially through automatic writing.

Sheehan says that the purpose of Green Hope Farm is to demonstrate how the angelic, elemental and human kingdoms can work harmoniously together and with God. The angelic kingdom holds the vision and divine plan for the place, and imbues the human kingdom with love and inspiration. The elementals bring the divine plan into physical form, using humans as their "hands and feet."

There are three principal angels who work closely with Sheehan and others engaged in the work: Thela, Sheehan's primary contact; RAPHAEL, who holds the energy of love at the land; and Immanuel, who holds the energy of wisdom. In addition, input is provided by Ascended Masters and by Pan, chief of the nature spirits.

**Deva departing the gardens, top of photo (reprinted courtesy of Molly Sheehan)**

The gardens are carefully planned according to geometric shapes, and careful planning also goes into what will be planted and when. Geometric shapes are believed to be crucial, for they determine the different healing energies that will manifest. Shapes change every season. Visitors attest to sensing the different energies, and some persons have reported experiencing the healing of physical disorders after spending time in the gardens.

Some of the produce is used to make essences, similar to Bach Flower Remedies. Many of these are said to facilitiate the development of higher powers of consciousness.

**Further reading:**
Guiley, Rosemary Ellen. "Behold the Kingdom of the Nature Gods, Parts I and II. *FATE*, May 1994, pp. 46–55; June 1994, pp. 37–41.

**Grigori** See SONS OF GOD.

**guardian angel** An angel who is attached to a person from birth to death, providing constant guidance, protection, and companionship. The concept of guardian spirits is ancient and universal; guardian angels are particularly prominent in Catholicism.

The Judeo-Christian guardian angel evolved from the guardian beings of other cultures, such as the *fravishis* of ZOROASTRIANISM and the *kari-bu* of the Babylonians. The latter were winged half-beast, half-human creatures whose special function was to guard temples, homes and buildings. The Greeks had their daemons and the Romans their genii (see GENIUS). In tribal societies, guardian spirits and

**Victorian postcard of guardian angel and children**

spirit guides are an approximate equivalent of the guardian angel.

Guardian angels are not expressly named in the Bible, but the concept of personal angels is established in various passages. In the first book of Genesis (32:1), we find that "Jacob went on his way and the angels of God met him," implying that he had personal angels protecting him on his journey. In Psalm 91:11–13, we are told that God "will give his angels charge of you to guard you in all your ways. On their hands they will bear you up, lest you dash your foot against a stone. You will tread on the lion and the adder, the young lion and the serpent you will trample under foot."

In Acts 13:6–17, St. Peter, imprisoned by Herod, is freed by an angel who wakes Peter up, causes the chains to fall off of him, and takes him outside. Peter thinks only that he is having a vision. Once he is in the street the angel vanishes, and Peter realizes that the experience was real. He refers to the angel as one of God's: "Now I am sure that the Lord has sent his angel and rescued me from the hand of Herod and all that the Jewish people were expecting" (13:11). But when Peter shows up at the house of Mary, mother of John, people mistake him (apparently) for his own personal angel. Rhoda the maid announces he is at the gate, but the people present in the house say, "You are mad. . . . It is his angel!" (13:15) Peter convinces them it is himself in the flesh.

Jesus also refers to the personal angels of children: "See that you do not despise one of these little ones; for I tell you that in heaven their angels always behold the face of my Father who is in heaven" (Matthew 18:10–11).

The church fathers agreed about the existence of personal, or guardian, angels. For example St. Basil the Great, citing Matthew 18:10–11, said that "each one of the faithful has an Angel who directs his life." St. John Chrysostom concurred. They disagreed, however, over whether pagans and the unbaptized were entitled to guardian angels, and also when exactly a guardian angel assumed his duties with regard to a human's life. ORIGEN, commenting on Matthew, believed that only the faithful receive guardian angels, and at one time even opined that adults in general do not have them, because Jesus referred only to children. Saints Basil and Cyril of Alexandria likewise believed that only the faithful qualified. St. Jerome made no distinction between souls of the righteous and souls of sinners, but agreed with St. Basil that mortal sin would put guardian angels "into flight." St. Ambrose said that God sometimes withdraws a guardian angel in order to give someone the "opportunity" to struggle alone, and thus gain more glory. St. Thomas AQUINAS qualified that view by stating that he did not believe a guardian angel would completely abandon a person, but might leave temporarily. Some church fathers believed that the guardian angel was installed at baptism, while others, such as Aquinas, Jerome, and St. Anselm, believed that the angel appears at birth.

The Catholic church has taught, from the Middle Ages on, that every person has a guardian angel. There are no exceptions for any reason, whether of race, age, religion, sex or virtue. Even the most wicked people on the earth have guardian angels. While guardian angels protect and guide, their ultimate purpose is to enlighten and help the soul to achieve salvation (thus it could be argued that the wicked need guardian angels more than the righteous). Hebrews

1:14 states: "Are they [angels] not all ministering spirits sent forth to serve, for the sake of those who are to obtain salvation?" And 1 Timothy 2:4 notes that God "desires all men to be saved and to come to knowledge of the truth."

The Catholic church teaches that guardian angels watch over humanity as a shepherd watches his flock. Jacob's ladder (Genesis 28:12) provides testimony to this; his dream shows angels descending from heaven to protect and ascending to sing praise to God (see JACOB). Angels are joyful, and happy to promote the welfare of human souls, for it is the will of God and angels serve God. The church further teaches that the dignity of one's angel depends on the dignity of the person. Ordinary Christians have one of the lower order of angels, while priests, bishops, kings, etc. have nobler spirits to guard them. Feasts of the guardian angels are observed on October 2 and in some places on the first Sunday of September.

There are six basic ways in which guardian angels help people:

1. *They put good thoughts into minds, and move will to what is good.* Although angels manifest when necessary, such as their appearance to the shepherds at Bethlehem to announce the birth of Jesus and their appearances at His tomb and after His ascension, guardian angels generally influence us without beeing seen or heard. They accomplish this through "secret impulse," or what otherwise would be described as intuition. They incite pious and salutary thoughts and desires and, when necessary, fear of God's judgment. Guardian angels correct us when we stray.

2. *They pray with us and for us, and offer our prayers and our good works to God.* It is not that God doesn't hear us when we pray, but the angels mingle our prayers with theirs and thus make them "more acceptable to God." Aquinas, who wrote extensively on angels, observed that angels help us obtain all the benefits that we receive from God.

3. *They protect in danger.* Certainly guardian angels rescue us from the dangers that beset us in the physical world, but their chief task in this regard is to protect us from the "snares of the devil." It is urged that the care of our guardian angels is solicited at all times, especially before a journey (see RAPHAEL) or the start any new enterprise.

4. *They reveal the will of God.* Among the biblical examples of this are Abraham's attempt to sacrifice ISAAC, in which an angel stays his hand at the moment of slaughter (Genesis 22:11–12); the angel who interprets the word of God for the prophet Zechariah in the Book of Zechariah; and Gabriel's annunciation to Mary of the birth of Jesus (Luke 1:28–38). The appearance of angels in such circumstances often causes fear initially, but that soon gives way to joy and consolation. With evil angels, the effect is the reverse: they engender feelings of consolation at first, which then disintegrate into fear and confusion. The way to obtain the protection of guardian angels is to imitate them by living a holy life, to honor them and to always invoke their aid. They are attracted to innocence; evil drives them away just as smoke drives away bees. The church advocates that people express their appreciation to their guardian angels.

5. *They receive and protect the soul at the moment of death.* Origen states that the "celestial escort" receives the soul at the moment it leaves the body. The guardian angel guides it to the afterworld, protecting it from the onslaught of demons who attempt to steal it away to hell. This role of psychopomp overlaps with that of the official ANGEL OF DEATH, one of the many titles held by MICHAEL. The biblical basis for this belief can be found in Luke 16:22, concerning the death of the beggarman Lazarus: "The poor man died and was carried by the angels to Abraham's bosom." (The rich man who refused to feed Lazarus, meanwhile, died and went to hell, and was refused mercy by Abraham.)

According to Catholic belief, if the soul goes to purgatory, the guardian angel visits it frequently to bring relief and comfort. When the soul becomes purified of all debt of sin, the guardian angel will, at the request of MARY, Queen of Angels, fly it to heaven, accompanied by jubilant martyrs and choirs of angels.

Numerous liturgical prayers to guardian angels ask for their presence at the hour of death.

6. *Guardian angels praise God.* Angels continuously sing the glory of God, and encourage humans to do the same.

Various popes have publicly acknowledged their close relationship with their guardian angels, and have advocated that others cultivate the same (see Popes PIUS XI, PIUS XII and JOHN XXIII).

The literature of the Christian saints contains numerous encounters with guardian angels (see ANGELOPHANY). Descriptions speak of guardian angels who were not always cheerful but capable of remonstration, and, in accordance with the opinion of St. Ambrose, even withdrawal of presence whenever the saints in question acted in a displeasing or ungodly manner (see St. FRANCES OF ROME).

St. Francis de Sales and St. Paul of the Cross, prior to preaching, would silently address the guardian angels of everyone present, and ask that the listeners be well disposed to what they were about to say.

Padre Pio (a popular Italian priest renowned for his bilocations and healings, but not canonized), following the advice of Pius XII, had a constant and close relationship with his guardian angel. Lore has it that God used to the angel to make it possible for Pio to understand foreign languages he had not learned, and to have clairvoyant knowledge of secrets within the heart (especially useful to him when hearing confessions). Pio would tell people that whenever they were in need of his prayer, they should address his guardian angel through their guardian angels. One story goes that a busload of pilgrims, en route to San Giovanni Rotondo where Pio lived, got caught at night in a violent lightning storm in the Apennine mountains. They followed his advice and weathered the storm unscathed. When they arrived the next day, and before they could tell their story, Pio announced that he had been awakened by his guardian angel during the night and had prayed for them.

Similarly, Theresa Neumann (not canonized) used her guardian angel (she saw hers and the guardian angels of others standing off to the right of their human charges) to discover whatever she needed to know about the secrets and hidden lives of her visitors.

Aquinas acknowledges that the mere presence of our angels influences us for the better; however, if we are not aware that we are being enlightened, then we are not enlightened. St. Ignatius of Loyola observed that the more we advance ourselves spiritually, the more we are able to discern the subtle influences of our angels, and thus the more receptive we are to their help. St. John of the Cross opined that when we attain higher spiritual levels, we no longer need the mediation of angels, but obtain our enlightenment directly from God. Not only are angels no longer necessary, but words, forms and images fall away as well.

People are not the only recipients of guardian angels; the early church fathers assigned a particular angel to the stars and everything in the heavens, to everything in the natural world, and to the elements. Aquinas thought that to be rather exaggerated, but opined that there were guardian angels for every species of living things, and for nations, cities, churches and communities. The heads of state and church thus had two guardian angels, one for themselves and one for their offices. Earlier, Clement of Alexandria supported the idea of guardian angels for countries and cities, but said they "perchance" might be assigned to some individuals as well.

The existence of guardian angels of nations is established in Deuteronomy 32:8: "When the Most High gave to the nations their inheritance, when he separated the sons of men, he fixed the bounds of the peoples according to the number of the sons of God." (The term SONS OF GOD is a reference to angels.) Other biblical references to guardian angels of nations refer to them as "princes." Daniel 10:13 refers to the "prince of Persia" and to the archangel Michael as "one of the chief princes."

St. Paul's vision of the "man of Macedonia" in Acts 16:9 is widely interpreted as referring to the guardian angel of Macedonia: "And a vision appeared to Paul in the night: a man of Macedonia was standing beseeching him and saying, 'Come over to Macedonia and help us.'"

Modern popular thought sees guardian angels as being ever-present and ever-loving beings. See DEVOTIONAL CULTS.

**Further reading:**
Huber, Georges. *My Angel Will Go Before You*. Westminster, Md: Christian Classics, 1983.
Parente, Fr. Pascal P. *The Angels: The Catholic Teaching on the Angels*. Rockford, Ill.: Tan Books and Publishers, 1973. First published 1961.
*St. Michael and the Angels*. Rockford, Ill.: Tan Books and Publishers, 1983. First published 1977.
*The Catechism Explained*. Rockford, Ill.: Tan Books and Publishers, 1921.

**The Angel of Hope (reprinted courtesy of U.S. Library of Congress**

**guardian spirit** A spirit that protects individuals, tribes and clans, or provides magical or shamanic power. In terms of their abilities, guardian spirits are the approximate equivalent of angels; however, they usually have animal forms, which stems from a deep belief that humans and animals are related to one another.

The purpose of guardian spirits is to help in the spiritual development of a person, and to provide sources of spiritual and psychic power. Other names for them are totems, power animals, spirit helpers, tutelary spirits (in Siberian shamanism), assistant totems (among Australian Aborigines), "spirits of the head" (used by the Vasyugan of Siberia), and *nagual* (used among Mexican and Guatemalan shamans, from the Aztec term *nahualli*).

Guardian spirits are considered to dwell literally within the body, rather than exist externally. Unlike the GUARDIAN ANGEL, who comes to one at birth and remains with one until death, guardian spirits may change during the course of a person's life, depending on spiritual development and needs.

Like angels, guardian spirits represent the human conscious and the unconscious, what is obvious and what is hidden. They are sources of knowledge, wisdom and inspiration, and help human beings to connect to otherworldly realms. As intermediaries between the physical world and the Creator, or "Great Mystery," they are sources of power that can be tapped by the individual.

Guardian spirits can shapeshift to other forms, including human, when necessary. This somewhat parallels the ability of angels to appear disguised as human beings (however, angels are often ascribed a human appearance, anyway). The innate animal form of a guardian spirit represents the collective power of an entire species or genus, which has magical powers that enables the guardian spirit to perform extraordinary feats. Guardian spirits can converse with humans, regardless of their form.

Beliefs about guardian spirits vary. In many tribes it is more important for males to have guardian spirits than females. Such spirits are acquired during rites of passage into adulthood (which are more elaborate for males than for females) and during vision quests. Males who do not acquire guardian spirits will suffer weakness and failure in life.

Some tribal societies have totem guardian spirits which protect entire tribes or clans on both a collective and individual basis.

In shamanic cultures, shamans must acquire guardian spirits, who empower them with magical powers, in order to function in their roles. The guardian spirits share much in common with angels in terms of their powers and roles. The guardian spirit serves as the shaman's "power animal," or his alter ego. When the shaman enters an altered state of consciousness he merges with his power animal and uses it for guidance. It accompanies him on his journey to the Underworld, where he searches for sick or lost souls, or on his mystical ascents to the sky, where he goes to obtain revelation and prophecy.

Guardian spirits do not remain with a shaman throughout his life, but change as the shaman grows spiritually and acquires new powers.

The term "spirit helpers," also found in shamanic cultures, generally refers to minor powers with specialized functions, as the healing of specific illnesses or diseases. The spirit helpers are used collectively by a shaman, who in turn works with his guardian spirit, or power animal.

Communication with the guardian spirit is made through ecstatic dancing, in which the dancer enters a trance state and assumes the form of the animal, and also through drumming and chanting, and in meditation.

**Further reading:**

Eliade, Mircea. *Shamanism*. Princeton, N.J.: Princeton University Press, 1964.

Harner, Michael. *The Way of the Shaman*. New York: Bantam, 1986.

Hultkrantz, Ake. *The Religions of the American Indians*. Berkeley, Calif.: University of California Press, 1979. First published 1967.

**Hagar** The Egyptian handmaid of Sarai (Sarah), wife of Abram (ABRAHAM), was aided by an ANGEL OF THE LORD in her times of distress. The story is told in the Old Testament Book of Genesis 14 and 21.

Sarai is old and childless when she suggests to Abram, who is 86, that he conceive children through her maid, Hagar. Abram agrees. When Hagar becomes pregnant, she considers herself better than her mistress, Sarai. Enraged, Sarai curses Abram. He tells his wife to do as she pleases with Hagar. Sarai punishes the maid, who flees into the wilderness.

As Hagar rests by a spring, an ANGEL OF THE LORD appears to her and inquires where she has come from, and where she is going. When Hagar replies, the angel instructs her to return to Sarai and submit to her punishment. As reward, the angel says he will "so greatly multiply your descendants that they cannot be numbered for multitude" (Genesis 16:10). He also tells her she will bear a son, and should name him Ishmael. "He shall be a wild ass of a man, his hand against every man and every man's hand against him; and he shall dwell over all his kinsmen" (Genesis 16:12).

Hagar calls the angel "a God of seeing," and wonders, "Have I really seen God and remained alive after seeing him?" (Genesis 16:13). The spring becomes known as Beer-laharoi, which means "the well of one who sees and lives."

Hagar follows the angel's instructions. Her troubles, however, are not over; the story resumes in Genesis 21.

Fourteen years later, Sarai bears a son, ISAAC, following a visit by three angels. By the time Isaac is weaned, Sarah (as she was renamed by God) frets that his inheritance will be threatened by Ishmael. She orders Abraham (as he is renamed) to cast out Hagar and Ishmael. Abraham does not wish to do so, but he is reassured by God that Ishmael shall have his own nation. So, Abraham packs up some bread and water and sends the two off into the wilderness of Beersheba.

When the water runs out, Hagar sets Ishamel under a bush. Certain they will die, she cries outloud that she cannot bear to look upon the death of her child. Ishamel begins to cry. God hears the weeping. An angel calls from heaven to Hagar, "What troubles you, Hagar? Fear not; for God has heard the voice of the lad where he is. Arise, lift up the lad, and hold him fast with your hand; for I will make him a great nation" (Genesis 21:17–18).

To Hagar's astonishment, she sees a water well. They have plenty of water, and survive. Ishmael grows up and becomes an expert archer. Hagar secures for him an Egyptian wife, and Ishmael lives in the wilderness of Paran.

A haloed angel shows Mary Magdalene, Salome and Mary the empty tomb of Jesus

The moral of this tale is to call upon your inner strength to survive adversity. The role of the angel here is not to rescue, but to call attention to self-reliance.

**Further reading:**
Ginzburg, Louis. *Legends of the Bible*. Philadelphia: The Jewish Publication Society, 1992.
Margolies, Morris B. *A Gathering of Angels*. New York: Ballantine Books, 1994.

**Halaliel** See Edgar CAYCE.

**halo** The halo became a standard feature in sacred art of the angel and of all heavenly beings by the fourth century C.E. The halo signifies divine radiance, and marks membership in the Kingdom of Light—nearness to God.

The ancient Egyptians, Greeks, Indians and Romans used halos to depict supernatural force, mystical states and superior intellect. In Egypt and Greece the halo was associated with the sun and with resurrection. In the Eleusinian mysteries the sacrificed and reborn god, usually Dionysus, was portrayed with a halo.

In Christian art the saints, Jesus and the Virgin Mary wear halos, as do the angels.

In the East, crowns and headdresses substitute for halos, but bear the same significance. A halo or crown also can be

**The archangel Michael weighs souls of the dead (by Johann Weissenburger, *Ars Moriendi*, 1514)**

seen as the radiance of the crown chakra, which is prominent in persons of advanced spiritual development.

See WINGS.

**hell**    The underworld, which in Christianity is the eternal home of Satan and the fallen, demonic angels, as well as of the souls of all sinners. The name "hell" comes from the Scandinavian death goddess Hel, whose name refers to her home.

The concept of hell, or a place where souls go after death, probably predates written history. The first extant accounts of a Land of the Dead appear on Sumerian clay tablets found in the valley of the Tigris and Euphrates rivers in what is modern-day Iraq. The peoples from that area—Sumerians, Akkadians, Babylonians and Assyrians, collectively called Mesopotamians—have underworlds that share many of those characteristics that reappear in later civilizations and religions: mountain barriers, rivers, boats and boatmen, bridges, gates and guardians, an important tree. Hell, or the Land of the Dead, is somewhere in the Great Below.

The most famous Babylonian epic is *Gilgamesh*, in which Inanna, the Queen of Heaven and Earth (Queen Istar in Akkadia and Astarte in Assyria, both goddesses of fertility),

goes to visit her sister Ereshkigal, the ruler of the dead. Inanna seems destined to stay below, until her faithful vizier petitions Ereshkigal to free his mistress. Reluctantly, Ereshkigal lets her go, provided she can provide ransom. Inanna sends her lover, Dumuzi, who then must perpetually stay below for six months and return to the Great Above for six months.

This descent story closely resembles the Greek myths of Demeter and Persephone, Orpheus and Eurydice; the Egyptian stories of Isis and Osiris; the Roman myth of Ceres and Prosperpina; and the harrowing of hell by Christ after the Crucifixion. Such accounts mirror the perpetual changes of season and the resurrection of the soul.

The idea of there being judgment after death may have originated with the Egyptians. In order to reach paradise, or Sekhet Hetepet, the body and soul travel by the boat of Ra, the sun, along the river of the Milky Way, much as later Greek souls navigated the River Styx. Upon disembarking, the dead must pass through seven gates, each with a gatekeeper, watcher and herald, then enter the Hall of Justice. Thoth, god of wisdom, prosecutes the case of the soul before Osiris the Judge, and the soul may defend itself. Eventually Anubis places the petitioner's heart on the scales of justice, and if the heart sinks lower than a feather from the headdress of Maat, goddess of truth, the soul is eaten by the horrid monster Ammit. Christian parallels are St. Peter as gatekeeper of heaven, and the archangel MICHAEL as psychopomp and weigher of souls.

ZOROASTRIANISM, founded by the prophet Zoroaster (Zarathustra) in Babylon, profoundly affected the development of the Judeo-Christian conception of hell. Zoroastrianism introduced dualism into religion, with the forces of good continually battling the forces of evil. The divine Good, Ahura Mazda ("wise lord"), lives in the Great Above with his seven *Amahraspand*, or angels. Angra Mainyu, or Ahriman ("evil spirit"), the Lord of Lies, dwells under the earth and sends out his *daevas*, or devils, to torment the world. Law, love and light oppose darkness, chaos, filth and death in an epic struggle for man's soul.

In another powerful parallel to Christianity, Zoroaster taught that there will be a final cosmic battle between Good and Evil, and that Evil will be conquered. A savior named Soshyans, born of a virgin impregnated by Zoroaster, will harrow hell, forgive sinners, and facilitate a universal resurrection of the body and reunion with the soul. Hell will be destroyed and the kingdom of God will reign forever.

Similarly, Isaiah 7:14, 9:6 says, "Behold, a young woman shall conceive and bear a son, and shall call his name Immanuel . . . and his name will be called 'Wonderful Counselor, Mighty God, Everlasting Father, Prince of Peace.'" Revelation 20:7–10 says:

> And when the thousand years are ended, Satan will be loosed from his prison and will come to deceive the nations which are at the four corners of the earth . . . to gather them for battle; their number is like the sand of the sea. . . . And the devil who had deceived them was thrown into the lake of fire and brimstone where the beast and the false prophet were, and they will be tormented day and night for ever and ever.

By the Middle Ages, hell had become a place of unspeakable horror in Christianity, building upon New Testament references. Most of the Gospel references to hell occur in Matthew, wherein Jesus warns his listeners over and over again about the certainty of damnation for those who do not believe. Matthew 13:41–42 states: "The Son of man will send his angels and they will gather out of his kingdom all causes of sin and all evildoers, and throw them into the furnace of fire; there men will weep and gnash their teeth."

Central to the Christian concept of damnation was the Fall, both the descent into hell by Lucifer and his angelic followers and the fall out of Paradise of Adam and Eve. Jesus also descended into hell to harrow the souls of the just, but ascended in the Resurrection. Eventually the concepts of death, hell, Satan and sin became merged, so that no one would be spared unless he or she had truly believed and lived a godly life. The idea of Original Sin became so strong that few in medieval times expected to go to heaven.

But rather than dismissing hell as an expected eventuality, the church spent a great deal of time trying to frighten people into renouncing the devil. Priests lavishly detailed hell's fires and punishments, and religious art and drama portrayed the many heinous aspects of Satan's minions. The most colorful aspect of such religious theater was the "Hellmouth," or the entryway into the pit of hell. Whereas a ladder might represent heaven, the Hellmouth was an elaborate creation, usually a papier-maché beast's head with wide jaws which opened and closed with winches. Smoke, flames, foul smells and noise emitted from the yawning contrivance, and actors playing demons would dance out on stage from the opening. Very low humor accompanied the antics of the devils. The Hellmouth's finest moment came when Christ descended through its fetid doorway to release the Old Testament prophets.

Medieval authors wrote extensively on hell. Many took apocalyptic visits through the Great Below, describing in gruesome detail the terrors to be found there and identifying contemporary sinners, usually politicians, tax collectors and corrupt church officials, as some of Hell's more colorful and deserving inhabitants.

Certainly the most famous literary visit to hell was Dante Alighieri's in the *Inferno* (c. 1300), wherein DANTE is led by the Roman poet Virgil through the nine levels of hell, narrowing to the final center at Satan himself. The architecture of Dante's *Inferno*, coupled with the author's extensive knowledge of classical mythology and his involvement in Renaissance Italy's turbulent politics, make his the most exhaustive and fascinating portrait of hell. But although the church embraced his vision, Dante's presentation of Hell as allegory, not revelation, paved the way for later intellectuals to reject hell's threat entirely.

By the late sixteenth and early seventeenth centuries the Jesuits had reformed hell into a less dramatic place, devoid of cavorting demons. Instead they made it into a fiery landscape overrun with diseased, repugnant, foul-smelling peasants, merchants, aristocrats and all types of sinners, crowded together (in a favorite image of the day) like grapes in a wine press. Many of the inhabitants were heretics, Protestants, scientists and any other group who had tested the waters of the Reformation.

The English poet John MILTON redefined hell yet again in his mammoth work *Paradise Lost*. Unlike the vision-literature of the past, which concentrated on the tortures of damnation,

Milton fleshed out the story of Lucifer's battle with God and the Fall of Adam and Eve. Lucifer is a proud man, jealous of the power God gives to His Son, and he chooses to fight God rather than obey. When he loses, Lucifer turns his wiles upon innocent Man. Milton's hell is dark and dreary, inhospitable, both frozen and fiery, a parched desert. It is a cavernous underworld, more notable for its separation from God than for its diabolic creatures.

Although fire-and-brimstone preachers still thundered from seventeenth- and eighteenth-century pulpits against sin, death and hell, exhorting their congregations to seek salvation, many intellectuals of the 1700s came to view hell as more Miltonian than Dantean. The mystic Emanuel SWEDENBORG described hell as being a place peopled with monsters and monstrous activities, but one created by those humans who had chosen lives of evil and self-love rather than a place into which sinners were cast. Evil itself was Satan and hell, so there was no need for a separate devilish leader. Sinners made their own misery.

In the nineteenth century, the Industrial Revolution led many to speculate that life itself was hell on earth. There was so much filth, poverty, degradation and economic disparity that many saw no reason to fear a worse place after death. If there was no longer a social contract, no accountability, then anything was possible, even the cruel fantasies of the Marquis de Sade, the horror of Bram Stoker's vampiric count, or even the ghoulish experiments of Mary Shelley's Dr. Frankenstein. In protest against their ugly surroundings, the Romantic poets sought to revive the shining gods and heroes of classic mythology, but they still equated hell with the ravages of misgovernment and poverty they saw all around them.

In modern times, some groups and individuals optimistically reject any and all notions of hell, saying that a just and loving Christ will save all people, not just the godly elect, and that there could be no hell for a loving God. Some follow a Swedenborgian bent, believing that hell is what a person enters when he or she rejects love and charity. Others believe that at death souls go neither to heaven nor hell but simply into the abyss of nothingness.

See also LITERATURE AND ANGELS.

**Further reading:**
Chua-Eoan, Howard G. "Sympathy for the Devil," *Time*, December 27, 1993, pp. 60–61.
May, Herbert G. and Bruce M. Metzger, eds. *The Oxford Annotated Bible with the Apocrypha*, Revised Standard Version. New York: Oxford University Press, 1965.
Swedenborg, Emanuel. *Heaven and Hell*, translated by George F. Dole. New York: Swedenborg Foundation Inc., 1976.
Turner, Alice K. *The History of Hell*. New York: Harcourt Brace & Co., 1993.

**Hinduism** Hindu cosmology acknowledges not only major and minor deities (*devas* or shining ones), but numerous other intelligences: demigods, spirits, attendants, and a host of infernal and celestial beings. Each *deva* has its different forms and aspects. Hinduism is in essence a nondual system, and thus does not share the Christian conception of absolute evil. For the Hindu aspirant the stages of development that one has yet to confront appear luminous, angelic and can be represented as divinities, while contacts with the stages left behind hamper progress and appear obscure and evil. The difference between gods (*sura*) and antigods (*asura*) is therefore not one of kind but of degree. According to the aspirant's choices, certain powers will be obstacles or helpers, demons or angels, drag one down or inspire and liberate. The *asuras* are associated with powerful instincts and attachments that keep human beings within the power of Nature.

*Asura* is a much-discussed term associated with pre-Vedic India, that is, the time before the Aryans began to arrive in the third millennium B.C.E. Later mythology explains the change in the status of the *asuras* in a fashion similar to that of the fall of the angels in Judeo-Christian story. As they multiplied they became jealous of the *devas* and proud; a series of struggles with the gods followed, and they gradually became incorporated with the demons, spirits and ghosts worshiped by the aboriginal tribes, as well as non-Vedic gods of the other Indian populations. However, the functions of *devas* and *asuras* are more mixed than in the Judeo-Christian belief system. Indeed, the *asuras* can win boons from the gods by penance, and if they repent they may end up as great devotees or benefactors of mankind.

Hindu metaphysics takes up questions of "reality" in those ancient Sanskrit scriptures, the Vedas and the Upanishads. The Vedic seers stated what Buddhists, Plato, the Neoplatonists, Sufis and Christian mystics were to observe centuries later: that deities are both projections of our minds and objectively outside us. These divine and/or infernal beings are experienced as outside one's individual ego, but as the consciousness expands, one realizes the god's true nature to be that of the unbounded Consciousness in which everything exists; the gods are apprehended to be within us, as is everything else in the universe. The infinitely complex web of relationships that is the universe operates through a network of correspondences that connects each part to the whole and links the subtle to the gross levels. The system operates as a vast hologram. Thus each deity, itself an aspect of the universal Consciousness, is at the same time intimately associated with particulars through its connections with elements, senses, names, sounds, colors, diagrams, symbols etc. Traditionally, a devout believer will worship three kinds of deities: the local deity, the family deity and the personal deity.

To the Hindu, the distinction between myth and history, legend and fact, is arbitrary, for the outer world of "reality" and the inner world of "imagination" are equally real, continuously influencing and shaping each other, being mutually interdependent polarities in a unified field that is itself the dream of the Divine. The epic poems the *Puranas*, the *Ramayana* and the *Mahabharata* contain all aspects of Hindu lore—religious, ritual, spiritual, mystical, scientific, philosophical, legal and historical—in their thousands of legends and stories.

Once Vishnu promised the defeated gods the elixir of immortality (*amrita*) if they would temporarily cooperate with the demons and churn the ocean of milk. From this churning rose the elixir, which the gods drank gleefully. Everyone is at some time affected by Rahu "the seizer," who tries to swallow the sun and moon at eclipses because they prevent him from drinking the *amrita* when the ocean is churned. As the ascending node of the moon, Rahu causes many problems in the astrological realm, vitally important for Hindus.

The demoness Vatapi ill-treated sages and was defeated by Agastya, the holy man who brought Vedic rites to South India. A famous victory for good was the defeat of the genie king Mahisha, who took the form of a buffalo, symbol of death, and was decapitated by the warlike goddess Durga. Like many demons, Ravana, the epitome of egotism and greed and the adversary of Rama, could change his form at will. At the climax of the *Ramayana* he almost defeats Rama in single combat, but eventually Rama's magic weapon prevails.

The two main names of the gods, *sura* and *deva*, have also a number of secondary meanings, all indicative of godly qualities: *krda* (play), *vijigisa* (supremacy), *vyapara* (relation), *dyuti* (light), *stuti* (praise), *moda* (joy), *mada* (ecstasy), *svapna* (dream), *kanti* (radiance), *gati* (movement).

The main kinds of *asuras* are *daityas* (genii), *danavas* (giants), *kalakanjas* (stellar spirits), *kalejas* (demons of Time), *khalins* (threshers), *nagas* (serpents), *nivata-kavacas* (wearers of impenetrable armor), and *raksasas* (night wanderers). Serpent kings and queens, *nagas* are half-snake, half-human. They are beautiful, richly adorned and dangerous, and they defend their sumptuous underground cities fiercely against both gods and men. They are the guardians of the scriptures and esoteric knowledge, and often they live underwater.

Beyond the solar sphere are immense spheres that no longer belong to the world of man, representing the transcendent aspects of the Cosmic Being, the boundless powers from which universes are born, the Unknowable. The higher principles, the higher gods, dwell in these supersolar worlds known as "the spheres of the stars." Mountains, trees, rivers, animals have in them a common yet multiple life, and are guided by conscious beings who are attendants of the earth goddess.

The Adityas (sovereign principles) are the sons of the Primordial-Vastness (Aditi), which is the primal power, the unbroken totality, the boundless heaven. The twelve sovereign principles generally are given as Mitra (solidarity), Varuna (fate), Aryaman (chivalry), Daksa (ritual skill), Bhagra (the inherited share), Amsa (the gods' given share), Tvastr (craftsmanship), Savitr (the magic power of words), Pusan (prosperity), Sakra (courage), Vivasvat (social laws) and Visnu (cosmic law). The regents of the directions are: east/Indra (power, courage), south/Yama (justice, lord of dead), west/Varuna (knowledge), north/Kubera (wealth), northeast/Siva (purity), southeast/Agni (ritual sacrifice), southwest/Surya (the sun) and/or Nirrti (misery), and northwest/Vayu (life, health).

All of these gods and demigods have beings under them who intervene in human affairs under their various dominions of influence. For instance Kubera, god of wealth, has dominion over the *yaksas* (the speedy ones, spirits of the earth), guardians of the earth's treasures. Legend has it that Kubera and the *yaksas* were originally *asuras* (antigods), but withdrew from the *raksasas* (night wanderers).

The Maruts and the Rudras are the divinities of the subtle world, the middle sphere, or sphere of space, situated between earth and sky. The Rudras appear as faithful companions of Rudra-Shiva (an aspect of the third person of the Hindu Trinity, Shiva). They are his friends, his messengers, whom everyone fears. The Rudras are not celestial aristocrats but the working class of heaven. The Maruts (immortals) are a restless, warlike horde of flashy young men, the embodiment of heroism and youthful exuberance.

In time the Vedic polytheistic universe became organized under the Trinity of Brahma the Immense Being, Vishnu the Redeemer, and Shiva the Destroyer/Transformer. Hindu metaphysics associated them with cohesion (Vishnu), disintegration (Shiva), and balance (Brahma). In addition, the tension between the opposites, the creative aspect of divinity, Shakti, the all-pervading divine Energy, had been personified in the great goddess since the early *Rig Veda*. The Trinity was thus one of the divine couples: Brahma and Sarasvati (the Flowing One, goddess of speech, poetry, music, representing the union of power and intelligence); Vishnu and Lakshmi (Fortune, the power of multiplicity); Shiva and Shakti (all pervading active energy), Parvati (Daughter of the Mountain, peaceful, permanent energy, ether personified), and Kali (Power-of-Time); sub-aspects of the gods and goddesses were personified in further versions of the couples.

One manifold name of the goddess as Star, Golden Embryo—the cosmic location from which the world develops—and the power of hunger (not just for food, but for transcendence) is Tara, who also is worshiped by Jains and Buddhists. Minor forms of the goddess were *yoginis* (ogresses or sorceresses, powers of realization), *dakinis* (female imps, eaters of raw flesh), *grahis* (seizers, witches who cause new babies to die), *bhairavis* (fearful ones, servants of Durga and Siva), and *sakinis* (able ones, female attendants of Durga). *Dakinis* have important functions in Tantric Buddhism, far more elevated than in Hindu lore.

A panoply of demigods (*devatas*), spirits and fabulous creatures also have been featured since earliest Hindu times. The *ghandarvas* (fragrances, or celestial harmonies) and *apsaras* (essences, or unmanifest potentialities) are the celestial beings born of the centripetal *sattva* tendency, the tendency toward light. They are minor forms of Vishnu. The *apsaras* are essences of the waters, forms that take shape within the causal ocean. In later myth they are represented as water nymphs, eternally young women who are the courtesans and dancers of heaven. They are also called the women of the gods (*surangana*) and the daughters of pleasure (*sumad-atmaja*). They are depicted as uncommonly beautiful, with lotus eyes, slender waists, and large hips and breasts. Through their languid postures and sweet seductiveness they rob those who see them of their wisdom and intellect. *Apsaras* have been known on several occasions to have been sent by the gods to lure from their austerities ascetics who might endanger their supremacy, the most famous such *apsara* being Menaka, who succeeded in bringing down the great sage Vishwamitra.

The number of *apsaras* is large; one source records thirty-five million. They choose lovers from among the dead fallen on the battlefield. They have the power to change their form, are fond of playing dice, and give luck to those whom they favor. They produce madness, and the *Atharva Veda* provides charms against them.

The *ghandarvas* are said to possess limitless sexual power and to be attracted by women. They play the part of lovers, giving or refusing fecundity. Varuna is said to have regained his virility by an aphrodisiac provided by a *ghandarva*. *Ghandarvas*' vibrations soothe and nourish the earth plane. Amorous intelligences, the *ghandarvas* love scented oils and incense, and have given the gift of music to mankind. Their preferred instrument is the *vina*, whose sweet tones refine the emotions of love and devotion.

The *charanas* ("wanderers") are the bardic historians of the heavens. Their speciality is to recount ancient tales, sing the praises of heroes, and teach the arts of dance, at which they excel.

The attendants of Siva are the Ganas, which include all the minor deities that are counted in groups: the Adityas, the Rudras, and the Vasus, which are respectively the divinities of the sky, the atmosphere, and the earth. In addition there are the Visvadevas, the ten Universal Principles, the Satisfied (Tusitas), the sixty-four Shining Ones (Abhasvaras), the forty-nine divinities of the winds (Anilas), the Princely Ones (Maharajikas), and the Means-of-Realization (Sadhyas).

Realized human beings who have attained liberation are known as Siddhas. They are perfect and blessed spirits, also defined as divinities, but there remains a difference between beings who have become deities after having been through the bondage of life and gods eternally unbound. The human being may dissolve into Basic Nature, while a divinity is forever free.

Ribhus are men who attain immortality by performing with skill a large number of propitiatory rites; they are guardians of the ritual sacrifice, clever craftsmen who dwell in the solar sphere. Vidyadharas resemble men but have magic powers and can change form as they fancy. Generally, they are benevolent aerial spirits. They can marry humans, who then themselves become Vidyadharas.

Village-angels (*grama-devata*) and village-goddesses (*grama-kali*) are local tutelary deities. The latter are also divinities of forests. Many temple guardians are fabulous hybrids, *yalis*, often the heraldic emblem of the temple builder. They combine the attributes of various powerful creatures—dragons, elephants, lions, horses—and usually are shown destroying enemies, with the pop-eyes of a god expecting blood sacrifices. Tree spirits (*yukshis*) abound in both Hindu and Buddhist art, as fertility icons and protagonists in myths and legends.

**Further reading:**

MacKenzie, Donald A. *Indian Myth and Legend*. Boston: Longwood Press, 1978.

Shearer, Alistair. *The Hindu Vision*. London: Thames and Hudson, 1993.

Zimmer, Heinrich. *Myths and Symbols in Indian Art and Civilization*. Princeton, N.J.: Princeton University Press, 1946.

## Hodson, Geoffrey (1886–1983)

**Hodson, Geoffrey** (1886–1983)  English clairvoyant and Theosophist who wrote more than forty books on the occult and, most especially, angels and nature spirits. Geoffrey Hodson believed he was contacted by the angels in the mid-1920s, and he spent much of the rest of his life trying to see angels and understand their universal wisdom.

Hodson was born on March 12, 1886 in Wainfleet, Lincolnshire, England to a family of yeomen farmers. He was the oldest of five children. When he was 15, his family suffered hard times, and he was forced to quit school and go into business to earn a living.

During his childhood years, he had several psychic experiences that showed natural clairvoyant abilities. Perhaps these experiences led to his early interest in metaphysics. He sampled Spiritualism, but it did not appeal to him. Around 1912, he heard Theosophist Annie Besant lecture on "The

Great White Brotherhood," and decided to join the Theosophical Society lodge in Manchester. He later became an important figure in the society.

From 1914–1918, Hodson served as an infantry trooper for the British in World War I. In 1919, he resumed a civilian life, marrying Jane Carter, whom he had met during his military training. The couple lived in Preston.

The Hodsons would take frequent trips to the countryside, researching local fairy and nature spirit lore. These experiences opened Hodson's awareness of the angelic realms.

In 1924, Hodson began a series of clairvoyant experiments at the behest of the London Research Group of the Theosophical Society. He and his wife moved to London. For the next five years, he worked in the clairvoyant diagnosis and occult treatment of disease. He invoked divine and angelic aid for patients. Also, he used his clairvoyance in researching angelology, embryology, anthropology, geology, psychology, physics and astronomy.

In 1929, Jane fell ill with multiple sclerosis. Her illness, however, did not prevent the couple from touring America for three years, during which time Hodson lectured and pursued studies of occultism and Native American history and archaeology.

Hodson's fame as a clairvoyant spread, and international lecture invitations arrived. The couple traveled around the world. Hodson distinguished himself in the 1960s when he used his clairvoyance on fossils found in South Africa.

**Deva (Copyright 1979 by Robert Michael Place. Used by permission)**

The Hodsons settled permanently in New Zealand. Jane's health deteriorated, and she died on October 27, 1962, in Auckland. Hodson later married Sandra Chase, a friend of the couple who took care of Jane during her long illness.

Hodson's later years were full of international travel, lecturing, research and writing. He wrote forty-seven books, plus scores of articles and pamphlets. He became active in animal welfare rights. From 1953 to 1955 and in 1961, he served as director of studies of the Theosophists' School of the Wisdom in Adyar, India. He was awarded the Theosophical Society's Subba Row gold medal for his contributions to theosophical literature.

Hodson began his angel research in 1921. In 1924 or 1926 (Hodson gives both dates in two different books), he was sitting quietly on a hillside in Sheepscombe, Gloucestershire, gazing at the countryside. Through meditation Hodson hoped to enter nature's hidden life and see fairies, gnomes and other spirits at work. Suddenly the skies were filled with light, and his consciousness was completely subsumed by that brilliant radiance. Gradually he became aware of a shape, a "Heavenly Being," within that light, who blended its mind with Hodson's to impart the wisdom of the universe. Hodson claimed he was completely awake and able to write. The Being, who called itself Bethelda, was godlike, beautiful and majestic, yet at the same time quite passive and impersonal.

Bethelda explained to Hodson the organization of the Heavenly Host, their purposes and activities, and the close relationship angels have to man—even though most of mankind is completely blind to the angels' ministrations. The angels stand ready at all times to foster cooperation between themselves and mankind to uplift the human race. But, Bethelda told Hodson, man must quietly listen and watch. If man's consciousness melds with that of Nature, concentrating on purity, simplicity, directness and impersonality, he will perceive the angels, for they are always there. Angels have no personality separate from the Divine Will, and are ministers and messengers of the Divine Ideation. They were present before mankind and are not the spirits of deceased humans.

In Hodson's book *The Brotherhood of Angels and Men*, published in 1927, he organized the angels into the following categories, groupings he believed were the easiest to contact by man and the most beneficial.

The Angels of Power are those able to teach men and women how to release the deeper levels of spiritual energy within them and to inspire them to infuse their entire lives with the angels' fiery and motivating energy. These angels are attracted to ceremonial and religious functions and use such gatherings as channels for their power. If the mental attitudes of all participants in a ceremony are in harmony, the angels' ability to transmit this energy is increased.

The Angels of Healing are these that work tirelessly to heal the sick and injured, stand ready to provide a healing touch, suffer with those who are dying, and offer consolation to the bereaved. Healing angels serve under RAPHAEL, whom Hodson identified as an archangel. Unfortunately, too few healing angels actually get the chance to help mankind, for overcoming the barriers erected by mankind's closed minds and hearts dissipates the energy necessary for healing.

The Guardian Angels of the Home are those that delight in man's labors, the laughter of children, the warmth and security of shelter and sustenance. They guard against danger and disease, against strife and discord, and hear each simple prayer. Harmony and love are their watchwords.

The Builder Angels are those that supervise the creation of all forms and worlds, from the greatest planetary system to the smallest grain of sand. They take on the universal Archetypes, the patterns for all life forms, and aid in the incarnation of each being. Angelic organization is quite hierarchical, and builder angels especially have their assigned levels of work and responsibility.

At the point of human conception, the angels take the divine emanations from the Word and attach the cells of the person's physical and his etheric, or spiritual, bodies together. At childbirth, Builder Angels working under their Queen help mothers to deliver children in joy, not pain. Hodson does not identify the Queen as the Virgin Mary per se, but describes her as a Holy One who has won freedom from the burdens of the flesh and ascended to the Angel Hosts. In the name of Him (most probably Christ) whom she bore long ago, she uplifts all womanhood and stands ready, through her angelic assistants, at every human birth.

The Angels of Nature breathe life into the Builders' creations. This order's hierarchy includes the lower nature spirits, such as brownies, sylphs, undines, gnomes and salamanders, who control agriculture, the growth of fruit and flowers, the formation of earth and minerals, water and fire. Hodson said that if man would only understand these spirits' presence and influence, he could learn to control the weather and other natural disasters.

The Angels of Music embody the creative Word of God and the expression of His divine Voice. They sing God's Word, sounding like a million harps or the rolling of the sea. Their songs emanate from the center of the Universe in great, glorious waves, giving harmony to the world and providing the radiance of light and sound which is the Voice of God. Their mission is to pour forth this heavenly music; it is up to mankind to hear.

The Angels of Beauty and Art express the perfect beauty of the Absolute Divinity that is in everything. They help the Builders to hone and perfect each form so that even more loveliness is revealed. Beauty is eternal, and one of God's most treasured offerings. Each time mankind attempts to create anything, no matter how insignificant, that object or act should be judged beautiful. And when that search for the beautiful becomes man's permanent aspiration, he comes closer to the angels at the Hand of God.

Bethelda told Hodson that in order to foster this brotherhood between angels and men, humans must take the initiative. For their part, the angels always are ready and eager to work with mankind. But in order to build a bridge of communication, first there must be more humans willing to try. They must be quiet and listen to Nature, approaching it from within as well as from without. They must practice such angelic communication daily, always choosing the path to the highest sensibility.

Ceremony and ritual are very important. Supplicants would be wise to set up a shrine exclusively for the invocation of the angels, decorated with religious symbols, pictures of the

Geoffrey Hodson (reprinted courtesy of Theosophical Publishing House)

holy ones in each religion, flowers and candles—flowers and a single beautiful object at the very least. Prayers of invocation should be offered in the morning, and those of thanksgiving at night. Communicants must be completely clean and pure, much as any priest should be. In *The Brotherhood* Hodson provides simple prayers for contacting each order of angels and suggests that supplicants wear certain colors associated with the orders, much as the priests and priestesses of Santería and Candomblé do when they call upon their orishas, or gods (see ORISHAS): rose and soft green for the Guardian Angels, deep sapphire blue for the Healers, sky blue for the Builder Angels associated with childbirth, white for both ceremony and Angels of Music, apple green for the Nature Angels, and yellow (the color of wisdom) for the Angels of Beauty and Art.

Much as Virgil guided DANTE through hell and purgatory, Bethelda revealed different types of angels to Hodson, who continued to see angels and nature spirits long after Bethelda departed. Hodson claimed that Mountain Gods in the Sierra Nevada range of California were colossal, rising 30 to 60 feet in height. They were surrounded on every side by brilliantly colored auric forces, resembling wings emanating from a golden center, which changed color as the energy ebbed and flowed. Each had a visible face with a broad brow, wide-set eyes and a square jaw. Fire Lords, masters of the salamanders (nature spirits of fire are called "salamanders" after mythical beings, especially lizards or reptiles, which were thought to be able to live in fire), stood like enormous human blast-furnaces. Bethelda guided Hodson through their searing flames unscathed. Storm Angels, who resembled bats and had terrifying expressions, controlled the elemental forces. Gods of gold appeared as feminine in shape, with radiating auras that resembled flaxen hair.

Bethelda taught Hodson about the angels' mental communications and their use of auric color to convey emotion. Rose is the color of love. Illustrations by Ethelwynne M. Quail of all the angels and nature spirits Hodson has described appeared in his book *The Kingdom of the Gods*.

The angels, said Hodson, ask only to receive love from mankind, and to have humans always seek the highest, the best, the most beautiful, the most loving and giving in all their endeavors. Angels are eager to impart the Divine Fire of healing, power and beauty. Through humanity's search for the angels, Hodson concluded they will develop patience, peace, wisdom, joy, vision, thoroughness, unity and complete knowledge of the Self and its oneness with the Divine.

**Further reading:**

Hodson, Geoffrey. *The Brotherhood of Angels and Men*. Wheaton, Ill.: The Theosophical Publishing House, 1982.
———. *The Kingdom of the Gods*. Adyar, Madras, India: The Theosophical Publishing House, 1972.
"Geoffrey Hodson—Man of Words 1886–1983," *Theosophy in New Zealand*, Vol. 44, No. 2, April–June, 1983, pp. 38–40.

**hosts**  See CHOIRS.

**hours, angels of**  See PLANETARY ANGELS.

# I

**Ialdabaoth**   See GNOSTICISM.

**Iblis**   In Persian and Arabic lore, Iblis is the equivalent of Satan or the Devil. Variations of his name are Eblis and Haris.

In Islamic lore, Eblis was known as AZAZEL, and once was one of the most exalted of angels, serving as treasurer of Paradise. But when God created Adam and commanded the angels to worship him, he refused, and was cast out of heaven along with a band of his followers. They all became JINN.

**Ibn 'Arabi**   See ISLAMIC ANGELOLOGY.

**Intelligences**   Types of astral powers, or intercessors of God, that appear in various mythologies.

From prehistory to the present, humans have entertained the concept that higher beings, souls or minds rule the stars and planets and influence happenings on Earth. Mediterranean and Middle Eastern astronomy, astrology and mythology were indistinguishable. Pythagoras and his followers practiced an astral religion. Plato aligned the myths of his culture, including a metaphysics of "spheres" or ascending and descending worlds, with his philosophy of consciousness and the soul. Aristotle designated those incorporeal beings that sustain the spheres as "secondary movers." He also agreed with Plato that certain aspects of human consciousness exceed the bodily "scientific" parameters that he so carefully began to define. The astral religion of "the cradle of civilization" was retained in Judaic, Christian and Islamic versions of GNOSTICISM and Hermeticism as the three main theologies diverged, with the parallelism and correspondences of the physical and spiritual spheres being a recurring theme.

The application of the term "Intelligences" has changed radically through the history of philosophy. It can be tracked in two primary directions, which retain the elements of its prehistoric roots: (1) a panoply of astral powers; and (2) intercessors of God who influence human thought and imagination.

The astral "Powers" (Greek *archons*, a term prevalent in Gnosticism) retain a celestial connotation. They were part of the cosmogony of St. PAUL, and were included in the hierarchy of angels plotted by PSEUDO-DIONYSIUS and ascribed to Christian theology through St. Thomas AQUINAS. What some have called "Active Intelligences" are non-corporeal intercessory entities that activate the imaginal (extended by some to prophetic and mystical) dimensions in human consciousness, opening to the Divine. This second line was developed by the Neoplatonists, Islamic Theosophists (see ISLAMIC ANGELOL-

OGY), and Maimonides (see JUDAIC ANGELOLOGY). Systemic connections between spirit and psyche have been further explored in modern archetypal psychology, spearheaded by the farflung studies and speculations of Carl G. JUNG.

### PLATO (427?–347 B.C.E.)

Several passages from the works of Plato convey his ideas and his eloquence on this subject:

> In the heaven which is above the heavens . . . there abides the very being with which true knowledge is concerned; the colorless, formless, intangible essence, visible only to mind, the pilot of the soul. The divine intelligence, being nurtured upon mind and pure knowledge, and the intelligence of every soul which is capable of receiving the food proper to it, rejoices at beholding reality once more. . . . (*Phaedrus* 247). The rest of the souls are also longing after the upper world and they all follow, but not being strong enough they are carried around below the surface . . . and many of them are lamed or have their wings broken. . . . and all of them after a fruitless toil, not having attained to the mysteries of true being, go away, and feed upon opinion [appearance] (*Phaedrus* 248).

> Now when the Creator had framed the soul according to his will, he formed within her the corporeal universe, and brought the two together, and united them centre to centre. . . . The body of heaven is visible, but the soul is invisible, and partakes of reason and harmony, and being made by the best of intellectual and everlasting natures, is the best of things created (*Timaeus* 37). God invented and gave us sight to the end that we might behold the courses of intelligence in the heaven, and apply them to the courses of our own intelligence which are akin to them. . . . (*Timaeus* 48).

### ARISTOTLE (384–322 B.C.E.)

Plato's most famous student, Aristotle, differs remarkably in style and tone. Secondary movers (of the heavenly bodies, that is, secondary to the Prime Mover, or God) are explained thus in *Metaphysics*, XII, 8:

> Since that which is moved must be moved by something, and the first mover must be in itself unmovable, and eternal movement must be produced by something eternal and a single movement by a single thing, and since we see that besides the simple spatial movement of the universe, which we say the first and unmovable substance [the Prime Mover, "a substance which is eternal and unmovable and separate from sensible things" (XII, 7, 1073a)] produces, there are other spatial movements—those of the planets—which are eternal. . . . Each of these movements also must be caused by a substance both unmovable in itself and eternal. . . . Evidently, then, there must be substances which are of the same number as the

movements of the stars, and in their nature eternal, and in themselves unmovable. . . .

In *De Anima* II, V, 417b, Aristotle provides his understanding of soul, and like Plato, situates it in the large universal context: ". . . what actual sensation apprehends is individuals, while what knowledge apprehends is universals, and these are in a sense within the soul." In Book III, 4, 429a, he says:

> mind in order . . . to dominate, that is, to know, must be pure from all admixture. . . . It too, like the sensitive part, can have no nature of its own, other than that of having a certain capacity. Thus that in the soul which is called mind (by mind I mean that whereby the soul thinks and judges) is, before it thinks, not actually any real thing. For this reason it cannot reasonably be regarded as blended with the body; if so it would acquire some quality, e.g. like warmth or cold . . . as it is, it has none. It was a good idea to call the soul "the place of forms."

(See St. PAUL for that key Christian pastor and theologian's treatment of the cosmic forces of his Judaic and Hellenic culture, and his sense of how Christ's incarnation will transform them.)

### *PLOTINUS (205?–270)*

An Egyptian who taught philosophy in Rome, whose works were well known and often quoted by ST. AUGUSTINE, Plotinus revered Plato. He is the first and most influential of a group of philosophers known as the Neoplatonists. Plotinus developed Plato's and Aristotle's ideas in the context of his own mystical vision, which was strongly tinged with Gnosticism. It was Plotinus who coined much of the terminology passed on into the Middle Ages and the Renaissance. The Divine Thought (Greek *ho Nous*, variously translated Mind, Divine Mind, Intellect or Intelligence) is a sort of mediation to human beings of the Unknowable One, and connotes the highest reality actually knowable. Universal Intelligence contains all particular intelligences, and the totality of the Divine Thoughts known in the language of Plato as Ideas or Ideals. "Intelligence" or "Intelligible" applies to various expressions of the Divine Thought or *Nous*.

Plotinus rejects the notion that astral Intelligences influence human life. He first recalls various citations of Plato (*Philebus* 30): "Whence comes our soul unless the body of the universe, which contains elements like those in our bodies but in every way fairer, had also a soul?" and says

> There is no absurdity or impossibility in the notion that the soul in the earth has vision; we must consider that it is the soul of no mean body; that in fact it is a god, since certainly Soul must be everywhere good. [But] it is impossible that the will of the stars, a doom for the All, any deliberation among them, should be held responsible for the fate of their inferiors. It is foolish to think that such beings engage in human affairs (IV *Ennead* I, iv, 26).

Plotinus quotes Heraclitus, Empedocles and Plato on the descent of the soul into the body as being akin to an imprisonment or entombment in a cave (determined by necessity), from which the ascent begins back to the Divine Source, breaking the fetters of sense and mind to reclaim more and more of one's true nature. Plotinus believes that there is a great range of accessibility to the Divine Mind among humans, and that as one ascends one is guided by more and more powerful Intelligences.

Plotinus's student Porphyry wrote a *Life of Plotinus*, in which he tells a story about an Egyptian priest who arrived in Rome and offered to evoke a visible manifestation of Plotinus's presiding spirit. Plotinus readily consented, and the evocation was made. A Divinity appeared, not a being of the spirit ranks, and the Egyptian exclaimed: "You are singularly graced! The guiding spirit within you is none of the lower degree, but a God." Thus Plotinus had for indwelling spirit a Being of a more divine degree, and he kept the eye of his own divine spirit ceaselessly turned toward that inner presence. It was this preoccupation that led him to write his treatise. "On Our Tutelary Spirit," an essay that sought to explain the differences among spirit guides:

> What, then, is the spirit (guiding the present life and determining the future)? The Spirit of here and now. And the God? The God of here and now. Spirit; God; This in act within us conducts every life; for even here and now it is the dominant of our nature. It is the Prior of the individual spirit, presiding inoperative while its secondary acts; so that if the acting force is that of the sense-life, the tutelary spirit is the rational being, while if we live by that rational being, our tutelary spirit is the higher being.
>
> The words "you shall yourselves choose (your presiding spirit)" [Plato, *Republic* 617D] are true; for by our mode of life we elect the spirit loftier than that life. It is not when life is ended that it conducts us; it operates during the lifetime. . . . For the Soul is many things; and each of us is an Intellectual Cosmos, linked to this world by what is lowest in us, but by what is highest to the Divine Intellect. By all that is intellective we are permanently in the higher realm, but at the fringe of the intellectual we are fettered to the lower.
>
> Our tutelary spirit is not entirely outside of ourselves, is not bound up with our nature, is not the agent in our action; it belongs to us as belonging to our soul, as "the power which consummates the chosen life"; for while its presidency saves us from falling deeper into evil, the direct agent within us is something neither above nor equal to it, but under it; man cannot cease to be characteristically man. Our souls must have their provinces according to their different powers; released, each will inhabit a star consonant with the temperament and faculty within constituting the principle of the life. Emancipated souls have transcended the spirit-nature and the entire faculty of birth and all that belongs to this visible world ("On Our Tutelary Spirit," III *Ennead*, 3).

### *PSEUDO-DIONYSIUS*

A Christian Neoplatonist of the late fifth to early sixth century, PSEUDO-DIONYSIUS follows the drift of Plotinus. He believes that the process of interpreting biblical and liturgical symbols constitutes the first step on the ascent to God. The primary purpose of symbols is to uplift the faithful from the realm of sense perception to the realm of the intellect. Furthermore, Pseudo-Dionysius holds a conception of the Intelligences much like that of his pagan predecessors; mainly, that it is through the angelic beings in the hierarchy of the universe that all spiritual enlightenment of humans is mediated. The final goal of this uplifting through all symbols and concepts is union with God, also expressed as deification, or "theosis"—being as much as possible like and in union with God.

### *ISLAMIC THEOSOPHISTS*

When the works of Plato and Aristotle were translated into Syriac and then into Arabic, they entered a fertile and contentious Islamic intellectual world, with a division between what became Sunni and Shi'a versions of Islamic theology. (See ISLAMIC ANGELOLOGY.) In brief, to follow through with the applications of Intelligences, one branch of Islamic thought, the Neoplatonic angelology of Avicenna (980–1037), was dominated by "the Active (or agent) Intelligence," that "Angel of humanity" who is identified with the Holy Spirit and the Angel GABRIEL as the Angel of Knowledge and Revelation. Far from regarding this figure as a rationalization, a reduction of the Spirit to the intellect, the Islamic theosophists following Avicenna (and the Gnostic, Hermetic, and Neoplatonic lines) looked upon the Angel as intimately related to the spiritual existence of humanity.

This Intelligence is the tenth in the hierarchy of the Cherubim or pure separate Intelligences, and this hierarchy is paralleled by the secondary hierarchy of the Angels, who are the Souls which move the celestial Spheres; at every degree of these hierarchies couples or *syzygai* are formed between them. These celestial Souls, exempt from sense perception and its deficiencies, possess Imagination; they are indeed Imagination in its pure state. They are par excellence the Angels of this intermediate world, where prophetic inspiration and theophanic visions have their place. The Intelligence, or Holy Spirit, is the source from which human souls emanate, the source at once of their existence and their light. All knowledge and all reminiscence are a light projected by the Intelligence upon the soul. Through the Intelligence the human individual is attached directly to the celestial Pleroma, without the mediation of any teacher or ecclesiastical reality. This radical spiritual autonomy of the individual alarmed the orthodox, and created an adverse reaction to the Avicennan line led by Averroes (1126–1198).

During the process of translation into Arabic of the Greek and Latin classes, Plotinus's last three *Enneads* had been wrongly attributed to Aristotle; thus the Gnostic and Neoplatonic thoughts of Plotinus surrounded the name of Aristotle for several hundred years. Averroes was instrumental in correcting this error. He wished to restore authentic Aristotelianism, and severely criticized the Neoplatonism of Avicenna. In addition to the Active Intelligence, which is separate and unique, he accepts the existence of a human intelligence independent of the organic world, but this intelligence is not the individual. The individual is identified with the perishable; what can become eternal in the individual pertains exclusively to the separate and unique Active Intelligence. Averroes also excludes from his cosmology the entire second angelic hierarchy, that of the celestial Angel-Souls, governing the world of the active Imagination, the world which is the scene of visionary events, of symbolic visions, and of the archetypal persons to whom the esoteric meaning of Revelation refers. Averroes was inspired by the idea that all minds have not the same degree of discernment; to some men the literal aspect, the *zahir*, is addressed, while others are capable of understanding the hidden meaning, the *batin*. He knew that if what only the latter can understand were revealed to the former, the result would be psychosis and social disaster. All this is similar to the arcane discipline of Gnosticism, which survived in Sufism.

One of those who gained the best insight into the scope and resonance of the problem of the Intelligence raised in medieval philosophy was Abu'l-Barakat, (*d.* 1165), a pro-foundly original Jewish thinker who converted to Islam toward the end of his life. He envisioned neither the separate Active Intelligence, one for all, nor an active Intelligence immanent in each individual, but a plurality of separate and transcendent active Intelligences, corresponding to the specific divergences among the multitude of souls. "Some souls . . . have learned everything from invisible guides, known only to themselves. . . . The ancient Sages . . . taught that for each individual soul, or perhaps for a number of souls with the same nature and affinity, there is a being of the spiritual world who, throughout their existence, adopts a special solicitude and tenderness toward that soul or group of souls; it is he who initiates them into knowledge, protects, guides, defends, comforts them, brings them to final victory, and it is this being whom the Sages called the 'Perfect Nature.' And it is this friend, this defender and protector, who in religious language is called the 'Angel.'"

### *MAIMONIDES*

Finally, Maimonides (1135?–1204), the great Jewish rabbi and legal scholar educated in Islamic Spain, was well acquainted with the works of Plato, Aristotle, the Neoplatonists, Avicenna and Averroes. He held that Intelligences are pure form, existing in their own plane, that of the angels, which is arranged in a causal hierarchy. Angelic Intelligences are the medium through which humans experience prophecy and vision (see JUDAIC ANGELOLOGY). Maimonides, following Aristotle's definition of *phantasia* so as to link dreams and imagination, argues that the nature of individual minds has something to do with the ability to "pick up" veridical dreams, and that their external sources lie in the movements of the spheres, which have an effect upon consciousnesses that are tuned into them. All this means is that some people are able to work out partially, for the most part intuitively and without consciously thinking about it, how the world will change and develop over a period. They grasp the future course of events, perhaps in the form of a dream.

Maimonides points out that dream and prophecy both involve the seeing of aspects and the reception of experiences which, unlike most imagination, are not under the control of the people involved. Maimonides presents this process as being almost entirely a natural phenomenon, but his sense of "nature" was a complex system like that of Avicenna, concentric spheres interconnecting and relating. Maimonides did not lay out a mystical system per se, as did the Islamic Theosophists. His inclination was to leave "mystery" alone and define as closely as possible what was intelligible, humbly ceding to the Angelic Intelligences a role in facilitating the prophetic and visionary aspects of human "intelligence."

**Further reading:**
Corbin, Henry. *Avicenna and the Visionary Recital.* Trans. Willard R. Trask. Princeton, N.J.: Princeton University Press, Bollingen Series LXVI, 1960, 1988.
Corbin, Henry. *Creative Imagination in the Sufism of Ibn Arabi.* Trans. Ralph Manheim. Princeton, N.J.: Princeton University Press, Bollingen Series XCI, 1969.
*The Essence of Plotinus.* Trans. Stephen MacKenna., ed. Grace H. Turnbull. New York: Oxford University Press, 1948.
Leaman, Oliver. *Moses Maimonides.* New York: Routledge, 1990.
*A Plato Reader.* Trans. B. Jowett., ed. Ronald B. Levinson. Boston: Houghton Mifflin, 1967.

Rorem, Paul. "The Uplifting Spirituality of Pseudo-Dionysius," *Christian Spirituality*, Vol. I. Ed. Eivert Cousins. New York: Crossroads, 1985.

**Isaac**    In the Old Testament, the son of ABRAHAM and Sarah, whose life is saved by an intervening ANGEL OF THE LORD.

Genesis 22 tells how God tests Abraham's obedience by ordering him to take Isaac to the Mount of Moriah and there sacrifice him to the Lord. Abraham does as ordered, binding Isaac and placing wood on him for a sacrificial fire. He raises his knife to slit the boy's throat, but at the last moment the Angel of the Lord intervenes and stops the sacrifice. Verses 10–12 state:

> Then Abraham put forth his hand, and took the knife to slay his son. But the angel of the Lord called to him from heaven, and said, "Abraham, Abraham!" And he said, "Here am I." He [the angel] said, "Do not lay your hand on the lad or do anything to him; for now I know that you fear God, seeing you have not withheld your son, your only son from me."

Abraham then spies a ram caught in the thicket, and he sacrifices it to the Lord instead.

Verses 15–18 reitereate God's earlier covenenant with Abraham (Genesis 15:17):

> And the angel of the Lord called to Abraham a second time from heaven and said, "By myself I have sworn, says the Lord, because you have done this, and have not withheld your son, your only son, I will indeed bless you, and I will multiply your descendants as the stars of heaven and as the sand which is on the seashore. And your descendants shall possess the gate of their enemies, and by your descendants shall all the nations of the earth bless themselves, because you have obeyed my voice."

In rabbinic literature, a midrash from the eighth century tells the interesting story of what happened to Isaac at the moment he was about to be slain. Abraham's knife touches the boy's throat and at that moment, his soul flies out of his body and rises into heaven. There angels take him to the celestial academy of Shem and Eber. He remains there for three years studying the Torah as a reward for his suffering. All of the treasuries of heaven are opened to him: the treasuries of prayer, souls, ice and snow, as well as the palaces of heaven, the celestial Temple that has existed since creation, and the "Chambers of the Chariot" (perhaps a description of the throne of God). Isaac is shown his past lineage on earth, as well as the future generations that will come from Abraham. The End of Days also is revealed.

Meanwhile Abraham stands frozen, his hand upraised. Though three years pass for Isaac, only a single breath transpires for Abraham. The instant the angel speaks and tells him not to lay a hand on the lad, Isaac's soul returns to his body. When he is back in his body, Isaac realizes that the dead will have future life and exclaims, "Blessed is He who quickens the dead!" Abraham unbinds the boy and he arises as if reborn.

Christian influence is apparent in this story, which underscores the theme of death and resurrection. Howard Schwartz, scholar of Jewish literature, points to the parallel between the three years of Isaac in heaven and the three days that passed between Jesus' death and resurrection.

The story also resembles modern-day accounts of the NEAR-DEATH EXPERIENCE. There is the ascent to heaven and the meeting with angels; the revelation of mystical secrets; the life-review; the revelation of the future and the end of times. The distortion of time also is characteristic of an NDE. Near-death experiencers often feel that time is expanded or stretched, and that what takes place during their encounters occurs over a much longer period of time than what actually passes on earth.

**Further reading:**
Schwartz, Howard. *Gabriel's Palace: Jewish Mystical Tales*. New York: Oxford University Press, 1993.

**Isaiah**    One of the great prophets of the Old Testament, whose call to duty involved a grand vision of the heavenly court attended by seraphim, the highest of angels (see CHOIRS). Isaiah received his call in 740 B.C.E., the year Uzziah, King of Judah, died. He prophesied for forty years, and had the ear of kings.

In Isaiah 6:1–8, the prophet describes his initial heavenly vision:

> I saw the Lord sitting upon a throne, high and lifted up; and his train filled the temple. Above him stood the seraphim; each had six wings: with two he covered his face, and with two he covered his feet, and with two he flew. And one called to another and said: "Holy, holy, holy is the Lord of Hosts; the whole earth is full of his glory."
>
> And the foundations of the thresholds shook at the voice of him who called, and the house was filled with smoke. And I said: "Woe is me! For I am lost; for I am a man of unclean lips, and I dwell in the midst of a people of unclean lips; for my eyes have seen the King, the Lord of hosts!"
>
> Then flew one of the seraphim to me, having in his hand a burning coal which he had taken with tongs from the altar. And he touched my mouth, and said: "Behold, this has touched your lips; your guilt is taken away, and your sin is forgiven." And I heard the voice of the Lord saying, "Whom shall I send, and who will go for us?" Then I said, "Here I am! Send me."

God then endorses Isaiah as a messenger and instructs him to make people listen to the word and warnings of God.

The main thrust of Isaiah's many prophecies was that the nation must depend on God alone, and God will judge all who turn away from him. However, he also said that God loves to forgive. Isaiah prophesied the coming of the Messiah (9:6) and the creation of new heavens and new earth (65:17–25) in which "the wolf and the lamb shall feed together."

See ANGELOPHANY.

**Further reading:**
Alexander, Pat (ed.) *The Lion Encyclopedia of the Bible*. Batavia, Ill.: Lion Publishing, 1986.
*The New Oxford Annotated Bible with the Apochrypha*. Herbert G. May and Bruce M. Metzger, eds. New York: Oxford University Press, 1977.

**Islamic angelology**    The Koran establishes angelology as the second of the five Islamic articles of faith (Divine Unity, Angels, Messengers [Prophets], Revealed Books, Day of Resurrection). Every believer knows from the Koran (Surah 35.1) that the angels are subtle and luminous bodies provided with two, three, four or more wings. They can assume various forms; they are endowed with perfect knowledge and have power over their acts. Their ministry is to glorify God; they manifest themselves to the Prophets and their spiritual heirs (*wasi*), in order to signify a divine communication to them.

To say more of them, for example to affirm the transcendence of the angel through the *ta'wil* (return to the Origin, taking place in a vertical dimension), to carry back the notion of angels to that of INTELLIGENCES and the Souls of the heavenly spheres, to the powers of nature or to the human faculties—all that, according to official doctors of Islamic theology, is foolhardiness, straying from the right road. Though in Islamic revelation the angel and angelology decentralized the monotheistic universe, scholars and holy men who applied angelology to metaphysics, psychology, cosmology, and mystical practice provoked alarm, incomprehension, and even open hostility in the legalists.

Paradoxically, the immense spiritual wealth of Islamic angelology, probably the most elaborate and subtle of all sources worldwide, was constituted by commentary from saints and scholars outside Islamic orthodoxy, or at least considered controversial, primarily in Shi'ite prophetology and some sects of Sufism. It is also evident from scholarly research that both Judaic and Islamic angelology have historic connections to ZOROASTRIANISM, preserved in Judaic, Christian and Islamic forms of GNOSTICISM and many schools of Hermeticism, none of which is included in orthodox belief or practice in any of the key theologies. But before this material is treated, it is possible to sum up general Islamic beliefs and practices regarding angels.

### GENERAL ISLAMIC BELIEFS ABOUT ANGELS

Ibn Majah states that Muslims believe the angels (*malak* or *mal'ak*) are of a simple substance created of light, endowed with life, speech and reason. The angels are sanctified from carnal desire and the disturbance of anger; they do not disobey God, and they do what God commands of them. "Their food is the celebrating of God's glory, their drink the proclaiming of God's holiness, their conversation the commemoration of God, their pleasure worship of God," according to Ibn Majah.

The difference between angels and *jinn* is a difference of species. The *jinn*, or *jann* or *genii*, sometimes described as *shayatin*, are considered to be created of liquid fire. They are good as well as bad, and they can be converted, as one Koranic verse indicates: "It has been revealed to me that a company of the Jinn gave ear, then they said 'We have indeed heard a Koran wonderful, guiding to rectitude'" (Surah 72). This may be an echo of the epistle of James: "the devils have faith like that, and it makes them tremble" (James 2:19). The *jinn* are self-propagating, and would seem to be quite similar to Greek genii or daemons.

Four of the angels are archangels, or as they are called in Arabic, Karubim (Cherubim), namely: Jabra'il or Jibril (GABRIEL), the angel of revelations, who dictated the Koran to Mohammed; Mika'il or Mikal (MICHAEL), the patron of the Israelites; ISRAFIL, the angel who will sound the trumpet at the last day; and Izra'il or Azra'il, the ANGEL OF DEATH. Angels are said to be inferior to human prophets because all the angels were commanded to prostrate themselves before Adam (Surah 2.32). Seven prophets are believed to have carried Revelation forward: Adam, Noah, ABRAHAM, MOSES, David, JESUS and MUHAMMAD, the last often referred to simply as the Prophet.

According to Sufi teacher Abdul Karim Jili, the highest angel is identified with the Spirit mentioned in the Koran. He is made from God's light, and "from him God created the world and made him His organ of vision in the world." He is the Divine Command, chief of the Kerubim, axis of creation. He has eight major forms, great Angels who bear the Throne, and all other angels are created from him "like drops from the ocean." He is also the eternal "prophetic light" from which all prophets derive their inner being; the breath or spirit sent to Mary to conceive Jesus; and Muhammad in his perfect manifestation.

Jili, in describing the angel as the "Muhammadan light," says that God creates from his faculties the Archangels and Angels, who in turn preside over the principles of the universe. From his heart comes Israfil, the mightiest of the Angels; from his intelligence Gabriel, treasurer of Divine Knowledge. From his judgment comes Azrael (Azrail), the ANGEL OF DEATH. From his *himma* (spiritual aspiration) comes Michael, who metes out the fate of all things. From his Thoughts come all the celestial and terrestrial Angels (i.e. "the souls of the spheres and of mankind"). From his Imagination comes the very stuff of the universe itself, which is "Imagination within Imagination within Imagination." From his Soul or Ego come both the sublime and contemplative angels, SATAN and his hosts.

The angels intercede for humans: "the angels celebrate the praise of their Lord, and ask forgiveness for the dwellers on earth" (Surah 42.3). In addition a GUARDIAN ANGEL looks after each person all through life, with duties of giving assistance against unbelievers, and is permitted to intercede if necessary. "Each hath a succession of angels before him and behind him, who watch over him by God's behest" (Surah 13.12). "He is the supreme guard over his servants, and sendeth forth guardians who watch over you, until, when death overtaketh any one of you, our messengers receive him and fail not" (Surah 6.61).

Two other angels (though not Koranic) are known by name, Munkar and Nakir, who visit the graves of the newly-buried as soon as the funeral party has returned. They are charged with examining the dead person with regard to belief. Other angels who have special functions are Ridwan, the angel in charge of heaven, sometimes called the "Treasurer of the Garden," even the "Door-Keeper" of the Garden, which may connect in some way to the cherubim in Genesis keeping the way of the Tree of Life with a flaming sword (Genesis 3:24).

Every believer is attended by two recording angels called the Kiramu'l katibin. One has its station on the right, the one who contemplates and dictates; the other has its station on the left, the one who records. Like the angels of Jacob's vision, sometimes they come down to humans, sometimes they mount to heaven. The text adds: It is said that among their number are those to whom the human being is entrusted, and whom the Holy Book calls "Guardians and Noble Scribes" (82.10–11). The recording angels are acknowledged daily in the Muslim prayer ritual, the Salat. Esoteric treatments of these *kiramu'l katibin* will be touched upon shortly.

Both of the names Satan and Devil are Koranic, and Satan originally was a good angel but on declining to share in the worship of Adam, he was expelled from Paradise. He is often mentioned with the adjective "the Stoned" following. This is Koranic and most probably has reference to the *Jamrah*, the throwing of stones at three Shayatin during the Pilgrimage rites.

There is one Surah in the Koran (53) in which one appears to Muhammad "terrible in power"; this passage fomented debate on the question of who was appearing, God or an angel, in Islam as it did in Christianity (see ANGEL OF THE LORD). Regarding angelic choirs, there is an almost parallel allusion to the heavenly host at Bethlehem in Surah 97. And when it comes to military assistance, the Koran promises three to five thousand angels to believers. "Is it not enough for you that your Lord aideth you with three thousand angels sent down?" (Surah 3.120). Judaic, Christian and Islamic "legions of angels" all evoke the Dead Sea War Scroll, which describes "the warrior angels [who] gird themselves for battle; they are marshalled in serried ranks and mustered for the day of combat." Other Qumrum [Dead Sea Scroll] documents mention a subdivision of angels into five classes, angels concerned with plagues, and others who mediate judgment or are divine agents for protection, punishment, revelation, or the offering of praise.

Parallels abound between the Islamic and biblical visions of the last judgment (see REVELATION). On the Day of Resurrection the four bearers of the throne (like the four living creatures in Revelation) will be raised to eight. They parallel the cherubim of Isaiah 6:2, even to their description: those who "bear the Throne and those round about it, proclaim the praises of their Lord, and believe in Him" (Surah 40.7). "Upon the day when the Spirit and the angels stand in ranks . . . thou shalt see angels encircling about the throne" (Surah 68.77).

## ISLAMIC SECTS

With the death of Muhammad in 632, prophecy itself came to an end. There will be no other prophet. The question arises then: How does the religious history of humanity continue on after the Seal of the Prophets? This question, and the answer to it, are essentially what constitutes the religious phenomenon of Shi'ite Islam, which is founded on a prophetology amplifying into an Imamology, in some Shi'ite sects constituted by twelve Imams (teachers/holy guides), and in others seven. In the Sunni branch of Islam, which took precedence, four Imams, founders of the four juridical rituals of Sunni Islam (Hanbalite, Hanafite, Malakite, Shafi'ite), are credited with being the heirs of the prophets and the Prophet, Muhammad.

The key difference between the dominant, legalistic Sunni branch of Islam, and Shi'ism, can be approached by a quote from the eleventh-century Iranian philosopher Nasir-i Khusraw: "positive religion (*shari'ah*) is the exoteric aspect of the Idea (*haqiqah*), and the Idea is the esoteric aspect of positive religion. . . . Positive religion is the symbol (*mithai*); the Idea is that which is symbolized (*mamthui*). The exoteric aspect is in perpetual flux with the cycles and epochs of the world; the esoteric aspect is a divine Energy which is not subject to becoming." One of the key Shi'ite premises is the polarity between *shari'ah* and *haqiqah*; its mission is the continuation and the protection of the spiritual meaning of the divine revelations, that is to say their hidden, esoteric meaning.

Philosophical thought in Islam moves in two counter but complementary directions in the *ta'wil*. Forms are thought of as being in space rather than in time; the world is perceived not as evolving in a horizontal and rectilinear direction, but as ascending; the past is not behind us but beneath our feet. From this axis stem the meanings of the divine Revelations; according to the Shi'ite approach to the esoteric, each of these meanings corresponds to a spiritual hierarchy, to a level of the universe that issues from the threshold of metahistory. Thought can move freely, unhindered by the prohibitions of any dogmatic authority. On the other hand it must confront the *shari'ah*, should the *shari'ah* at any time repudiate the *haqiqah*.

The literalists of the legalistic religion, the doctors of the Law, repudiated these ascending perspectives. Thus the organic link, the bipolarity of *shari'ah* and *haqiqah*, was broken, and the purely juridical interpretation of Islam was consolidated. The *batin* (hidden meaning) isolated from the *zahir* (literal aspect), rejected, even, produced a situation in which philosophers and mystics were out of line, their position increasingly compromised while the orthodox legalists, whose knowledge was wholly exoteric, reigned over a popular social sect. The foregoing material on angels is common knowledge in that popular sect. What follows is known by few, constituting the esoteric inheritance of Islam, preserved in the immense corpus of the Shi'ite Imams and many other unorthodox mystical philosophers.

## HIGHLIGHTS OF ESOTERIC ISLAMIC ANGELOLOGY

### Prophecy

The Imams list and explain four categories of prophecy as a continuation of the Prophets/Messengers and Revealed Books. First, there is the prophet or *nabi* who is a prophet only for himself, and not obliged to proclaim what is received. Second, there is the *nabi* who hears the voice of the angel while dreaming but does not see the angel in a waking state, and is likewise not sent to proclaim his vision to anyone. Third is the category of the prophet who has the vision or perception of the angel not only while sleeping, but in the waking state. This prophet may be sent to bring light to a more or less numerous group. This is the *nabimursal*, the prophet-messenger. Fourth, within the *nabimursal* are the seven great prophets (Adam to Muhammad) whose mission (*risalah*) is to proclaim a *shari'ah*, a new divine law that abrogates the one preceding it. According to the Shi'ite idea of the cycle of prophecy, only the *shari'ah* or legislative kind of prophecy has come to an end with Muhammad's death, while the esoteric prophecy continues.

The mission of the Messenger (prophet) includes the waking vision of the angel, a vision whose modality is something different from sense perception, properly called *wahy*, divine communication. To explain this inner vision, the parallel is made between the light of the sun being necessary for the eye to see, as is the light of the Angel-Intelligence for the human intellect to know. The Angel-Intelligence is identified with the Angel of Revelation, the Holy Spirit or the Angel Gabriel, and also called the Pen (*qalam*) because it is the intermediary cause between God and humankind to actualize knowledge in the heart, as the pen mediates between writer and paper. Knowledge through God is actualized only through the angels, the esoteric interpretation of Surah 42.50–51: "It is not vouchsafed to any mortal that God should speak to him save by communication from behind a veil, or by sending a messenger."

Another metaphor often used to explain the role of the Angel-Intelligence is that of mirrors, from the divine mirror to the mirror of the heart. The veil between the two mirrors is lifted, sometimes because it is removed by hand, as the philosophers try to do, sometimes because the wind begins to blow, or by divine grace (angel). The mirror also often has been used as a metaphor for the imagination, a third faculty of knowledge lying between sense perception and pure intellection, and also attributed to carefully distinguished angelic intervention through symbolic forms. The images, symbolic forms selected by the angel to further the ascent of the soul up the *ta'wil*, guide the soul even after the body dies, according to some visionary accounts.

### ANGELIC PREHISTORY AND ESOTERIC HISTORY

Similar to the worldview of Christian GNOSTICISM, one sect of Shi'ite gnostics, the Ismaili community, explains human esoteric history as a recovery from a catastrophic prehistoric mistake made by an angel, namely the Third Intelligence, *Adam ruhani*, the celestial spiritual Adam, angel-archetype of humanity, who refused to respond to the summons of the First Intelligence, remained motionless in a state of bedazzlement, and finally recovered only to realize he had been overtaken, delayed, had fallen behind himself, and was now the Tenth Intelligence. This interval of time in stupor he must redeem, corresponding to seven other Intelligences, who are called the Seven Cherubim, the Seven Divine Worlds, who assist the Angel-Adam to come to himself.

This delay introduces into a being of light an alien dimension which expresses itself in the form of an opaqueness. Each archangelic Intelligence in the Pleroma contains a Pleroma of innumerable forms of light. All the forms that composed the Pleroma of the celestial Adam were immobilized with him in the same delay. He communicated to them the eternal summons and in varying degrees of obstinacy and rage they rejected him; this denial darkened the essential ground of their being, which had previously been purely incandescent. The Angel-Adam realized that if they remained in the pure spiritual world they would never free themselves of their darkness, and thus he made himself the Demiurge of the physical cosmos, as the instrument through which the Forms that had once been of Light would find their salvation.

Through several cycles of rulership of the three dimensions of cosmic space, the first human being arose like a plant growing out of the earth, to be distinguished from both his celestial archetype (the spiritual Adam, the Third Intelligence who became the Tenth), and from the partial Adam who inaugurated our present cycle. He is described as the integral primordial Adam (*Adam al-awwal al-kulli*), and he is surrounded by twenty-seven companions, who in physical forms are the faithful humanity of the Tenth Angel, whose fidelity is manifested by their physical and spiritual superiority over all other humans of other climes. The first earthly Adam is simultaneously the epiphanic (manifest) form and the veil of the celestial Adam. He is the founder of the permanent esoteric hierarchy, uninterrupted from cycle to cycle, up to and since Islam.

After having invested his successor, the first Adam was transferred to the Pleroma, where he succeeded the Tenth Angel, the celestial Adam, who himself rose with the entire hierarchy of Intelligences to a level higher. This ascending movement will not cease until the Third Angel Intelligence

has regained the sphere of Second Intelligence. The cycle of epiphany was followed by one of occultation (necessitating the arcane sciences and philosophy, for most of humanity was unworthy of the revelations), which was followed by a new cycle of epiphany and so on in rotary succession. This will continue until the ultimate Resurrection of Resurrections, which will be the consummation of our Aion and will restore humanity and its Angel to their initial state.

### VISIONARY RECITALS OF AVICENNA AND AL-SUHRAWARDI

It is possible here only to skim the surface of esoteric Islamic angelology, but the mystical richness of this lore can be grasped through a brief encounter with two masters of the visionary recital (an Islamic literary/prophetic form in which the Angel addresses the human seeker). Ibn Sina (988–1037), popularly called Avicenna in the West, was well known to St. Thomas AQUINAS and other medieval scholars, and generally considered an Islamic Neoplatonist (see INTELLIGENCES). Avicenna's *Recital of Hayy ibn Yaqzan* uses a frame story of the journey into the Orient—that is, of the soul's return to its "home" under the conduct of its Guide, its celestial Self.

This metaphoric journey aligns with angelology the emanation of origin, spheres of existence, and the subtle dynamics of the soul. There are the Archangels or pure Intelligences, the Kerubim (Cherubs). There are the Angels who emanate from them and who are the moving Souls of the celestial spheres. There are the human souls, or "terrestrial angels," who move and govern earthly human bodies. In this recital one is aware of the kinship and homology between heavenly and human souls, *animae coelestis* and *animae humanae*. Human souls are in the same relation to the Angel from whom they emanate and who is the Tenth of the Kerubim, as is each Soul to the Intelligence from whose thought its being is an emanation. Hence it is in imitation of the *anima coelestis* that the terrestrial angel or *anima humanae* will realize its angelicity, which is still virtual precisely because terrestrial. But unlike the *anima coelestis*, the human soul can be false to its being, transgress its limits, and develop the demonic virtuality in itself. It is the realm of the human soul that is the dwelling place of the demons, the Iblises (see IBLIS) and the *devs*. It is for the human soul to decide whether its angelic or demonic virtuality is to flower in it.

In esoteric terms, the two Recording Angels can be thus explained: The human intellect is guided by the Angel, who is the partner of the intellect and who needs it for his own divine service (*Hayy ibn Yaqzan*, chapt. 25). The practical intellect is the terrestrial angel on the left who "writes," or executes, what is dictated by the angel on the right.

Celestial souls and human souls share the function of ruling and governing physical bodies. To do this they must imagine. The whole immense world of the imaginable, the universe of symbol (*'alam al-mithal*), would not exist without the soul. But here the Celestial Souls possess a superiority; their bodies are made of celestial matter, and because unlike human imaginations theirs are not dependent on sensible knowledge, their imaginations are true. Since the imagination can be angel or demon, it is essentially the first alternative that is realized in the *animae coelestis* and through them, in human souls. The love between the angelic intelligence and the soul is compared not only to the affection between parent and child, between master and disciple, but to the reciprocal love of lovers. The celestial souls offer themselves as models to be imitated; the human soul is to hear and obey. These two complementary aspects define the journey into the Orient, in the terms of the *Recital of Hayy ibn Yaqzan*, as "travelling in company with the Angel."

Below the greater Orient of the pure cherubinic Intelligences, the schema of Israq places an intermediate Orient, the world of symbols, which is the "clime" of the celestial Angels or Souls. It is these who inspire, who make visible to the Imagination as organ of metamorphoses, the symbolic visions that come to prophets and theosophic Sages. If the Prophet Muhammad received his revelations from the Angel Gabriel, it is nonetheless true that, for each mystical Sage, joining himself with the Angelic Intelligence (the speculative name of the Angel Holy Spirit) is each time equivalent to becoming the "seal of prophecy."

To raise itself step-by-step toward the world of Pure Intelligence, through the successive states in its posthumous state, the soul must be enveloped in the subtle celestial body that will have been organized for it by the Images, the symbols, and the dreams dispensed by the celestial Souls. The world of symbols and of archetypal Images is also the world of remembrance, and it is the celestial souls who preserve the traces of all particular things (compare with Carl G. JUNG's concept of ARCHETYPES). The relation of the soul to the Active Intelligence is expressed with unmistakable clarity as the relation of child to parent, and although the visionary system is formidable in its complexity, the tone of the mystic Sage is never intellectual or rational, but always one of an exquisite love and tenderness.

Ibn 'Arabi (1163–1240) developed a philosophical description of the functions of image, symbols and dreams dispensed by the celestial Souls that attracted attention in the West as another version of Platonism. But Ibn 'Arabi also offers visionary recitals in his voluminous writings, testimonies of the mental, emotional, and physical subtleties of Sufi yoga to cultivate the whole being of the seeker in the ascent through the *ta'wil*.

The Persian visionary Shihabal al-Din al-Suhrawardi (1145–1234) held that because Avicenna lacked knowledge of Zoroastrianism, his work was incomplete. The effects of al-Suhrawardi's "theosophy of Light" have been felt in Iran down to our own time. One of its essential features is that it makes philosophy and mystical experience inseparable: A philosophy that does not culminate in a metaphysic of ecstasy is vain speculation; a mystical experience that is not grounded on a sound philosophical education is in danger of degenerating and going astray. Iranian Islam also preserved the objective existence of the intermediate world, the world of subsistent Images ('alam al-mithal) or immaterial bodies, which al-Suhrawardi calls the cosmic "Intermediate Orient," and at the same time it preserved the prerogative of the Imagination, which is the organ of this intermediate world, and the specific reality of the events, the theophanies, enacted in it, a reality in the fullest sense, though it is not the physical, sensory, historical reality of our material being.

This world is the scene of al-Suhrawardi's symbolic dramaturgy. His work includes a complete cycle of Recitals of Initiation in Persian, which are continuations of the Avicennan Recitals. Their titles are suggestive—"The Recital of the Occidental Exile," "The Purple Archangel"—his theme always being the Quest, a progressive initiation into self-knowledge as knowledge that is neither the product of abstraction nor the re-representation of the object through the intermediary of a form, of a Species, but a Knowledge identical to the Soul itself, to the personal existential subjectivity, and which is essentially life, light, epiphany, awareness of self. Representative knowledge, of the abstract or logical universe, does not even approach the present unitive, intuitive knowledge—an illumination (*ishraq huduri*) which the soul, as a being of light, causes to shine upon its object. The soul's epiphany to itself constitutes the epiphanic or Oriental Presence (*hudur ishraqi*). To the degree with which it tears itself away from the Darkness of its Occidental exile, the human soul causes itself to be present by the very act of self-awareness. This is the case for all the beings of light in all the worlds and inter-worlds.

In *The Familiar of the Mystical Lovers* (*Mu'nis al-'Ushshaq*) Suhrawardi dramatizes three beings proceeding from the meditation of the First Archangel (the Intelligence) bearing the names Joseph, Zulaykha and Jacob and representing respectively Beauty, Love and Sadness reflecting upon his being. Sadness (Jacob) corresponds to the heaven whose subtle matter "materializes" the thought of a nonbeing; it measures the zone of shadow, the distance that always intrudes between the Love and Beauty to which it aspires—that is, between the celestial Angel and the Angel-Cherub. But at the same time this heaven, this Sadness, is the instrument that allows the Soul, by the roundabout way of a long pilgrimage, to approach that Beauty, to attain the goal of its desire, just as by moving its heaven, the Soul tends toward the Angel from whom it emanates. The same nostalgia at the heart of the mystic is likewise the secret of celestial physics.

Suhrawardi claims to have seen in a vision the primordial Flame which is the source of those epiphanies, those "dawn splendors" that revealed to him the authentic "Oriental Source." This is the "Light of Glory" that the Avesta names as the Xvarnah (*khurrah* in Persian, or *farr, farrah* in Parsi), the effulgent majesty of the beings of light, and it is also the energy which conjoins the being of each being, its "personal angel," and its destiny. Al-Suhrawardi represents it as the eternal radiance of the Light of Lights, from which emanates the first Archangel, whom he calls by his Zoroastrian name of *Bahman*. The relationship that eternally unfolds between the Light of Lights and the First Emanant is the archetypal relationship between the first Lover and the Beloved, exemplified at all levels of the procession of being, establishing all beings in pairs. By engendering each other out of their irradiations and reflections, the hypostases of Light become countless in number. Intimated beyond the fixed stars of Peripatetic or Ptolemaic astrology lie innumerable marvelous universes. Contrary to what was to happen in the West, where the development of astronomy eliminated angelology, here it is angelology taking astronomy beyond the classical schema within which it was confined.

The world of these Pure Lights is organized into a threefold hierarchy. From the initial relationship between the Light of Light and the First Emanated Light, through the multiplication of the intelligible dimensions which compound with each other, there proceeds eternally the universe of the Primordial Ruling Lights. These form a descending hierarchy which al-Suhrawardi calls "the longitudinal Order" and are universes of the Archangels, whom he calls "the supreme sovereign lights," the world of the Mothers, where a twofold event takes place in being. On the one hand their positive dimensions (dominion, independence, active contemplation) produce a new Order of Archangels who are no longer each other's causes but who are equal amongst themselves in the hierarchy of Emanation and form the latitudinal order. These are archangel archetypes of "lords of species," identified with the Platonic archetypes—not as realized universals but as hypostases of Light. The names of the Zoroastrian archangels and some of the angels are expressly mentioned. This latitudinal Order also includes the angel of humanity, the Holy Spirit, Gabriel, the active Intelligence.

On the other hand the negative intelligible dimensions of the longitudinal order (dependence, passive illumination, love as intelligence) produce the Heaven of the Fixed Stars. The innumerable stellar individuations of this Heaven are so many emanations which materialize, in a still wholly subtle celestial matter, that part of nonbeing which conceals their being that emanates from the Light of Lights.

Finally, from this second order of Archangels there emanates a new Order of Lights, through the intermediary of which the Archangel archetypes govern and rule over the Species, at least in the case of the higher species. These are the Angel-Souls, the *animae coelestis* and *animae humanae* of Avicenna's angelology. Every species is an icon of its angel, a theurgy effected by this angel in the *barzakh* (the inter-world, the *mundus imaginalis*, everything that is body, everything that is a screen and an interval, which is of itself Night and Darkness). It is an act of light by the Angel, but it does not combine materially with the Darkness, and from this stems al-Suhrawardi's notion of potential being, matter, substantial forms, and so on, a perception of the world through a metaphysic of essences aligned with a complex angelology.

**Further reading:**

Bishop, Eric F. F., "Angelology in Judaism, Islam and Christianity," *Anglican Theological Review*, Vol XLVI, January 1964.

Corbin, Henry. *Avicenna and the Visionary Recital*. Trans. William R. Trask. Princeton, N.J.: Princeton University Press: Bollingen Series LXVI, 1960, 1988.

———. *Creative Imagination in the Sufism of Ibn 'Arabi*. Trans. Ralph Manheim. Princeton, N.J.: Princeton University Press: Bollingen Series XCI, 1969.

———. *History of Islamic Philosophy*. Trans. Liadain Sherrard. London: Kegan Paul International, 1993.

Klein, F. A. *The Religion of Islam*. London: 1906, 1971.

Nasr, Seyyed Hossein. *An Introduction to Islamic Cosmological Doctrines*. Boulder, Colo.: Shambhala, 1978.

——— (ed.). *Islamic Spirituality*. New York: Crossroad, 1987.

**Israfil** Angel prominent in Islamic lore, though not named in the Koran. The name Israfil means "the burning one." Israfil serves as the angel of resurrection who blows the trumpet on Judgment Day—to bring of his own demise, for he and other angels supposedly will be destroyed in the universal conflagration that will be unleashed.

According to lore, Israfil served as a companion to the prophet MUHAMMAD for three years before being succeeded by GABRIEL.

A well-known Islamic story says that Allah dispatched MICHAEL, GABRIEL, Israfil and AZRAEL to the four corners of the earth, to get seven handfuls of dust for the creation of Adam. However only Azrael, the Angel of Death, was able to accomplish this.

**Further reading:**

Davidson, Gustav. *A Dictionary of Angels*. New York: The Free Press, 1967.

**Izra'il** The Islamic ANGEL OF DEATH. His name is mentioned in the Koran, and his characteristics and duties are elaborated upon by commentators. He is one of the four principal archangels of Islamic angelology. In Hebrew lore, he is known as Azrael, whose name means "whom God helps."

While the angel ISRAFIL breathes life into souls, Izra'il takes breath away. He is associated with writing, in the idea that writers "take away" ideas from the realm of thought and cause them to fall into the world of matter.

On the macrocosmic level, Izra'il represents the human soul. He removes the soul from the world and delivers it to God's forgiveness, and thus the soul is displayed in a nobler form. In this respect, Izra'il is considered the bringer of good news, because he helps the soul on its path to spiritual perfection.

Azrael is supposed to be the biggest of the angels, with his shape pleasing to the believer, in order to facilitate the release from life. Sufi teacher Abdul Karim Jili says that Azrael appears to the soul in a form provided by its most powerful metaphors. He may even manifest invisibly, "so that a man may die of a rose in aromatic pain"—or of a rotting stench. When the soul sees Azrael it "falls in love," and its gaze is thus withdrawn from the body as if by seduction. Great prophets and saints may be invited politely by Azrael in corporeal form, as he did to MOSES and MUHAMMAD.

When the Sufi poet Rumi lay on his deathbed, Azrael appeared as a beautiful youth: "I am come by divine command to inquire what commission the Master may have to entrust to me." Rumi's human companions almost fainted with fear, but the Sufi master replied: "Come in, come in, thou messenger of my King. Do that which thou art bidden, and God willing thou shalt find me one of the patient."

Islamic angelology holds that Azrael is another form of RAPHAEL, and possesses 70,000 feet and 40,000 wings. He has as many eyes and tongues as there are people. Arabic mythology tells that Azrael constantly writes and erases in a large book. The writing brings birth and the erasing brings death.

Still another story, regarding the creation of Adam, has Azrael fulfilling a crucial task. The angels MICHAEL, Gabriel and ISRAFIL do not produce seven handfuls of earth necessary to make Adam; Azrael does. Thus, he is endowed with the power to separate the soul from the body.

In Islamic occult lore, Izra'il exists in the seventh heaven, is associated with the planet of Saturn (ruler of time and associated with death), and governs the spleen.

See DEATHBED APPARITIONS.

**Further reading:**

Barnstone, Willis, ed. *The Other Bible*. San Francisco: Harper-SanFrancisco, 1984.

Davidson, Gustav. *A Dictionary of Angels*. New York: The Free Press, 1967.

Klein, F. A. *The Religion of Islam*. London: 1906, reprint 1971.

Nasr, Seyyed Hossein (ed.). *Islamic Spirituality*. New York: Crossroad, 1987.

# J

**Jacob** Among the most discussed and most inexplicable of biblical stories is the one containing what is probably the most striking encounter of an angel with a biblical personage: the patriarch Jacob (son of ISAAC and Rebekah) wrestling all night with the angel in Genesis 32:22–31. Jacob's dream while sleeping on a stone pillow, in which he sees a ladder of angels ascending and descending from heaven (Genesis 28:10–17), is a powerful image that has fascinated people throughout the ages.

### JACOB'S LADDER

After stealing his twin brother Esau's birthright with the aid of his mother Rebekah, Jacob leaves to escape his father Isaac's shame and Esau's wrath. Rebekah suggests that he go to her brother. On his way to his uncle Laban's country, Jacob stops for the night, taking a stone as his pillow. He dreams: "a ladder was there, standing on the ground with its top reaching to heaven; and there were angels of God going up it and coming down." (Genesis 28:12). Next in the dream Jabob hears the voice of Yahweh explaining his high spiritual destiny: This land will be the dwelling of his innumerable descendants, and Yahweh never will desert him. When he wakes up Jacob calls the place Bethel, the gate of heaven, anoints the stone pillow with oil and sets it up as a monument, with which he promises faithfulness and to give a tenth of his wealth to Yahweh in return for his preservation and safe return to his father.

There are many rabbinic and midrashic comments on this dream and its context. Some note the union of the land and the people destined for it, signified by Jacob's placing his head on the stone. Some rabbis interpret the ladder as a symbol of the angels' constant interventions and frustration with the previous patriarchs from the beginning of creation up until this point, when Jacob at last is found worthy. Jacob's acceptability is signified by the choice of him as the model for the man-faced angel on the chariot of EZEKIEL. Some saw the ladder as a political allegory, a prophecy of the ascent and descent of Israel that was to come.

In John 1:51, Jesus tells his disciples "I tell you most solemnly, you will see heaven laid open and, above the Son of Man, the angels of God ascending and descending." Maimonides (*Guide of the Perplexed*, II) interpreted the ladder as representing the hierarchy of the INTELLIGENCES. A glimpse of angelic activities, particularly the image of a ladder, denoted the interdependence of the angelic hierarchies, and was an obvious interpretation in angelology. Analogies were applied to stages of spiritual ascent for human seekers, for example by Bonaventure (see MONASTICISM, CHRISTIAN).

**Angels on Jacob's ladder**

Various scholars since have taken the ladder to represent every kind of correspondence, system, and parallelism between worlds and planes of being, ranging from the esoteric motto "as above, so below" to the rough model of eighteenth-century science, "the Great Chain of Being."

### JACOB WRESTLING WITH THE ANGEL

After working for fourteen years in order to win Rachel, the bride of his choice (having had first to marry Leah because of Laban's deception), fathering twelve sons and working many more years with the help of the ANGEL OF THE LORD to gain great flocks of his own (Genesis 31:11), Jacob departs from Laban with all his wives, children, and flocks of livestock to return to his father and the unknown factor, his brother Esau. "While Jacob was going on his way angels of God met him, and on seeing them he said 'This is God's camp,' and he named the place Mahanaim" (Genesis 32:2–3). Jacob has sent a party out to meet Esau, and has found that Esau is coming to meet him with four hundred men. After taking the usual precaution when entering someone's territory of sending gifts ahead to Esau, and praying, Jacob leaves everyone on one side of the river Jabbok (literally *yeabheq*, "strove") and goes alone to the other side.

> And there was one [literally, "a man"] that wrestled with him until daybreak who, seeing that he could not master him, struck him in the socket of his hip, and Jacob's hip was dislocated as he wrestled with him. He said, "Let me go, for day is breaking." But Jacob answered "I will not let you go unless you bless me." He then asked, "What is your name?" "Jacob," he replied. He said, "Your name shall no longer be Jacob but Israel, because you have been strong against God, you shall prevail against men." Jacob then made this request; "I beg you, tell me your name," but he replied, "Why do you ask my name?" And he blessed him there. (Genesis 32:24–29)
>
> Jacob named the place Peniel, "Because I have seen God face to face," he said "and I have survived." The sun rose as he left Peniel, limping because of his hip. That is the reason why to this day the Israelites do not eat the sciatic nerve which is in the socket of the hip; because he had struck Jacob in the socket of the hip in the sciatic nerve. (Genesis 32:30–32)

It is not surprising that this dramatic scene has spurred so much commentary from Judaic, Catholic and Protestant theologians, biblical scholars, and literary critics. Its complex symbolism and enigmas challenge the usual boundaries of interpretation. Graves and Patai say:

> The widely differing midrashic views of this wrestling match between Jacob and the "man" whom he afterwards identifies with God, are all prompted by pious embarrassment. God, the transcendental God of Judaism, could never have demeaned himself by wrestling with a mortal and then begging to be released from his hold. In any case, if He loved Jacob so well, and was so perfectly loved in return, why should they have struggled? And if the adversary was only an angel, should he be identified with GABRIEL or MICHAEL, or rather with the fallen angel SAMAEL?

However, the metaphor of a pious man struggling with God in prayer and forcing Him to grant a blessing easily gained currency. The name "Israel" means "El [God] strives against my enemies," and derives in no small sense from the receiving of the new name and new status after having striven with God and not having been vanquished.

Another midrash presents Esau as Jacob's unknown adversary at Peniel, in which case this struggle would be a continuation of the one that began even in the womb, a vying over primacy and territories. Jacob did indeed win, and seal his victory by giving rich expiatory gifts to his brother, who thereupon vacates the land (Genesis 36:6–8).

Along those lines, Midrash Rabbah identifies the assailant as being Esau's guardian angel. The implication is that Jacob knew with whom he was wrestling, and was reassured by his success that he would have nothing to fear from his imminent reunion. The reason the angel is required to depart before dawn is that he is required to be present among the heavenly host to praise God. "Let your brothers praise him,"

objects Jacob, to which the angel replies that if he does not praise God today, the angels will not let him do so tomorrow. According to this midrash the injury to Jacob was only temporary.

Early Christian exegesis identified the angel who wrestled with Jacob as a figure of Christ. Jacob's victory, which was with the angel's consent, indicated that the Jews would appear to overcome Christ during his Passion. St. AUGUSTINE understands the name Israel to mean "seeing God," and this will be the reward of the saints. The paradox that Jacob emerges from the encounter both blessed and lame points forward to the fact that some Jews will believe in Christ and others will reject him (*City of God* XVI.39).

Maimonides treats Jacob's wrestling match as he treats other angelic visitations, as a prophetic vision (see JUDAIC ANGELOLOGY and ANGEL OF THE LORD). Furthermore, he posits that the passage "the angels met him [Jacob]" (Genesis 32:2) is a foreshadowing of the wrestling match. A sympathetic interpretation of this prophetic visionary approach by Maimonides is provided by Hillel of Verona, who discusses Jacob's struggle with the angel thus:

> There was no doubt whatsoever that the struggle was literally real . . . I will never believe though, that the angel was a body with joints and arms, but it happened like this: the angel, by means of a spiritual divine power, created in the air surrounding Jacob motions of thrust and pressure, through which the particles of air were violently moved and by their movement forced the body of Jacob, by pressing and coercing it as in the thrust of wrestling . . . to move to and fro. . . . But the angel himself appeared to him, in truth, only in a "prophetical vision." . . . Thus the story of this event is literally true, as the real happenings were combined with the prophetical vision.

In his lectures on Genesis of 1542–44, Martin Luther rejected the Jewish interpretations as well as the allegories of his Christian predecessors. He assumes that the assailant is Christ even though Jacob thinks it is a man, and that the assailant had tried to convince Jacob that the promises to him had been revoked. Anguish over this caused Jacob to fight at a level beyond what was his normal physical strength and enabled him to overcome his opponent. The request for a blessing is a demand that the assailant revoke the earlier suggestion that Jacob had been forsaken by God and is without hope. Only when Jacob's name is changed does Jacob realize who his opponent was, and that during his struggle he has been close to Heaven as well as Hell. In his joy at dawn he exclaims that he has seen God. In terms of theology, the meaning of the incident for Luther is that there is a dark side to the nature of God, and it is a mystery which the aspiring soul must encounter and struggle with, holding tenaciously to faith.

John Calvin regards the incident as a vision, and states that Jacob was wounded so that the content of the vision would leave a permanent visible mark on him. God knew what the outcome would be, of course, so strictly speaking Jacob did not overcome God. Calvin holds that if God fights with us, he provides us with the means of resistance. Thus God fights both against us and for us.

Whereas the eighteenth century tended to rationalize the story and the early nineteenth century romanticized it, the most recent trends in reading it have been to look at myth, symbol and narrative structure, incorporating more developed linguistic and historical materials. Karl Ellinger, for instance, assumes that the Yahwist (one of the authors of one of the two schools who wrote/compiled Genesis) was building on an ancient story that believed in demons of the night. The Yahwist interpolated Jacob's prayer (Genesis 32:9–12), and the divine attack on Jacob by Yahweh was the answer to that prayer. Ellinger argues that for the Yahwist the story was not about Jacob's struggle with God, but about God's struggle with Jacob. God is the real subject of the story, who in answer to Jacob's prayer, wrestles with him in judgment and in His graciousness gives Jacob a new name, and new courage to face the future. Literary deconstruction was applied to Genesis 32 by Roland Barthes so as to elegantly outline its layers of possible meaning, but Barthes arrived no closer to a definite sense of what had happened or who the wrestler was meant to be.

One midrash suggests that GABRIEL may have been the angel who wrestled with Jacob. This wrestling with Gabriel accords with the Islamic mystical attribution of Gabriel as the personal Holy Spirit who is the initiator and guide of the aspirant's spiritual ascent (see INTELLIGENCES; ISLAMIC ANGELOLOGY). According to the symbolic exegesis of the Jewish mystic Joseph Ben Judah, the intellective soul struggles to be united with the Angel, with the Active Intelligence, until the rising of the light, at which time the soul emerges, delivered, from the darkness that imprisoned it. This is a combat not with an Angel but *for* the Angel, for the Angel in turn needs the response of a soul if its being is to become what it has to be.

**Further reading:**

Corbin, Henry. *Creative Imagination in the Sufism of Ibn' Arabi*. Trans. Ralph Manheim. Princeton, N.J.: Princeton University Press, 1969.

Graves, Robert, and Patai, Raphael. *Hebrew Myths*. New York: Doubleday Anchor Books, 1964.

Leaman, Oliver. *Moses Maimonides*. London and New York: Routledge, 1990.

Luther, Martin. *Luther's Works*. St. Louis: Concordia, 1971.

Maimonides. *Guide of the Perplexed*. Abridged. Introduction by Julius Guttmann. London: East and West Library, 1952.

Rogerson, John. "Wrestling With the Angel: A Study in Historical and Literary Interpretation," *Hermeneutics, the Bible, and Literary Criticism*. Eds. Ann Loades and Michael McLain. New York: St. Martin's Press, 1992.

**Jacob's ladder**   See JACOB; DREAMS.

**Jahoel (also Jehoel, Shemuel, Kemuel, Yaoel and Metatron)**   A member of the ANGELS OF THE PRESENCE, who mediates the ineffable name of God. The name Jahoel may have been an early form of METATRON.

Jahoel is said to be chief of the seraphim (a job also held by Seraphiel), and governs heavenly singing. He is responsible for holding in check LEVIATHAN, the monster of evil who will swallow the souls of sinners on Judgment Day.

**Jesus**   Angels are prominent in the story of Jesus. The ANGEL OF THE LORD announces the coming birth of his forerunner John the Baptist to John's father Zechariah, instructing him on the name and upbringing (Luke 1:11–22). The angel says "I am GABRIEL who stand in God's presence," and strikes Zechariah dumb because he has doubted the message. Gabriel was sent to Mary in the sixth month of Elizabeth's pregnancy with John (Luke 1:26–38), to tell her not only of her own conception of Jesus, "Son of the Most High," but also that her cousin Elizabeth is with child. When John is circumcised, Zechariah regains his speech after he follows the angel's instructions by writing on a tablet that the child is named John.

The angel of the Lord appeared to the shepherds the night Jesus was born (Luke 2:9–14) and announced his birth; a "great throng of the heavenly host" then appeared to sing praises to God.

The angel of the Lord also appeared to Joseph in a dream before the birth of Jesus, explaining that Mary had conceived by the Holy Spirit (Matthew 1:20–21); again to warn him to take Mary and Jesus away to Egypt to avoid the wrath of Herod, which would unleash the slaughter of Innocents (Matthew 2:13); once again to tell Joseph it was safe to return to Israel (Matthew 2:19); and finally to remove for safety to Galilee (Matthew 2:23).

In Matthew 4 and Luke 4, Satan tempts Jesus in the wilderness, quoting Psalm 91, "He will put you in his angels' charge," to persuade Jesus to prove he is the Son of God by throwing himself off a parapet. After Jesus expels Satan from his presence, "angels appeared and looked after him" (Matthew 4:11). In Matthew 18:10 Jesus tells his disciples "never despise any of these little ones [children], for I tell you that their angels in heaven are continually in the

*The Agony in the Garden* (Albrecht Dürer, 1508)

presence of my Father in heaven." This passage is one of the key scriptural proofs for the belief in guardian angels. John 5:4 relates that at the pool of Bethzatha (Bethesda) "at intervals the angel of the Lord came down into the pool and the water was disturbed, and the first person to enter the water was cured."

In the garden on the Mount of Olives, after Jesus had prayed about his ensuing Passion and death, "an angel appeared to him, coming from heaven to give him strength" (Luke 22:43). Soon Jesus was taken prisoner by the high priests' servants. Jesus tell his disciple, who has just cut off the ear of one of the guards: "Put your sword back. . . . Do you think that I cannot appeal to my Father, who would promptly send more than twelve legions of angels to my defense? But then would the scriptures be fulfilled that say this is the way it must be?" (Matthew 26:51–55). (Luke 22:51 adds that Jesus healed the man's severed ear.) John identifies the disciple who did the cutting of the ear as being Simon Peter (John 18:10).

After Jesus was buried, on the third day the women went to the tomb and according to Matthew 28, "all at once there was a violent earthquake, for the angel of the Lord, descending from heaven, came and rolled away the stone and sat on it. His face was like lightning, his robe white as snow." The guards were so shaken, so frightened of him, that they were like dead men. But the angel spoke and said, "There is no need to be afraid. . . . He has risen." Mark says that simply "a young man in a white robe" (16:5–6) has told them that Jesus has risen. Luke says (24:4–5) "two men in brilliant clothes suddenly appeared at their side" and told them the news. In John 20:11–14, Mary Magdalene finds "two angels in white sitting where the body of Jesus had been, one at the head, the other at the feet." They speak with her just before Jesus appears to her.

A controversy arose in Christian theology about the identity of the angel of the Lord. Some insisted that it was none other than the pre-incarnation Christ, and many theologians have not questioned this concept, which would place Christ in this persona ubiquitously throughout the Old Testament. The continued presence of angel messengers titled "Angel of the Lord" in the New Testament has not entered into the discussion.

(See also SONS OF GOD, an epithet which in Genesis was associated with fallen angels, but eventually became a title identified with Jesus Christ.)

**jina**   See TANTRIC BUDDHISM.

**jinn (also djinn or ginn)**   In Arabic and Islamic lore, a type of spirit being that became demonized in Christianity. Like the DAEMON, *jinn* can be either good or evil. They possess supernatural powers, and can be conjured in magical rites to perform various tasks and services. A *jinnee* (singular) appears as a wish-granting "genie" in many Arabic folktales.

In pre-Islamic lore the *jinn* are malicious, are born of fire, and are not immortal. They live with other supernatural beings in the Kaf, a mythical range of emerald mountains that encircles the Earth. They like to roam the deserts and wilderness. Usually they are invisible, but they have the power to shapeshift to any form, be it insect, animal or human.

Islamic theology absorbed and modified the *jinn*; some became beautiful and good-natured. According to lore they were created two thousand years before Adam and Eve, and are equal to angels in stature. Their ruler, IBLIS, refused to worship Adam, and so was cast out of heaven along with his followers. Iblis became the equivalent of the Devil, and the followers all became demons.

King Solomon used a magic ring to control *jinn* and to protect himself from them. The ring was set with a gem, probably a diamond, that had a living force of its own. With the ring, Solomon branded the necks of the *jinn* as his slaves.

One story tells that a jealous *jinnee* (sometimes identified as ASMODEUS) stole Solomon's ring while he bathed in the river Jordan. The *jinnee* then seated himself on Solomon's throne at his palace and reigned over his kingdom, forcing Solomon to become a wanderer. God compelled the *jinnee* to throw the ring into the sea. Solomon retrieved it, and punished the *jinnee* by imprisoning him in a bottle.

According to another story, Solomon brought *jinn* to his crystal-paved palace, where they sat at tables made of iron. The Koran tells how the king made them work at building palaces and making carpets, ponds, statues and gardens. Whenever he wanted to travel to faraway places, the *jinn* carried him there on their backs.

*Jinn* appear in tales such as "Aladdin's Lamp" in *Arabian Nights*, in which they carry out the wishes of a master who learns the magic that will command them. In "Aladdin's Lamp," the "genie" imprisoned in the lamp is derivative of the *jinnee* imprisoned in the bottle by Solomon.

See DEMON.

**Further reading:**
de Givry, Emile Grillot. *Witchcraft, Magic and Alchemy.* New York: Dover Publications, 1971. First published 1931.

**Joan of Arc** (1412–1431)   French peasant girl, known as "the Maid of Orleans," whose communion with saints and an angel led her to become a military hero of France. Her success was short-lived, for her enemies succeeded in executing her as a heretic. Her story is especially interesting to scholars because of the extensive documentation of her trial, in which she was interrogated at depth about her visions and voices.

Joan was born to a farming family in Domremy, a village between the Champagne and Lorraine districts. At the time, France was torn by civil war and had an unstable throne. Henry V of England had invaded and was claiming the crown of the insane King Charles VI. Charles VII, or the Dauphin, put up no resistance. Joan's mission, guided by her supernatural aides, appears to have been ensuring the coronation of the Dauphin and the defeat of the English.

At the age of thirteen she began to experience visions and voices. At first it was a single voice accompanied by a brilliant light. Other voices manifested. They instructed her to "be a good girl, and go often to church." The voices then began to intervene often in her life, and to be accompanied by forms that Joan identified as the archangel St. MICHAEL and saints Catherine and Margaret. The voices usually came to her during a waking state, but sometimes they roused her from sleep. Sometimes they were unintelligible. They manifested almost daily.

Over time the voices gave Joan more instructions and predictions of the future, and revealed her mission. She was to

*Joan of Arc* (Jules Bastien-Lepage, c. 1879; reprinted courtesy of Metropolitan Museum of Art, New York, gift of Erwin Davis, 1889)

take up arms like a man, raise the English siege of Orleans, and see that the Dauphin was crowned king of France. The voices told her that she would be wounded in battle, and that a great victory would be won over the English within seven years.

When Joan protested to the voices that she could not possibly accomplish these things, the voices replied, "It is God who commands it." The voices became so insistent that she finally sought an audience with Robert Baudricourt, who commanded the king's forces in the town of Valcouleurs. Baudricourt dismissed her with laughter.

But when one of her prophecies later came true—a serious defeat for the French in battle—Baudricourt agreed to send her to the Dauphin. For protection she traveled in male clothing, something that later would contribute to her demise.

She had an audience with the Dauphin on March 8, 1429. He purposely disguised himself, but she recognized him instantly. She impressed him because she knew his daily personal prayer to God, which she had received from the voices. She persuaded him about her mission, and asked for troops to lead to Orleans.

Court advisors considered her a lunatic, so Charles sent her to a council of theologians for interrogation. They found no quarrel with her, and sent her back to Charles. According to Joan, Charles accepted her not because of the clergy, but because she had presented him with a divine sign. She said Michael had accompanied her to her meeting with Charles, and had bowed to him and presented him with a marvelous crown. The angel had told him that with Joan's help, the English would be banished from France.

Charles gave her troops, which she led into battle against the English at Orleans, flying a special standard that bore the words "Jesus: Maria" and a representation of the Eternal Father being presented a fleur-de-lis by two angels.

Joan raised the siege of Orleans in May 1429, and won another important campaign against the English on the Loire River. Charles was crowned Charles VII on July 17 of that year. In gratitude, he ennobled Joan and her family. Among the people, she was hailed as the savior of France.

Despite the victories, the English retained a firm hold on Paris and parts of Normandy and Burgundy. Joan attempted to wrest control of Paris, but she was ordered to retreat before the battle was decided. She then attempted to raise the English siege of Compeigne on May 23, 1430, but she was wounded, unhorsed and captured. The duke of Burgundy, an ally of the English, imprisoned her in the tower of Beaurevoir castle. Joan attempted to escape twice by jumping out of the tower—against the instructions of her saints—and was apprehended. For several months, she languished in the tower; Charles VII never made a single effort on her behalf. The English, still stung by their defeat at her hands, persuaded the duke of Burgundy to sell her to them for 10,000 francs. She was delivered to the bishop of Beauvais, an English ally.

Joan was imprisoned in Castle Rouen. At first she was placed in an iron cage, and then she was chained to a bed and watched around the clock by guards. On February 21, 1431, she appeared before an ecclesiastical tribunal, who interrogated her about her visions, voices, wearing of male clothing, and faith in the Church. Joan honestly described her communication with the saints and said that she could see, hear, kiss and embrace them. When it came to answering questions, Joan demurred until she was permitted to do so by her voices. She admitted to hearing them daily. The tribunal declared her revelations diabolical; she also was vehemently denounced by the University of Paris.

Joan's interrogators were especially interested in why she thought her spirits were saints rather than demonic deceptions. Had she been given a sure sign? A consultant to the investigations, the bishop of Lisieux, had stated that prophets should be believed only if there were accompanying signs, miracles and references to scriptures. A sign would be something imprinted on the physical world, which could be perceived by at least one of the five senses and could be verified independently (see references to Michael's apparitional hand and footprints under MICHAEL).

Joan could offer no such evidence. She said she knew her spirits were good because they always helped her. She could identify Michael, she said, by his angelic speech and language. However, she also admitted that initially she was uncertain that it was indeed Michael; she was afraid; she saw him many times before she knew it was Saint Michael.

The interrogators were not impressed by the alleged sign given to Charles, for no testimony was forthcoming from the court as to the verity of what she claimed. Joan's world may have been full of visions, voices, apparitions and a crown, but no one else could—or would—verify the truthfulness of it all.

From the outset the interrogators were inclined to believe that Joan's experiences were of evil spirits, and they relentlessly attempted to link them with fairies (because fairies were pagan, they were evil in the view of the church). Joan

testified over and over again that the spirits filled her with joy and guided her. When Michael appeared, she said, she felt carefree and not in a state of mortal sin; she was always unhappy to see him depart. The spirits even kissed and embraced her, she said. The alleged physical contact repulsed the interrogators, who associated that too with evil. Furthermore they were put off by the spirits' instruction to her to wear men's clothing and to ignore many of their questions. Ultimately what sealed her fate was her spirits' counsel to fight the English.

Joan was charged with seventy counts of sorcery, witchcraft, divining, pseudo-prophecy, invoking of evil spirits, conjuring, being "given to the arts of magic," and heresy. The charges of sorcery and witchcraft could not be substantiated, and were dropped. The remaining charges were reduced to twelve, chief among them being heresy, the wearing of men's clothing and the ability to see apparitions. She remained unrepentant and refused to recant, even when threatened with torture. On May 24, 1431, she did make a partial recantation before a large, jeering crowd at the cemetery of St. Ouen. She was sentenced to life in prison. But upon returning to her cell, she resumed male dress. She declared again that the voices were from God, and that God had sent her on her mission.

She was accused again of dressing as a man on the instructions of her saints. (Some modern historians speculate that guards stole her own clothing and left her nothing but men's clothing to wear.) On May 28, 1431, Joan was condemned as a relapsed heretic. On May 30 she recanted her confession and was excommunicated from the church. She was burned at the stake the same day in Rouen.

According to legend her heart refused to burn, and the executioner discovered it whole in the ashes. The ashes were cast into the Seine.

Nearly twenty years after her execution, at the behest of Joan's mother and two brothers, Charles VII initiated an investigation into her rehabilitation. The report, written in 1449, takes a much more sympathetic view of her experiences. It emphasizes as a virtue, not a sin, her willingness to accept the counsel of her saints, her distaste for violence, and the accuracy of her prophecies. It also emphasizes that she possessed five saintly virtues that were deemed signs at the time: humility, willingness to accept counsel, patience, accuracy and charity. It notes her lack of fear whenever she dealt with her spirits, which various experts throughout the centuries had stated was characteristic of a good rather than an evil person.

Pope Calixtus III annulled her sentence in 1450. She was canonized in 1920 by Pope Benedict XV. A national festival in her honor is held in France on the second Sunday in May. Her feast day is May 30.

Frederic W. H. Myers, a founder of the Society for Psychical Research in 1889 in London, hypothesized that Joan's visions and voices were externalizations of her own inner voice coming from her subconscious, which Myers called "the subliminal self." He compared her saint-guides to the *daimon* of Socrates, an inner voice Socrates credited to a guiding spirit that had been with him from childhood (see DAEMON). Joan's case, Myers said, exhibited characteristics of motor automatism, in which voices are accompanied by an "overwhelming impulse to act in obedience to them."

**Further reading:**
Christian, William A., Jr. *Apparitions in Late Medieval and Renaissance Spain*. Princeton, N.J.: Princeton University Press, 1981.
Myers, Frederic W.H. Myers. *Human Personality and Its Survival of Bodily Death, Vols. I & II*. New ed. New York: Longmans, Green & Co., 1954. First published 1903.
*One Hundred Saints*. Boston: Little, Brown & Co., 1993.
Pernoud, Regine. *Joan of Arc: By Herself and Her Witnesses*. New York: Dorset, 1964. First published 1962.

**John XXIII** (1881–1963)    Pope John XXIII (1958–1963) maintained a deep and abiding faith in guardian angels, thanks to the influence of Pope PIUS XI. John XXIII often used his radio addresses to exhort followers never to neglect devotion to their guardian angels, who, he said, stand ready at all times to help. He particularly urged parents to educate their children that they were not alone but always in the company of their guardian angels.

Like Pius XI, John XXIII brought his guardian angel into all his dealings with other persons, especially those with whom he was having trouble. He followed the advice given to him by Pius XI and asked the guardian angels of both him and the other person to work out an accord between them on the angelic level, which then would manifest on the physical level. Even if no difficulties were present, John XXIII always at least acknowledged and paid respect to all guardian angels present at any meeting or gathering. He often acknowledged to his secretary how his guardian angel had inspired him to do various things. He confided to a Canadian bishop that his angel had given him the idea to call the Second Vatican Council in 1962, which became the high point of his pontificate.

John XXIII was warm and outgoing, and one of the best-loved popes of modern times. He worked for world peace, dialogue with other faiths, and social welfare causes around the world.

**Further reading:**
Huber, Georges. *My Angel Will Go Before You*. Westminster, Md.: Christian Classics, 1983.

**Judaic angelology**    In biblical and rabbinic tradition, the heavenly intermediary forces are called angels. Parts of the tradition consider the angels to be only intermediary; other parts clearly believe in their intercessory nature.

Judaic angelology preceded, as did the religion itself, the Christian and Islamic versions. All three religions also evidence strong influence from ZOROASTRIANISM, to which part of the Jewish population was exposed during the Babylonian captivity in the seventh century B.C.E. In pre-exilic times angels belonged to popular rather than prophetic Judaic religion, but after the exile in 560 B.C.E. angels spring into prominence, seen distinctively in EZEKIEL and Zechariah. These were far surpassed by the later developments in DANIEL and ENOCH, which feature a highly developed hierarchy of angels.

In the time in which the Jews were in touch with the Persian religion, not only was a complete system of angels developed, but the abstract idea of angels and spirits, and names and numbers for spirits, distinctly paralleled Zoroastrian conceptions. For example, at this time, Yahweh was represented as surrounded by a great multitude of angels who do his bidding. Among these are the archangels,

sometimes called Watchers and Holy Ones (Daniel 4:13, 17, 23; I Timothy 5:21; Enoch 12; 2, 4; 14:1; 15:1, 8), sometimes distinctly referred to as the seven holy angels (Tobit 12:15; Enoch 20; Revelation 8:2). Similarly, seven Holy Ones compose the Zoroastrian Amahraspands, with Ahura Mazda as the leader of the six Amesha Spenta (or Amahraspands), the Bounteous Immortals. It was only after Persian influence that names were given to archangels. Enoch names the entire seven, and other long lists of angels occur in other later literature, including the Talmud 48 and 56. These angel names are Hebrew, with the exception of one Persian deva, ASMODEUS. Derived from the concept of the *fravashi* in Zoroastrianism—the souls of the deceased, the protecting spirits of the living, and other protective genii (see GENIUS)—were the Jewish guardian angels, and perhaps the good angels of the second book of Maccabees. Finally, the personifications of Wisdom in Job and Proverbs, and still more strongly in the later Wisdom literature (see SOPHIA), suggest those of the Amesha Spenta in the *gathas* of the Avesta.

Later the Jewish historian Philo of Alexandria (30 B.C.E.–45 C.E.) blended ideas from the Old Testament and Greek philosophy, which equally inspired him. He framed the concept of powers, logic and angels as agents between God and the world. The Logos is their sum collectively, through whom God deals with the world and with humans. The manner in which the second-greatest of the Amesha Spenta, Vayuman (Good Thought, Good Mind), is spoken of in the Avesta is often strikingly parallel to expressions used of the Logos by Neoplatonism, the stream into which Philo's cosmology and angelology entered (see INTELLIGENCES) from Judaism.

All three major Western religions honor the texts of the Old Testament as divine revelation. They share roots in Middle Eastern history and mythology—especially Zoroastrian, as has just been sketched—and Semitic languages (angel/messenger is *mal'ak* in both Hebrew and Arabic).

Also shared is the belief in the presence of an evil force, a disobedient angel, an adversary of God (Hebrew *satan*), who wreaks havoc on the human plane, and in this connection a shared concept of the origin of evil in the theological sense. In both the Koran and the Bible, angels are sent to strengthen believers, succor them here and in eternity, undertake military assistance (Joshua 5:13–15; 2 Kings 19:35, John 20:11–13), punish disbelievers, intercede for humans, act as guardian angels, and mete out God's judgment on the last day. Both Islamic and Judaic angelology forbid the worship of angels, although there is confusion in the Old Testament surrounding the often-worshipped ANGEL OF THE LORD: is it God, angel or human? St. PAUL condemns the worship of angels (Colossians 2:18); ORIGEN also takes up this point.

The references to angels in the Old Testament did not prevent the aristocratic Jewish intellectual Sadducees in ancient Israel from denying the existence of angels. Their major differences with the other line of belief, the Pharisees—who believed in resurrection, angel, and spirit—are made dramatically apparent in Acts 23:1–11 when Paul is brought before the Sanhedrin. The resurrection of the body and the doctrine of angels were not part of Jewish teaching until a comparatively late date. From the text it is apparent that the Sadducees still rejected both, while Paul and the Pharisees, who were in agreement about all three, did eventually prevail.

The majority of Jews, however, from post-exilic times onward, had not only affirmed the existence of angels but also conjured up notions about angels that went far beyond what scriptural references warranted. Unique to Judaism were its age-old oral tradition of law and its folklore, in addition to thousands of years of written commentary in the Talmudic and Midrashic literature. Graves and Patai's *Hebrew Myths*, subtitled "Stories of Cosmic Forces, Deities, Angels, Demons, Monsters, Giants and Heroes—Interpreted in the Light of Modern Anthropology and Mythology," compiles this Judaic lore exhaustively. Separate entries in this book treat of key Old Testament angels and angel-connected stories and themes: MICHAEL, GABRIEL, RAPHAEL, SAMAEL, LUCIFER/SATAN, ABRAHAM, JACOB, Ark of the Covenant, MOSES, TOBIT, ENOCH, DANIEL, JOB, EZEKIEL, the ANGEL OF THE LORD and SOPHIA, which deals with the Wisdom literature. New Testament entries include JESUS, PAUL and REVELATION.

Moses ben Maimon, known as Maimonides (1135–1204) the greatest medieval Jewish philosopher, took Judaic angelology in a new direction. He was born in Cordoba and wrote his works in Arabic using Hebrew characters. He was also a rabbi, physician and legal scholar. His significance to the Jewish community rests largely upon the breadth of his work on law. His *Mishneh Torah* (Code of Law) systemized the Oral Law, until then lacking overall organization, which he derived from Islamic models for jurisprudence. All his works, and especially the *Guide of the Perplexed*, are credited with aligning Judaism and philosophy. Specifically, he articulated a worldview coherent with a logical and natural understanding of the universe of his time (via Islamic Aristotelian philosophy, which Jewish intellectuals of his time and place absorbed without qualms), then showed how that worldview was actually implicit in the biblical and rabbinic tradition. Published in the 1190s, *Guide of the Perplexed* quickly was translated into Hebrew and thus influenced Jewry worldwide. In the early 13th century a Latin translation profoundly influenced Albert the Great and his most famous pupil, St. Thomas AQUINAS, who often cites Maimonides's works, respectfully calling him "the rabbi."

Like Aquinas, Maimonides believed in using philosophical method to determine the extent to which the power of human thought can grasp metaphysical truth, with the Bible considered the repository of all the great metaphysical questions as well as divine revelation. As Maimonides understood it, the philosophical interpretation of the Bible does not import any extraneous ideas into the Bible, but instead reveals the true and real meaning present in the text. Maimonides combined faith in the power of the human mind with a profound awareness of the limits of human understanding. Maimonides's theory about angels illustrates this.

In Chapter 2 of his *Code of Law* he takes up the topic of angels. He begins by identifying knowledge and love of God as one and the same phenomenon. With this he establishes the priority of sound philosophical knowledge as a commandment of God and as an act of piety for any religious Jew. He begins his exposition of the structure of the universe, indicating that it is divided into three parts: the sub-lunar world, the supernal realm, and the Intelligences which exist as pure form only. This last realm he identifies as that of the angels. He then labels all corporeal description of the angels as contained in the biblical and rabbinical tradition as metaphors. Finally he sets forth his views that the Intelligences are arranged in a causal hierarchy.

In six brief paragraphs, Maimonides sets forth his basic view that (1) the beings which are intermediate between God and creation are the pure-form Intelligences and the heavenly bodies; (2) that these beings are arranged in a causal hierarchy; and (3) that the corporeal imagery of the tradition must be treated as metaphors. Next he attempts a fusion of philosophy and tradition, a philosophical exegesis of the sources on the subject of angels. He draws up a list of the ten "main" angels, arranges them in hierarchical ranking, and identifies the last of them as the intellectual link between humankind and God. Lastly he describes the intellectualist function of God, the angel-Intelligences, and the human intellect.

The text of paragraph seven reads as follows: "The variation in the names of the angels is according to their rank. They are therefore, called: Hayyot ha-Qodesh, they are the highest of all; Ofannim, Er'elim, Hashmallim, Serafim, Mal'akhim, Elohim, Bene'Elohim, Keruvim, and Ishim. All these ten names by which the angels are called correspond to

**Michael holding the cube of Metatron (reprinted courtesy of Jayne M. Howard)**

their ten ranks. The rank, above which there is no other rank except God, may He be blessed, is the rank of the form called Hayyot [ha-Quodesh]. Therefore, it is said of them, in prophecy, that they are beneath the throne of glory. The tenth rank is that of the form called Ishim. They are the angels which speak to the prophets and which appear to them in the prophetic vision. Therefore, they are called Ishim [humans] for their rank is close to that of the intellect of humans."

All the names as well as the pronouns that refer to them individually are in plural form, implying that since the action of God (or any one angel) always involves the action of the whole chain of spiritual and physical being, the names must be understood as plural. Each Intelligence emanates another Intelligence and a sphere with its own body, intellect, and soul (*GP*, II.4, 10, 11). This list is considerably shorter than the long list of angel-names in biblical and rabbinic literature. One rabbi responded: "That the angels are only ten in number is the opinion of the philosophers . . . but it is not the opinion of the divine Sages, may their memory be a blessing, who walk in the Torah of God, relying on the truth of the Scripture." However, Maimonides' solution here became canonical and appears in all subsequent literature.

The Hayyot ha-Quodesh are the First Intelligence (*hayyat* is the term for the spheres). Maimonides derived the term from the rabbinic daily liturgy, the mystical Merkabah tradition (referring to Ezekiel's chariot) and Talmud. Offanim is a homonym referring to the second Intelligence and to the four elements. In its first sense it too is derived from the rabbinic daily liturgy and the mystical Merkabah tradition. In its second sense, it is drawn from Ezekiel 1 and 10. The Arabic translation renders the word as "the one, who possesses faces."

The third Intelligence is Er'elim, which the Arabic renders as "the raised noble ones." Hashmallim is very abstruse and has received much commentary. The reference is to the fourth Intelligence. It may be the border of the Intelligences, between the above (God) and the below (the physical universe). It may be the channel of intermittent communication. It may be a deliberate obfuscation. The Arabic translation renders it as "the one who possesses lights and translucency." Seraphim from Isaiah 6:2 and the rabbinic daily liturgy and Talmud, the fifth Intelligence, is rendered "the one who inflames, who causes fear and veneration of Him." Mal'akhim might be used for all the angels-Intelligences or for the sixth Intelligence only. It points to Jacob's dream (Genesis 28:12), which Maimonides interpreted as referring to the hierarchy of the Intelligences.

Elohim may refer to the providential activity of God. It is rendered "the ruling governor." Bene'Elohim is drawn from Genesis 6:1–4, Job 1:6, 2:1; 38:7; and Psalms 29.1: "sons of God." Keruvim is not only the ninth Intelligence, but refers to human intellect and the heavenly spheres. Finally, the Ishim are the Agent Intelligences or Active Intellect, the prophetic and mystical contact with humanity.

Maimonides departed from the traditional view by divesting a large part of the miracles reported by the Bible of their supernatural character or by denying their reality. He accepted the miracle as the means by which God realizes His purposes in the world, but he seriously questioned the kinds

of miracles in the Bible that verge on the folkloric. He denied the type of miracle in which God, or his messengers the angels, talk to men as equals. Some of the miracles he treated as natural events. Numerous others he divested of their external reality, seeing them as nothing but experiences of revelation to the prophets (and in his theory of prophecy, visions and dreams constitute essential revelations to the prophets). This applied above all to the biblical stories in which angels appear in bodily form.

Maimonides accepted the existence of angels, but as indicated above, he identified the angels with the Intelligences, which according to Aristotle oversee the movement of the spheres, and whose functions Maimonides extended to facilitate prophetic and visionary experience in humans. These beings, he believed, could as little appear in bodily form as God himself. Therefore, Maimonides concluded wherever in the Bible angels appear bodily, only prophetic vision could be intended. Thus Maimonides dispensed with the naive idea of miracles and the naive form of angels (and also demons).

Maimonides pointed to several stories of the Bible to explain how prophetic vision was occurring and not an actual appearance of God or angel; for example the visit to Abraham of three men (Genesis 18), the wrestling of Jacob with the angel (Genesis 32:25) and the story of Balaam and the ass (Numbers 22:21–35). Referring to Daniel, Maimonides says, "The speech of the angel to him and his setting him upright, all this happened in a vision of prophecy. In a state such as this the senses too cease to function, and the overflow in question comes to the rational faculty and overflows from it to the imaginative faculty so that the latter becomes perfect and performs its function" (*Guide of the Perplexed*). When things happen through the agency of angels, and when God is said to have spoken to someone, these events all take place "in a dream or in a vision of prophecy" (*GP* II, 41; 386).

Maimonides repeats this point several times, emphasizing that "it should by no means occur to your thought that an angel can be seen or that the speech of an angel can be heard except in a vision of prophecy or in a dream of prophecy," to which he added, rather threateningly to the literalist, "you can draw inferences from what I have mentioned as to what remains of the things that I have not mentioned" (*GP* II 42; 390). "Even where there is no direct reference to the presence of an angel or a vision or a dream when we come to passages in which God apparently spoke directly to people, we should understand that the reference to a dream or vision is implicit in such a passage" (*GP* II, 46; 404). All such apparent communication requires some form of intermediation by the imaginative faculty (*GP* II, 45; 403). Indeed, Maimonides is rather sharp with literalists of passages in which someone is ordered to do something by a divine source: "Only those weak in syllogistic reasoning fancy with regard to all this that the prophet tells that he was ordered to do certain things and hence did them" (*GP* II, 46; 405).

Therefore it seems clear that when Maimonides talks about angels existing, he is using a special sense of the idea of existence. Although he starts (in *GP* II, 6) with the positive statement that "the fact that angels exist does not require that a proof deriving from the Law be brought forward . . . for the Torah has stated this in a number of passages," he later states

"Midrash Qoheleth has the following text: 'When man sleeps, his soul speaks to the angel, and the angel to the cherub. Thereby they have stated plainly to him who understands and cognizes intellectually that the imaginative faculty is likewise called an angel and that the intellect is called a cherub'." "Soul" generally is taken to mean "common sense," the faculty which first receives the impressions of the five senses and passes them onto the imagination (the angel). Common sense provides the imagination with sense impressions, which then are passed on in the form of images to the intellect, where they are transformed into intellectual concepts.

A critic of Maimonides, Isaac Abrabanel, held that prophecy is not a natural event but a miracle divinely brought about by God; dreams and prophecy are quite different things (cited by Leaman). Maimonides's predecessor Avicenna (see ISLAMIC ANGELOLOGY) discussed this problem, and rather ambiguously referred to angels as existing in both an absolute sense and relatively to us; his account accords with Maimonides's distinction between actuality and prophecy. The prophetic message is "real," but the angelic appearance is just that: an impression which helps the recipient to understand the message.

**Further reading:**
Blumenthal, David R. "Maimonides on Angel Names," *Hellenica and Iudaica*. Ed. A. Caquot. Paris: Editions Peeters, 1986.
Carter, George William. *Zoroastrianism and Judaism*. New York: AMS Press, 1970.
Graves, Robert, and Patai, Raphael. *Hebrew Myths*. New York: Doubleday Anchor Books, 1964.
Leaman, Oliver. *Moses Maimonides*. London and New York: Routledge, 1990.
Maimonides. *Guide of the Perplexed*. Abridged. Introduction by Julius Guttmann. London: East and West Library, 1952.
Maimonides. *Guide of the Perplexed*. Trans. S. Pines. Chicago: University of Chicago Press, 1963.
Maimonides. *Mishne Torah*. Ed. J. Cohen. Jerusalem: Mossad Harav Kook, 1964.

**Jung, Carl Gustav** (1875–1961)   One of the most influential minds of the twentieth century, Carl G. Jung was a scientist and practicing psychiatrist, whose collected works comprise twenty volumes. Jung was unique among scientists in several ways. First, he possessed immense learning in ancient and modern world mythology, Eastern and Western mysticism, including alchemy and GNOSTICISM, poetry, music, art and architecture, anthropology, worldwide varieties of religious and spiritual experience and practice. Even more remarkable, however, his attention to his own inner life gives his descriptions of humanity's psychic dynamics a unique, experientially informed dimension. Most important of all, Jung never subscribed to the chief supposition of his age, that science and religion are incompatible. In discussing a mental patient with an imaginary cancer, Jung noted that the whole notion of the individual as maker of his psychic condition has been of relatively recent coining. "Not so very long ago even highly civilized people believed that psychic agencies could influence our minds and feelings. There were ghosts, wizards, and witches, daemons and angels, and even gods, who could produce certain psychological changes in human beings" (*Collected Works* [*CW*] 11, 20).

*A SUMMARY OF JUNG'S LIFE*
Jung was born on July 26, 1875, in Kesswil, Switzerland, and grew up in Klein-Huningen near Basel. In early childhood he began to visit mystical realms in dreams. He felt he had two personalities. One was a wise old man who stayed with him and had an increasing influence on his thought throughout his entire life.

Jung experienced precognition, clairvoyance, psychokinesis, and hauntings. His psychic sensitivity may have been hereditary, for both his mother and maternal grandmother were known as "ghost seers."

Jung began to take serious interest in occult phenomena in 1898. In 1900 he decided to become a psychiatrist, and did his medical training at Basel. Throughout his career the paranormal played a significant role in his vision of humanity's psychic realm.

He married in 1903. In 1906 he published one of his most significant early works, *The Psychology of Dementia Praecox*.

Jung became interested in mythology around 1909, the year he resigned a post at Burgholzki Mental Clinic, where he had been practicing for nine years. Also in 1909 he traveled to the United States with his mentor, Sigmund Freud, and received an honorary degree from Clark University in Worcester, Massachusetts. (Jung also received honorary doctorates from Harvard in 1936, Oxford in 1938, and the University of Geneva in 1945.)

In 1910 he was appointed permanent president of the International Congress of Psycho-Analysis. Jung resigned this position in 1914, one year after he also resigned a professorship at the University of Zurich.

From 1907 to 1913, Jung was greatly influenced by Freud, but they parted company over diverging viewpoints, especially concerning the spiritual aspects of the psyche. The break with Freud had a profoundly disturbing effect on Jung, and he suffered a six-year-long breakdown during which he had psychotic fantasies. He was labeled a "mystic" and was shunned by his peers. During this phase of Jung's life, he experienced numerous paranormal phenomena, described below.

Following his emergence from this period, Jung pursued work on his own theories. One of the most important was his general theory of psychological types, first published in 1921. He distinguished two basic psychological types, extroverts and introverts, who could be grouped according to four basic functions: thinking, feeling, sensation and intuition. Other significant theories include the anima (feminine principle) and animus (masculine principle), psychic images which exist in everyone as feminine and masculine aspects; the collective unconscious; and archetypes. Of symbols, Jung termed them "an intuitive idea that cannot yet be formulated in any other or better way." Of dreams, he maintained that they are the private property of the dreamer and seek a private language that only the dreamer can interpret; some dreams, however, come from the collective unconscious and belong to all mankind.

Jung was intensely interested in GNOSTICISM, particularly its SOPHIA or wisdom. This interest, joined with an interest in alchemy, paved the way for a modern revival of interest in the spiritual dimensions of both subjects. Jung also became intensely interested in mandala symbolism.

In 1944, Jung suffered a heart attack. He recovered, and later recounted a near-death experience (NDE) in which he attained a mystical understanding of the meaning of his life. In the aftermath, he experienced a remarkable transformation in which he felt he was in the happy state felt by the unborn. He had a vision in which he was Adam and a Jew, and his nurse was his Magna Mater, who proceeded to teach him the mystery of the *hieros gamos*, or sacred marriage with the divine.

After the death of his wife, Jung built a castle of stone on newly acquired property in Bollingen, Switzerland. He carved numerous alchemical and mystical symbols into the stone. The ongoing building and altering of his Tower signified for him an extension of consciousness achieved in old age. The Tower and its symbolic role in his life is a leitmotif in Jung's writings. During his retirement at Bollingen, Jung reworked many earlier papers and developed further his ideas on many topics.

In *Aion* (1951), Jung summarized the roles of the "archetypes of the unconscious" and commented on the Christ image as symbolized in the fish. While there may not be a Jungian Christology per se, Jung's work had a major influence on Christian scholarship. Religious themes are developed by Jung in another major work of the period, "Answer to Job" (1952), as well as in *Mysterium Coniunctionis* (1955–56), which concerns alchemy. In the latter, his last masterpiece, he states that he was satisfied that his psychology was at last "given its place in reality and established upon its historical foundations."

Jung believed in reincarnation and was influenced by *The Tibetan Book of the Dead*. He believed that his own incarnation was due not to karma, however, but to a passionate drive toward understanding in order to piece together mythic conceptions. He feared greatly for the future of mankind, and said that our only salvation lay in becoming more conscious. He believed his work proved that the pattern of God exists in every person.

Three days before he died, Jung had the last of his visionary dreams, and a portent of his own impending death. In the dream, he became whole. Present in the dream was a significant symbol, a tree's roots interlaced with gold, the alchemical symbol of completion. When he died in his room in Zurich on June 6, 1961, a great storm arose on Lake Geneva and lightning struck a favorite tree of his.

Jungian principles have been found to be applicable to nearly all academic disciplines, from mythology to religion and from quantum physics and to nearly all aspects of modern life. His prolific writings have been collected into twenty volumes plus a supplement.

### VISIONARY EXPERIENCES

During his lifetime Jung concealed the origins of his discoveries. He said that everything he wrote was based on empirical evidence, indicating that no matter how esoteric or mystical much of his work appeared, it always rested on experience drawn from the psychiatric and psychological field. His heirs have not released the corpus containing Jung's original experiences of the unconscious. But after his death and the publication of his autobiographical fragments entitled *Memories, Dreams and Reflections*, progressively more daring revelations began to emerge from his disciples. His posthumous letters and notes disclosed that between 1912 and 1917 Jung underwent a period of psychic intensity that involved a tremendous flooding of his consciousness from

within by forces which he called archetypal, but which previous ages would have declared to be divine and demonic.

He called this cycle of experiences his *Nekyia*, using the term with which Homer described the descent of Odysseus into the underworld. His handwriting changed to a style used in the fourteenth century, and he painted with pigments he himself made. According to eyewitnesses, Jung had bound his most beautiful scriptures and paintings in red leather, which became known as "the Red Book," and they fell into two distinct categories. Some were bright and angelic, while others were dark and demonic in form. One document that has surfaced from this period, entitled *Seven Sermons to the Dead*, purports to be dictated by the second-century Gnostic Basilides in Alexandria (see ABRAXAS and GNOSTICISM). Thus there is evidence to support a claim that much if not all of Jung's scientific work may be based on visionary revelations, on the order of Emanuel SWEDENBORG, Jakob BOEHME, William BLAKE, Rudolf STEINER, Islamic theosophists such as Avicenna and al-Suhrawardi (see ISLAMIC ANGELOLOGY), and all the mystics from around the world whose works he knew so well.

Jung described the human psyche as a circular whole with four functions: thinking, sensing, feeling and intuiting. Most people have a preferred function, with at least one auxiliary. Hence the empiricist would mostly think about sensations; the theorist think about intuitions; the aesthete feel about intuitions; and the sensualist feel about sensations. While the clients who came to him for therapy varied widely in the balance of these functions, Jung had a general diagnosis for Western culture: It was overly dominant in its thinking function. Technological man had gained the whole world and lost his soul:

> At the end of the second millennium the outlines of a universal catastrophe became apparent, at first in the form of a threat to consciousness. This threat consists in giantism—in other words, a hubris of consciousness—in the assertion: "Nothing is greater than man and his deeds." The otherworldliness, the transcendence of the Christian myth was lost, and with it the view that wholeness is achieved in the other world. (*Memories, Dreams and Reflections* [*MDR*], 328)

In the context of the Judeo-Christian myth, Jung found the role of angels remarkable in their pointing to a disturbance on "the other side," that is, in the unconscious. He calls the fall of the angels

> a premature invasion of the human world by unconscious contents. The angels are a strange genus: they are precisely what they are and cannot be anything else. They are in themselves soulless beings who represent nothing but the thoughts and intuitions of their Lord. Angels who fall, then, are exclusively "bad" angels. These release the well-known effect of "inflation," which we can also observe nowadays in the megalomania of dictators; the angels beget with men *a race of giants* which ends by threatening to devour mankind, as is told in the Book of ENOCH.

The self-realization of God in human form, to rectify the situation, picks up for Jung the Old Testament and Gnostic idea of the divine marriage and its consequences; the possibility of "Christ within us" means that

> the unconscious wholeness penetrated into the psychic realm of inner experience, and man was made aware of all that

entered into his true configuration. This was a decisive step, not only for man, but also for the Creator—Who, in the eyes of those who had been delivered from darkness, cast off His dark qualities and became the *summum bonum*. (*MDR*, 328)

Jung saw the task of middle and later age as being the achievement of insight, wholeness, and spiritual depth, the rounding out of the psyche, which he called "the individuation process." If the conscious mind does not pay attention to the hints that the unconscious brings before it, the individuation process will continue.

The only difference is that we become its victims and are dragged along by fate towards that inescapable goal which we might have reached walking upright, if only we had taken the trouble and been patient enough to understand in time the meaning of the numina that cross our path. The only thing that really matters now is whether man can climb up to a higher moral level, to a higher plane of consciousness, in order to be equal to the superhuman powers which the fallen angels have played into his hands. But he can make no progress with himself unless he becomes very much better acquainted with his own nature. (*CW* 11, 746).

Unconscious wholeness therefore seems to me the true *spiritus rector* of all biological and psychic events. . . . Attainment of consciousness is culture in the broadest sense, and self-knowledge is therefore the heart and essence of this process. The Oriental attributes unquestionably divine significance to the self, and according to the ancient Christian view self-knowledge is the road to knowledge of God. (*MDR*, 325)

Jung's concept of the unconscious was much more elaborate than Freud's. There was a personal unconscious of dimmed memories and repressed materials; a transpersonal or collective unconscious at a deeper level, evidenced by emotions and visions erupting from its depth; and a fathomless part beyond. By "collective unconscious" Jung meant "the inherited possibility of psychical functioning . . . namely . . . the brain structure." This shared human heritage was quite unlike the dark chaos of impulse which Freud had posited. Jung's unconscious had a primordial structure and coherence, like a burial chamber of priceless antiques whose luster is revealed by the light of consciousness probing the darkness of the womb.

One cannot directly observe the unconscious mind, but persistent hints are given of its archetypal structure. For Jung, archetypes were primordial psychic processes transformed into images where consciousness can grasp them, but only elusively via symbol and metaphor.

The primordial images [archetypes] are the most ancient and the most universal "thought-forms" of humanity. They are as much feelings as thoughts; indeed, they lead their own independent life rather in the manner of part souls, as can easily be seen in those philosophical or Gnostic systems which rely on perception of the unconscious as the source of knowledge. The idea of angels, archangels, the "principalities and powers" of St. PAUL, the archons of the Gnostics, the heavenly hierarchy of Dionysius the Areopigate, all come from the perception of the relative autonomy of the archetypes. (*CW* 7, 104)

Jung quotes an alchemical lexicon's definition of *meditatio* as "an inner dialogue with someone unseen. It may be God,

when He is invoked, or with himself, or with his good angel." He continues: "The psychologist is familiar with this 'inner dialogue'; it is an essential part of the technique for coming to terms with the unconscious" (*CW* 12, 390). In another alchemical context, Jung says that

the angel, as a winged or spiritual being, represents, like Mercurius, the volatile substance, the pneuma, the disembodied. Spirit in alchemy almost invariably has a relation to water or to the radical moisture, a fact that may be explained simply by the empirical nature of the oldest form of "chemistry," namely the art of cooking. The steam arising . . . conveys the first vivid impression of "metasomatosis," the transformation of the corporeal into the incorporeal, into spirit or pneuma (*CW* 13, 101).

In short, the angel or spiritual being is an archetype who mediates and activates the spiritual inner power into the conscious being.

A striking example of an archetype that Jung calls "a symbol of the immortal self" is the Koranic figure Khidr, the "long-lived one" who is analogous to Elijah, Osiris, a Second Adam, a counselor. Jung tells of the headman of a safari he met in East Africa, a Somali raised in the Sufi faith. "To him Khidr was in every way a living person, and he assured me that I might at any time meet Khidr . . . in the street in the shape of a man, or he might appear to me during the night as a pure white light. . . ." The man had dreamed of Khidr and respectfully saluted him, and a few days later his wish for employment had been fulfilled. Jung says this shows how even in our own day, the archetype lives on in the religion of the people. "The position assigned to him by dogma [Surah 18] was, according to my Somali, that of *maleika kwanza-ya mungu*, 'First Angel of God,' a sort of 'Angel of the Face,' an *angelos* in the true sense of the word, a messenger" (*CW* 91, 250). (Compare INTELLIGENCES and ISLAMIC ANGELOLOGY.)

Jung suggests that the Holy Spirit/Angel Gabriel is within; the immortal self is being mediated by the archetypal figure of Khidr; this the Islamic theosophists would not deny. What they would call the divine mirroring of the angel Intelligence in the human imagination, Jung calls the accessing of the human unconscious through the primordial structures of archetype and myth. "Only here, in life on earth, where the opposites clash together, can the general level of consciousness be raised. That seems to be man's metaphysical task—which he cannot accomplish without 'mythologizing.' Myth is the natural and indispensable intermediate stage between unconscious and conscious cognition" (*MDR*, 311).

See also ARCHETYPES.

**Further reading:**

Guiley, Rosemary Ellen. *Harper's Encyclopedia of Mystical and Paranormal Experience.* San Francisco: HarperSanFrancisco, 1991.

Hoeller, Stephan A. *The Gnostic Jung and The Seven Sermons of the Dead.* Wheaton, Ill.: Quest Books, 1982.

Jung, Carl G. *Collected Works.* Ed. Sir Herbert Read. Trans. R. F. C. Hull. Princeton: Bollingen Series XX Vols, 1–20, 1958 ff.

Jung, Carl G. *Memories, Dreams and Reflections.* Ed. Aniela Jaffe, trans. Richard and Clara Winston. New York: Pantheon, 1961.

# K

**Kabbalah**   See JUDAIC ANGEOLOGY; MAGIC, ANGELS IN.

**kari-bu**   See CHOIRS; GUARDIAN ANGEL.

**Kelly, Edward**   See John DEE; MAGIC, ANGELS IN.

**Kemuel**   See ANGELS OF DESTRUCTION; MOSES.

**Leviathan** One of the demonic angels who is associated with the primordial deep of the seas. In rabbinic lore, Leviathan (a Hebrew name means "that which gathers itself together in folds") is associated with the RAHAB, angel of the sea. Leviathan is personified as an enormous whale who is impervious to all weapons.

In Job, Leviathan is a sea demon. In Jonah, Leviathan is a whale who swallows Jonah and keeps him in its belly for three days, until God orders Jonah to be vomitted up. In Isaiah, Leviathan is the "fleeing serpent" and "twisting serpent," "the dragon that is in sea," whom God will slay at the end of time (27:1).

Both Leviathan and BEHEMOTH were created on the fifth day.

**Lilith** In Jewish, Christian and Islamic mythology, Lilith is a winged female demon of the night who flies about searching for newborn children to kidnap or strangle, and sleeping men to seduce in order to produce demon sons.

Lilith evolved from Babylonian and perhaps Sumerian demonologies, which included male and female evil spirits that molested children. Lilith figures prominently in Jewish demonology.

Lilith has a female face, wings and long hair. She flies about at night with a horde of demons, using tens of thousands of names to disguise herself. She visits women in childbirth and sleeping men, from whose nocturnal emissions she creates her demon sons.

There are different versions of the story of how Lilith came into being. According to one, she encountered Adam after his split with Eve, and had sexual relations with him that produced the demon sons who fill the world. According to another version she was the first woman to have sexual relations with Adam, and thus was his wife. Lilith demanded equality with Adam, and failing to get it she left him in anger. She said the Ineffable Name of God and flew off into the air. Adam complained to God that his wife had deserted him. God then sent three angels, Sanvi, Sansanvi and Semangelaf (in some accounts, Snwy, Snswy and Smnglf), to bring Lilith back to Eden. The angels found her in the Red Sea, and threatened her with the loss of one hundred of her demon children every day unless she returned to Adam. She refused, and was punished accordingly. Lilith took revenge by launching a reign of terror against women in childbirth, newborn infants—particularly males—and men who slept alone. She was forced, however, to swear to the three angels that whenever she saw their names or images on an amulet, she would leave infants and mothers alone.

This story has Christian versions, in which the name of Lilith varies and the angels are replaced by the saints Sines, Sisinnios and Synodoros.

Another Kabbalistic story tells that Lilith became the bride of SAMAEL (SATAN). She will exist until the Messianic day, when God will cleanse evil from the face of the earth.

Various charms and amulets protected the vulnerable against her predations. Women in childbirth were protected by amulets bearing not only the names of the three angels but also their form, wings, hands and legs, which were affixed to all four walls of the birthing room. The incantation "To her that flies in rooms of darkness—pass quickly quickly Lil[ith]" was said to protect homes. New marriages were protected from Lilith by the tossing of four coins on the marriage bed and saying "Adam and Eve" and "Avaunt thee, Lilith!"

As late as the eighteenth century, it was a common practice in many countries to protect new mothers and infants with amulets against Lilith. Male infants were vulnerable for the first week of life; girls for the first three weeks. Sometimes a magic circle was drawn around the lying-in bed, with a charm inscribed with the names of the three angels, Adam and Eve, and the words "barring Lilith" or "protect this newborn child from all harm." Sometimes amulets with such inscriptions were placed in all corners of and throughout the bedchamber. If a child laughed in its sleep, it was a sign that Lilith was present. Tapping the child on the nose made the demon go away.

Men who had nocturnal emissions believed they had been seduced by Lilith during the night, and had to say incantations to prevent the offspring from becoming demons. Lilith was believed to be assisted by succubi in her bloodthirsty nocturnal quests, and these gathered with her near the "mountains of darkness" to frolic with Samael. The *Zohar* describes Lilith's powers as being at their height when the moon is on the wane.

Lilith also could be repelled by the saying of any of her numberless names. The basis for this comes from the story (probably Christian Byzantine in origin) about how the prophet Elijah confronted her as she was en route to attack a woman's newborn son, and "to give her the sleep of death, to take her son and drink his blood, to suck the marrow of his bones and to eat his flesh." Elijah forced her to reveal some of her names. Then he excommunicated her.

Lilith probably is related to the Judeo-Hellenistic demon Obizoth, who is repelled by an amulet bearing one of the mystical names of the archangel RAPHAEL.

According to Islamic mythology, her sexual relations with her infernal husband, IBLIS, created the demonic JINN.

Lilith-like demons appear in mythologies around the world. She also is associated with other characters in legend and myth, including the Queen of Sheba and Helen of Troy. In medieval Europe she often was portrayed as the wife, concubine or grandmother of Satan. In the late seventeenth century she was described as a screech owl (probably originating from a reference in Isaiah), blind by day, who sucked the breasts or navels of young children or the dugs of goats.

Some of Lilith's best-known names are:

Abeko, Abito, Abro, Abyzu, Ailo, Alu, Amiz, Amizo, Amizu, Ardad Lili, Avitu, Batna, Bituah, Eilo, Gallu, Gelou, Gilou, 'Ik, 'Ils, Ita, Izorpo, Kalee, Kali, Kakash, Kea, Kema, Kokos, Lamassu, Odom, Partasah, Partashah, Patrota, Petrota, Podo, Pods, Raphi, Satrina(h), Talto, Thiltho, Zahriel, Zefonith.

**Further reading:**
Davidson, Gustav. *A Dictionary of Angels*. New York: The Free Press, 1967.

Mercatante, Anthony S. *An Encyclopedia of World Mythology and Legend*. Frenchs Forest, Australia: Child & Associates Publishing, 1988.

Scholem, Gershom. *Kabbalah*. New York: Dorset Press, 1987. First published 1974.

**Lindbergh, Charles** (1902–1974)   The man who was first to fly solo nonstop across the Atlantic Ocean may have done so with the help of angels. On his flight from New York to Paris in 1927, Charles Lindbergh had profound mystical experiences, which he kept secret for twenty-six years. Lindbergh then revealed that vaporous beings had appeared to aid him; while he did not call them "angels," they can be interpreted as such.

Lindbergh did not mention his supernatural experiences in his first book about the flight, *We, Pilot and Plane*, published later in 1927. He did in *The Spirit of St. Louis*, published in 1953, and he discussed it again in *Autobiography of Values*, published posthumously in 1977. His reluctance reflects in part the prevailing lack of social acceptance of such experiences.

The historic flight took thirty-three and a half hours. As he related it, Lindbergh had to remain alert at all times; there was no such thing as automatic pilot, and to doze off at the controls meant certain death by plummeting into the ocean. At one point over the Atlantic, fatigue and tension altered Lindbergh's perception of reality. By the ninth hour, he felt both very detached from and very near to the world below, and it made him think of "the nearness of death" and "the longness of life."

Lindbergh slipped into an altered state of consciousness that to him seemed both wakefulness and sleep. He was conscious of being three elements: body, which was fatigued; mind, which made decisions; and spirit, a driving force that told him sleep was not needed, and that his body would be sustained through relaxation.

While he was in this twilight state, he became aware that the fuselage behind him was filled with ghostly presences that were humanlike but vaguely outlined, transparent and seemingly weightless. They did not appear suddenly. One moment, they were not present, another moment they were,

as if they had always been there. Lindbergh, who felt caught in some "unearthly age of time," was not surprised or afraid. In *The Spirit of St. Louis* he states:

> Without turning my head, I see them as clearly as though in my normal field of vision. There's no limit to my sight—my skull is one great eye, seeing everywhere at once.
>
> These phantoms speak with human voices—friendly, vaporlike shapes, without substance, able to vanish or appear at will, to pass in and out through the walls of the fuselage as though no walls were there. Now, many are crowded behind me. Now, only a few remain. First one and then another presses forward to my shoulder to speak above the engine's noise, and then draws back among the group behind. At times, voices come out of the air itself, clear yet far away, traveling through distances that can't be measured by the scale of human miles; familiar voices, conversing and advising on my flight, discussing problems of my navigation, reassuring me, giving me messages of importance unattainable in ordinary life.

The ability of the spirits to appear and disappear; their friendly demeanor and helpful advice; and their imparting of mystical wisdom "unattainable in ordinary life" are all characteristic of angelophanies, as well as encounters with other types of spirit beings. Lindbergh seemed to associate them, however, with the dead, for he often wondered whether he had crossed the boundary between life and death and was in the land of the dead.

As his altered state continued, Lindbergh felt weightless himself, independent of physical laws: "I'm almost one with these vaporlike forms behind me, less tangible than air, universal as aether. I'm still attached to life; they, not at all; but at any moment some thin band may snap and there'll be no difference between us."

Lindbergh also offers a description of the beings that makes them sound archetypal: "The spirits have no rigid bodies, yet they remain human in outline form—emanations from the experience of ages, inhabitants of a universe closed to mortal men. I'm on the borderline of life and a greater realm beyond, as though caught in the field of gravitation between two planets, acted on by forces I can't control, forces too weak to be measured by any means at my command, yet representing powers incomparably stronger than I've ever known."

Lindbergh acknowledged that at another time, these visions would would have startle him, but he felt so separated from earthly life that they seemed normal:

> [The] emissaries from a spirit world are neither intruders nor strangers. It's more like a gathering of family and friends after years of separation, as though I've known all of them before in some past incarnation. . . . They belong with the towering thunderheads and moonlit corridors of sky. . . . What strange connection exists between us? If they're so concerned with my welfare, why didn't they introduce themselves before?

Here again is another characteristic of an angelophany: the appearance of angels only at a moment of great need, and when the percipient is in an altered or receptive state of consciousness.

Says Lindbergh: "I live in the past, the present, and the future, here and in different places, all at once. Around me are old associations, bygone friendships, voices from ancestrally distant times."

If Lindbergh had lived in another era, he might have immediately interpreted the helping beings as angels. Instead, he struggled to place them in a context he could understand.

The experience changed his views about life after death. He said that death no longer seemed final, but rather the entrance to a "new and free existence which includes all space, all time."

**Further reading:**

Lindbergh, Charles. *The Spirit of St. Louis*. New York: Charles Scribner's Sons, 1953.

Murphy, Michael, and Rhea A. White, *The Psychic Side of Sports*. Reading, Mass.: Addison-Wesley, 1978.

**literature and angels**   Probably no theme in literature is more universal than "Know thyself." From Oedipus to Socrates through Hamlet and Faust, characters who act out the human quest for self-knowledge have dealings, real or metaphoric, with the gods, angels and demons, and spirits of every stripe. Indeed, song and story have consistently provided humanity with a zone of vicarious informative experience to help them cope with the "other side" (including the other side of oneself). The theme of human self-knowledge forever enacts a struggle between forces, sometimes good and evil, sometimes light and dark, but art provides a safer distance from which to examine their own experience. The epic sagas that have come down to us each "justify the ways of God to man," as John Milton's argument goes in *Paradise Lost*, sometimes complementing the religious and philosophical status quo and sometimes challenging it.

In the twentieth century the angelic and demonic applications for "knowing oneself" moved from the province of religion to that of psychology, a shift that Carl G. JUNG helped to facilitate. Archetypal psychology, led by James Hillman, finds poetry and narrative processes to be better analogies for the psyche than Freud's scientific model. Much modern literature and literary theory now occupies zones of interpretive relativity, but demonic and angelic imagery inherited from the ages still pervades the human psyche in cultures worldwide.

*EPIC PERSPECTIVE*

If the modern reader allows for a bit of leverage, all the gods and demigods of classical literature can be interpreted as angels of varying rank, especially as Greek mythology begins with a war in heaven, just as in Judaic legend. Further back, the Hindu *Ramayana* pits the avatar Rama against the demon Ravana. The most famous section of the *Mahabharata* is the *Bhagavad-Gita*, the "song of God," actually a conversation between Krishna, the charioteer, and Arjuna, the peerless Pandava archer, on the battlefield at Kurukshetra. Two intermarried families whose members are guided by certain gods or swayed by demonic beings have assembled to fight it out after many generations of strife and treachery, and Krishna briefs Arjuna on the cosmic situation before the conch shell blows to signify the battle's start.

Whereas Hindu and Greek myth allowed the gods to have intercourse and produce offspring with humans, the Judaic storyline eliminates these "abominations" with Noah's flood. (See SEX AND ANGELS.) Hindu and Buddhist deities are still very much alive in rituals today, including in parts of the epic *Gita* and the Sanskrit *sutras*, the oldest literature in the world. The members of the Greek pantheon and a few latecomers such as Dionysus are referred to, invoked, adored in hymns, and featured prominently in the works of Aeschylus, Sophocles and Euripides, the dialogues of Plato, the Homeric hymns, and of course the *Iliad* and the *Odyssey*.

The intervention of Apollo, Aphrodite, Ares, and Athena in the Trojan War, the arrival of Hermes or Iris with messages, appear to be similar to the comings and goings of the ANGEL OF THE LORD and GABRIEL in the Old and New Testaments. The plots of both the *Iliad* and the *Odyssey* are driven by rivalries among the gods; throughout the epics, intercessory actions of the gods abound. Whereas Athena is the special goddess who guides and protects Odysseus, Venus is the mother-guardian angel of Aeneas in Virgil's epic *The Aeneid*, with several appearances of the "messenger with wings," Mercury.

The *Aeneid*'s underworld provided DANTE ALIGHIERI with a working model for the Christian inferno he molded in his *Divina Commedia* in the early fourteenth century. Both *El Cid* and the *Chanson de Roland* invoke the Christian angels during their battles. The German *Nibelungenlied* (to be taken up in the nineteenth-century operas of Richard Wagner) with its fairies, nymphs, and demons, and the Anglo-Saxon *Beowulf* both convey folk cosmology before the advent of Christianity. *Beowulf* shows the dawning of a Christian revisioning of the local demonic "genii," as the Christlike heroes Beowulf and Wiglaf destroy Grendel and his mother. The epic romances of

**Angel offering inspiration (reprinted courtesy of U.S. Library of Congress)**

the Italian Renaissance by Vegio, Sannazaro, Vida and Tasso include interventions by the Christian archangels. Ariosto's early-sixteenth-century *Orlando Furioso* includes an irreverent treatment of Michael's assistance to the Christians in their battle against the Moors.

In English writings prior to JOHN MILTON's epic treatment of the fall of Adam and Eve in *Paradise Lost* and the redemption in *Paradise Regained*, Shakespeare's ghosts, witches and genii (Ariel and Caliban in *The Tempest*) are less interesting to angelology than Edmund Spenser's elaborate allegorical universe. In his *Faerie Queene* (1590), good and evil forces are cloaked in angelic and demonic symbolism derived from Celtic, Arthurian, Anglo-Saxon and French-Norman folklore; Catholic and Protestant politico-theology; and literary allusions from the classics, Dante and the Italian epic romance writers, especially Ariosto's *Orlando Furioso*.

Milton was steeped in the works of his fellow Calvinist, calling Spenser "my original," and "a better teacher than Scotus or Aquinas," since Spenser's mission as a poet was to embody moral lessons in beautiful imaginative forms, Milton's aspiration exactly. There is a striking analogy between Milton's interpretation of the struggle of forces involved in Adam's fall and the representation of virtue under trial in the person of Sir Guyon (*Faerie Queene*, Book II). Both advocate temperance, interpreted in light of Platonic ethics as the supremacy of the rational over the passionate principle in the soul. Spenser's *Fowre Hymns* ("Of Heavenly Love" and "Of Heavenly Beautie") are spectacular cosmic visions going beyond the common stock of ancient, medieval, and Renaissance philosophy, invoking Platonic Ideas and INTELLIGENCES and the nine choirs of angels (Hymn 4). "Love, lift me up upon thy golden wings,/ From this base world unto thy heaven's height,/ Where I may see those admirable things/ Which there thou workest by thy sovereign might (Hymn 3)." The "Mutabilitie Cantos" of the *Faerie Queene* (Book VII, Cantos 6 and 7) present an elevated parallelism between physical nature, human nature, and Heaven, complete with Spenserian versions of the Greek pantheon.

Several lesser-known English religious epic poets, known as "Spenserians," also influenced Milton, namely Giles and Phineas Fletcher. Phineas Fletcher's *Apollyonists*, and its Latin counterpart *Locustae*, include a representation of Satan as a majestic and defiant being. The theme of Giles Fletcher's *Christ's Victory in Heaven* is the same as that of Book III of *Paradise Lost*, except that Milton places the heavenly debate over man's fate into the mouths of the Father and the Son.

### LYRIC POETRY

Although angels receive recognition, along with Mary and the other saints, in medieval and Renaissance court and folk lyrics, some seventeenth- and eighteenth-century English poets reached truly celestial heights in image and melody (see MUSIC AND ANGELS). Milton's youthful lyric "On the Morning of Christ's Nativity" (1645) and mature "At a Solemn Music" (1673) both aspire to recreate the music and magic of the angelic presence. "Ring out ye Crystall spheres,/Once bless our human ears,/ (If ye have power to touch our senses so)/ And let your silver chime/ Move in melodious time;/ And let the Base of Heav'ns deep Organ blow,/ And with your ninefold harmony/ Make up full consort to the Angelic symphony" ("Nativity" 24–33). "O may we soon again renew the Song,/ And keep in tune with Heav'n, till God ere long/ To his celestial consort us unite,/ To live with him, and sing in endless morn of light" ("Solemn Musick" 40–44).

Milton's Catholic contemporary Richard Crashaw (1612–1649) wrote two famous lyrics celebrating angels. "Musick's Duell" parallels a lute player's song with the angelic music of the spheres. "In the Holy Nativity" the shepherds sing of their vision of the angels. Crashaw also wrote two poems about St. Teresa of Avila's visionary experiences. "The Flaming Heart" attempts to recapture the saint's visitation by a Seraphim: "O sweet incendiary! . . . By all thy dower of Lights and Fires;/ By all the eagle in thee, all the dove . . . /By all thy brim-fill'd bowls of fierce desire/ By thy last Morning's draught of liquid fire. . . ."

Several of the metaphysical poets have left us unique angelic poems. In George Herbert's "Easter Wings" the verses actually form wings. John Donne's "The Dream" brings celestial qualities to the bed of lovers, and "The Relique" refers to the asexuality of the lovers' guardian angels. Donne's "Anniversary Poems," on the death of a young girl, survey the upper and lower realms and find her soul to be so pure that she has "Tutelar Angels" assigned to each of her limbs (Second Anniversary, 43–45). In "Holy Sonnet 5" Donne says "I am a little world made cunningly/ Of Elements and an Angelike spright" and in "Holy Sonnet 7" he cries "At the round earth's imagin'd corners, blow/ Your trumpets, Angels. . . ." Thomas Traherne's "Wonder" recounts heaven from the point of view of a soul: "How like an Angel came I down!" Henry Vaughan's "The Retreate," "Peace," and especially "The World" convey the elevated consciousness of a mystical partnership with angels.

John Dryden's "Ode in Honour of St. Cecilia's Day" is a symphonic gathering of classical and Christian images relating to music in praise of the patron saint of music. He repeats "He [the old pagan musical god] rais'd a Mortal to the Skies;/ She [St. Cecilia] drew an Angel down."

With the Romantic poets of Germany, France, Italy and England, another wave of mythological symbolism and supernatural, magical and mystical experiences was layered into literature, with otherworldly beings galore. For the scientifically informed Percy Bysshe Shelley, angels of every rank, nymphs, demons, vampires and the like, symbolized not only themselves but also emotions, psychic forces, and even physical forces. A recursive loop back to classical mythology, refigured by the romantic sensual drive and mystical bent, was the preoccupation of many poets such as Friedrich Holderlin in *Hyperion*, John Keats in *Hyperion* and *Endymion*, Shelley in *Prometheus Unbound* and legions of others. After all, in those days a good education still covered the Greek and Latin classics.

Shelley was haunted "by the awful shadow of some unseen Power," passionately convinced of the living presence of "that Light whose smile kindles the universe," and he asserted an intimate relationship between this "interfused and over-ruling Spirit" and the souls of individual human beings. Man does not have to stand alone. "I vowed that I would dedicate my powers/ to thee and thine. . . ." The "phantoms of a thousand hours" are called upon to bear witness "that never joy illumed my brow/ Unlinked with hope that thou wouldst free/ This world from its dark slavery" ("Hymn to Intellectual Beauty").

Byron's verse drama *Cain* was one of many Romantic works that reapproached the topic; good and evil, in this case via the characters the ANGEL OF THE LORD and LUCIFER. Another work of Byron's, "Heaven and Earth," is a "mystery" based on Genesis 6:2 (see SONS OF GOD and SEX AND ANGELS), with Samuel Taylor Coleridge's line from "Kubla Khan" used as an epigraph: "And woman wailing for her demon lover," a theme which Coleridge might have treated fully had he developed the fragmentary "Christabel," and which Keats did develop in "La Belle Dame Sans Merci." Commenting on this theme in Byron, Jung said: "as a power which transcends consciousness the libido is by nature daemonic; it is both God and devil." (See also ABRAXAS.)

Coleridge intended to write a critical essay on the supernatural as a preface to *The Rime of the Ancient Mariner*, but he did not leave one. William Wordsworth and Coleridge's plan for the *Lyrical Ballads* (1798; second ed. 1800) was to treat of natural and supernatural experiences, with Coleridge covering the latter. In *Biographia Literaria*, Chapter XIV, Coleridge speaks of this project and states that his objective was "to transfer from our inward nature a human interest and a semblance of truth sufficient to procure for these shadows of imagination that willing suspension of disbelief for the moment, which constitutes poetic faith." The *Rime* certainly achieved that purpose, with demonic figures of Life in Death, tutelary spirits of the oceans, and much more. His gloss specifies that when the bodies of the mariners come to life again, it happens not by the souls of the men, not by daemons of earth or middle air, but by a blessed troop of angelic spirits, sent down by the invocation of their guardian saints." Coleridge's translation of Burnet's *Archaeologiae Philosophicae* provides a nice credo for the Western intellectual with an open imagination: "I easily believe that there are more invisible Natures than visible ones in the universe. But who will explain to us the rank, relations, characteristics and powers of each? What do they do? Where do they live? The human mind has always circled around the knowledge of these things, but never achieved it."

### VISIONARY LITERATURE

Yet hundreds of poets, saints and mystics, Taoist, Buddhist, Islamic and Hindu, as well as tribal visionaries, have in fact achieved and recorded such knowledge. The Koran was dictated to Muhammad by GABRIEL, according to legend. The visionary recitals of Ibn Sina, Ibn Arabi, al-Suhrawardi and others purport to have been literally recited to them by angels (see ISLAMIC ANGELOLOGY). Native American shaman Black Elk's vision at age nine, as recorded at the end of his life, was two angelic figures who showed him the shaman's world. The works of Rumi, Kabir, Sri Aurobindo, Rabindranath Tagore, William BLAKE, William Butler Yeats and his friend A.E. (George William Russell) reveal a familiarity with multiple worlds and beings.

In the West, Gnostic and Hermetic lore is believed by some to have been preserved in the Grail cycle, a series of medieval and Renaissance documents set in a magic time and place, the spiritual Britain. In the introduction to his Grail Romance, Robert de Boron claims that the work was given to him by the Angel of the Lord. The book then vanished. In order to find it again he journeyed through the Angelic World and followed the Questing Beast through a visionary landscape.

To a certain extent, all good poets have some visionary/intuitive capacity, and all of the great ones possess an integration of language, inner vision and energy, which they may or may not attribute to angels or higher beings. Probably Yeats and Blake are the best exemplars of this capacity in the English language, and Goethe and Rainer Maria Rilke in German (see GOETHE). Rilke's *Duino Elegies*, extraordinary poems even in translation, are about the human longing for transcendence and use angels as their unifying symbol. When a friend tried to persuade Rilke to undergo psychotherapy, he wrote back: "I am afraid it would exorcise my angels along with my demons."

**Further reading:**
Chessman, Harriett Scott, ed. *Literary Angels*. New York: Fawcett Columbine, 1994.
Hillman, James. *Archetypal Psychology*. Dallas, Texas: Spring Publications, 1983.
Greene, Thomas. *The Descent from Heaven: A Study of Epic Continuity*. New Haven: Yale University Press, 1963.
Sugg, Richard P., ed. *Jungian Literary Criticism*. Evanston, Ill.: Northwestern University Press, 1992.
Wilson, Peter Lamborn. *Angels*. New York: Pantheon Books, 1980.

**loa**   See ORISHAS.

**Lot**   See SODOM AND GOMORRAH.

**Lucifer**   Angel erroneously equated with SATAN. The name means "bearer of light" or "bearer of fire," "Son of the Morning" or "Morning Star." In Hebrew, Lucifer is Helel ben Sahar: "Bright Son of the Morning." Rabbinical literature of the fourth and fifth centuries C.E. describes him as SAMAEL, the highest of those angels around the throne of God and created above the seraphim. He was distinguished from all his other angelic brethren by possessing twelve wings.

There is only one reference to Lucifer in the Bible, in Isaiah 14:12–15: "How you are fallen from heaven, O Day Star, son of Dawn! How you are cut down to the ground, you who laid the nations low! You said in your heart, 'I will ascend to heaven; above the stars of God I will set my throne on high; I will sit on the mount of assembly in the far north; I will ascend above the heights of the clouds, I will make myself like the Most High.' But you are brought down to Sheol [the underworld], to the depths of the Pit."

The Old Testament writers did not distinguish fallen angels from other angels; *satan* was a common noun used to denote an adversary. But St. Jerome, one of the church fathers (c. 347–420) identified the Isaiah passage with Satan, the leader of the fallen angels. From that time on "Lucifer" became one of the names of the Devil. The identification was further reinforced by John MILTON who made Lucifer the protagonist of *Paradise Lost*.

The eighteenth-century mystic Emanuel SWEDENBORG denied the existence of any Satan or demon. He attributed all power to the Divine True and Good, or the Lord, and claimed that there was no controlling devil responsible for hell. He said that while a literal reading of Scripture seemed to tell the story of Lucifer's fall, in reality "devil" and "Satan" simply mean hell, the place of evil and falsehood chose by those who go down the path of self-love and lack of charity. For Swedenborg, "Lucifer" meant "people from Babylon."

**Further reading:**
Every, George. *Christian Mythology*. London: The Hamlyn Publishing Group Ltd., 1970.
Swedenborg, Emanuel. *Heaven and Hell*. Trans. George F. Dole. New York: Swedenborg Foundation Inc., 1976.
Turner, Alice K. *The History of Hell*. New York: Harcourt Brace & Co., 1993.

**Luther, Martin**    See PROTESTANT ANGELOLOGY.

**Maclean, Dorothy** (1920– ) A founder of FINDHORN, whose mediumistic abilities enabled her to communicate with angels and devas. Maclean relayed the beings' instructions for growing unusual produce in a harsh Scottish climate, and also spread their teachings about humankind's co-creative relationship with the spirit world.

Dorothy Maclean was born on January 8, 1920, in Guelph, a small town in Ontario, Canada. She had no particular psychic gifts as a child; these were to develop in adulthood through years of spiritual study and practice.

Maclean studied business at the University of Western Ontario, and after graduation in 1940 became a secretary for the British Intelligence Service. Her work took her from Toronto to New York City, and she was chaperoned by the woman who was to become her spiritual mentor, Sheena Govan, a Quaker whose parents had founded an evangelical movement, the Faith Mission. Maclean's job eventually took her to Panama, South America and England. In Panama she met an Englishman, John Wood, also working for the intelligence service. Though he was distant and somewhat secretive about himself, Maclean felt compelled to accept his proposal of marriage. After they were married, she discovered that John followed Sufi teachings. She became immersed in the study and practice of these herself, as well as other philosophies practiced by other spiritual groups, particularly after the couple moved to England.

Through these studies, Maclean learned to develop her spiritual attunement to the still center within, and to practice telepathic communication with people around the world. Govan taught her about unconditional love, and Sufi teachings taught her about "love in action," or seeking to do everything in life with purity of heart for the greater glory of God.

The marriage was emotionally unsustaining, and Maclean began to see that her best course of action would be to express an unconditional love for Wood and set him free. She focused a great deal of energy on achieving that state. One day she suddenly had her first awareness of the God within. It changed her life, and set the stage for her subsequent experiences at Findhorn.

Maclean also was influenced by Govan, who had a substantial following in the United Kingdom. Govan introduced Maclean to many people, including Peter and Eileen Caddy, with whom Maclean would later establish Findhorn. Peter Caddy, a Royal Air Force officer, was steeped in Rosicrucianism and its teachings on the power of positive thought. He had been married to Govan for five years; Govan had terminated the marriage, but they retained a close relationship.

Dorothy Maclean (reprinted courtesy of Dorothy Maclean)

After her divorce from Wood, Maclean worked as a secretary on Fleet Street in London. She began to get inner promptings to write down her inspirations. She showed these to Govan, who recognized her budding mediumistic gifts and encouraged her to develop them by channeling spiritual messages for others. Following Govan's guidance, Maclean quit her secretarial work to live "according to God's will." She worked as a kitchen maid and then as a mother's helper—a most humbling change, but one that taught her to trust that she would be led to do what God intended her to do.

Scandal struck Govan when publicity arose over news that a man had left his family to be with her. The press in Scotland hounded Govan's group, whom they dubbed "the Nameless Ones" because the group had no name. The group disbanded.

Maclean joined up with the Caddys in Glasgow. They spent six years working at the Cluny Hill Hotel, a Victorian resort open only during the summer. Maclean served as secretary and receptionist. The hotel flourished, and the Caddys and Maclean spent their spare time working on spiritual attunement and telepathically communicating around the world in the "Network of Light," a loose collection of people who shared similar spiritual ideals and who had telepathic abilities. They also communicated with "space beings," who said they were alien beings from elsewhere in the universe, and with the "Masters of the Seven Rays," who were highly developed humans who had undertaken to aid humanity in its spiritual quest.

Maclean and the Caddys moved to another hotel in Scotland but could not repeat their success—they were fired in 1962. Their only recourse was to band together four miles away at Findhorn, a small fishing village located on an inhospitable strip of the north Scottish coast, where the Caddys lived in a caravan with their three children. The Caddys and Maclean scraped out a living. Peter began to cultivate a garden, with mixed success.

In May 1963, Maclean, in her daily meditation, received an unusual message about the "forces of Nature." She learned that one of her jobs was to attune and harmonize with those forces, who would be friendly in their greeting to her. Peter interpreted this as meaning that she could receive guidance from Nature on what to do in the garden. This was immediately affirmed in her next meditation, with the following message, told in Maclean's autobiography *To Hear the Angels Sing*.

> Yes, you can cooperate in the garden. Begin by thinking about the nature spirits, the higher overlighting nature spirits, and tune into them. That will be so unusual as to draw their interest here. They will be overjoyed to find some members of the human race eager for their help.
>
> By the the higher nature spirits I mean the spirits of differing physical forms such as clouds, rain, vegetables. The smaller individual nature spirits are under their jurisdiction. In the new world to come these realms will be open to humans—or should I say, humans will be open to them. Just be open and seek into the glorious realms of Nature with sympathy and understanding, knowing that these beings are of the Light, willing to help but suspicious of humans and on the lookout for the false. Keep with me and they will not find it, and you will all build towards the new.

Maclean did as instructed, and so began a long and fruitful relationship with the angelic and devic kingdoms. The first nature spirit to come into her awareness was what she called the "Pea Deva," which she described as holding the archetypal pattern in place for all the peas in the world. Her primary contact was the "Landscape Angel," who acted as control and had a broad, holistic outlook. The Landscape Angel often facilitated communication with other beings. All communications were on the inner planes.

Initially Maclean did not know what to call the beings with whom she came in contact. She thought them to be angels, but to her the term "angel" conjured up hackneyed religious and pop-culture images. These beings seemed too glorious. She settled on the term "deva," though in talking about them she used the terms "angel," "deva," and "nature spirit" interchangeably. Later in life she felt that "angel" better expressed the beings she experienced.

With the advice of the devas (Maclean's favored term during her Findhorn years), Peter's garden grew lush and robust. They produced bumper crops of produce, some of fantastical size, which they sold in the local community. Agricultural experts, who examined the produce and the soil, could not explain their success. When they began to publicly acknowledge their spiritual help others were attracted to Findhorn, and they established a spiritual colony. After a couple of years Peter no longer needed angelic messages, but had learned enough from them to work the garden. Maclean worked in the office and continued to receive varied messages from the devas, expanding her own consciousness. She was able to contact the devas of animals, stones and inanimate objects ("machine devas").

Maclean left Findhorn in 1973, and commenced work as a writer and lecturer. She settled for a time in the High Sierras of California to work on her autobiography. She joined up with about fifteen other Findhorn veterans, including mystic David Spangler. They called themselves the Lorian Association, and lived for a while in the San Francisco Bay area. They offered public performances of talks, songs and dance drawn from their Findhorn experiences.

In 1976, Maclean returned to Canada and lived in Toronto for eight years. She then moved to Issaquah, Washington, near Seattle, where Spangler and other members of the Lorian Association had moved. She occasionally revisits Findhorn to deliver workshops and lectures.

After returning to North America, Maclean began to attune to angels of cities and countries (see PSEUDO-DIONYSIUS). These experiences gave her insights into the characters and group destinities of collections of humans.

Her autobiography, *To Hear the Angels Sing*, was published in 1980. In it, Maclean acknowledges the uncertainties and doubts that accompanied her experiences with the angelic realm. At Findhorn she often feared that she would pose the wrong questions on behalf of Peter, or not get the information straight. Sometimes she was skeptical of her own abilities and results, and worried that others would think her strange.

Nonetheless, Maclean's own spiritual understanding deepened tremendously due to her Findhorn experiences, and she passed this wisdom on to others. She provided a unique look into the workings of the angelic and devic kingdoms. Though she was by no means the first to have extensive contact with these realms, she was able to gain a large public platform thanks to the success and popularity of Findhorn.

Maclean realized that to attune to angels and devas is to attune to one's own higher self, the God-essence that dwells within each soul. Finding the God within is the important achievement, she said; angels are a subsidiary part of that attunement. She acknowledged that all perceptions received are colored by the recipient, in terms of beliefs, biases, vocabulary, the subconscious and other factors.

Maclean described devas as "the builders of our world. Embodiments of creative intelligence, they wield or transmute what we might call energy (vibrating waves or particles in patterns) into increasingly more 'physical' structures (including emotional and mental structures) and finally into what we call matter (which is pattern in space). They build vehicles for the expression of life on all levels: mineral, vegetable, animal, human and suprahuman." The beings she encountered were not small in relative stature, as one might think of fairies and elves; some, she said, were awesome beings whose scope stretched into the infinite universe. Her primary contacts were the overlighting angels/devas of a species, rather than the spirits that tend to individual life-forms.

The devas told Maclean to think of plant life in terms of light and of vital patterns of energy. She learned that everything can be viewed in the same way—including humans. The devas hold these patterns in place so that form can manifest. According to Maclean, the devas do their work with joy and love, despite the counterproductive acts of humankind that destroy their work. They are wary of humans, but most seem willing to help if a sincere plea is put to them. Humans, they said, must be the ones to initiate contact with their realms, and then they will respond. They said that frequently humans enter the devic realms without knowing it, for fleeting moments. Such occasions are walks in nature, for example, where one is suddenly uplifted with euphoric feelings.

The devas also told Maclean that human beings ultimately have greater powers than they, but also more limitations, the latter being imposed by our destructive thoughts and ways. Humans cannot access their true powers of creativity because they have cut themselves off from the divine source of power, God. The devas emphasized the need to approach everything from the standpoint of love, which opens one to knowledge of the unity of all things.

Maclean said that through her contact with the angelic/devic realms she was able to unify her higher and lower selves into a wholeness. She connected with the God-source within, and learned that humans can truly create their own reality in a joyous partnership not only with each other but with the higher realms as well.

**Further reading:**
Hawken, Paul. *The Magic of Findhorn*. New York: Bantam Books, 1976.
Maclean, Dorothy. *To Hear the Angels Sing*. Hudson, N.Y.: Lindisfarne Press, 1990. First published by Lorian Press, 1980. Second ed. by Morningtown Press, 1988.

**magic, angels in**   The invocation of both good and evil angels plays a prominent role in the Western tradition of ceremonial magic. Important uses of the names of angels are as the inscription of names on amulets, and the speaking of names so as to invoke angels or the qualities they represent.

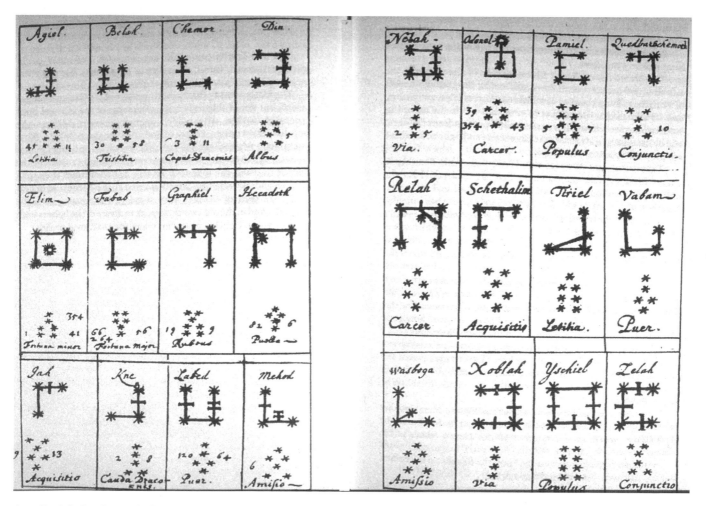

**Angelic alphabet for magical purposes**

Magic is the harnessing of supernatural powers and beings, such as angels and demons, and the powers of nature, to effect change in the physical world. Some paths of ceremonial magic work for inner, i.e., spiritual change. The harnessing is accomplished through ritual that expands consciousness and directs the will.

The term magic derives from the Greek *magus*, which means "sorcerer." Many systems of magic exist, each with its own procedures, rules and proscriptions. Magic is neither "white" nor black," but reflects the intent of the magician.

Anthropologist Bronislaw Malinowski defined magic as having three functions and three elements. The functions are to produce, protect and destroy; the elements are spells or incantations, rites or procedures, and the altered state of the magician. Altered states are accomplished through fasting, meditating, chanting, visualizing symbols, sleep deprivation, dancing, staring into flames, inhaling fumes, taking drugs, etc.

In the Western tradition, the Greeks developed two systems of magic, low and high. Low magic was the sorcery of spells and potions provided for a fee. This acquired an unsavory reputation for fraud by the fifth century B.C.E. High magic involved working with spirits, and was esteemed much like religion.

With the Christianization of Europe, low magic began to be persecuted as witchcraft. High magic, a mix of Hermetic and Kabbalistic lore, flourished in the Middle Ages and Renaissance, probably as a reaction against the growing power of the Church-state, which proscribed all magic outside the bounds of religious miracles. Magic was discredited by the scientific revolution of the seventeenth century, but interest was revived in the nineteenth century by occultists such as Francis Barrett and Eliphas Levi, whose respective works *The Magus* (1801) and *Dogma and Ritual of High Magic* (1856) were influential.

The effects of dualism on magic can be seen by the twelfth century. Prior to that it would have been difficult to distinguish many magical rituals from religious rituals. With the growth of dualism, the distinction between good and evil spirits affected magic, the magician's view of the spirit world, and the external world's view of magic in general. Now everything in the cosmos was governed not just by a spirit, but by a good spirit and an evil spirit.

While magic is worked through ritual, merely going through the motions is not effective. An initiate learns how to develop great powers of concentration and visualization and to acquire knowledge of the natural forces of the universe, the ability to enter into controlled altered states of consciousness, and the ability to direct the will toward a goal. This internal power is channeled through ritual and through the use of magical implements and invocations. The use of "names of power," or names of specific spirits, releases powerful vibrations that open the door between the physical realm and the realm of the spirits, enabling the magician to cross over, or to communicate with spirits. (See NAMES OF ANGELS.)

### ANGELS IN KABBALISTIC MAGIC
The manipulation of the physical and spiritual worlds through use of the names of God and of angels is particularly important in kabbalistic magic. The Kabbalah does not expressly forbid magic but various kabbalistic writings warn of the dangers of it, and state that only the most virtuous persons should perform magic, and do so only in times of public emergency and need, never for private gain. How strictly these admonitions were followed is uncertain, as an extensive literature exists on what is called the "practical Kabbalah," an important source to Western magic in general. The practical Kabbalah evolved from about the fourteenth century onward, reaching a peak in the Renaissance. A master of practical Kabbalah was called a *ba'al shem* ("master of the name") and was adept at making amulets, invoking angels or demons, and exorcising evil spirits.

Practical Kabbalah is complex; its relationship to angels includes the use of many angelic alphabets, secret codes of communication whose mythical origin is probably the *Book of Raziel* (see RAZIEL). The earliest such language is the "alphabet of METRATON." Other alphabets are attributed to MICHAEL, GABRIEL, RAPHAEL and other angels. In form some resemble cuneiform, while others are related to early Hebrew or Samaritan script. They are called "eye writing" in kabbalistic literature, because the letters are formed by means of lines and circles resembling eyes. Such letters are found on amulets and in texts. Divine names, such as the names of God and of angels, have many functions, including the evocation of automatic writing for revelation.

So-called "black magic" is called "apocryphal science" in the Kabbalah. It is strictly forbidden, and only theoretical knowledge is permitted. According to the *Zohar*, those who choose to practice it become sorcerers who journey to the "mountains of darkness" where live the fallen angels Aza and AZAEL, to study under a sorcerer-witch. In the Bible, the archetypal sorcerer is Balaam.

Regardless of the type of magic practices, the granting of visions (*giluy einayim*) as a result of it is considered to be a rare phenomenon. One vision might be the ability to perceive angelic eye-writing, which constitutes the invisible letters spelling out secret thoughts and deeds and hovers over the head of every person. Adepts also may see haloes around the heads of the righteous, the brief appearance of the Tetragrammaton (YHVH, the unspeakable name of God) in fiery letters, and visions of angels. The latter are explained in this way: The angel's form is imprinted on the ether. Seeing an angel is considered to be a reward for one's having purified the corporeal body. Sorcerers who deal with demons have comparable experiences with the fallen angels.

See John DEE.

**Further reading:**
Cavendish, Richard. *The Black Arts*. New York: Perigee Books, 1967.
Guiley, Rosemary Ellen. *The Encyclopedia of Witches and Witchcraft*. New York: Facts On File, 1989.
McLean, Adam (ed.). *A Treatise on Angel Magic*. Grand Rapids, Mich.: Phanes Press, 1990.
Scholem, Gershom. *Kabbalah*. New York: Dorset Press, 1987. First published 1974.

**Maimonides**   See JUDAIC ANGELOLOGY.

**mansions of the moon**   In occult lore and magic, the moon is accorded twenty-eight mansions, or spheres of influence, based upon its twenty-eight-day cycle of phases.

Each mansion is governed by an angel, has positive or negative influences over certain activities, and is ascribed talismans for working specific kinds of magical spells. In magical ritual, the magician calls upon the appropriate ruling angel of the mansion involved to help effect the spell.

The mansions of the moon are fixed in the eighth sphere of heaven. As the moon wanders the sky, it obtains the powers and virtues of the signs of the Zodiac and the stars contained in them. Each mansion measures twelve degrees, fifty-one minutes and nearly twenty-six seconds, according to the Kabbalists.

The mansions, their names, their ruling angels, their zodiac signs, and their influences are as follows:

**First Mansion**
*Name*: Alnath (horns of Aries)
*Angel*: Geniel
*Zodiac sign*: Aries
*Influences*: Causes prosperous journeys; creates discords; helps in the giving of medicines, especially laxatives

**Second Mansion**
*Name*: Allothaim or Albochan (belly of Aries)
*Angel*: Enediel
*Zodiac sign*: Aries
*Influences*: Helps in the finding of treasures and the holding of captives; aids voyages, sowing and planting; hinders purging and vomiting

**Third Mansion**
*Name*: Alchaomazon or Athoray (showering or Pleiades)
*Angel*: Anixiel
*Zodiac sign*: Aries
*Influences*: Profitable to sailors, hunters and alchemists

**Fourth Mansion**
*Name*: Aldebaram or Aldelamen (eye or head of Taurus)
*Angel*: Azariel
*Zodiac sign*: Taurus
*Influences*: Causes the destruction and hindrances of buildings, fountains, wells, gold mines and the flight of creeping things (insects), and begets discord

**Fifth Mansion**
*Name*: Alchatay or Albachay
*Angel*: Gabriel
*Zodiac sign*: Taurus
*Influences*: Helps the return from a journey and the instruction of scholars; confirms edifices; gives health and goodwill to persons of quality

**Sixth Mansion**
*Name*: Athanna or Alchaya (little star of great light)
*Angel*: Dirachiel
*Zodiac sign*: Gemini
*Influences*: Helps hunting, the besieging of towns and the revenge of princes; destroys harvests and fruits, hinders the operations of physicians

**Seventh Mansion**
*Name*: Aldimiach or Alazarch (arm of Gemini)
*Angel*: Schliel
*Zodiac sign*: Gemini
*Influences*: Confirms gain and friendship, is profitable to lovers, destroys magistracies

**Eighth Mansion**
*Name*: Alnaza or Anatrachya (misty or cloudy)
*Angel*: Amnediel
*Zodiac sign*: Cancer
*Influences*: Causes love, friendship and the society of fellow travelers; drives away mice, afflicts captives and confirms their imprisonment

**Ninth Mansion**
*Name*: Archaam or Arcaph (eye of the Lion)
*Angel*: Barbiel
*Zodiac sign*: Cancer-Leo
*Influences*: Hinders harvest and travelers, puts discord between humans

**Tenth Mansion**
*Name*: Algelioche or Albegh (neck or forehead of the Lion)
*Angel*: Ardifiel
*Zodiac sign*: Leo
*Influences*: Strengthens buildings, promotes love and benevolence, helps against enemies

**Eleventh Mansion**
*Name*: Azobra or Ardaf (hair of the Lion's head)
*Angel*: Neciel
*Zodiac sign*: Leo
*Influences*: Good for voyages, gain by merchandise and redemption of captives

**Twelfth Mansion**
*Name*: Alzarpha or Azarpha (tail of the Lion)
*Angel*: Abdizuel
*Zodiac sign*: Leo
*Influences*: Gives prosperity to harvests and plantations, is good for the bettering of servants, captives and companions; hinders seamen

**Thirteenth Mansion**
*Name*: Alhaire (Dog stars, or wings of Virgo)
*Angel*: Jazeriel
*Zodiac sign*: Virgo
*Influences*: Aids benevolence, gain, voyages, harvests and freedom of captives

**Fourteenth Mansion**
*Name*: Alchureth or Arimet, Azimeth, Althumech or Alcheymech (spike of Virgo)
*Angel*: Ergediel
*Zodiac sign*: Virgo
*Influences*: Causes the love of married folk; cures the sick; is profitable to sailors; hinders journeys by land

**Fifteenth Mansion**
*Name*: Agrapha or Algrapha (covered or covered flying)
*Angel*: Atliel
*Zodiac sign*: Libra
*Influences*: Helps in the extracting of treasures and the digging of pits; assists in divorce, discord and the destruction of houses and enemies; hinders travelers

**Sixteenth Mansion**
*Name*: Azubene or Ahubene (horns of Scorpio)
*Angel*: Azeruel
*Zodiac sign*: Scorpio
*Influences*: Hinders journeys, wedlock, harvest and merchandise; prevails for redemption of captives

**Seventeenth House**
*Name*: Alchil (crown of Scorpio)
*Angel*: Adriel
*Zodiac sign*: Scorpio
*Influences*: Betters a bad fortune; makes love durable; strengthens buildings; helps seamen

**Eighteenth Mansion**
*Name*: Alchas or Altob (heart of Scorpio)
*Angel*: Egibiel
*Zodiac sign*: Scorpio
*Influences*: Causes discord, sedition, conspiracy against princes and mighty ones and revenge from enemies; frees captives; helps edifices

**Nineteenth Mansion**
*Name*: Allatha or Achala (tail of Scorpio)
*Angel*: Amutiel
*Zodiac sign*: Scorpio
*Influences*: Helps in the besieging of cities, the taking of towns, the driving of humans from their places, the destruction of seamen and the perdition of captives

**Twentieth Mansion**
*Name*: Abnahaya (a beam)
*Angel*: Kyriel
*Zodiac sign*: Sagittarius
*Influences*: Helps in the taming of wild beasts and the strengthening of prisons; destroys the wealth of societies; compels a person to come to a certain place

**Twenty-first Mansion**
*Name*: Abeda or Albedach (a desert)
*Angel*: Bethnael
*Zodiac sign*: Capricorn
*Influences*: Good for harvest, gain, buildings and travelers; causes divorce

**Twenty-second Mansion**
*Name*: Sadahacha, Zodeboluch or Zandeldena (a pastor)
*Angel*: Geliel
*Zodiac sign*: Capricorn
*Influences*: Promotes the flight of servants and captives in their escape; helps the curing of diseases

**Twenty-third Mansion**
*Name*: Zabadola or Zobrach (swallowing)
*Angel*: Requiel
*Zodiac sign*: Capricorn
*Influences*: Helps divorce, the liberty of captives; promotes health to the sick

**Twenty-fourth Mansion**
*Name*: Sadabath or Chadezoad (star of fortune)
*Angel*: Abrinael
*Zodiac sign*: Aquarius
*Influences*: Aids the benevolence of married people and the victory of soldiers; hurts the execution of government and prevents its being exercised

**Twenty-fifth Mansion**
*Name*: Sadalabra or Sadalachia (butterfly or spreading forth)
*Angel*: Aziel
*Zodiac sign*: Aquarius
*Influences*: Favors besieging and revenge; destroys enemies; causes divorce; confirms prisons and buildings; hastens

messengers; conduces to spells against copulation; binds a human being so that he or she cannot perform a duty

**Twenty-sixth Mansion**
*Name*: Alpharg or Phragal Mocaden (first drawing)
*Angel*: Tagriel
*Zodiac sign*: Aquarius–Pisces
*Influence*: Causes union and the health of captives; destroys buildings and prisons

**Twenty-seventh Mansion**
*Name*: Alchara or Alyhalgalmoad (second drawing)
*Angel*: Atheniel
*Zodiac sign*: Pisces
*Influences*: Increases harvest, revenues and gain; heals infirmities; hinders buildings; prolongs prison sentences; causes danger to seamen; helps to cause mischief to anyone

**Twenty-eighth Manson**
*Name*: Albotham or Alchalcy (Pisces)
*Angel*: Amnixiel
*Zodiac sign*: Pisces
*Influences*: Increases harvest and merchandise; secures travelers through dangerous places; makes for the joy of married people; strengthens prisons; causes the loss of treasures.

See MAGIC, ANGELS IN.

**Further reading:**
Barrett, Francis. *The Magus*. Secaucus, N. J.: The Citadel Press, 1967. First published 1801.
McLean, Adam (ed.). *A Treatise on Angel Magic*. Grand Rapids, Mich.: Phanes Press, 1990.

**Marian apparitions**   Visions or supernatural manifestations of the Blessed Virgin Mary. The experiences are accompanied by other paranormal phenomena, such as visions of angels, heavenly music and singing, miraculous healing, luminosities, and on the part of the percipients, extrasensory perception, prophesying and mediumship. The apparitions tend to be apocalyptic in nature, with Mary exhorting people to prayer and righteous living, and to the building of churches in her honor. She also warns of dire consequences if people continue in their sinful ways. She bestows secret prophecies on a select few who perceive her (frequently children). In this respect Mary has taken over the primary functions of the prophets of old, who were transported to heaven to receive the same admonitions and prophecies from God. But Mary, out of her love for humanity and her loyalty to those devoted to her, is able to intercede with an angry God on humanity's behalf.

Marian apparitions have been reported worldwide over the centuries, but only eight have been deemed authentic by the Catholic church. In the latter twentieth century, reports of Marian apparitions escalated dramatically. Two major reasons behind this increase are the Catholic church's acceptance of Mary's assumption into heaven as an article of faith in 1950, thereby raising her spiritual stature; and the general trend toward apocalyptic thinking with the approach of a new millennium. The latter involves a need to turn to a spiritual savior figure.

The Catholic church holds that religious apparitions are mystical phenomena permitted by God. Both corporeal and incorporeal apparitions are recognized, and are mentioned

NUESTRA SEÑORA DE GUADALUPE.
OUR LADY OF GUADALUPE.

Our Lady of Guadalupe (reprinted courtesy of U.S. Library of Congress)

in both Old and New Testaments of the Bible. Marian apparitions are not accepted as articles of faith, but those which are deemed authentic are celebrated. The church is painstaking in its investigation of Marian apparitions.

Authentic sightings approved by the church are: Guadalupe, Mexico, 1531; Paris, 1830; La Salette, France, 1846; Lourdes, France, 1858; Knock, Ireland, 1879; Fatima, Portugal, 1917; Beauraing, Belgium, 1932–33; and Banneaux, Belgium, 1933. Appearances of angels are especially associated with four of those (Paris, Guadalupe, Knock and Fatima), and with numerous unauthenticated sightings as well.

At Guadalupe, Mary's appearances were accompanied by heavenly singing, and one of her miraculous signs involved an angel. She appeared five times to Juan Diego, a middle-aged Aztec convert to Catholicism. The first episode occurred in the predawn one morning, as Juan was on his way to attend Mass. He suddenly heard a heavenly choir, and then a lady's voice calling out to him by name. Diego then saw a woman standing in a luminous cloud of mist iridescent with rainbow hues. She identified herself immediately as Mary.

On another occasion Mary appeared and told Diego to pick flowers, despite the fact that it was too cold a time of the year. Miraculously, he found a garden of roses at a site where

no flowers had grown before. He followed her instructions to wrap the flowers in his cape and take them to the bishop. Unwrapped, the cape was imprinted with a beautiful image of the Immaculate Conception: a woman with the sun and stars, standing on a new moon, with an angel at her feet. The cape remains preserved at the shrine built at Guadalupe.

In Paris, the percipient was Catherine Laboure, a nun with the Sisters of Charity in the Rue du Bac. She entered the convent in 1830, shortly before the sighting. Within a few days of her arrival she had a vision of the heart of St. Vincent, glowing above a case containing some of his relics. She prayed to St. Vincent and to her GUARDIAN ANGEL to be granted a vision of Mary, her greatest ambition.

On July 18, Laboure was awakened at 11:30 P.M. by the sound of her name being called. She saw a child of about four or five years of age with golden hair, whom she took to be her guardian angel. The angel told her to go to the convent chapel; upon arrival, she found it brilliantly lit. Mary appeared at midnight and delivered her customary messages of exhortation to prayer, the appointment of Laboure to a mission that would require her suffering, and various prophecies.

Mary appeared to Laboure again on November 27 in a glorious vision while Laboure was praying in the chapel at about 5:30 P.M. She told Laboure to have a medal struck of her vision, and that all who wore it would receive graces. Laboure was not able to do this until six months before her death in 1876. The medal, called "the Miraculous Medal," is now worn by millions worldwide.

At Fatima in 1917—the most dramatic of the authenticated sightings—three children were paid three visits by an angel who identified itself as the Angel of Portugal, who acted as an annunciating figure. Mary then appeared to the children: Lucia dos Santos, ten, and her two cousins, Jacinta and Francisco Marto, seven and nine respectively. The two girls saw a "young lady" and heard her speak; the boy saw her but did not hear her speak. The children said the lady was dressed in white and stood above a small tree. She asked them to return to the same place at the same hour of the same day for six consecutive months. Tens of thousands of spectators showed up at the appointed time and place to witness the six apparitions.

At the final sighting on October 13, a crowd of 50,000 or more gathered in the rain. Mary appeared to the children and told them to build a chapel in her honor. She said she was the "Lady of the Rosary," and that people must say the rosary daily. Then the rain stopped, and a phenomenon now known as the "miracle of the sun" occurred. The sun appeared suddenly through a rift in the clouds and seemed to spin, throwing off multicolored light. It appeared to plunge to the earth, giving off heat, and then returned to normal in the sky.

A devotional cult to the Angel of Portugal, the guardian angel of the state, was sanctioned by the Catholic church (see DEVOTIONAL CULTS).

Lucia wrote four memoirs between 1935 and 1941. In her *Second Memoir* she made the new claim that she and her cousins had been visited by an angel in 1916. This "Angel of Peace," as he identified himself, taught the children a special prayer, and said that the hearts of Jesus and Mary were attentive to them. Lucia described him as looking to be about fourteen or fifteen years of age, whiter than snow,

N. S. DE MISERICORDIA, CON SUS TRES MARTI.<br>
VENERADOS EN SU ERMITA DE LA VILLA DE REUS.

Marian apparition at Reus, Spain

transparent as crystal, and quite beautiful when the sun shone through him. She warned the other two that the visit must be kept secret (secret visits, messages and prophecies are an integral part of Marian apparitions, and conform with apocalyptic experiences).

On a second visit the angel urged them to pray constantly to God, and said that the hearts of Jesus and Mary had "designs of mercy" on them. He instructed them to turn everything they could into a sacrifice offered to God, which would be reparation for the sins that offend God and supplication for the conversion of sinners. The angel said that if they did this, their country would have peace. He then identified himself as the Angel of Portugal. He ended his visit by telling them to bear the suffering that God would send them.

On a third visit, the angel gave them communion. Lucia received the consecrated host, and Jacinta and Francisco were allowed to share the chalice.

At Knock, Ireland, Mary, other figures, and perhaps angels were seen on August 21, 1879, by fifteen people by the village chapel at dusk. Besides Mary there were figures of St. Joseph, and a bishop or St. John the Evangelist (accounts differ). There also was an altar, above which was a lamb with a halo of gold stars; behind the lamb was a cross. Mary had her hands raised in prayer. Although it was raining, no rain fell where the apparition appeared. One witness, Patrick Hill, was eleven years old. Interviewed again in 1897, he embell-

ished his account with visions of winged angels who fluttered in the air for some ninety minutes.

In 1961, apparitions appeared at San Sebastian de Garabandal in northern Spain; they are unauthenticated. The sightings involve the archangel MICHAEL, who, like the Angel of Portugal at Fatima, gave the witnesses communion. The case began on June 18 when four girls reported that they had seen an angel. Over the next two weeks, the angel made nine appearances. In the two years following, there were more than two thousand reports of Marian apparitions by the girls.

One of the chief documents is the *Diary* of one of the witnesses, Conchita Gonzalez, who was twelve at the time. She began to write the account in September of 1962 and finished it in 1963.

According to Gonzalez, she and the other seers were stealing apples on June 18—and arguing over whether it was right to do so—when a beautiful figure appeared, brilliant in light. The girls told others about this angel, and were ridiculed by some. The girls returned to the spot the next day to pray, but the angel did not reappear. Gonzalez was consoled by a voice that night which assured her that she would see the angel again. The angel did appear on the following day, causing some disbelievers to recant.

Others joined them in prayer at the site, and over the next eleven days the girls had various ecstasies and eight more sightings of the angel, in front of numerous witnesses who could not see the phenomena themselves. On six of the eight appearances, the angel only smiled at the girls. On June 24, he appeared with a sign beneath him; they could only remember that the first line began with "Hay" and the second line contained roman numerals.

On July 1 the angel appeared with the sign again and spoke for the first time, telling the girls that he had come to announce the arrival of Mary on the following day. Mary appeared on July 2, accompanied by two angels who looked like twins. One was Michael—the angel who had been appearing to them; the other was not recognized (Gonzalez never said how she was able to identify the angel as Michael). On Mary's right side was a large eye of God.

During these and other visions the girls were subjected to crude experiments by researchers, to test their ecstatic states by measuring their sensitivity to pain. During the June 25 appearance of the angel, Gonzalez was dropped on her knees, pricked and scratched with needles and subjected to strong electric light, none of which broke her trance or made her feel any pain.

On May 18, 1962, the girls began to announce that they had been receiving communion from Michael. Mari Loli was the first to make the claim. She said Michael had told her he would give her communion while the local priest was absent. The four girls said that from then on they received frequent communions from the angel.

Gonzalez said that Michael used unconsecrated hosts in order to teach them how the host should be received. One day the angel told them to fast, and to bring another child along as a witness. He then gave them consecrated hosts. These reports generated much controversy. Priests said that angels did not have the ability to consecrate a host. Gonzalez took this objection to Michael, who then told her he had taken consecrated hosts from tabernacles on earth. Nonetheless, some people doubted the story.

Prior to their public admission of communion from Michael, the girls were witnessed going through gestures of putting their hands together, sticking out their tongues and swallowing, all of which now made sense. After the admission, numerous photos were taken of them receiving invisible communion.

On June 22, 1962, the angel told Gonzalez—who had been asking for a miracle as a sign of proof—that during the next communion God would perform a miracle through the angel's intercession by making a host visible on her tongue. (Until then, Gonzalez had never realized that no one else could see the hosts given them by the angel). She told the angel that this would be a tiny miracle, and he laughed. On July 18, a host appeared on her tongue and was seen by witnesses.

Though the girls later retracted some of their statements about their experiences, believers were not dissuaded. Even the retractions seemed to be part of the overall experience, with Gonzalez's diary claiming that Mary had predicted that retractions would be made. Supporters of the apparitions at Garabandal have worked to try to convince the Catholic church to authenticate the sightings.

See ANGELOPHANY; MARY.

**Further reading:**

Arintero, Juan. *Mystical Evolution in the Development and Vitality of the Church, Vol. I.* St. Louis: B. Herder, 1949.

Attwater, Donald. *A Dictionary of Mary.* New York: P.J. Kennedy, 1960.

McClure, Kevin. *The Evidence for Visions of the Virgin Mary.* Wellingborough, England: The Aquarian Press, 1983.

Zimdars-Swartz, Sandra L. *Encountering Mary.* Princeton, N.J.: Princeton University Press, 1991.

**Mary**  The mother of Jesus has numerous titles, among them "Queen of Angels," "Our Lady of the Angels" and "Queen of Martyrs." She also is called "Blessed Virgin," "Virgin Mary" or simply "Our Lady." Early church councils, including those at Ephesus in 431 and at Chalcedon in 451, gave her the title *Theotokos* ("God-bearer"); the title "Mother of God" is widely used, especially among Catholics. Devotion to Mary is a vital part of the Catholic liturgical life, especially in the Eastern Orthodox churches.

According to Catholic doctrine, Mary's Immaculate Conception makes her the one exception to the state of Original Sin (the state in which all humankind is born, due to the fall of Adam and Eve). Because Mary was destined to be the mother of Christ, God infused her soul with grace at the moment of her conception in the womb of her mother, St. Anne, which freed her from lust, slavery to the Devil, depraved nature, darkness of intellect and other consequences of Original Sin. Her Immaculate Conception is announced by the archangel GABRIEL (Luke 1:26–38). Gabriel tells her that the Holy Spirit will come upon her in order that she may to conceive her Son.

The idea of the Immaculate Conception was rejected by St. Thomas AQUINAS in the thirteenth century. Many modern theologians, challenging doctrines, consider the Immaculate Conception to be symbolic and not literal.

Similarly, the church sanitized her sexuality in general. Besides conceiving Jesus without human intercourse, she became "the Virgin" who never defiled her body with sexual

**Mary and Jesus (Albrecht Dürer)**

intercourse—despite the fact that the Bible refers to Jesus' brothers and sisters.

Furthermore, Mary did not die as a mere mortal, but was raised from the dead by Jesus and assumed into heaven as a live woman (the Assumption became an article of faith in 1950). In other lore, her death is announced by the archangel MICHAEL.

Mary and her proper place in Christian theology have been a subject of much controversy over the centuries. She absorbed the characteristics of previous pagan goddesses, thus fulfilling that universal need for worship of a Mother-figure which otherwise is curiously absent from Christianity. Early church fathers attempted to discourage worship of her by saying that God would never be born of a woman. For the first five centuries after Christ, Mary was depicted as lower in status even than the Magi, who were graced by haloes in sacred art. The Marianite sect, which considered her divine, was persecuted for heresy. In the early fourth century, Constantine I ordered all goddess temples destroyed and forbade the worship of Mary, so that she would not overshadow her Son. The people, however, refused to accept Christianity without the worship of Mary. She was prayed to as a mother who intercedes for her children. By the sixth century she had been given a halo in art, and by the ninth century she had been designated the Queen of Heaven. By the eleventh century she had eclipsed Jesus in popularity as the savior of mankind, and the great Gothic cathedrals were built to her greater glory.

In Catholic tradition Mary reigns in the splendor of heaven, where angels behold her glory and are ravished at the sight of her. She is second only to Jesus in suffering, and so commands the obedience of the angelic host. It may be Michael who leads the good angels in the celestial war against evil (see REVELATION), but he is under the command of Mary. The Queen of Paradise may even be considered to be the Mother of Angels, since she loves them and treats them as her own children. The Precious Blood shed by Jesus is the song of angels, the light of Mary, and the jubilee of her woes.

Countless visions of Mary have been reported worldwide; the numbers rose dramatically in the latter part of the twentieth century. The Catholic church has authenticated only a handful of them (see MARIAN APPARITIONS). Numerous saints have seen VISIONS of Mary, often accompanied by angels. Frequently she exhorts people to pray, to counter the evil loosed in the world.

In Catholic tradition an unnamed Bernadine sister had a vision in which she saw the desolation wrought by evil. She heard Mary tell her that the time had come to pray to her as the Queen of the Angels, to ask her for the assistance of the angels in fighting the foes of God and men. The sister asked why Mary, who is so kind, could not send the angels without being asked. Mary responded that she could not because prayer is one of the conditions God requires for the obtaining of favors. Mary then communicated the following prayer, which is part of the many devotions to Mary:

> August Queen of Heaven! Sovereign Mistress of the angels! Thou who from the beginning hast received from God the power and mission to crush the head of Satan, we humbly beseech thee to send thy holy Legions, that, under thy command and by thy power, they may pursue the evil spirits, encounter them on every side, resist their bold attacks and drive them hence into the abyss of eternal woe. Amen.

Several feast days are observed in Mary's honor: the Immaculate Conception, her Nativity, Purification, Annunciation and Assumption. The most popular devotion to Mary is the rosary, which is the saying of fifty "Hail Marys," five "Our Fathers," and five doxologies ("Glory be to the Father . . .") while meditating on specific traditional mysteries. This association with the rosary stems from apparitions of Mary seen at Fatima, Portugal, in 1917, in which she identified herself as the Lady of the Rosary and asked that believers say the rosary every day.

Ex-canonical works such as the Book of John the Evangelist refer to Mary as being an angel herself. The Apochryphal New Testament says that she is the angel sent by God to receive the Lord, who enters her through the ear.

**Further reading:**

Arintero, Juan. *Mystical Evolution in the Development and Vitality of the Church, Vol. I.* St. Louis: B. Herder, 1949.

Attwater, Donald. *A Dictionary of Mary.* New York: P.J. Kennedy, 1960.

*St. Michael and the Angels.* Rockford, Ill.: Tan Books and Publishers, 1983. First published 1977.

Warner, Marina. *Alone of All Her Sex: The Myth and the Cult of the Virgin Mary.* New York: Vintage, 1983.

**Mastema (also Mansemat)**   The angel of adversity, whose role is similar to that of SATAN, as adversary of God and tempter of humankind.

Mastema is called the "Father of Evil." He appears in the pseudepigraphal Book of Jubilees, and in *The Zadokite Fragments and the Dead Sea Scrolls.* Noah prayed to God to imprison all evil spirits, but at Mastema's behest, God granted the angel one-tenth of all demons to be committed to his service. Thus, Mastema roams about testing the faith of human souls.

Mastema is credited with assisting Egyptian sorcerers against MOSES and Aaron, and is said to be the one who attempts to kill Moses in Exodus 4:24.

**Further reading:**

Davidson, Gustav. *A Dictionary of Angels.* New York: The Free Press, 1967.

Ronner, John. *Know Your Angels.* Murfreesboro, Tenn.: Mamre Press, 1993.

**Meister Eckhardt**   See MONASTICISM, CHRISTIAN.

**Melchizadek (also Melchisedek; Melchisedec)**   A king and priest in the Old Testament, who elsewhere in angel lore is associated with angels. His name means "the god Zedek is my king," and he is described in the New Testament as the "king of righteousness" and the "king of peace."

In Genesis 14:18–20, Melchizedek is identified as the king of Salem (Jerusalem), who blesses Abram (see ABRAHAM) after a battle. Abram then tithes to the king. Psalm 110:4 declares, "You are a priest forever after the order of Melchizedek." These words are echoed in the New Testament book of Hebrews (5:6–10), in which Jesus is declared the high priest successor, "Thou art a priest forever, after the order of Melchizedek" for offering the sacrifice of his life. Hebrews 7:1 says that Melchizedek has not father or mother or geneaology, "and has neither beginning of days nor end of life, but resembling the Son of God he continues a priest forever."

2 Enoch says Melchizadek is the supernatural son of Noah; midrashim also identify him as a son of Noah, and the feeder of the beasts aboard the Ark. Phoenician mythology identifies him as the father of the seven ANGELS OF THE PRESENCE. Early Greek writers called him a virtue and prince of peace.

**Further reading:**

Davidson, Gustav. *A Dictionary of Angels.* New York: Free Press, 1967.

**Mephistopheles**   One of the seven great princes of Hell, and a stand-in for Satan in legend and literature. Mephistopheles means in Hebrew "he who loves not the light."

Mephistopheles is best-known for the part he plays in the legend of Dr. Johann Faust, which has been turned into plays, poems, operas and symphonies. The story concerns the way in which vanity can lead to easy seduction by the devil. Perhaps the best-known of these artistic creations is GOETHE's *Faust.*

According to the story, Faust lives in fifteenth-century Weimar, Germany, where he is an astrologer, alchemist and magician. In his youth he exhausted all the knowledge of his time, and so he turned to sorcery. Now in old age, he is bitter and disillusioned. Using his skill in sorcery, he conjures up Mephistopheles in the name of BEELZEBUB. The demon is friendly and consoling. Faust conjures him a second time, and Mephistopheles promises him all the worldly pleasures and sensations he desires—in exchange for his soul at the end of twenty-four years' time. Faust agrees.

For the next twenty-four years, Faust lives a splendid life. He has youth, wealth, magical powers and the satiation of all his physical desires. He can magically transport himself anywhere in the world, conjure up any woman, have anything. Then the demon comes to collect his due.

Goethe allows redemption for Faust. He has the doctor seduce a young woman named Margaret. She bears a child, but is so overcome with shame that she kills it. She is arrested and imprisoned, and in prison she becomes insane.

Faust, meanwhile, continues to live the high life. He conjures up Helen of Troy. Mephistopheles takes Faust on an adventure and shows him the creation of the universe, and the secrets of the homunculus (an artificial man created by magic).

Faust tries to save Margaret, but to no avail. She goes to her death, and her sacrifice redeems them both.

**Further reading:**
Hyatt, Victoria, and Joseph W. Charles. *The Book of Demons*. New York: Fireside, 1974.

**Metatron**  In Judaic lore, one of the greatest of angels. In the various accounts about Metatron, scarcely an angelic duty or function is not related to him. Primarily he sustains the physical world, and carries Jewish prayers through nine hundred heavens to God. He is an important angelic figure in the Kabbalah (specifically the *Zohar*), the Talmud, and the PSEUDEPIGRAPHA. Metatron apparently absorbed characteristics originally ascribed to the angel JAHOEL.

Metatron stands at the top of the Tree of Life as the Angel of the Lord. He also is identified with the "tree of knowledge of good and bad," which means he embodies both human and angelic perfection. This enables him to be an excellent interface between the two realms, but his success depends on the righteousness of humans. The good deeds of people generate a spiritual energy that literally vitalizes Metatron, and without it he grows weak and less effective.

Metatron also is the representative of God who led the tribes of Israel through the wilderness, and probably he is the dark angel who wrestled with Jacob. He is sometimes identified as the angel who stays the hand of Abraham as he is about to sacrifice his son Isaac, and he is credited with ordering the angelic announcement of the coming of the Flood (see URIEL). Metatron also is said to have given the wisdom of the Kabbalah to humanity.

The etymology of "Metatron" is unclear. Possibly the name itself was intended to be a secret, and may have been produced through a glossolalia-type of altered state of consciousness. Glossolalia is speaking in tongues, and is perhaps best known for the part it plays in charismatic religions. According to the *Zohar*, the name of Metatron is the equivalent of Shaddai, one of the names of God. This association is derived from the mystical numerology called gematria, which assigns a numerical value to each letter in the Hebrew alphabet. Names and words that have the same numerical value have a mystical connection. Both Shaddai and Metatron equal 314. As another aspect of God, Metatron is sometimes called the "shining light of the Shekinah" and he "whose name is like that of his Master." Eleazor of Worms

Metatron (Copyright 1995 by Robert Michael Place, from *The Angels Tarot* by Rosemary Ellen Guiley and Robert Michael Place. Reprinted courtesy of HarperSanFrancisco)

speculated that "Metatron" comes from the Latin term *metator*, which means a guide or measurer, an apt description of this important angel.

Metatron is sometimes called "the Prince of the Countenance," meaning he is the chief of those angels who are privileged to look upon the face of God. Other Judaic literature ascribes more than one hundred alternative names to Metatron. In some early accounts he is called "the lesser Yahweh," implying that he might be a second God. However the Talmud points out that Elisha received proof that Metatron was merely an angel, and thus could be punished, because he received sixty "strokes with fiery rods."

Descriptions of Metatron speak of a being or pillar of fire with thirty-six pairs of wings and myriad eyes. His face is more dazzling than the sun. He serves as God's ANGEL OF DEATH, instructing Gabriel and Samael which human souls to take at any given moment. The flames that issue from him create legions of angels.

According to one legend Metatron originally was the human prophet ENOCH, who was so righteous that God transformed him directly into an angel, turning his flesh into flames, his intestines into fire, and his bones into embers and giving him 365,000 fiery eyes. As Enoch had been a scribe, so Metatron continues on as a heavenly scribe, residing in the seventh heaven and logging all celestial and earthly events.

Among Metatron's other significant duties are minister to the Throne of Glory, where sits God; High Priest of the Heavenly Temple (a role also ascribed to the archangel MICHAEL); minister of wisdom, who holds the secrets to all divine affairs; and minister of the guardian angels of the "seventy peoples of the world." In addition, he teaches those prematurely dead children who arrive in Paradise.

According to the *Zohar*, Enoch was able to be transformed into Metatron because the divine spark lost by Adam in the Fall entered Enoch. Since mortals cannot contain the divine spark of perfection, it was then necessary for God to take Enoch into heaven and turn him into an angel.

**Further reading:**

Davidson, Gustav. *A Dictionary of Angels.* New York: The Free Press, 1967.

Guiley, Rosemary Ellen. *Angels of Mercy.* New York: Pocket Books, 1994.

Margolies, Morris B. *A Gathering of Angels.* New York: Ballantine Books, 1994.

Ronner, John. *Know Your Angels.* Murfreesboro, Tenn.: Mamre Press, 1993.

Scholem, Gershom. *Kabbalah.* New York: Dorset Press, 1987. First published 1974.

**Michael**   The most prominent and greatest angel in Christian, Hebrew and Islamic lore. His name in Hebrew means "who is like God" or "who is as God." Michael is Chaldean in origin. In angelologies, his chief roles are many: He is warrior, protector, healer, guardian. He holds numerous offices in heaven: He is chief of the virtues and archangels (see CHOIRS), a prince of the presence (see ANGELS OF THE PRESENCE), and the angel of repentance, righteousness, mercy and salvation. Some of his roles overlap with those of the other two great archangels of Christian lore, GABRIEL and RAPHAEL. In Christian art, Michael usually is portrayed in warrior garb, holding a sword and scales and trampling SATAN.

### BIBLICAL REFERENCES

Michael is mentioned by name in DANIEL, Jude and REVELATION. In Daniel he is the guardian angel of the people of God (Israel). In Daniel 10:13, Michael is named and described as "one of the chief princes, and in Daniel 10:21, "one having the appearance of a man" tells Daniel ". . . there is none who contends by my side except Michael, your prince." In Daniel 12:1, the prophecy of "the time of the end" states that "At that time shall arise Michael, the great prince who has charge of your people. And there shall be a time of trouble, such as never has been since there was a nation till that time; but at that time your people shall be delivered, every one whose name shall be found written in the book." (This is a reference to the Israelites' departure from Egypt, led by MOSES and guided by a pillar of cloud during the day and a pillar of fire at night [Exodus 33ff]. In Exodus 23:20, God promises to send his angel before them. Though Michael is not named here, it is widely interpreted that he is that angel.)

In Jude 9, the archangel Michael contends with Satan over the body of MOSES (according to Jewish lore, Satan wishes to reveal the tomb of the prophet in order to seduce the Israelites into the sin of idolatry; Michael, obeying God, concealed the tomb).

In Revelation 12:7–12, Michael and his legions battle Satan and his forces in heaven, and Satan is thrown down.

Numerous other biblical references to "the angel of Yahweh" and "the ANGEL OF THE LORD" are interpreted as meaning Michael. Besides Exodus, another example is found in Zechariah 3:1–2, which tells of an angel of the Lord who confronts Satan before God and the high priest Joshua.

### CHRISTIAN LORE

In Catholic devotion there is no greater angel than Michael; the Catholic church refers to him as "Prince of the Heavenly Hosts." Churches were built and dedicated to him from the fifth century onward. So intense was adoration of Michael that many devotional cults sprang up all over Europe, peaking in popularity in the late Middle Ages. Devotion to Michael (as well as to Gabriel and RAPHAEL) today is still encouraged by the Catholic church through DEVOTIONAL CULTS, prayer and mass.

Michael is the guardian angel of the Hebrew nation. Michael wages ceaseless war against the forces of Satan. He is the special defender of Christians (and particularly Catholics) and the church. Satan trembles at the mere mention of his name, and all the angels of heaven bow down before him in obedience. Michael inspires fidelity to God. St. Francis de Sales wrote that veneration of Michael is the greatest remedy against despising the rights of God and against insubordination, skepticism and infidelity.

At mass, Michael presides over the worship of adoration to the Most High, and sends to God the prayers of the faithful, symbolized by the smoke from incense. The prayer to St. Michael, asking him to defend Christians in battle, is a condensed form of the general exorcism against Satan and evil spirits composed by Pope Leo XIII.

One of his important duties is as psychopomp to the dead, guiding the souls of the newly departed to the afterlife. In this capacity he resembles the Greek/Roman god Hermes/Mercury and the Egyptian god Thoth. Michael weighs the souls for righteousness. He is associated with benevolent aspects of the ANGEL OF DEATH and has the ability to shapeshift when he comes to take a soul away (see ABRAHAM). In lore, Michael is the angel designated to appear to Mary to announce her death.

In Catholicism, Michael guards the gates of purgatory and has pity on the souls therein. Legends tell of prayers made to Michael for souls in purgatory; he appears and takes them into heaven.

Michael shares with Raphael special healing duties, a function naturally associated with him as protector of the general welfare. Catholic tradition holds that Michael caused a medicinal spring to appear at Chairotopa near Colossae; anyone who bathed there and invoked the Blessed Trinity and Michael was said to be cured. Michael also caused a healing spring to appear from a rock at Colossae. Pagans attempted to destroy it by directing a stream against it, but Michael split the rock with lightning, giving a new bed to the stream and sanctifying the waters forever.

Michael was considered the great heavenly physician at Constantinople, and is credited with banishing a pestilence in Rome during the days of St. Gregory the Great.

Michael has two feasts days: May 8, which commemorates the dedication of a basilica in honor of him on the Salarian Way about six miles outside of Rome, and September 29, known as Michaelmas.

### APPARITIONS OF MICHAEL

There have been numerous apparitions of Michael reported over the centuries, usually on or near mountaintops. One of the most famous sites is the Michaelion church near Constantinople, erected in the fifth century by the emperor Constantine. At the command of MARY, Queen of the Angels, Michael came to the aid of Constantine in his battle against the pagan emperor Maxentius. Constantine built the church for Michael in gratitude. After its completion Michael appeared there to the emperor and said, "I am Michael, the chief of the angelic legions of the Lord of hosts, the protector of the Christian religion, who while you were battling against godless tyrants, placed the weapons in your hands." Miracles attributed to Michael have been reported at the Michaelion over the centuries.

Another famous apparition of Michael appeared to the Bishop of Siponto on Mount Gargano in Apulia, near Naples, Italy, during the reign of Pope Gelasius (492–496). A shrine erected in the cave of the apparition attracted hordes of pilgrims. In the seventh century the shrine was at a peak of popularity, due in part to a Lombard victory over the Saracens in 663 that was attributed to the help of Michael. According to lore the Lombards, who went to the shrine to give thanks for their victory, found the imprint of Michael's foot near the south door of the temple.

In France, Michael has appeared on Mont St. Michel, where a sanctuary was erected.

In Spain, where the cult of Michael peaked in popularity in about the thirteenth century, one of the best-known apparitions was the 1455 appearance to a shepherd about halfway between Navagamella and Fresnedillas, in the foothills of the Sierra de Guadarrama. The sighting was investigated in 1520, when some of the witnesses were still alive, and also in 1617.

According to testimony, Michael appeared late one afternoon in 1455 on a holm-oak tree and a rockrose plant, to shepherd Miguel Sanchez. Michael told the shepherd not to be frightened, but to tell others that a shrine should be erected on the site and a brotherhood founded, both in honor of the angelic messengers. Sanchez protested that no one would believe him, but Michael insisted that he tell his employer. "I will make them believe you so they build a shrine here to the holy angels," he said. He then made an imprint of his hand on the tree.

However, Sanchez did not tell the story. A few days passed, and one morning he awakened crippled. His legs were folded in a bizarre manner, so that the backs of his calves touched his thighs and his heels touched his buttocks. His employer, Pedro Garcia de Ayuso, tried unsuccessfully to cure him with herbs and oils. At last Sanchez told of his vision. Garcia de Ayuso consulted with authorities, and they carried the shepherd to the site of the apparition. There they found the handprint on the tree trunk. It was considered

proof, and plans were made immediately for construction of a chapel. A mass was said there for the shepherd's health; when it was completed, he was cured. Sanchez was named keeper of the shrine.

(Compare to MARIAN APPARITIONS.)

### HEBREW LORE

Rabbi Shimon ben Laqish (Midrash Konen) names the seven Heavens as follows: Wilon, Raqi'a, Shehaqim, Zebhul, Ma'on, Makhon, and 'Arabhoth. They are all fixed and vaulted over earth, one above the other. Wilon, the lowest, shades the uppermost earth from the heat, but at sundown Wilon is rolled back to enable the Moon and stars to shine from Raqi'a, the Second Heaven.

According to the Hagiya, in Shehaqim a pair of millstones grind manna for the righteous; in Zebhul are found the heavenly Jerusalem, the Temple, and the altar upon which the Archangel Michael offers sacrifices; in Ma'on, hosts of ministering angels hymn God's mercy all night long but fall silent at dawn, thus allowing Him to hear His praises sung by Israel below; Makhon contains storehouses of snow and hailstones, lofts of dews and rains, chambers of storms, and caves of fog; in 'Arabhoth abide Justice, Law and Charity, the treasures of Life, Peace and Blessing, the souls of the righteous, the souls of the yet unborn, the dew with which God

**Michael subduing Satan**

will revive the dead, the chariot seen by Ezekiel in a vision, the ministering angels, and the Divine Throne.

Legend holds that the two primeval monsters, LEVIATHAN and BEHEMOTH, will murder each other, but variations predict that God will send Michael and Gabriel against both creatures and that when they fail to dispatch either, God will shoulder the task Himself.

Some midrashim state that God commands the archangel Michael to "bring me dust from my sanctuary" to make Adam. Others say that God disdains to fetch Adam's dust himself and sends an angel instead, either Michael to Mount Moriah, or Gabriel to the world's four corners. Nevertheless Earth opposes the angels, knowing she will be cursed on Adam's account, and God stretches forth his own hand to gather it.

Some midrashim say when Cain kills Abel, he tries to bury the corpse, but Earth spews it up again and cries, "I will receive no other body until the clay that was fashioned into Adam has been restored to me!" At this Cain flees, and Michael, Gabriel, Uriel and Raphael place the corpse upon a rock, where it remains for many years without corrupting. When Adam dies these same archangels bury both bodies at Hebron side by side, in the very field from which God had taken Adam's dust.

The midrashim say that the fallen angels AZAEL and Shemhazzi (see SONS OF GOD) cause such wickedness on earth among the Canaanites that the four archangels tell God, and God sends Raphael to bind AZAEL hand and foot, heaping jagged rocks over him in the dark Cave of Dudael, where he now abides until the Last Days. Gabriel destroys the Fallen Ones by inciting them to civil war. Michael chains Shemhazzi (see SEMYAZA) and his fellows in other dark caves for seventy generations. Uriel becomes the messenger of salvation who visits Noah.

One midrash says that when Jacob and Esau are in Rebekah's womb and fight, Michael intervenes on Jacob's behalf and saves him from death. SAMAEL intervenes on behalf of Esau. Rabbinic lore says that Gabriel and Michael were witnesses to the contract in which Esau sold Jacob his birthright.

The Testament of Abraham, a Greek text that is part of the PSEUDEPIGRAPHA, relates that when Michael comes to fetch Abraham's soul, the patriarch boldly insists on seeing the whole world. God commands Michael to let Abraham ride across the heavens in a chariot drawn by cherubim, and so his wish is fulfilled. Yet Abraham still is reluctant to die. God then sends the ANGEL OF DEATH disguised as a fair youth, and when his true aspect is revealed Abraham faints in horror. Death draws out Abraham's soul through his fingers. Michael wraps it in a divinely woven kerchief and conveys it to Heaven.

The Yalqut Genesis and the Pirqe Rabbi Eliezer say that it is Michael who fights with JACOB at Peniel. When God asks Michael, "What have you done to my first-born son?" Michael answers, "I shrank a sinew in your honor." God says, "It is good. Henceforth, until the end of time, you shall have charge of Israel and his posterity! For the prince of angels should guard the prince of men; fire should guard fire, and head should guard head!"

Hebrew midrashim and folklore sources tell us that when Jacob's daughter Dinah is raped by the Canaanite Sechem, she gives birth to a daughter. Her brothers wishes to kill the child but Jacob restrains them and puts a silver disk about her neck, laying her underneath a thornbush (hence her name "Asenath" for the bush). Michael in the shape of an eagle takes off with Asenath to Egypt and leaves her beside God's altar, where a priest finds her and adopts her. Many years later, when Joseph saves Egypt from famine, he makes a trip throughout Egypt and the women throw him tokens of gratitude. Asenath throws him her silver disk and he recognizes it. Knowing she must be his own niece, he marries her.

## ISLAMIC LORE

The Moslems relate that the angels Gabriel, Michael, Israfil and Azrael bring dust from the four corners of the world, and with it Allah creates the body of Adam. To form his head and heart, however, Allah chooses dust from a site at Mecca, where the Holy Ka'aba later rises. Mecca is the navel of the earth for Moslems, as Mount Moriah is for the Hebrews and Delphi for the Greeks.

Michael's wings are emerald-green and covered with saffron hairs. Each hair contains a million faces that speak a million dialects, all imploring the pardon of Allah. When Michael cries over the sins of the faithful, his tears create cherubim.

## STEINER AND MICHAEL

According to Rudolph STEINER, human evolution has been under the guidance of Michael as the Spirit of the Age since 1879. The consciousness of humankind as a whole crossed in the last century the Threshold that separates the world of nature grasped by the senses from the spiritual world that manifests within the human soul.

In those who progress to active thinking it will be possible to make Inspiration the determining element of soul. This is what Michael's "rulership" of this millennial age really means. Michael does not work so much for the initiate as for those who wish to understand spiritual investigations. Michael stands cosmically behind man. For it is not Michael himself who wages the battle, but human devotion and the resulting image of Michael, or what Steiner calls "the Michaelmas Imagination." Because Michael won the battle over the Dragon in 1879, the spiritual will more and more lay hold of humanity, and spiritual truth will take root among men, although it will not become the general conviction.

In a series of lectures delivered in October of 1923 on the Four Seasons and the Archangels, Steiner outlined his ideas on the Michaelmas Imagination. At Michaelmas (September 29) we celebrate the sulfurizing and meteorizing process in man: everything that opposes love of ease, opposes anxiety, encourages the unfolding of inner initiative and free, strong, courageous will. This is the Festival of Strong Will. The renewal of the whole soul-disposition of humankind should be celebrated at Michael Festival, one that renews the whole inner man. Michael's look in autumn is that of guidance, like a pointer, as though wishing not to look inward, but outward into the world. His gaze is positive, active. And his sword, forged out of cosmic iron, is held so that at the same time he indicates to men their way.

Michael's gold-woven, silver-sparkling raiment comes from what is formed in the heights through the upward-raying silver and gold that flows to meet it, from the transmutation by the sun's power of the silver sparkling upward from the earth. As autumn approaches we see how the silver given by the earth to the cosmos returns as gold, and the power of this transmuted silver is the source of what happens in the earth during winter.

In the spring Michael is below, working through the earth from the other hemisphere, coming to meet mankind with his positive gaze; showing the way into the world and glad to draw the eyes of men in the same direction as he stands close to mankind, the complement of Raphael in spring.

**Further reading:**

Christian, William C. Jr. *Apparitions in Late Medieval and Renaissance Spain*. Princeton, N.J.: Princeton University Press, 1981.

Davidson, Gustav. *A Dictionary of Angels*. New York: The Free Press, 1967.

Graves, Robert, and Patai, Raphael. *Hebrew Myths*. New York: Doubleday Anchor, 1964.

Schroff, Lois. *The Archangel Michael*. Herndon, Va.: Newlight Books, 1990.

Steiner, Rudolf. *The Four Seasons and the Archangels*. Bristol, England: The Rudolf Steiner Press, 1992.

**Milton, John** (1608–1674)   Considered one of the greatest poets in the English language, John Milton is best known for his epic poem *Paradise Lost*. He also wrote various political and religious treatises, served in Cromwell's Commonwealth, and fought with both the established Church of England and its reformers.

Born in 1608 to a family in comfortable circumstances, Milton attended Cambridge University and studied Latin, Greek and the other classics. Like most of his contemporaries, Milton was well versed in religious subjects and firmly believed in the actuality of angels. They figure as prominently in the literature of the time as the mythical gods. One of his earliest poems, "Ode on the Morning of Christ's Nativity," describes the angels who announce Christ's birth as harbingers of light bringing an end to the darkness of sin and evil—an ironic twist, when one remembers that Lucifer's name meant "bearer of light." The angels also fill the world with song and harmony, providing the medieval philosophers with their "music of the spheres."

But it is in *Paradise Lost* that he most fully describes the angels and their circumstances. Milton wrote his epic poem after the Restoration of King Charles II to the English throne, a period in which Milton's total blindness and his political ties to the Commonwealth left him with little to do but write the verses he had long planned to write.

The poem recounts the story of Lucifer's rebellion, and the rapture of Adam and Eve in the Garden of Eden and their eventual shame and expulsion. Milton explains in great detail—some of it based on Judeo-Christian literature and some drawn from his own imagination—the characteristics of the angels, the accounts of the great battles between Lucifer's armies and the followers of God, the overwhelming beauty of Eden, and man's fall from grace. Most of the discourse on the angels occurs as a conversation between Adam and the archangel RAPHAEL, who had been sent by God to warn Adam and Eve of the devil's temptations. Eve prepares a feast for Adam and Raphael, and they talk of the Fall, God's grace, and what angels are like over the meal.

Raphael tells Adam that angels are the link between humans and God: "pure, Intelligential substances" rather than rational beings. They are intuitive, with great knowledge that encompasses reason. In many ways, particularly physically, angels resemble man, but their bodies are made of ether, which Milton identified as the "fifth element": non-solid, with a liquid texture. As such they are pure spirit compared to man but "natural" to God, since He created them.

Angels have all five of man's senses, but they experience taste, smell, sight, hearing and touch with their whole beings and not through particular organs. They eat, enjoy music, delight in tastes, smells and sounds, and even have sexual intercourse—an angelic talent original to Milton.

Angels cannot be in more than one place at the same time, but they travel at unimaginable speeds. They also are able to assume any size or shape, and either gender. Angels live on planets and have been called stars. They exist as agents of divine providence, ministering to man on God's behalf, or as agents of perversion if they have followed LUCIFER.

But most of all angels are winged, shining and beautiful. In Book V, verses 277–284, Milton describes Raphael as he descends into the Garden:

**Lucifer reigning over the souls of sinners (John Baptist Medina for *Paradise Lost*, 1688).**

*A Seraph winged: six wings he wore, to shade*
*His lineaments divine; the pair that clad*
*Each shoulder broad, came mantling o'er his breast*
*With regal ornament; the middle pair*
*Girt like a starry zone his waist, and round*
*Skirted his loins and thighs with downy gold*
*And colors dipped in Heaven; the third his feet*
*Shadowed from either heel with feathered mail*
*Sky-tinctured grain.*

Another characteristic of angels is their invulnerability. Each side inflicts great pain upon the other during the battles of the rebellion, but does not suffer any longer than a moment. In Book VI, verses 326–334, Lucifer marvels at his brief agony:

*Then Satan first knew pain,*
*And writhed him to and fro convolved; so sore*
*The griding sword with discontinuous wound*
*Passed through him; but the ethereal substance closed*
*Not long divisible, and from the gash*
*A stream of nectarous humor issuing flowed*
*Sanguine, such as celestial spirits may bleed,*
*And all his armor stained, erewhile so bright.*

Traditional Judeo-Christian writings organized the angels in complicated hierarchies:

| Seraphim | Dominions | Principalities |
|----------|-----------|----------------|
| Cherubim | Virtues | Archangels |
| Thrones | Powers | Angels |

Milton rejected these rankings, organizing the angels into three degrees or choirs. Lucifer often refers to the above-mentioned nine hierarchies when speaking of his minions; the titles are more expressions of Lucifer's power and his exercise of authority than actual rankings. Milton also described many of the leading angels as Archangels, whereas Michael often is designated the only Archangel (Lucifer was probably an Archangel before his fall). These divinities rule the four corners of the world. Milton's Archangels are

*Michael*: the first in command of God's army
*Gabriel*: second in command; bearer of annunciation to Mary
*Uriel*: viceroy of the sun
*Raphael*: God's chief minister

Other loyal angels in God's service are

*Abdiel*: a seraph meaning "servant of God." Abdiel alone stood up to Lucifer when he boasted of his victory
*Ithuriel*: a cherub, "discovery of God"
*Uzziel*: like Uriel, the "eye of the Lord" and "strength of God"
*Zephon*: "searcher of secrets"
*Zophiel*: "spy of God"

See LITERATURE AND ANGELS.

**Further reading:**
Arthos, John. *Dante, Michaelangelo and Milton*. London: Routledge and Kegan Paul, 1963.
Bush, Douglas, ed. *The Portable Milton*. New York: The Viking Press, 1949.

**Nun experiencing an angel in prayer**

Elledge, Scott, ed. *John Milton: Paradise Lost, An Authoritative Text*. New York: W. W. Norton & Co., 1975.

**monasticism, Christian**   The role of angels in the contemplative experience of the West can be traced into late medieval times through the teachings and lives of the great saints, many of whom were founders and leaders of monastic communities: the saints AUGUSTINE, FRANCIS OF ASSISI, Bernard of Clairvaux, Bonaventure, Thomas AQUINAS, Catherine of Siena and TERESA OF AVILA.

In both East and West, each religion or sect of any size created communities separated from society where seekers could lead a life of single-minded spiritual aspiration. Or, holy persons living in solitude attracted disciples, and small communities would grow around these teachers. Both kinds of Eastern monasticism were established hundreds of years before Western monasticism, which began to develop in the last centuries before Christ. In the West, Jewish "monks" were Essenes, a community with which John the Baptist probably associated. Gnostics and other sects were practicing monastic life at the same time as such Desert Fathers of the Church as St. Anthony of Egypt (250–350), who started out as a hermit and ended up leading a community.

St. Pachomius (c. 290–350) was an Egyptian Copt who, after his conversion to Christianity while in the Roman army, spent some years in retreat with another hermit. He was praying alone in the desert of Tabenna when an angelic figure spoke to him and told him to found a monastery according to the rule the angel would give. His companion helped him to build what would become the first Christian cloister. A wall surrounded the humble structure as a symbol of the monk's separation from the world, and no stranger was allowed beyond a certain point, leaving "the inner sanctum" unsullied. Pachomius's "Angelic Rule," one of the major monuments of early Christian literature, was innovative in one major fact: It was a binding commandment, akin to a law. After living as a novice for a number of years, each monk accepted the rule as an unalterable canon of life.

But Christian monasticism was most profoundly influenced by St. Augustine (354–430), whose teachings on angels coincided with monastic spirituality. Monks were disposed to think of themselves as a group chosen for the heavenly city. As Augustine said, the terrestrial church has only a partial vision of God, while the celestial church enjoys the full vision of God. The monks grounded their theories of contemplation on this distinction. As the counterparts of the angels, monks occupied a special place at the heart of the church universal. They bore witness to the bliss which awaits the pure of heart; their penances and ascetic practices prepared them for the incorporeal life of angels. In a sense monks *were* angels here and now. Early monks frequently defined their vocation as the angelic life, insofar as they were detached, pure and devotional. Poverty, chastity and obedience were rooted in angelic reality, as angels had no bodily needs and served God unceasingly. Indeed, in accordance with Christ's words (Matthew 22:30; Mark 12:25; Luke 20:35–36) that the blessed will be "like the angels in heaven," people regarded human celibacy as the prime correlative between angels and men.

Augustine developed this connection in his tract *Holy Virginity*, where he praises virginity as *vita angelica*, angelic life, "a sharing in the life of the angels and a striving for endless immortality here in this perishable flesh." Practicing continence dedicated to God means "reflecting on the life of heaven and of the angels amid this earthly mortality." Thus whoever has taken a vow of celibate chastity, whether a man or woman, must "live on earth the life of the angels," and begin to be on this side of the grave what other Christians "will be only after the resurrection." He saw further resemblances to the angelic life in the way the celibate direct their senses and their efforts to "what is eternal and immutable," and in their zeal for performing works of virtue, "so that they show to earth how life is lived in heaven." Following from this, Augustine developed the theme of the "heavenly life," *vita coelestis*, a psychology of living on earth with one's eyes turned upward. The contemplation (*vita contemplativa*) of God practiced in the monastery would in time proceed to freedom from passion; the monks, like angels, would be immersed in happiness derived from divine truth and beauty while still in this world.

Probably the most mature expression of an Augustinian monastic approach to angels is to be found in the works of St. Bernard of Clairvaux (1090 or 1091–1153), who tirelessly exhorted his monks to seek angelic help in their prayer-lives. Bernard assumes that true monks are destined to take the places of fallen angels. The connection between monks and angels is closer than the connection between angels and Christian humankind. He likens the celibate monk or nun to the Bride in the Song of Solomon: "Her life bears witness to her origin and to the dignity of her nature and her homeland. . . . She is chaste just like the angels, and that in the flesh of a fallen race, in a frail body that the angels do not have. . . . What can be a clearer sign of her heavenly origin than that

she retains a natural likeness to it in the land of unlikeness, than that as an exile on earth she enjoys the glory of the celibate life, than that she lives like an angel in an animal body?" (*On The Song of Songs, II*) This exhortation and others like it for women to identify with the angels inspired a wave of anorexia in the fourteenth and fifteenth centuries among pious young women who renounced human food to delight and savor the food of the angels. The first of these was Catherine of Siena (1347–80), who died at the age of thirty-three after subsisting for some years only on communion wafers.

The Augustinian view that the elect on earth were making their way toward the empty spaces left in the angelic hierarchies by reprobate angels persisted. Since the translation by Erigena of PSEUDO-DIONYSIUS in the ninth century, monastic writers often had compared the ascent of the contemplative soul to the angelic hierarchies. Typically the various angels of the nine choirs were rendered analogous to the different stages of the soul's upward progress. The myriad angels, furthermore, were to lend special assistance to the soul.

The great Franciscan St. Bonaventure (c. 1217–1274), a contemporary of Aquinas, attempted to synthesize the Augustinian and Dionysian legacies of angels with man's spiritual life. Bonaventure made a series of analogies between the soul's ascent to God and the structure of angelic hierarchies. The intersecting point of the two hierarchies is the love of God, a goal which deviates from the Dionysian stress on knowledge. The seraphim, who have their replica in St. Francis, correspond to the soul's unitive way. The most angelic members of the church militant are those who have perfectly "hierarchized" their souls, and only Francis of Assisi achieved this perfect correspondence. The Franciscan mission is to teach others how to model their lives on Francis, the archetype of Christ.

This sense of the angelic elect differs sharply from Bernard's cloistered monks in contemplation. In his mystical works Bonaventure almost always refers to the angelic hierarchies as ontological models of how true contemplation should work. He rarely alludes to the soul as living in eternal bliss among the angels. Whereas Augustine emphasizes the equality of men and angels—here potential, there actual—Bonaventure thinks that the importance of angels lies in how each angelic level represents a phase in the soul. Nor does Bonaventure use Augustine's pastoral ploy of imaging vacancies in the angelic ranks in order to prod Christians onward to a transcendent goal. For Augustine, meditation on angels would lead to rejection of worldly things, whereas for Bonaventure, angels assist man in seeing God in all His creatures. Reflection on the angels results not in flight from the world but in the sanctification of its beauty.

Within a generation of Bonaventure's death the Rhineland mystics had greatly contracted man's ties to angels. Of all the early Rhineland mystics Meister Eckhardt (1260?–1327) has the most to say about the function of angels in the spiritual life. This Dominican largely bypassed the monastic legacy of imitating the angels either in their actions or their nature. He centers instead on the biblical notion of the angel as *messenger*. For Eckhardt the angels' function is less to bring the soul up to God, than to bring

God down to the soul. Bonaventure utilized Dionysian hierarchies to show how the soul can ascend to God through contemplation. Eckhardt uses the same hierarchies to show how God can descend into man.

For Eckhardt, ultimately the soul does not become angelic, since the angel after all is merely a creature. Rather, the soul becomes like God. It seeks angelic aid only in its initial stages of perfection, because in those stages it requires images and intermediaries in order to strip itself of the creaturely. But the whole point of this phase is to convince the soul that it does not require images. The purpose of angelic help is simply to allow the soul to reflect on its own "spark," which alone will render it God-like. Indeed, the soul can become more divine than the angel. The angels' task is established for all eternity; the soul alone can become one with God. When God decides to penetrate a soul, it must be empty of all creatures, angels included. The angels' work is service. The grace of the Holy Spirit in the soul is a "face of God." In a sense, God simply will not tolerate any creatures to aid Him in this special work. No angel is noble enough for God's birth in the human heart, where He makes her like Himself in grace.

Eckhardt's angelology was a response to the desire for a theology of contemplation united to the structures of traditional monasticism. Bernard considers the contemplative life to be impossible without a monastic setting. Eckhardt deems the setting irrelevant, unless it is in some way actually detrimental to perfection. Elect souls require only grace, not prescribed rules of ascetic conduct. Eckhardt also reacted against Bonaventure's overt ecclesiological system—making exact correspondences among the diverse hierarchies: visible church, angels, and the contemplative soul. For Eckhardt the illumination of the angels is only the preparation for the soul's intellect to "spark." The three highest choirs of angels—thrones, cherubim and seraphim—are analogues to the soul's reception of knowledge, quietude and love of God.

The monastic literature of angelology and contemplation reached its apex in the twelfth century with Bernard. The waning of monastic culture after 1200 (with the rise of new orders such as the Franciscans and Dominicans, who were not cloistered) accords with a lessening of interest in Augustinian angelology. Bonaventure typified this new trend, and Meister Eckhardt exemplified a move toward speculative mysticism. For Augustine's monks the angels had been integral mirrors of their identity; Augustine's heavenly city would reward the pilgrim with angelic status. By contrast, Eckhardt's City of God exists primarily in the heart of the contemplative.

**Further reading:**

Bell, Rudolph. *Holy Anorexia*. Chicago: University of Chicago Press, 1985.

Gilson, Etienne. *The Philosophy of St. Bonaventure*. London: Sheed and Ward, 1940.

Nigg, Walter. Trans. Mary Ilford. *Warriors of God: The Great Religious Orders and Their Founders*. New York: Alfred Knopf, 1959.

Renna, Thomas. "Angels and Spirituality: The Augustinian Tradition to Eckhardt." *Augustinian Studies*, Vol. 16. Villanova University, 1984.

Walshe, M., ed. *Meister Eckhardt*. London: Watkins, 1981.

Zumkeller, Adolar. Trans. Edmund Colledge. *Augustine's Ideal of the Religious Life*. New York: Fordham University Press, 1986.

**Mons, angels of**    Incident during World War I in which Allied soldiers reportedly were aided by heavenly soldiers, and England's patron saint, St. George, mounted on horseback. The visions were not limited to British and French troops. Several captured Germans allegedly asked about the horsemen or the leader on a white horse. Whole battalions apparently retreated in fear. According to some German reports, the soldiers fell back against what appeared to be thousands of troops, not the two small Allied regiments.

The incident occurred during the battle of Mons, Belgium, on August 26–27, 1914. The Allies had only two regiments posted there, while surrounded by the better-equipped Germans. Outmanned and outgunned, the Allies expected to be slaughtered, but although they suffered numerous losses, the numbers were many fewer than expected. Many in the companies believed their retreat was saved by hundreds of mounted, armoured soldiers—spirits of the English victors at the battle of Agincourt in 1415—who came between them and the German army. Others saw or heard St. George, described as a yellow-haired man riding a white charger.

Public interest in the stories was tremendous, despite the fact that they sounded suspiciously like the plot of a fictional story, "The Bowmen," written by novelist Arthur Machen and published in the London *Evening News* barely a month after the battle, on September 29, 1914. In Machen's story, a British soldier, overwhelmed at Mons, recalls a Latin motto he once read on a plate in a vegetarian restaurant. The motto read, *Adsit Anglis Sanctus Georgius*, "May St. George be a present help to the English." No sooner had the desperate soldier invoked the motto than he heard voices roaring the same plea and adding other medieval calls for courage and preservation. The soldier looked beyond his trench and saw long lines of mounted bowmen, who shot swarms of arrows at the advancing Germans. The enemy fell by the thousands, but the German staff found no wounds on their fallen comrades.

Although Machen belatedly took credit as the only source of the angelic stories, claiming they could all be traced to his fictional tale, his protestations could not stem the increasing flood of accounts that God had taken an active stand on behalf of the Allies. Indeed, in his field notes of September 5, Brigadier-General John Charteris of the British Expeditionary Force referred to stories among his men about angelic sightings at Mons—at least three weeks before the publication of Machen's story.

Reports of angelic intervention at Mons died out about October 1914 but revived later the following spring. On April 30, the Roman Catholic newspaper *The Universe* printed an anonymous account from a supposedly reputable Catholic officer about an experience of another officer at Mons. It seemed that this second officer and about thirty of his men were trapped in a trench when they decided to make a run for it rather than be slaughtered by the advancing Germans. Yelling "St. George for England!", the men were met by a large company of bowmen who led them in a charge on the enemy's trenches. Later, a captured German prisoner asked who was the officer seated on a great white horse. The officer who told this story to the first Catholic officer said he did not see St. George but did see the archers. Again, the German dead showed no wounds.

**Angels at the Battle of Mons**

In the May 15, 1915, issue of the parish magazine of All Saints Parish, Clifton, England, a Miss Marrable, daughter of the canon, was reported to have met two officers (although she did not know their names) who claimed they had witnessed the angelic intervention. One officer said that when the angels appeared, the German cavalry horses reared in fright and ran in all directions, no matter how determinedly the riders tried to force their horses to continue the charge.

In the same month, the Spiritualist newspaper *Light* ran a piece recounting a sermon reportedly preached by the Rev. Fielding Ould, vicar of St. Stephen's in St. Alban's. Rev. Ould heard a story from three sources whom he believed reputable, as follows: A sergeant had often visited a branch of the Young Men's Christian Association, in which hung a picture of St. George slaying the dragon. Later, during the battle of Mons, the sergeant repeated the legend of St. George to his beleaguered men, telling how St. George was the patron saint of England and the war cry of English soldiers for centuries. Facing the advancing Germans, the men shouted "Remember St. George for England!" Shortly the Germans hesitated in their charge, then turned around and fled. One of the prisoners left behind told his captors of the horsemen in armor who led the Allies' charge—surely they were not Belgians!

On June 9, 1915, *Bladud, The Bath Society Paper* ran several accounts, always anonymous, of other soldiers who witnessed the same phenomenon. One officer wrote that his sol-diers had fled to a place where they could stand against the Germans, even though they expected death. But instead of seeing the advancing German cavalry they saw a troop of angels and the German horses stampeding in terror. A captain in charge of German prisoners said that the Germans felt there was no use in fighting the English, for the Germans had seen angels fighting above and in front of the Allied lines, both at Mons and Ypres. Another group of German prisoners attested that they had surrendered because of the hosts of soldiers in the Allied ranks, but in truth there were only two English and French regiments.

In an interview published August 12, 1915, in the London *Daily Mail*, a wounded lance-corporal told that he and his battalion were in retreat from Mons on August 28, 1914. The weather was hot and clear, and the Allied forces were waiting for the Germans to charge. While the corporal was standing guard with some others, an officer ran up to them in great agitation and asked if they'd seen anything. The guards thought he meant German soldiers, but instead the officer took the men to see something in the night sky. There was a strange light in the sky that was distinctly outlined and separate from moonlight. As the men watched, the light became brighter and more clearly defined, revealing three shapes. The one on the center had outstretched wings, and all three wore long, loose golden garments. These spirits hovered above the German lines for about an hour then disappeared.

Phyllis Campbell, a nurse who served behind the lines at Mons, contributed the following to the *Occult Review* in August 1915, a year after the battle. Campbell reported that many of the wounded, particularly the French Catholics, requested pictures of saints and angels to comfort them. Following the retreat at Mons, many of the soldiers were in an exalted state, and one British soldier, a fusilier from Lancashire, asked for a picture of St. George. The fusilier claimed he had seen St. George on a white horse leading the British troops at Vitry-le-François. Another soldier, injured in the leg, corroborated the fusilier's claims and said that St. George had led the charge at Vitry with his sword upraised. French troops maintained the figure was St. MICHAEL or JOAN OF ARC. Campbell claimed to hear the story again later from a priest, two officers and three Irish soldiers.

In her booklet *Back of the Front*, Miss Campbell reported that many severely wounded soldiers, who should have been screaming in pain, were strangely calm, saying that they'd seen a great man on a white horse fighting on their behalf. Miss Campbell claimed that she'd submitted her accounts of the visions at Mons to the *Occult Review* before Machen's story appeared in late September 1914, but no record exists of any submission.

In a letter written by an unnamed lieutenant colonel to Machen, which ran in the *Daily Mail* September 14, 1915 (the lt. colonel's name was supposedly known to editors of the *Daily Mail* but withheld), perhaps the most believable account appeared about the angelic archers. The officer wrote that after the battle of Le Cateau on August 26, 1914, he and two other officers were riding along the column of their division during the night of August 27. Although weary, the officer did not believe that he nor the others had lost their mental faculties. While talking and joking to keep awake, the lt. colonel became conscious of two large bodies of cavalry riding in squadrons in the fields on both sides of the road. The lt. colonel did not remark on the horsemen but watched them for about twenty minutes. They marched in step with his horse and were going in the same direction.

The other two officers had also stopped talking, and at last one of them asked the lt. colonel if he'd seen anything in the fields. All three saw the same sight and determined to take a small party out to reconnoitre. But as soon as the men approached the cavalry, the night grew darker and the horsemen disappeared. The lt. colonel admitted to exhaustion, but said that several witnessed the same phenomenon, a situation he believed unlikely due simply to fatigue.

On August 24, 1915, the *Daily Mail* printed what it believed was the first account of angels at Mons that could be substantiated by a named witness. Private Robert Cleaver, of the First Cheshire Regiment, supposedly signed an affidavit in the presence of a G. S. Hazlehurst stating that he had seen the angels of Mons with his own eyes. Private Cleaver described the angels as a flash of light that confused the German cavalry and caused their lines to crumble. Unfortunately, when Mr. Hazlehurst checked with the headquarters of the Regiment at Salisbury, he found that Private Cleaver had not joined the Regiment until August 22, 1914, and did not post out to France until September 6. He therefore never fought at Mons.

Private Cleaver's story ran along similar lines to previously reported accounts about mysterious clouds and lights.

As early as February 14, 1915, *Light* had run an account by another unnamed officer about the strange cloud that rose up between the German and English lines. In the May 5 *Light*, a General N. stated that while his rearguard was under heavy German fire, a luminous cloud or bright light appeared between the armies. Within the cloud he saw moving shapes, but he could not tell if they were figures. Again the German horses reared and fled, saving the English from certain death.

The paper reported that another young officer—still anonymous—saw the cloud as well, convincing him that the Allies were destined for eventual victory. In a fourth story, a soldier saw a golden cloud appear between the English and German lines, enabling him to save a child who was trapped by the gunfire. In this case the cloud was accompanied by a man on a big horse, similar to the reports of St. George.

Other accounts of divine intervention included the appearance of a great cloud as well, either black or luminous, which came between the Allies and the Germans. Some of these clouds appeared to have bright beings within them. Some witnesses reported seeing true angels, with wings and flowing robes, either coming between the two sides or fighting beside or above the British and French. Other reports told of the "Comrade in White," a figure who walked the battlefields in complete calm and safety to bring aid and comfort. In some accounts the comrade was identified as Jesus Christ.

In the May 15, 1915, *Light*, a Mrs. F. H. Fitzgerald Beale of Mountmellick, Ireland, wrote that a soldier of the Dublin Fusiliers, who had returned home wounded, had seen a black cloud at Mons. The cloud was so thick that it shielded the English lines completely. Mrs. Beale also reported that every soldier who had returned home had told her that a crucifix placed on a home or building was always saved even if everything around it burned.

For some, aid and comfort did not come with a host of angels but through the offices of one man. In the June 9, 1915, issue of *Bladud* referred to above, a Dr. R. F. Horton wrote that several wounded soldiers had told him of a "Comrade in White" who walked the battlefields, even during shelling, to rescue and heal the injured. Then a Miss Stoughton wrote about the experience of her sister, who was an army nurse. The nurse said many soldiers had related seeing the "Comrade in White," who they believed to be the Lord Himself.

Perhaps the most moving story was printed in the June 1915 issue of *Life and Work* magazine. An unnamed soldier wrote that after an especially heated battle a man in white walked among the wounded completely unfazed by sniper fire and shells. He seemed to be everywhere at once. The soldier said that later that day he was shot in both legs while charging the German trenches, and lay in a shell-hole until after dark. As night fell, he heard quiet, firm footsteps and saw the gleam of the man's white clothing. The Germans opened fire, but the stranger stretched out his arms in entreaty and then bent over and lifted the injured soldier. The soldier said he must have fainted, for when he awoke he had been carried to a little cave by a stream. The man was tenderly washing his wounds.

Then the soldier slept; when he awoke, he looked to see what he could do to help his rescuer. He found him kneeling in prayer, and was surprised to see that his hands were injured and bleeding. The man said they were old wounds that had been bothering him lately. When the soldier saw that the man's feet were bleeding as well, he realized with a shock that he had been saved by Christ.

In August 1915, Machen published a compendium of his war tales entitled *The Bowmen and Other Legends of the War*. In the introduction, Machen carefully explained the development of the Angels at Mons as his own fiction. A little later, Harold Begbie published *On the Side of the Angels: The Story of the Angels at Mons—An Answer to 'The Bowmen.'* Begbie collected all the accounts he could find and tried to show that no matter whether the visions were true or false they were not simply creations of Machen.

But the strangest twist on the stories of Mons came from the German side in an article published by the London *Daily News* on February 17, 1930. According to a Colonel Friedrich Herzenwirth, a former member of the Imperial German Intelligence Service, the soldiers actually witnessed visions of soldiers and angels. But instead of heavenly intervention the images were movies projected upon the foggy white cloudbanks over Belgium. Col. Herzenwirth said the object of the mission was to create mass hysteria and terror. He ruefully admitted that if the Kaiser's officers had foreseen that the visions would strengthen the Allies' resolve, rather than weaken it, they would have tried other propaganda. He believed some of the British forces realized the trick but used it to their advantage. The next day, the *Daily News* reported that a highly placed member of the German War Intelligence Department had told the paper's Berlin correspondent that he knew of no Col. Herzenwirth and that the entire story was a hoax.

The last "firsthand" account of angels on the battlefields of World War I appeared in *Fate* magazine in May 1968. The magazine reported on a letter from Rev. Albert H. Baller of Clinton, Massachusetts, who had spoken about UFOs to a group of engineers in New Britain, Connecticut, in the mid-1950s. Rev. Baller reported that during the lecture, one of the engineers said that he'd been in the trenches near Ypres in August 1915 when the Germans launched the first gas attack. At that time none of the soldiers knew of this new, deadly weapon and were unprepared to defend themselves. The troops panicked and ran, with many overtaken by the gas. Suddenly a figure came walking out of the gaseous mist wearing a uniform of the Royal Medical Corps but without any protection from the poison. He spoke English with a French accent.

Around his waist the man had a belt with hooks holding tin cups, and he carried a bucket of what looked like water. He slid into the trench and began removing the cups, dipping them into the liquid and telling the soldiers to drink quickly. The engineer received one of the cups, and remembered that the drink was almost too salty to swallow. But anyone who did drink the liquid was saved from any lasting effects from the gas. Rev. Baller regretted that he did not remember the engineer's name.

Was Machen responsible for the Angels of Mons, or did all these people really experience an angelic visitation? Nearly anyone who could corroborate the stories of angels at Mons is now dead, and accounts from the time are anonymous and unproven. In any case, if the tales did no more than boost the morale of the wounded, they served their purpose.

**Further reading:**

Cavendish, Richard, ed. *May, Myth & Magic: The Illustrated Encyclopedia of Mythology, Religion and the Unknown*, Vol. 11. New York: Marshall Cavendish Ltd., 1985, p. 2963.
Gibbs, Nancy. "Angels Among Us," *Time*. December 27, 1993, p. 61.
McClure, Kevin. *Visions of Bowmen and Angels: Mons 1914*. St. Austell, Cornwall, England: The Wild Places, ca. 1992.

**Mormonism**  Better known as the Church of Christ of Latter-day Saints, the Mormons grew from six original members in 1830 to three million in the 1990s. The Joseph Smith family had experienced dramatic economic ups and downs, migrating from Vermont to New Hampshire and finally to upper New York in the 1820s. Joseph Smith, Sr., had received visions. When in 1823 his son Joseph Smith, Jr., reported receiving visions and instructions from an angel called MORONI, the father and the rest of the large close family, now located in Palmyra, New York, were receptive and believed his account.

Joseph Smith, Jr.,'s testimony about this series of events, which led him to believe that he had been chosen by God to restore the true church of Christ and that all other Christian groups were apostate, constitutes the introduction to *The Book of Mormon*, allegedly written by Mormon, a prophet-historian from the ancient Middle East. "The crowning event recorded in The Book of Mormon is the personal ministry of the Lord Jesus Christ among the Nephites soon after his resurrection. It puts forth the doctrines of the gospel, outlines the plan of salvation, and tells men what they must do to gain peace in this life and eternal salvation in the life to come. After Mormon completed his writings," the introduction continues, "he delivered the account to his son Moroni, who added a few words of his own and hid up the plates in the Hill Cumorah. On September 21, 1823, the same Moroni, then a glorified, resurrected being, appeared to the Prophet Joseph Smith and instructed him."

Moroni's first visit to Joseph Smith, Jr., after the rest of the family in the crowded cabin had gone to sleep, was chiefly characterized by whiteness and brilliance, his "robe of most exquisite whiteness beyond anything earthly I had ever seen . . . and his countenance truly like lightning." Moroni repeatedly told Smith about lost scriptures preserved on plates buried nearby.

With the plates were two magical stones attached to a silver breastplate, construed by some as eyeglasses, called Urim and Thummin, which enabled Smith to translate the scriptures by 1827, after which the angel took the golden tablets away.

Smith and first three men and then another eight, hereafter official witnesses, testified to the existence of the scripture, inscribed in a strange language on gold plates. It is reported that of the first three, Oliver Cowdery and David Whitmer believed they saw an angel descend on a light bearing the plates and confirming the authenticity of the translation. Martin Harris did not claim to have had the vision, but accepted that Smith had seen the angel. Several days later eight men—four Whitmer brothers and their brother-in-law Hiram Page, with Joseph Smith, Sr., and two more of his sons, Hyrum and Samuel—were shown the plates, which they "did handle with our hands." "Seen and hefted," the plates were taken up to heaven by an angel.

Supporters took the text of the translation to a publisher in Mentor, Ohio, and it appeared as *The Book of Mormon* in 1830. The work quotes heavily from the authorized version of the English Bible and is couched in a similar style. It purports to tell the story of the true church of Christ on the American continent after it migrated from Jerusalem. "After thousands of years [from the destruction of the Tower of Babel] all were destroyed except the Lamanites, and they were the principal ancestors of the American Indians," states the introduction to the 1981 version of *The Book of Mormon*.

Mormonism underwent almost continual shifts as it started to grow under the patronage of converts. Smith Jr. continued to receive new visions and revelations, and added these dimensions to Mormon proscriptions in the 1830s and 1840s; dissenters rebelled against some of these and either left the fold voluntarily or were expelled. Meanwhile, outsiders and the law of the land often challenged the sect on business, political, moral or religious grounds. Joseph Smith, Jr., was killed in an attack on the Mormons' Nauvoo, Illinois, outpost in 1844. A brief summary of some of the most notable Mormon beliefs, particularly in relation to the angels and celestial hierarchies, will give an idea of the uniqueness of this sect.

### MORMON BELIEFS AND PRACTICES

The New England settlers who became the first Mormons emerged from a long-standing group of separatists or radicals who lived on the fringes of Calvinist Puritan orthodoxy. They were well prepared for the Mormon message because they asked questions, held spiritist universalist views, and were predisposed to the occult and magical.

This was coupled with a yearning for the ancient church, a stream of thought called *restorationism*, which went back to the Middle Ages. This theme had been picked up by each Protestant declaration of independence and even Catholic revolutions, such as that of the Franciscans. Mormonism spoke to the revulsion with the "ordinary" or "gentile" church, and the passion to possess dogmatic purity in Joseph Smith's discovery and translation from an ancient language of golden scriptures buried at the time of the Tower of Babel.

Among this separatist fringe in the eighteenth-century New England area were also "Immortalists," who believed in human divinization, and those who practiced "spiritual wifery" or "the new covenant of spiritual union." There were strange sects who met behind closed doors and were rumored to do all manner of things. One 1793 report stated that a Nat Smith of Hopkinton, Massachusetts, "proceeded to assume and declare himself to be the Most High God and wore a cap with the word GOD inscribed on its front. His Great Chair was a Holy Chair. . . . He had a number of Adorers and Worshippers, who . . . believed he was the Great God."

Treasure-divining was a central dimension of the radical perfectionism of the New Israelite movement, which emerged in Rutland County, Vermont, at the end of the 1790s and which had a direct link to Mormonism. Nathaniel Wood, one of its leaders, prophesied after his excommunication that he had literal descent from the Lost Tribes of Israel, had a special dispensation; his family and followers began work on a temple and divined for gold "to pave the streets of the New Jerusalem" and expected that a destroying angel would bring down earthquakes and plagues on the "gentiles."

Money-diggers would locate buried treasure through divination and attempt to retrieve it. Joseph Smith, Sr., had taken part in some of these expeditions, four of which were officially reported in affidavits by subsequent researchers. Martin Harris, one of the eleven official witnesses to the golden plates, reported that Joseph Smith, Jr., said Moroni "told him he must quit the company of the money-diggers." An 1826 trial record shows that Joseph Smith, Jr., had taken part in a treasure hunt using a certain stone. Richard L. Bushman, a sympathetic biographer, said that Smith Jr. had gotten involved because he was pressured by neighbors, his own father, and by poverty.

In treating the elements from a culture of magical practice that contributed to Joseph Smith's messages and methods, John Brooke cites treasure-divining or money-digging along with witchcraft, conjuring, counterfeiting, alchemy and Freemasonry. John L. Brooke's thesis is that Smith "began his engagement with the supernatural as a village conjurer but transformed himself into a prophet of the 'Word,' announcing the opening of a new dispensation. Then, moving beyond his role as prophet and revelator, Smith transformed himself and the Mormon priesthood into Christian-hermetic magi, a role previously manifested in the medieval alchemist, the Renaissance hermetic philosopher (see MUSIC AND ANGELS), and the perfectionist sectarians of the Radical Reformation."

Mystical trances producing visions of angels and saints, prophecy and the like, performed in the inner sanctum, were offered to the faithful, following the tradition of alchemy and Kabbalah that the human soul can break free from the elemental sphere of the earth and ascend through lesser celestial and supercelestial heavens of the planets, the stars, and the angels to communicate directly with the divinity. In May 1829 John the Baptist appeared to Smith and Oliver Cowdery, and they received from him divine appointments as First and Second Elders of the new church. They claimed that John the Baptist had conferred on them the Levitical, or Aaronic Priesthood. Conferred on "every worthy male member," eventually starting with boys twelve years old, these offices provided the semblance of an egalitarian order for white males in the church. Welcomed as deacons, teachers, and priests, the Aaronic Priesthood held "the keys of the ministering of angels." They were to watch over the church, teach the gospel, and perform baptisms.

In February 1832 Smith revised Genesis and reproduced the three heavens of the Kabbalah and hermeticism in the three Mormon heavens, the telestial, terrestrial and celestial. Both hermeticism and Mormonism celebrate the mutuality of spiritual and material worlds, precreated intelligences, free will, a divine Adam, a fortunate, sinless Fall, and the symbolism and religious efficacy of marriage and sexuality. And as in hermeticism, Adam, "the father of all, prince of all, that ancient of days," would occupy a central position in the Mormon cosmology. In fact, this divine Adam was also eventually equated with MICHAEL the archangel by Brigham Young in April 1852:

When our Father Adam came into the garden of Eden, he came into it with a celestial body, and brought Eve, one of his wives, with him. He helped to make and organize this world. He is Michael, the Archangel, the Ancient of Days! about whom holy men have written and spoken—he is our Father and our God, and the only God with whom we have to do.

In stark contrast to Reformation Calvinists, who stand before their omnipotent God sinful and powerless inheritors of Adam's original sin at the Fall, hermeticism promised divine power to mortal man as magus, restored to the powers of Adam in Paradise before the Fall. Freemasonry too presented a mythology where the divine Adam in the Garden of Eden communed directly with God and the angels in a state of perfection. Hermeticism and Mormonism both rejected original sin and advocated free human will. Mormonism explicitly rejected Calvinism in its advocacy of universal salvation and the freedom of the will.

Smith's authority as "Seer and Revelator" was announced in April 1830 and confirmed in September. In February and March 1831, Smith issued a series of revelations that began to establish sacramental and institutional strictures, including the collective economy called the United Order of Enoch, or the Law of Consecration. The Council of Twelve Apostles was established in February 1835. In granting priestly powers "to seal up the Saints," Joseph Smith gave the Mormon hierarchy the same authority that the hermetic a'chemist assumed: human means to immortality, indeed divinity. The men of the hierarchy, initiated into these rituals in the long attic rooms of the new temple in Kirtland, Ohio, in March 1836, testified that "they were filled with the Holy Ghost, which was like fire in their bones," and fell into visions and prophecy. Smith had visions of Adam and Abraham, and of his deceased brother Alvin in the celestial kingdom. This experience inspired a revelation that informed the practice of baptism for the dead, begun six years later.

Joseph Smith made this revelation on July 12, 1843, at Nauvoo, Illinois:

> [I]t shall be done unto them all things whatsoever my servant hath put upon them, in time and through all eternity; and shall be of full force when they are out of the world; and they shall pass the angels and the gods, which are set there, to their exaltation and glory in all things, as hath been sealed upon their heads, which glory shall be a fullness and a continuation of the seeds forever and ever.
>
> Then shall they be as gods, because they have no end. . . . Then shall they be above all, because all things are subject to them. Then shall they be gods, because they have all power, and the angels are subject to them. (Brooke, 3)

By 1845 a successor of Smith, John Haven, had welcomed the first group of children who were to stand in for deceased ancestors, who would then become immortal Mormons by being baptized after death.

Smith's theology thus promised a radical departure from traditional Protestant Christianity. The Mormon cosmos promised universal salvation for humanity and divinity to the Mormon faithful. As a Mormon proverb later put it, capturing the doctrines of both eternity and divinization: "As man is now, so once was God; as God is now, man may become." Human salvation and Mormon divinity would be structured in a radically new configuration of the invisible world, three ascending kingdoms replacing the duality of heaven and hell.

Being endowed in the temple was the first of many secrets that would allow a Mormon to ascend toward godhead. By April 1844 only sixty-six people had been given the induction ceremony. Celestial marriage would seal a couple for eternity, and only those who had been granted eternal marriage would be allowed to ascend to the third heaven. On May 28, 1843, Smith was sealed to his wife Emma Hale for "time and eternity." Eternal marriage—and godhead—was guaranteed only by the marriage sealing added to the temple endowment. In heaven, Mormons without sealed eternal marriages would occupy the lowest degree of glory in the celestial kingdom, where they would simply be ministering angels, servants to those of higher degrees, and condemned to an unexalted existence, without prospect of progression toward and in divinity.

Finally, someone had to have authority to bestow these privileges on the uninitiated and to receive the ultimate reward. This was the high priesthood to which John the Baptist had initiated Joseph Smith and Oliver Cowdery. By 1846 almost six hundred Mormons had been given a second anointing to give the kingly patriarchal powers "to seal up the Saints to eternal life." The reward of the second anointing was a virtually unconditional guarantee of godhead in the highest degree of the celestial kingdom.

In announcing a new dispensation, in assuming the revelatory powers of a prophet, in blurring the lines between spirit and matter, and in promising godhead to the faithful, Smith defied not only the established and evangelical churches, but even the most ardent contemporary advocates of the imminences of the millennium. The growth of the Mormon sect, its persecution and eventual triumph under Brigham Young, who led 30,000 of the faithful to a permanent settlement in Utah, are part of American history and folklore. The modern Church of Latter-day Saints has a very large following and a vigorous campaign of proselytization.

**Further reading:**

*The Book of Mormon: An Account Written by the Hand of Mormon Upon Plates taken from the Plates of Nephi.* Translated by Joseph Smith, Jr. First published 1830. Salt Lake City, Utah: The Church of Christ of Latter-day Saints, 1981.

Brooke, John L. *The Refiner's Fire: The Making of Mormon Cosmology, 1644–1844.* New York and Cambridge, England: Cambridge University Press, 1994.

Bushman, Richard L. *Joseph Smith and the Beginnings of Mormonism.* Urbana and Chicago: University of Illinois Press, 1984.

Paul, Erich Robert. *Science, Religion, and Mormon Cosmology.* Urbana and Chicago: University of Illinois Press, 1992.

**Moroni** As God's heavenly messenger to Joseph Smith, Jr., founder of the Church of Jesus Christ of Latter-day Saints, or Mormonism, Moroni brought Smith the story of Christ's work in the New World. These accounts were inscribed in an ancient hieroglyphic code on golden tablets, and buried near Smith's home in western New York State. Smith's translations, collected into *The Book of Mormon*, form the other sacred texts, besides the Bible, of the church.

The younger Smith was not the first member of his family to receive messages from divine spirits, however. Around 1811 the Smiths were living in Vermont, eking out a subsistence living as farmers. Both Joseph Sr. and his wife Lucy had come from more comfortable situations, and they deeply

ENTERED ACCORDING TO ACT OF CONGRESS IN THE YEAR 1886, BY C. C. A. CHRISTENSEN, EPHRAIM, UTAH.

The angel MORONI delivering the plates of the BOOK OF MORMON to JOSEPH SMITH jun.
September 22d 1827.

**Moroni delivering the plates of *The Book of Mormon* to Joseph Smith Jr. (reprinted courtesy of U.S. Library of Congress)**

resented their neighbors' hostility and contempt as a result of the Smiths' current poverty. Joseph and Lucy associated such attitudes with prevailing religious thought, which equated ill fortune with bad intentions, sin and even evil—in other words, the Smiths must be getting what they deserved.

Joseph Sr. began to have revelatory dreams which vividly showed his contempt for organized churches. The elder Smith later recounted that a heavenly messenger whom he described as an "attendant spirit" came to him with a box representing "true religion." When Smith tried to open the box, wild animals—which Smith took to represent the various established sects—rushed to attack him, and he dropped the box.

Later the attendant spirit returned and took Smith through a desolate area into a beautiful valley. In his dream, Smith gathered his large family around a tree which bore delicious fruit, much like the Tree of the Knowledge of Good and Evil in Eden. But instead of leading to sin and banishment, the fruit of this tree represented God's pure love for all those who keep His commandments. Smith was enraptured.

But his joy was marred by observing a large building in the distance, filled with finely dressed men and women who laughed contemptuously at the Smith family, much as the Smiths' neighbors had done. The angel told Joseph that the

building represented Babylon, the center of evil in the Book of Revelation, and that the finely dressed people inside despised God's true saints and would fall from His grace. Such black-and-white depictions of salvation, especially when the saved are the poor and downtrodden, characterize a school of thought known as Christian Primitivism.

Around 1815, Joseph and Lucy moved their family to Oneida County (now Ontario County) in western New York State, to try their luck in a new area. During the nineteenth century Oneida County was inflamed by one religious movement after another—from Presbyterians, Methodists and Baptists to great revival preachers like Charles Grandison Finney, and from groups like the Oneida Perfectionists to Millerites and Spiritualists. So many ideas caught fire in the area that locals called it the Burned-Over District.

By 1820–21, another revival was in progress among the Presbyterians, Methodists and Baptists, with fire-and-brimstone preachers of each sect exhorting sinners to confess and avoid the religious lies of the other two groups. Most of the Smith family chose Presbyterianism, but Joseph could not make up his mind. Described as a literal thinker, he prayed for divine guidance to select the one church that was right.

According to Joseph Smith, Jr.'s, own account in *The Pearl of Great Price*, a pillar of light descended from the heavens bringing two Personages, as Smith called them, ostensibly God the Father and one whom He called "my Beloved Son." These Personages told Smith to choose no existing denomination, for they were all wrong, and like his father before him he would be shown the true Church.

Smith reports that he was reviled and persecuted for his visions, but they did not stop. On the night of September 21–22, 1823, his room was filled with a brilliant white light revealing an angel, called Moroni, who appeared as a messenger from God. Moroni told Smith that he had helped to write, then bury, a history written on gold plates by his father Mormon, of an ancient people descended from Israel who had lived and died in America. Most biblical scholars maintain that God created the angels as a separate population, but Moroni apparently became an angel after death.

He told Smith that around 600 B.C.E., God forewarned the Hebrew prophet Lehi of the coming captivity in Babylon. Lehi gathered his family and followers and fled Jerusalem, wandering in the wilderness for many years until they reached the sea. With divine guidance, Lehi's family built a boat and sailed to what is now America. Upon arriving, a long-simmering family argument split Lehi's sons into two factions. Those who were righteous and obeyed God followed Nephi (Nephites); those who chose evil followed Laman (Lamanites). Each side won or lost wars for supremacy until Christ appeared to them after the Resurrection. He reunited the Nephites and Lamanites, chose twelve disciples, and instituted a 200-year period of peace, prosperity and service to God.

But by the time Lehi's descendants had been in America for a thousand years, both factions had become corrupt and oblivious to the prophet's warnings. As the Lamanites, a fierce, dark-skinned people, were exterminating the Nephites in yet another war circa 421 C.E., the prophet and general Mormon engraved an abridged history of his people on golden plates, using Egyptian-like hieroglyphics. Shortly before he was killed, Mormon entrusted the plates to his son Moroni, who added to the history and then buried the plates in the Hill Cumorah before he too died. Victorious but without the benefit of contact with the gentler, white Nephites, the Lamanites became even more fierce. They forgot their history, Moroni told Smith, and eventually became the native Americans discovered by Columbus.

Moroni ended his narrative by telling Smith that God had chosen him to retrieve these plates, translate their stories with the accompanying seer stones, and resurrect the church to prepare for the latter days (before the Second Coming). The angel appeared to Smith three times that night, repeating the story and his instructions verbatim, and again the next day. The angel revealed the plates' hiding place—the above-mentioned Hill Cumorah, miraculously near Smith's Manchester, New York, home—but forbade him to dig up the plates until four years from that date. Although eager to verify his vision, Smith did as he was told, retrieving the golden plates, the seer stones called the Urim and Thummim, and the breastplate upon which they were fastened on September 22, 1827.

Smith created a sensation when he brought home these golden plates covered in Egyptian-style hieroglyphics. He had had a reputation for finding things, maybe mythic treasures, by using a seer or "peep" stone (a crystal ball), but this prize and his revelations were too much for most of his neighbors. To avoid harrassment, Smith and his new wife Emma went to Harmony, Pennsylvania, to translate the plates. Martin Harris, a sympathetic farmer who had given the Smiths $50 to move, left his wife and family to follow the Smiths and help with the plates' translation.

By the spring of 1828, Smith and Harris had transcribed 116 pages of manuscript, which Harris begged Smith to let him take home and show to his wife. Previously Harris had taken a sample of Smith's translation to New York, where Professor Charles Anthon had identified the characters on the plates as Egyptian, Chaldean, Assyrian and Arabic. Although warned by Moroni to guard the plates, stones and translation, Smith allowed Harris to take the manuscript—the only copy—which he then reportedly lost.

By April 1829, Smith had started over. He was still translating when Oliver Cowdery appeared, an itinerant schoolteacher who had heard of Smith's work from Smith's parents in Manchester. Intrigued, Oliver became his scribe, and the work was finished by the end of the year. David Whitmer, an early convert to Mormonism, said that Smith would put the stones in his hat and pull it around his face to simulate darkness. Then a character would appear, as if on parchment, accompanied by the English translation. Smith would read the translation to Cowdery, who wrote it down, then another character would appear in the hat. *The Book of Mormon*, hence the church's familiar name, was published in March 1830.

Once the translation of the first plates was complete, Moroni supposedly reclaimed the plates and stones, with many of the later plates still sealed. The angel never again appeared to Smith or any of his followers.

**Further reading:**

Crim, Keith, general ed. *Abingdon Dictionary of Living Religions.* Nashville: Abingdon Press, 1981.

Guiley, Rosemary Ellen. *Harper's Encyclopedia of Mystical and Paranormal Experience.* San Francisco: HarperCollins, 1991.

Melton, J. Gordon. *Encyclopedic Handbook of Cults in America.* New York and London: Garland Publishing Inc., 1986.

Moore, R. Laurence. "The Occult Connection? Mormonism, Christian Science and Spiritualism," *The Occult in America*, John Godwin, ed. New York: Doubleday, 1982.

Shipps, Jan. *Mormonism: The Story of a New Religious Tradition.* Urbana, Ill.: University of Illinois Press, 1985.

Smith, Joseph Jr. trans., *The Book of Mormon.* Salt Lake City: The Church of Jesus Christ of Latter-day Saints, 1986.

Smith, Joseph Jr. *The Pearl of Great Price.* Salt Lake City: The Church of Jesus Christ of Latter-day Saints, 1972

Winn, Kenneth H. *Exiles in a Land of Liberty: Mormons in America 1830–1846.* Chapel Hill: The University of North Carolina Press, 1991.

**Moses**   Biblical patriarch and great leader of the Israelites who received the Ten Commandments and other moral rules from God, and who had various encounters with angels.

The infant Moses was cast adrift in a basket in bulrushes in Egypt. He was found and raised as an Egyptian by the daughter of the king. The Egyptians' cruelty toward Israeli slaves angered him, and he killed an Egyptian overseer, an act which forced him to flee from Egypt. He lived as a shepherd in the desert and married a daughter of Jethro.

Forty years went by. One day, Moses was out grazing his flocks on Mount Horeb, and he came upon a burning bush. According to Exodus 3:2–5:

> And the angel of the Lord appeared to him in a flame of fire out of the midst of the bush: and he looked, and lo, the bush was burning, yet it was not consumed. And Moses said, "I will turn aside and see this great sight, why the bush is not burnt." When the Lord saw that he turned aside to see, God called to him out of the bush, "Moses, Moses!" and he said, "Here am I." Then he said, "Do not come near; put off your shoes from your feet, for the place on which you are standing is holy ground."

God told Moses he had heard the crying and suffering of the enslaved Israelites. He told Moses to return to Egypt and petition the pharaoh to let the Israelites go, and to lead his people to the "Promised Land."

Moses, along with his brother, Aaron, did as directed, but the pharaoh refused, insisting on a miracle. Aaron turned his staff into a serpent, but still the pharaoh refused. Advised by the Lord, Moses and Aaron warned the pharaoh that the Egyptians would be punished with ten plagues unless the Israelites were released. The pharaoh still was unmoved, and plagues of vermin, pests, pestilence, storms and darkness swept the land.

The final plague was the death of the first-born of every family and every animal in Egypt. God instructed the Israelites how to mark their homes with the blood of a sacrificed lamb, so that they would be passed over (the origin of the Passover). The deaths were carried out by the destroying angel. (See ANGELS OF DESTRUCTION.)

The pharaoh then released the Israelites. Moses, guided by an angel, led them to Canaan. God helped Moses to part the waters of the Red Sea to give them easy passage. When they reached Mt. Sinai, Moses went up the mountain, where he was given the Ten Commandments by God.

A modern interpretation of the angel in the burning bush is that Moses had a NEAR-DEATH EXPERIENCE (NDE). His long years in the desert—a place of spiritual transformation—may have prepared him for a marked change in consciousness. The bush might be akin to the dazzling white light seen

**Moses beholding the Messiah and the Great Mystery (Jakob Boehme, *Mysterium magnum*)**

in NDEs. The instructions to liberate the Israelites might be compared to the life-review in an NDE, and to the new sense of mission (usually spiritual) that many NDErs feel after their experience. Moses may have attained a state of ultra-consciousness on the mountain, and his personality may have been altered so that he became a charismatic leader and lawgiver to his people.

The incident involving receipt of the Ten Commandments also involved angels, according to some accounts. The Bible says only that the Lord comes down to the top of Mount Sinai and calls Moses to the top, and Moses goes up (Exodus 19:20). The mountain is shrouded in a mystical smoke and fire that makes the entire mountain top appear to burn. A rabbinic story from the ninth century relates that Moses ascends on into heaven.

According to the story, when Moses reaches the top of Mount Sinai he sees a cloud floating there and steps inside it. He is at once in the presence of a great light similar to that of the burning bush. The cloud bears him up to heaven, and he loses track of time. The cloud stops at the gate of the firmament and he gets out. The angel Kemuel, who guards the gate, admonishes him for trying to enter heaven. Moses tells the angel he has come to receive the Torah, and instantly the gate opens. Seeing that it is God's will, Kemuel allows Moses to come through. The angels, who were not happy to see the creation of humanity, likewise are not happy to see the Torah being passed into human hands.

Moses travels to the river Rigyon, made of fire that consumes both angels and humans. Angels of destruction greet him and try to incinerate him with their breath of fire. Moses cries out to God ("Master of the Universe") for help, and a wave of fire rises up and obliterates the angels.

When other angels see Moses, they too cry out to God for help. God tells them that he has come for the Torah, prompting the angels to protest, "You created the Torah before You created the world. How can such a precious treasure pass into the hands of a mere man?" God replies, "It was created for that very purpose."

God pulls Moses up to Paradise. Moses apprehends God on his throne, and behind Him an angel so big that Moses is terrified. This is the angel SANDALPHON who, God explains, weaves garlands out of the prayers of Israel. Calmed by God, Moses relaxes. He watches as Sandalphon finishes a garland, and immediately it rises of its own accord to rest on the head of God. This sets in motion mighty forces. The heavenly hosts shake with awe, the wheels of the throne revolve, and the creatures of the Chariot roar out like lions, "Holy holy is the Lord of hosts."

God too is weaving. He tells Moses that he weaves the crowns of the letters of the Torah, so that one thousand years into the future they will be interpreted by Rabbi Akiba ben Joseph. Moses is then shown a vision of the rabbi studying the Torah, and saying he learned it from Moses at Mount Sinai. In this way Moses is given to comprehend the legacy he will bestow upon future generations.

God opens the portals of heaven and reveals himself to the people of Israel, who fall down and die of fright. God then dispatches a dew of Resurrection, which revives the souls of the righteous as it will at the End of Days. All are revived.

God then assigns 120 myriad angels to act as a sort of GUARDIAN ANGEL to the people of Israel. Each person receives two angels, one to keep the heart beating and the other to raise the head so that the glory of God can be perceived.

While the portals are open and the people below can hear, God transmits the Torah to Moses for the next forty days. This becomes written law. For forty nights, He explains to Moses what he has transmitted. This becomes oral law, revealing the seventy meanings of every word of the Torah.

When the task is done, a cloud takes Moses back to the top of Mount Sinai, and he delivers the word to the people.

See also ANGEL OF THE LORD; ANGELS OF THE PRESENCE, NEAR-DEATH EXPERIENCE.

Compare to ISAAC.

**Further reading:**

*The New Oxford Annotated Bible with the Apochrypha.* Herbert G. May and Bruce M. Metzger, eds. New York: Oxford University Press, 1977.

Schwartz, Howard. *Gabriel's Palace: Jewish Mystical Tales.* New York: Oxford University Press, 1993.

Steinmetz, Dov, M.D. "Moses' 'Revelation' on Mount Horeb as a Near-Death Experience," in *Journal of Near-Death Studies,* 11(4) Summer 1993, pp. 199–203.

## Mount Moriah, angel of  See ISAAC.

## Muhammad (c. 570 or 571–632)

The Messenger of God and the Prophet of Islam received his call to prophecy via dreams in which either God or the archangel GABRIEL appeared to him. Muhammad is believed by followers to be the last of all divine revelations before the end of the world. His name means "the Praised one" or "he who is glorified." According to tradition there are 200 names for Muhammad, such as "Joy of Creation," "Beloved of God," etc. Mention of his name customarily is followed by one of several invocations, such as "God bless him and give him peace."

Muhammad was an inspired prophet and religious reformer in the Semitic (and biblical) tradition, preaching holy war and the triumph of justice. The religion he founded borrows much from Judaism and Christianity. By some accounts he was illiterate, which make a case for his having obtained wisdom directly from God in revelations rather than copying Judaism and Christianity. However, Muhammad was a businessman prior to becoming a prophet, and it is likely that he was at least semiliterate. Nonetheless it is not likely that he actually read Judeo-Christian literature, though he had heard some of the stories contained therein.

Muhammad preached a God that is both personal and transcendent. He accepted Jesus as the Messiah, and the Immaculate Conception of Mary and the Virgin Birth. However, he believed that Judaism and Christianity had distorted God's revelations to Moses and Jesus, and that the pagan Arabs lived in ignorance of God's will. He reformed Arabic religion and life, and established Islam as the "original" word of God.

Only two dates are certain in Muhammad's life: the year of his emigration from Mecca to Medina, 622, and the year of his death, 632. The primary source of information on his life is the Koran (Qu'ran), the holy book of Islam given to him by Allah (God) in a series of revelations.

Muhammad was born in Mecca between 567 and 572, most likely in 570 or 571. His lineage was traced back to Ishmael and ABRAHAM. His father died prior to his birth and he was made a ward of his grandfather, Abd al-Muttalib, the founder of the pagan Hashimite tribe of the Quryash of Mecca, a cult of idols. Muhammad was given to a Beduin foster mother to be raised in the desert.

According to one account, two men dressed in white appeared one day, when the boy was four or five and was out shepherding lambs. They threw him down, opened his chest, and stirred their hands around. In later years Muhammad said that the men were angels who had come to wash a dark spot from his heart with snow; thus was he purified of original sin. Muhammad also had an unusual and large mark between his shoulders. Ringed by hair, it was supposed to be the "Seal of Prophecy," the sign of the last Divine Messenger to the world.

Muhammad returned to Mecca while still a young child. Eventually he became a businessman dealing in skins and raisins. At the age of twenty-five he married Khadijah, who was nineteen years his senior. She bore either two or three sons, who died in infancy, and four daughters.

Muhammad began to feel the call of spirit in 610, when he reached forty years of age. He withdrew to the mountains near Mecca to pray and meditate. He began to receive a series of divine revelations. They are not given in order in the Koran, and it is difficult to ascertain which occurred first. It is likely that he had at least several revelations before those dealing with the Koran began. In Suras 53 and 81:17–19, Muhammad describes two visions that apparently had occurred to him in the past. He is approached by a mysterious male figure first "on the high horizon" and then near a lotus tree by "the garden of the dwelling"; Muhammad describes himself as the figure's servant (the second experience, in which Muhammad was transported to another realm, clearly was visionary). The descriptions suggest that the figure is God; it was later in Muhammad's career that he interpreted this figure as that of Gabriel. Muslim interpreters also have favored Gabriel.

It was not until after Muhammad moved to Medina in 622 that he interpreted any of his revelations as coming from Gabriel. This may have been motivated by criticism directed at him, that he was not a true prophet because God had not sent down his angels to him. His critics called him "jinn-possessed." (See JINN.)

However, during his Mecca ascetic period, Muhammad did receive many revelations that came to him in dreams and in heavy, torporous trances. These revelations continued throughout the rest of his life.

One of his visionary experiences involved an ascent to heaven (a prerequisite for any prophet). He is taken to the Temple Mount in Jerusalem astride the mythical beast Buraq, and then to the seventh heaven and then to God, where, it was later said, he began to receive the Koran. Another tradition holds that first the angels Michael and Gabriel appear and open his breast and wash his heart (a retelling of the alleged childhood event), removing doubt, polytheism, error and pre-Islamic belief and instilling within it faith and wisdom. Then Gabriel takes Muhammad to the heavens. In the first heaven he meets Adam; in the second heaven John and Jesus; in the third heaven the patriarch Joseph; in the fourth heaven the prophet Idris; in the fifth heaven Aaron; in the sixth heaven Moses; and in the seventh heaven Abraham. From there he is taken to Paradise, where God gives him revelations, including fifty daily prayers. On his descent, Moses urges Muhammad to ask God to reduce the number of prayers. He does so five times, until the number is reduced to five.

Another tradition describes Muhammad's introduction to the Koran as beginning in a dream. One night the Angel Gabriel appears as the Messenger of Allah. He brings a coverlet of brocade upon which there is writing. He presses it upon Muhammad and says, "Recite!" Muhammad asks, "What shall I recite?" The angel says only, "Recite!" They engage in this exercise several times, and then Gabriel finally gives him what later became the opening lines of Sura 96:

> Recite in the name of thy Lord who created,
> Who created man of blood coagulated.
> Read! Thy Lord is most beneficient,
> Who taught by the pen,
> Taught that which they knew not to men.

Muhammad reads the coverlet and Gabriel departs. When he awakens he hears words that seem to be written on his heart: "O Muhammad, you are the Apostle of God and I am Gabriel."

Regardless of exactly how it happened, the first night of Koran revelations is referred to as the "Night of Power." According to Muslim tradition, the Koran was revealed gradually over the rest of Muhammad's life, in nearly daily trance states, with the final revelation coming just months before his death in 632. The Koran totals 6,666 verses and forms the doctrine of Islam. Muhammad himself never explicitly stated that this was how he received it. The Koran states that it was sent from God gradually so that it could be recited to people at intervals.

Three years after the first revelation, Muhammad began to call himself a prophet and to preach to his own clan, the Hashimites, that if they did not worship God instead of their idols they would be punished. The followers of the new religion were called Muslims, which is derived from a term that means "they that surrender to God."

Muhammad was successful in converting many people, which engendered hostility from the Quryash, who guarded the Ka'bah stone in Mecca. Conflict then arose. The Quryash banned commerce with the Hashimites and began persecutions of the Muslims, driving them out. Muhammad went to Yathrib in 622, now observed as the year in which the Islamic era began. Yathrib became the first Islamic state and became known as Medina, "the city of the Prophet."

A holy war erupted. Muhammad, aided by legions of angels, eventually prevailed, destroying the idols at the Ka'bah. Within weeks, Mecca officially converted to Islam. There followed conversions all over Arabia.

In March 632, Muhammad led a farewell pilgrimage to Mount Ararat, where he delivered the last revelation of the Koran. The new religion was named Islam ("surrender" or "reconciliation") and the law of Islam was established. Muhammad died on June 8, 632, and was buried in his house. His death was followed by a period of confusion and civil wars.

Islam seeks to restore the pre-Fall state of the Garden of Eden, in which man in his essence was perfect and capable of perceiving God in the Unseen. Its fundamentals are the Five Pillars: the profession of faith; the canonical prayer or worship; the fast; the legal tithe; and the pilgrimage.

See ISLAMIC ANGELOLOGY.

**Further reading:**

Dermenghem, Emile. *Muhammad and the Islamic Tradition.* Woodstock, N.Y.: The Overlook Press, 1981. First published 1955.

Lippman, Thomas W. *Understanding Islam: An Introduction to the Moslem World.* New York: New American Library, 1982.

Peters, F.E. *Muhammad the and Origins of Islam.* Albany, N.Y.: State University of New York Press, 1994.

**Munkar**   See ISLAMIC ANGELOLOGY.

**music and angels**   "Music is well said to be the speech of angels," wrote Goethe. From ancient times, sound and ceremonial song have linked the bodily senses to the mystical, and have brought near to us the presence of God and angels. The Vedas, yogas of Tantrism, HINDUISM, Sufism and Taoism include chant, song and music as key elements. The vibratory metaphor corresponds to gradations of gross, subtle and ethereal realms, each the domain of higher beings invoked with their tone. Each of the chakras in the human subtle energy field is ruled by a "goddess" who can be intoned through her mantra. In the West another pervasive notion of angels and music, related to the Eastern vibratory metaphor, thrived for millennia among theologians and philosophers, namely that the celestial spheres were analogous to angelic hierarchies and created the music of the spheres. For them, music was a mathematics made audible through mystical and magical powers.

Further, in every sect music is an essential component of ritual and liturgy. Music in all known cultures—ancient or modern, Eastern or Western—begins as an oral tradition. The Jewish cantor, the priest who sings the Mass, and the Muslim muezzin, who calls the faithful to prayer five times a day, are single unaccompanied voices. The purity and power of a

Nineteenth-century songsheet (reprinted courtesy of U.S. Library of Congress)

human voice in pure chant evokes the ancient sense of the *logos* implicit in the term *theologia*, a poetic utterance about God. For over a thousand years it was believed that the divine office chanted by monks—"angels in training" on earth—participated in the continual angelic chorus praising God.

The connection between artistic inspiration and angels, mythologically embodied in the Muses, suggests attunement with a divine source. Countless musicians, artists and poets have described the experience of being seized by the muse and "shown" or "given" a work. Wolfgang Amadeus Mozart, for example, could compose one work while transcribing another. In a letter he described how his compositions came to be:

> Whence and how do they come? I do not know and I have nothing to do with it. Those which please me, I keep in my head and hum. . . . Once I have my theme, another melody comes linking itself to the first one, in accordance to the needs of the composition as a whole. Then my soul is on fire with inspiration, if, however, nothing occurs to distract my attention. . . . The work grows; I keep expanding in conceiving it more and more clearly until I have the entire composition finished in my head though it may be long. Then my mind seizes it as a glance of my eye a beautiful picture of a handsome youth. It does not come to me successively, with its various parts and worked out in detail, as they will be later on, but it is in its entirety that my imagination lets me hear it.

### LITURGY

The Jewish morning service contains some ancient prayers (*yoser*) which scholars have traced back to the Essenes and resemble *The Litany of the Angels* found among the Dead Sea Scrolls. Jewish folklore claimed that as the devout chanted their prayers, choirs of angels accompanied them. The Sanctus of the Christian Mass continued this motif. *The Litany of the Angels* consists of two brief fragments. The first is based squarely on the vision of EZEKIEL (1 and 10) and depicts the angels rising in their several ranks to praise God aloft on His Chariot/Throne (Merkabah). The second sets forth a series of blessings evidently conceived as the angelic counterpart to the Priestly Benediction (Numbers 6.24–27) recited in the Temple of old and now a staple element of all Jewish public worship.

*The Litany*, though fragmentary, conveys the celestial hierarchy's presence in sound as well as vision:

> While they are soaring aloft, there sounds a murmur of angel voices . . . and the lifting of their wings is accompanied by a clamor of joyous song. It is the murmur of angels blessing the Chariot-like Throne above the firmament of the cherubim, while they themselves, from below the place where the Glory dwells, go acclaiming in joyous song the splendor of that radiant expanse. . . . Like fiery apparitions are they, spirits most holy, looking like streams of fire, in the likeness of burnished metal or of lustrous ware; clothed in garments opalescent, a riot of wondrous hues, a diffusion of brightness; live angelic spirits, constantly coming and going beside the glorious wonderful Chariot. Amid all the noise of their progress sounds also the murmured intonation of blessings, and whenever they come round, they shout their holy hallelujahs.

The conflict between the Angels of Mercy—Sandalphon's army—and Satan's host on Rosh Hashanah and Yom Kippur, the days of awe and judgment, is dramatically expressed in the Hineni, a prayer in which the cantor, leading the congregation, pleads with God that he "rebuke Satan and keep him from blocking the ascent of my prayers . . . and may all the angels who are assigned to prayers convey my prayer before the throne of your glory."

The Sanctus of the Mass has direct links to several biblical passages describing the unceasing glorification of God by the angels. REVELATION 4.8 combines Ezekiel 10's prophetic vision, of the Cherubim of the heavenly court who carry the throne and cry praise of God unendingly, with the prophetic vision of the seraphim in the temple in Isaiah 6. The same passage became the heart of the prayer of sanctification (the Kedoshah) which is a vital part of every Jewish prayer service. ST. PAUL tells the Ephesians (1.21): "thou art exalted high above all principalities and powers, all virtues and dominations, and above every name that is known, not in this world only, but in the world to come."

Therefore both Jewish and Christian worship is no merely human occasion. The angels and the entire universe take part in it. The songs of the church are the counterparts of heavenly songs and, corresponding to the manner of participation in the heavenly song, the spiritual life of the church is incorporated in that of heaven. The Epistle to the Hebrews 12:18 declares that Christians approach the festive assembly in which countless angels, the citizens of the heavenly city, and the souls of just men made perfect take part. It was also assumed that the laity's song was of a lower order than that of the monks. ORIGEN said "to man, the singing of psalms is appropriate; but the singing of hymns is for angels and those who lead a life like that of the angels."

Christian liturgists were conscious from the beginning of the heavenly hierarchy linking up with the church. In the first thousand years of monasticism, the orders of angels were believed to be literally augmented by priestly and monastic orders that resembled them. Thus their singing of the praises of God at the eight daily offices (matins at midnight; lauds at daybreak; terce, sext, and nones during the working day; vespers at sunset; and finally compline before retiring) was in accompaniment of the angels. Monastic inner mental discipline included concentration on the song of praise of the angels, enabled by silence much of the time, broken only by song in some orders.

For a millennium, the only music heard in the Christian churches, East and West, was vocal, specifically chant. Every community or individual church developed its own localized chant repertoire, which it passed on orally from generation to generation. Among the more prominent versions were Byzantine, Celtic, Gallician (French), Mosarabic (Spanish), Benevental (lower Italian), Ambrosian (Milanese) and Gregorian for Rome. The earliest notation of the music dates from the eighth century.

By the ninth century the Mass liturgy was firmly established, and church composers had begun to experiment with ways to embellish it. Polyphony—music with two or more different yet related melodic parts—started to develop in the West because of a single factor, the development of notation, the written record of spontaneous or intentional embellishments of a given melody. By the thirteenth century hundreds of harmonic polyphonic liturgical pieces were on record, mostly centered in France. But polyphony created a conservative reaction, with Cistercian and Dominican orders forbidding it in services. In 1324 Pope John XXII issued a bull against it.

By then polyphony had crept into secular music, which also had developed the use of varied instruments and received Eastern influences by way of the Crusades. By the fourteenth century, settings of the Mass for polyphonic choruses and solos were common. In the Renaissance, fully instrumented polyphonic pieces with female voices were established, and "classical" music was well launched, with Palestrina (c. 1525–1594) and Monteverdi (1567–1643) leading the way into the Baroque. A great deal of composition, into the twentieth century, continued to be liturgical, but the exclusive embodiment of the angelic connection in monophonic chant was over. In late Renaissance England, Tavener, Tallis, and others developed polyphonic choral music for cathedral and university choirs. This took hold, and remains to this day remarkably angelic-sounding.

## MUSIC OF THE SPHERES

The Hermetic tradition, rooted in ancient astronomy and particularly the mystic brotherhood of Pythagoras, codified all science, art, and law for its initiates under the principle of cosmic harmony. Plato demonstrated in the *Timaeus* that music and mathematics could be used to explain every terrestrial phenomenon. The notion of angelic INTELLIGENCES guiding the heavens resonates in the pervasive metaphor "the music of the spheres," nicely articulated by Plotinus:

If the stars pass a blessed existence in their vision of the life inherent in their souls, and if, by force of their souls' tendency to become one, and by the light they cast from themselves upon the entire heavens, they are like the strings of a lyre which, being struck in tune, sing a melody in some natural scale . . . if this is the way the heavens, as one, are moved, and the component parts in their relation to the whole, then the life of all things together is still more clearly an unbroken unity. (IV *Ennead* II, iv, 8)

Early Christian theologians such as Origen and Clement, steeped in Hermetic, Gnostic, and Platonic lore, identified the celestial musical ratios of astral religion with the Word of God, arising from the ambiguity of the Greek word *logos*. "Theologia" in older Greek meant a poetic utterance about God, and thus could mean not merely science but also the Logos—especially the sublime integration of sound and sense—of the bards of yore. Clement conceived of Jesus as a song consummating the harmony of all things, "and on this many-voiced instrument of the universe He makes music to God, and sings to the human instrument." St. AUGUSTINE composed *De musica* in the fifth century, the first in a long line of scholarly theoretical treatments of the Pythagorean theme. St. Thomas AQUINAS asserted that "everything that moves in nature is moved by the Ruler; the angels transmit the motion to the spheres." *The Liturgy of St. Mark* is one of many medieval musical tractates that begins with a reference to the music of the spheres. The concept was that the Church's praise tunes in to the praises of the cosmos; the place of music in Church worship accords with the sort of praise offered by sun, moon, and stars. The harmony of the spheres rings out, the angel sound resounds, the liturgy of the Church has found its voice.

Clement, second-century Bishop of Alexandria, also described processions of ancient Egyptian priests singing magic hymns by Hermes (the Greek god who guides and brings messages to souls), and named Hermes Trismegistus as the author of the *Corpus Hermeticum* (supposedly lost, to be rediscovered by Renaissance humanists). Until the seventeenth century the *Corpus* was universally believed to date from the earliest era of human history. In *The City of God* Augustine affirms this unequivocally: "As for morality, it stirred not in Egypt until Trimegistus's time, who was indeed long before the sages and philosophers of Greece." Generations of would-be magi believed that it contained all the essential esoteric lore, including the invocation by music of all the angelic and demonic realms.

In 1460 Cosimo de' Medici obtained an almost complete manuscript of the *Corpus* and contracted the brilliant classicist Marsilio Ficino to translate it. Ficino occupies an essential position in the chain of musical philosophers, for he also translated the key works of Plato and the Neoplatonists. Ficino was a great believer in sympathetic magic, and he detailed principles of musical magic, combining stars with their corresponding celestial virtues. Ficino himself composed astrological music, which has not survived, based on the essential congruity between the music of the spheres, the music of the human organism, and ordinary music making, emphasizing the sympathetic relationship between the human soul and the cosmic spirit, reflected in the perfect proportions of instrumental music to which the human organism responds so profoundly. Ficino postulated that music concerts possess a living spirit analogous to the human soul and the cosmic spirit. Other Renaissance philosophers, such as Giordano Bruno and Tommaso Campanella, followed

Ficino's lead. Campanella believed, however, that "if there is harmony in the heavens and in the angels, it is of a different order"; that is, our instrumental music is in no way comparable; if the celestial music exists, we are incapable of hearing it.

Astronomer and mathematician Johannes Kepler (1571–1630) wrote the summa on this theme, the fifth book of his *The Harmony of the Universe.* Kepler explicitly acknowledges Pythagoras and Plato as his conceptual masters, and adheres closely to their idealistic schema of a universe ruled by perfect mathematical music. For Plato and Cicero and the scholastics, the music of the spheres consisted only of scales but Kepler added the dimension of polyphony, with simultaneity as an essential component. The Geneva-born Jesuit antiquarian Athanasius Kircher published *Musurgia universalis* in 1650, an encyclopedia of music applying the music of the spheres governed by seraphic Intelligences to a critique of music in his time, including the new Baroque musical styles and the still-emerging opera, as well as the older polyphonic music.

For another Pythagorean, Sir Isaac Newton, the first to use logarithms in musical calculations, Greek mythology was an integral part of his natural philosophy. He used language similar to that of Pythagoras and Plato on the theme of the musical universe: "the soul of the world, which propels into movement this body of the universe visible to us, being constructed of ratios which created from themselves a musical concord, must of necessity produce musical sounds from the movement which it provides by its proper impulse, having found the origin of them in the craftsmanship of its own composition." Newton saw in the perfect order of music the most apt analogue of the orderly cosmos. After Newton, the great theme vanishes until one last flowering in the Masonic movement of the eighteenth century, climaxed in Mozart's opera *Die Zauberflöte* (*The Magic Flute,* 1791) Johann Sebastian Bach, a learned man, was familiar with the theme of the harmony of the spheres. In *Bach and the Dance of God,* Wilfred Mellers states: "As rational Enlightenment encroached, Bach ballasted his faith with hermetic truths that could be demonstrated, in terms of music, with an exactitude that leaves verbal language helpless; what results from Bach's *demonstratio* of the transcendental unity of number is liberation and joy."

### ANGELIC THEMES IN MUSIC
Almost every major composer has written sacred music, i.e., for the liturgy, even if he is better known for other genres. Furthermore, mathematical purity and cosmic scope—the element of the music of the spheres—are recurrent qualities of most great musical works. The Baroque "doctrine of the affections" held that the purpose of music was to illustrate or imitate various emotional or affective states. Musicologist Joscelyn Godwin states that this was "the very basis of early opera, as well as one of the unquestioned assumptions of later composers such as Bach and Handel." Spiritual tuning of "the human instrument" through a recursive mythological loop was an obvious agenda in Wagner's *Ring* cycle of operas, where many degrees of intervening spirits and demons abound, and for the several dozen musical treatments of Goethe's *Faust* (see LITERATURE AND ANGELS), notably Donizetti's *Fausta* (1832), Gounod's *Faust* (1859)—once the world's most popular opera—and Berlioz's *The Damnation of Faust* (1846, first staged 1893).

An angelic chorus occurs in the last movement of Gustav Mahler's Symphony #8 in E Flat ("Symphony of a Thousand"). The closing of Goethe's *Faust* is the text. The angelic chorus also finds its way into hundreds of Christmas carols and sacred works. The angel blows the trumpet of the Last Judgment in art, literature, instrumental works, spirituals and sacred songs. The angelic orchestra was a popular Renaissance and Baroque theme. (See ART AND ANGELS and LITERATURE AND ANGELS.) Various angelic motifs recur in popular music, art, and story through the ages: the intervention of angels in human life for assistance (the guardian angel) and inspiration (the Muse); angelic beauty or sweetness comparable to that in a human lover; the appearance of an angel or demon as an omen; a struggle with an angel or demon; the angel or demon lover. In these days of computer indexes, hundreds of angel song titles can be accessed, attesting to music's continued archetypal link between humanity and the mystical realms.

**Further reading:**
Anderson, E. *The Letters of Mozart and His Family.* Third ed. New York: Norton, 1990.
Gaster, Theodor H. *The Dead Sea Scriptures.* Third ed. Garden City, N.Y.: Anchor/Doubleday, 1976.
James, Jamie. *The Music of the Spheres.* New York: Grove Press, 1993.
Peterson, Eric. *The Angels and the Liturgy.* New York: Herder and Herder, 1964.

**mysterious stranger**   An angel who appears in the form of a human being to intervene in the affairs of mortals, usually those who are in distress. The mysterious stranger is one of the more common and more dramatic manifestations of angels.

Characteristics of angelic mysterious strangers vary, though there are common elements that occur in most episodes. Mysterious strangers can be male or female, and of any race. Most often they are male—usually a fresh-looking, cleancut youth. They are invariably well dressed, polite and knowledgeable about the crisis at hand. Often they are calm but they can be forceful, and know just what to do. They do speak, though they talk sparingly, and they will even take hold of the people in distress. They eat food. They are convincingly real as flesh-and-blood humans. However, once the problem has been solved, the mysterious stranger vanishes. It is that abrupt and strange disappearance that makes people question whether they have been aided by a mortal or an angel. Upon reflection, the arrival of the mysterious stranger—suddenly, out of nowhere, or in the nick of time—adds credence to the angel-as-stranger belief.

Perhaps the first notable mysterious strangers of record are the three angels, disguised as men, who visit ABRAHAM, as reported in Genesis 18. The angels have been dispatched by God to destroy the wicked cities of Sodom and Gomorrah. En route, they visit Abraham's tent on the plains of Mamre. He welcomes them and gives them water to wash their feet, the shade of a tree for rest, and food. He stands by while the angels eat a meal of curds, milk, cakes and the meat of a calf. The angels tell Abraham, who is 99, that his 90-year-old wife, Sarah—who had been barren her entire life—will bear a child the following spring. Abraham and Sarah do not believe it, but Sarah does indeed conceive and bear a son, Isaac. The moral of this tale is to always be kind to strangers, who may be disguised angels and emissaries of the Lord.

In the apocryphal Book of Tobit, probably written in the second century B.C.E., the archangel RAPHAEL appears as a mysterious stranger to guide Tobias on a journey (see TOBIT).

An example of a modern mysterious stranger and a medical rescue is the following story from *Angels of Mercy* by the author. The story concerns a woman who lives in California:

> I was in a hospital suffering from some rare throat virus that caused me to cough so violently, I would begin to strangle. During one of those fits in the middle of the night, I called for a nurse. No one came right away, and I began to panic, for I couldn't breathe.
>
> Suddenly the door flew open and a short, stocky nurse came bursting in, and with a voice of authority said, "Close your mouth and breathe through your nose." When I gestured that no air would come through my nose, she clamped her hand over my mouth and shouted, "Breathe!" And, breathe I did and I stopped choking. Her next words were, "Just can't understand why they haven't taught you that." And out she went.
>
> Because I wanted to thank her, the next morning I asked the nurse who was it who was on night duty. When she asked me to describe her, she looked puzzled and said that description didn't fit anyone on their staff, but she would check on it.
>
> Later, the head nurse came in and asked me to describe the nurse again. She said there was no one employed there who came close to my description. When I asked why they hadn't instructed me on what to do when I began to strangle, they said they had never heard of the method.
>
> The doctor's response to the experience was interesting. He knew about the method, but why he hadn't told me, I'll never know. But he whispered in my ear, "I think you met an angel." By then, I was convinced I had.

Another compelling example is reported in *Touched By Angels* by Eileen Elias Freeman. The encounter involves an American woman who, with her three small children, undertakes a stressful trip to Germany to join her military husband. She speaks little German. Upon arrival, her husband is nowhere to be found, and the woman feels stranded. Unbeknownst to her, her husband has suffered an injury in an auto accident. At the depths of her despair she is suddenly approached by a well-dressed man in a business suit and fedora, who speaks English. He calls the military base for her, and tells her about her husband's accident. He pulls out a thermos of coffee from his briefcase for her to drink, and calmly tells her how to catch a train for the military base. He takes her to the ticket window and explains her situation in German to the clerk. He hails her a taxi, tells her what the fare will be, and how to pay it.

At the train station, the woman and her children board a train. She looks out the window and, to her astonishment, sees the businessman who helped her. He boards the car and tells her they have gotten on the wrong train. He picks up all of their heavy luggage as though the cases were empty, and shepherds them off and onto the right train. He bids them goodbye, and the woman watches him go through the exit that leads to the platform. She leans out her window to thank him again, but he never appears. There was nowhere for him to go but the platform, and he has mysteriously vanished.

One of the distinguishing features of this case is that the mysterious stranger is black, like the woman and her children. Certainly, in a foreign country, assistance and reassurance provided by someone of the same race is welcome and comforting.

One need not be in dire straits to have a mysterious stranger appear on the scene, as the following story from an Illinois woman, reported in *Angels of Mercy*, illustrates:

> I went into a local electronics store with my son, who had his newly purchased shortwave radio. He had been having difficulty receiving certain channels, and believed there was a problem with the radio. We began a discussion with the store manager. My son began to explain the problem, but the manager cut him off, trying to make it sound like my son didn't know how to operate the radio. The more my son tried to object, the more insistent the manager became.
>
> Suddenly, out of nowhere, this young man appeared at the register where we were standing, and intervened. He had something in his hand to purchase and said very quietly, yet with knowledge, that my son had a point. He proceeded to explain very calmly to the manager what the problem was. Not only did he solve the problem, but suddenly the manager was much nicer. Then the man purchased the item in his hand. It was *crystals* for a shortwave.
>
> I was just dumbfounded. The young man wished us a nice day and left the store. A couple of seconds later, I rushed out the door to thank him, but he was *gone*. He literally disappeared. The store is in the middle of the block, so you would still be able to see someone walking down the sidewalk. Obviously, this was not an ordinary human. I still get chills when I think about it.

A frequent type of mysterious stranger intervention is the "roadside rescue," in which a mysterious stranger arrives to help a motorist stranded on a lonely road at night, or injured in an accident in an isolated spot.

Not all people who say they are aided by angels report mysterious strangers. Some hear clear but disembodied voices, feel invisible hands, or sense unseen presences. It is not known why angels manifest as humans in some cases and not in others. Modern angelologists hypothesize that the appearance of a mysterious stranger may in fact be the least unsettling form of angelic intervention. Many persons undergoing stress are more likely to respond to the aid of what appears to be a friendly fellow human being. Perhaps the shock of an obviously supernatural intervention would only serve to intensify the crisis.

**Further reading:**

Freeman, Eileen Elias. *Touched by Angels*. New York: Warner Books, 1993.

Guiley, Rosemary Ellen. *Angels of Mercy*. New York: Pocket Books, 1994.

Howard, Jane M. *Commune with Angels*. Virginia Beach, Va.: A.R.E. Press, 1992.

*The New Oxford Annotated Bible with the Apochrypha*. Herbert G. May and Bruce M. Metzger, eds. New York: Oxford University Press, 1977.

Smith, Robert C. *In the Presence of Angels*. Virginia Beach, Va.: A.R.E. Press, 1993.

# N

**Nakir** See ISLAMIC ANGELOLOGY.

**names of angels** Since antiquity, the proper names of angels have been believed to hold great mystical and magical power. The names of angels reflect their official duties or roles in the cosmic schema of things; each letter shines a divine light that can be meditated upon and contemplated. Angel names are "names of power" used in prayers and incantations and on amulets to help the mortal person gain access to the mysteries expressed by the name. They also provide protection against the forces of darkness.

Most angel names in Judeo-Christian lore are Hebrew. The "-el" at the end of the names is a suffix meaning "God"; thus angels are "of God."

Only three angels are named in Christian scripture: MICHAEL, GABRIEL and RAPHAEL (the latter's name appears in the Book of Tobit, which is part of the Catholic Bible). However, ex-canonical works belonging to the APOCHRYPHA and PSEUDEPIGRAPHA, as well as other sources, are rich in angel names, among them the archangel URIEL. The Catholic church does not permit the use of any proper names of angels other than Michael, Gabriel and Raphael. All names from apocryphal writings were rejected by Pope Zachary in 745, and again by a synod at Aix-la-Chapelle, France, in 789.

The concept of "names of power" dates to the ancient Egyptians, Greeks, Hebrews, Assyrians, Essenes and Gnostics, all of whom believed that incredible power could be unleashed by the vibrations of spoken words. The Egyptians invented names of power for magical rituals, which were passed into texts absorbed into Western culture. Names of power play a prominent role in Jewish mysticism.

The Merkabah, Jewish mysticism that preceded the Kabbalah (c. 100 B.C.E.–1000 C.E.), emphasized the importance of names of power as a way of ascending through the layers of heavens to the throne-chariot of God (see EZEKIEL). The names of angels and the secret names of God intermingle in the literature, and some names are not distinguished as referring specifically to one or the other.

The Essenes, a Jewish sect that existed at about the time of Jesus, had a mystical literature both magical and angelological in content. Persons were required to take an oath of secrecy never to reveal angel names, lest they be abused for evil purposes. The Gnostics, too, had rites of initiation that involved secret names of archons and aeons. (See GNOSTICISM.)

The most powerful of all the names of power is the Tetragrammaton, the personal name of God in the Old Testament. It is given as YHVH, the Hebrew letters *yod, he, vau, he*. The numerical values assigned to these letters add up to ten, which in Hebrew numerology represents the basic organizing principle in the universe. So powerful is the Tetragrammaton that for centuries it was seldom spoken. As early as the time of Jesus, it was whispered only on Yom Kippur by a high priest within the inner sanctuary of the temple. In the scriptures substitute words were used, such as "Adonai" or "Adonay" or "Elohim" (the latter term also is interpreted as the name of an angel or of a rank of angels). The exact pronunciation of the Tetragrammaton is not known; the most accepted is "Yahweh." A common variation is "Jehovah."

The power of a name was determined through gematria, a system for discovering the truths and hidden meanings behind words. Gematria is a means of interpreting the Torah, each letter of which has its own divine significance, but it also is used to refer to a general way of mystically interpreting names.

In gematria, numerical values are assigned for each letter of the alphabet. The numerical values of words are totaled, and interpreted in terms of other words with the same numerical value. In this manner names can be related to other names, and names can be related to passages in Scripture.

The first known use of gematria dates to the Babylonian king Sargon II, in the eighth century B.C.E.. Sargon built the wall of Khorsabad exactly 16,283 cubits long, because that was the numerical value of his name. The ancient Greeks used gematria to interpret dreams; the system also appears in the literature of the Magi. The Gnostics applied it to the names of the deities ABRAXAS and Mithras, equating them because they both added up to 365. The Gnostic cosmology conceives of 365 aeons or celestial spheres; thus Abraxas is the chief of aeons.

The early Hebrews used gematria to interpret Scripture; the first reference to the term in rabbinic literature appears in the second century. Early Christians borrowed the technique to ascertain that the dove is the symbol of Jesus: the Greek word for "dove," *peristera*, adds up to 801, and so do the Greek letters of alpha and omega, which represent the Beginning and the End.

The Kabbalists did much to develop gematria into various complex methods; one Kabbalistic tract alone lists seventy-two different methods.

See MAGIC, ANGELS IN; METATRON; SCHEMHAMPHORAS.

**Further reading:**

Connolly, David. *In Search of Angels*. New York: Perigee Books, 1993.
Parente, Fr. Pascal P. *The Angels: The Catholic Teaching on the Angels*. Rockford, Ill.: Tan Books and Publishers, 1973. First published 1961.
Scholem, Gershom. *Kabbalah*. New York: Dorset Press, 1974.

**nature spirit** In mythologies around the world, a type of being who dwells in the nature kingdom. In the Western tradition, nature spirits are under the dominion of the angel kingdom. Nature spirits are to earth what angels are to heaven and humans. They possess supernatural powers, and watch over the well-being of all things in nature, animal, plant and mineral.

Nature spirits come in countless types, shapes, sizes and dispositions. Some are regarded as being benevolent toward humans, while others are mischievious or malevolent. Some are human-like in appearance, while others assume the shapes of animals, half-human half-animals, or fabulous-looking beings.

Nature spirits tend to stay in one spot: They remain attached to a thing or place in nature, such as trees, rivers, plants, bogs, mountains, lakes, etc. (See GENIUS.)

Kabbalists assigned four angelic princes to rule over the four winds and over the four quarters of the world. MICHAEL rules the east wind, RAPHAEL the west wind, GABRIEL the north wind, and ARIEL the south wind. According to Francis Barrett, a nineteenth-century English occultist, "every one of these spirits is a great prince, and has much power and freedom in the dominion of his own planets and signs, and in their times, years, months, days and hours; and in their elements, and parts of the world, and winds."

Barrett also observed that, in counterbalance to the heavenly angels, there are evil spirits who also rule the four winds and four quarters like kings: Urieus over the east, Anaymon over the south, Paymon over the west, and Egin over the north. (The Hebrew names are, respectively, Samael, Azazel, Azael and Mahazuel.)

See also DEVA.

**Further reading:**
Barrett, Francis. *The Magus.* Secaucus, N.J.: The Citadel Press, 1967. First published 1801.

**near-death experience (NDE)** Mystical-like phenomena experienced by individuals who come close to death, or who clinically die and then return to life. The near-death experience (NDE) usually involves beings of bright light identified by some as angels.

The term "near-death experience" was coined by Dr. Raymond Moody, the first American physician to document and study the phenomena. His initial research was published in 1975 in *Life After Life.* Moody found that few people would talk openly about an NDE out of fear of ridicule, and medical professionals tended to dismiss such episodes as hallucinations. Within two decades, NDEs were common media fare, as well as the subject of serious scientific inquiry. It is estimated that some 15 million people in the United States have had an NDE; children as well as adults report them.

Moody, along with other NDE researchers including Kenneth Ring, psychologist and founding member of the International Association of Near-Death Studies, have identified several traits common to NDEs, some or all of which may be experienced by any one person:

- A sense of being out-of-body, looking down on one's self and others who try to resuscitate the body
- Cessation of pain and a feeling of bliss or peacefulness

Angel guiding the spirits' flight (reprinted courtesy of U.S. Library of Congress)

- Traveling down a dark tunnel toward a brilliant light at the end
- Meeting glowing beings who appear to be angels, Jesus, or other religious figures
- Meeting dead friends and relatives
- Seeing a life-review
- Seeing visions of the future
- Undergoing a judgment of one's life that is rendered not by God, angels, or any being but by one's self
- Feeling reluctant to return to life

Skeptics explain NDEs as a hallucination brought about by a lack of oxygen; the release of endorphins, the body's own painkillers; or increased levels of carbon dioxide in the blood. NDE researchers counter that drug-induced experiences can parallel an NDE but lack the mystical, noetic quality of the NDE, which brings about profound life changes after return. Invariably NDErs lose their fear of death, have a diminished interest in material pursuits, and begin to lead more spiritual lives. Some change their careers. Some experience psychic openings and prophecy. Some feel evangelistic, and want to impart to others the importance of love.

Nearly 97 percent of all reported NDEs are described as positive. A small minority say they do not see heaven, but see hell and demonic figures.

The beings of light seen in an NDE (which may or may not be identified as "angels"—cultural and religious conditioning appear to be influencing factors) initially are formless light, and gradually take on a human-like form made of brilliant light or clothed in brilliant white robes. Generally they do not have wings. They radiate an all-encompassing, intense love that fills the person with joy and peace.

The beings function as both guide and gatekeeper. They take the person along on their journey as far as they can go, usually to a threshhold such as an entrance or a bridge to a building or beautiful garden, or simply to a place that the person intuitively knows marks the final boundary between life and death. The beings then tell their charges that they must go back because they have unfinished business. Sometimes they ask their charges if they wish to stay or return. Most people say they wish to stay, but usually a relationship, such as that to a spouse or a child, pulls them back to the realm of the living.

In many instances souls of the dead, rather than angelic-like beings, function as guides and gatekeepers.

Researchers such as Ring have suggested that the NDE is a form of enlightenment or "gateway to a higher consciousness," and could have a transformative effect on the entire planet if enough people have similar experiences. Ring further has said that one does not have to die in order to experience similar enlightenment, or at least to assimilate the lessons of an NDE.

In fact the NDE may be a modern mechanism for the ongoing transmission of spiritual wisdom and truths, and the maintaining of social order. From antiquity, the mythologies of the world have included stories of otherworld journeys by heroes, sages and prophets. These visionary quests and journeys are laden with archetypal figures and symbols; the central characters themselves are archetypes. The heroes are accompanied by guide figures (angels or beings comparable to angels), and ascend to heaven or descend to the underworld. They encounter strange beings, have adventures, and learn the secrets of the cosmos. They are given laws, moral codes and spiritual truths to deliver to others upon their return. (See ENOCH; MOSES; MUHAMMAD.) This theme appears not only in mythology but in literature as well (see DANTE), and also is documented in real-life NDEs from earlier times.

In ages past, communities and social groups relied upon visionary figures as their intermediaries to other realms. The increase of NDEs into a wider pool of population, as well as the increased reporting of other kinds of "exceptional human experiences" (episodes of psi, out-of-body travel, mystical experience, kundalini awakenings and the like) show a trend toward individuals becoming visionaries in their own right. Rather than obtain wisdom secondhand from a sage, the individual has his or her own direct experience of God.

Carol Zaleski, a religion lecturer at Harvard, has compared stories of otherworld visions and journeys found in medieval Christian literature with modern NDE accounts, and published her results in *Otherworldly Journeys*. She says that the modern NDE stories, like their medieval counterparts, provide a way for individuals to incorporate a "religious sense of the cosmos" into their scientific/secular understanding. The NDE functions as one way in which the religious imagination mediates the search for ultimate truth.

Ring has found numerous parallels between the NDE and the UFO encounter. In some UFO encounters, extraterrestrials, who arrive in brilliant light, take humans on cosmic trips and impart prophecies and wisdom to take back to Earth. Some contactees consider the ETs to be angels, and some ufologists contend that ancient descriptions of angels and gods descending from the sky actually were visitations by ETs. However, most UFO episodes are negative; some involve abductions and unpleasant medical procedures. Seen from a mythological standpoint, the UFO encounter could be the demonic side of the NDE.

There also are similarities between the NDE and MARIAN APPARITIONS, or visions of the Blessed Virgin MARY. In Marian apparitions, formless light gradually assumes shapes interpreted as being angels and Mary. Paranormal phenomena occur (such as the spinning sun at the Fatima apparitions in Portugal in 1917), and visionaries are imparted wisdom and given instructions for relaying information to others. They are told or shown visions of the future. The wisdom exhorts people to a more spiritual life, including prayer.

Visions of the future seen in NDEs, UFO encounters and Marian apparitions generally are apocalyptic: massive cataclysms, earth-changes, economic woes, wars and upheavals in society. All of these in turn are parallel with apocalyptic visions of the end of days given to various biblical and other prophets (see ENOCH; ISAAC) and contained in REVELATION. One of the major functions of angels is to usher in the "end times" and Judgment Day, to quell the forces of evil, and to separate the souls of the righteous and the sinners and escort them to their appropriate afterlife.

Philosopher Michael Grosso observes that the "end times" is an archetype deeply imbedded within our collective unconscious, and that history shows a pattern of a rise in apocalyptic experiences at the approach of major calendar milestones, such as the end of a century or millennium. These experiences, and the increased interest in angels as of the late twentieth century, may be part of a broad psychic shift on a collective level, marking a new era of expanded consciousness, especially of a spiritual nature.

See also ANGEL OF DEATH; DEATHBED VISIONS.

**Further reading:**
Grosso, Michael. *The Final Choice*. Walpole, N.H.: Stillpoint, 1985.
Moody, Raymond A., Jr., *Life After Life*. Georgia: Mockingbird Books, 1975.
———. *Reflections on Life After Life*. Harrisburg, Pa.: Stackpole Books, 1977.
———. *The Light Beyond*. New York: Bantam Books, 1988.
Ring, Kenneth. *Life At Death*. New York: Coward, McCann & Geoghegan, 1980.
———. *Heading Toward Omega*. New York: William Morrow, 1984.
———. *The Omega Project*. New York: William Morrow, 1992.
Zaleski, Carol. *Otherworld Journeys: Accounts of Near-Death Experience in Medieval and Modern Times*. New York: Oxford University Press, 1987.

**Nike** The Greek winged goddess of victory was an early inspiration for the winged angel. The Greeks associated Nike with Athena, the queen of heaven and the goddess of wisdom, skill and warfare; Athena sometimes was worshipped as Athena Nike. In particular Nike embodied victory in athletics, music and especially battle. She appeared to the victorious on the battlefield, to whisper the favors of the gods. The Romans called her Victoria or VICTORY.

See WINGS.

**numbers of angels**    The question of how many angels are in existence has been pondered by theologians and occultists for centuries. Various formulae have been applied to ascertain the exact numbers of angels.

Early writings refer only to infinite numbers of angels—their ranks are so vast as to be beyond calculation. The biblical prophet DANIEL had a vision of heaven in which at least one hundred million angels appeared: "a thousand thousands served him, and ten thousand times ten thousand stood before him." The prophet ENOCH, in his travels to heaven, observed "angels innumerable, thousands of thousands, and myriads and myriads." Enoch's description is echoed in the New Testament BOOK OF REVELATION, authored by John of Patmos.

In the Kabbalah, the *Zohar* states that six hundred million angels were created on the second day of creation, but adds that other angels were created on other days for other purposes. In the third century, the Jewish scholar Simon ben Lakish related angels to the seven heavens of Enoch and the signs of the zodiac. There were a total of 1.06434 quintillion angels, he said, organized into hosts, camps, legions, cohorts and myriads.

In Islam, the Koran states only that "numerous angels are in heaven." However, an Islamic tradition about the archangel MICHAEL holds that Michael is responsible for creating 700 quadrillion cherubim alone. The archangel is said to be covered with saffron hairs, each of which has a million faces and each face a million eyes, from each of which fall 700,000 tears, each of which becomes a cherub.

According to Clement of Alexandria, one of the early fathers of the Christian church, the stars were angels. The Roman Catholic church declared that the numbers of angels were fixed at the time of creation. ORIGEN, a Christian theologian who was anathematized by the church, questioned that, and said that angels in fact "multiply like flies."

In the Middle Ages, speculation on the numbers of angels reached a peak. St. Thomas AQUINAS said that every person on earth has a guardian angel, but that the total ranks of angels were much greater. Albert the Great, a Dominican monk who was a teacher to Aquinas, said that each of the nine CHOIRS of angels had 66,666 legions, each of which had 6,666 angels, for a total of nearly 4 billion angels. Other medieval scholars placed the total number of the heavenly host at 301,655,722, of which 133,306,668 were fallen.

Many modern angelologists believe that the question of the numbers of angels is moot: There are as many angels in the universe as are necessary. Even in the 1600s, the folly of angel-counting was recognized. Thomas Heywood, an English playwright, said that counting angels would "grow from ignorance to error." The rhetorical question, "How many angels can fit on the head of a pin?" points to the medieval preoccupation with trying to answer an ultimately futile question.

See Johann WEYER.

**Further reading:**
Connolly, David. *In Search of Angels*. New York: Perigee Books, 1993.
Godwin, Malcolm. *Angels: An Endangered Species*. New York: Simon & Schuster, 1990.
Ronner, John. *Do You Have a Guardian Angel?* Murfreesboro, Tenn. Mamre Press, 1985.

**Opus Sanctorum Angelorum**   See DEVOTIONAL CULTS.

**Origen** (c. 185–254 C.E.)   Ardent Christian theologian and apologist in a time of intense religious turbulence, Origen wrote extensively about angels and their roles, influencing other theologians who came after him.

Several Roman persecutions of Christians highlighted Origen's life. He was born in Alexandria, then the center of Hellenic culture and a hotbed of GNOSTICISM. Thus it was inevitable that he would absorb some views from those quarters, which may explain in part why Origen's theology became controversial in later centuries for being if not heretical, at least dangerously unorthodox.

Origen's linguistic expertise was outstanding, he worked for thirty years on an authoritative edition of the Old Testament with his *Hexapla*, a huge set of documents that contained six parallel columns of the Hebrew and Greek textual versions.

He describes a complex angelology in *De Principiis* ("of first principles"). This work consists of a coherent system of Christian teaching about God and the cosmos, to refute Gnostic dualism, and a pioneer attempt to explain his methods for attaining an accurate interpretation of the Bible. He was exploratory rather than dogmatic, and his speculations later were turned against him.

### A SUMMARY OF ORIGEN'S LIFE

Origen was born *c.* 185 C.E. in Egypt, and he is recognized as the first of the church fathers to be born into a Christian family. His father Leonides reportedly was martyred in the persecution of Alexandrian Christians under the Roman emperor Septimus Severus in 202. Tradition records that Origen's mother restrained her son at this time from seeking the glory of martyrdom, by hiding his clothes so as to keep him indoors. The oldest of seven children, Origen became a teacher of Greek in order to support his bereaved family. He quickly achieved recognition and success within the church as an instructor of catechumens (adult converts in training for baptism).

Another story that has perpetually followed Origen is that he castrated himself in young manhood, an act of zeal occasionally attested to in this period of the early church. Whether this is true or not, Origen has retained a centuries-long reputation for saintly asceticism and chastity, and an appetite for hard work that earned him the nickname Adamantius. (In his later life he wrote a commentary on St. Matthew in which he deplores fanatics who take a literal interpretation of Matthew 19:12, which observes that some men make themselves eunuchs for the sake of the Kingdom of Heaven.)

One of Origen's admirers, Ambrosius, became the patron of his *Hexapla*, hiring for him seven scribes of the biblical text and seven transcribers of Origen's dictation. Oriegen was loved and revered in Palestine, Phoenicia, Greece and Arabia. He traveled frequently to explain and defend Christian doctrine, and to teach educated prospective converts. Much of this debate and instruction also was pursued in his writing, only a fraction of which survives in reliable texts. The *Hexapla* was lost, and the original Greek *De Principiis* is available only in fragments, forcing scholars to use a Latin translation "expurgated" of heresy in 398 by Rufinus.

Origen's long productive years in Alexandria were ended by the hostility of the bishop Demetrius over Origen's having been ordained a presbyter during his travels in Palestine. Another persecution of Alexandria by Rome also was underway, this time by Caracalla. Thus Origen moved to Ceasarea in Palestine in 231. There he continued to teach, preach and write. During the Decian persecution (249–250) he was imprisoned and tortured in an unsuccessful attempt to make him denounce his faith. His physical health may well have been broken by this suffering: he died shortly thereafter at Tyre (*c.* 253–54), where a marble monument marked his grave until the thirteenth century.

### ANGELOLOGY

(All quotes from Origen are from *De Principiis*, unless otherwise indicated.)

**Cosmology**

> Before the Aeons existed all spirits were pure; demons, souls and angels alike all served God and did what he commanded them. The devil was one of them. He had free-will and wanted to set himself up against God, but God cast him down. All the other powers fell with him. The biggest sinners became demons, lesser ones angels, the least archangels. . . . Other souls were not sinful enough to be made demons but were too sinful to be made angels. These God punished by making the world, binding them to bodies and putting them into it. Although these spiritual creatures, then, all had the same nature, God made some of them demons, some angels, and some men. That does not mean that he is a respecter of persons. No, what he did was in keeping with their sins. If it were not so, and if the soul had no previous experience, how is it that we find men blind from birth, before they could possibly have sinned, and why do others go blind although they have done nothing wrong?

This passage from Book II of *De Principiis* contains the basis of Origen's cosmology: The variety of beings and bodies issues from the use of free choice by all rational beings made *before* the creation of the world—before matter, before bodies. One of Origen's most controversial tenets is his belief that even heavenly bodies, planets and stars were once pure spiritual beings, made material through their free choice of evil. Two of Origen's beliefs presented here were later considered heretical by some; his belief in (1) a pure, incorporeal plane that preceded the physical (this concept is basic to Platonism and Gnosticism); (2) a system similar to what in Sanskrit the Hindu sages called "karma": fate doled out to souls "in keeping with their sins" in past lives (suggesting reincarnation) or, according to Origen, previous planes of existence.

Origen believed that God carefully planned this cosmos in such a way that after the Fall His free creatures could recover their original sinless status by interacting with one another in all their diversity. Along with this diversity Origen also sees mutability, the possibility of ascent or descent with progress or the lack of it.

Origen divides the whole creation into three main classes, corresponding to those of ST. PAUL: (1) the *coelestia* (angels, stars and planets), closest to God and with the two main tasks of helping to govern the systems and aiding their inferiors; (2) the *terrestria*, the human race, who are helped by the first class and are thus enabled to recover their lost happiness; (3) the wicked angels, who are incapable of being cured, at least in this world, and who try to inhibit human souls in their upward progress. These three classes represent not compartments set in concrete, but rather different degrees of the same downfall.

Origen believes that Christ's incarnation and redemption made possible the return of all beings to their beginning: "through the goodness of God, the unity of the Holy Spirit and surrender to Christ, they will all be brought to a single term, which will be like their beginning. . . . Because God's judgments are proportionate to the good and bad behavior of individuals and to their merits, some will receive the rank of angel in the world to come, some power or command over others, some a throne from which to rule over others, some dominion over servants. Those who have not fallen beyond redemption will be guided and helped by those just mentioned." The idea that some humans could ascend to angelic status shocked later thinkers.

Conversely, Origen postulated that "some of those now subject to the powers of evil [devils] . . . will fairly soon fill up the places left vacant among the human race, either in the space of one world or in several," thence to attain angelic status once more and go back to their unity of the beginning. The prospect of devils being purified by rising to human and then back to angelic rank, as well as the possibility of "several worlds," jarred subsequent churchmen.

Origen's spirituality stems from this cosmology. He represents the soul as dynamically caught up in a test of will between good and evil spirits. Evil rests not in the body, he argues adamantly against both Platonists and Gnostics, who view the flesh as the seat of evil. Evil rests in the will; bodiliness is a consequence of the Fall. "We men acquired our bodies because of the sins we had committed, and the lights of the heavens were given their bodies for the same reason.

Thus, some shine more and others less. Contrariwise, the demons were given aerial [made of ether] bodies because their sins were graver." One day, Origen asserts, corporeality will come to an end and there will be an *apocatastasis*, a return to a purely spiritual state.

God's overarching goal is to enable each soul to return to Him under his own free will, and He has arranged everything so as to further that goal. The angels have postponed their personal enjoyment to assist those who are not as good as others. God will allow some to plunge deeper into evil; in Origen's image, the abscess of evil must be allowed to burst. (In Gnosticism, a similar concept has been called a "homeopathetic" doctrine of salvation.) Some souls cannot be saved in this world; God defers these souls' acceptance of grace to another world, but meanwhile uses them as a means of tempting the saints. Thus the role of angels in their mission to govern humans, and also that of demons in their allowance to tempt humans, are both part of the play of the divinely planned cosmos.

**Duties of Angels and Demons**

Origen was well informed on Jewish angelology and the Book of Enoch (see ENOCH), and he had looked carefully at angelic interventions in both Old and New Testaments. He firmly rejects the Hellenistic and Gnostic idea that the angels created the cosmos. But he is in accord with the widespread belief that angels have hierarchical duties in running that cosmos. "There are angels in charge of everything, of earth, water, air and fire . . . used by the Logos as instruments to regulate the movements of the animals, the plants, the stars."

Elsewhere he mentions "the virtues who preside over the earth and the seeding of trees, who see to it that springs and rivers do not run dry. . . ." In response to a pagan philosopher, Celsus, he states that whereas the Greeks call daimons (see DAEMON) the protectors that preside over nature, the Christians call them angels. In another place he states that Christians honor angels, but do not worship them as pagans worship the daimons. These nature functions Origen accords to the lowest order of angels.

*Angels of Nations*

Origen believes that higher angels preside over human societies. He follows the precedent of the Bible, in telling how God assigned the nations their inheritance in accordance with the number of the angels of God. Origen says that after the fall of the Tower of Babel people were "handed over to angels, who harried them in varying degrees, according to the distance they had gone from the Orient [the true Light], and they were to remain under them until they had atoned for their folly." Each group was given a language and led to a dwelling place according to what it deserved.

Were these angels of nations good or bad? Origen was aware of the biblical ambiguity, and came to the conclusion that every nation had two angels attached to it. Are the bad angels those who punish a nation on God's behalf? Origen also considered the notion in the Book of Enoch that after the assignments were made, some of the angels turned traitor. Origen does not arrive at a clear definition of the bad angels of the nations, but those bad angels certainly were considered to be the instigators of idolatry, because they urged people to worship them rather than God.

The angels of nations are called "princes" by Origen. He associates them with the occult sciences practiced in the various nations, mentioning Egyptian, Chaldean, Persian, Greek and Hindu versions. Origen says that "in the prophet EZEKIEL the Prince of Tyre is obviously a spiritual power. These and the other Powers of this world have each some special science of their own, and they all teach their respective dogmas and opinions to men." He thinks that these spirits intend no harm, but act on the belief that what they teach is true.

This power of angels over nations was withdrawn after Christ came. The good angels welcomed the change; they had toiled long in the pagan nations with little to show for their efforts. Origen associates these with the shepherds on the night of Jesus birth, indicating an allegorical reading of the Gospels. The shepherds stand for "angels [of nations] to whose care men are entrusted. . . . It was to them that the [messenger] angel came and announced the . . . coming of the true Shepherd" (from *Homily on Gospel of St. Luke*). There was a transition period before they were to be relieved of their duties, in which great conversions to Christ were easily accomplished by the angels. Origen comments that this happened in Macedonia and in Egypt.

However it was quite different for the bad angels, the "princes of the world." Conversion for them was not impossible, but most went against Christ. Origen quotes Paul in Ephesians 6:12: "It is not against flesh and blood that we enter the lists; we have to do with princedoms and powers, with the *cosmocratores*." In Origen's own time the "princes and powers of idolatry" were still constantly challenging Christians on a life-and-death basis.

Israel was the one nation that went on worshiping the true God as it had done from the beginning. Origen believed that the nation of Israel kept the original language of the world. They stayed where they were originally, but their subsequent slavery and banishment and eventual diaspora were the result of their sins.

*Guardian Angels*
The question of guardian angels takes one into the area where Origen especially ministered as a teacher of new Christians: the sacramental and spiritual life. As soon as a person converts and gives himself to Christ, as soon as he renounces Satan and his following, Christ hands the soul over to an angel. Origen teaches that "every one of the faithful, we are told, however insignificant he may be in the Church, is assisted by an angel, and Christ is our witness that these angels behold the Father's face continuously." In another place he says that "every human soul has an angel who guides it like a brother." Origen uses this comforting concept constantly, in guiding people in the spiritual life. When Christ came into the world, myriad angels descended to assist him in his work by becoming guardian angels.

Just like the nations, every individual has a good and a bad angel of his own, according to Origen. A battle is fought over every soul, and as long as humans worship idols, angels can do nothing. They cannot look freely upon the Father's face. But when a person becomes a Christian, "no matter how insignificant I may be, my angel is free to look upon the Father's face. If I am outside the Church, he dare not do so."

Children receive spiritual direction from angels, who suggest to them good thoughts and desires, but maturing souls are capable of gaining instruction directly from Christ. Origen reminds the faithful: "God allows the opposing forces to fight against us, because he wants us to get the better of them. The function of bad angels is to tempt the just and put them to the test." Christ himself battled Satan many times, illustrating the reality of the struggle at the highest level.

This inner drama, of a conflict of will in each individual between good and bad spirits in ascending degree of tests, was investigated by subsequent Christian thinkers and continues to be to this day. It is an archetypal motif that appears in virtually all spiritual traditions, many of which Origen had knowledge of, but many of which he did not.

There is a feedback loop built into all angelic activity: However much progress they cause human beings to make, to that degree their own progress and bliss increase. "Whether the angels look on God's face always, or never, or only sometimes, will depend on the merits of those whose angels they were," says Origen. The angels also collaborate with the Apostles and the churches' shepherds, the bishops. Every church possesses both a visible bishop and an invisible angel. And if a Church is faring badly, so too are its angels. Origen stresses the identity of earthly and angelic authority: "the same functions are shared by an angel and a man and they are both perfectly good bishops."

Origen envisioned an angel "encamped beside those who fear the Lord," and further thought that if many faithful were assembled, so also would their angels be. "Thus, when the saints are assembled, there will be two Churches, one of man and one of angels." Each church and bishop has an angel, and each person; therefore, assembling for worship in a church brings great angelic forces to bear.

Origen also believes that specific hierarchies of angels are present during the practice of each of the sacraments. At the moment in which the priest immerses a child in baptismal water, the angels immerse the soul in the Holy Ghost. Higher echelons of angels are particularly involved in the sacramental life of the soul, with the Eucharist being a significant turning point.

Both Origen's devotion and his spiritual and intellectual breadth can be appreciated from the standpoint of his angelology. Although conservative church thinkers of later generations have found intolerable Origen's inclusiveness and hopefulness—his view that even the fallen angels may well be redeemed by grace in another world—his open-ended mental constructs were the natural concomitants of being an excellent scholar interacting with educated people from many different cultures in the Alexandria of his day. Since his death he has found many admirers in addition to the detractors, simply because he dared to ask large questions and posit creative answers, many of which have been reapproached in the light of his contribution.

**Further reading:**
Danielou, Jean. *Origen*. Translated by Walter Mitchell. New York: Sheed and Ward, 1955.
Crouzel, Henri. *Origen*. Translated by A. S. Worrall. San Francisco: Harper & Row, 1989.
Chadwick, Henry. *Early Christian Thought and the Classical Tradition*. New York: Oxford University Press, 1966.
Cross, F. L. *The Early Christian Fathers*. London: Gerald Duckworth & Co., 1960.

**orishas** The archetypal deities worshipped by followers of Santería and Candomblé. Closely related to devas and other nature spirits, orishas also are angels. Within Vodun, they are called the *loa*.

The orishas came to the New World with the West African slaves, principally from the Yoruban tribes along the Niger River. Forced to convert to Catholicism, the slaves worshipped their gods in secret, eventually seeing in them many characteristics of the Catholic saints and using the saints as covers for the African deities. Years later, the Spanish and Portuguese masters became fascinated with Yoruban magic and religion and embraced Santería (from *santo*, the Spanish word for saint), syncretizing it with their Catholic faith.

Like many other ancient and contemporary religions, particularly those practiced in the East, Santería and Candomblé acknowledge a Supreme, an Absolute, but find worship of such a distant, impersonal force too inaccessible. Instead, practitioners call on a pantheon of deities, each associated with a force of nature or ability to affect events and circumstances.

In Yoruban, *orisha* literally means "head-calabash," and is the term for "god." Each worshipper "chooses a head" or selects an orisha as spirit guide, a guardian angel who protects and promotes the interests of the petitioner. Selection is based on personality commonalities and the sense of energy one feels in a particular setting sacred to an orisha: the mountains, the ocean, the forests, the rivers. Occupations have patron orishas, as do those individuals involved in parenting, healing or fortune-telling. Once a practitioner has chosen an orisha—or more exactly, the orisha has chosen his devotee—care is given to show deference to the orisha's desires, favorite colors and foods, special days and worship preferences.

The orishas originate from a complicated cosmogony, wherein great tragedy and sexual passion explain their existence and temperament. One of the most popular orishas is Yemaya or Yemanja (Iemanja in Portuguese), the mother of many of the orishas and patron of the oceans and motherhood. Every year on January 1, thousands of Brazilians flock to the oceanside to ask Yemanja's blessing. A small boat decorated with candles, flowers and statues of the saints is set adrift in the waves. If the boat sinks, then Yemanja has again accepted her devotees' offering.

Her son Chango (Xango) is the god of fire and thunder, and supervises warfare and great sexual passion. Oshun (Oxum), Chango's sister and mistress, governs marriage, romantic love and money. Ochosi (Oxossi) is the god of hunters, birds and wild animals, and dwells in the forests. Omolu (Omulu), the god of contagious diseases, has the power to begin and end epidemics. And Yansan (Iansa) controls wind, lightning and storms.

Another important orisha is Eleggua, the god of entryways, doors and roads, who permits the other orishas to come to earth. All homes keep an image of Eleggua behind the door to serve as gatekeeper. In Candomblé, worshippers pray to the Exus, similar in function to Eleggua but more like primal forces of nature who act as divine tricksters and messengers to the gods, a function of traditional angels. Eleggua has many manifestations, and some of them are called Eshus as well. The Eshus or Exus can be benign or malignant. King Exu often is identified with LUCIFER, and works with BEELZEBUB and ASTAROTH to become Exu Mor (death) and Exu of the Crossroads. At his worst he is Exu of the Closed Paths, a wicked demon who closes off all paths to prosperity, love, success and health.

Theosophy also closely identifies angels with particular facets of nature, assigning gods responsibility for the mountains, rocks, animals, plants, seas, fire, wind and storms. Lower nature spirits such as brownies and sylphs work under these angels, tending to the more menial details of nature's care. In his book *The Brotherhood of Angels and Men*, Theosophist Geoffrey HODSON described several categories of angels, each with particular powers and responsibilities similar to those of the orishas: angels of power, of healing, of the home, of building, of nature, of beauty, of music and the arts. Each of Hodson's angels has favorite colors, places and sacred objects and prefers certain modes of worship, just as do the orishas.

Whether angels or orishas, these devic spirits have one goal: to receive love from man, and to guide him in his quest for perfect spiritual oneness with nature and with God.

**Further reading:**

Altman, Nathaniel. "The Orishas: Communing with Angels in the Candomble Tradition of Brazil," *Angels & Mortals: Their Co-Creative Power*, compiled by Maria Parisen. Wheaton, Ill.: Quest Books, The Theosophical Publishing House, 1990.

Guiley, Rosemary Ellen. *Harper's Encyclopedia of Mystical and Paranormal Experience*. San Francisco: HarperSanFrancisco, 1991.

Hodson, Geoffrey. *The Brotherhood of Angels and Men*. Wheaton, Ill.: The Theosophical Publishing House, 1982.

———. *The Kingdom of the Gods*. Adyar, Madras, India: The Theosophical Publishing House, 1972.

**Pachomius, St.**   See MONASTICISM, CHRISTIAN.

**Padre Pio**   See GUARDIAN ANGEL.

**Paul, St.**   Born Saul, in the city of Tarsus in Asia Minor around 10 C.E. of Jewish parents of the tribe of Benjamin, educated in Jerusalem in the school of the Pharisees, Paul zealously persecuted the infant Christian sect until his conversion on the road to Damascus around 34. A vision of the risen Jesus told him that he had been chosen as the apostle to the pagans (Acts 9:3–16). This is precisely what the renamed Paul was for the rest of his life, interrupted only by shipwrecks and imprisonment. He traveled the eastern Mediterranean world from Jerusalem to Rome, throughout Greece and Asia Minor, preached, converted, established communities and churches, and thereafter, when he could not revisit them or send another close disciple, rendered them pastoral care through the Epistles. The Acts of the Apostles (generally ascribed to St. Luke, a close companion of Paul) and his own letters form two sources from which the facts and chronology of his life can be constructed. He was martyred in Rome in 67.

The Epistles were not meant to be doctrinal treatises, but reflections on situations occurring in the particular church to which Paul was writing. The Epistles reveal Paul's syntheses of Christian belief, philosophy and practice, as he himself understood these through the channel of his love of Christ. The story is told against the backdrop of his astounding conversion; his hearing Jesus' voice and being struck blind. He voiced his constant sense of Christ's leading him, and he urged the faithful to follow his degree of faith inwardly and outwardly to "new life" in spite of the Judaic, Hellenic, Roman and other political, religious and cultural realities of their time. The Epistles quickly became canonical and appear in Christian liturgy along with the Gospels. Their complexities have proved endlessly fascinating to biblical scholars, who dispute full authorship by Paul of several sections and whole epistles. It is now generally conceded that the Epistle to the Hebrews was not written by Paul himself; several of his close followers have been suggested as authors. The field of biblical scholarship has always been linguistically challenging. The Epistles were preserved in Greek, which becomes highly relevant when discussing Paul's angelology.

### ANGELOLOGY

Paul believed that human beings were influenced by spirits good, evil and neutral. The source of his cosmology of "Angels" and "Powers" was the Judaism in which he was educated, which he built upon in the service of his theology of salvation.

The good spirits were angels (*angeloi*); once he refers to *archangelos* (1 Thessalonians 4:16). The word *malak* in Hebrew translates into *angeloi* in Greek, and means messenger/representative. God sends such to earth on salvific missions. They have served as intermediaries in the giving of the Law (Galatians 3:19). They are associated with the Second Coming and the Final Resurrection in 1 Thessalonians 4:16. They are usually portrayed as good, as in 1 Corinthians 13:1, "If I speak in the tongues of men and of angels." References to their role can be ambiguous, as in the puzzling reference in 1 Corinthians 11:10: "the woman ought to have on the head a sign of subordination [lit. "authority"] because of the angels." Another enigmatic statement appears in 1 Corinthians 6:3: "Do you not know we are to judge angels?" Evil can be dis-

**The conversion of St. Paul**

guised as angels (Galatians 1:8, 2 Corinthians 11:14). Romans 8:38 mentions angels among the cosmic forces that can drive the faithful away from the love of God: "neither death nor life, no angel, no prince, nothing that exists, nothing still to come, not any power, or height or depth, nor any created thing, can ever come between us and the love of God made visible in Christ our Lord." This passage also is relevant to the meanings Paul attributes to Powers, "heights" and "depths," which will be addressed shortly.

In 2 Corinthians 12:7 an angel of Satan has been sent to harass Paul. Ho Satanas, a transliteration of the Hebrew *satan*, appears ten times in the Pauline corpus. Ho Diabolos occurs as well. In 2 Corinthians 4:4 Satan is called "the god of this age." The functions of these Satan/Diabolos figures agree with those of the Judaic tradition: Accuser (2 Corinthians 2:11; Ephesians 4:27); Tempter (1 Corinthians 7:5; 2 Corinthians 11:3; 11:14, Ephesians 6:11); Executor (1 Corinthians 5:5; 2 Corinthians 12:7). Satan is God's adversary, who opposes himself to the spreading of the Gospel (2 Corinthians 4:4), interferes with the apostolic plans of Paul (1 Thessalonians 2:18), ensnares men (1 Timothy 3:7), will help the Lawless One to seduce the world (2 Thessalonians 2:9), but whom God finally will crush (Romans 16:20). In 1 Corinthians 10:20f, the demons appear in the precise sense of the false gods whom the pagans worship through their idolatry (see ORIGEN). In 1 Timothy 4:1 the demons are deceitful spirits, whose doctrines will seduce the people of later times. Paul takes over the Jewish tradition on evil spirits by neglecting to ask questions about the origin of angelic evil.

"Powers" appear in Paul under five names: Archai ("Rulers"), 8 times; Exousiai ("Authorities"), 7 times; Dynameis ("Powers"), 3 times; Kyriotetes ("Lordships"), twice; and Thronoi ("Thrones"), once. These Powers appear particularly in the Epistles of Paul's captivity: Colossians 1:16, 2:10, 2:15; Ephesians 1:21, 3:10, 6;12; but also they are met in 1 Corinthians 15:24; Romans 8:38; 2 Thessalonians 1:7. Peter also names "Authorities" and "Powers" next to Angels (1 Peter 3:22). The Colossians and Ephesians were especially prone to worry about these mighty "Powers" associated with heavenly bodies in their local cultures. Their functions were those of government, as can be seen from the names. In the Old Testament and the Book of ENOCH, God's practice of entrusting nations to an angel was established.

For Paul, some of these spirits appear to be mortal enemies. In 1 Corinthians 2:6–8, the "Princes of this age" (*Archontes tou aionos toutou*) have "crucified the Lord of Glory." This context clearly suggests that human authorities are manipulated by superior powers who influence the world. "The Prince of this world" translates from *Archon tou kosmou toutou* in John 14:30; 16:11.

There is reason to deduce, however, that Paul shared the astrological idea of his place and time that the Cosmos was ruled by celestial powers. For example in Ephesians 2:2 he mentions "the Prince (*archon*) of the authority (*exousia*) of the air." And in Ephesians 6:12 the *archai* and *exousiai* are explained by "the world rulers of this darkness," and "the spiritual hosts of evil in the heavens." It is from heaven that the *archai* operate over the human world, and not like the Angels who intervene through individual missions or who rule over particular atmospheric phenomena, but as superior authorities who direct the course the world from above. In principle they do it through God's authority; they are created by God in Christ (Colossians 1:16); but they have lost their original power and will cede it under the new regime set in motion by Christ's incarnation (1 Corinthians 2:6; 15:24; Colossians 2:10). This evolution holds true of government and economy on earth too (1 Corinthians 13:8–10).

There is no punishment here, but reordering. If the princes of this world have crucified Jesus, it was because they knew not his true identity. The powers and principalities do not know everything; it is only now that they discover the mystery of salvation that was previously hidden from them. Paul says that he has been "entrusted with this special grace, not only of proclaiming to the pagans the infinite treasure of Christ, but also of explaining how the mystery is to be dispensed. Through all the ages, this has been kept hidden in God, the creator of everything. Why? So that the Sovereignties and Powers should learn, only now, through the church, how comprehensive God's wisdom really is, exactly according to the plan which he had from all eternity in Christ Jesus our Lord" (Ephesians 3:9–11).

However, Paul also conveys a sense of animosity against the Powers, first of all directed against the doctors of Colossae; by their legal observances do they not even worship angels (Colossians 2:18). They keep in force systems abolished by Christ and leave to the heavenly Powers authority which they no longer have. The doctors are guilty, but one gets the impression that the Powers themselves willingly accept the situation and encourage these marks of homage. Something similar happens in the case of the Powers for Paul. One feels here that the world is held in thrall by demonic Powers: "Put God's armor on so as to be able to resist the devil's tactics. For it is not against human enemies that we have to struggle, but against the Sovereignties and Powers who originate the darkness in this world, the spiritual army of evil in the heavens" (Ephesians 6:12).

**Further reading:**
"Introduction to the Letters of St. Paul," *The Jerusalem Bible*. Garden City, N.Y.: Doubleday and Company, 1966.
Knox, W.L. *St. Paul and the Church of the Gentiles*. Cambridge, England: Cambridge University Press, 1939.
Caird, G.B. *Principalities and Powers: A Study in Pauline Theology*. New York Oxford University Press, 1966.

**Perelandra**   Garden and nature research center, similar in concept to FINDHORN, in which humans work in cooperation with angelic beings.

Perelandra was founded by Machaelle Small Wright and her partner, Clarence Wright, in Virginia. In 1974, Machaelle Wright opened psychically, and in 1976 she began to communicate with overlighting intelligences in nature, which are known variously as devas, angels, nature spirits and elementals. These intelligences provide guidance in the creation and cultivation of gardens.

The name Perelandra is taken from the science fiction novel by C. S. Lewis about Venus, which he calls Perelandra and is the planet of perfection. It is visited by two Earth men, one good and the other evil. The good man moves within the harmony of Perelandra, while the evil one moves in destruction. Wright felt the name appropriate for their woodsy site, which still retained a spark of perfection despite the damage done to it by previous owners. The site is located on about twenty-two acres near Jeffersonton, Virginia, about sixty miles southwest of Washington, D.C.

See GREEN HOPE FARM.

**Further reading:**
Atwater, P.M.H. "Perelandra: Cooperating Co-creatively with Nature," *New Realities*, May/June 1988, pp. 17–20.
Wright, Machaelle Small. *Behaving as if the God in All Life Mattered.* Jeffersonton, Va.: Perelandra, 1987.

**Phanuel**   Angel sometimes identified as being one of the four primary archangels along with MICHAEL, GABRIEL and RAPHAEL. Phauel often is equated with URIEL, as well as with Ramiel (also known as Jeremiel).

Phanuel appears in the Ethiopic Book of Parables. He governs the repentance of those who aspire to eternal life, and fends off "the Satans." In early Hebrew times his name was invoked for protection against evil spirits.

**philangeli**   See DEVOTIONAL CULTS.

**Pius XI** (1857–1939)   Pope Pius XI (1922–1939) publicly acknowledged his personal relationship with his GUARDIAN ANGEL during a time when angels were out of fashion in popular culture. He said he prayed to the angel every morning and evening—and throughout the day, if necessary.

As a young man, Achille Ratti was impressed by St. Bernard's assertion that it is humanity's duty to respect, love and trust one's guardian angel. When Ratti became Pope Pius XI, he took the advice to heart, and his faith in his guardian angel came to play a role in all the good deeds he accomplished in life, he said.

Pius XI confided to Monsignor Angelo Roncalli, who later became JOHN XXIII, that angels helped him in his many delicate diplomatic dealings. Prior to a meeting with someone whom he needed to persuade, he would pray to his guardian angel, making his best case, and asking him to take it up with the guardian angel of the other person. Sometimes Pius XI would himself invoke the guardian angel of the other person, asking to be enlightened as to the other's viewpoint. Once the two angels had reached an understanding, he told Roncalli, the situation involving himself and the other person became smoother.

Pius XI was renowned for his diplomatic activity. He brought about the Lateran Treaty, signed in 1929. This concordat between the Holy See and Italy ended a dispute over papal sovereignty and created Vatican City as the new sovereign state. The treaty also recognized Roman Catholicism as the only state religion in Italy.

Pius XI actively opposed fascism, communism and the Nazi party. He championed social reform and greater participation by the lay public in religion, as well as the rights of native cultures and "Oriental" Catholics.

Pius XI recommended to others that they pray to their guardian angels as well. He especially sought out people on the front lines: diplomats, teachers, missionaries and the like. These individuals, who in turn influenced the lives of many others, were especially in need of angelic guidance, he said.

**Further reading:**
Huber, Georges. *My Angel Will Go Before You.* Westminster, Md.: Christian Classics, 1983.

**Pius XII** (1876–1958)   Pope Pius XII (1939–1958) was a champion of angels, especially the GUARDIAN ANGEL. Yet unlike Popes PIUS XI and JOHN XXIII, he did not reveal his own personal dealings with angels.

In an encyclical in 1950, Pius XII stated that it was a mistake to question whether angels are "real beings"—this was erroneous thinking that could undermine church doctrine. He urged people to renew their devotion to angels. On October 3, 1958, a few days before his death, he gave an address to a group of American tourists in which he reminded them of the existence of an invisible world populated with angels:

Did Christ not say, speaking to little children, who were so loved by his pure and loving heart: "Their angels always behold the face of my Father who is in heaven." When children become adults, do their guardian angels abandon them? Not at all.

The hymn at first vespers in yesterday's liturgy told us, "Let us sing to the guardian angels of men, heavenly companions, given to the Father by our frail nature, lest we succumb to the enemies who threaten us." This same thinking is to be found time and time again in the writings of the Fathers of the Church.

Everyone, no matter how humble he may be, has angels to watch over him. They are heavenly, pure and splendid, and yet they have been given to us to keep us company on our way:

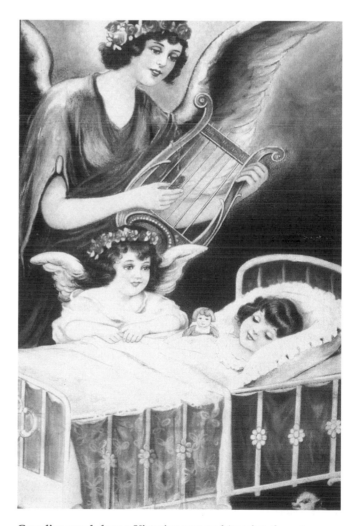

**Guardian angel, from a Victorian postcard (reprinted courtesy Jayne M. Howard)**

they have been given the task of keeping careful watch over you so that you do not become separated from Christ, their Lord.

And not only do they want to protect you from the dangers which waylay you throughout their journey: they are actually by your side, helping your souls as you strive to go ever higher in your union with God through Christ.

. . . We do not want to take leave of you . . . without exhorting you to awaken, to revive your sense of the invisible world which is all around us . . . and to have a certain familiarity with the angels, who are forever solicitous for your salvation and your sanctification. If God wishes, you will spend a happy eternity with the angels: get to know them here, from now on.

**Further reading:**
Huber, Georges, *My Angel Will Go Before You*. Westminster, Md.: Christian Classics, 1983.

**planetary angels**   In occult lore, there are seven angels who govern the seven planets known to the ancients (considered the seven planets of astrology as well). The seven planets rule hours throughout the day and night. Thus, the angel associated with a planet also rules certain times.

The English occultist Francis Barrett states in his book *The Magus* (1801) that the planetary angels "are those seven spirits which always stand before the face of God, to whom is entrusted disposing the whole celestial and terrene kingdoms which are under the moon: for these (as the more curious theologians say) govern all things by a certain vicissitude of hours, days and years; as the astrologers teach concerning the planets which they are set over, which Mercurius Trismegistus calls the seven governors of the world, who, by the heavens as by instruments, distribute the influences of all the stars and signs upon their inferiors."

The planetary angels are charged with the movements of the planets through the heavens, and their places in the universe. According to Barrett, the angels and their assignments are:

Sun—Michael
Moon—Gabriel
Mercury—Raphael
Venus—Anael
Mars—Samael
Jupiter—Sachiel
Saturn—Cassiel

**Further reading:**
Barrett, Francis. *The Magus*. Secaucus, N. J.: The Citadel Press, 1967. First published 1801.

**Plato**   See INTELLIGENCES.

**Plotinus**   See INTELLIGENCES.

**poetry and angels**   See LITERATURE AND ANGELS.

**powers**   See CHOIRS.

**Pravuil**   In the Book of Enoch, the wise archangel who keeps all the records of heaven. God summoned Pravuil to present the records to Enoch, and to instruct him in writing down everything he saw and heard during his trip to heaven. See ENOCH.

**princes**   See GUARDIAN ANGEL; ORIGEN.

**Princes of the Countenance**   In apocalyptic literature, such as the Ethiopic Book of Enoch, a group of angels who are privileged to look upon the face of God. Of these, META-TRON is the most important. According to the Kabbalah, the function of the Princes of the Countenance is "to exalt and arrange the throne in a befitting manner."

**Further reading:**
Scholem, Gershom. *Kabbalah*. New York: Dorset Press, 1987. First published 1974.

**principalities**   See CHOIRS.

**Protestant angelology**   The Protestant revolt began in the sixteenth century with Martin Luther's Ninety-Five Theses, nailed on the door of Wittenberg Cathedral in 1517, and Henry VIII's 1534 Act of Supremacy, declaring himself the head of the Church of England. The founders of the various lines of Protestantism—Anglican, Lutheran, Calvinist—discarded some church dogma and much ecclesiastical law, modified practices for both clergy and laity, yet retained a great deal of both dogma and practice. Protestantism kept church dogmas on angels relatively intact.

The church had made an official statement on the subject of angels at the Fourth Lateran Council in 1215, about fifty years before St. Thomas AQUINAS formulated his elaborate commentaries on angels. All the implications of the first sen-

**Martin Luther triumphing over the monk's devil (Matthew Gnidius, *Dialogi*, 1521)**

tence of the book of Genesis, expounded at great length by St. AUGUSTINE in Book XII of his *Confessions*, were made explicit in the statement of the Council:

> God is "creator of all things visible and invisible, spiritual and corporeal; who by his almighty power, together at the beginning of time, formed out of nothing the spiritual creature and the corporeal creature, that is, the angelic and the terrestrial; and then the human creature, composed of both body and spirit. For Satan and the other devils were created by God, and created good in nature; it is of themselves they have become evil." They "fell into sin of their own free will," and are "eternally damned."

The Council of Trent, held intermittently by the church between 1545 and 1563 in response to the Protestant Reformation, added to the last article above the following article of dogma: that "the first man, Adam, sinned at the devil's instigation . . . passed into the devil's powers, and with him the human race that was descended from him." This focus on Satan's strength, and the human susceptibility to his wiles, was a recurrent Protestant theme.

Martin Luther (1483–1546) led the parade of Protestant theologians who made much of human corruption and the constant presence of Satan and the devils under his command. He wrote that

> the acknowledgement of angels is needful in the church. Therefore godly preachers should teach them logically. First, they should show what angels are, namely, spiritual creatures without bodies. Secondly, what manner of spirits must be spoken of, not created evil by God, but made so by their rebellion against God, and their consequent fall; this hatred began in Paradise, and will continue and remain against Christ and his church to the world's end. . . . The devil is also near and about us, incessantly tracking our steps, in order to deprive us of our lives, our saving health, and salvation. But the holy angels defend us from him, insomuch that he is not able to work up to such mischief as willingly he would.

In *The Institutes of Christian Religion*, John Calvin (1509–1564) points his readers' attention to this "concise information concerning the nature of devils; that at their creation, they were originally angels of God, but by degenerating have ruined themselves, and become the instruments of perdition." Calvin does not neglect to add perspective on the struggle of good and evil. Satan "can do nothing against God's will and consent." Satan "attempts those things which he thinks most opposed to God," but "God holds him tied and bound with the bridle of his power," so that he can do "only those things which are divinely permitted."

Calvin's treatment of angels is limited to what can be deduced from his perusal of sacred Scripture, saying this is "what the Lord has been pleased for us to know concerning his angels." He begins to embody the conservative Protestant belief more explicitly when he enjoins us "not to speak, or think, or even desire to know, concerning obscure subjects, anything beyond the information given us in the Divine word." He cautions us, in reading Scripture, "to investigate and meditate upon things conducive to edification; not to indulge curiosity or the study of things unprofitable."

Calvin's comments on angels are accompanied by Scripture pertinent to the question at hand. For example, here is the first sentence of the section of his *Institutes of the Christian Religion* (XIV, 6.), subtitled "The angels as protectors and helpers of believers":

> Scripture strongly insists upon teaching us what could most effectively make for our consolation and the strengthening of our faith: namely, that angels are dispensers and administrators of God's beneficence toward us. For this reason, Scripture recalls that they keep vigil for our safety, take upon themselves our defense, direct our ways, and take care that some harm may not befall us.

This is followed by citation and comments on no less than a dozen passages.

On the question of "whether individual angels have been assigned to individual believers for their protection, I dare not affirm with confidence," Calvin begins, and explains his reservations. In Matthew 18:10, although

> Christ hints that there are certain angels to whom their safety [the children] has been committed . . . from this I do not know whether one ought to infer that each individual has the protection of his own angel. We ought to hold as a fact that the care of each one of us is not the task of one angel only, but all with one consent watch over our salvation. . . . If the fact that all the heavenly host are keeping watch for his safety will not satisfy a man, I do not see what benefit he could derive from knowing that one angel has been given to him as his especial guardian. Indeed, those who confine to one angel the care that God takes of each one of us are doing a great injustice both to themselves and to all the members of the church; as if it were an idle promise that we should fight more valiantly with these hosts supporting and protecting us round about! (XIV, 7) (See GUARDIAN ANGEL.)

Calvin takes pains (XIV, 8) to repudiate Aquinas's elaborate speculative treatment of angels and their number and form (as in *Summa Theologica* I, cvi–cviv), arguing that there is no scriptural evidence for any of it. Regarding the position of Aquinas that the number of angels vastly surpasses the number of material things, Calvin disagrees: "Let those who venture to determine the number of angels examine on what foundation their opinions rest." This question belongs to "that class of mysteries, the full revelation of which is deferred to the last day."

As far as the angelic hierarchy is concerned, Calvin considered PSEUDO-DIONYSIUS, Aquinas's chief source, unreliable, remarking that

> no man can deny that great subtlety and acuteness is discovered by Dionysius, whoever he was, in many parts of his treatise on the Celestial Hierarchy; but if any one enters into a critical examination of it, he will find the greatest part of it to be mere babbling. . . . A reader of that book would suppose that the author was a man descended from heaven, giving an account of things that he had not learned from the information of others, but had seen with his own eyes. But Paul, who was "caught up to the third heaven" [2 Corinthians, XII, 1], not only has told us no such things, but has even declared that it is not lawful for men to utter the sacred things which he had seen.

Erasmus and Luther, before Calvin, had disputed on stylistic and theological grounds Pseudo-Dionysius's claim to be the Areopagite who encountered St. Paul. The incipient Protestant movement, with its distaste for the kind of theoretical expertise evinced by Aquinas and others' work on angels, delighted in the exposure of the imposter, used it to discredit the Scholastics' pretense to being Christian, and moved to dismantle the elaborate system of medieval Doctors of the Church like Bonaventure (see MONASTICISM, CHRISTIAN), who had argued that the hierarchy of the angels was a prototype of the hierarchy of the church.

Karl Barth, a leading twentieth-century follower of Calvin, comments that Aquinas's angelology "offers us a classic example of how not to proceed in this matter. . . . In the matter of angels it is better to look resolutely and exclusively in a different direction than to try to look at the Bible and other sources of knowledge at the same time." If we do that, "our philosophy will spoil our theology, and our theology our philosophy. . . . Holy Scripture gives us quite enough to think about regarding angels." He also accords with Calvin's denunciation of Pseudo-Dionysius, dismissing him as "one of the greatest frauds in church history," but adds that "within its limits his work is one of those original and masterly ventures which do not often occur in the history of theology" (Church Dogmatics, Vol. III, Part 3, "The Kingdom of Heaven").

Calvin warned against the "superstition which frequently creeps in, to the effect that angels are ministers and dispensers of all good things to us . . . and what belongs to God and Christ alone is transferred to them" (XIV, 10). He discusses the difficulties Paul had with this worship of angels, a holdover from pagan philosophy and practice. "Farewell, then, to that Platonic philosophy of seeking access to God through angels, and of worshipping them with intent to render God more approachable to us. For that is what superstitious and curious men have tried to drag into our religion from the beginning and persevere in trying, even to this day" (XIV, 12).

Calvin held that Scriptural evidence concerning the reality of angels required us to reject the notion that they were merely symbolic—visions or voices experienced by men. "So many testimonies of Scripture cry out against this nonsense that it is a wonder such crass ignorance could be borne with" (XIV, 9). The same "trifling philosophy" is refuted concerning devils (XIV, 19).

The warfare of the Kingdom of God against the kingdom of Satan is a theme frequently presented by Calvin. "All that Scripture teaches concerning devils aims at arousing us to take precaution against their stratagems and contrivances, and also to equip ourselves with those weapons which are strong and powerful enough to vanquish these most powerful foes" (XIV, 13). Nevertheless, "we ought to accept as a fixed certainty the fact that he [Satan] can do nothing unless God wills and assents to it" (XIV, 17). The Christian elect, the true believers, are assured of victory in this holy war, according to Calvin. "God does not allow Satan to rule over the souls of believers, but gives over only the impious and unbelievers, whom he deigns not to regard as members of his own flock, to be governed by him." Satan "is said to blind all those who do not believe in the gospel [2 Corinthians 4:4]. Again, to carry out his 'work in the sons of disobedience' [Ephesians 2:2], and rightly, for all the impious are vessels of wrath. . . . As believers are recognized as the children of God because they wear his image, so are those rightly recognized to be the children of Satan from his image, into which they have degenerated" (XIV, 18).

It is easy to infer some characteristics of Calvinism from the remarks of its offshoot. The line of this branch of Protestantism gave birth to Puritanism, of which John MILTON was a devout follower, and which was brought to North America in some strict versions with some of its first English settlers.

Two American Protestants who practiced Puritanism in seventeenth-century New England illustrate the ongoing metamorphosis of angelology that was set in motion by the Protestant revolt. Samuel Willard (1640–1707) was acting president of Harvard College for several years, and author of several books on divinity. He believed that the human was a unique being who spans the cosmological divide between the visible, inconstant world of animals and the invisible, constant world of angels. The "most pure and subtle matter" of angelic beings is nonetheless matter; even though they are "perpetual and aeviternal," they are still creatures. "They are capable of torment; they are not a mere act, as God is, but have a protention; they are quantity and not infinite" (Compleat Body of Divinity). The "rational soul" of human beings positions them at the juncture of earth and heaven, matter and spirit; with the body rooted in the inconstant world of terrestrial beings and the soul sharing with the angels the celestial sphere of constant natures, both are constitutive and both are "essential" to humanity (Compleat Body).

Willard also believes that there are a multitude of real demons, but ordinarily he refers to them as if they were one being, the devil, or Satan, or "the god of the world," created by God but turned evil by the angelic revolt in the courts of heaven. Satan exercises power through "man's consent," which is derived mostly from that erroneous sense of "self-sovereignty" which humans have that they can master life, and assisted by a "spy watching its season and advantage within human concupiscence" (Mercy Magnified).

Poet Edward Taylor (c. 1642–1729) emigrated from England in 1668, graduated from Harvard College in 1671, and served as a minister on the western Massachusetts frontier until his death. Taylor's theology in most respects followed a straight enough Calvinist line. However, he extended the Protestant tendency to diminish the importance of angels to a belief, stated again and again, that humankind, partaking intimately of God's own being through Christ, must now stand even higher than angelic nature in the scale of creation, being "little lower than God":

> Give place ye holy Angells of Light. Ye Sparkling Stars of the Morning. The Brightest Glory, the Highest Seate in the Kingdom of Glory . . . belong to my nature and not to yours. I cannot, I may not allow it You, without injury to Mine own Nature, and Indignity and Ingratitude to my Lord, that hath assumed it into a Personal Conjunction with his Divine Nature and seated it in the Trinity [Christographia]. I'le Claim my right: Give place, ye Angells Bright./ Ye further from the Godhead stande than I. . . . Gods throne is first and mine is next: to you/ Only the place of Waiting-men is due. ("The Experience")

Scholars have traced Taylor's deifying tendencies to Christian mysticism and some of the early Christian fathers, St. Augustine and ORIGEN among them, who wrote with excitement about humanity's ascent to participation in the divine nature. This helps to explain the optimism that sets him apart from many of his "doom and gloom" Puritan contemporaries.

Taylor may have been influenced by a textual conflict. Whereas the King James Version translation of a line in Psalm 8 reads "a little lower than the angels," the Geneva Bible offered more support for the revised chain of being with its rendering: "a little lower than God." Modern commentators point out that the Hebrew *elohim* translates in the plural as "gods," members of Yahweh's divine council. But the Hebrew words for angels, "*malak*" and "*elohim*," had a much wider range of application than can be pinned down by English (see JUDAIC ANGELOLOGY).

Another consideration is the early Christian polemic against angel worship taken up by St. Paul and continued by Calvin, as foregoing citations attest. *The Book of Concord*, written by Luther and still dogma of the modern Evangelical Lutheran church, also speaks to this issue:

> Although the angels in heaven pray for us (as Christ himself also does), and although saints on earth, and perhaps also in heaven, do likewise, it does not follow that we should invoke angels and saints, pray to them, keep fasts and vigils for them . . . serve them in still other ways, regard them as helpers in time of need, and attribute all sorts of help to them, assigning to each of them a special function, as the papists teach and practice. This is idolatry. Such honor belongs to God alone.

Luther and Calvin illustrate plainly the fact that Reformed theologians had little incentive to inquire into any perhaps benign, non-human mysteries of the invisible world, scornful as they were of Roman Catholic notions that heavenly messengers might act as intercessory agents or objects of prayer. A few isolated works, such as Increase Mather's *Angelographia* (Boston, 1696) discussed the real, present influence of good angels in the lives of saints. But on the whole for Protestants, the angels' post-biblical functions paled before the importance to God of humanity's struggle against the Devil to achieve divine identity as the elect of Christ.

**Further reading:**
Barth, Karl. *Church Dogmatics.* Edinburgh: T & T Clark, 1960.
Calvin, John. *Institutes of the Christian Religion.* Ed. John T. McNeill, trans. Ford Lewis Battles. Philadelphia: Westminster Press, 1960.
Gatta, John J. "Little Lower than God: Super-Angelic Anthropology of Edward Taylor." *Harvard Theological Review,* Vol. 75 (July 1982), pp. 361–368.
Lowrie, Ernest B. *The Shape of the Puritan Mind: The Thought of Samuel Willard.* New Haven: Yale University Press, 1974.
Martin Luther. *Table Talk,* Vol. 54. Ed. and trans. Theodore C. Tappert. Philadelphia: Fortress Press, 1967.
———. *The Book of Concord: The Confessions of the Evangelical Lutheran Church.* Ed. and trans. Theodore C. Tappert. Philadelphia: Fortress Press, 1959.

**pseudepigrapha**   A collection of inspired Jewish and Jewish-Christian works that are not part of the canon. Some of these writings contain detailed information about angels not found in the Scriptures.

Pseudipigraphical works were written primarily between 200 B.C.E. and 200 C.E. Done anonymously by multiple authors, their authorship sometimes was attributed to legendary figures. There are two types of pseudepigrapha, the Palestinian (written in Aramaic or Hebrew) and the Alexandrian (written in Greek).

In angelology, probably the most important pseudepigraphical work is the Book of Enoch, attributed to the prophet ENOCH, who was transported to the heavens by angels. The secrets of the universe were revealed to him, which he wrote down. For his holy labors, God transformed Enoch into the angel METATRON. The Book of Enoch addres-

ses the origin of evil, the nature and duties of angels, the pre-existent Messiah, and the nature of Gehenna-Hell and Paradise, among other subjects. Sections referred to as "the book of celestial physics" describe how angels rule the seasons, time, elements, planets and stars.

The Book of Enoch is also called 1 Enoch or the Ethiopian Enoch. It is part of the Palestinian Pseudepigrapha, and is preserved in its entirety in Ethiopic translation. Parts of it exist in Greek and Latin, and in Aramaic fragments found at Qumran, where the Dead Sea Scrolls have been excavated.

Unlike the APOCRYPHA, which is not referenced in the New Testament, the Book of Enoch is quoted in Jude 20:14–15.

**Further reading:**
Laurence, Richard (transl.). *The Book of Enoch the Prophet.* San Diego, Calif.: Wizards Bookshelf, 1976.
*The New Oxford Annotated Bible with the Apochrypha.* Herbert G. May and Bruce M. Metzger, eds. New York: Oxford University Press, 1977.

**Pseudo-Dionysius**   Pseudonymous early Greek writer who wrote extensively on Christian mysticism and on the heirarchies and nature of angels. Pseudo-Dionysius, also erroneously known as Dionysius (or Denis) the Areopagite (whom St. PAUL converted in Athens), may have been a Syrian clergyman, or perhaps even more than one person. The exact dates of his writings are unknown, although it is believed that they date to the fifth or sixth centuries C.E. His works include *The Celestial Hierarchy, The Mystical Theology, The Ecclesiastical Hierarchy* and *The Divine Names.* These writings had a profound influence on medieval Christian thinkers, including St. Thomas AQUINAS and St. John of the Cross, and on writers such as John MILTON and DANTE.

St. John of the Cross perhaps most eloquently expressed the essential Pseudo-Dionysian idea when he said in his poetry that he pursued knowledge by means of unknowing. This *agnosia,* "without knowing," is the opposite of *gnosis* and symbolizes a state of innocence. Pseudo-Dionysius believed that union with God is achieved when body and mind are "dead" and the spirit functions beyond time. Thus one attains "divine darkness," that is, one knows God by knowing nothing.

Pseudo-Dionysius follows the Platonic and Neoplatonic pattern tradition of devotion to the number three. He conceives of all reality in triadic hierarchies. In his work *The Celestial Hierarchy,* he presents an angelic kingdom of nine levels, the names of which he took from biblical tradition. Following the thought of the day he divides these into three realms, each of which contains three orders, each of which is further broken down into three levels of intelligences. In each group of three, the function of the first (top) level is perfection or union, that of the second level, illumination, and that of the third level, purification. This triadic arrangement provides a means for the divine, or spirit, to descend into matter, and for matter to ascend to divinity.

A hierarchy, says Pseudo-Dionysius, is "a sacred order, a state of understanding and an activity approximating as closely as possible to the divine." The goal of a hierarchy "is to enable beings to be as like as possible to God and to be at one with him." Thus, through the angelic hierarchy, humankind has a way of reaching up to God and sharing in the Light that emanates from Him.

**The archangel Gabriel appearing to Mary**

Pseudo-Dionysius says that angels are nearer to God than are humans, "since their participation in him takes so many forms." He elaborates:

> Their thinking processes imitate the divine. They look on the divine likeness with a transcendent eye. They model their intellects on him. Hence it is natural for them to enter into a more generous communion with the Deity, because they are forever marching towards the heights, because, as permitted, they are drawn to a concentration of an unfailing love for God, because they immaterially receive undiluted the original enlightenment, and because, ordered by such enlightenment, theirs is a life of total intelligence. They have the first and most diverse participation in the divine, and they, in turn, provide the first and most diverse revelations of the divine hiddenness. That is why they have a preeminent right to the title of angel or messenger, since it is they who first are granted the divine enlightenment and it is they who pass on to us these revelations which are so far beyond us. (180A–B)

### RANKS OF ANGELS

At the center of the triadic angel kingdom is God, emitting rapid vibrations which slow as they move out from the source and become light. As these vibrations slow they become heat, and finally matter. Nine orders of celestial beings surround God, divided, as mentioned, into three triads. At any level the angels possess all of the powers of those beneath them but not of those above. The aim of each hierarchy—that is, group of three—is to imitate God so as to take on his form, states Pseudo-Dionysius. The task of each is "to receive and to pass on undiluted purification, the divine light, and the understanding which brings perfection" (208A).

The upper triad is composed of seraphim (love), cherubim (knowledge) and thrones. The entities of the upper triad are in direct contact with God. They receive "the primal theophanies and perfections," says Pseudo-Dionysius, which they then pass on to the middle triad. These three levels are so close to God as to be perfect and utterly pure: "They are full of a superior light beyond any knowledge and . . . are filled with a transcendent and triply luminous contemplation of the one who is the cause and the source of all beauty" (208C). The hymns of these angels, who dance ceaselessly around God singing his praises, are transmitted to humans by theologians.

The name *seraphim* means "fire-makers" or "carriers of warmth." Seraphim maintain an unfaltering heat of movement about the throne of God, and are able to hold undiminished both the light they have and the illumination they give out. They purify through fire and lightning, and have the ability to push away every shadow.

The name *cherubim* means "fullness of wisdom" or "outpouring of wisdom." They have the power to see and to know God; to contemplate the divine splendor in primordial power; and to pour out their wisdom to others.

The *thrones* transcend all earthly defects, and are forever separated from all that is inferior to them. They are free from passion and material interests, and can openly receive and bear God.

The middle triad consists of *dominions, powers*, and *authorities* (also called *virtues* in other hierarchies). These in turn pass God's word to the last triad.

The name *dominions* signifies a lifting up that is free of earthly tendencies. Dominions strive ceaselessly toward true dominion and the true source of all dominion, rejecting empty appearances and returning completely to God.

The *powers* exhibit a kind of masculine and unshakable courage in all that they do. They manifest a dynamic energy. Powers point to the transcendent power of God, the source of all power.

The *authorities* receive God in a harmonious and unconfused way, and point to the ordered nature of both celestial and intellectual authority.

The last triad, of principalities, archangels and angels, is responsible for communicating God's word to humans.

The *principalities* possess a godlike and princely hegemony, and set the example of behavior according to the highest principles.

The *archangels* commune with the principalities and bring about the unity of all the angels. They interpret and mediate divine pronouncements and announce them to the angels.

The *angels* are closest in the celestial hierarchy to human beings, and transmit what they receive from higher up in the form of enlightenment and wisdom.

### NUMBERS OF ANGELS

Pseudo-Dionysius reflects on the numbers of angels cited in the Bible (Daniel 7:10 and Revelation 5:11), "a thousand

**A power (Toome, in Heyward's *Hierarchy of the Blessed Angels*, 17th c.)**

times a thousand and ten thousand times ten thousand." He is inclined not to take these numbers literally, but to interpret them as meaning simply that the true number of angels is innumerable and unknowable, surpassing the limits of human numbering. (See NUMBERS OF ANGELS.)

### FORMS OF ANGELS

It is no accident that angels most often are described as "flames," "fiery" and "beings of fire or lightning," says Pseudo-Dionysius. Fire represents the Word of God: it passes undiluted through everything, lights up everything, and yet remains hidden at the same time. It cannot be looked upon, changes with its own activity, and bestows itself upon all who come near it. It rises up and penetrates deeply.

Pseudo-Dionysius says it is also appropriate to give human descriptions to angels, for there is much in the human form that symbolizes the divine attributes of angels. For example, eyes symbolize the power to gaze up toward the light of God, and shoulders, arms and hands signify acting and achieving. The fact that most angels depicted as humans are given an almost adolescent amount of vigor, Pseudo-Dionysius believes, shows the perennial vigor of living power.

Similarly, the clothing and accoutrements given to angels also are laden with symbolism. Priestly raiments connote the capacity to guide others spiritually to the divine, while the scepter shows the sovereignty and royal power with which angels guide. Spears show discriminating skill, and sharpness of power. One needs only to use one's own "dis-

cerning mind" to interpret all of these symbolisms, Pseudo-Dionysius says.

Additionally, it is appropriate to describe angels as elements of nature, such as wind and clouds. Wind symbolizes the ability to move about freely and to be anywhere quickly; clouds symbolize being filled in a transcendent way with hidden light. (Clouds and fire figure prominently in biblical descriptions of angels, the ANGEL OF THE LORD, and God himself).

**Further reading:**

Barnstone, Willis, ed. *The Other Bible.* San Francisco: HarperSan-Francisco, 1984.

*Pseudo-Dionysius: The Complete Works.* New York: Paulist Press, 1987.

**putti** Secular child figures with wings, which began to appear in early Renaissance Christian art, in addition to winged adult angels. The putti also are called "cherubs," a term not to be confused with the mighty cherubim named in Scripture.

Putti became popular in idyllic scenes from the New Testament, especially the Nativity and the childhood of Christ. Essentially they represent innocence and purity. Usually they are depicted in pairs, or in happy flocks that form an entourage for Christ. Like the Italian *amorini*, they often are shown dancing and making music.

**Three putti with shield and helmet (Albrecht Dürer, c. 1500)**

Putti were inspired both by EROS, the god of love, and by the Roman EROTES, funerary winged boys. Although putti are not angels, their use in Christian art increasingly identified them with angels, and contributed to the overall decline in the importance of the angel in theological thought.

See WINGS.

**Further reading:**
Berefelt, Gunnar. *A Study on the Winged Angel: The Origin of a Motif.* Stockholm: Almquist & Wiksell, 1968.

**Raguel** Angel assigned to watch over the good behavior of other angels, and prominent in the Book of Enoch. The name "Raguel" means "Friend of God." Variations are Raguhel, Rasuil, Akrasiel, Suryan and Rufael.

According to the prophet ENOCH, Raguel is the archangel who transports mortals to the heavens—a task also attributed to the angel ANAFIEL. Enoch say that Raguel is the Angel of the Earth. He also is a guardian of the second heaven, which is ruled by the archangel RAPHAEL and is a penal colony where fallen angels await judgment. There Raguel is instrumental in meting out justice to erring angels.

The Apochryphal *Revelation of John* tells of God calling upon the services of Raguel in the Judgment, after the separation of the sheep from the goats: "Then shall He send the angel Raguel, saying: Go, sound the trumpet for the angels of cold and snow and ice, and bring them together every kind of wrath upon them that stand on the left."

In 745, Pope Zachary, at a church council, reprobated (condemned) Raguel, along with various other angels. Pope Zachary termed Raguel a DEMON "who passed himself off as a Saint," a curious verdict on an angel whose task it is to make sure other angels do not fall from grace.

**Further reading:**
Laurence, Richard, trans. *The Book of Enoch the Prophet.* San Diego, Calif.: Wizards Bookshelf, 1976.

**Rahab** An ANGEL OF DEATH and destruction, sometimes synonymous with BEHEMOTH and LEVIATHAN. Rahab (the name means "violence") is the demon of insolence and pride.

He also rules over the primordial sea, and is not always malevolent. Rahab's name can be invoked through magic to obtain the assistance of the sea. Jewish mystical tales tell of Rahab obligingly offering up treasures and possessions lost in shipwrecks, in response to incantations invoking his holy name. In one story he retrieves an evil amulet that was sunk in the seas, which a rabbi then uses to exorcise the curse of a witch.

Jewish lore has it that God destroyed Rahab for refusing to part the upper and lower waters at creation. Apparently he was resurrected, for God destroys him again for chasing the Israelites across the parted Red Sea. In a benevolent act, Rahab rescues *The Book of Raziel*, containing all knowledge and mystical secrets, after the other angels have cast it into the sea to prevent it from being used by humans (see RAZIEL).

**Further reading:**
Davidson, Gustav. *A Dictionary of Angels.* New York: The Free Press, 1967.
Schwartz, Howard. *Gabriel's Palace: Jewish Mystical Tales.* New York: Oxford University Press, 1993.

**rainbow** See WINGS.

**Ramiel** An angel with various apocalyptic functions. He is described in the Enochian writings as both a fallen angel and one of the seven angels who stand before God; in the Sybylline Oracles he is one of five angels who lead souls to judgment; the others are URIEL, Arakiel, Samiel and Aziel. Ramiel also is known as Remiel, PHANUEL, Jeremiel and Yerahmeel.

In the apocalyptic 2 Baruch, part of the PSEUDEPIGRAPHA, Ramiel is the angel of visions who interprets Baruch's experiences. Baruch (a scribe to Jeremiah in the Bible, but a prophet in 2 Baruch) has a dialogue with God in which he receives revelations, including the coming of the Messiah. Ramiel, in speaking of the coming, terms the Messiah as "bright lightning" (*The Other Bible*, pp. 510–511):

*When he has brought low everything in the world*
*and on the throne of his kingdom, for that whole sage, sits down in peace,*
*then joy will be revealed*
*and also rest.*
*Healing will descend in dew,*
*disease will withdraw,*
*and worry and pain and lamentation will be unknown to men*
*and felicity will cover the earth.*
*No one will die untimely*
*nor will adversity strike.*
*Judgments, reviling, contention, revenge,*
*blood, passion, envy, hatred*
*will all be condemned and removed.*
*For those are the evils that fill the world*
*and trouble man.*
*Wild beasts will leave the forests and minister to men,*
*and asps and dragons will come out of their holes and serve a little child.*
*Women will no longer feel pain when they bear*
*nor suffer torment when they yield the fruit of the womb.*
*And in those days reapers will not grow weary*
*nor builders feel toil*
*and their labors will advance swiftly*
*and serenely,*
*for in that time the corruptible will vanish*
*and the incorruptible will have its beginning,*

*to which good things belong,*
*far from evil and near the immortal.*
*This is bright lightning who came after the last waters.*

**Further reading:**
Davidson, Gustav. *A Dictionary of Angels*. New York: The Free Press, 1967.
Barnstone, Willis, ed. *The Other Bible*. San Francisco: HarperSanFrancisco, 1984.

**Raphael**    One of the principal angels in Judeo-Christian angelologies, accorded the rank of archangel. Raphael's name originates from the Hebrew *rapha*, which means healer or doctor, thus Raphael is "the shining one who heals"; also "the medicine of God." Often he is connected with the symbol of healing, the serpent. He is entrusted with the physical well-being of the earth and its human inhabitants, and is said to be the friendliest of the angels.

Raphael is not mentioned by name in the Protestant Bible, but he does play a prominent role in the Book of TOBIT, part of the Catholic but not part of the Hebrew canon. There, Raphael teaches the arts both of healing and of exorcism. He acts as a guide and companion on a journey, thus making him the angel of travel and safety.

Raphael has numerous titles and duties. He is counted among the seven angels who stand before God mentioned in REVELATION, and is part of four orders of angels: seraphim, cherubim, dominions and powers (see CHOIRS). He is the angel of the evening winds, guardian of the Tree of Life, and the angel of prayer, peace, joy, light and love.

In kabbalistic lore, Raphael is charged with healing the earth. He is one of the ten sephiroth of the Tree of Life. He is believed to be one of the three angels who visit ABRAHAM, though he is not named as such in Genesis. He is credited with healing Abraham of the pain of his circumcision, and JACOB of his wounded thigh due to the fight with the dark adversary.

According to several rabbinic sources, a pearl hung on Noah's ark which indicated when day and night were at hand. Others say this light came from a sacred book Noah was given by the archangel Raphael, bound in sapphires and containing all knowledge of the stars, the art of healing, and the mastery of demons. Noah bequeathed this to Shem, who passed it to Abraham. It went on through to Jacob, Levi, Moses, Joshua and Solomon.

The presence of this book of wisdom in the early Babylonian myth of the flood strengthens the view, according to some scholars, that ENOCH, whom the angels helped to write a book of wisdom, was really Noah, and references to Raphael perhaps really were references to RAZIEL, the angel who is keeper of the cosmic book of secrets.

The apocryphal Book of Enoch terms Raphael one of the "watchers" (see SONS OF GOD) and a guide to the underworld.

Catholic devotional lore contains numerous stories about the deeds of Raphael. St. Cyriaca (also called Dominica), who was martyred under the emperor Maximilian in the fourth century, was addressed by Raphael during her tortures. The angel, identifying himself by name, said that he had heard her prayers, and congratulated her on her courage. Because of her suffering she would glorify the Lord. Sister Mary Francis of the Third Order of St. Francis, who lived during

**Tobias and the Angel (Andrea del Verrocchio, c. 1480; reprinted courtesy of the National Gallery, London)**

the late eighteenth century, was frequently ill. She was told on one occasion by the angel that he would heal her—and he did. She and others were witnesses to a smell of sweet perfume, which she attributed to the presence of Raphael. The angel also is credited with healing others of various afflictions, including epilepsy, and of providing protection during journeys.

Raphael's feast day is October 24.

Rudolph STEINER associated Raphael with the "Easter imagination." Steiner's spiritual practice blended the senses, imagination, inspiration and intuition, and used imaging, poetry and all the arts to express his teachings. He gave a series of lectures in October 1923 on the four seasons and the archangels that illustrates his method beautifully. The following details about Raphael are interwoven with the cosmic and natural processes indicated by the change of seasons.

Easter celebrates the death and resurrection of the Redeemer, and the figure of Raphael comes before us in dramatic guise as the Physician, Magician, and Hermes-like mediator who arouses in us the rightful approach, through reverence and worship, to what the Easter imagination is.

In spring Raphael is found up above with his deeply thoughtful gaze, with his staff of Mercury, which now in the airy heights has become something like a fiery serpent, a serpent of shining fire, no longer resting on the earth, but as though held forth, using the forces of the air, mingling and combining fire, water and earth so as to transmute them into healing forces, working and weaving in the cosmos. In autumn Raphael brings to humans the healing forces which he has first kindled in the cosmos. Raphael, with deep wisdom in his gaze, leans on the staff of Mercury, supported by the inner forces of Earth.

**Further reading:**

Davidson, Gustav. *A Dictionary of Angels.* New York: The Free Press, 1967.

O'Sullivan, Fr. Paul. *All About the Angels.* Rockford, Ill.: Tan Books and Publishers, 1990. First published 1945.

Steiner, Rudolf. *The Four Seasons and the Archangels.* Bristol, England: The Rudolf Steiner Press, 1992.

**Raziel**   The angel charged with guarding the secrets of the universe. The name "Raziel" means "secret of God" or "angel of mysteries." Variations of the name are Saraquel, Ratziel, Akrasiel and Gallizur. Raziel figures prominently in kabbalistic and rabbinic lore, and in the writings of ENOCH.

In the Kabbalah, Raziel is the archangel assigned to guard the second sephiroth, Cochma, on the Tree of Life. He also is the chief of the THRONES. He is credited with being the author of *The Book of the Angel Raziel,* a medieval text that may actually have been written by Eleazar of Worms or Isaac the Blind.

According to legend, Raziel was ordered by God to give the book to Adam. God, taking pity on Adam, wanted to give him the book so that he could gaze into the mirror of all existence and see the face of God, and himself as an image of God. The book contained all celestial and earthly knowledge, as well as the secret to decoding 1,500 keys to the mystery of the world, keys which were not even explained to the other angels. Jealous at being left out of the cosmic secrets, other angels stole the book from Adam and threw it into the sea. God ordered RAHAB, the Angel of the Sea, to retrieve it and return it to Adam. It later was passed to the prophet ENOCH, where much of it was incorporated into the book of Enoch. Reportedly, an oral version of *The Book of the Angel Raziel* exists in kabbalistic tradition.

Although the keys in the book are not understood by any other angel, Raziel nonetheless is said to stand on the peak of Mount Horeb every day and proclaim the secrets to humankind.

**Further reading:**

Davidson, Gustav. *A Dictionary of Angels.* New York: The Free Press, 1967.

Godwin, Malcolm. *Angels: An Endangered Species.* New York: Simon & Schuster, 1990.

**recording angels**   Angels who are charged with keeping track of all events, celestial and earthly. Babylonians called the recording angel Nabu or Nebo; in Arabic mythology, the name is Moakkibat. The Book of Enoch tells of PRAVUIL, keeper of heavenly records.

In Islam every believer is attended by two angels, called the Kiramu'l katibin, "Guardians and Noble Scribes" (Surah 82.10–11). The one on the right contemplates and dictates; the other on the left records. The closing of the Muslim daily prayer ritual, the *salat*, acknowledges their presence. The general or exoteric explanation of these angels is that they constantly watch and record each person's good and bad actions. Upon death, the life's record is given to AZRAEL, the ANGEL OF DEATH.

The esoteric meaning of Islam's recording angels can be interpreted thus: The human intellect is the partner of the

Above: Angelic writing from the Book of Raziel, Netherlands 17th Century. Taking compassion on Adam, God sent Raziel to give him a book so that he might look into the mirror of existence and so see the Divine Face and himself so illuminated as an image of God. It is reported that an oral version still exists within the traditions of the Kabalah.

**The Book of Raziel**

angel, the "traveling companion" who is guided by the angel and whom, on his side, the angel needs in order to solemnize his divine service, that is, to irradiate Forms and thereby to rise toward his Principle. The practical intellect is analogous to the terrestrial angel on the left, whose duty it is to write— that is, to act and execute—what is dictated by the angel whose place is on the right.

See ISLAMIC ANGELOLOGY.

**Remiel**   The angel charged with leading souls to Judgment. The name "Remiel" means "Mercy of God." Remiel also is called the "Lord of Souls awaiting Resurrection." Variations of the name are Ramiel, Phanuel, URIEL, Yerahmeel and Jeremiel.

In the writings of the prophet ENOCH, Remiel is identified both as one of the seven archangels who stand before God and as one of the fallen angels. As an archangel, he is charged with spreading the instructions of all seven archangels. He also presides over thunder, as does URIEL.

Remiel is the angel of "true visions." In the Apocalypse of Baruch, he gives Baruch his vision of victory over the army of Sennacherib, and sometimes he is said to be the angel who actually destroys the army (as is the archangel MICHAEL).

**Further reading:**

Godwin, Malcolm. *Angels: An Endangered Species.* New York: Simon & Schuster, 1990.

Laurence, Richard, trans. *The Book of Enoch the Prophet*. San Diego, Calif.: Wizards Bookshelf, 1976.

**Revelation, Book of**   In this, the final book of the New Testament, which foretells the second coming of Christ, the end of the world, the Last Judgment, Armageddon and the establishment of a New Heaven and a New Earth, angels of intricate symbolic power figure prominently. Although a common tradition attributes the book to the apostle John, there is vigorous scholarly debate as to the true author. Moreover, it is not agreed that the author of Revelation is also the author of the Gospel and Epistles of John. There are many stylistic and linguistic differences between the five Johannine writings, but there are striking similarities as well.

Scholars agree that early readers of Revelation were well versed in the sort of symbolic allegory and imagery in which the book was written, able to read the language of myth because they knew well the traditions of Jewish apocalyptic writings and Greek and Roman literature. Yet decoding that symbolic language two thousand years later is no easy task. How much contemporary historical allegory is present? Is the author working with a numerological system? Does he use a symbolic code? As far as John's angels are concerned, their functions are consistent with the cosmology of the times. (See JUDAIC ANGELOLOGY.)

Here we consider the varied angels and their functions in Revelation. This is by no means a summary of the whole book, which presents arrays of elaborate allegories relevant to early Christian history, prophecy, and theology.

In 1:1, God "sent his angel [literally, messenger] to make it known to his servant John, and John has written down everything he saw and swears it is the word of God and the witness of Jesus Christ." "Messenger" is ambiguous; it could be Jesus. In 1:12, John sees seven gold lamps which are the seven churches, and seven stars are their heavenly counterparts (angels). In 1:20, the angels of the seven churches accord with the Jewish belief that individuals, nations and communities had angels that were responsible for them (Exodus 23:20). (See ORIGEN.)

John addresses his letters not to the bishops but to the angels, and holds them responsible for the faults of the communities they represent. In John's worldview heaven and earth are equally parts of the physical universe that God created; they belong inseparably together, and everything on earth, including evil, has its counterpart in heaven. When the old order is finally destroyed, John foresees a new heaven and a new earth.

In 4:5, in his vision of the heavenly altar, John sees "seven flaming lamps burning, the seven Spirits of God," the seven angels of the presence attend the Lamb (Christ; cf. Tobias 12:15; Zechariah 4:10; Luke 1:26). In 4:6–8, "Four animals . . . with six wings and eyes all the way round as well as inside . . . never stopped singing." These are the four angels responsible for directing the physical world. Four symbolizes the physical world. Their many eyes symbolize God's omniscience and providence. The angels give unceasing glory to God for his creation. The figures of lion, bull, man, and eagle suggest all that is noblest, strongest, wisest, most swift in the created world. Ever since the early Christian theologian Irenaeus first interpreted them thus,

**Heavenly war between good and evil angels (Gustave Doré)**

these four creatures have been associated with the four Evangelists.

In 5:11 we find, "In my vision, I heard the sound of an immense number of angels gathered around the throne . . . ten thousand times ten thousand . . . shouting" praises of the Lamb. In 7:1:

> Next I saw four angels, standing at the four corners of the earth, holding the four winds of the world back. . . . Then I saw another angel rising where the sun rises, carrying the seal of the living God; he called in a loud voice to the four angels whose duty was to devastate land and sea: "Wait until we put the seal on the foreheads of the servants of our God."

In 8:2–5:

> Next I saw seven trumpets being given to the seven angels who stand in the presence of God. Another angel, who had a golden censer . . . filled it with the fire from the altar, which he then threw down on the earth; immediately there came peals of thunder and flashes of lightning, and the earth shook.

Verses 8:6–12 state that the seven angels who hold the seven trumpets are now ready to sound them. The first brings hail and fire; a third of the earth is burnt up. The second drops a great mountain on fire into the sea, which turns into blood. The third causes a huge star to fall from the sky, burning rivers and springs. This is the star called Wormwood; the water turns bitter. The fourth blasts a third of the sun and a third of the moon and a third of the stars.

Verses 9:1–11 state:

> Then the fifth angel blew his trumpet, and I saw a star [one of the fallen angels] that had fallen from heaven onto the earth, and he was given the keys to the shaft leading down to the Abyss [where the fallen angels were imprisoned pending their ultimate punishment]. . . . The smoke from the Abyss darkened the sun and out of the smoke dropped locusts who attacked any man who was without God's seal on their foreheads. . . . Their tails were like scorpions', with stings, and it was with them that they were able to injure people for five months. Their emperor was the Angel of the Abyss, whose name in Hebrew is ABADDON, or Apollyon in Greek [Destruction, or Ruin].

In 9:13–19 the sixth angel blows his trumpet, and a voice speaks to the sixth angel and says "Release the four angels that are chained up at the great river Euphrates." These are released to destroy a third of the human race: Their horses had lions' heads, and out of them came fire, smoke and sulfur. In 10:1–7, a powerful angel descends, a scroll in his hand. It announces that when the seventh angel blows his trumpet God's secret intention will be fulfilled.

In Verse 12:7 war breaks out in heaven; MICHAEL with his angels attacks the dragon, the primeval serpent, known as Satan, who fights back with his angels, but they are defeated and driven out of heaven. Satan is hurled down to earth and his angels are hurled down with him.

In verse 14:6–11 another angel flies overhead, sent to announce the Good News of eternity to all who live on the earth by announcing the Last Judgment. A second angel follows, announcing that Babylon has fallen. A third angel says that those who followed the beast will be tortured in the presence of the Lamb and his holy angels, and the smoke of their torture will go on for ever and ever. In 14:14–20, four angels with sickles gather in the harvest.

In Chapters 15–16, seven angels bring the seven plagues that are the last "because they exhaust the anger of God." They all have harps, and are singing the hymn of Moses and the Lamb. One of the four animals gives the seven angels seven golden bowls, filled with the anger of God. Now the seven angels give the last seven plagues: sores; death of the sea creatures; rivers turned to blood; sun scorching people with flames; the throne of the beast turned to darkness and people cursing with pain; beasts come from the Euphrates for the battle of Armageddon; and a violent earthquake and falling hail, destroying everything.

In Chapters 17–18, angels tell John about the famous prostitute the Whore of Babylon, the beast yet to come, and the fall of Babylon. In 19:17–21, John sees an angel standing in the sun who announces to the birds, "Come and get ready to eat the flesh of kings, heroes, generals, horse and riders." Then is fought the first battle of the end: the rider Faithful and True conquers the beast and his army, and the birds gorge on their flesh.

The beast and the Whore are titanic forms of evil in the world. The beast is associated by John with the Roman empire of his own day, but also has characteristics of all four empires of Daniel's vision (13:1–2). The Whore is Babylon the great, but also bears the allegorical names of Sodom and Egypt and the character of Jerusalem (9:8; 14:8; 17:5). Each has in its own way the power to delude the whole world, apart from those who are protected from such delusion by the seal of God (13:8,14; 14:8; 17:2; 18:3). The essence of evil is deceit and counterfeit. Satan is "the deceiver of the whole world" who misleads men by telling lies about God. The beast is the Antichrist, the false Messiah, who makes blasphemous claims to deity.

In 20:1–15, an angel throws the beast into the Abyss and chains him up for a thousand years. After a thousand years Satan will come again to rally his forces, Gog and Magog, for another great war against the saints. But fire will come down and consume them. The devil will be thrown into the lake of fire and sulphur where the Beast and the false prophet are, and their torture will be never ending. Anyone whose name is not found in the Book of Life will be thrown into the burning lake.

In Chapters 21–22, a new heaven and a new earth are now revealed to John by angels. The holy city has twelve gates, each guarded by an angel. An angel measures the city and gates and walls with a gold measuring rod. An angel shows John the river of life, flowing crystal-clear down the middle of the street. Finally the angel tells John that all he has written is sure and will come true, and happy will be those who treasure the prophecy of this book. He reminds John that he too is a servant, just as John is. The epilogue (22:16) states: "I, Jesus, have sent my angel to make these revelations to you for the sake of the churches."

**Further reading:**

Bowman, J. W. "Book of Revelation" in *The Interpreter's Dictionary of the Bible*. New York: Abingdon Press, 1962.

Caird, G. B. *A Commentary on the Revelation of St. John the Divine*. New York: Harper & Row, 1966.

Glasson, C. F. *The Revelation of John*. Cambridge, England: Cambridge University Press, 1965.

**Ridwan** See ISLAMIC ANGELOLOGY.

**ritual** See ART, ARCHITECTURE AND RITUAL, ANGELS IN.

# S

**Samael** A Gnostic god and, in Judaism, the evil angel who comes to be identified with SATAN. Samael actually is the name of a kingdom of the Aramaens, in the area of Syria in the second millennium B.C.E. A variation of the name is Sammael.

Some mythologists have associated this name with "Dread God," a Semitic version of the Asiatic Sama, Samana, or Samavurti, the "Leveller." The Sama Veda called him a storm god, clothed in black clouds.

Samael is a name that arises several times within GNOSTI-CISM. In one Gnostic text, SOPHIA (originally a high angel, or AEON) confronts her imperfect son Ialdabaoth, who in another reading is her "shadowed" creation (an abortion of her wish to create on her own), who has subsequently created angels to create this world. Ruling them he thinks he is the ruler of all, sufficient unto himself. Sophia tells him: "You are wrong, Samael."

The name Samael means "the blind god." Blindness is a theme that runs through Gnosticism, for which ignorance not willful sin, is the seat of evil. In another Gnostic text Ialdabaoth casts Adam and Eve, and the serpent who tempted them, out of paradise after they have eaten of the tree of Gnosis (Knowledge of Good and Evil). The serpent then uses the angels begotten upon Eve by the planetary powers to bring into existence six sons. These sons, along with himself, become seven earthly demons; the serpent is called Michael or Sammael. The concept of seven evil demons is a very old one in the East, and a demonic connotation lingers around this name.

In Hebrew demonology, the name Samael first appears in the story of the fall of the angels in the Ethiopic Book of Enoch 6. Samael also is identified as the ANGEL OF DEATH, the head of all devils, and the chief of all tempters. He leads the rebel armies of angels in heaven.

Prior to the fall, Samael is higher than the mighty seraphim. He has twelve wings. His duties include being in charge of all nations, except Israel, over which he shall have power only on the Day of Atonement. Then he will war with the archangel MICHAEL, the guardian of Israel. The war will last until the end of days, when Samael will be handed over to Israel in shackles.

Samael is described as flying through the air, with one long hair streaming from his navel. As long as the hair remains intact, he will reign. Samael, however, does not know the way to the Tree of Life. He is the angel who governs the planet Mars.

He has three brides, LILITH, Namaah and Agrat bat Mahlat, an angel of prostitution.

**Further reading:**
Scholem, Gershom. *Kabbalah*. New York: Dorset Press, 1987. First published 1974.

**Sandalphon (also Sandalfon)** A giant angel who in rabbinic lore is a weaver of prayers, and the twin brother of the mighty METATRON. The name means "co-brother."

In rabbinic lore, Sandalphon is so big that his size strikes fear into the heart of MOSES when the prophet is taken into heaven to receive the Torah. There he finds the angel weaving garlands out of the prayers of Israel, which place themselves on the head of God upon completion. In addition he fights SAMAEL (Satan) endlessly, a job he shares with the archangel MICHAEL. He also determines the sex of the unborn.

Sandalphon's abode is placed variously in the third, sixth and seventh heavens in rabbinic literature, and in the fourth heaven in Islamic lore.

**Santería** See ORISHAS.

**Sariel** Identified in various sources as an archangel, a fallen angel, a seraph. The name "Sariel" means "God's command." Variations of the name are Suriel, Suriyel, Zerachiel, Saraquel and even URIEL.

The earliest references to Sariel are in the Qumrun literature, in which he is mentioned along with the archangels MICHAEL, GABRIEL and RAPHAEL. His name sometimes is confused with that of Uriel. Sariel is not found in works of the APOCRYPHA or PSEUDEPIGRAPHA, and receives only a few mentions in rabbinic literature, usually as overseer in the sixth heaven.

Sariel sometimes is identified as the Lord's ANGEL OF DEATH, and as the angel who taught MOSES all his knowledge. Sariel also delivered instructions on hygiene and cleanliness to Rabbi Ishmael, and is credited with being an angel of healing, like Raphael. Sariel is one of the ANGELS OF THE PRESENCE.

The prophet ENOCH said that Sariel was one of the seven archangels (ranking fifth in line), but one of the fallen host as well.

Sariel is among the SONS OF GOD, and taught the course of the moon to humanity. He also governs the zodiac sign of Aries (see ZODIAC ANGELS), and figures in ceremonial magic as protection against the evil eye (see MAGIC, ANGELS IN.).

**Further reading:**
Barrett, Francis. *The Magus*. Secaucus, N.J.: The Citadel Press, 1967. First published 1801.
Godwin, Malcolm. *Angels: An Endangered Species*. New York: Simon & Schuster, 1990.

**Satan** In Christianity, a fallen angel who is the prince and embodiment of all evil, and who is committed to tempting humanity into sin and thus condemning them into everlasting hell. The name *Satan* means "adversary," "opponent" or "obstacle" in Hebrew.

Originally, among the Hebrews, Satan was not so thoroughly evil. In fact, he was not even any one angel in particular. Rather, the term *satan*, with a lowercase "s," was a common noun applied to any obstacle or adversary. The Israelites, who were engaged in constant struggles, demonized their enemies in the forms of monstrous beasts. But as time went on the term *satan* became applied to enemies, with an increasingly malevolent tint.

Hebrew storytellers as early as the sixth century B.C.E. used a supernatural character called a *satan*, by which they meant any of God's angels—the *bene ha-elohim* ("sons of God")—whom God dispatched to block or obstruct human activity. Sometimes the blocking was a good idea, if the human characters were following a sinful path.

In the Bible, the term *satan* appears for the first time in Numbers 22:23–35. God sends an ANGEL OF THE LORD to act as a satan to block the journey of BALAAM, who has displeased God. When Balaam's ass sees the satan standing in the road, she balks, causing Balaam to strike her three times. The angel of the Lord reveals himself, and Balaam promises to do what God tells him through his emissary, the satan.

In the Book of Job a character named Satan, who seems to have the job of roaming the earth and keeping an eye on humans, torments JOB to test his faith. This Satan is described as one of God's loyal servants.

At about this same time in history—about 550 B.C.E.—the term *satan* was being utilized by Hebrew writers when describing internal strife among the Israelites. In 1 Chronicles 21, we find a satan who convinces King David to number his people against the wishes of God, causing God to send a destroying angel to kill 70,000 Israelites by means of the plague (despite the fact that David repents).

So too does Zechariah use the term *satan* to describe internal conflicts among the Jews. He also shows Satan as being hostile in his opposition to Joshua (Zech. 3:1–2).

Radical dissenters among the Israelites began to use the term *satan* more and more to characterize their own Jewish opponents, whom they viewed as obstacles to their objectives. They also used other terms including the names of wicked angels. All of these became associated with evil enemies: Satan, BEELZEBUB, SEMYAZA, MASTEMA, AZAZEL and Belial. The name Satan was applied more than any other. Stories about angels who sinned and fell from heaven were applied to Jewish opponents. Satan as a figure became increasingly prominent as a personality, one of evil.

Satan became identified with the fallen angels called Watchers (see SONS OF GOD). There are different versions as to how these angels fell out of favor. One is that they lusted after mortal women and were thrown out; the other is that they voluntarily descended to Earth to teach humankind (somewhat like the Titans of Greek lore), where they cohabited with women and thus were cast into a pit of darkness. The leaders of the Watchers are Semyaza and Azazel. The Enochian writings tell of God sending the four archangels RAPHAEL, GABRIEL, URIEL and MICHAEL to slay the giant offspring of the Watchers (the *nephilim*) and attack the Watchers themselves. Raphael binds Azazel and casts him into a pit. The Book of Jubilees says that one-tenth of the Watchers were spared by God so that they might be subject before Satan,

Satan (Gustave Doré)

their leader, on earth. (The Book of Jubilees also castigates Jews who do not keep themselves separate from Gentiles; the conflicts that arose were attributed to Satan, Belial or Mastema, all of whom represented the enemy within.)

The story of the Watchers underwent many transformations, and was influential among the Christians. The casting out of sinful angels, who became the demons of hell under a prince of evil, formed a crucial part of Christian theology. Satan became identified with LUCIFER primarily from a passage in Isaiah 14:12–15: "How you have fallen from heaven, bright morning star. . . ." "Bright morning star," or more literally "bright son of the morning," was translated into Latin as Lucifer.

Christian thought also was influenced by the Essenes, a Jewish sect that coexisted briefly with Christianity. The Essenes saw themselves as "sons of light" who battled the "sons of darkness." Both forces were ruled by princes. However the Essenes did not personify these princes, but instead saw them as universal principles.

The writers of the Gospels portrayed Satan as having been cast out of heaven for sin (in Luke 10:18 he falls like lightning), a being of evil who opposes God and Jesus. Jews who did not follow Jesus were cast in the role of agents of Satan (later, any Gentiles who opposed Christians fell into the same camp). Jesus was cast as the focal point in the war between God's forces of Good and Satan's forces of Evil. His resurrection is a victory over Satan; thus those who follow Christ cannot lose in the great cosmic battle for souls.

Throughout the New Testament, the name of Satan is associated only with evil. He is called: "accuser of the brethren" in Revelation 12:10; "adversary" in 1 Peter 5:8; "Beelzebub" in Matthew 12:24; "the Devil" in Matthew 4:1; "the enemy" in Matthew 13:39; "the evil one" in 1 John 5:19; "the father of lies and a murderer" in John 8:44; "the god of this age" (i.e., of false cults) in 2 Corinthians 4:4; "a roaring lion" (in terms of destructiveness) in 1 Peter 5:8–9; a "tempter" in Matthew 4:3; and a "serpent" in Revelation 12:9.

Among his evil acts described in the New Testament are: tempting believers into sin (Ephesians 2:1–3; 1 Thessalonians 3:5); tempting believers to lie (Acts 5:3); tempting believers to commit sexually immoral acts (1 Corinthians 7:5); accusing and slandering believers (Revelation 12:10); hindering the work of believers in any way possible (1 Thessalonians 2:18); waging war against believers (Ephesians 6:11–12); inciting persecutions against believers (Revelation 2:10); opposing Christians with the ferociousness of a hungry lion (1 Peter 5:8); and fostering spiritual pride (1 Timothy 3:6).

The role of Satan as the agent of evil became magnified over time. By the Middle Ages, Satan, as the Devil, was believed in as a real, potent being who possessed terrible supernatural powers and was intent upon destroying man by undermining his morals. In this pursuit he was aided by his army of evil demons. Satan's machinations were a driving force behind the Inquisition, which persecuted any enemy of the Christian church—moral, political, ethnic, social or religious—as being one of Satan's disciples.

Modern views of Satan vary. Fundamentalists tend to view him as a real being of pure evil, whose trickster tactics will trip up the unwary. His avowed purpose is to thwart the plan of God by any means possible. He fosters false prophets, teachers, Christs and apostles.

Others believe in Satan more in terms of the Essenes' idea of a cosmic principle, the shadow aspect of light. According to the Catholic church, the devil's objective is to ruin the church. He is given special powers by God to try people, in order that they may have an opportunity to be cleansed. By keeping the Ten Commandments and steering clean of all sin, one stays out of the devil's reach. God also permits evil spirits to possess people who have sinned.

See also REVELATION.

**Further reading:**

Pagels, Elaine. *The Origin of Satan.* New York: Random House, 1995.

Rhodes, Ron. *Angels Among Us.* Eugene, Oreg.: Harvest House Publishers, 1994.

Russell, Jeffrey Burton. *The Devil: Perceptions of Evil from Antiquity to Primitive Christianity.* Ithaca, N.Y.: Cornell University Press, 1977.

———. *Lucifer: The Devil in the Middle Ages.* Ithaca, N.Y.: Cornell University Press, 1984.

**Schemhamphoras**  Seventy-two angels who bear the Names of God, and are used in invocation and in magic.

The Schemhamphoras function as names of power. The concept of "names of power" dates to the time of the ancient Egyptians, Greeks, Assyrians and Gnostics, as well as the Hebrews, who believed that incredible power could be unleashed through the sound vibrations of words. The Egyptians invented names of power for magical rituals, which were passed into texts absorbed into Western culture.

The most powerful of all the names of power is the Tetragrammaton, the personal and sacred name of God in Hebrew Scripture. The Tetragrammaton is usually expressed as YHVH, the Hebrew letters *yod, he, vau, he.* The exact pronunciation of the Tetragrammaton is not known; the most commonly accepted is "Yahweh." A common variation is "Jehovah." So awesome is the Tetragrammaton that for centuries it was considered to be ineffable and was rarely spoken. As early as the time of Jesus, it was whispered only on Yom Kippur by a high priest in the inner sanctuary of the Temple in Jerusalem. In the sacred texts, substitute names of power were used, such as "Adonai" or "Adonay" or "Elohim," and the names of the Schemhamphoras.

The Schemhamphoras and the verses associated with them are as follows:

1. *Vehujah:* Thou, O Lord, art my guardian, and exaltest my head.

2. *Ieliel:* Do not remove thy help from me, O Lord, and look to my defense.

3. *Sirael:* I shall say so to the Lord, Thou art my guardian, my God is my refuge, and I shall hope in him.

4. *Elemijel:* Turn, O Lord, and deliver my soul, and save me for Thy mercy's sake.

5. *Lelahel:* Let him who lives in Zion sing unto the Lord, and proclaim his goodwill among the peoples.

6. *Achajah:* The Lord is merciful and compassionate, long-suffering and of great goodness.

7. *Mahasiah:* I called upon the Lord and he heard me and delivered me from all my tribulations.

8. *Cahatel:* O come let us adore and fall down before God who bore us.

9. *Haziel:* Remember Thy mercies, O Lord, and Thy mercies which have been forever.

10. *Aladiah:* Perform Thy mercies upon us, for we have hoped in Thee.

11. *Laviah:* The Lord liveth, blessed is my God, and let the God of my salvation be exalted.

12. *Hahajah:* Why hast Thou departed, O Lord, so long from us, perishing in the times of tribulation.

13. *Jezalel:* Rejoice in the Lord, all ye lands, sing, exult, and play upon a stringed instrument.

14. *Mebahel:* The Lord is a refuge, and my God the help of my hope.

15. *Hariel:* The Lord is a refuge for me, and my God the help of my hope.

16. *Hakamiah:* O Lord, God of my salvation, by day have I called to thee, and sought Thy presence by night.

17. *Leviah:* O Lord our Lord, How wonderful is Thy name in all the world.

18. *Caliel:* Judge me, O Lord, according to Thy loving kindness, and let not them be joyful over me, O Lord.

19. *Luviah*: I waited in hope for the Lord, and He turned to me.

20. *Pahaliah*: I shall call upon the name of the Lord, O Lord, free my soul.

21. *Nelakhel*: In Thee also have I hoped, O Lord, and said, Thou art my God.

22. *Jajajel*: The Lord keep thee, the Lord be thy protection O Thy right hand.

23. *Melahel*: The Lord keep thine incoming and thine outgoing from this time forth for evermore.

24. *Hahajah*: The Lord is well pleased with those that fear Him and hope upon his mercy.

25. *Haajah*: I have called unto Thee with all my heart and shall tell forth all Thy wonders.

26. *Nithhaja*: I shall acknowledge Thee, O Lord, with all my heart, hear me, O Lord, and I shall seek my justification.

27. *Jerathel*: Save me, O Lord, from the evil man and deliver me from the wicked doer.

28. *Sehijah*: Let not God depart from me, look to my help, O God.

29. *Rejajel*: Behold, God is my helper, and the Lord is the guardian of my soul.

30. *Omael*: For Thou art my strength, O Lord. O Lord, Thou art my hope from my youth.

31. *Lecabel*: I shall enter into the power of the Lord, my God, I shall be mindful of Thy justice only.

32. *Vasariah*: For the word of the Lord is upright, and all His works faithful.

33. *Jehuvajah*: The Lord knows the thoughts of men, for they are in vain.

34. *Lehahiah*: Let Israel hope in the Lord from this time forth and for evermore.

35. *Chavakiah*: I am joyful, for the Lord hears the voice of my prayer.

36. *Manadel*: I have delighted in the beauty of Thy house, O Lord, and in the place of the habitation of Thy glory.

37. *Aniel*: O Lord God, turn thy power towards us, and show us Thy face and we shall be saved.

38. *Haamiah*: For Thou art my hope, O Lord, and Thou hast been my deepest refuge.

39. *Rehael*: The Lord has heard me and pitied me and the Lord is my helper.

40. *Jejazel*: Why drivest Thou away my soul, O Lord, and turnest thy face from me?

41. *Hahahel*: O Lord, deliver my soul from wicked lips and a deceitful tongue.

42. *Michael*: The Lord protects thee from all evil and will protect thy soul.

43. *Vevaliah*: I have cried unto Thee, O Lord, and let my prayer come unto Thee.

44. *Jelabiah*: Make my wishes pleasing unto Thee, O Lord, and teach me Thy judgments.

45. *Sealiah*: If I say that my foot is moved, Thou wilt help me of Thy mercy.

46. *Ariel*: The Lord is pleasant to all the world and His mercies are over all His works.

47. *Asaliah*: How wonderful are Thy works, O Lord, and how deep Thy thoughts.

48. *Michael*: The Lord hath made thy salvation known in the sight of the peoples and will reveal His justice.

49. *Vehael*: Great is the Lord and worthy to be praised, and there is no end to his greatness.

50. *Daniel*: The Lord is pitiful and merciful, long-suffering and of great goodness.

51. *Hahasiah*: Let the Lord be in glory forever and the Lord will rejoice in His works.

52. *Imamiah*: I shall make known the Lord, according to His justice, and sing hymns to the name of the Lord, the greatest.

53. *Nanael*: I have known Thee, O Lord, for Thy judgments are just, and in Thy truth have I abased myself.

54. *Nithael*: The Lord hath prepared His seat in heaven and His rule shall be over all.

55. *Mebahiah*: Thou remainest for ever, O Lord, and Thy memorial is from generation to generation.

56. *Poltal*: The Lord raiseth up all who fall and setteth up the broken.

57. *Nemamiah*: They who fear the Lord have hoped in the Lord, He is their helper and their protector.

58. *Jejulel*: My soul is greatly troubled, but Thou, O Lord are here also.

59. *Harahel*: From the rising of the Sun to the going down of the same, the word of the Lord is worthy to be praised.

60. *Mizrael*: The Lord is just in all his ways and blessed in all his works.

61. *Umbael*: Let the name of the Lord be blessed from this time for evermore.

62. *Iahael*: See, O Lord, how I have delighted in Thy commandments according to Thy life-giving mercy.

63. *Anaviel*: Serve ye the Lord with gladness and enter into His sight with exultation.

64. *Mehikiel*: Behold the eyes of the Lord are upon those that fear Him and hope in His loving kindness.

65. *Damabiah*: Turn, O Lord, even here also, and be pleased with Thy servants.

66. *Meniel*: Neither leave me, Lord, nor depart from me.

67. *Ejael*: Delight in the Lord and He will give thee petitions of thy heart.

68. *Habujah*: Confess to the Lord, for He is God, and His mercy is forever.

69. *Roehel*: The Lord is my inheritance and my cup and it is Thou who restorest mine inheritance.

70. *Jabamiah*: In the beginning God created the heaven and the earth.

71. *Hajael*: I shall confess to the Lord with my mouth and praise Him in the midst of the multitude.

72. *Mumijah*: Return to thy rest, my soul, for the Lord doeth thee good.

See NAMES OF ANGELS.

**Further reading:**

McLean, Adam, ed. *A Treatise on Angel Magic*. Grand Rapids, Mich.: Phanes Press, 1990.
Scholem, Gershom. *Kabbalah*. New York: Dorset Press, 1987. First published 1974.

**seasons, angels of**   In occult magical lore, various angels are associated with the seasons of the year. Their names are to be invoked at appropriate times for ritual purposes. Occultist Francis Barrett gives the associations as follows (names of seasonal angels and the heads of the season signs):

*Spring*
Angels: Caracasa, Core, Amatiel, Commissoros
Head of sign of spring: Spugliguel
*Summer*
Angels: Gargatel, Tariel, Gaviel
Head of sign of summer: Tubiel
*Autumn*
Angels: Tarquam, Guabarel
Head of sign of autumn: Torquaret
*Winter*
Angels: Amabael, Cetarari
Head of sign of summer: Attarib

Rudolph STEINER also associated angels with seasons, and ascribed the seasonal and angelic qualities to stages of spiritual growth in humankind. He began with MICHAEL (autumn) and then moved to GABRIEL (winter), RAPHAEL (spring) and URIEL (summer).

**Further reading:**

Barrett, Francis. *The Magus*. Secaucus, N.J.: The Citadel Press, 1967. First published 1801.
Steiner, Rudolph. *The Four Seasons and the Archangels*. Bristol, England: The Rudolf Steiner Press, 1992.

**Semyaza (also Shemhazi, Shamayza)**   A leader of the fallen angels, one of the SONS OF GOD who cohabits with women. According to lore, Semyaza cohabited with one of Eve's daughters and produced two sons who ate every day one thousand each of camels, horses and oxen. As punishment for his sins, he hangs upside down in the constellation Orion, suspended between heaven and earth.

**seraphim**   See CHOIRS.

**sex and angels**   Varieties of angelic and demonic entities interact sexually with humans in myth and scriptures worldwide. *Dakinis* assist yogic aspirants in transforming their sexual energy into spiritual energy; (see TANTRIC BUD-

DHISM); *apsaras*, irresistible heavenly courtesans, can seduce high masters from the path (see HINDUISM); Plato berated the lusts of DAEMONS characterizing EROS as a daemon, not a god. The two key Christian theologians, St. AUGUSTINE and St. Thomas AQUINAS, both stated that demons can have sexual intercourse with humans. Augustine followed the trend started by the Jewish theologian Philo in identifying the SONS OF GOD of Genesis 6 with the fallen angels. In *The City of God* 15–23 Augustine says "incubi . . . have often behaved improperly towards women, lusting after them and achieving intercourse with them." Aquinas described how the same demon may first assume the form of a woman as a succubus—to extract by some means or another seed from a man, then to change into the form of a man—an incubus—to deposit this seed in a woman's womb. These notions of demons coupling with humans were rigorously pursued in the centuries-long frenzy of witch hunting, trials and burnings.

GNOSTICISM embraced the principle of the opposites and their creative conflictual relationship (see ABRAXAS), taking both ascetic and libertine approaches to the divine mystery of sexuality. As in Taoism and Tantrism, ritualized and sanctified sex was part of some practices. The creative duality principle applied among the aeons (angelic rulers of spheres), who participated in "matings" (syzygies) from which emanated other aeons. Gnostics spoke of the ultimate salvation of both psychic and spiritual elements in the ascent of the Gnostic upward through the 365 spheres. When the soul reached the Mother and she received her bridegroom, each soul as well would receive its angels as bridegrooms, enter the bridal chamber, and come toward the beatific vision. They would become aeons and enter into aeonic marriages partaking of the cosmic syzygy.

When the Christian fathers debated how the angels fell, some suggested it was by carnal lust of the "sons of God" for "the daughters of men," which produced the race of abomination that God had to destroy through the Flood. Although most concluded that the sin of the fallen angels was one of pride and continued to debate the details of that egotism, some believed that fallen angels became corporeal because of their sin. It was held universally that unfallen angels were uncorporeal and hence unsexed beings. Partaking of perpetual bliss in the beatific vision, they were far above such gross desires and practices of humans as eating, excretion and sexual activity.

Christian MONASTICISM began a trend that survives in the celibacy of Roman Catholic clergy, namely, the superiority of virginity to marriage and parenthood. The Virgin Mother was worshipped and prized above all other saints. The life of the sexually continent was an exact imitation on earth of the life of the angels, according to Augustine's monastic scheme. (Martin Luther, a former Augustinian monk, blamed the demons for the nocturnal emissions of monks which almost daily prevented the monks from being able to celebrate mass, and preferred the "holy estate of matrimony, where thou [God] dost wink at our infirmity.")

Stuart Schneiderman's *An Angel Passes* is a fascinating application of the symbolic linguistic principles of Jacques Lacan to Christian angelology, reviewing all ancient, medieval and modern sources on angels and sex. He finds that by establishing in human society the primacy of unsexed beings (i.e., by nuns and priests imitating angels) a "huge invisible upheaval among the powers of heaven" took place. The polytheistic universe of the pagan pantheon (and Zoroastrianism, Gnosticism, Tantrism, Hinduism, etc.), where pairs of gods, angels, and demigods mated and fought, was replaced by one of "a mother and son [both virgins] reigning as king and queen, as bridegroom and bride, undivided, fulfilled, pronouncing one final judgment. . . . Those who inherited the angels from Old Testament and pagan sources were faced with the task of taking beings who were ruled or defined by their relation to Eros and reconstituting them in function of Christ." The principle of Eros is dynamic dualism, the principle of Christ holds everything to be one in the mind of God. The current upsurge of interest among Christian societies in Eastern religions, analytic and archetypal psychology (see Carl G. JUNG), and angels may reflect a need to readjust this imbalance in symbol systems and cosmology.

**Further reading:**
Grant, Robert. "Gnostic Spirituality." *Christian Spirituality I: Origins to 12th Century*, Bernard McGinn and John Meyendor, eds. New York: Crossroad, 1987.
Schneiderman, Stuart. *An Angel Passes: How the Sexes Became Undivided*. New York: New York University Press, 1988.

**Shelley, Percy Bysshe**   See LITERATURE AND ANGELS.

**Solomon**   See ANGEL OF DEATH; DEMON.

**Sodom and Gomorrah**   One of the best-known biblical tales of destruction by an angel (see ANGELS OF DESTRUCTION) is that of the evil cities of Sodom and Gomorrah, related in the Book of Genesis.

In Genesis 18, the prophet ABRAHAM, visited by three angels, learns after their departure for Sodom that God intends to destroy the cities of Sodom and Gomorrah because "their sin is very grave" (18:20). Abraham asks if God will destroy the righteous along with the wicked. He asks God if the cities would be spared if fifty righteous people could be found within them. God agrees. Abraham then bargains God down to forty-five, then thirty, and finally ten righteous people. But no such ten can be found.

Two of the angels who visited Abraham (one is often identified as GABRIEL) arrive in Sodom in the evening and are met by Lot, Abraham's nephew, who offers them food and shelter. They say they prefer to spend the night in the street. He entreats them, and they enter his house and partake of a feast of food (by some accounts, it only *appears* to Lot that the visitors eat—see EATING). Lot's hospitality is not as generous as that of Abraham. He serves the angels unleavened bread, and is not as attentive as his uncle.

The men of Sodom surround the house and demand that Lot produce the two visitors; it is implied that their intent is to sexually abuse the visitors. Lot offers them his daughters instead. The men attempt to break down the door. The angels hold the door fast, and strike the intruders blind.

The angels then inform Lot that Sodom is about to be destroyed because of the wickedness of its inhabitants, and that he should gather his family and flee. Lot attempts to warn the two men who are about to marry his two daughters, but they think he is joking.

At dawn, the angels tell Lot to take his wife and two daughters and flee, and to not look back, lest they be destroyed along with the city. They are charged not to look behind them as they flee. Lot fears for his safety, and begs the angels to spare a small city called Zoar, where he decides to go. The angels agree.

During their flight, Lot's wife looks behind her and is turned into a pillar of salt. The rest of the party is safe. Then God rains down fire and brimstone upon Sodom and Gomorrah: "the smoke of the land went up like the smoke of a furnace" (19:28).

Christian and Jewish theologians have disagreed over whether Lot was addressed by God or two angels; the question of what happened to the third angel also has been debated. Three angels visit Abraham but only two are said in Genesis to depart for Sodom. The third party sometimes is identified being the Lord.

The sexual interest in the angels shown by the men of Sodom is a reversal of the sexual interest in humans attributed to angels (see SONS OF GOD). Such human-angel intercourse is met with punishment and downfall.

**Further reading:**
*Harper's Bible Commentary*. James L. Mays, gen. ed. San Francisco: HarperSanFrancisco, 1988.
*The New Oxford Annotated Bible with the Apochrypha*. Herbert G. May and Bruce M. Metzger, eds. New York: Oxford University Press, 1977.

**Smith, Joseph, Jr.**   See MORMONISM; MORONI.

**Sons of God**   Genesis 6:1–4 contains an obscure passage from one of the two sources of the Pentateuch: "The sons of God, looking at the daughters of men, saw they were pleasing, so they married as many as they chose." Yahweh was not pleased at the mixture of his spirit with flesh, and limited their lifetime to one hundred and twenty years. "The Nephilim were on the earth at that time (and even afterwards) when the sons of God resorted to the daughters of man, and had children by them. These are the heroes of days gone by, the famous men." This parallels several mythic fragments, including the popular Hebrew story of the Nephilim, a race of Titans of eastern legend, born of the union between gods and mortals.

This myth is variously developed in the Apocrypha and in midrashim. In one story, two angels in confidence with God, Shemhazai (see SEMYAZA) and AZAEL, were permitted by God to descend to earth to determine if man is worthy. When they arrived they were overcome with lust and begot monsters upon women. Shemhazai repented; he was turned into the constellation called Orion by the Greeks. Azael, far from repenting, still offers women ornaments, cosmetics and clothing so that they can lead men astray. For this reason on the Day of Atonement, Israel's sins are heaped onto the annual scapegoat, which is thrown over a cliff to Azael.

In another version of the story, the "inspecting angels" first turn themselves into precious stones, which are stolen by covetous men. Then the angels take human shape and are subject to human lust. Angels are thus chained to Earth, unable to resume their spiritual shapes. Another astrological story tells of a virgin who resists the Fallen ones. She asks them first to lend her wings, whereupon she flies to heaven and takes sanctuary at the Throne of God, who transforms her into the constellation Virgo—or some say, the Pleiades.

According to the *Zohar* Genesis, the Sons of God won that name because the divine light out of which God had created their ancestor, SAMAEL, shone from their faces. The Daughters of Men, they say, were children of Seth, whose father was Adam, not an angel, and their faces therefore resembled our own. Later Judaism and most early ecclesiastical writers identify the "sons of God" with the fallen angels; but from the fourth century onward, as the idea of angelic natures becomes less material, the church fathers reverse the order in the *Zohar* Genesis, commonly taking the "sons of God" to be Seth's descendants and the "daughters of men" to be Cain's.

The Jewish historian Josephus (38–100 C.E.) interpreted it thus: "The angels of God now consorted with women, and begot sons on them who were overbearing and disdainful of every virtue, such confidence had they in their strength."

Genesis 6 does not present this episode as a myth, nor does it render judgment; it records the anecdote of a race of supermen simply to serve as an example of the increasing human malice that provoked God into sending the Deluge.

The version told by the Book of Jubilees is that many of the sons of God were attracted to women. They decided to disobey God, descend to Earth, and take the women as wives. This act had many problematic consequences. It was a sin of hubris—a mixture of pride and lust. It also resulted in a mixing of the spiritual with the material, which was strictly forbidden by God. The sons of God imparted to their wives angelic knowledge not meant to be shared with humans, such as the secrets of growing herbs, working with minerals, working enchantments and other magic.

The union between the angels and the daughters of Eve resulted in unnatural offspring. These Nephilim, or "fallen ones," were gigantic, destructive creatures. They required great amounts of food, and when food ran out they would eat humans and even each other. God sent the Great Flood to eliminate these abnormal beings and preserve the human race. However, there was a second occurrence of these creatures in Canaan, and Israel was charged with destroying them. The destruction was incomplete, and many got away, their fate unknown.

The fate of the rest of the Watchers was to be held prisoner forever. Their leader, AZAZEL, was cast by the archangel RAPHAEL into a dark pit (either in the earth or in the fifth heaven), where he will remain until Judgment Day, when he will be cast into fire.

The prophet ENOCH said that during his trip to the many layers of heavens, he witnessed a penal colony in the fifth heaven, where gigantic angels known as the Grigori (Watchers) were being kept prisoner.

A holy order of Grigori are said to reside in the second heaven. The Grigori are eternally silent. Some of the Grigori and their teachings to humanity are:

- *Armaros*: the resolution of enchantments
- *Araquiel* or *Arakiel*: the signs of the earth
- *Azael*: the making of knives, swords, shields, ornaments and colors for the beautifying of women (cosmetics)
- *Baraqijal* or *Baraqel*: astrology

- *Ezequeel* or *Ezekeel*: knowledge of the clouds
- *Gadreel*: introduction of weapons of war
- *Kokabel* or *Kawkabel*: the science of the constellations
- *Penemue*: writing; and sharing the secrets of wisdom with children
- *Sariel*: the course of the moon
- *Semyaza*: enchantments, root-cuttings
- *Shamsiel*: signs of the sun

The title "Son of God" appears elsewhere in the Old Testament and in the New Testament. It does not necessarily mean natural sonship, but a sonship that is merely adoptive, i.e., which is a result of God's deliberate choice to set up a very intimate relationship between God and his creature. In this sense the title is given to angels (Job 1:6), to the Chosen People (Exodus 4:22), to individual Israelites (Deuteronomy 14:1), to their leaders (Psalms 82:6). When the title was applied to the Messiah (1 Chronicles 17:13; Psalms 2:7) it does not imply that he is more than man, nor is there reason to suppose that it had deeper significance when the expression was used by Satan (Matthew 4:3, 6) or by the possessed (Mark 3:11; 5:7; Luke 4:41), still less when used by the centurion (Mark 15:39; Luke 23:47).

Nevertheless, the title "Son of God" can bear a more profound meaning of sonship in the full sense of the words. Jesus clearly insinuated this meaning when he spoke of himself as "the Son" (Matthew 21:37) ranked above the angels (Matthew 24:36). These assertions, coupled with others that speak of the Messiah's divine rank (Matthew 22:42–46) and of the heavenly origin of the "Son of Man," assertions finally confirmed by the resurrection, have endowed the expression "Son of God" with that strictly divine significance which was later given it in St. PAUL (Romans 9:5).

**Further reading:**

Davidson, Gustav. *A Dictionary of Angels*. New York: The Free Press, 1967.

Godwin, Malcolm. *Angels: An Endangered Species*. New York: Simon & Schuster, 1990.

Graves, Robert, and Patai, Raphael. *Hebrew Myths*. New York: Doubleday Anchor, 1964.

Introductions and Notes. *The Jerusalem Bible*. Garden City, N.Y.: Doubleday, 1966.

**Sophia**   An important figure in GNOSTICISM, where she is the youngest of the AEONS (high angels ruling an aeon, or sphere of the universe), very much involved in the creation of this world and early human history. Sophia also is the figure of Divine Wisdom (in Greek, *sophia* means wisdom), and has a literary and iconographic history recorded in the Hebrew Bible, Hellenic Judaism, and early Christian literature. These two strains of an anciently derived, powerful feminine being named "Sophia" have somewhat merged in contemporary feminist spirituality.

### THE GNOSTIC SOPHIA

The Gnosticism entry in this book covers some of that cult's myths of creation and the origin of the human condition, stories pervaded by angels of varying pedigrees, degrees of enlightenment and ignorance, and thus full of mixed motives. These myths have long been recognized as derivative, and many have been traced to their ancient sources. One notable link is with the Egyptian goddess Isis (key Gnostics were Egyptian). Isis iconography has many links with Gnostic names and motifs, for example ABRAXAS. Parallels have been drawn between the wanderings and tears of Isis in search of Osiris, and the lovers' ultimate reunification and transformation, and the wanderings and tears of Sophia seeking "the Father" (the Unknown God) and ultimately being united with the Logos (Christ, the Father's son). Like Isis, the mother goddess of the Gnostics encompasses what for humanity are opposites: She is at once virgin and mother, father and mother, prostitute and virgin, male and female, whole and part, self and other.

Scholarly study of the Nag Hammadi Coptic documents (discovered in upper Egypt in 1945 and first published in English in 1977), suggests that there was a decline in the prestige of the personified Sophia, as one moves from the earlier non-Christian documents (that is, those with a pagan or Jewish bias) to the later Christianized Gnostic documents. For example, in the early Jewish–Gnostic *Apocalypse of Adam*, the life-giving principle of salvation is given to Adam by the Holy Eve, whereas in a late Christian tractate the male spirit is presented as being the necessary agent of the feminine soul's salvation. Non-Christian Gnostic texts (*Apochryphon of John, the Second Stele of Seth*, the *Second Treatise of the Great Seth*) for the most part portray Sophia as being the preeminent female AEON in the divine realm. In *On the Origin of the World*, the mythological presentation is almost entirely set within feminine imagery, from the formation of the world by Pistis Sophia and the creation of Eve before Adam to the destruction of the world through the mindless fury of an unnamed goddess.

In the pagan letter *Eugnostos the Blessed*, Sophia appears as Agape (Love), Aletheia (Truth), Syzygos (Consort), Mother of the Universe, and Sige (Silence). In both extant versions of this document Sophia is described as part of the androgyne Sophia/Immortal Anthropos. Without the female and male aspects of the form of God that this androgyne carried, subsequent creation would not take place, for it is only from their union that another male-female being, Savior/Pistis Sophia results, and from their union, six androgynous spiritual beings are generated. The unions of these twelve entities reveal seventy-two powers, and the resultant 360 powers are regarded as the 360 days of the year. A parallel revelatory discourse, the *Sophia of Jesus Christ*, follows the elaborate cosmology and naming of *Eugnostos* and adds material from another myth (which suggests a Christian author) about Sophia's independent culpable activity, wherein she is a fallen feminine deity in need of the male spirit of Christ for her salvation.

### SOPHIA AND THE WISDOM LITERATURE

In theological circles today there is much debate as to how to understand the personified Sophia of the "Wisdom Literature" in Hebrew Scripture: Proverbs 1–9, Sirach 24, Job 28 and the Wisdom of Solomon, to name the better-known texts. Some Hebrew scholars contend that this body is a foreign intrusion. Some have seen links to the various wisdom goddesses of the Near East, especially Isis, or another Egyptian goddess, Ma'at. Sophia obviously was in great part a symbol of the learning tradition within Israel, a patriarchal society. Therefore some consider it naive to link the rise of

Sophia in the Hebrew scriptures with some shift in attitudes toward the subordination of women. To a large extent Sophia came into being because the wisdom tradition of the Hebrew faith itself needed such a mythic figure to represent its response to the challenge posed by the Hellenistic world starting *500* B.C.E.

The Book of Proverbs encompasses the whole field of wisdom, from the cosmic to the virtues of a capable wife. Wisdom was brought forth at the very beginning of God's creation (*Proverbs 8*); she witnessed and has knowledge of all matters. She is God's eternal companion. She is a lover, ceaselessly seeking men; she builds a house, prepares a feast, sends maids to invite all to "walk in the way of understanding" (Proverbs 9:6). Wisdom, beloved of man, also is the beloved of God. In this way she mediates the gulf between humanity and God. By loving wisdom, the scholar forms an attachment to the cosmic world. In the apocryphal Solomon, Chapters 10 and 11, the writer retells the sacred history of the Hebrew people from Sophia's point of view. In this version of the stories of Adam and Eve, Cain and Abel, Noah, ABRAHAM and Lot, JACOB, Joseph and MOSES, Sophia takes the place of man as the designer and controller of history.

The image of Wisdom evolved during the Hellenic period into the powerful image of Sophia, the divine wisdom of the book of Ben Sirach. She is figured forth as a tree or plant, in accord with her connection to creation (Sirach 24:12–19). She also is identified with the Hebrew law (Sirach 24:23–25; Baruch 3:37–4:2). Men devoted themselves to the service of Sophia, abandoning family ties. Rabbinic Judaism identified Wisdom with Torah. But Judaism made the search for Wisdom a communal affair (within the community of men) and avoided individual celibate devotion, quite a different spiritual path from that followed by Christians in love with God. (See MONASTICISM, CHRISTIAN.)

Biblical scholars agree that the Wisdom literature was a late entry into the scriptures, but they can find no direct source for Sophia. Why did Sophia emerge? Theories range from her being an invention of Hebrew theologians to her being the outbreak of a long-suppressed female valence in the Hebrew religion. This latter idea is abetted by the appearance in the Kabbalah of Shekinah, a Jewish version of the concept of Shakti in Hinduism: the female partner/soul of God. Scholars also have been unable thus far to determine which segment of Hebrew society or culture was particularly dedicated to the study of Sophia. Since Solomon is named as author of some of the Wisdom literature, some suggest it was the product of philosophers in the court of that monarch. But this theory does not hold up well, for during the probable time of its composition there was no king in Israel and the material does not speak to the concerns of such an elite. The fact that a good part of the Wisdom literature exists only in the Greek language attests to a strong influence on Jewish scholars of the Greek devotion to philosophy (*philo*, love, of *sophia*, wisdom). In addition, Greek culture did not lack female figures of stature such as the goddess Athena, comparable to Sophia.

### SOPHIA IN CHRISTIAN SCRIPTURES

A whole series of New Testament texts identifies Jesus with Sophia. In Corinthians 2:6–8 ST. PAUL says:

> But we still have a Sophia to offer to those who have reached maturity; not a philosophy of our age, it is true, still less of the

masters of our age, which are coming to an end. The hidden Sophia of God which we teach in our mysteries is the Sophia that God predestined to be for our glory before the ages began. She is a Sophia that none of the masters of this age have ever known.

John's gospel portrait of Jesus is fully comprehensible only in the context of the role Sophia had played in Greek and Hebrew tradition. In John 1:1–3, for instance, "In the beginning was the Word . . .," the meaning of "Word" corresponds to the meaning of Sophia in the Hebrew scriptures. Jesus's declarations of who he is ("You are of this world; I am not of this world" [John 8:23–24] and [12:44–48] "I, the light, have come into the world, so that whoever believes in me need not stay in the dark any more") remind one of Sophia's about herself, summed up in Sirach 24: "Sophia speaks her own praises, in the midst of her people she glories in herself." The model of the self-proclaiming teacher does not exist in the Hebrew scriptures outside of Sophia.

The other gospels contain references that lean heavily on Sophia: Matthew 11:16–19 (Luke 7:31–35); Luke 10:21f; Matthew 23:34–36 (Luke 11:49–51) and Matthew 23:37–39 (Luke 13:34f). There is a remarkable parallel between Matthew 11:28–30, where Jesus says "Come to me . . . shoulder my yoke and learn from me," and Sirach 51:26, "Put your necks under her yoke, and let your souls receive instruction" and Sirach 6:25, "Give your shoulder to her yoke."

When one remembers how readily the Gnostics embraced Sophia, and how as Christianity developed, Gnosticism became one of its more serious rivals, it is not surprising that this presence of Sophia in the New Testament was downplayed. As the early Christians were compiling the documents for the New Testament, the Gnostics were pushing the Jesus–Sophia identification, emphasizing that "gnosis" saved humanity rather than Jesus' suffering and death.

As a footnote to the Christian fate of Sophia, it should be noted that Eastern Orthodoxy adored Sophia, and erected in Constantinople her greatest shrine in the sixth century C.E. It was one of the wonders of the world: the Church of Holy Sophia (Hagia Sophia). The church was embarrassed by this magnificent monument and created a saint named Sophia, whose tenuous story lacked even a date. Catholic scholars now aver that the church of Hagia Sophia was never dedicated to the Great Mother in any form, not even that of a female saint. They would have us believe that its name (which in Greek clearly means "Holy Female Wisdom") really means "Christ, the Word of God."

*SOPHIA IN ARTS AND PHILOSOPHY*

The appeal of Sophia is especially apparent in Goethe's *Faust*, where the artist conflates qualities of Isis, Mary, Sophia and Helen of Troy. The final words of the poem are "And so the eternal feminine leads us upward." The goddess Isis, and Egyptian mysteries, found their way into Masonic rituals; it has been suggested that those rituals are derived from some of the literary works in question. The Isaic mysteries were the inspiration for Mozart's *The Magic Flute*, and so interested Goethe that he wrote *The Second Part of the Magic Flute* in 1798.

In the philosophy of Jakob BOEHME (1575–1624), a major influence on William BLAKE, Sophia represented not only Wisdom, the mystical spouse, half of the androgynous

Adam, but also the Virgin of Light, identified with Logos. After the death of his fiancée, Novalis (1772–1801) recorded in his journal an entry called "Christ and Sophia." His *Hymns to the Night* (1800), with their stunning sensuality, represent the triumph of the nocturnal and feminine side of being.

*SOPHIA AND FEMINIST SPIRITUALITY*

This survey of where and how versions of Sophia appeared in virtually all religious contexts a few thousand years ago, should make clear her great attraction to contemporary Western women, free at last to pursue not only their educations and their lives but their souls' journey without the fear of patriarchal dominance.

Neo-pagan, Jewish and Christian feminists all find inspiration in the myths, texts, motifs and compelling presence of Sophia, the Wisdom-Woman goddess.

**Further reading:**

Arthur, Ruth Horman. *The Wisdom Goddess: Feminine Motifs in Eight Nag Hammadi Documents*. Lanham, Md.: University Press of America, 1984.

Attwater, Donald. *The Penguin Book of Saints*. Baltimore: Penguin Books, Inc., 1965.

Cady, Susan; Ronan, Marian; and Taussig, Hal. *Sophia: The Future of Feminist Spirituality*. San Francisco: Harper & Row, 1986.

Frymer-Kensy, Tivka. *In The Wake of the Goddess: Women, Culture and the Biblical Transformation of Pagan Myth*. New York: Fawcett Columbine Books, 1992.

Good, Deirdre J. *Reconstructing the Tradition of Sophia in Gnostic Literature*. Atlanta: Scholars' Press, 1987.

King, Karen, ed. *Images of the Feminine in Gnosticism*. Philadelphia: Fortress Press, 1988.

Legge, Francis. *Forerunners and Rivals of Christianity*. New Hyde Park, N.Y.: University Books, 1964.

*Mythologies*. Compiled by Yves Bonnefoy. Chicago: University of Chicago Press, 1991.

**Sorath**   See Rudolph STEINER.

**Spangler, David**   See FINDHORN.

**Spenser, Edmund**   See LITERATURE AND ANGELS.

**spirit guide**   Mythologies around the world include nonphysical beings who function as guides and protectors, and who provide inspiration. Angels fall into this broad category of supernatural beings. Other spirit guides might be spirits of the dead, semidivine entities, or beings with animal shapes such as those found in shamanic cultures. Modern psychology might look upon such a guide as being an aspect of one's own Higher Self or one's subconscious.

It is widely believed that one or more primary spirit guides appear at birth. These remain close during a person's life, and assist in the transition at death (compare to GUARDIAN ANGEL and GUARDIAN SPIRIT). In addition to primary spirit guides, secondary spirit guides may appear on the scene for temporary periods.

Spirit guides also can appear at any time in life, especially if mediumistic abilities open suddenly. Such spirit guides, usually souls of the dead, ostensibly communicate with the medium so as to relay information to others. The primary spirit guide to a medium is called a "control," who apparently monitors the access of other entities to the medium.

A "spiritual guide" (reprinted courtesy of U.S. Library of Congress)

Like angels, spirit guides can manifest in physical form, appear in dreams, and communicate via the inner voice.

**Further reading:**
Myers, Frederic W.H. *Human Personality and Its Survival of Bodily Death*, Vols. I & II. New ed. New York: Longmans, Green & Co., 1954. First published 1903.

**spirit helper**   See GUARDIAN SPIRIT.

**spirits of form**   See Rudolph STEINER.

**star of Bethlehem**   The bright star that guided the three Magi to the Christ child, as told in the New Testament, can be interpreted as being an angel rather than a star.

The Gospel of Matthew tells of the star seen by the Magi in the east, which went before them as a beacon and guided them to the infant Jesus in Bethlehem. The light moves about in a fashion uncharacteristic of a star but in keeping with other biblical descriptions of guiding angels as being lights, lightning, stars and flames.

The Book of Judges tells how stars played a role in a victory by Israel, and the Book of Job speaks of the morning stars singing together. The Book of Isaiah mentions the angel LUCIFER, whose name means "bearer of light" or "son of the morning." Revelation describes angels as being stars. The apocryphal Book of ENOCH describes angels of fire, with eyes like burning lights. Seraphim, the angels closest to God, are "fire-makers." Such burning lights appearing in the sky could have been described by the ancients as stars. Angels are associated or equated with stars in various philosophical writings.

See also Jakob BOEHME; JESUS; ORIGEN.

**Further reading:**
Mattingly, Terry. "Was it a star or an angel guiding Magi to Bethlehem?" *Seattle Times*, Dec. 25, 1993, p. A19.

**Steiner, Rudolf** (1861–1925)   Philosopher, artist, scientist and educator whose "spiritual science," called *anthroposophy*, blends many strands of occult lore into an esoteric Christian frame. Rudolph Steiner's teachings about Higher Beings, INTELLIGENCES, angels and the four major archangels—MICHAEL, GABRIEL, RAPHAEL and URIEL—are extensive.

*A SUMMARY OF STEINER'S LIFE*
Steiner was born to Austrian parents on February 27, 1861, in Kraljevic, then part of Hungary and now in Yugoslavia. His father, a railway clerk, hoped that Rudolph would become a railway civil engineer, but an early manifestation of psychic gifts set him on a different path. Steiner began to experience clairvoyance at the age of eight; throughout his life he taught as one who regards his experience as authoritative, although he did not intend the results of his spiritual research to be considered infallible. At the age of nineteen he was initiated by an adept whose identity was never revealed. In 1886 he was hired by the Specht family to tutor four boys, one of whom was autistic. His exceptional tutoring enabled the boy to finish school and become a medical doctor. Later, one wing of Steiner's activity was his development of the Waldorf schools—the first was established in Stuttgart in 1919—now the largest nonsectarian system of education in the world. The Waldorf system also addresses the needs of retarded children.

Rudolph Steiner (used by permission of the Anthroposophic Press, Hudson, N.Y. 12534)

Steiner found that he was in rapport with the Theosophical Society, becoming the secretary of the German branch in 1902. However he withdrew about ten years later, after becoming disillusioned with what he termed the "triviality and dilettantism" of many members. He questioned Annie Besant's cultist championship of Jiddu Krishnamurti as the next Messiah, believed that cofounder Helena P. Blavatsky had distorted occult truths, and ultimately concluded that it was not possible to build a spiritual science on Eastern mysticism.

In 1913 Steiner formed the Anthroposophical Society, taking some members with him from the Theosophists. He described his path as one leading to spiritual growth on the four levels of human nature: the senses, imagination, inspiration and intuition. In Dornach, near Basel, Switzerland, he established the Goetheanum, a school for esoteric research, where he intended to produce Goethe's dramas and his own mystery plays. The building was burned to the ground in 1920 but rebuilt in 1922, and now serves as the international headquarters for the organization.

In the twenty-five years before his death in 1925, Steiner traveled around Europe and Great Britain giving more than six thousand lectures. His published works include more than 350 titles, most of which are collections of lectures. His key works outlining his occult philosophy are *Knowledge of the Higher Worlds and Its Attainment* (1904–1905), *Theosophy: An Introduction to the Supersensible Knowledge of the World and the Destination of Man* (1904) and *An Outline of Occult Science* (1909).

### SPIRITUAL SCIENCE AND PHILOSOPHY

The intent of Steiner's philosophy is practical: He aimed at nothing less than the transformation of the individual, and thereby of society. Although Steiner drew heavily from the natural science works of Johann Wilhelm von GOETHE (which he edited in his university years) and the idealist epistemology of Johann Gottlieb Fichte (on whose scientific teachings Steiner wrote his doctoral dissertation), his was a radical commitment to experience and the solution of cultural problems. Steiner's first two philosophical works, *Truth and Knowledge* (1892) and *Philosophy of Freedom* (1894), argue that thinking can and must be developed as a liberating activity, one that grasps the most immediate particular by penetrating to its essential spiritual core. Steiner strives to lead the thinker to experience the practical and transformative power of original thinking in relation to the empirical world. He insists that ideas—one's own ideas generated by thinking freed from convention—make all the difference.

For Steiner, the ills of the world are largely attributable to the human failure to achieve a mode of thinking that is suffused with heart and will, which he refers to synonymously as "free" or "spiritual." Steiner is committed to "true civility": intuition, and action on ideals, in service of the artistic, the scientific, the educative. In *Knowledge of the Higher Worlds and Its Attainment*, Steiner insists that every individual can develop a spiritual, transformed consciousness:

> There slumber in every human being faculties by means of which one can acquire for oneself a knowledge of higher worlds. Mystics, Gnostics, Theosophists—all speak of a world of soul and spirit which for them is just as real as the world we see with our physical eyes and touch with our physical

hands. At every moment the listener may say to himself: that, of which they speak, I too can learn if I develop within myself certain powers which today still slumber within me. (p. 1)

At the age of forty Steiner felt that he was ready to speak publicly about his spiritual philosophy, his clairvoyant experiences, and what he had learned from them. By this time he had gained much experience in the nonphysical realms through profound meditation. Steiner claimed to have access to the Akashic Records, from which he had learned the true history of human evolution. He said that at one time humankind was more spiritual and possessed supersensible capabilities, but lost them on the descent to the material plane. At the nadir of human descent, Christ arrived and provided the opportunity to reascend to higher spiritual levels. For Steiner the life, death, and resurrection of Christ were the most important events in the history of humankind and the cosmos. The Gospels, however, did not contain the complete story.

### HIGHER BEINGS AND THE MILLENNIUM

Steiner wrote that Christ has, since the mystery of Golgotha, become the Spirit of the Earth, and yet He comes from regions beyond the earth. If we are stirred only by what belongs to the earth, we can never develop our Spirit Self. We lay the first seeds of this when we Christianize science, for it is Christ who brings the forces we need from outside the earth. "Progressive Angels," in whom the power of Christ is working, will teach that the substance of the world, even to the minutest particle, is permeated with the spirit of Christ, and he will be found working in the very laws of chemistry and physics. Two new impulses are arising, moral love and confidence in one another. Pure love, stronger than ever before, will have to be given wings within us. We must meet the other person as an ever-changing riddle, who evokes confidence in his or her own way from the very depths of our soul.

According to Steiner, the initiate comes to know the Spiritual Beings active behind phenomena, both the divine hierarchies that are already preparing spiritually that which will later descend to become physical events, and the powers which oppose them. In addition there are elemental beings who are the earthly servants of these higher beings, both in nature and in humans. The initiate can see what they are doing, and discovers that the truly creative Gods have their workplace within the human skin, in the inner organs, and that what permeates these will develop the form of the future. The initiate sees how past phases in the evolution of humanity will emerge again in metamorphosed form during the involution, the respiritualization of the earth, and how we already work with these germinal forces when we are in the depths of sleep, preparing not only our own next incarnation but also the future of the earth—though only that which is great and cosmic, not the details.

In *Spiritual Values*, Steiner states that

> of all that the Spirit has to accomplish on Earth through man, by far the greater part is accomplished during sleep.... Whilst we are asleep, lofty Spiritual Beings work upon the human soul, with the object of bringing man to his full and complete evolution in Earth existence.... (p. 47) [E]very night man grows out into the Cosmos. Just as here on Earth we are connected with the plants, with the minerals, with the

air, so are we connected in the night with the constellations of the fixed stars. From the moment we fall asleep, the starry heavens become our world, even as the Earth is our world when we are awake. (p. 48)

Dreams carry the experience of the cosmos through the threshold of the astral into the physical body, gathering images and feelings that vibrate with cosmic residue.

### THE ELOHIM: THE SPIRITS OF FORM

Seen from Steiner's spiritual perspective on human evolution, the original divine forces under the rulership of the Being known as Jehovah (Jahve, Yahweh), one of the Elohim or Spirits of Form, lost control. But Christ brought to Earth at the time of Golgotha the forces of the other six Elohim, who together with Jehovah had created man in their own image and breathed into him the living soul. And the first of these forces for the future starts to become active in those who receive the new Christ impulse mediated by spiritual science. The events of the present time are part of a greater battle behind the scenes between Wisdom/SOPHIA—all the forces of the past that have created us under the guidance of Jehovah, and Love—and the great forces of the other six Elohim which work creatively into the future. Only through the rhythmic swing of the pendulum between Wisdom and Love will the future be rightly formed. The Hierarchies intend for us only that to which we contribute from now on in full consciousness, and we have to go through both inner and outer soul-battles that make us strong.

### MICHAEL: THE SPIRIT OF THE AGE

Steiner reported that during the last century the consciousness of humankind as a whole crossed unconsciously the Threshold that separates the world of nature, grasped by the senses, from the spiritual world that manifests within the human soul. In consequence, human thinking, feeling and willing are no longer fully coordinated. This shows itself in many ways; for example, in increasing mental illness and in the incidence of violence. But in complete contrast, the opportunity is now open for spiritual perception in clear waking consciousness.

Furthermore, since 1879 human evolution has been under the guidance of MICHAEL, as Spirit of the Age. As ruler of the Cosmic Intelligence, the coordinator of the divine INTELLIGENCES in the heavenly bodies, he enables the person who applies intelligence and reasoning to reports of the spiritual world to grasp these through his understanding. Michael inspires the will to do so, and also spreads the impulse of cosmopolitanism that is so characteristic of the millennium.

In those who progress to active thinking, it will be possible to make Inspiration the determining element of soul. This is what "Michael rulership" really means. Michael does not work so much for the initiate as for those who wish to understand spiritual investigations. Michael stands cosmically behind man, while within man there is an etheric image that wages the real battle through which we can become free. Because Michael won the battle over the Dragon in 1879, the spiritual will lay hold of humanity more and more, and spiritual truth will take root among men although it will not become the general conviction. Steiner predicted that before the end of the twenty-first century, buildings would arise all over Europe dedicated to spiritual aims.

### ANGELIC ASSISTANCE

While science and technology "can only apprehend the corpse of reality" at the same time the old Christian spirituality is falling apart and cannot be repaired. The possibility of help from Spiritual Beings has not been lacking, but this is now dependent on the cooperative activity of the individual. States Steiner: "The doors to the Spiritual world now stand open, and the gods will immediately help if we turn to them. But their laws require them to deal with free men, not puppets." Furthermore, Luciferic and Ahrimanic beings constantly interact to challenge Angelic forces in human thought, sense and will, making each individual's esoteric discrimination or "spiritual science" a crucial skill to learn and practice. In a lecture given on October 9, 1918 (*The Work of the Angels in Man's Astral Body*), Steiner described how throughout this century the Angels have been seeking to implant three impulses in people before 2000 C.E., and how these impulses must turn to harm if they are not taken up with precisely this esoteric discrimination in each individual's will.

First, the Angels bring a strong impulse toward brotherhood, based on a deep interest in others and the inability to be happy so long as the other is unhappy; its obverse is the pernicious misuse of sexuality that rebels against brotherhood and shows itself in rape or in terrorism that has no respect for innocent bystanders. Secondly, Angels bring recognition of the hidden divinity in the other, so that each meeting becomes a sacred rite, the sharing of ideas a communion without need of church; its obverse is a taste for medicants or drugs that damage health, and soul-numbing addiction that only serves drug barons. Thirdly, Angels bring us the possibility of gaining spiritual insight through thinking; its obverse unleashes tremendous mechanical forces in the service of egoism, dramatically evident in dangerous leaders and cutthroat business practices.

Steiner remarked on April 4, 1912, that "without new spiritual impulses, technology will not only dominate outer life, but will overpower and numb us, driving out the religious, philosophical, artistic, and even ethical interests in the higher sense—men will turn into something like living automata." This lack of spirituality also made humans susceptible to the evil being spread over the earth through the influence of malevolent forces.

### LUCIFERIC AND AHRIMANIC BEINGS

As illustrated above, Steiner discovered that while some beings encourage the advancement of humankind's spiritual consciousness, others urge the separation of humanity from each other and the earth through unbridled egoism and private ecstasy. These spirits Steiner labeled Luciferic for their negative impact. Still others wish people to remain mired in a materialistic, mechanistic world. These last spirits Steiner called "Ahrimanic" beings, after the Persian personification of evil. He links Lucifer with air and warmth, Ahriman with earth and cold, and traces through the changes of seasons (and the elemental spirits of the Earth, which can serve the purposes of destructive Higher Beings as well as those fostering human spiritual evolution), another manifestation of the eternal struggle between them.

Steiner faced serious inner battles with these forces, declared his salvation to be through his immersion in the mysteries of Christ (not to be confused with any formal Christian religion), and warned that the spiritual path to higher consciousness entailed such battles. He noted that people strongly resist taking responsibility to fight on the inner plane, preferring to project the battle out onto imagined enemies. Every thousand years as a new millennium approaches, Luciferic and Ahrimanic beings make particularly strong attacks on human progress because of heightened fears of Armageddon and an end to the world. Thus the Luciferic and Ahrimanic beings find humans even more susceptible to spiritual debasement, mental slavery and mass hysteria.

Steiner would concur with Carl G. JUNG that the profoundest challenge to our age is to grasp with full intensity the polarity between Lucifer and Ahriman (see ABRAXAS). Modern consciousness has inherited a polarity between God and the devil, heaven and hell, but we need to understand that to strive toward paradise—willfully and forthwith—is just as bad for a person as to do the opposite. We must recognize that our true nature can be expressed only through dynamic equilibrium. On the one side we are tempted to soar into the fantastic, the ecstatic, the falsely mystical; on the other side we are dragged down by the prosaic, the arid, the dull and sterile.

Chaos, in which Luciferic and Ahrimanic forces participate, is necessary for human evolution, but is also highly antisocial. Steiner's commitment to "higher civility" spurred his reappraisal of human relations. At Dornach, a sculpture shows the Representative of Man standing between Lucifer and Ahriman. Whereas at present we see the other person superficially, Steiner would have us see each person as a special form of balance between Lucifer and Ahriman. We will gain this capacity by paying attention in retrospect to those who have educated, befriended, even injured us—often in a very helpful way. It is here that social impulses arise in time to perceive the head, the gait, the movements of another as an image of his/her eternal spiritual being. Steiner said on October 10, 1916, that as a rule we do not encounter anyone we have not met in previous incarnations. Likes and dislikes are great enemies of real social relations. Condemning a person obliterates a karmic relationship entirely, postponing it to a next incarnation, and no progress can be made.

Steiner explains that Ahrimanic beings are highly intelligent, extraordinarily clever and wise. They act behind the veil of nature and work to destroy the human physical organism. When we enter their world, destruction, hatred, or the like arise within us. Sensuous urges and impulses are enhanced. They move to destroy others without any benefit to ourselves. They replace thinking by all kinds of lower organism powers, especially the impulse to lie.

The Luciferic beings foster egoism within us, and have a passion for creating and bringing things into existence. Steiner insists that future evolution will be endangered if these two beings are not recognized. The clear, exact thinking required to pursue spiritual science counteracts the superficial phrases Ahriman uses to dull thought. Each individual must cease to grovel in the inner life, acting out of temperament or an obscure feeling of affiliation to some group; instead one's inner life derives from the pendulum of Love and Wisdom, revealing the deeper connections of life around us.

## SORATH

Steiner also perceived other beings beginning to generate evil with a far mightier force than Lucifer and Ahriman. One is Sorath, the Sun-Demon of Revelation. Steiner says that toward the millennium, spiritual people will be able to see the Sun-Genius, the etheric vision of Christ, and Sorath will foment opposition to belief in this phenomenon, arising around the year 1998 in numerous men who are possessed by him, exhibiting intensely strong natures, with raving tongues, destructive fury in their emotions, and faces which outwardly look animalized. They will mock that which is of a spiritual nature. In the mystery of 666, or Sorath, is hidden the secret of black magic. The power by which the Sun-Genius overcomes Sorath is MICHAEL, who has the key to the abyss and the chain in his hand (*The Apocalypse of St. John*).

## THE FOUR SEASONS AND THE ARCHANGELS

In October 1923 Steiner gave five lectures at Dornach, later published separately as *The Four Seasons and the Archangels: Experience in the Course of the Year in Four Cosmic Imaginations*. Details about each archangel's qualities tied to the seasons, and more of the qualities of the imagination Steiner linked to each, will be found in the separate entries on MICHAEL, GABRIEL, RAPHAEL and URIEL. This material, a symphony-like treatment of the divine continuity in the four movements of the seasons for Earth, Higher Beings, Elemental Beings, human consciousness, and spiritual skills and lessons, alchemy with its minerals and colors, Christian liturgy, mythology, Goethe's poetry and his own iconography, reveals how deeply imaging and aesthetics manifest Steiner's spiritual integration. Indeed, he describes each season in the context of how he would produce a mystery play about it—what colors, images he would choose—and suggests how these iconic choices embody some esoteric meanings. His colored chalk drawings accompanied the lectures and were reproduced in the volume.

### Autumn—Michael

Steiner starts with autumn, Michaelmas (feast September 29). Michael Imagination, like Michael, wields a sword of iron, iron in the blood and strength in the spirit. At Michaelmas we celebrate the sulfurizing and meteorizing process in man—everything that opposes love of ease, opposes anxiety, encourages the unfolding of inner initiative and free, strong, courageous will. Michaelmas is the Festival of Strong Will. The renewal of the whole soul-disposition of humankind should be celebrated at Michael Festival, one that renews the whole inner man.

### Winter—Gabriel

Next is the Christmas Imagination; Gabriel is its angel. At Christmas we celebrate the birth of the Redeemer, but Steiner ties the earth to the Mother: Mary or Demeter. In fact at one point he calls the Christmas Imagination the Mary Imagination. Gabriel always has been the angel most closely connected with Mary, present at many of the stages leading to the birth of Jesus, and the messenger who announced to humans its glorious new synthesis.

In the depths of winter the earth, in relation to the cosmos, is self-enclosed, as if it were cut off from the cosmos. During the winter the earth is wholly earth, with a concentrated earth-nature. In high summer the earth is open to the cosmos, lives with the cosmos, and in between, spring and autumn hold Earth in balance with the cosmos.

The picture of Mother and child celebrates the festival of earth gravity, enclosure and inner shelter. The depths of winter show us the connection of the cosmos with man, with man who takes up the birth-forces of the earth. The picture of Mary with the child arises out of the cosmos itself.

### Spring—Raphael

Easter Imagination brings Raphael, the Physician Angel. At Easter we celebrate the death and resurrection of the Redeemer. The figure of Raphael comes before us in dramatic guise as the mediator who arouses in us the rightful approach, through reverence and worship, to what the Easter Imagination is.

The activation of Earth in spring, Steiner notes, activates both Luciferic and Ahrimanic powers; the former try to take up the etheric into their own being, the latter try to ensoul the earth with astrality. The risen Christ stands triumphant between reddish Ahriman under his feet and the Luciferic blue/yellow power hovering above that seeks to draw the upper part of man away from the earth. Raphael takes on a Hermetic/Healer stance with a mercurial staff; sulfur and phosphorous are both present for combustion. The Easter

The archangel Michael: the Spirit of the Age (reprinted courtesy of U.S. Library of Congress)

Imagination celebrates transformation for healing, for the world-therapy that lives in the Christ principle.

### Summer—Uriel

Finally, the St. John (the Baptist, feast June 24) Imagination of high summer, with creative, admonishing Uriel presiding, is a festival of pervading radiant Intelligence, sulfuryellow and fire-red, of consolidated Imagination of Cosmic Understanding. At the height of summer, the elemental spirits soar upward and weave themselves into Uriel's realm, the shining Intelligence above.

Uriel, the representative of the weaving cosmic forces, appears in summer, seeking to embody himself in a vesture of light. Uriel's own intelligence arises fundamentally from the working together of the planetary forces supported by the working of the fixed stars of the zodiac. At midsummer the Trinity reveals itself out of the midst of cosmic life, cosmic activity. Steiner says "it comes forth with inwardly convincing power if . . . one has first penetrated into the mysteries of Uriel."

### TRINITY OF HEAVEN, EARTH, AND CHRIST

Steiner's Trinity is not of Father, Son and Holy Ghost. He says that at midsummer "we behold the outcome of the working together of Spirit Father and Earth Mother, bearing so beautifully within itself the harmony of the earthly silver and the gold of the heights. Between the Father and the Mother we behold the Son. Thus arises the Trinity Imagination, which is really the St. John Imagination. The background is Uriel, the creative, admonishing Uriel. . . ."

### INTERPLAY OF THE ARCHANGELS

If we want to arrive at an understanding of man's circumstances and situation in the world, Steiner says, we must seek it in the interworking of those Beings who appear in conjunction with these pictures (the "mystery play" images for each of the Imaginations and Archangels). If we know what is going on secretly in the products and beings of nature, we learn to recognize their therapeutic power. From MICHAEL, GABRIEL, RAPHAEL and URIEL stream out forces through the cosmos that enter man as formative force. In general Gabriel's forces are nourishing powers, Raphael's are healing; Uriel gives forces of thought, and Michael gives forces of movement.

One of the interplay factors is that whatever is permeated by Ahrimanic influences during one season is transformed into healing powers at another season. Thus the Archangels and Imaginations of one season are present strongly as the "counterpoint" of another. Their complementarity can be illustrated thus:

*Winter*: Gabriel above, Uriel below.
*Spring*: Raphael above, Michael below.
*Summer*: Uriel above, Gabriel below.
*Autumn*: Michael above, Raphael below.

In winter, after Uriel has made his way round the earth, his forces stream up through the earth and come to rest in our heads. Then these forces, which at other times are outside in nature, work through us to make us citizens of the cosmos. They actually cause an image of the cosmos to arise in our heads, illuminating us so that we acquire human wisdom. In this connection man is truly a microcosm against a macrocosm.

While during autumn Michael is the cosmic Archangel above, at Michaelmas it is Raphael who works in human beings—Raphael who is active in the whole human breathing system, regulating it and giving it his blessing. Up above we have the powerful Michael Imagination, with the sword forged from meteoric iron, the garment woven out of Sungold and shot through with the earth's silver-sparkling radiance, while Raphael below is working in man, aware of every breath that is drawn, of everything that flows from the lungs into the heart and from the heart through the whole circulation of the blood.

While Gabriel manifests as Christmas Imagination he is the cosmic Spirit; we have to look above to find him. During the summer Gabriel carries into man all that is brought about by the plastic, formative forces of nourishment. At midsummer they are carried into man by the Gabriel forces streaming through the Earth, when it is winter on the other side of Earth.

Michael reaches his height in autumn, and in spring his forces penetrate up through the earth and live in all that comes to expression in man as movement and the power of will, enabling him to walk and work and take hold of things.

Steiner was influenced by Goethe's *Faust* (which borrows from a much older source), which describes angels ascending and descending and develops the theme of the Archangels passing to each other their "golden vessel" containing the special healing powers. For example, Raphael passes it to Uriel, whereby the healing forces are made into the forces of thought. Michael receives from Uriel the thought-forces, and through the power of cosmic iron, out of which his sword is formed, transforms these thought forces into the forces of will, which become in man the forces of movement.

Steiner's voluminous talents as artist, philosopher, spiritual teacher, and "scientist of the invisible" have only been touched upon here. He presents a sweeping, mystical, visionary system that ties into the anxieties of our time, showing how the Angelic realms are intertwined with our inner and outer lives.

**Further reading:**

McDermott, Robert A. Ed. and Intro. *The Essential Steiner*. San Francisco: Harper & Row, 1984.

Sheperd, A.P. *Rudolf Steiner: Scientist of the Invisible*. Rochester, Vt.: Inner Traditions International, 1954, 1983.

Steiner, Rudolf. *An Autobiography*. New trans. Blauvelt, N.Y.: Rudolf Steiner Publications, 1977.

———— *The Four Seasons and the Archangels*. Bristol, England: The Rudolf Steiner Press, 1992.

———— *Planetary Spheres and Their Influence on Man's Life on Earth and in the Spiritual Worlds*. London: Rudolf Steiner Press, 1982.

**Swedenborg, Emanuel** (1688–1772)  A scientist and mystic, Emanuel Swedenborg believed that he communicated with God and His angels directly through a series of visions. He described in great detail the structure and hierarchy of both heaven and hell and the transitional place spirits go after death before choosing their eventual home. He stressed that mankind is totally free to select either heaven or hell, and that only through man's humanity can God truly be revealed. Swedenborg's books on these revelations met with derision and rejection during his lifetime, yet they influenced the works of nineteenth- and twentieth-century philosophers and theologians.

Swedenborg was born in Stockholm on January 29, 1688, the second son of the Lutheran Bishop of Skara. The family name was then Swedberg; the father changed it to Swedenborg when they became part of the nobility in 1719. The elder Swedenborg served for many years as a professor at the University of Uppsala, and Emanuel studied Latin, Greek, other European and Oriental languages, astronomy, geology, metallurgy, anatomy, mathematics, economics and other sciences there from age eleven to twenty-one. After graduation he traveled to Holland, Germany and England, where he met the astronomers Edmund Halley and John Flamsteed. By the time of his return to Sweden in 1716, his reputation brought him to the attention of King Charles XII, who named him a special assessor to the Royal College of Mines. Fascinated by the mining industry, Swedenborg turned down the opportunity to teach at Uppsala.

Although Swedenborg attempted to marry twice, neither young lady accepted him, and he devoted himself to work instead. In 1718 he invented a device to carry boats overland for a distance of fourteen miles. He worked on designs for submarines and air-guns, which could fire sixty or seventy rounds without reloading, and even dabbled in flying machines. In 1734 he wrote the *Opera Philosophica et Mineralia*, in which he described his "nebular hypothesis" as the basis for planet formation—ideas often erroneously attributed to Immanuel Kant. For the next ten years, Swedenborg wrote various treatises on animals, mineralogy, geology, creation and anatomy. But not until the publication of *Worship and the Love of God* in 1745 did Swedenborg turn his attention completely to the study of religion and God's revelations.

Swedenborg began to have ecstatic visions in 1743. Up to that time he hadn't given much thought to spiritual matters, although he had argued that the soul existed. Suddenly he was overcome with revelations about heaven and hell, the work of angels and spirits, the true meaning of Scripture and the order of the universe. Although Swedenborg maintained that he was fully conscious during the visions, he could remain in a trance for up to three days. It appears that he had the unusual ability to remain for prolonged periods in a hypnagogic state, the twilight phase that occurs just before the onset of sleep. In this state of consciousness one receives vivid images and voices, and it is possible to interact with these in ways much less difficult than those utilized in the dream state.

Swedenborg was so convinced that God had selected him to be His spiritual emissary that he quit his post as assessor in 1747, at age fifty-nine, and went on half-pension to devote himself fully to the Lord's work.

Swedenborg's theses revolved around two main points: that it is only through the eyes of mankind that God is truly revealed (although at no time did Swedenborg presume that God had exhausted all His revelations), and that man, through free will, creates his life and the eventual choice of heaven or hell. Men and women are completely at liberty to pursue lives devoted to love of the Divine and charity toward the neighbor, or to glorify self-love and evil. By so doing they make their own heaven or hell. Choices are final.

Immediately after death, the soul goes to an intermediary state called the "Spirit World" (somewhat akin to purgatory, only more temporary), in which one must confront one's "true affections." That is, what matters in the afterlife is not what one thinks or knows, but what one intends and does. After reconciling these matters, the soul naturally drifts toward its real nature, heaven or hell. In the Spirit World, as in heaven and hell, it is impossible to deceive others or to hide one's true nature.

Heaven for Swedenborg little resembles the sylvan paradise usually found in religious literature. Instead the angels who live there—all of them former humans, not separately created beings—live much as they had done on earth. They have faces, arms and legs, eyes, ears, noses and hair; they live in houses similar to their earthly domiciles, grouped into communities, towns and cities; they wear clothing; they speak and write; they eat food; they marry; never idle, they organize into different governments and perform useful occupations; they play, listen to music and generally live no differently from "natural," as opposed to spiritual, man. They have no sense of time, however, only of varying states of faith, intelligence, love and wisdom. As the angels progress into higher states they appear to grow older but tend to resemble young adults once they have accepted the Lord's love and wisdom. In heaven, spatial relativity is unknown as defined on earth. Those in similar states are near to each other, and those of dissimilar states are farther apart.

Angels of the inmost heaven exist solely as expressions of Divine Will and Love, taking no credit for any thought or action separate from the Lord. No matter which way they turn they always face east, the direction of the rising sun and thereby the Light of the Divine. They hear, speak and see more keenly, for as spiritual beings they understand so much more than humans, especially the universal language of all angels. Such complete life in the Lord yields immeasurable bliss and joy, often expressed as completely innocent delight.

All children are admitted to heaven, whether or not they were baptized. Baptism does not signify salvation but merely the need to be reborn in the Divine. In fact all people, not just Christians, are accepted into heaven if they have lived lives of love and charity. Once in heaven, the angels instruct them in the ways of the Lord. Even the rich, often thought excluded at the expense of the poor and meek, are welcome if the intent of their lives has been divinely inspired.

Perhaps because he was lonely in his bachelorhood, Swedenborg gave special emphasis to the state of married love in heaven. He explained that true married love is the total bonding of two minds into one, the blending of discernment and intent, the expression of the good and the true. To the extent that such a complete bond exists that couple becomes one angel, for an angel represents the good and the true together. And since each angel is a heaven in miniature with all the angels constituting all the heavens, married love is itself heaven.

All these things Swedenborg claimed came from discussions with the angels, which he recorded with a scientist's detachment and attention to detail. He realized that few would accept his visions as true revelations, but would instead accuse him of blasphemy or insanity. But he did not care, firmly asserting that he had heard, seen and spoken to God's heavenly representatives. He recounted his revela-

tions in several weighty tomes, including the eight-volume *Arcana Coelestia*. Other titles were *Apocalypse Explained*, *Conjugial Love*, *Divine Love and Wisdom*, *Divine Providence*, in 1758 his most famous, *Heaven and Hell*, and *Spiritual Diary*.

The Swedenborgian Hell differed greatly from the eternal fire of damnation propounded by the preachers of his day. Rather it is quite a modern place, peopled by those who choose self-love and evil rather than Divine love and truth. The Lord casts no one into Hell but instead works steadfastly through his angels to save that soul. Those who embrace evil and falsehood make their own Hell.

Hell's denizens continue their earthly lives and habits, much as Swedenborgian angels do, but with the continual threat of punishment if they exceed acceptable levels of vice and corruption. Retribution is the only restraint on their evil natures. There is no fallen Lucifer or Satan leading this gang of rogues. "Lucifer" and "Satan" themselves mean hell, and there is no devil in charge, for all the spirits in hell are former human beings. Because they have chosen malice and darkness, their faces are distorted into monstrous, repulsive shapes. They live in gloom yet appear to be burned by the fire of their own hatred. They speak with anger and vengefulness, they crave each other's company, and shrink back in loathing and pain from the approach of an angel. The constant clash of their falsehoods and senses produces a sound like the gnashing of teeth. The openings, or "gates," of hell are numerous and omnipresent, but they are visible only to those spirits who have chosen that path. Inside, hell resembles cavernous, bestial lairs, with tumbledown homes and cities, brothels, filth and excrement. Other hells may be barren deserts.

In any of these three worlds, time does not exist as it does on earth, Swedenborg says. It is measured by changes of state. Space also is different; spirits of like mind are "near" to each other, whatever their actual "location."

Swedenborg exerted tremendous influence on later nineteenth-century thinkers, especially Ralph Waldo Emerson and William BLAKE. Emerson greatly admired Swedenborg but found heaven and hell as Swedenborg described them deadly dull. Emerson also chafed under the premise that once a human had made his choice for heaven or hell there was no turning back, no atonement nor redemption. Blake initially embraced Swedenborgianism but eventually rejected it along with other examples of the Age of Reason. His "The Marriage of Heaven and Hell" satirized *Heaven and Hell* as a means of direct revelation, yet the idea of a clearly defined other world continued to influence Blake's art and writing.

After his death in 1772, some of Swedenborg's followers established various churches and societies to study and put forth the mystic's theories. The Church of the New Jerusalem was founded in England in 1778 and in the United States in 1792. The so-called New Church did not consider itself a separate religion but a help to further enlightenment. The Swedenborg Society was established in 1810 to publish translations of Swedenborg's books, create libraries, and sponsor study and lecturing. Spiritualists embraced Swedenborg's concept of the spirit's survival after death and the possibility of communication with the spirits. Like Swedenborg, they rejected reincarnation.

Helen Keller loved Swedenborg's writings and urged everyone to tackle his complicated and dense works. Many proponents of the New Age agree with Swedenborg's idea that hell is what you make it.

Swedenborg became enamored with England when he first visited there as a young man, and he spent most of his later years there. He died at the age of 84 and was buried in London.

**Further reading:**

Guiley, Rosemary. *Harper's Encyclopedia of Mystical and Paranormal Experience*. San Francisco: HarperSanFrancisco, 1991.

Lachman, Gary. "Heavens and Hells: The Inner Worlds of Emanuel Swedenborg," *Gnosis*, No. 36, Summer 1995, pp. 44–49.

Stanley, Michael, ed. "Angelic Nature: From Works of Emanuel Swedenborg," *Angels & Mortals: Their Co-Creative Power*, compiled by Haria Parisen. Wheaton, Ill.: Quest Books, The Theosophical Publishing House, 1990.

Swedenborg, Emanuel. *Heaven and Hell*, trans. George F. Dole. New York: Swedenborg Foundation Inc., 1976.

Turner, Alice K. *The History of Hell*. New York: Harcourt Brace & Co., 1993.

**take-away apparition**   See DEATHBED VISIONS.

**Tantric Buddhism**   The Tantric system of enlightenment arose in pre Vedic India, and remains a version of yogic practice in India with teachers and initiates. It rests on the worship of the mother goddess as Shakti, who imbues the world with power. The name derives from the *tantras*, Sanskrit texts written centuries after the primordially based teachings had been formulated. It combined with Buddhism in other Asian countries, was eventually suppressed and disappeared in China and Japan, but it is still widely practiced in the Buddhist monasteries of Nepal, Bhutan and Tibet.

Tantric practice consists in learning how to transmute bodily sexuality into a complete union with the Shakti. There can be no doubt that sexual intercourse was used in original Tantric practice, both as a way of transmitting initiations through a line of female power-holders and as a basis for meditative ritual. It is known that the great poet-saint Milarepa was initiated partly through intercourse with a disciple of his teacher Marpa, and some of the most sacred texts of this branch of Buddhism, for example, the Hevaira Tantra, give clear instructions for the way the sexual ritual is to be performed. Its human practitioners become at the outset respectively *herukas* (heroes) and yoginis (female yogis) or *dakinis* (in Tibetan *khadomas*, or female "sky-goers"). *Dakinis* are female partners whose names sometimes clearly identify them as forms of Wisdom, much as SOPHIA did in Gnostic and Judaic mysticism.

As in the practices of yoga in HINDUISM, GNOSTICISM, Sufism (see ISLAMIC ANGELOLOGY), and other paths, the Tantric system employs a complex symbolism played upon the imagination to further the aspirant's progress. The sexual rituals, actual and imaginative, on which the imagery is based depend on a special technique of activating a subtle body within the mediator's physical body, with its own inner pattern of energies and channels, named and personified by "deities of the mandala," entities scarcely distinguishable from gods, goddesses, angels and demons. Meditators evoke and visualize many orders of metaphysical principles, focusing on them through mantras and images of the deities. In the mystical context the distinctions between "real" and "unreal" are never sharp, certainly not as meaningful as the results of practice.

The mandala is one of the principal layouts used in all Tibetan mysticism and art. Monks and nuns select *tankas*, portable mandalas, for their practice. The mandala consists of a circle with divisions radiating from the center, some-times interpreted as the petals of the lotus, indicating that the figures on the periphery are unfoldings from the center. Each mandala is meant to be set up and followed through, stage by stage, around its layout, beginning with its eastern or southern quadrant and ending at its center. Once the mandala has been visualized and vitalized, it may be infolded and returned to the center. Mandalas of different lineages of deities may have varying numbers of petals.

Union of the male and female eventually becomes Buddha-Nairatma, which equals Enlightenment in union with Void. This is the subtle meaning of *Om mani padme Hum*. *Om* is the ancient Sanskrit invocation of the Supreme Reality; *mani* means "jewel" or "diamond," the *vajra* ("thunderbolt" and "diamond"—two condensed metaphors for the energy of the Void in which all opposites are reconciled, and also the erect male sexual organ—the "jewel" is thus condensed transcendent semen); *padme* means the "lotus," long associated with the female genitals, specifically of the Goddess who gives birth to the world, and in the Buddhist context, to spiritual insight into the appearance and disappearance of phenomena; *Hum* invokes energetic power.

*Jinas* are the energy-wisdom symbols, proceeding from the center and subdividing to produce all the mental creations that constitute the abstract and concrete contents of the universe. Each of the *jinas* stands not only for a kind of wisdom-energy but also for one kind of faulty sense perception to be remedied. In some mandalas they are shown interacting with the five kinds of wisdom, their partners the Bodhisattvas, the archetypal personifications of total compassion and metaphysical insight. The female forms have the following names: the Sovereign Lady of the Void (center), the All-Seeing (east), the No-Otherness (south), She of the White Raiment (west), and the Savioress (north).

Sometimes all the figures in the mandala are depicted in wrathful aspect, with haloes of flame, gruesome ornaments and hideous mein, dancing upon corpses. In this form the mandala portrays the universe with the five wisdoms clouded by the passions or delusions of sentient beings, which result from the operation of Avidhya (not seeing). They do not represent divine wrath, their functions being quite unlike those of the medieval Christian demons. Their purpose is not to torture sinners but to overcome evil, their clenched teeth and ferocious expressions exertions of all their strength in the battle against passion and delusion. Furthermore, these wrathful aspects are essential to the Tantric concept of non-duality; beauty and ugliness are two aspects of every object of perception. One more reason for the wrathful spirits is the belief that, when one dies, forty-nine days must be spent in the *bardo,* or intermediate state that precedes rebirth. During that time one encounters thought-forms emanating from one's own consciousness that have the appearance of wrathful deities or demons. Familiarity with the mandala will help to disperse fear of them.

*Dakinis* (or *khadomas*) are always portrayed in female form. They are representations of the forces welling up in the aspirant by which one is driven to master the hostile array of cravings, passions, and delusions and transform them into the winged steeds that will carry one forward to Enlightenment. The *dakini* is the universal urge to Enlightenment as it acts within the person. Often ferocious in appearance, they are reminiscent of the dread Hindu goddess Durga. It is usual for an adept to take one of the *dakinis* as a personal symbol of communication with divine wisdom (similar to the functions attributed to the Active Intelligence in medieval thought). By uniting with one's *dakini,* one penetrates the true meaning of doctrines too profound to yield to everyday consciousness.

*Yidams* are deities adopted by individuals as their mentors and guardians. When an initiate enters upon the path, the lama will select a *yidam* well suited to his special requirements. If one has fierce passions to subdue, the *yidam* will be one of the wrathful deities. Someone who is in emotional distress will be assigned a comforter, one who supports with chaste devotion. The adept may in imagination be warmly intimate with his *yidam,* but this love must be idealized. The twenty-one *taras* are the most frequently encountered *yidams.* Each has subtly different correspondences with psychic realities; the green, white and red *taras* are usually selected. Sometimes the *yidam* is equated with the *dakini* or even the guru. A devotee of the green *tara,* for example, might invoke her with the words: "*guru, yidam, dakini, maha arya tarayeh*!"

Imaginative visualization was elaborated into enormous and complex sequences. Much Tibetan art is intended to provide a basis for such visualizations. The procedure consists of the meditator calling on personified spiritual principles by name, invoking their mantras, and then visualizing their presence as intensely as possible so as to identify with them. A great collection of these *sadhanas* (meditations), the Sadhanamala, ("Garland of Sadhanas") had seen compiled in India by about 600 C.E. Each personification has its own color, posture, number of heads and arms with meaningful gestures (*mudras*), and symbolic objects. Broadly speaking, they represent energy-principles condensed into persons. Here is an example:

> The worshipper should conceive himself as Vajravarahi whose completion is red like the pomegranate flower, who has two arms, one face, three eyes, dishevelled hair, and who is endowed with the six favorable symbols. Her essence is the five spiritual knowledges and her nature is the pleasure of *Sahaja* [supreme spiritual conjunction]. In her right hand she holds the vajra *gri-gug* [flaying knife], in her left a skull-cap full of blood, with a trident impaling heads in the crook of that arm. She stands in the *Pratyahlida* [dance] posture and tramples on the fierce Kalaratri. She wears a garland of freshly severed heads and licks the blood that trickles from them.

Actual gods and demons who belong to the six orders of sentient beings are also depicted in outer parts of the man-dala. It is taken for granted in most Asian countries that there are all kinds of supernatural beings, the highest of which are called gods. Whether spoken of as gods, angels or demons, such beings are empowered to help the aspirant only to a limited extent. For instance, Buddhists are free to worship the gods associated with certain mountains or localities, or not.

**Further reading:**
Blofeld, John. *The Tantric Mysticism of Tibet.* New York: E. P. Dutton & Co., 1970.
Rawson, Philip. *Sacred Tibet.* London: Thames and Hudson, 1991.
Sogyal Rimpoche. *The Tibetan Book of Living and Dying.* Ed. Patrick Gaffney and Andrew Harvey. New York: HarperSanFrancisco, 1992.

**Taylor, Edward**   See PROTESTANT ANGELOLOGY.

**Teresa of Avila, St.** (1515–82)   One of the great Christian mystics and the founder of the Discalced Carmelite Order, whose authoritative works on prayer remain classics to the day. Teresa of Avila also had astounding experiences involving angels. Her books are *Life,* her autobiography (1565); *The Way of Perfection* (1573), about the life of prayer; and *The Interior Castle* (1577), her best-known work, in which she presents a spiritual doctrine using a castle as the symbol of the interior life.

She was born Teresa de Cepeda y Ahumada, to a noble family, on March 28, 1515, in or near Avila in Castile. Her mother died when she was 15, which upset her so much that her father sent her to an Augustinian convent in Avila. Her exposure to the monastic life convinced her that she wanted to become a nun, but her father forbade it as long as he was living. At about age 20 or 21 she left home and secretly entered the Incarnation of the Carmelite nuns in Avila. Her father dropped his opposition.

In 1538, soon after taking the habit, Teresa began to suffer from ill health, which she attributed to the change in her life and diet. It was through her chronic and severe afflictions that Teresa discovered the power of prayer, which enabled her to heal herself and which then became the focus of her spiritual life and her writings.

In her autobiography, *Life,* Teresa comments on her "many ailments" during her first year in the convent, including increasingly frequent fainting fits and heart pains so severe that others became alarmed. She was often semiconscious or unconscious altogether. She opined that these problems were sent by God, who was offended at her innate "wickedness." Rather, she may have suffered from malaria.

Teresa's health failed to the point where a grave was dug for her at her convent. She astonished everyone by recovering on her deathbed. She remained bed-ridden for eight months, and spent the next three years regaining her health. It was not until she reached the age of forty that the principal symptoms of her illness finally disappeared. Later, she credited the power of prayer and the intercession of St. Joseph with her recovery.

Throughout her monastic life, Teresa was blessed with numerous ecstatic experiences. She did not seek them out, but considered them a divine blessing. She spent long periods in the prayer of quiet and the prayer of union, during which she often fell into a trance and at times entered into mystical flights in which she felt as if her soul was being lifted out of her body. She likened ecstasy to a "delectable death," saying that the soul becomes awake to God as never before when the faculties and senses are "dead."

Teresa likened prayer to the cultivation of a garden. She outlined four steps for the watering of the garden so that it would produce fruits and flowers, which are the measure of the prayer's progress in love.

The first and simplest step is meditation, which Teresa said is like drawing water from a deep well by hand, in that it is slow and laborious.

The second step is taken through quiet, when the senses are stilled and the soul can then receive some guidance; thus, the prayer gets more water for the energy expended. The soul begins to lose its desire for earthly things.

The third step is taken through the prayer of union, in which there is contact between the prayer and God, and there is no stress. The garden, in fact, seems to be self-watered, as though from a spring or a little stream running through it. Teresa confessed that she had little understanding herself of this step. The senses and mental faculties, she said, could occupy themselves only and wholly with God.

The fourth step is taken by God himself, raining water upon the garden drop by drop. The prayer is in a state of perfect receptivity, loving trust and passive contemplation. Physically, the prayer faints away into a kind of swoon, Teresa said; her description resembles the trance states described by mystics of many faiths.

Teresa often came out of deep prayer states to find herself drenched in tears. These were tears of joy, she attested. Mystics in modern times also experience this.

She made such rapid progress in her prayer that she was concerned that she was being deceived by the devil, because she could neither resist the favors when they came nor summon them. Rather, they came spontaneously. Since she considered herself to be a weak and wicked person, she feared she was vulnerable to the influence of the infernal.

Teresa sought out spiritual counsel in an attempt to allay her fears. Some of her advisors agreed that such favors could be experienced by a weak woman, and fueled her fears of devilish interference. One, more objective advisor told her to put the matter before God by reciting the hymn "Veni, Creator" as a prayer. This she did for the better part of a day, at which point a rapture came over her so strong that it nearly carried her away. She said, in her autobiography, *Life*:

> This was the first time that the Lord had granted me this grace of ecstasy, and I heard these words: "I want you to converse now not with men but with angels." This absolutely amazed me, for my soul was greatly moved and these words were spoken to me in the depths of the spirit. They made me afraid therefore, though on the other hand they brought me much comfort, after the fear—which seems to have been caused by the novelty of the experience—had departed. (p. 172)

Her greatest experience with an angel occurred in 1559 and is known as "the transverberation of St. Teresa." "Transverberation" means "to strike through"; the mystical episode involved an angel piercing her heart with an arrow of love. In *Life*, Teresa says:

> Beside me, on the left hand, appeared an angel in bodily form, such as I am not in the habit of seeing except very rarely. Though I often have visions of angels, I do not see them. They come to me only after the manner [of intellectual vision]. But it was our Lord's will that I should see the angel in the following way. He was not tall but short, and very beautiful; and his face was so aflame that he appeared to be one of the highest rank of angels, who seem to be all on fire. They must be of the kind called cherubim, but they do not tell me their names. I know very well that there is a great difference between some angels and others, and between these and others still, but I could not possibly explain it. In his hands I saw a great golden spear, and at the iron point there appeared to be a point of fire. This he plunged into my heart several times so that it penetrated to my entrails. When he pulled it out, I felt that he took them with it, and left me utterly consumed with the great love of God. The pain was so severe that it made me utter several moans. The sweetness caused by this intense pain is so extreme that one cannot possibly wish it to cease, nor is one's soul then content with anything but God. This is not a physical, but a spiritual pain, though the body has some share in it—even a considerable share. So gentle is this wooing which takes place between God and the soul that if anyone thinks I am lying, I pray God, in His goodness, to grant him some experience of it. (p. 210)

Teresa was so affected by this experience that she vowed to do everything in a manner that would be perfect and pleasing to God.

In 1562 Teresa founded a convent in Avila with stricter rules than those which prevailed at Carmelite monasteries. Her aim was to establish a small community that would follow the Carmelite contemplative life, especially its unceasing prayer. She was met with great opposition, but in 1567 she was permitted to establish other convents. She dedicated herself to reforming the Carmelite order. At the age of fifty-three she met the twenty-six-year-old John Yepes (later known as St. John of the Cross), who became one of her allies and worked to reform the male Carmelite monasteries. After a period of turbulence within the Carmelites from 1575 to 1580, the Discalced Reform was recognized as separate.

By 1582, Teresa had founded her seventeenth monastery, at Burgos. Her health was now broken, and she decided to return to Avila. The rough journey proved to be too much, and upon arriving at the convent Teresa went straight to her deathbed. Three days later, on October 4, 1582, she died. The next day the Gregorian calendar went into effect, dropping ten days and putting her death on October 14. Her feast day is October 15. Teresa was canonized in 1662 by Pope Gregory XV, and she was declared a Doctor of the Church—the first woman to be so honored—in 1970 by Pope Paul VI.

**Further reading:**

*The Life of St. Teresa of Avila by Herself*. J.M. Cohen, trans. London: Penguin Books, 1987.

*One Hundred Saints*. Boston: Little, Brown & Co., 1993.

**theophany**   See ANGELOPHANY.

**Theosophy**   See DEVA.

**Theliel**   See EROS.

**thrones**   See CHOIRS.

**Tobit, Book of**   Apochryphal story establishing the healing ministry of angels. Tobit tells how the archangel

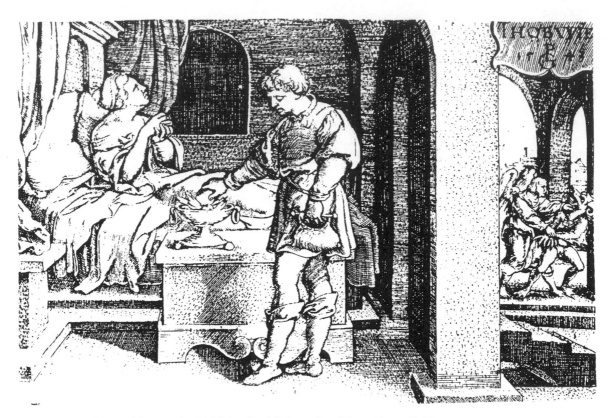

**Tobias burning magical fish, enabling Raphael (*right*) to banish Asmodeus (Georg Pencz, 1540)**

RAPHAEL, whose name means "the shining one who heals," provides magical formulae for healing. The story underscores the concept that angels do not act on their own but are emissaries of God, and that they have no physical form but can create the appearance of form for the benefit of humans.

The Book of Tobit was originally written in Hebrew or Aramaic, probably in the second century B.C.E. The story concerns a pious man named Tobit and his son, Tobias. It takes place in the late eighth century B.C.E. in the Assyrian capital of Nineveh, where the people of Northern Israel have been taken captive. The storyteller is Tobit himself, who is instructed by Raphael to write an account of the events that happen to him, his son and others.

By his own description, Tobit was a model of piety, walking "in the ways of truth and righteousness." He gave money, food and clothing to the poor. He defied Sennacherib the king by burying his fellow Israeli dead, whose bodies were left in the open by their captors.

On one occasion Tobit, who was fifty years old, was just sitting down to dinner when he learned of another corpse that needed burying. He left his meal and attended to the body. He was defiled from handling the corpse and so did not return home that night, but slept by the wall of the courtyard. He left his face uncovered.

Unbeknownst to Tobit, sparrows were perched on the wall, and their droppings fell into his eyes, rendering him blind. He sought help of various physicians, to no avail. His wife was forced to work to earn money.

After eight years, Tobit, depressed and in despair, begged God to let him die. In preparation for death he called in his only son and told him to journey to Media, where he had left some money in trust with another man. He instructed Tobias to find a man to accompany him on the journey, and he would pay the man's wages for his time and trouble.

While this drama was unfolding in Nineveh, another was taking place in Media. There, a young woman named Sarah was possessed by the demon ASMODEUS, "the destroyer." Sarah had been given to seven men in wedlock, but the demon had killed them all on their wedding night, before the marriages could be consummated. Sarah's parents, Raguel and Edna, feared that they would never marry off their only daughter.

God heard the prayers of both Tobit and Raguel, and dispatched Raphael to heal Tobit's blindness and exorcise the demons from Sarah.

When Tobit went looking for a man to accompany him on the trip to Media, he found Raphael, who appeared as a human and introduced himself as Azarius, the son of one of Tobit's relatives. They struck a deal for wages and departed.

The first evening they camped along the Tigris River. Tobias went down to the river to wash, and a giant fish jumped up and threatened to swallow him. Raphael told him to catch it, which he did with his hands, and threw it up on the bank. Raphael said, "Cut open the fish and take the heart and liver and gall and put them away safely." Tobias did this. They then roasted and ate the rest of the fish.

Tobias asked the angel of what use were the saved parts. Raphael replied, "As for the heart and the liver, if a demon or evil spirit gives trouble to any one, you make a smoke from these before the man or woman, and that person will never be troubled again. And as for the gall, anoint with it a man who has white films in his eyes, and he will be cured."

As they neared their destination, Raphael told Tobias that they would stay in the house of Raguel, and that he should take Sarah as his wife. Understandably, Tobias was not thrilled to learn that seven prospective husbands had all died at the hands of the demon. But the angel assured him, "When you enter the bridal chamber, you shall take live ashes of incense and lay upon them some of the heart and liver of the fish so as to make a smoke. Then the demon will smell it and flee away, and will never again return. And when you approach her, rise up, both of you, and cry out to the merciful God, and he will save you and have mercy on you. Do not be afraid, for she was destined for you from eternity. You will save her, and she will go with you, and I suppose you will have children by her."

The events came to pass as the angel predicted. Tobias was offered the hand of Sarah in marriage, and a contract was drawn up immediately. In the bridal chamber, Tobias followed Raphael's instructions for exorcising Asmodeus. The demon fled to "the remotest parts of Egypt" (the traditional home of magic and witchcraft), where Raphael bound him up.

After a fourteen-day wedding feast, Tobias, his bride and Raphael returned home to Tobit. Tobias anointed his father's eyes with the gall of the fish, and Tobit's sight was restored. In gratitude, he and Tobias offered Raphael half of the monies that Tobias had retrieved from Media.

The angel then revealed his true self to the men. "I am Raphael, one of the seven holy angels who present the prayers of the saints and enter in the presence of the glory of the Holy One," he said. He told Tobit that he had been ever-present with him, and had taken his prayers for healing to God. He urged the men to praise and thank God, and to lead righteous lives.

Tobit and Tobias were alarmed to be in the presence of an archangel, and fell to the ground in fear. But Raphael assured them that no harm would befall them. "For I did not come as a favor on my part, but by the will of our God," he said. "Therefore praise Him forever. All these days I merely appeared to you and did not eat or drink, but you were seeing a vision. And now give thanks to God, for I am ascending to him who sent me. Write in a book everything that has happened." Raphael vanished.

The Book of Tobit remains one of the most popular books in the Apochrypha, illustrating the Jewish values of prayer and piety, and the moral vibrancy of its folklore as well.

**Further reading:**
Guiley, Rosemary Ellen. *Angels of Mercy*. New York: Pocket Books, 1994.
*The New Oxford Annotated Bible with the Apochrypha*. Herbert G. May and Bruce M. Metzger, eds. New York: Oxford University Press, 1977.

**Torah** See JUDAIC ANGELOLOGY; MOSES.

**totem** See GUARDIAN SPIRIT.

**trees, sacred** Trees, especially the oak, have long been revered, even worshipped as sacred objects. Sacred trees are the dwelling places of various spirits and deities, who can be petitioned for oracles. The Druids especially worshipped the oak, and listened in the oaks for the rustling of wind in the

leaves and the chirpings of birds, to interpret their meaning. Parts of sacred trees were used in medical remedies and healing rites.

The ancient Hebrews also practiced tree-worship, especially of the oak and terebinth. Such trees were inhabited by spirits called Benat Ya'kob, or "daughters of Jacob." Shrines were erected at certain trees, and religious prostitution also was practiced. This worship and these practices were denounced by early biblical prophets such as Hosea, Ezekiel and Isaiah. The Old Testament tells of angels who appear at the sites of sacred oaks and/or terebinths. In these episodes the angels can be seen as substitutes for pagan tree-spirits.

In Genesis, the first recorded appearance of God to ABRAHAM was through an angel at a sacred oak or terebinth (the names for both are similar to each other in Hebrew and have caused confusion in translations) at Shechem. Abraham erected an altar to God at the site. Abraham also lived among the sacred trees of Mamre at Hebron, where he erected another altar to God. It was there that three angels, disguised as men, visited him one day when he was en route to destroy Sodom and Gomorrah. He extended them his hospitality, feeding them as they rested beneath a large terebinth. In return the angels forecast the birth of a son to the elderly Abraham and his elderly wife.

An angel of the Lord came down from heaven and sat underneath a sacred oak or terebinth of Ophrah. GIDEON, who was threshing wheat, stopped to feed the stranger lamb meat, and broth and unleavened cakes. The angel turned away the food and told Gideon to lay the meat and cakes on a rock and pour the broth over them. The angel then touched the rock with his staff, causing it to burst into flames and consume the food. The angel vanished, and Gideon built an altar to God at the site.

The sacred tree of Mamre and its site became an object of adoration for centuries, according to early historians. Eusebius, bishop of Caesarea, reported that the spot was revered as divine by the local population, in commemoration of Abraham as the founder of Israel. The three angels also were worshipped, and pictures of them and other idols were placed under the tree. However, a pilgrim of Bordeaux, who wrote the *Itinerary of Jerusalem*, said in 333 that the tree itself no longer existed at that time, but the site was worshipped. St. Jerome (c. 347–420?), a church father, also implied that the tree was no longer standing.

Every year until the time of Constantine and perhaps later, a festival was held at "the oak of Mamre" during the summer, attended by the local people and by distant Phoenicians and Arabs as well. According to the church historian Sozomenus:

> Very many also assemble for trade, to buy and sell; for every one sets great store on the festival. The Jews do so because they pride themselves on Abraham as their founder; the Greeks do so on account of the visit of the angels; and the Christians do so because there appeared at that time to the pious man One who in after ages made himself manifest through the Virgin for the salvation of mankind. Each, after the manner of his faith, does honor to the place, some praying to the God of all, some invoking the angels and pouring wine, or offering incense, or an ox, or a goat, or a sheep, or a cock. For every man fattened a valu-

able animal throughout the year, vowing to keep it for himself and his family to feast upon at the festival on the spot. And all of them here refrain from women, either out of respect to the place or lest some evil should befall them through the wrath of God, though the women beautify and adorn their persons specially, as at the festival, and show themselves freely in public. Yet there is no lewd conduct, thought the sexes camp together and sleep promiscuously.

The idolatry, "unclean sacrifices," and sexual behavior enraged the emperor Constantine (288?–337, *r.* 310–337), a convert to Christianity. Constantine declared that all idols should be burned and the altar at the site overturned. In a letter to Eusebius he said that "the spot shall be adorned with the pure building of a basilica, in order that it may be made a meeting-place worthy of holy men."

**Further reading:**
Frazer, Sir James G. *Folklore in the Old Testament*. New York: Avenel Books, 1988. Abridged ed.

**tutelary spirit**   See ANGEL; GUARDIAN SPIRIT; INTELLIGENCES.

**Uriel** In noncanonical literature one of the most important angels, described variously as an archangel, a seraph and a cherub. The name "Uriel" probably means "Fire of God" or "God is my light."

Uriel is portrayed as a stern and punishing angel. The prophet ENOCH said that he is head of the seven archangels and presides over Tartarus or Hell, where he pursues the punishment of sinners. According to the *Apocalypse of St. Peter*, this punishment consists of burning sinners in everlasting fire and hanging blasphemers by their tongues over unquenchable fires. On Judgment Day he will break the brazen gates of Hades and assemble all the souls before the Judgment Seat.

Uriel also served as a guide to Enoch on his trip through the layers of heavens.

As a cherub, Uriel is said to guard the Gate of Eden with a fiery sword in hand. The Book of Enoch describes him as the angel who "watches over thunder and terror." He also appears as a "benign angel" who attacks Moses for not observing the circumcision rite of his son, a role also credited to GABRIEL.

Uriel is among the angels identified as the dark angel who wrestles with Jacob. In the Prayer of Joseph, part of the PSEUDEPIGRAPHA, Uriel states, "I have come down to earth to make my dwelling among men, and I am called Jacob by name." The exact meaning of this statement is not clear, but it suggests that Uriel may have become Jacob, thus making him the first angel of record to become a mortal.

Various Hebrew sources relate the story that when Cain killed Abel and tried to bury the corpse, Earth spewed it up again and cried, "I will receive no other body until the clay that was fashioned into Adam has been restored to me!" At this Cain fled, and MICHAEL, GABRIEL, Uriel and RAPHAEL placed the corpse upon a rock, where it remained many years without corrupting. When Adam died, these same archangels buried both bodies at Hebron side by side, in the very field from which God had taken Adam's dust.

The midrashim say that the fallen angels Azael and Shemhazzi (see SONS OF GOD) were causing such wickedness on earth among the Canaanites that the four archangels told God, and God sent Raphael to bind Azael hand and foot, heaping jagged rocks over him in the dark Cave of Dudael, where he now abides until the Last Days. Gabriel destroyed the Fallen Ones by inciting them to civil war. Michael chained Shemhazzi and his fellows in other dark caves for seventy generations. Uriel became the messenger of salvation who visited Noah. Dispatched by METATRON, he warns Noah of the coming Flood.

Uriel (from *The Angels Tarot* by Rosemary Ellen Guiley and Robert Michael Place reprinted courtesy of HarperSanFrancisco)

Like Metatron, Uriel also is credited with giving the gift of the Kabbalah to humanity. He is said to have led Abraham out of Ur, and interpreted prophecies for the benefit of humanity. In the pseudepigraphical Fourth Book of Ezra,

Uriel reveals heavenly mysteries to Ezra and answers weighty questions about evil and justice. He serves as a guide of the luminaries.

Uriel appears in Qumrun scrolls, the *Gospel of Barnabas*. By the name SARIEL this archangel is designated one of the four leaders of the "War of the Sons of Light and the Sons of Darkness," a section of another of the Dead Sea Scrolls, *The Triumph of God*. The human warriors are given exact instructions on who is to fight where, with weapons described carefully. There are four subdivisions, and each is to have the name of his archangel inscribed on his shield.

A church council in Rome in 745 reprobated (condemned) Uriel, but later reinstated him as Saint Uriel. He is often portrayed as holding a flame in his open hand.

**Further reading:**

Davidson, Gustav. *A Dictionary of Angels*. New York: The Free Press, 1967.

Gaster, Theodor H. *The Dead Sea Scriptures*, third ed. Garden City, N.Y.: Anchor/Doubleday, 1976.

Godwin, Malcolm. *Angels: An Endangered Species*. New York: Simon & Schuster, 1990.

Margolies, Morris B. *A Gathering of Angels*. New York: Ballantine Books, 1994.

# V

**Victory**   The winged Roman goddess of victory, adopted from the similar Greek deity, NIKE, served as a model for the winged angel of Christian art.

Victory symbolizes invincibility. In mythology she is the daughter of Pallas and Styx. The Romans used her as a symbol of the invincibility of their own empire, and she became the protector of the Roman city and state. But as emperors and others converted to Christianity, Victory kept her place alongside Christian imagery, such as angels. Like angels, Victory acted as a messenger of the gods, especially bestowing news of victory in battle.

In art, Victory is shown as an obviously female figure, with prominent breasts. Usually, one breast is exposed from the flowing tunic; sometimes she is portrayed naked with a mantle. She is crowned with laurel. She holds medallions and palm branches, which Christian artists borrowed for their angels. Her image appears in funerary art, ceremonial and triumphal art, statuary, and on coins.

While Victory joined winged angels in art of the Roman Empire beginning in the fourth century, she never became confused with angels, nor became an angel. She was always distinguished from them by her female form. It was not until the Renaissance that Christian artists began to portray angels as females.

See WINGS.

**virtues**   See CHOIRS.

**visions**   See ANGELOPHANY.

**Vodun**   See ORISHAS.

**village-angel**   See HINDUISM.

**Watchers**  See DANIEL; SONS OF GOD.

**Weyer, Johann** (1515–1588)  German physician who opposed the torture and execution of alleged witches during the Inquisition and who cataloged the demons of hell.

Johann Weyer was born to a noble Protestant family in Brabant. He studied medicine in Paris and became a physician, serving as a court physician to the Duke of Cleves in the Netherlands. His sympathy for witches was influenced by one of his teachers, the famous occultist Agrippa von Nettesheim, who had successfully defended an accused witch only to suffer personally for it.

Weyer believed in the devil and his legions of demons, but did not believe that witches were empowered by the devil to harm humankind. Nor did he believe stories of flying through the air and attendance at sabbats in which the devil was worshiped and babies were eaten. He thought that belief in witchcraft was caused by the devil, and that the church ironically served the cause of the devil by promoting belief in the evil power of witches.

In his book *De praestigiis daemonum* (1563), Weyer gave a rational analysis of reports of alleged witch activity, and concluded that most witches were deluded and mentally disturbed old women, outcasts of society who were fools, not heretics. Some might wish to inflict harm on their neighbors, but were powerless to do so. If harm occurred coincidentally, they believed in their delusion that they had brought it about. He did believe that some witches served Satan and did harm people, but not through supernatural means. He urged the church to forgive those who repented or, at most, to levy fines upon them.

Weyer successfully discouraged witchhunting in much of the Netherlands for a while, but was forced out by the Catholic governor, the duke of Alba. His book had almost the opposite effect of what he had intended. He was savagely denounced by critics such as Jean Bodin and King James I, both of whom advocated the extermination of witches. James's authoring of his anti-witch treatise, *Daemonologie*, was done in response to Weyer and another witch sympathizer, Reginald Scot. Bodin urged that copies of Weyer's book be burned. Others wrote books refuting Weyer, and these helped to stimulate more witch hunts. Weyer himself was accused of being a witch.

Weyer then turned his attention to cataloging the realms of hell, just as theologians had cataloged the realms of heaven. In 1568, he published the *Pseudo-Monarchy of Demons*, an inventory and description of Satan's legions. He cited 7,405,926 devils and demons organized in 1,111 divisions of 6,666 each,

**Johann Weyer**

ruled over by 72 princes. Later the Lutheran church thought his estimate too low, and raised the census of the demonic population to 2,665,866,746,664, or roughly 2.6 trillion.

See DEMON.

**Further reading:**

Ankarloo, Bengt, and Gustav Henningsen, eds. *Early Modern European Witchcraft: Centres and Peripheries*. Oxford, England: Clarendon Press, 1990.

Russell, Jeffrey B. *A History of Witchcraft*. London: Thames & Hudson, 1980.

**Williard, Samuel**  See PROTESTANT ANGELOLOGY.

**wings**  The image of angels as humanlike beings with wings—so prevalent in modern thought—did not become fixed in art until the fourth century C.E. The evolution of the wing closely follows theological thought on angels.

Wings denote spirituality and divine purpose, speed, and the ability to mediate between the physical and nonphysical realms. The endowment of wings on spiritual beings is an ancient idea, but one that developed in the West more so than in the East. Eastern deities, saints and spiritual beings move about without the benefit of wings, which are not necessary to navigate in the world of illusion. In art they are shown descending from the sky or hovering in the air, held up by the weightlessness of their own divinity.

### HISTORY OF THE WINGED ANGEL

In the ninth century B.C.E., the Assyrians began to place wings on the shoulders of their protective geniuses, despite the fact that their bodies seemed too heavy and muscle-bound for celestial flight. These divine beings were depicted in art as being human figures with wings. The *kari-bu*, a half-human, half-animal figure that guarded buildings, also had wings. The ancient Egyptians also employed wings, such as the human-headed bird that represents the *ba*, the eternal part of the soul.

Probably the greatest influences on the winged angel came out of Greek and Roman mythology. NIKE, the winged goddess of victory, was adopted as Victoria or VICTORY by the Romans. To the Romans she symbolized the invincibility of the Roman Empire, a trait borrowed by the Christians and converted to represent the invincibility of Christ. In art, the Winged Victory customarily was depicted with one breast exposed, and sometimes naked with a mantle of drapery flowing around her. Her image was adopted into sacred art in Egypt and Syria.

The Christian angel was inherited from the Hebrews. However, the Jews prohibited figurative representations of their religious concepts. The canonical scriptures give scant information on the appearance of angels. The Bible describes the seraphim and cherubim as having wings, but otherwise says that angels "came," "stood" or "went" without offering details as to how they moved about. Angels appeared as lightning and flame (see ENOCH; MOSES) and as humanlike beings (see ABRAHAM; TOBIT; JACOB) that passed for mortals. Even the angels of the New Testament are not described as winged. GABRIEL, in announcing the birth of Jesus to Mary, merely "comes in" and "departs." The angel who announced the birth of Jesus to the shepherds just appeared "suddenly" and "came upon them" in the night. Thus, early angel art portrayed angels as ennobled, ethereal male humans without wings.

Though angels played an important role in Christian piety from a very early stage, it was not until 325 that the Council of Nicea made belief in angels a part of dogma. This stimulated theological discussions and writings on angels, including the matter of angels' flight. Art followed the direction that the Church fathers pointed toward. The winged, hovering angel evolved dramatically during the fourth century, creating a formula that dominated art throughout the sixth century. This formula reappeared again in Carolingian art (eighth century) and the Romanesque art of Italy and southern France

Angel with swanlike wings announcing birth of Jesus

(mid-eleventh to mid-twelfth centuries). By the end of the fourth century, Christian artists had turned to the pagan religions for inspiration. They borrowed heavily from the Greek idea that divinity has shape and is humanlike, and from the Roman image of Victory. However, they refrained from frank nakedness and sexuality. Their angels were adult males but without pronounced sexual characteristics—almost androgynous in appearance—and were fully clothed, with a standard tunic and mantle. Their wings often were not pronounced in size or detail. By the end of the fifth century the winged, hovering angel had become standard, even in Persian art that was absorbed into Islam (Persian angels tend to have smaller, thinner wings than Christian angels).

The formulaic angel—winged, male, clothed in flowing tunic and mantle—sometimes appeared in the early centuries alongside images of Victory and the EROTES in funerary art. Yet it was readily distinguished from those figures by its maturity, clothing, and lack of sexual features. Angels were often shown in pairs, holding wreaths with the medallion of Christ or the cross of Christ, or other ceremonial symbols. Generally, however, angels were reserved for depiction of the central themes in Christianity and not the mundane affairs of humans.

The purposes of these winged angels included demonstration of their role as

- Divine messengers of God, sent to execute the will of God
- Guardians of, and attendants to, Christ
- Guides of the soul to eternity, or heaven
- Important participants in ceremonies
- Heralds of the Last Judgment

By the fourteenth century, theological interest in angels had peaked and begun to decline. The Inquisition focused attention on fallen angels—the demons who tempted people into sin and witchcraft. These beings were given ugly, batlike wings by artists. The Reformation of the sixteenth century further diminished the importance of the heavenly angel.

This decline was mirrored in changes in angel art. Renaissance artists began to portray angels as male youths and especially women, signifying that angels no longer held central stage in theology. Ironically, this shift produced some of the greatest and most beautiful angel art: depictions of glorious beings with enormous, elegant, wings and exquisite, flowing garments. Artists turned to birds such as the eagle and the swan for their models of wings. They gave them rainbow hues. The rainbow is a symbol of the bridge to heaven, and underscores the angel's role as intermediary between heaven and earth.

The Renaissance image of the angel remains imbedded in our collective mind as what an angel "should" look like, and dominates modern renditions of angels. Today, angels in art are just as likely to be feminine as masculine; children often are used as models as well (see PUTTI).

### WINGED ANGELS IN MODERN ENCOUNTERS

Despite what we think angels "should" look like in art, most modern anecdotal reports of real-life encounters with angels do not involve beings with wings (see ANGELOPHANY). Visual apparitions usually are of balls of white or white-gold light, or of columns or pillars of light that vaguely resemble or suggest human form. Sometimes such figures seem to be wearing flowing, glowing white drapery that suggests the shape of wings, but without clear definition.

The so-called mysterious stranger is an intervening figure that passes for a human being, like the three "men" who came and visited Abraham and the "man" who accompanied Tobias on his journey.

**Further reading:**

Berefelt, Gunnar. *A Study on the Winged Angel: The Origin of a Motif.* Stockholm: Almquist & Wiksell, 1968.

Guiley, Rosemary Ellen. *Angles of Mercy.* New York: Pocket Books, 1994.

Highet, Gilbert. "An Iconography of Heavenly Beings," *Horizon,* Vol. III, No. 2, November 1960, pp. 26–49.

**witches**   See DEMONS.

**wormwood**   According to the Book of REVELATION, Wormwood is the name of a fallen angel who will bring plagues upon the earth during the end times. The name Wormwood means "bitterness," and is derived from the Latin term *absinthium*.

Revelation tells of the end times of the world. It says that God sits on his throne, holding a huge book fastened by seven seals. When Christ breaks the seals, each releases a disaster upon the earth. The seventh and last seal brings seven disasters, each ushered in by the trumpet blast of an angel.

Wormwood is a star (angel) that falls from heaven at the trumpet blast of the third angel, and poisons many waters of the earth, causing multitudes to die. Revelation 8:10–11 states:

> The third angel blew his trumpet and a great star fell from heaven, blazing like a torch, and it fell on a third of the rivers and on the fountains of water. The name of the star is Wormwood. A third of the waters became wormwood, and many men died of the water, because it was made bitter.

**Yazata**  See ZOROASTRIANISM.

**yidam**  See TANTRIC BUDDHISM.

# Z

**Zechariah** See ANGEL OF THE LORD; JESUS.

**zodiac angels** In occult lore, twelve angels assigned to rule over the twelve houses of the zodiac.

In *The Book of Secret Things*, written in the late Middle Ages by occultist Johannes Trithemius, the signs and their respective governing angels are set forth as follows:

*Aries the Ram:* Malahidael or Machidiel
*Taurus the Bull:* Asmodel
*Gemini the Twins:* Ambriel
*Cancer the Crab:* Muriel
*Leo the Lion:* Verchiel
*Virgo the Virgin:* Hamaliel
*Libra the Scales:* Uriel or Zuriel
*Scorpio the Scorpion:* Barbiel
*Sagittarius the Archer:* Advachiel or Adnachiel
*Capricorn the Goat:* Hanael
*Aquarius the Water-Carrier:* Cambiel or Gabriel
*Pisces the Fishes:* Barchiel

The association of angels with the zodiac probably is borrowed from similar associations of governing deities with the signs made by the Chaldeans or Babylonians, who formalized the Zodiac *c.* 3000 B.C.E.

Francis Barrett, a noted English occultist of the nineteenth century, drew a connection between the angels of the zodiac and the twelve angels mentioned in the Book of REVELATION. In John of Patmos's vision of the holy city of New Jerusalem, descending from the heavens, there is a high wall with twelve gates, each of which is guarded by an unnamed angel.

In ceremonial magic, the names of zodiac angels are invoked in rituals pertaining to astrological influences. The angels are petitioned for help in effecting spells and enchantments.

**Further reading:**
Barrett, Francis. *The Magus.* Secaucus, N.J.: The Citadel Press, 1967. First published 1801.

**Zoroastrianism** Zoroaster (the Greek version of the Persian Zarathustra), the prophet from whom the ancient Iranian religion took its name, was born perhaps as early as 650 B.C.E. The most ancient documents from which scholars have worked are fragmentary and difficult to translate. Controversy has raged as a result of the lack of evidence on

**Gemini, the Twins, depicted as angels (Hyginus, *Poeticon Astronomicon,* 1504)**

even when and where Zarathustra lived. Rudolph STEINER maintained that the first prophet named Zarathustra lived earlier than recorded history, and that subsequent followers were named for him. Hence, documents attributed to Zarathustra have been dated hundreds of years apart. One of them comprised the *Gathas*, songs or odes of the sacred book of Zoroastrianism, the Avesta, containing the religion's central doctrines.

Zoroastrianism established a dualistic cosmology in which the conflict between the forces of good and evil is played out on a hierarchical scale of spiritual and material spheres. Such dualism was a dramatic departure from the polytheism of the *Yashts*, a document similar to the song-cycle of the earliest Indo-Aryans, the *Rig-Veda* (see HINDUISM), but the common origins of the two religions are obvious from the fact that the demigods of the *Yashts* share names with the Hindu pantheon and later reappear as Zoroastrian angels.

As a direct result of Zoroastrian reform, the gods and demigods called *devas* in the *Veda* were demonized, and the other class of deity called *ahura* by Iranians and *asura* by the

Indians were eliminated, with the exception of Ahura Mazda (later called Ohrmazd), who was elevated to the status of the one true God from whom all other divinities proceeded. Over and against the God stood Angra Mainyu (Hindu Aryaman), later Ahriman, the Destructive Spirit. Life on earth was presented as a battle between Ahura Mazda and his attendant powers on one hand and Angra Mainyu and his demonic hordes on the other. For Zarasthustra it was a very real battle, since *deva* worshippers were still adherents of the traditional religion, and these he roundly identified with all that is evil.

Against Ohrmazd stands Ahriman. (Steiner used the name Ahriman to represent a specific negative force in his spiritual system applied to the millennium 2000 C.E.). In the *Bundahishn*, or Book of the Primal Creation, is recounted the following story. The two antagonists had always existed in time, but when Ohrmazd first chanted the *Ahunvar* (True Speech), the key prayer of Zoroastrianism (similar to "In the beginning was the Word," opening the Gospel of St. John), it revealed to Ahriman that all was really lost, and his annihilation was certain. Assaulted by this truth, Ahriman fell unconscious for three thousand years while Ohrmazd created the universe, the two worlds (spiritual and material), as a weapon with which to defeat Ahriman. An unorthodox document called the *Zurvan* indicates that early creation myths varied or were altered, for in the Zervanite version Ahriman creates first the Lying Word (the exact opposite of the *Ahunvar*) and then Akoman, the Evil Mind, which he could not do if he were unconscious.

By origin a spiritual being, the human soul, in the shape of what the Zoroastrians call *fravashi* or *fravahr*, preexists the human body. Both body and soul, however, are creatures of Ohrmazd, and the soul is not eternally preexistent as in many Eastern religions. Humankind belongs to God and to God will return. On earth each individual is free to choose good or evil, and if one chooses evil it is an unnatural act, because humans are begotten by Ohrmazd and his wife/daughter Spandarmat, the Earth. The orders of creation, interplaying spheres of beings and their adversaries, the drama of Gayomart, the first Primal Man, who mates with Ahriman's "Demon Whore"—all are highly reminiscent of GNOSTICISM and the myths surrounding SOPHIA. Zoroastrian myth is full of the archetypes Carl G. JUNG found active in the human psyche four thousand years later (see ABRAXAS); for example, the Terrible Mother (the Demon Whore) versus the Good Mother (Spandarmat). Humans, their thoughts, their acts, are in the forefront of the archetypal fray.

Since Zoroastrian and Hindu origins predate the historical record, it is reasonable to assume that their cosmologies and psychodynamic patterns reflect earliest human experience, thought and practice. Furthermore, the angelologies of the Western religions—Judaism, Christianity and Islam, both the Orthodox and Gnostic versions—each flowered in the Middle East, took the one preceding and accreted new elements, and resonated heavily with Zoroastrian angelology. Most particularly consistent is the opposition of God and Satan, played out in battles of the heavenly hosts against the demons. The Book of Job illustrates the early Jewish tradition in which SATAN was God's servant. Under Persian influence, after the seventh century B.C.E. captivity of the Jews in Babylon, Satan came to be regarded as the cosmic enemy of God, parallel to Ahriman.

Zoroastrianism accepts evil as a fact, not a problem, maintained Mardan-Farrukh in the ninth century C.E. A searching sage who returned to Zoroastrianism after exploring many other sects, he argued that once you admit the reality of evil, then God is responsible for it unless evil is an eternal principle coexistent with God and irreconcilably opposed to Him. Monotheistic systems cannot reconcile "evil" and/or the meaningless behavior of God. According to the Zoroastrian, the Moslem God is not good, neither does he pretend to be, while the Christian God advertises himself as good and plainly is not. The error of Manichaeism—that the body is composed of the substance of evil, a view which infected Christianity and Islam—is to the Zoroastrian unnatural, perverted and blasphemous.

For Zoroastrians neither evil nor creation is mysterious, and there is no problem of evil because it is a separate principle and substance standing over against the good God and threatening to destroy him. The duration of this conflict is limited; Ohrmazd will defeat Ahriman. God needs man's help in his battle with the "Lie," as the principle of evil is frequently called in the ancient documents. Evil is not identified with matter, as was the case with the Manichees. Rather, the material world is the handiwork of God, a weapon fashioned by the Deity with which to smite the Evil One. The world is the trap that God sets for the Devil, and in the end Ohrmazd will deal Ahriman the death blow. Both are accompanied by subsidiary created spirits.

Ohrmazd is helped by the six Amahraspands (or Amesha Spenta), Bounteous Immortals, which correspond to archangels. Each adopts one of the material creations, after Ohrmazd adopts Man. The names of the six are personifications of abstract concepts or virtues:

1. Vahuman: Good Thought, Good Mind

2. Artvahisht: Best Righteousness or Truth

3. Shahrevar: the Choice Kingdom, Material Sovereignty

4. Spandarmat: Bounteous Right-Mindedness, Wisdom in Piety, who is in fact identified with the earth

5. Hurdat: Health, Wholeness, Salvation

6. Amurdat: Life or Immortality

These six were created by Ohrmazd to aid him through their creative and organizing activity; by preference he acts through their ministering hands. They receive special worship in ritual and are said to descend to the oblation on paths of gold. Each has a specific character and sphere. Vahuman was Ohrmazd's first creation and his chief promoter. He welcomes the blessed souls, leads Zarathustra to Ohrmazd, is invoked for peace, and had special charge over useful animals. Artvahisht personifies divine law and order, and rules all fires. Shahrevar personifies Ohrmazd's might, majesty, regal power and triumph, and presides over metals, his signs and symbols. Spandarmat is daughter of Ohrmazd and heaven; she personifies religious harmony and piety and presides over the earth, which manifests her bounty. Hurdat and Amurdat are two feminine archangels always mentioned together. The first personifies complete health and perfection, and the other immortality.

They are the promised reward of the blessed after death, in paradise. Their charges are water and plants, respectively. Each holy one has a month assigned in its honor, a special day as a holy day, and a flower as an appropriate emblem. The Amahraspands are everywhere in the Zoroastrian system, and probably originated with the prophet himself.

Beneath the six stand the Yazatas, "adorable beings" who serve like the Amahraspands, are legion, and are divided into heavenly (spiritual) and earthly (material) subcategories. Ohrmazd himself leads the spiritual and Zarathustra the material Yazatas. They have assignments similar to the celestial INTELLIGENCES and the daemons of water, air, fire, and earth. The first month of the year is dedicated to the *fravishi*, who encompass not only individual human souls and guardian angels, but also local genii (see GENIUS).

Ahriman is served by a host of demons, most of which are personified vices such as concupiscence, anger, sloth, and heresy, but there are six arch-demons who oppose the Amahraspands. Against Vahuman is set Akoman, the Evil Mind. Against Artvahisht is Andra (Hindu Indra), against Shahrevar is Saru (the tyrant), against Spandarmat is Naoghatya (arrogance), and against Hurdat and Amurdat are Taru and Zarika, evil hunger and evil thirst. The arch-fiends aim to destroy the work and influence of the good spirits. The *Bundahishn* states that they are assisted by "demons, too, who are furies in great multitude. They are demons of ruin, pain, and growing old, producers of vexation and vile revivers of grief, the progeny of gloom and vileness, who are many, very numerous, and very notorious."

Because Zoroastrians believe that their role in this world is to cooperate with nature and to lead a virtuous life, no religion has been so opposed to all forms of asceticism and monasticism. It is their bound duty to marry and rear children, for the simple reason that human life on earth is a sheer necessity if Ahriman is to be defeated. Similarly, Zoroastrianism makes a positive virtue of agriculture, making the earth fruitful, strong and abundant in order to resist the Enemy, who is the author of disease and death.

There is a rigid dogmatism with regard to preserving the purity of the body, the care of useful animals, agricultural practice, and strict ritual observance. Celibacy is both unnatural and wicked.

On the moral plane all the emphasis is on righteousness or truth and on doing good works, for deeds are the criterion by which alone one is judged after parting this life on the "Bridge of the Requiter," the bridge of Rashn the Righteous, who impartially weighs each soul's good and evil deeds. If there is a preponderance of good, the soul proceeds to Heaven, but if evil, it is dragged off to Hell. There is a place where one goes if the good and evil deeds are exactly equal, but the comparison with Purgatory is inexact because "the place of the mixed" is not a place of purgation but of mild correction, in which the only pains suffered are those of heat and cold. The Zoroastrian Hell is like the Christian Purgatory, in that the punishment is only temporary. The final purgation from sin takes place at the Last Judgment at the end of time. The stain left by sin is purged from all souls, and from this all without exception emerge spotless. No one is punished eternally for sins committed in time.

Sin is viewed as a sheer perversity; it is a failure to recognize who is your friend and who is your enemy. In Zoroastrianism God is one's friend and Ahriman is the enemy, from whom all evil and suffering proceed. Thus, for a Zoroastrian to admit that God even permits evil is tantamount to attributing to him qualities which are indeed proper to Ahriman, equivalent to changing God into a demon. Monotheists have been deceived in this way, and this represents a genuine triumph for Ahriman, for besides being the Destroyer, he is also the Deceiver, the Liar, and his deception takes the form of persuading men that evil proceeds from God. But his triumph is short-lived, for in the end all human souls, reunited with their bodies, return to Ohrmazd, who is their creator and father.

The Islamic conquest of Iran in the seventh century sent all other sects into disarray; many Zoroastrians went east to India, where they are called Parsis. Today there are only about 150,000 followers, of whom most live in and around Bombay, India.

**Further reading:**

Dhalla, Maneckji Nusservanji. *History of Zoroastrianism*. New York and Oxford: Oxford University Press, 1938. Reprint AMS Press, 1977.

Zaehner, R.C. *The Dawn and Twilight of Zoroastrianism*. New York: Putnam, 1961.

# BIBLIOGRAPHY

Adler, Mortimer J. *The Angels and Us.* New York: Collier Books/Macmillan, 1982.

Alexander, Pat. ed. *The Lion Encyclopedia of the Bible.* Batavia, Ill.: Lion Publishing, 1986.

Allison, Alexander W., et. al. *The Norton Anthology of Poetry*, Third ed. New York: W. W. Norton & Co., 1983.

Altman, Nathaniel. "The Orishas: Communing with Angels in the Candomble Tradition of Brazil," in *Angels & Mortals: Their Co-Creative Power*, Maria Parisen, comp., Wheaton, Ill.: Quest Books, Theosophical Publishing House, 1990.

Anderson, E. *The Letters of Mozart and His Family*, third ed. New York: Norton, 1990.

Ankarloo, Bengt, and Gustav Henningsed, eds. *Early Modern European Witchcraft: Centers and Peripheries.* Oxford: Clarendon Press, 1990.

Arintero, Juan. *Mystical Evolution in the Development and Vitality of the Church, Vol. I.* St. Louis: B. Herder, 1949.

Arthos, John. *Dante, Michaelangelo and Milton.* London: Routledge and Kegan Paul, 1963.

Arthur, Ruth Horman. *The Wisdom Goddess: Feminine Motifs in Eight Nag Hammadi Documents.* Lanham, Md.: University Press of America, 1984.

Attwater, Donald. *The Penguin Book of Saints.* Baltimore: Penguin Books, Inc., 1965.

———. *A Dictionary of Mary.* New York: P.J. Kennedy, 1960.

Atwater, P. M. H. "Perelandra: Cooperating Co-creatively with Nature," *New Realities*, May/June 1988, pp. 17–20+.

Augustine. *Confessions.* F. J. Sheed, trans. New York: Sheed and Ward, 1943, 1970.

———. *The City of God.* Trans. Marcus Dods, George Wilson and J.J. Smith. Introduction by Thomas Merton. New York: Modern Library, 1950.

Barnstone, Willis, ed. *The Other Bible.* San Francisco: HarperSan-Francisco, 1984.

Barrett, Francis. *The Magus.* Secaucus, N.J.: The Citadel Press, 1967. First published 1801.

Barrett, William. *Death-Bed Visions: The Psychical Experiences of the Dying.* Wellingborough, Northhamptonshire: The Aquarian Press, 1986. First published 1926.

Barth, Karl. *Church Dogmatics*, Edinburgh: T & T Clark, 1960.

Battenhouse, Roy W., ed. *A Companion to the Study of St. Augustine.* New York: Oxford University Press, 1955.

Beasley-Murray, G. R. "The Interpretation of Daniel 7," *The Catholic Biblical Quarterly*, Vol. 45, No. 1, January 1985.

Bell, Rudolph. *Holy Anorexia.* Chicago: University of Chicago Press, 1985.

Berefelt, Gunnar. *A Study on the Winged Angel: The Origin of a Motif.* Stockholm: Almquist & Wiksell, 1968.

Bishop, Eric F. F. "Angelology in Judaism, Islam and Christianity," *Anglican Theological Review*, Vol XLVI, Jan. 1964.

Blavatsky, H.P. *The Secret Doctrine.* Pasadena, Calif.: Theosophical University Press, 1977. First published 1888.

Blofeld, John. *The Tantric Mysticism of Tibet.* New York: E. P. Dutton & Co., 1970.

Blumenthal, David R. "Maimonides on Angel Names," *Hellenica and Judaica.* A. Caquot, ed. Paris: Editions Peeters, 1986.

*The Book of Mormon: An Account Written by the Hand of Mormon Upon Plates taken from the Plates of Nephi.* Joseph Smith, Jr., trans. First published 1830. Salt Lake City, Utah: The Church of Christ of Latter-day Saints, 1981.

Bourke, Vernon J. *Wisdom from St. Augustine.* St. Thomas, Texas: Center for Thomistic Studies, 1984.

Bowman, J. W. "Book of Revelation" in *The Interpreter's Dictionary of the Bible.* New York: Abingdon Press, 1962.

Bramley, William. *The Gods of Eden.* San Jose: Dahlin Family Press, 1989.

Brooke, John L. *The Refiner's Fire: The Making of Mormon Cosmology, 1644–1844.* New York and Cambridge, England: Cambridge University Press, 1994.

Brown, Peter. *Augustine of Hippo.* Berkeley: University of California Press, 1967.

Burckhardt, Titus. *Alchemy: Science of the Cosmos, Science of the Soul.* London: Stuart and Watkins, 1967.

Bush, Douglas, ed. *The Portable Milton.* New York: The Viking Press, 1949.

Bushman, Richard L. *Joseph Smith and the Beginnings of Mormonism.* Urbana and Chicago: University of Illinois Press, 1984.

Cady, Susan; Ronan, Marian; Taussig, Hal. *Sophia: The Future of Feminist Spirituality.* San Francisco: Harper & Row, 1986.

Caird, G.B. *Principalities and Powers: A Study in Pauline Theology.* Oxford University Press, 1966.

———. *A Commentary on the Revelation of St. John the Divine.* New York: Harper & Row, 1966.

Calvin, John. *Institutes of the Christian Religion.* Ed. John T. McNeill, trans. Fred Lewis Battles. Philadelphia: Westminster Press, 1960.

Carter, George William. *Zoroastrianism and Judaism.* New York: AMS Press, 1970.

*The Catechism Explained.* Rockford, Ill.: Tan Books and Publishers, 1921.

Cavendish, Richard. *The Black Arts.* New York: Perigee Books, 1967.

———. *Visions of Heaven and Hell.* London: Orbis Publishing, 1970.

Cavendish, Richard, ed. *Man, Myth & Magic: The Illustrated Encyclopedia of Mythology, Religion and the Unknown.*, Vol. 11. New York: Marshall Cavendish Ltd., 1985, p. 2963.

Cellini, Benvenuto. *Autobiography.* New York: P.F. Collier, c. 1910.

Chadwick, Henry. *Early Christian Thought and the Classical Tradition.* New York: Oxford University Press, 1966.

Chessman, Harriett Scott, ed. *Literary Angels.* New York: Fawcett Columbine, 1994.

Christian, William A., Jr. *Apparitions in Late Medieval and Renaissance Spain.* Princeton: Princeton University Press, 1981.

Chua-Eoan, Howard G. "Sympathy for the Devil," *Time*, December 27, 1993, pp. 60–61.

Cicciari, Massimo. *The Necessary Angel.* Albany: State University of New York Press, 1994.

Clark, Mary T. *An Aquinas Reader*. New York: Fordham University Press, 1988.

Connolly, David. *In Search of Angels*. New York: Perigee Books, 1993.

Corbin, Henry. *Avicenna and the Visionary Recital*. Trans. William R. Trask. Princeton University Press: Bollingen Series LXVI, 1960, 1988.

———. *Creative Imagination in the Sufism of Ibn 'Arabi*. Trans. Ralph Manheim. Princeton University Press: Bollingen Series XCI, 1969.

———. *History of Islamic Philosophy*. Trans. Liadain Sherrard. London: Kegan Paul International, 1993.

Crim, Keith, general ed. *Abingdon Dictionary of Living Religions*. Nashville: Abingdon Press, 1981.

Cross, F.L. *The Early Christian Fathers*. London: Gerald Duckworth & Co., 1960.

Crouzel, Henri. *Origen*. A.S. Worrall, trans. San Francisco: Harper and Row, 1989.

Danielou, Jean. *Origen*. Walter Mitchell, trans. New York: Sheed and Ward, 1955.

Dante Alighieri. *The Divine Comedy*. John Ciardi, trans. New York: W. W. Norton & Co., 1961.

———. *La Vita Nuova*. Barbara Reynolds, trans. Harmondsworth, Middlesex, England: Penguin Books, 1969.

Davidson, Gustav. *A Dictionary of Angels*. New York: The Free Press, 1967.

Davies, Brian. *The Thought of Thomas Aquinas*. Oxford: Clarendon Press, 1992.

De Givry, Emile Grillot. *Witchcraft, Magic and Alchemy*. New York: Dover Publications, 1971. First published 1931.

Dermenghem, Emile. *Muhammad and the Islamic Tradition*. Woodstock, N.Y.: The Overlook Press, 1981. First published 1955.

Dhalla, Maneckji Nusservanji. *History of Zoroastrianism*. New York and Oxford: Oxford University Press, 1938, reprint AMS Press, 1977.

Downing, Barry H. *The Bible & Flying Saucers*. New York: Lippincott, 1968.

Eliade, Mircea. *Images and Symbols*. Princeton: Princeton University Press, 1991. First published 1952.

———. *The Myth of the Eternal Return*. Princeton: Princeton University Press, 1971. First published 1954.

———. *Shamanism*. Princeton, N.J.: Princeton University Press, 1964.

Elledge, Scott, ed. *John Milton: Paradise Lost. An Authoritative Text*. New York: W. W. Norton & Co., 1975.

Engle, David. *Divine Dreams*. Holmes Beach, Fla.: Christopher Books, 1994.

*The Essence of Plotinus*. Stephen MacKenna, trans., Grace H. Turnbull, ed. New York: Oxford University Press, 1948.

Evans, Hilary. *Gods, Spirits, Cosmic Guardians: A Comparative Study of the Encounter Experience*. Wellingborough, Northamptonshire: The Aquarian Press, 1987.

Every, George. *Christian Mythology*. London: The Hamlyn Publishing Group Ltd., 1970.

Field, M. J. *Angels and Ministers of Grace: An Ethno-Psychiatrist's Contribution to Biblical Criticism*. New York: Hill & Wang, 1971.

Findhorn Community. *The Findhorn Garden*. New York: Harper & Row Perennial Library, 1975.

Fowler, Raymond. *The Watchers*. New York: Bantam Books, 1990.

Frazer, James G. *Folklore in the Old Testament*. Abridged ed. New York: Avenel Books, 1988.

———. *The Golden Bough*. New York: Avenel Books, 1981. First published in 1890.

Freeman, Eileen Elias. *Touched by Angels*. New York: Warner Books, 1993.

Frymer-Kensy, Tivka. *In The Wake of the Goddess: Women's Culture and the Biblical Transformation of Pagan Myth*. New York: Fawcett Columbine Books, 1992.

Gaster, Theodor H. *The Dead Sea Scriptures*. Third ed. Garden City, New York: Anchor/Doubleday, 1976.

Gatta, John J. "Little Lower than God: Super-Angelic Anthropology of Edward Taylor." *Harvard Theological Review*, Vol. 75 (July 1982), pp. 361–368.

Gibbs, Nancy. "Angels Among Us," *Time*, December 27, 1993.

Gilchrist, Cherry. "Dr. Dee and the Spirits," *Gnosis*, No. 35, Summer 1995, pp. 33–39.

Gilson, Etienne. *The Philosophy of St. Bonaventure*. London: Sheed and Ward, 1940.

———. *The Christian Philosophy of St. Thomas Aquinas*. L. K. Shock, trans. New York: Random House, 1966.

Ginzburg, Louis. *Legends of the Bible*. Philadelphia: The Jewish Publication Society, 1992.

Glasson, C. F. *The Revelation of John*. Cambridge: Cambridge University Press, 1965.

Godwin, Malcom. *Angels: An Endangered Species*. New York: Simon & Schuster, 1990.

Goethe, Johann Wolfgang von. *Faust*. Cyrus Hamlin, ed., Walter Arendt, trans. New York: Norton, 1976.

Good, Deirdre J. *Reconstructing the Tradition of Sophia in Gnostic Literature*. Atlanta: Scholars Press, 1987.

Gordon, Anne. *A Book of Saints*. New York: Bantam Books, 1994.

Graham, Billy. *Angels: God's Secret Agents*. New York: Doubleday & Co., 1975.

Grant, Robert. "Gnostic Spirituality." *Christian Spirituality I: Origins to 12th Century*, Bernard McGinn and John Meyendor, eds. New York: Crossroad, 1987.

Grant, Robert J. *Are We Listening to the Angels?* Virginia Beach, Va.: ARE Press, 1994.

Graves, Robert, and Patai, Raphael. *Hebrew Myths*. New York: Doubleday Anchor Books, 1964.

Greene, Thomas. *The Decent From Heaven: A Study of Epic Continuity*. New Haven: Yale University Press, 1963.

Grosso, Michael. *The Final Choice*. Walpole, N.H.: Stillpoint, 1985.

———. *The Millennium Myth: Love and Death at the End of Time*. Wheaton, Ill.: Quest Books, 1995.

———. "The Cult of the Guardian Angel," in *Angels and Mortals: Their Co-Creative Power*, compiled by Maria Parisen. Wheaton, Ill.: Quest Books, Theosophical Publishing House, 1990.

———. "UFOs and the Myth of the New Age," *ReVision*, Vol. 11, No. 3, Winter 1989, pp. 5–13.

Guiley, Rosemary Ellen. *Angels of Mercy*. New York: Pocket Books, 1994.

———. *The Encyclopedia of Witches and Witchcraft*. New York: Facts On File, 1989.

———. *Harper's Encyclopedia of Mystical and Paranormal Experience*. San Francisco: HarperSanFrancisco, 1991.

———. *The Miracle of Prayer: True Stories of Blessed Healings*. New York: Pocket Books, 1995.

———. "Behold the Kingdom of the Nature Gods," Parts I and II. *Fate*, May 1994, pp. 46–55; June 1994, pp. 37–41.

Halewood, William H. *Angels: Messengers of the Gods*. London: Thames and Hudson, 1980, 1994.

———. *Six Subjects of Reformation Art*. University of Toronto Press, 1982.

Harner Michael. *The Way of the Shaman*. New York: Bantam, 1986.

*Harpers Bible Commentary*. James L. Mays, gen. ed. San Francisco: HarperSanFrancisco.

Hawken, Paul. *The Magic of Findhorn*. New York: Bantam Books, 1976.

Heick, O. W. *A History of Christian Thought*. Philadelphia: Fortress Press, 1965.

Highet, Gilbert. "An Iconography of Heavenly Beings," *Horizon*, Vol. III, No. 2, Nov. 1960, pp. 26–49.

Hillman, James. *Archetypal Psychology*. Dallas, Texas: Spring Publications, 1983.

Hodson, Geoffrey. *The Kingdom of the Gods*. Adyar, Madras, India: The Theosophical Publishing House, 1972.

Hodson, Geoffrey. *The Brotherhood of Angels and Men*. Wheaton, Ill.: The Theosophical Publishing House, 1982.

Hoeller, Stephan A. *The Gnostic Jung and The Seven Sermons of the Dead*. Wheaton, Ill.: Quest Books, 1982.

Holmyard, E.J. *Alchemy*. Mineola, N.Y.: Dover Publications, 1990. First published 1957.

Howard, Jane M. *Commune with Angels*. Virginia Beach, Va.: A.R.E. Press, 1992.

Huber, Georges. *My Angel Will Go Before You*. Westminster, Md.: Christian Classics, 1983.

Hultkrantz, Ake. *The Religions of the American Indians*. Berkeley: University of California Press, 1979. First published 1967.

Humann, Harvey. *The Many Faces of Angels*. Marina del Rey, Calif.: DeVorss Publications, 1991.

Hyatt, Victoria, and Joseph W. Charles. *The Book of Demons*. New York: Fireside, 1974.

"Introduction to the Letters of St. Paul," *The Jerusalem Bible*. Garden City, N.Y.: Doubleday and Company, 1966.

Introduction and Notes, *The Jerusalem Bible*. Garden City, New York: Doubleday, 1966.

James, Jamie. *The Music of the Spheres*. New York: Grove Press, 1993.

Jonas, Hans. *The Gnostic Religion*, Second ed. Boston: Beacon Press, 1963.

Jung, Carl G. *Collected Works*. Sir Herbert Read, ed., R. F. C. Hull, trans. Princeton: Bollingen Series XX. Vols. 1–20, 1958 ff.

———. *The Archetypes and the Collective Unconscious*. Second ed. Bollingen Series XX. Princeton: Princeton University Press, 1968.

———. *Memories, Dreams and Reflections*. Aniela Jaffe, ed., Richard and Clara Winston, trans. New York: Pantheon, 1961.

King, Karen, ed. *Images of the Feminine in Gnosticism*. Philadelphia: Fortress Press, 1988.

Klein, F. A. *The Religion of Islam*. London, 1906, reprint 1971.

Knox, W.L. *St. Paul and the Church of the Gentiles*. Cambridge: Cambridge University Press, 1939.

Kramer, Heinrich, and James Sprenger. *The Malleus Maleficarum*. London: John Rodker, 1928.

Laccarriere, Jacques. *The Gnostics*. Translated by Nina Rootes. New York: City Lights, 1989.

Lachman, Gary. "Heavens and Hells: The Inner Worlds of Emanuel Swedenborg," *Gnosis*, No. 36, Summer 1995, pp. 44–49.

Laurence, Richard, trans. *The Book of Enoch the Prophet*. San Diego, Calif.: Wizards Bookshelf, 1976.

Leaman, Oliver. *Moses Maimonides*. London and New York: Routledge, 1990.

Legge, Francis. *Forerunners and Rivals of Christianity*. New Hyde Park, N.Y.: University Books, 1964.

Levey, Judith S. and Agnes Greenhall, eds. *The Concise Columbia Encyclopedia*. New York: Columbia University Press, 1983.

*The Life of St. Teresa of Avila by Herself*. J. M. Cohen, trans. London: Penguin Books, 1987.

Lindbergh, Charles. *The Spirit of St. Louis*. New York: Charles Scribner's Sons, 1953.

*The Lion Encyclopedia of the Bible*. Pat Alexander, ed. Batavia, Ill.: Lion Publishing Corp., 1986.

Lippman, Thomas W. *Understanding Islam: An Introduction to the Moslem World*. New York: New American Library, 1982.

Little, Gregory L. *People of the Web*. Memphis: White Buffalo Books, 1990.

Lowrie, Ernest B. *The Shape of the Puritan Mind: The Thought of Samuel Willard*. New Haven: Yale University Press, 1974.

Luck, Georg. *Arcana Mundi: Magic and the Occult in the Greek and Roman Worlds*. Baltimore: Johns Hopkins University Press, 1985.

Lukas, Georg. *Goethe and His Age*. New York: Grosset and Dunlap, 1969.

Luther, Martin. *The Book of Concord: The Confessions of the Evangelical Lutheran Church*. Theodore C Tappert, ed. and trans. Philadelphia: Fortress Press, 1959.

Luther, Martin. *Luther's Works*. St. Louis: Concordia, 1971.

———. *Table Talk*, Vol. 54 Theodore C. Tappert, ed. and trans. Philadelphia: Fortress Press, 1967.

MacDonald, William Graham. "Christology and the 'Angel of the lord'". *Current Issues in Biblical Patristic Interpretation*. G.F. Hawthorne and Merrill Tenney, eds. Grand Rapids, Mich. Erdman, 1975.

MacGregor, Geddes. *Angels: Ministers of Grace*. New York: Paragon House, 1988.

MacKenzie, Donald A. *Indian Myth and Legend*. Boston: Longwood Press, 1978.

Maclean, Dorothy. *To Hear the Angels Sing*. Hudson, N.Y.: Lindisfarne Press, 1990. First published by Lorian Press, 1980. Second ed. by Morningtown Press, 1988.

Maimonides. *Mishne Torah*. J. Cohen, ed. Jerusalem: Mossad Harav Kook, 1964.

———. *Guide of the Perplexed*. Abridged. Introduction by Julius Guttmann. London: East and West Library, 1952.

———. *Guide of the Perplexed*. S. Pines, ed and trans. Chicago: University of Chicago Press, 1963.

Margolies, Morris B. *A Gathering of Angels*. New York: Ballantine Books, 1994.

Mattingly, Terry. "Was It a Star or an Angel Guiding the Magi to Bethlehem?" *Seattle Times*, Dec. 25, 1993, p. A19.

May, Herbert G., and Bruce M. Metzger, eds. *The Oxford Annotated Bible with the Apocrypha*, Revised Standard Version. New York: Oxford University Press, 1965.

McClure, Kevin. *The Evidence for Visions of the Virgin Mary*. Wellingborough, England: The Aquarian Press, 1983.

———. *Visions of Bowmen and Angels: Mons 1914*. St Austell, Cornwall, England: The Wild Places, c. 1992.

McDermott, Robert A. ed. and Intro. *The Essential Steiner*. San Francisco: Harper & Row, 1984

McInerny, Ralph M. *A First Glance at St. Thomas Aquinas*. Notre Dame, Ind.: Notre Dame University Press, 1990.

McLean, Adam, ed. *A Treatise on Angel Magic*. Grand Rapids, Mich.: Phanes Press, 1990.

Mellor, Anne Kostelanetz. *Blake's Human Form Divine*. Berkeley: University of California Press, 1974.

Melton, J. Gordon. *Encyclopedic Handbook of Cults in America*. New York and London: Garland Publishing Inc., 1986.

Mercatante, Anthony S. *An Encyclopedia of World Mythology and Legend*. French's Forest, Australia: Child & Associates Publishing, 1988.

Moody, Raymond A. *The Light Beyond*. New York: Bantam Books, 1988.

———. *Reflections on Life After Life*. Harrisburg, Pa.: Stackpole Books, 1977.

———. *Life After Life*. Georgia: Mockingbird Books, 1975.

Moore, R. Laurence. "The Occult Connection? Mormonism, Christian Science and Spiritualism," *The Occult in America*. John Godwin, ed. New York: Doubleday, 1982.

Murphy, Michael and Rhea A. White, *The Psychic Side of Sports*. Reading, Mass.: Addison-Wesley, 1978.

Myers, Frederic W.H. *Human Personality and Its Survival of Bodily Death*, Vols. I & II. New ed. New York: Longmans, Green & Co., 1954. First published 1903.

*Mythologies*. Compiled by Yves Bonnefoy. Chicago: University of Chicago Press, 1991.

*The New Oxford Annotated Bible with the Apocrypha*. Herbert G. May and Bruce M. Metzger, eds. New York: Oxford University Press, 1977.

Nigg, Walter, Mary Ilford, trans. *Warriors of God: The Great Religious Orders and Their Founders*. New York: Alfred Knopf, 1959.

Nosr, Seyyed Hossein. *An Introduction to Islamic Cosmological Doctrines*. Boulder, Colo.: Shambhala, 1978.

Nosr, Seyyed Hossein, ed. *Islamic Spirituality*. New York: Crossroad, 1987.

Oliphant, Mrs. *Francis of Assisi*. London: Macmillan and Co., Ltd., 1898.

*One Hundred Saints*. Boston: Little, Brown & Co., 1993.

Osis Karlis. *Deathbed Observations by Physicians and Nurses*. Monograph No. 3. New York: Parapsychology Foundation, 1961.

Osis, Karlis, and Erlendur Haraldsson. *At the Hour of Death*. Rev. ed. New York: Hastings House, 1986.

O'Sullivan, Fr. Paul. *All About the Angels*. Rockford, Ill.: Tan Books and Publishers, 1990. First published 1945.

Pagels, Elaine. *The Gnostic Gospels*. New York: Random House, 1979.

———. *The Origin of Satan*. New York: Random House, 1995.

Parente, Fr. Pascal P. *The Angels: The Catholic Teaching on the Angels*. Rockford, Ill.: Tan Books and Publishers, 1973. First published 1961.

Parisen, Maria, comp. *Angels & Mortals: Their Co-Creative Power*. Wheaton, Ill.: Quest Books, The Theosophical Publishing House, 1990.

Parish, James Robert. *Ghosts and Angels in Hollywood Films*. Jefferson, N.C.: McFarland & Company, 1994.

*Patristic Interpretation*. G.F. Hawthorne and Merrill Tenney, eds. Grand Rapids, Mich.: Erdman, 1975.

Paul, Erich Robert. *Science, Religion, and Mormon Cosmology*. Urbana and Chicago: University of Illinois Press, 1992.

Pernoud, Regine. *Joan of Arc: By Herself and Her Witnesses*. New York: Dorset, 1964. First published 1962.

Peters, F. E. *Muhammad and the Origins of Islam*. Albany, N.Y.: State University of New York Press, 1994.

Peterson, Eric. *The Angels and the Liturgy*. New York: Herder and Herder, 1964.

*A Plato Reader*. B. Jowett, Ronald B. Levinson, ed., Boston: Houghton Mifflin, 1967.

*Pseudo-Dionysius: The Complete Works*. New York: Paulist Press, 1987.

Randolph, Vance. *Ozark Magic and Folklore*. New York: Dover Publications, 1964. First published 1947.

Rawson, Philip. *Sacred Tibet*. London: Thames and Hudson, 1991.

Renna, Thomas. "Angels and Spirituality: The Augustinian Tradition to Eckhardt." *Augustinian Studies*, Vol. 16. Villanova University, 1984.

Remy, Nicolas. *Demonolatry*. Secaucus, N.J.: University Books, 1974. First published in 1595.

Rhodes Ron. *Angels Among Us*. Eugene, Oreg.: Harvest House Publishers, 1994.

Ring, Kenneth. *Heading Toward Omega*. New York: William Morrow, 1984.

———. *Life At Death*. New York: Coward, McCann & Geoghegan, 1980.

———. *The Omega Project*. New York: William Morrow, 1992.

Robinson, James, M. ed. *The Nag Hammadi Library in English*. San Francisco: Harper & Row, 1977.

Rogerson, John. "Wrestling With the Angel: A Study in Historical and Literary Interpretation," *Hermeneutics, the Bible, and Literary Criticism*. Ann Loades and Michael McLain, ed. New York: St. Martin's Press, 1992.

Ronner, John. *Know Your Angels*. Murfreesboro, Tenn.: Mamre Press, 1993.

———. *Do You Have a Guardian Angel?* Murfreesboro, Tenn.: Mamre Press, 1985.

Rorem, Paul. "The Uplifting Spirituality of Pseudo-Dionysius," *Christian Spirituality*. Vol. I. Eivert Cousins ed. New York: Crossroads, 1985.

Russell, Jeffrey Burton. *The Devil: Perceptions of Evil from Antiquity to Primitive Christianity*. Ithaca, N.Y.: Cornell University Press, 1977.

———. *Lucifer: The Devil in the Middle Ages*. Ithaca, N.Y.: Cornell University Press, 1984.

———. *A History of Witchcraft*. London: Thames and Hudson, 1980.

Schneiderman, Stuart. *An Angel Passes: How the Sexes Became Undivided*. New York University Press, 1988.

Scholem, Gershom. *Kabbalah*. New York: Dorset Press, 1987. First published 1974.

Schroff, Lois. *The Archangel Michael*. Herndon, Va.: Newlight Books, 1990.

Schwartz, Howard. *Gabriel's Palace: Jewish Mystical Tales*. New York: Oxford University Press, 1993.

Seligmann, Kurt. *The Mirror of Magic*. New York: Pantheon Books, 1948.

Shearer, Alistair. *The Hindu Vision*. London: Thames and Hudson, 1993.

Sheperd, A.P. *Rudolf Steiner: Scientist of the Invisible*. Rochester, Vt.: Inner Traditions International, 1954, 1983.

Shipps, Jan. *Mormonism: The Story of a New Religious Tradition*. Urbana, Ill.: University of Illinois Press, 1985.

Singer, June. *Seeing Through the Visible World: Jung, Gnosis, and Chaos*. San Francisco: Harper & Row, 1990.

Smith, Robert C. *In the Presence of Angels*. Virginia Beach, Va.: A.R.E. Press, 1993.

Snugg, Richard P., ed. *Jungian Literary Criticism*. Evanston, Ill.: Northwestern University Press, 1992.

Sogyal Rimpoche. *The Tibetan Book of Living and Dying*. Patrick Gaffney and Andrew Harvey, eds. New York: HarperSanFrancisco, 1992.

Spangler David. *Revelation: The Birth of a New Age*. Elgin, Ill.: The Lorian Press, 1976

*St. Michael and the Angels*. Rockford, Ill.: Tan Books and Publishers, 1983. First published 1977.

Stanley, Michael, ed. "Angelic Nature: From Works of Emanuel Swedenborg," *Angels & Mortals: Their Co-Creative Power*, compiled by Maria Parisen. Wheaton, Ill.: Quest Books, The Theosophical Publishing House, 1990.

Steiner, Rudolf. *An Autobiography*. New trans. Blauvelt, N.Y.: Rudolf Steiner Publications, 1977.

———. *The Four Seasons and the Archangels*. Bristol, England: The Rudolf Steiner Press, 1992.

———. *Planetary Spheres and Their Influence on Man's Life on Earth and in the Spiritual Worlds*. London: Rudolf Steiner Press, 1982.

Steinmetz, Dov, M.D. "Moses' 'Revelation' on Mount Horeb as a Near-Death Experience," in *Journal of Near-Death Studies*, 11(4) Summer 1993, pp. 199–203.

Stoudt, John Joseph. *Jacob Boehme: His Life and Thought*. New York: Seabury Press, 1968.

Sugrue, Thomas. *There Is a River: The Story of Edgar Cayce*. New York: Holt, Rhinehart & Winston, 1942.

Swedenborg, Emanuel. *Heaven and Hell*. George F. Dole, trans. New York: Swedenborg Foundation Inc., 1976.

TeSelle, Eugene, *Augustine the Theologian*. New York: Herder and Herder, 1970.

Thompson, C. J. S. *The Lure and Romance of Alchemy*. New York: Bell Publishing, 1990. First published 1932.

Turner, Alice K. *The History of Hell*. New York: Harcourt Brace & Co., 1993.

Walsh, Michael, ed. *Butler's Lives of the Saints*, Concise Edition. San Francisco: Harper & Row, 1985, pp. 314–320.

Walshe, M., ed. *Meister Eckhardt*. London: Watkins, 1981.

Weeks, Andrew. *Boehme: An Intellectual Biography*. State University of New York Press, 1991.

# INDEX

Boldface numbers indicate article titles. *Italic* numbers indicate illustrations.